BUDGETING

Profit Planning
and Control

Fifth Edition

PRENTICE-HALL SERIES IN ACCOUNTING

Charles T. Horngren, Editor

BUDGETING

Profit Planning and Control

Fifth Edition

GLENN A. WELSCH, CPA

The Peat, Marwick and Mitchell Co.
Professorship in Accounting, Emeritus
The James L. Bayless Chair in Free Enterprise, Emeritus
The University of Texas at Austin

RONALD W. HILTON, Ph.D.

Professor of Accounting
Cornell University

PAUL N. GORDON, CPA

Partner
Peat Marwick Main & Co.

PRENTICE HALL, Englewood Cliffs, NJ 07632

LIBRARY OF CONGRESS
Library of Congress Cataloging-in-Publication Data

Welsch, Glenn A.
    Budgeting : profit planning and control. -- 5th ed. / Glenn A.
Welsch, Ronald W. Hilton, Paul N. Gordon.
        p.   cm. -- (Prentice-Hall series in accounting)
    Includes bibliographies and index.
    ISBN 0-13-085754-8
    1. Budget in business.   I. Hilton, Ronald W.   II. Gordon, Paul N.
III. Title.   IV. Series.
HG4028.B8W45 1988
658.1'54--dc19   88-4030
                                                  CIP

Editorial/production supervision and interior design: Maureen Wilson
Cover design: Diane Saxe
Manufacturing buyer: Ed O'Dougherty

 © 1988 by Prentice-Hall, Inc.
A Division of Simon & Schuster
Englewood Cliffs, New Jersey 07632

Materials from the Certificate in Management
Accounting Examinations, copyright by the National
Association of Accountants, are reprinted and/or
adapted with permission.

Questions from the CPA exam, copyright by the
American Institute of Certified Public Accountants,
are reprinted with permission.

Excerpts from *Management Accounting,* published by
the National Association of Accountants, are used
with permission.

Printed in the United States of America

10 9 8 7 6 5 4 3 2 1

ISBN 0-13-085754-8 01

PRENTICE-HALL INTERNATIONAL (UK) LIMITED, London
PRENTICE-HALL OF AUSTRALIA PTY. LIMITED, Sydney
PRENTICE-HALL CANADA INC., Toronto
PRENTICE-HALL HISPANOAMERICANA, S.A., Mexico
PRENTICE-HALL OF INDIA PRIVATE LIMITED, New Delhi
PRENTICE-HALL OF JAPAN, INC., Tokyo
PRENTICE-HALL OF SOUTHEAST ASIA PTE. LTD., Singapore
EDITORA PRENTICE-HALL DO BRASIL, LTDA., Rio de Janeiro

Contents

3   THE PROFIT PLANNING AND CONTROL PROCESS   *71*

4   APPLICATION OF COMPREHENSIVE PROFIT PLANNING AND CONTROL   *121*

PART II   *Application of Profit Planning and Control*

5   PLANNING AND CONTROLLING REVENUES: SALES AND SERVICE   *171*

6 PLANNING AND CONTROLLING PRODUCTION: WORK-IN-PROCESS AND FINISHED GOODS INVENTORIES   *210*

7 PLANNING AND CONTROLLING PURCHASES AND MATERIALS USAGE: MANUFACTURING AND NONMANUFACTURING   *240*

8 PLANNING AND CONTROLLING DIRECT LABOR COSTS   *280*

15 PERFORMANCE EVALUATION AND MANAGEMENT CONTROL   *542*

16 ANALYSIS OF BUDGET VARIANCES   *569*

17 COORDINATING ACCOUNTING SYSTEMS WITH PROFIT PLANNING AND CONTROL   *593*

18 PERSPECTIVES AND OVERVIEW   *630*

APPENDIX:
PROBABILITY AND DECISION MAKING UNDER
UNCERTAINTY   *648*

INDEX   *655*

Schedules

(for Superior Manufacturing Company)

CHAPTER 11

CHAPTER 12

CHAPTER 13

CHAPTER 14

Preface

Comprehensive profit planning and control, or budgeting, continues to be of prime importance in virtually all organizations. For a thorough understanding of the profit planning and control process, students and managers need familiarity with all aspects of the goals, technical procedures, and effects of budgeting. Just as important, though, is an understanding of the broad organizational context within which budgets are prepared and used. The unique strength of this text is its thoroughly comprehensive and integrated approach to the topic of budgeting. It is the only book of which we are aware that covers all aspects of the budgeting process—from the details of preparing the many schedules that comprise a master budget to the fundamental managerial issues that are affected by the profit planning and control process.

The Fifth Edition of *Budgeting: Profit Planning and Control* is well-suited for each of the following uses:

- ☐ a one-semester or term course covering all aspects of comprehensive profit planning and control
- ☐ a supplementary text in a wide range of management, industrial engineering, financial management, and managerial accounting courses
- ☐ executive development programs
- ☐ a handbook for managers who are involved in or affected by the budgeting process

STRENGTHS OF THE FIFTH EDITION   This edition represents a major revision of the text. While all of the topics covered in the Fourth Edition have been retained in the book, the writing has been streamlined for clarity and conciseness. The current edition retains the comprehensive and practical approach of previous editions and also expands coverage in key areas. Some of the major changes in the Fifth Edition are listed below:

- ☐ *New author team:* Glenn Welsch, of the University of Texas at Austin, continues as lead

xvii

author, bringing his wealth of knowledge and experience in teaching, writing, and consulting in the budgeting area. Ronald Hilton, of Cornell University, brings a fresh perspective on the behavioral, economic, and quantitative issues that interact with the budgeting process. Paul Gordon, a Partner in Peat Marwick Main and Co., provides a practical perspective and real world focus that makes the text more relevant than ever.

☐ Significantly *expanded coverage* of budgeting for service-industry firms and nonprofit enterprises, behavioral issues in profit planning and control, economic effects of the budgeting process, and quantitative decision models as they relate to the planning and control process.

☐ *Real world illustrations* and cases. Numerous illustrations of budgeting practices and issues in well-known organizations are included in the Fifth Edition. Examples include 3M, Alcan Aluminum, JKL Advertising Agency, a public school district in suburban Rochester, ARCO, the city of Charlotte, UNISYS (formerly Burroughs), Wisconsin Life Insurance Company, University Community Hospital in Tampa, Celanese, Chesebrough Ponds, and Intel Corporation.

☐ The *comprehensive demonstration case* from previous editions has been updated and expanded. The Superior case now begins with a computer service and sales company and then develops into a full-fledged manufacturing firm. This comprehensive demonstration case is introduced in Chapter 1 and continues all the way through the text, illustrating every step and schedule in comprehensive profit planning and control.

☐ *Emphasis on leadership and the role of managers* in organizations from the chief executive officer to all levels of management. Throughout the entire text, issues in planning and control are discussed for all management levels. Moreover, the pervasive implications of behavioral issues at each level of the organization are discussed.

☐ *Additional cases and problems* have been added, and the old cases have been updated and revised. Many cases have been recast as service-industry cases, including banks, airlines, and insurance companies.

☐ *Computer applications* have been added to bring the book up to date in this important area.

☐ *Pedagogical features* that are new in the Fifth Edition include chapter summaries, a suggested reference list in each chapter, more graphs and exhibits, a modernized format with a larger page size, real world illustrations, and more discussion questions and cases.

☐ Coverage of *just-in-time manufacturing (JIT), material requirements planning (MRP),* and other contemporary topics as they relate to the budgeting process.

SUPPLEMENTS TO THE FIFTH EDITION   A strong supplements package is available to assist instructors in using the text. These include a Solutions Manual with suggested times for the assignment material and also suggestions on using the questions and cases. New in the supplements package are Twin®/Lotus® 1-2-3® Problem Templates to help students develop their computer skills as they relate to the budgeting process.

USING THE FIFTH EDITION   *Budgeting: Profit Planning and Control* is divided into three parts and can be used effectively in a variety of ways. Part I, which includes the first four chapters, discusses a foundation that is essential for a comprehensive profit planning and control system. Because it is an overview and because it introduces the comprehensive demonstration case, it pervades the remaining chapters and should be studied carefully. Part II, covering Chapters 5 through 13, contains a detailed discussion of the application of a typical PPC system for both manufacturing and nonmanufacturing businesses. Separate chapters discuss the primary areas of comprehensive profit planning and control. Part III covers Chapters 14 through 18. This last part of the book discusses some important concepts and techniques that are usually incorporated into a comprehensive profit planning and control program and the interrelationships of a profit planning and control program with the cost accounting system used.

Used as the text for a course in budgeting, the book presents the procedures and issues in budgeting in sufficient detail that it is not necessary for instructors to lecture on every point. This frees instructors to use valuable classroom time to enrich and elaborate on selected topics, supplement the text with personnel experiences or other readings, such as articles in the popular business press or academic journals, pose provocative questions to the class, and discuss the assigned cases and relate them to the overall process of profit planning and control. The authors devote approximately two-thirds of the class time in a semester to discussion of cases assigned in advance and other non-textbook assignments. The cases included in the text range from detailed, numerical cases to force students to "get their hands dirty" by actually performing detailed budgeting steps, to broad, thought-provoking cases. The cases require the student to think imaginatively, to identify a problem, to weigh the various factors bearing on it, to evolve alternatives, to take a position, and finally to be prepared to defend that position. In class students should be required to explain their points of view, to defend them, to understand and appraise the position espoused by their classmates, to recognize viable alternatives, and to decide what alternatives appear to be most realistic in light of the situation. Practice in doing these things helps to increase the competence of students in resolving problems as opposed to completing only a series of "cookbook" computations.

This book may also be used effectively as a supplementary text in a variety of courses. By directing the students' attention to specific topics and cases, the text can enhance the depth of any course dealing with issues in planning and control.

Finally, the book may be used effectively as a handbook for managers involved in or affected by the budgeting process. The systematic organization and sequencing of the text, coupled with its detailed, comprehensive, and continuing illustrations, make it easy for users to find a topic in the book and quickly grasp the important points needed to understand the topic.

ACKNOWLEDGMENTS   We are indebted to many people for their suggestions, constructive criticism, insights, and assistance. Several users of previous editions reviewed the Fifth Edition and made valuable suggestions on how to improve the text. Our thanks go to M. C. Althaus, Edward J. Bader, John J. Burnett, Richard J. Coppinger, Janet Daniels, Larzette G. Hale, Steven D. Hall, Donald Keller, John F. Lannan, Jeffrey E. Michelman, C. M. Paik, Ernest J. Pavlock, Ray M. Powell, Pierre Salmon, Robert E. Seiler, and J. O. Weisenberg.

Word processing, proofing, and problem-checking duties were competently performed by Bobbie M. Barnes, Janie Basher, Cristina De La Fuente, Barbara Guile, Thu H. Nguyen, and William Zacchaeus. We are grateful for their dedication and professionalism.

We are grateful to Peat Marwick Main & Co. for their support and contributions in the preparation of the text.

In addition, we thank the people at Prentice Hall: Irene Hess, Julie Warner, and Maureen Wilson.

We also extend our appreciation to those who have given us permission to include problems and exerpts from published articles in the text. Permission has been received from the Institute of Certified Management Accountants of the National Association of Accountants to use questions and unofficial answers from past CMA examinations. We received permission from the National Association of Accountants to include in our book exerpts from its publication, *Management Accounting.* We also received permission from the American Institute of Certified Public Accountants to include questions and unofficial answers from past CPA examinations. Finally, we gratefully acknowledge permission from Professor David Solomons to use one of his cases in the text.

In writing the Fifth Edition of *Budgeting: Profit Planning and Control,* we have strived to present the most comprehensive, practical, and readable resource possible in the area of profit planning and control. We will sincerely appreciate receiving comments from instructors, accountants, and managers who use the book.

GLENN A. WELSCH
RONALD W. HILTON
PAUL N. GORDON

BUDGETING

Profit Planning
and Control

Fifth Edition

1 The Management Process

INTRODUCTION AND PURPOSE   The two primary functions of the managers of an entity are planning and controlling operations. In business, government, and most other group activities, a planning and control system (also called managerial budgeting) is widely used in performing managerial planning and control responsibilities. The purpose of this chapter is to give an overview of the management process and to establish that process, along with the related organizational structure of the entity, as the foundation for an effective planning and control system.

We use the descriptive term **comprehensive profit planning and control** in this book. Other terms used in the same context are **business budgeting, managerial budgeting,** and **budgeting.** For our purposes, the term **comprehensive profit planning and control** is defined as a systematic and formalized approach for performing significant phases of the management planning and control functions. Specifically, it involves (1) the development and application of broad and long-range objectives for the enterprise; (2) the specification of enterprise goals; (3) a long-range profit plan developed in broad terms; (4) a short-range profit plan detailed by assigned responsibilities (divisions, products, projects); (5) a system of periodic performance reports detailed by assigned responsibilities; and (6) follow-up procedures. Throughout this chapter, we emphasize those aspects of the management process directly related to comprehensive profit planning and control.

THE ROLE OF MANAGEMENT   The effectiveness with which an entity is managed is usually recognized as the single most important factor in its long-term success. Success is measured in terms of accomplishment of the entity's goals. **Management** can be defined as the process of defining entity goals and implementing activities to attain those goals by efficient use of human, material, and capital resources. The **management process** is a set of interdependent activities used by the management of an organization to perform the following functions of management: planning, organizing, staffing, leading, and controlling.

Goal Orientation

Both business and nonbusiness endeavors must have objectives and goals. In business endeavors, the primary goal orientations are (1) return on investment and (2) contribution to the economic and social improvement of the broader environment. Likewise, nonbusiness endeavors have specific objectives, such as the accomplishment of a given mission within specified cost constraints. In both cases, it is essential that the managers of the endeavor, as well as other interested parties, know the objectives and goals. Otherwise, effective management guidance of the activities and measurement of the effectiveness with which desired activities are performed are impossible. Thus, the responsibilities of management to specify and articulate goals and objectives are fundamentally identical in business and nonbusiness enterprises. The broad responsibilities of management essentially conform to a common pattern, whatever the type of endeavor.[1]

People Orientation

The success of an enterprise—business or other organization—depends on the people associated with the enterprise. These people include both the managers and the other employees, because all of these individuals are significantly involved in the attainment of enterprise objectives. Thus, "people" constitute the most critical part of management—not land, buildings, equipment, or materials. Developing an effective staff, providing a positive working climate, and positively motivating people determine in large measure, the success of most enterprises.

   The importance of involving people in the management process at 3M was expressed by the company's chief executive officer in the following excerpt from an article in *Management Accounting*. The Minnesota Mining and Manufacturing Company (3M) was cited by Peters and Waterman as being one of the world's most effective companies in their book *In Search of Excellence*.[2]

[1]William E. Thomas, *Readings in Cost Accounting, Budgeting and Control,* 6th ed (Cincinnati: South-Western Publishing, 1983), Reading No. 6, "Defining Goals—A Behavioral Approach," by Robert L. Morasky, pp. 85–94.

[2]Thomas J. Peters and Robert H. Waterman, *In Search of Excellence* (New York: Warner Books, 1982).

> ### PEOPLE ORIENTATION AT 3M
>
> "As our business grows, it becomes increasingly necessary to delegate responsibility and to encourage men and women to exercise their initiative. This requires considerable tolerance.
>
> "Those men and women to whom we delegate authority and responsibility, if they are good people, are going to want to do their jobs in their own way. These are characteristics we want and should be encouraged as long as their way conforms to our general pattern of operation.
>
> "Mistakes will be made, but if a person is essentially right, the mistakes he or she makes are not as serious in the long run as the mistakes management will make if it is dictatorial and undertakes to tell those under its authority exactly how they must do their job.
>
> "Management that is destructively critical when mistakes are made kills initiative, and it's essential that we have many people with initiative if we're to continue to grow."[3]

THE FUNCTIONS OF MANAGEMENT AND THE MANAGEMENT PROCESS   The management of an enterprise requires the continuing performance of certain managerial responsibilities. These responsibilities collectively are often called the **functions of management.** Although their designations vary, these functions are widely recognized by both academic scholars and professional managers. In our discussion of profit planning and control, we use the terminology and definitions of the management functions described by a prominent author essentially as follows:[4]

1   **Planning** is the process of developing enterprise objectives and selecting a future course of action to accomplish them. It includes (a) establishing enterprise objectives, (b) developing premises about the environment in which they are to be accomplished, (c) selecting a course of action for accomplishing the objectives, (d) initiating activities necessary to translate plans into action, and (e) current replanning to correct current deficiencies.

2   **Organizing** is the process by which employees and their jobs are related to each other to accomplish enterprise objectives. It consists of dividing work among groups and individuals, and coordinating individual and group activities. Organizing also involves establishing managerial authority.

3   **Staffing and human resource management** is the process of assuring that competent employees are selected, developed, and rewarded for accomplishing enterprise objectives. Effective staffing and human resource management also includes establishing a work climate in which employees are satisfied.

4   **Leading and interpersonal influence** is the process of motivating individuals (peers, superiors, subordinates, and nonsubordinates) or groups to assist willingly and harmoniously in accomplishing enterprise objectives (also called directing or actuating).

5   **Controlling** is the process of assuring efficient performance to attain the enterprise objectives. It involves (a) establishing goals and standards, (b) comparing measured performance against the established goals and standards, and (c) reinforcing successes and correcting shortcomings.

[3]Kathy Williams, "The Magic of Management Accounting Excellence," *Management Accounting*, (February 1986), p. 24.

[4]Adapted from Arthur G. Bedeian, *Management* (New York: Dryden Press, 1985), pp. 5 and 6.

The five functions of management collectively constitute the management process because they are concurrently and continuously being performed in managing an enterprise. The management process uses sequential linkages and feedback. For example, planning must precede organizing, and controlling should follow the other functions. For this reason, the management process is often diagramed as shown in Exhibit 1-1. Notice (a) the sequential linkages from planning to controlling and (b) the continuous feedback from functions 2, 3, 4, and 5 to planning. Continuous feedback is essential for improving performance and for replanning.

The five classifications shown in Exhibit 1-1 will be used for discussion purposes throughout this book. Primary emphasis will be given to planning and controlling because they constitute the main focus of a comprehensive profit planning and control system.

THE ESSENCE OF MANAGERIAL PLANNING   Planning is the first function of management shown in Exhibit 1-1. It is performed continuously because the passage of time demands both replanning and making new plans. Moreover, current feedback often necessitates newly planned actions to (a) correct performance deficiencies, (b) cope with unanticipated events that are unfavorable, and (c) take advantage of new developments.

Management planning is a process that includes the following five phases: (1) establishing enterprise **objectives** and goals, (2) developing

EXHIBIT 1-1

The Management Process

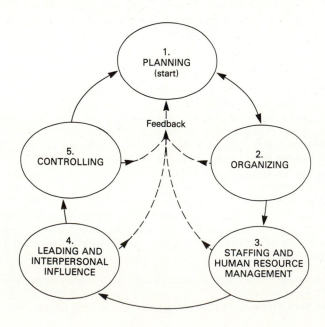

premises about the environment of the entity, (3) making **decisions** about courses of action, (4) initiating **actions** to activate the plans, and (5) evaluating **performance feedback** for replanning. Management planning provides the basis for performing the four other functions shown in Exhibit 1-1—organizing, staffing, leading, and controlling.

The importance of planning at the Alcan Aluminum Corporation was described by the company's chief executive officer in the following excerpt from an article in the *AMA Forum*.

PLANNING AT THE ALCAN ALUMINUM CORPORATION

The planning process, both short- and long-term, is the most crucial component of the whole system. It is both the foundation and the bond for the other elements because it is through the planning process that we determine what we are going to do, how we are going to do it, and who is going to do it. It operates as the brain center of an organization and, like the brain, it both reasons and communicates. [5]

The essence of management requires decisions of the highest order. Periodic decisions must be made about the entity's future courses of action, and corrections must be made to prior courses of action. Managerial decision making involves a significant managerial process.

The Decision-Making Process

Decision making involves a commitment or resolution to do or to stop doing an act, or to adopt or reject an attitude. [6] Sound decision making requires creativity and confidence. It is surrounded by risk, uncertainty, criticism, and second-guessing. It is important to understand that to do nothing about an issue or a problem is, in and of itself, a decision. Exhibit 1-2 shows the steps usually included in the decision-making process. The steps that seldom receive adequate attention are identification (2) and evaluation (6).

EXHIBIT 1-2

Steps in the Decision-Making Process

Step 1   Recognize a problem—A problem exists, a choice needs to be made, or there is an obstacle to attaining an enterprise goal.

Step 2   Identify alternatives—A systematic effort is made to identify the choices available. Usually a limited number of alternatives exist, constrained by time and money.

Step 3   Specify the sources of uncertainty—A careful analysis is made of the possible events that can occur. To the extent possible, probabilities or likelihoods may be associated with these events.

[5]Roy A. Gentles, "Alcan's Integration of Management Techniques Raises Their Effectiveness," *AMA Forum,* April, 1984, p. 32.

[6]Adapted from Jack Halloran, *Applied Human Relations, An Organizational Approach,* 2nd ed. (Englewood Cliffs, N.J.: Prentice-Hall 1983), p. 232.

Step 4   Select a criterion—The criterion is selected upon which the alternatives will be evaluated. Criteria such as profit, aggregate contribution margin, rate of return, or net present value may be chosen.

Step 5   Consider risk preferences—Consideration is given to the extent to which management is willing to select a risky alternative. Equivalently, management considers the trade-off between risk and return. How much higher return does a risky alternative need to provide in order to justify its inherent risk?

Step 6   Evaluate alternatives—In light of the choice set identified in step 2, the sources of uncertainty identified in step 3, the criterion established in step 4, and the risk preferences determined in step 5, determine the expected payoff associated with each alternative.

Step 7   Select the best alternative—The evaluation of alternatives in step 6, coupled with a careful consideration of the enterprise objectives and goals, results in the selection of an alternative.

Step 8   Implement the selected course of action—Appropriate actions are taken to initiate the chosen alternative. No decision will be effective unless effective actions are taken to make it a reality.

Sources: Adapted from Arthur G. Bedeian, *Management* (New York: *Dryden Press*, 1985), Chap. 7; and Joel S. Demski, *Information Analysis* (Reading, Mass,: Addison-Wesley, 1980), Chaps. 1 and 2.

SOME CONCEPTUAL VIEWS ABOUT THE ROLE OF MANAGEMENT

There are conceptual or philosophical disagreements as to the real **role of management** in both business and nonbusiness entities. A brief look at the extreme positions in these conceptual disagreements may add to our insights. One extreme pole has been labeled the market theory; at the opposite end of the spectrum is the planning and control theory.[7] These two opposing philosophies are presented in Exhibit 1-3. Notice that the **market theory,** in the extreme sense, views the managerial role basically as comprising **reactive decisions** that respond to environmental events as they occur. This view accords a passive role to management. In contrast, the **planning and control theory** views the management role essentially as an **active** one that attempts to condition the state of the enterprise. The latter theory emphasizes the planning function of management. The concept of comprehensive profit planning and control rests firmly upon the planning and control theory; that is, the primary success factor in an enterprise is the competence of management to plan and to control enterprise activities. This notion says that a management earns its bread and butter only if it can plan and control in ways that determine the long-range destiny of the enterprise. The foundation for profit planning and control, then, is that management must have confidence in its ability to establish realistic objectives and to devise efficient strategies to attain those objectives. The market theory argues very little for the concept of profit planning and control.

[7]The following three sources are highly recommended for their excellent conceptual exposition of these and numerous related theories mentioned throughout this book: Neil W. Chamberlain, *The Firm: Micro-Economic Planning and Action* (New York: McGraw-Hill, 1962); also by the same author and publisher: *Enterprise and Environment: The Firm in Time and Place* (1968); and Russell L. Ackoff, *A Concept of Corporate Planning* (New York: John Wiley, 1970).

In the real world, management operates somewhere between the two conceptual extremes represented in Exhibit 1-3. From time to time, some companies find themselves in situations where the noncontrollable variables appear dominant enough to determine the destiny of the firm. This observation is valid in many situations when viewed in the short run. However, such situations do not deny the planning and control theory. In practically all cases, an enlightened and imaginative management can manipulate many variables that will have a dominant impact on the long-range future success of the endeavor. For example, a competent management, finding itself in an environment (industry, market area, product line, geographical location, political situation) where the long-range destiny of the enterprise is dominated by the noncontrollable variables, will very quickly devise avenues for moving to environments where the controllable variables tend to dominate. Competent managers, and rational investors as well, generally are not interested in operating in an environment that is completely random. Thus, it would appear that the closer to the planning and control theory that a management operates, the greater the opportunities to reduce the randomness of events and the greater the significance of managerial competence.

EXHIBIT 1-3

Theoretical Views of the Role of Management

MARKET THEORY	PLANNING AND CONTROL THEORY
1. Management is solely at the whim of prevailing economic, social, and political forces (environment).	1. The future destiny of the enterprise can be manipulated; hence, it can be planned and controlled by the management.
2. As a consequence, management esentially fills the role of a fortune teller—reading the environment.	2. Good managers can contrive realistic ways to achieve the objectives.
3. When the environment is read, reactive managerial decisions are made.	3. Management can manipulate the controllable variables and plan for the noncontrollable variables.
4. Therefore, managerial competence (success) depends on an ability to read the environment and to react wisely.	4. Therefore, the quality of managerial planning decisions determines managerial competence.
Reactive (Ex Post) Decisions:	Active (Ex Ante) Decisions:
Management reads events that are happening and then reacts to them.	Management anticipates future events and plans for them.

Consistent with this conceptual view of the role of management, Fayol (one of the early perceptive observers of that role) wrote that all activities of an industrial undertaking could be divided into six categories:[8] (1) technical (production), (2) commercial (buying, selling, and exchange), (3) financial (search for and use of capital), (4) security (protection of property and persons), (5) accounting (including statistics), and (6) managerial activity. He very perceptively identified **managerial activity** (item 6 above) as the effort required to ensure accomplishment of the first five items. Fayol's managerial activity encompassed what is now called the planning and control functions of management.

The essence of planning and control rests upon some fundamental or philosophical views of the real role of management in an endeavor. In harmony with some of these views, profit planning and control rests upon the conviction that management can plan and control the long-range destiny of the enterprise by making a continuing stream of well-conceived decisions. The concept speaks to planned prosperity as opposed to unplanned happenstance. For long-range success, the stream of managerial decisions must generate plans and actions to provide the essential inflows that are necessary to support the planned outflows of the enterprise so that reasonable levels of profit and return on investment are earned. Continuing generation of profit by managerial manipulation of the inflows and outflows provides the substance of profit planning and control. These relationships are depicted in Exhibit 1-4.

Notice in Exhibit 1-4 that the essential inflows are people, capital, and materials and that they are generally cost-incurring factors. On the other hand, the planned outflows are products, services, and social contributions that the enterprise generates. The planned outflows of products and services generally are revenue-generating factors. The essential responsibility of management is to manipulate, through the management process, the planned combinations of inflows and outflows so that the long-range objectives of the enterprise are attained. In a profit-making situation, the principal measures of the accomplishment of long-range objectives are usually in terms of profit and return on investment. In the discussions that follow, manipulation of the relevent variables by management implies a stream of well-conceived decisions directed toward accomplishment of the specified long-range objectives of the enterprise. The managerial decisions must be both purposive and futuristic. By **futuristic** we mean that the important managerial decisions must be fundamentally concerned with the long-range future in contrast to spur-of-the-moment decisions. By **purposive** we mean that the stream of important managerial decisions must be primarily concerned with devising realistic strategies to attain those objectives. The stream of decisions should demonstrate implicit managerial self-confidence that the destiny of the firm can be effectively planned and controlled. Decision making requires imagination and courage; each major decision of management involves an effort to create or seize a positive opportunity or to escape the onset of decline.

[8]H. Fayol, *General and Industrial Administration* (London: Sir Isaac Pitman & Sons, 1949).

EXHIBIT 1-4

Planning Inflows and Outflows of an Enterprise

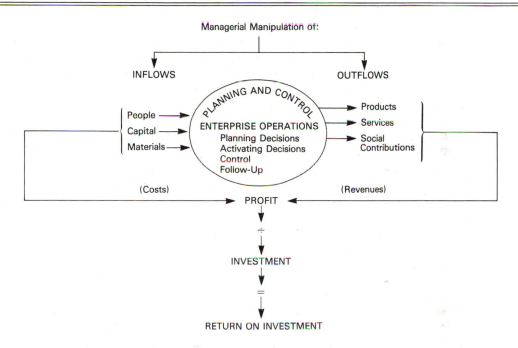

Fundamentally, then, managerial decision making entails the tasks of (1) manipulating the relevant **controllable variables** and (2) taking advantage of the relevant **noncontrollable variables** that may influence long-run operational success. Exhibit 1-5 shows how a management may initially—and periodically—approach the problem of identifying and evaluating the relevant variables for its organization. The analysis is designed to provide some initial insights essential to developing realistic plans and strategies for the enterprise. The relevant variables affecting the enterprise are presented in a three-way classification in Exhibit 1-5: external versus internal; time; and controllable versus noncontrollable. The last column, "Strategy and Planning Reference," provides a key to the plans and strategies with respect to each variable. Of particular relevance is the classification of each variable as to controllability or noncontrollability in the short-, intermediate-, or long-range time horizons. It is this classification that gives management insights into desirable strategies for the future. An especially salient generalization may be made at this point. The controllable variables are those that can be actively planned and controlled by management. In direct contrast, the noncontrollable variables cannot be influenced by management. Yet this does not mean that effective planning with respect to them is not possible. Significantly, the noncontrollable variables must be projected and "planned for" to take full advantage of their anticipated favorable consequences and to minimize their unfavorable consequences.

EXHIBIT 1-5

Identification and Evaluation of Relevant Variables

RELEVANT VARIABLES*	MANIPULATION BASIS						STRATEGY AND PLANNING REFERENCE
	SHORT-RANGE		INTER-MEDIATE		LONG-RANGE		
	C†	NC†	C	NC	C	NC	
External:							
Population		x		x		x	
GNP		x		x		x	
Industry sales		x		x	x		
Competitive activities		x		x		x	
Industry (in which to compete)		x		x	x		
Product lines, etc.		x	x		x		
Internal:							
Employees—quality		x	x		x		
Employees—quantity	x		x		x		
Capital–sources	x		x		x		
Capital—amount	x		x		x		
Research—nature		x	x		x		
Research—cost	x		x		x		
Advertising	x		x		x		
Productivity		x	x		x		
Pricing product		x	x		x		
Sales methods	x		x		x		
Production methods		x	x		x		
Operating costs—fixed	x		x		x		
Operating costs—variable, etc.	x		x		x		

*Illustrative only; classification unique to each situation.

†C—Controllable; NC—Noncontrollable.

Thus, we observe that managerial planning is necessary with respect to all the relevant variables. Herein lies a subtle trap. Many managers assume that they should plan for and consider primarily the controllable variables because "we can't do anything about the uncontrollable variables." To restate this important point in a different way, management, to be effective, must also anticipate the noncontrollable variables, evaluate their potential effects, and make plans consistent with those evaluations. Also, evaluation and analysis are crucial when determining the interrelationships between the controllable and noncontrollable variables. For example, the impact of certain noncontrollable variables on one or more of the controllable variables may be both significant and pervasive in a particular situation.

Two main types of management plans can be identified as follows:

TYPE	TIME DIMENSION	CHARACTERISTICS
Strategic (developed by top management)	Long-range	Focuses on enterprise objectives and overall strategies; affects all management functions; involves comprehensive and long-term consequences
Tactical or operational (developed participatively by all management levels)	Short-range	Refines the enterprise objectives to develop programs, policies, and performance expectations; involves timing that is intermediate-range to short-range; focuses on levels of assigned authority and responsibility; provides "budget information" for performance reports

Organizing

Organizing, as shown in Exhibit 1–1, is one of the basic phases of the management process. Organizing depends on the plans of the enterprise. It involves (a) subdivision of an enterprise into manageable work units (e.g., divisions and departments), (b) assignment or delegation of management responsibilities, and (c) definition of the locus of decisions. Typically, this is called organizational design or development of an organizational structure.[9] Exhibit 1-6 shows a composite organizational structure for a manufacturing company. This structure emphasizes the delegation of management authority and responsibility from the top of the company down. It is important because planning and controlling are implemented at each level in the organization. Notice the following characteristics of the structure in this organizational design:

a It is a composite organization structure because it shows the following (1) subdivision or scope of the responsibilities of each group, (2) departmentalization or horizontal division of the responsibilities, (3) delegation of the role of each staff group, and (4) delegation of line authority and responsibility to each group.

b There are two types of staff functions: (1) **advisory** and functional line authority limited to the areas of expertise (finance, personnel, and marketing) and (2) **specialized** expertise and guidance (public relations, legal, and engineering).

c There are four line-operating divisions, three byproducts (automobile, truck, and appliance) and one by geographical area (international operations).

d Each division has its own specialized engineering staff (only one is shown).

e Quality control in the appliance division is a staff function accountable to the division general manager. The Quality Control staff function is held accountable for quality control in the respective plants.

[9]Adapted from Charles N. Greene, Everett E. Adam, Jr., and Ronald J. Ebert, *Management for Effective Performance* (Englewood Cliffs, N.J.: Prentice-Hall, 1985), Chap. 11.

EXHIBIT 1-6
A Composite Organizational Structure

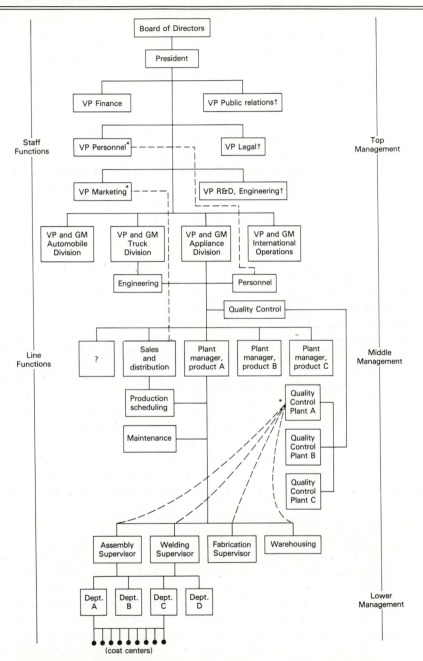

*Advisory and functional authority in their specialty areas.
†Specialized expertise and guidance.
—Functional authority and responsibility.

Source: Adapted from Charles N. Greene, Everett E. Adam, Jr., and Ronald J. Ebert, *Management: For Effective Performance* (Englewood Cliffs, N.J.: Prentice-Hall, 1985), p. 387.

Separate organization charts also are frequently prepared to indicate various relationships, such as reporting relationships, relationships between horizontal and vertical responsibilities, and flows of authority (downward and upward), as shown in Exhibit 1-7.

Most companies need both line and staff units. **Line managers** (units) contribute **directly** to the main objectives and goals of the organization. Therefore, they are in the "chain of command." Examples are production, purchasing, and distribution. Staff managers (units) contribute **indirectly** (but importantly) to the main objectives of the enterprise. Their primary contributions are providing advice and specialized expertise. Therefore, staff people are not in the chain of command. Examples of staff units are accounting, public relations, personnel, and legal.

EXHIBIT 1-7

Two Views of the Flow of Authority

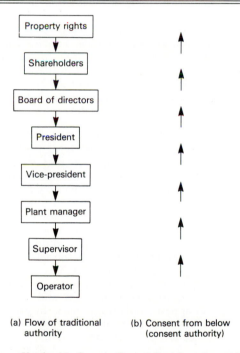

(a) Flow of traditional   (b) Consent from below
    authority   (consent authority)

Source: Adapted from Charles N. Greene, Everett E. Adam, Jr., and Ronald J. Ebert, *Management: For Effective Performance* (Englewood Cliffs, N.J.: Prentice-Hall, 1985), p. 362.

Staff units may be (a) advisory only, (b) primarily advisory, but with functional authority in their area of expertise, (c) required for consultation (e.g., legal), and (d) needed for selected line-staff approvals.

Organization structures should be supported with job descriptions for the manager of each organizational unit, as shown in Exhibit 1-8.

EXHIBIT 1-8

Job Description for a Production Control Manager

TITLE	Production Control Manager
REPORTS TO	Assistant Plant Manager
SPECIAL REQUIREMENTS	High school graduate, college degree preferred. Background in production classes, construction, machine capacities. Ability to understand specifications. Ability to coordinate and supervise.
SUPERVISORY RESPONSIBILITY	Assistant Production Control Manager, Production Control Supervisor, Production Control Schedulers, Clerks, Hourly Employees, and such other personnel as designed by Plant Manager.
JOB SUMMARY	Directs the activities of: scheduling plant production; procuring raw materials; and maintaining inventory for production and shipping.
DUTIES	Receive, review, enter and promise all orders. Schedule machinery, manpower and materials in such a way that the maximum amount of efficiency is obtained from the operating departments. Prepare production schedules in accordance with customer requirements and applicable specifications. Coordinate production control with technical and production operations and maintenance. Supervise procurement of raw materials and inventory control. Responsible for all production schedules including machine operation, overtime, vacation, etc. Prepare forthcoming schedules and advise Plant Manager, Production Manager, and Department Managers of these schedules. Supervise and coordinate packing, shipping, traffic, freight consolidation operations to ensure most economical freight rates and best delivery. Confer with sales offices. Follow up rush and delinquent orders. Confer with Plant Manager, Production Manager, and Plant Accountant in maintaining accurate backlogs by product class. Assist in operations report. Receive, review, and compile daily production reports of plant's progress per department. Perform special projects as required. Has authority to hire, fire, promote, demote, train, discipline and supervise employees under his or her jurisdiction. Responsible for plant safety, housekeeping, scrap and usage where applicable to his or her sphere of plant influence. Implement cost reduction and efficiency improvement programs. May be responsible for execution of Union agreement.

A well-defined organizational structure is important because it assigns authority and performance responsiblities in a systemic way.

The following factors influence organization structure.

INTERNAL FACTORS[10]

1   Conceptual view adopted—centralized decision making versus decentralized decision making with more delegation of authority
2   Span of control (the number of employees reporting to one supervisor)
3   Product diversity and kind of operation
4   Size of organization
5   Characteristics of the employees (professional, clerical, laborers)

EXTERNAL FACTORS[11]

6   Technology (how inputs are transferred to outputs)
7   Market characteristics (stability, scope, types of customers)
8   Environmental dependence (competition, legal constraints, regulatory, suppliers, and foreign effects)

Organization structure is fundamental to profit planning and control because both planning and control are directly related to the distribution of authority and responsibility throughout the enterprise. This distribution is typically formalized in the organization structure.

THE ESSENCE OF MANAGERIAL CONTROL   Control is the fifth, and last, function in the management process as shown in Exhibit 1-1. As with planning, controlling is performed continuously. Therefore, there are control processes that should always be operating in an enterprise. **Controlling** can be defined as a process of measuring and evaluating actual **performance** of each organizational component of an enterprise, and initiating **corrective action** when necessary to ensure efficient accomplishment of enterprise objectives, goals, policies, and standards. Planning establishes the objectives, goals, policies, and standards of an enterprise.

Control is exercised by using personal evaluation, periodic performance reports, and special reports. Another view identifies the types of control as follows:[12]

1.   Preliminary control   Used prior to action to ensure that
      (feed forward)   resources and personnel are prepared
                                   and ready to start activities.

[10]Adapted from Gary Dessler, *Human Behavior* (Reston, Va.: Reston Publishing, 1980), pp. 324–326.
[11]Adapted from Bedeian, *Management*, pp. 295-300.
[12]Adapted from Greene, Adam, and Ebert, *Managing for Effective Performance*, p. 522. Also see Thomas, *Readings in Cost Accounting, Budgeting and Control*, Reading No. 26, "Six Approaches to Preventive Management Control," by John C. Camillus, pp. 306–311.

2. Concurrent control
(usually periodic
performance reports)

Monitoring (by using personal observations and reports) of current activities
to ensure that goals are being met, and
policies and procedures are being
followed, during action.

3. Feedback control

Ex post action (preplanning) focusing
on past results to control future
activities.

A current control process, designed to help monitor the periodic activities
of a business and of each responsibility center (see Exhibit 1–6) has the following phases:

1   Compare actual performance for the period with the planned goals and standards.
2   Prepare a performance report that shows actual results, planned results, and any differ-
    ence between the two (i.e., variations above or below planned results).
3   Analyze the variations and the related operations to determine the underlying causes of
    the variations.
4   Develop alternative courses of action to correct any deficiencies and learn from the suc-
    cesses.
5   Make a choice (corrective action) from the set of alternatives and implement it.
6   Follow up to appraise the effectiveness of the correction; follow with feedforward for re-
    planning.

Subsequent chapters will illustrate the application of a control process in a
profit planning and control model.

Effective control requires **feedforward.** In other words, it is assumed that
objectives, plans, policies, and standards have been developed and communicated to those managers who have the related performance responsibilities.
Therefore, control must necessarily rest upon the concept of **feedback,** which
requires performance measurements and triggers corrective action designed to
ensure attainment of the objectives. When plans become operational, control
must be exercised to measure progress. In some cases, control also results in
the revision of prior plans and goals or in the formulation of new plans,
changes in operations, and reassignment of people. Control approaches must
be tailored to the characteristics of the operation and the organization structure.

An important aspect of control that is frequently overlooked is its relationship to the point of action. Control cannot be ex post facto; for example, an
expenditure already made or an inefficiency already committed cannot be un-
done. Therefore, effective control must be exercised at the point of action or at
the time of commitment. This concept implies that the manager responsible for
certain actions must engage in a form of prior control (ex ante); to do this, the
predetermined objectives, plans, policies, and standards must have been communicated to the manager and fully understood by the manager in advance.

With such information at hand, the manager is in a position to exercise control at the point of action. This fact emphasizes why the concept of feedforward is fundamental.

The comparison of actual results with planned goals and standards constitutes **measurement of the effectiveness of control** during a specified **past period.** This provides the basis for effective feedback. The facts shown in a performance report cannot be changed; however, the historical measurement may lead to improved control in the future. The significant concept here is that objectives, policies, and standards fulfill two basic requirements in the overall control process, namely: (1) feedforward—to provide a basis for control at the point of action, and (2) feedback—to provide a basis for measurement of the effectiveness of control after the action has taken place. Moreover, feedback is instrumental in replanning.

SOME BEHAVIORAL ASPECTS OF THE MANAGEMENT PROCESS   Behavior is the manner of conducting oneself. Top management must be concerned about the behavior at work of the other managers and employees. This means that managers often encounter behavior-modification problems. A broad perspective of some behavioral aspects of the management process is given in Exhibit 1-9. Management of the behavioral environment in an enterprise is both complex and subtle. All managers in an entity should be continually alert to the behavior at work of the employees under their supervision.[13] Behavioral management is complex and subtle because it must simultaneously deal with individuals, with groups, and with interpersonal relationships within groups.[14]

EXHIBIT 1-9

Some Behavioral Aspects of the Management Process

MANAGEMENT ACTIVITY	SOME CRITICAL BEHAVIORAL FACTORS
1. Planning (goals, standards, policies, etc.)	• Participation versus nonparticipation • Planning process • Communication of plans • Use of plans and standards
2. Organizing	• Organizational design • Delegation of authority and responsibilities (do they match?) • Job specifications • Line and staff conflicts

[13]This entire section was adapted from Gary Dessler, *Improving Performance at Work* (Reston, Va.: Reston Publishing, 1983). This is an excellent and practical book and we highly recommend it for further study of this important management topic. For a more academic approach to the subject, refer to Dessler's other book, *Human Behavior.*

[14]Also see Thomas, *Readings in Cost Accounting, Budgeting and Control,* Reading No. 7, "Behavioral Assumptions of Management Accounting," by Edwin H. Caplin, pp. 95–115.

3. Staffing
- Employment process
- Pay scales/incentives
- Evaluation of performance
- Job enrichment/career opportunities
- Future expectations of employees

4. Leadership (actuating)
- Style of leadership
- Attitude toward employees

5. Controlling (including performance evaluation)
- Method of setting goals and performance standards
- Meaning of goals and standards
- Method of measuring performance
- Methods of reporting and appraising performance
- Corrective action
- Rewards and punishment
- Follow-up activities
- Risk attitudes of managers
- Evaluation based on controllable performance
- Achieving goal congruence
- Provision of incentives

Schools of Thought about Behavioral Management

Historically, various schools of management thought have evolved as follows:

	SCHOOL AND PROPONENTS	APPROXIMATE TIMING	PRIMARY THRUSTS
1.	Classical (Taylor and Fayol)	Late 1800s	• Emphasis on technical efficiency • Workers treated as "givens" • Authority, top down; no participation
2.	Behavioral (Mayo, Roethlisberger, McGregor, Argyris)	1920s to 1950s	• Recognition of needs, wants, and desires of workers • Analysis of human behavior at work • Motivation of Theory X people to high performance by a favorable work situation, rather than only by financial rewards • Participation and reasonable autonomy
3.	Contingency (numerous proponents)	1950s to date	• Synthesis of the essential thrusts of the classical and behavioral schools—efficiency and behavioral • Recognition of increasingly complex management decisions

			• Recognition of contingency or situational view of organizations; management should take into account the kind of environment and tasks in the organization
			• Participation and lines of authority; line-staff distinctions
4.	Agency[15] (Jensen, Meckling, Ross, Holmstrom)	1975 to date	• An economist's view of an organization
			• Organization is viewed as a nexus of contracts among owners, managers, employees, suppliers, etc.
			• All parties are assumed to act rationally to maximize their own self-interest, as measured in economic terms
			• Different individuals have different information sets. Private information is used by its holder for economic gain
			• Emphasis on the construction of optimal contracts among all parties to (a) provide incentives for individuals to strive for organizational goals and (b) optimally share risk

Behavior Management Programs

Increasing recognition of the impact on productivity of behavioral motivation has resulted in **behavior management** (or **modification**) **programs.** Behavior management is a productivity-boosting technique that is intended to provide positive motivation through the use of rewards and punishment. **Behavior management** (also called **behavior modification, positive reinforcement,** or **conditioning**) is based on the idea that (1) behavior leading to a positive consequence (reward) tends to be repeated, while behavior that leads to a negative consequence (punishment) tends not to be repeated, and that (2) by providing the right rewards, one can change a person's behavior. Behavior management focuses exclusively on two things: on the worker's behavior and on the consequences of that behavior.

An assumption of behavior management is that actual behavior is more important than its psychological "cause" such as morale, personality, or needs. For example, if you tell a behavior management expert or behaviorist that one

---

[15]Michael C. Jensen and William H. Meckling, "Theory of the Firm: Managerial Behavior, Agency Costs and Ownership Structure," *Journal of Financial Economics* (**3**, 1976), pp. 305–60; Eugene Fama, "Agency Problems and the Theory of the Firm," *Journal of Political Economy* April 1980, pp. 288–307; Stephen Ross, "The Economic Theory of Agency: The Principal's Problem," *American Economic Review*, May, 1973, pp. 134–139; Bengt Holmstrom, "Moral Hazard and Observability," *Bell Journal of Economics*, Spring, 1979, pp. 74–91; and Stanley Baiman, "Agency Research in Managerial Accounting: A Survey," *Journal of Accounting Literature* (**1**, 1982), pp. 154–210.

of your salespeople has "too aggressive" a personality, he or she would probably respond by asking what specific behavior led you to believe this to be so. You respond by saying that the person calls prospective clients four or five times a day, often bothers them at home, and puts his feet on his desk when a client is in his office. To the behaviorist, these specific behaviors (calling clients at home and so on) are the sort of things that can and should be modified through behavior management. In contrast, some psychologists might instead try to change the salesman's personality on the assumption that making the person "less aggressive" would result in acceptable behavior. Similarly, if you tell a behaviorist that you want to improve the morale of your employees, the response would probably be, "Tell me what specific behaviors (like too many absences or poor-quality output) you have observed that lead you to believe you have a morale problem?" The behaviorist would then focus on changing those behaviors (through reward or punishment) rather than on boosting morale.[16]

Dessler emphasizes that behavior can be effectively changed only by changing the **consequences** of the behavior. Behavior management focuses on positive consequences called **reinforcements** (i.e., performance rewards such as praise, job enrichment, feelings of achievement, and bonuses), rather than negative consequences (i.e., punishment such as reprimands, demotions, firings, and salary cuts). However, there are times when punishment is needed to reduce **undesirable** behavior. Punishment must be (a) used carefully, (b) consistently applied, (c) administered to minimize attention by peers, (d) specifically related to a particular behavior, and (e) explained by talking about job behavior, not about people.

The steps involved in a behavior management program are shown in Exhibit 1-10.

Managing Behavior Through Economic Incentives

The economist's or agency theorist's view of behavioral management emphasizes the specification of a contract between the organization and the employee. This contract consists of the employee's explicit wage, salary, or bonus and also includes implicit characteristics such as promotions or job recognition. In specifying such a contract, the employee's attitudes toward money, work, and risk must be considered. The overall objective is to specify a contract with the employee so that the employee will expend maximal effort toward achieving organizational goals while at the same time the risks that the organization faces are collectively borne by all the organization's employees. This concept of risk sharing is important, since any organization operates in a world of uncertainty. Just as insurance companies allow risks to be shared among the policyholders through the collection of premiums and payment of claims, organizational contracts effectively allow employees to share the risks faced by their organization.

[16]Dessler, *Improving Performance at Work*, pp. 2–3.

EXHIBIT 1-10

Steps in a Behavior Management Program

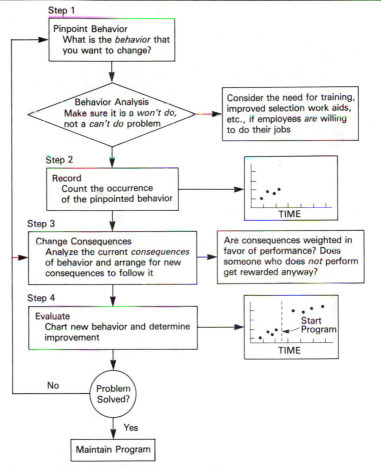

Source: Gary Dessler, *Improving Productivity at Work* (Reston, Va.: Reston Publishing, 1983), p. 10.

CHAPTER SUMMARY

1. The chapter started by defining
   a. Management as the process of defining entity goals and implementing activities to attain those goals
   b. The management process as a set of independent activities used by management to perform the five functions of management-planning, organizing, staffing, directing, and controlling
2. The essence of management includes (a) establishing enterprise objectives, (b) developing premises about the environment, (c) making decisions on courses of action, (d) initiating actions that translate plans into results, and (e) currently replanning to correct observed deficiencies.

3. Organizing involves (a) subdivision of an organization into management work units, (b) delegation of managerial responsibilities, and (c) determination of the locus of decisions.

4. Control is a process of measuring and evaluating actual performance and initiating corrective action. Planning and organizing establish the goals and standards with which control is implemented. Basically, control measures performance by comparing actual results with planned results and measuring variances above or below the plans.

5. Some behavioral aspects of the management process were discussed. The discussion emphasized positive and negative consequences with an emphasis on rewards versus punishment to change behavior. Behavior management programs, designed to increase productivity through rewards, were described. The economic or agency theory of organizations also was discussed. In this theory, the organization is veiwed as a nexus of contracts. Employees are motivated toward organizational goals through explicit and implicit contracts.

6. The chapter emphasized those activities in the management process that were most directly supportive of profit planning and control models.[17]

Comprehensive Demonstration Case

 *SUPERIOR COMPU-SERVICE*

After ten and one-half successful years of servicing computer equipment for an employer, H. T. Sparks started Superior Compu-Service on January 2, 19A. Sparks said that he "wanted to own a business that would keep up with advancing technology, be the boss, and get the profits." Superior Compu-Service would repair and service all kinds of personal computers and related hardware.

It is now December 31, 19C, and Sparks has decided to add electric typewriter and photocopier service to his business. Sparks has had no training or experience in management planning and control, nor is he familiar with accounting. A person was hired by the company during 19B to "take care of all clerical details, including bookkeeping." The company was moderately successful during the three years 19A–19C.

To finance expansion of current services and to add the new services, Sparks asked a local bank for a $300,000, three-year loan. To support the loan application, the bank loan officer asked Sparks to provide the following information:

1 A list and valuation of his personal assets and liabilities.

2 A summary of the company's 19A, 19B, and 19C income statement, balance sheet, and cash flow statement. The loan officer said that it might be necessary to have the 19C statement audited.

---

[17]A rich source for special study and a comprehensive bibliography is given in Robert S. Kaplan, *The Case for Case Studies in Management Accounting Research* (Boston: Harvard Business School, Working Paper, 9–785–001).

3 Information about his plans for organizing, staffing, and controlling the expanded company.

4 A two-year projection of revenues, profits, and cash flows.

Sparks will see the loan officer in about two weeks to discuss the information requested, and he hopes to get the loan approved. (Note: the local bank now has a number of "nonperforming" loans but does have money to lend.)

For the first time, Sparks has started thinking seriously about planning and control. After a get-acquainted meeting with a local consultant, Sparks has prepared the following information for the loan officer:

(1) Financial data about the business:

YEAR	ASSETS	DEBTS	NET WORTH	SERVICE REVENUE AMOUNT	SERVICE REVENUE INCREASE	PROFIT	ENDING CASH BALANCE
19A	$120,000	$20,000	$100,000	$ 90,000		$ 2,000	$ 6,000
19B	130,000	28,000	102,000	140,000	56%	7,000	12,000
19C	133,000	30,000	103,000	160,000	14%	10,000	20,000

(2) Personal assets not included above:

Residence, furniture, cars	$225,000
Savings	20,000
Debt	(80,000)
Total	$165,000

(3) Organizing, staffing, and control:

President—Sparks
Office manager (2 employees)—Davis (supervisor)
Computer repair manager (5 employees)—Olds (supervisor)
Buyer and stocking, parts (2 employees)—Bye (supervisor)
Planned:
  Typewriter and photocopier repair (4 employees)—Newton (supervisor)
  Promotion of new business (1 employee)

(4) Projected:

	COMPUTERS*		TYPEWRITERS AND COPIERS*		TOTAL
19D:					
Services	(+20%)	$192,000	(start)	$30,000	$222,000
Profit	(20%)	38,000	(3%)	1,000	39,000
Ending cash balance	(7%)	13,000	(7%)	2,000	15,000
19E:					
Services	(+30%)	$250,000	(+50%)	$45,000	$295,000
Profit	(20%)	50,000	(7%)	3,000	53,000
Ending cash balance	(7%)	18,000	(7%)	3,000	21,000

*Percentages based on service revenue.

Prologue

The purpose of this case is not to criticize Sparks, nor is it to decide the next step. The loan officer has deferred the loan decision and has not seen the above data. We will visit Sparks in some later chapters. The purpose of this case is to suggest a typical situation where the need for profit planning and control relates to the discussion in this chapter.

The following comments are appropriate now:

1   The use of percentages based on service revenue provides very rough projections.
2   The projected results are apt to be overly optimistic.
3   The effects of the loan, should it be approved, are not included in the data. Also, there is no information about how expenses were assigned in each line of service.
4   An organization chart may be useful.
5   A properly developed business plan would be a positive factor in the loan decision.
6   A profit planning and control program would be useful even in this small business.

Suggested References

BEDEIAN, ARTHUR G., *Management*, Chaps. 1, 2, 11, and 12. New York: Dryden Press, 1985.

DESSLER, GARY, *Improving Performance at Work*. Reston, Va.: Reston Publishing, 1983. Also a textbook by the same author and publisher, *Human Behavior*, 1980.

DONNELLY, JAMES H., JR., JAMES L. GIBSON, AND JOHN M. IVANCEVICH, *Fundamentals of Management*, 6th ed. Plano, Tex.: Business Publications, 1987.

GREENE, CHARLES N., EVERETT E. ADAM, JR., AND RONALD J. EBERT, *Management: For Effective Performance*, Chaps. 1, 2, and 11. Englewood Cliffs, N.J.: Prentice-Hall, 1985.

HALLOREN, JACK, *Applied Human Relations, An Organizational Approach*, 2nd ed. Englewood Cliffs, N.J.: Prentice-Hall, 1983.

WEBBER, ROSS A., MARILYN A. MORGAN, AND PAUL C. BROWNE, *Management*, 3rd ed. Englewood Cliffs, N.J.: Prentice-Hall, 1985.

Discussion Questions

1. Give the key elements in the definition of comprehensive profit planning and control.
2. What are the two primary goal orientations of a business?
3. List and briefly define the five functions of management.

4. Define decision making and list the eight steps in the decision-making process.

5. There are two opposites in respect to a conceptual view of the real role of management; these two extremes have been labeled market theory and planning and control theory. Explain the nature of these two opposing philosophies and indicate their significance.

6. Distinguish between controllable and noncontrollable variables.

7. Distinguish between strategic and tactical planning.

8. Define **organizing.**

9. Distinguish between line and staff authority and functions. How would a "director of planning" and a "VP of marketing" usually be classified?

10. What is a job description? How does it relate to organizing?

11. Explain the difference between three types of control: (a) preliminary, (b) concurrent, and (c) feedback.

12. Define behavior. Give five situations in which management is often faced with a behavior modification problem.

13. What are the primary thrusts of the following schools of thought about behavioral management—classical, behavioral, and contingency?

14. What is meant by a "Behavioral Management Program"? List the usual four steps in such a program.

CASE 1-1   *Decision maker for sale; call 711-1313*

Assume the following advertisement appeared in the Local Daily News:

FOR SALE OR RENT
DECISION-MAKING PERSONAL COMPUTER
Guarantees Good Decisions of All Kinds
Saves Your Time; No Worries;
Easy to Operate; No Hassles;
Scientific Method; No Errors;
GOOD TERMS—LOW PRICE
Call 711-1313

REQUIRED

1. How would you react to this ad?
2. Identify, discuss, and evaluate its implications for a business.

CASE 1-2   *Big GM—organization structure*

General Motors, one of the largest corporations in the United States, prepares an overall organization chart to show its basic organization structure (excluding subsidiaries) by product lines, by functions, and by territory (simplified for case purposes). GM manufactures and sells five product lines: Buick, Cadillac, Chevrolet, Pontiac, and Saturn. Typically, each product line has three major departments called Production, Distribution, and Finance. Territorial distribution regions for each function are Northern, Southern, Western, and Eastern.

REQUIRED

1. Draw an overall organization chart to show line authority and responsibilities. Start with stockholders.
2. List five more-detailed organization charts that GM may use to provide more-detailed structural relationships.
3. Explain how organization structure relates to (a) planning and (b) control.

CASE 1-3   *Four processes; interrelationships*

Chapter 1 discussed four different, but interrelated, processes as follows:

A. Functions in the Management Process:
   1.
   2.
   3.
   4.
   5.
B. Steps in the Decision-Making Process:
   1.
   2.
   3.
   4.
   5.
   6.
   7.
   8.

C. Phases in the Planning Process:
   1.
   2.
   3.
   4.
   5.
D. Phases in the Control Process:
   1.
   2.
   3.
   4.
   5.
   6.

REQUIREMENT 1

Complete the above outline by entering the functions, steps, and phases for each process. Following each one, add a few key words or phrases to provide a basis for elaboration. You may relate your discussion to a specific organization, such as a bank, an insurance company, a television manufacturer, a university, or a hospital.

REQUIREMENT 2

Be prepared to give a ten-minute oral presentation about any one of the processes. Also, be prepared to respond to relevant questions from your audience.

REQUIREMENT 3

Show the interrelationships among the four processes—management, decision making, planning, and control.

CASE 1-4   *Organizational conflict—a decision must be made*

Given below is a recently prepared summary organization chart for Ralston Company, Inc., a manufacturer of component parts for various computers. The company has been having product-quality problems evidenced by what the president believes is a very high and costly rejection rate at final inspection. The final inspections are made at the end of the production line by outside inspectors employed by the computer companies (customers).

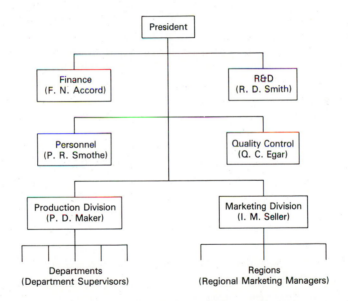

The outside inspectors have full authority to reject components. Rejected components are discarded because the customers will not accept "repaired units." Because of the increasing number of rejections, the Quality Control (QC) Group was expanded six months earlier to include three "Quality Control On-Line Inspectors." These employees spend most of their time inspecting along the production lines in the five production departments. They were told that they were responsible for seeing that defects are discovered when they occur (rather than at the end of the line by the outside inspectors).

This case focuses on one of the QC On-Line Inspectors, O. L. Reedy. Q. C. Egar has asked Reedy to come to his office for a conference. Here is the conversation:

EGAR: Reedy, the production manager, Maker, just called and asked me to straighten you out. He said that you are giving his department supervisors all kinds of trouble.

REEDY: What is his specific complaint?

EGAR: Well, mainly he said that you are giving his people orders and that you are slowing down the line by meddling too much. He said that he has told his people not to take any orders from you and for them to keep the line moving at the prescribed rate.

REEDY: Maker has never talked to me since the day I introduced myself, about six months ago, as an on-line inspector. He seems to avoid me intentionally.

EGAR: OK. Now tell me how you carry out your duties on a typical day.

REEDY: Well, first I lay on your desk a report of my inspections for the day before. I am careful to pinpoint things that might cause outside rejects. As I have written in numerous daily reports, many of the employees on the line are uninterested and careless about quality. All they want to do is put it through fast to meet their schedule and still have some loafing time during the day. They pay no attention to me when I notice poor quality, and they are very adept at covering up their defects. I have told the worst ones that it must be quality or else! Let's see. Next I make my plans for the day—what I will do "on the line." I usually return here to my desk around four o'clock.

EGAR: Well, that sounds OK. What do you think I should say to this big shot, Maker?

REEDY: I'm not sure about him, but we must find some way to spot quality mistakes when they first occur on the line. There is no point to completing a component that is already destined to be a reject.

EGAR: OK. I will think about it and call a meeting of all of the on-line inspectors. In the meantime, don't rock the boat.

REQUIRED

1. Should Egar have disciplined Reedy? Why?
2. Analyze the situation and identify the specific problem.
3. List some alternatives that should be considered to resolve the specific problem.
4. How should the alternatives be analyzed and evaluated?
5. Which alternative should be selected? Support your decision.
6. Give some guidelines for implementation.

CASE 1-5   *I'm sorry—OK?*

Jack Bigman is the supervisor of Food and Beverage Services at the South Florida Lodge. Bigman is concerned about worker Joe Little's performance on the job. The daily performance reports and Bigman's observations resulted in a conference with Joe. Essentially the supervisor said, "Joe, the system says that I have to talk to you about your job performance. It has never been very good, and it is not improving a bit. I think you can improve if you work hard and get the right attitude. Up front, I will say that I am going to discipline you, and this conference is first with a verbal warning that you are lazy, you waste time, and you have a poor attitude. If you do not improve soon, I will have to fire you. I'm sorry—OK?"

Joe: "OK."

REQUIRED

1. What did the supervisor do that was good or bad in terms of behavioral management?
2. Suggest ways in which the supervisor could have been more effective.

CASE 1-6   *Job enrichment, enriched!*

Southwest Airlines, Inc., is starting a job enrichment program to cultivate positive motivation among its employees. The consultant reminded the company president that a big, time-consuming, and costly program was not needed. "Instead," he said, "there are many ways to positively motivate your individual managers at all levels. For example, if a vice-president takes a supervisor to staff meetings from time to time, the supervisor will feel that the job has been enriched significantly."

The VP of finance and accounting, V. P. Bright, asked the accounting manager, A. M. Brown, to accompany him to the next VP staff meeting. Brown was inwardly very pleased because his job had suddenly become more interesting and challenging. After the meeting, he told the VP how much he appreciated the opportunity to attend and that he had derived some new perspectives from it. Bright responded, "We will do it often."

REQUIRED

Assume that Brown continued to attend the meetings of the VPs. In respect to the meetings, and aside from any monetary reward or promotion, what can Bright do to further enrich Brown's job? Be specific.

The Fundamentals
of Profit Planning
2 and Control

INTRODUCTION AND PURPOSE   Chapter 1 defined and discussed the management process—planning, organizing, staffing, leading, and controlling—as the basic foundation for comprehensive profit planning and control (abbreviated PPC for convenience). The emphasis in Chapter 1 was on management planning, organizing, and controlling because these are the management functions in which PPC is primarily applicable. To build upon Chapter 1, the purposes of this chapter are (a) to introduce the fundamentals of a comprehensive PPC program, (b) to explain the primary application features of PPC, and (c) to discuss the main advantages and some application problems of PPC.

OVERVIEW OF PPC   Comprehensive profit planning and control, as used in this book, is viewed as a process designed to help management effectively perform significant phases of the planning and control functions. The PPC model involves (1) development and application of broad and long-range objectives of the enterprise; (2) specification of enterprise goals; (3) development of a strategic long-range profit plan in broad terms; (4) specification of a tactical short-range profit plan detailed by assigned responsibilities (divisions, departments, projects); (5) establishment of a system of periodic performance reports detailed by assigned responsibilities; and (6) development of follow-up procedures.

Throughout this book, we use a **comprehensive** view of PPC (also called budgeting) rather than the narrow, traditional view of a budget as a clerically derived set of quantitative schedules prepared by an accountant, following the stereotyped reporting formats used in external financial statements. In past years, there has also been a tendency to view the budget primarily as a mathematical model for an organization developed by computer programmers. These views completely overlook the three most relevant aspects of the PPC concept:

(a) PPC requires major planning decisions by management, (b) PPC entails pervasive management control activities, and (c) PPC recognizes many of the critical behavioral implications throughout the organization. Viewed comprehensively, PPC is one of the more important approaches that has been developed to facilitate effective performance of the management process. The concepts and techniques of profit planning and control, as discussed in this book, have wide application in individual business enterprises, governmental units, charitable organizations, and virtually all group endeavors.

In modern-day businesses except in very small companies, it is virtually impossible for the top manager to have firsthand knowledge of all the relevant factors operating throughout a business. Nor can a single lower-level manager be expected to have the range of knowledge, experience, and competence to make all the decisions for the large segments of a company, either as a source of reliable information or as a participant in decision making. The quality of the judgments of the total management effort will continue to distinguish the better-managed and more successful companies. It is unlikely that clerical techniques, mathematical models, and simulations will substitute in major respects for managerial judgment in complex endeavors. These important tools, on the other hand, can be used to increase significantly the effectiveness of a management and to place managerial judgments on a more objective and informed foundation.

FUNDAMENTAL CONCEPTS OF PROFIT PLANNING AND CONTROL   The fundamental concepts of PPC include the underlying activities or tasks that must generally be carried out to attain maximum usefulness from PPC. These fundamentals have never been fully codified. As a basis for discussion, an outline of the fundamental concepts usually identified with PPC is given in Exhibit 2-1. Notice that this list does not include the mechanics of PPC. The mechanics of PPC involve such activities as the design of budget schedules, routine and repetitive computations, and clerical activities related to a PPC program.

Next, we discuss the application of a PPC program to the managerial planning and control functions, with special emphasis on the fundamentals listed in Exhibit 2-1.

EXHIBIT 2-1
An Outline of the Fundamental Concepts of Profit Planning and Control

---

1   A **management process** that includes planning, organizing, staffing, leading, and controlling (as shown in Exhibit 1-1)

2   A **managerial commitment** to effective management participation by all levels in the entity

3   An **organization structure** that clearly specifies assignments of management authority and responsibility at all organization levels

4   A management **planning process** consistent with the discussion in Chapter 1 (pages 3–7)

5 A management **control process** consistent with the discussion in Chapter 1 (pages 15–16)

6 A continuous and consistent **coordination** of all the management functions

7 Continuous feedforward, feedback, follow-up, and replanning through defined **communication channels** (both downward and upward)

8 A **strategic** (long-range) profit plan

9 A **tactical** (short-range) profit plan

10 A **responsibility accounting** system

11 A continuous use of the **exception principle**

12 A **behavioral** management program

MANAGEMENT PLANNING USING PPC

The fundamental purpose of management planning is to provide a **feedforward process** for operations and for control.[1] The concept of feedforward is to give each manager guidelines for making operational decisions on a day-to-day basis. The approved plans constitute the primary element of feedforward.

Planning is generally recognized as the most difficult task facing the manager, and it is one that is very easy to procrastinate. **Feedback** is also an important ingredient of both replanning and control. The characteristics of the seventh fundamental listed above—continuous feedforward and feedback—are shown in Exhibit 2-2.

Planning rests upon the view that the future success of an entity can be enhanced by continuous management action. It presupposes that an entity will be more successful, in terms of its broad objectives, with management actions to implement the **feedforward process** than it can if there is no activation by the management.[2]

Ackoff suggest that the management of an entity, during the early-stage planning process, should develop three different types of "projections" as follows:

1 A reference projection (the static case)—this involves an attempt to specify what the future state of the entity would be if nothing new were done; that is, if there were no planned intervention by the management.

2 A wishful projection (the highly optimistic case)—this involves a specification of "hopes and dreams" as to the future state of the entity; that is, essential fulfillment of all of the aspirations of the entity.

3 A planned projection (the most likely case)—this involves a specification of how closely the entity can attain the wishful projection realistically. The planned projection tends to be a realistic compromise between the reference and wishful projections. The planned projection specifies the planned objectives and goals (for example, the future state) to be attained during the time covered by the planning process.

---

[1]Ross A. Webber, Marilyn A. Morgan, and Paul C. Browne, *Management, Basic Elements of Managing Organizations*, 3rd ed. (Homewood, Ill.: Richard D. Irwin, 1985). Chapters 12 and 13 give an excellent discussion of planning.

[2]William E. Thomas, ed., *Readings in Cost Accounting, Budgeting, and Control*, 6th ed. (Cincinnati: South-Western Publishing, 1983), Reading No. 21, "Managing Through Feedforward Control," by Harold Koontz and Robert W. Bradspies, p. 249.

EXHIBIT 2-2

Feedforward, Feedback, and Replanning

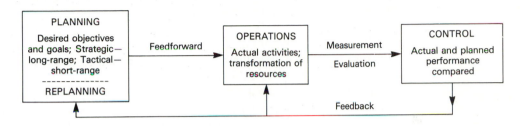

Some companies use a fourth type of projection, sometimes referred to as a "stretch projection." A stretch projection or budget is one that is attainable but will really push people and facilities to the limit. The essence of a stretch budget is, "What can the company achieve if it pulls out all the stops and maximizes attainable performance?"

The primary value in considering these different projections is to avoid including the elements of each as a mixture in the planned projection. Therefore, planning should start with a reference projection, coupled with a wishful projection, and conclude with a planning projection that represents a realistic management plan expressed in words and numbers.

Management planning is a continuous process because a planned projection can never be considered as the final and ultimate product. It must be revised as conditions change and new information becomes available.

From another viewpoint, management planning may be approached with complete informality at one extreme, or with complete formality at the other extreme. **Formality** means the extent to which (1) the planning process is structured (or systematized), and (2) the planning decisions are expressed in the form of written plans and standardized financial results (as in a budget). Numerous studies have shown that the better-managed companies strike a reasonable balance on this point, with a strong tendency toward a systematic approach to planning and expression of the results in a comprehensive profit plan and related documents. However, it is important to understand the hazards of overformalization.

Planning decisions are interdependent and must be partitioned in conformity with the operational or organizational subdivisions of the entity. Therefore, planning follows the lines of authority and responsibility in the enterprise. This subdivision means that there is a subset of planning decisions (and a consequent plan) for each manager in the entity (i.e., for each area of responsibility) from the highest to the lowest management levels. It makes possible effective and integrated application of the feedforward concept.

Each facet of planning must encompass an evaluation, or reevaluation, of the relevant variables (both the controllable and noncontrollable variables, as shown in Exhibit 1-5) because they will have significant impacts on the planning of realistic objectives and goals. The development of **enterprise objectives** is the most fundamental level of decision making in the planning process. Objectives state the desired broad, long-range future state of the enterprise. For example, the objectives for a manufacturing company should relate to such basic issues as breadth of product lines, quality of product, growth expectations, responsibilities to the owners, economic expectations, employee relationships and attitudes, and social responsibilities. Objectives express the desired future state and the end results of entity activities.

The next planning level is known as **goals,** which represent the broad objectives brought into sharper focus by explicitly specifying (a) time dimensions for attainment, (b) quantitative measurements, and (c) subdivision of responsibilities. For example, goals would explicitly state such items as the following: Three years from now the new product being developed with be introduced; the return-on-investment goal for next year will be 15 percent; and the profit goal for product A is 5 percent of sales for next year (i.e., the budget now being developed).

To establish the foundation for attainment of enterprise objectives and specific goals, management must develop **strategies** to be pursued by the entity. Strategies specify the "how"; they detail the plan of attack to be used in pursuing the goals operationally. For example, the strategies for a company may include expanding the current sales territory, reducing the selling price to attract higher volume, increasing the advertising, and financing the expansion with debt rather than equity.

Finally, the most detailed level of planning occurs when management **operationalizes** the objectives, goals, and strategies already established by incorporating them into the **profit plan.** A profit plan is a financial and narrative expression of the expected results from the planning decisions. It is called the profit plan (or the budget) because it explicitly states the goals in terms of time expectations and expected financial results (return on investment, profit, cost) for each major segment of the entity. Typical profit plans establish the content and format of the **internal-control reports** with respect to operations, inputs, outputs, and financial position developed by the entity for monthly performance reporting to the various levels of management.

Two concurrent profit plans typically are developed: one strategic (long-range) and one tactical (short-range). The **strategic profit plan** is broad, and it usually encompasses three or more years in the future. The **tactical profit plan** is detailed and encompasses a one-year time horizon—the upcoming year. These and some related concepts are summarized in Exhibit 2-3.

The development of strategic and tactical profit plans each year (Exhibit 2-3) is a process that involves managerial decisions and, ideally, a high level of managerial participation. One common scenario is depicted in Exhibit 2-4.

The planning function should vary in scope and intensity with the level of management. Top management has a much broader planning responsibility than lower management, and yet each level of management should have definite planning responsibilities. In contrast, control activities are more pervasive at the lower-management levels. A generalized expression of the relation-

EXHIBIT 2-3

Planning Relationships: Objectives, Goals, and Profit Plans

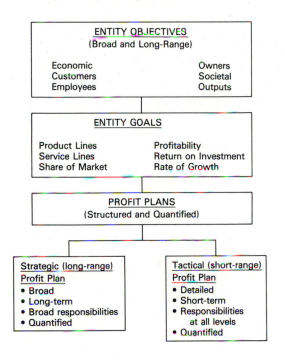

EXHIBIT 2-4

Developing Profit Plans

ACTIVITY	INFORMATION FLOW	APPROVAL SEQUENCE	PRIMARY PARTICIPANT
Entity Objectives	↓	↑	Board of Directors, Chief Executive Officer
Entity Goals, Planning Premises, and Strategies	↓	↑	Top-Management Group
Strategic (long-range) Profit Plan	↓	↑	Middle Managers
Tactical (short-range) Profit Plan	↓	↑	Operating Managers

ship between planning and control responsibilities related to the structural position of individual managers is shown in Exhibit 2-5.[3]

[3]Charles N. Greene, Everett E. Adam, Jr., and Ronald J. Ebert, *Management: For Effective Performance* (Englewood Cliffs, N.J.: Prentice-Hall, 1985), Chaps. 16 and 17.

EXHIBIT 2-5
Managerial Time Devoted to Planning Versus Control

Position	Proportion of Time Spent on
Chairman of the Board President Executive Vice-President Vice-President Division Head Department Head Assistant Department Head Supervisor Foreman Assistant Foreman Worker	The Planning Function The Control Function

TIME DIMENSIONS IN PPC   Whether an individual or an entity is idle or busy, time passes at the same rate. We seldom, if ever, have time to do all the things that we would like to do, nor do we have time to do many things as well as we would like. This is the plight of all managers. As a result, the planning function often suffers. Two important timing issues require careful attention if the planning function is to be carried out effectively. One relates to the concept of a planning horizon, and the other relates to the timing of planning activities. We will consider each briefly.

Planning horizon refers to the period of time into the future for which management should plan. In practically all situations, a need exists for a number of different planning horizons. The continuum of managerial decisions constitutes the totality of managerial planning. Each planning decision reflects a plan about future events, and the aggregate of all decisions constitutes the overall policies and plans of the organization. Decisions can affect only the future—the next minute, day, month, year, or series of years. No present decision can affect or change the past. Enterprise history cannot be changed, although it may be incorrectly recorded, reported, and interpreted. Because all managerial decisions are futuristic, each management is faced with the basic question of a **time dimension** in planning and decision making. The question is, How far into the future should the plans extend? This problem is complex because the time dimension is unique to the type of decision being made. For example, a sales manager, because of procrastination, may decide upon a basic promotional strategy on a last-minute basis, just in time to meet a particular publication deadline. Alternatively, a sophisticated sales manager will anticipate the major promotional decisions far enough in advance to permit adequate consideration and consultation with others prior to the commitment deadline. These simple examples demonstrate the need for an integrated and systematic approach to resolving the time dimension in planning and decision making. Without exception, major decisions made on a last-minute basis suffer from a lack of adequate supporting studies, analysis, evaluation, and consultation. Profit planning and control have evolved as a systematic approach to re-

EXHIBIT 2-6

Timing Dimensions in Profit Planning and Control

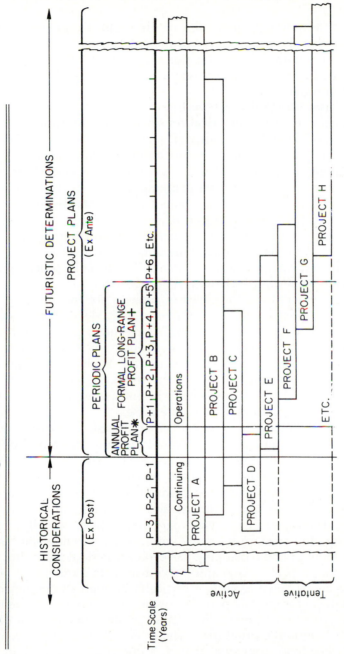

*Tactical plan.
†Strategic plan.

solve many aspects of the time dimension in planning and controlling operations.

Effective implementation of the profit planning and control concept requires that the management of the enterprise establish a definite time dimension for certain types of decisions. Exhibit 2-6 shows the time dimensions established by a well-known company for its comprehensive profit planning and control program.

Time-dimension perspectives in managerial planning require a clear-cut distinction between **historical** considerations and **future** considerations. Historical decisions and the results of operations in the past often constitute, in effect, the launching platform for future determinations. In this regard, Exhibit 2-6 shows a fundamental distinction between **project plans** and **periodic plans.** Classification of managerial planning into these two categories focuses on the need to make decisions and plans far ahead of activities.

Another time dimension relates to project planning. A continuing necessity exists for management to plan specific and identifiable projects (programs), each of which has a unique time dimension, because such projects entail commitments over variable time spans. The focus in **project planning** is on each separate project, which may represent either an operational or a nonoperational commitment. Examples of projects are the contemplated addition of a new machine, construction of a new plant, development and testing of a new product line, acquisition of another business, phasing out a current product, expansion of marketing to another geographical area, a research and development thrust, and a government contract. Such activities and programs should be planned over their life spans and should be viewed as special commitments. However, they must necessarily be integrated with the other activities, programs, and operations of the enterprise.

Periodic planning is the environmental necessity for management to plan, evaluate, and control operations within relatively short and consistent interim periods of time, such as one year. **Periodic plans** reflect calendar constraints that have been imposed by custom. Specifically, managers, owners, and other interested parties demand timetables; the result is **periodic** profit plans and performance reports and evaluations of the progress of an enterprise. Therefore, plans and progress reports are usually prepared by month, quarter, and year. In harmony with these environmental time constraints, the concept of periodic planning has evolved. Periodic planning represents a focus by time on profit plans and performance. In Exhibit 2-6, notice that periodic plans are depicted as cutting **vertically** through all the projects and continuing operations for specific periods of time. Also, notice that periodic plans encompass two subcategories—the **tactical** or **short-range profit plan** and the **strategic** or **long-range profit plan.** The exhibit shows what is commonly referred to as a "one-five" approach, that is, a one-year tactical (short-range) profit plan and a five-year strategic (long-range) profit plan. This arrangement is commonly used in industry today, although "one-three," "one-four," and "one-ten" arrangements are also used.

The concept of comprehensive profit planning and control encompasses a systematic and integrated approach to project planning, to tactical planning, and to strategic planning. Exhibit 2-6 shows one suggested time dimension; many variations are found in enterprises of various types. The time dimensions should be unique to the enterprise and should be designed to fit its particular needs and characteristics. Every management should develop a similar time-dimension chart for decision-making and planning purposes. Articulation and communication of the timing of profit planning and control activities in a form similar to Exhibit 2-6 is effective in most situations. A similar time-dimension chart, if viewed as a matter of basic policy, forces early consideration of major decisions and timely planning. This latter point is relevant because planning is generally recognized as the function on which management tends to procrastinate; it is so easy to "put off planning." In subsequent chapters of this book, application of these time-dimension concepts in profit planning and control will be illustrated and discussed in depth.

The Planning Calendar

Timing of planning activities suggests that there should be a definite management time schedule established for initiating and completing certain phases of the planning process. Managerial planning should be viewed as a continuous process at all levels of management. In day-to-day decision making, as well as in long-range matters, all levels of management must be continually reassessing the future, replanning, and revising prior plans in the decision-making process. However, certain aspects of planning are best accomplished in a formal way and on a definite time schedule. For example, Exhibit 2-6 depicts a "one-five plan" that requires the development of annual short- and long-range profit plans. This chart suggests that there should be a schedule of planning activities as a matter of management policy, frequently referred to as the **planning calendar** or **planning cycle.** Once management commits itself in this manner, procrastination in planning usually ends. Successful managers report that the absence of procrastination is an important benefit from a comprehensive profit planning and control program. In organizations where it was previously almost impossible to assemble management groups intact for planning sessions, it was found that after the adoption of a planning calendar, the planning sessions were usually given top priority. In many companies, executives will not make outside commitments during the critical phases of formal profit planning. Many companies that plan effectively report that for the first time both strategic and tactical planning are on a rational and timely basis. Nothing is more negative for effective profit planning than for management to issue a profit plan some time after the beginning of the period involved.

MANAGEMENT CONTROL USING PPC   The primary purpose of control is to ensure attainment of the objectives, goals, and standards of the enterprise. Control has many facets, such as direct observation, oral expression, narrative memoranda, policies and procedures, reports of actual results, and performance reports. Comprehensive profit planning and control focuses on performance reporting and evaluation of performance to determine the *causes* of both high and low performances.[4]

Performance Reporting

The essential characteristics of a PPC performance report are as follows:

1   Performance is classified by assigned responsibilities. The report must be in exact conformity with the organizational structure. There should be a separate report for each "box" on the organization chart in order to report performance by assigned authority and responsibility.

2   Controllable and noncontrollable items are designated. These two groups must be clearly differentiated because the manager's performance must be measured fairly (that is, only on the basis of items that the responsible manager can significantly influence).[5]

3   Timely reports are issued. For effective control, performance reports should be issued for interim time periods—that is, on a monthly, weekly, or, in some cases, daily basis. To be effective, performance reports must be given to the responsible managers and supervisors shortly after the end of the reporting period. Reports received weeks after the end of the reporting period are of little value. By that time the supervisor is involved in too many new problems to be much concerned about a set of historical events that cannot be changed.

This fundamental also carries the implication that control action, to be effective, must occur immediately after identification of the causes of the problem. The longer control action is deferred, the greater the unfavorable financial effect. Follow-up activities are desirable (a) to determine the effectiveness of control action and (b) to establish the basis for improvement in efficiency. As with control action, follow-up activities must be timely, and decisions based on the findings should be implemented as early as possible.

4   Emphasis is given to a comparison of actual results and planned results—the perfor-

---

[4]A. Thompson Montgomery, *Management Accounting Information* (Reading, Mass.: Addison-Wesley, 1979). Chap 2.

[5]Some people have argued that managerial performance evaluation should not be based only on controllable factors. The argument is based on economic theory and maintains that exclusion of noncontrollable items precludes risk-sharing opportunities that are in everyone's interest. By basing every manager's evaluation on the organization's outcome (e.g., profit) without regard to who controls the outcome, the risks faced by the organization are shared, as in an insurance setting. See Joel Demski, "Uncertainty and Evaluation Based on Controllable Performance," *Journal of Accounting Research* Autumn, 1976, pp. 230–45; or Stanley Baiman and James Noel, "Noncontrollable Costs and Responsibility Accounting," *Journal of Accounting Research,* Autumn, 1985.

The authors do not subscribe to this view. We maintain that a performance evaluation system should be based on performance measures that reflect outcomes that managers control or significantly influence. Any system that does otherwise will be rejected by managers as unfair and will likely have adverse behavioral consequences. For further discussion, see Robert S. Kaplan, *Advanced Management Accounting* (Englewood Cliffs, N.J.: Prentice-Hall, 1982), pp. 611–12.

mance report should designate the responsible manager and show actual results, planned results (standards), and the difference between them (variances). Performance reports also should call attention to the possible causes of variances when possible.

A typical performance report for a sales region is shown in Exhibit 2-7 (partially completed for illustrative purposes). An explanation of the possible causes of the variances would usually be attached to the report.

Responsibility Accounting

A **responsibility accounting** system is one of the fundamentals of PPC listed in Exhibit 2-1. Planning uses historical data, including past financial information, as one of its launching platforms. Control includes the measurement of performance by using actual results (see Exhibit 2-7), much of which must be provided by the accounting system. Actual results are compared with objectives, goals, and standards to determine variances (favorable or unfavorable) that shed light on performance. Therefore, the accounting system must be designed to provide financial information separately for each organizational unit, that is, by assigned authority and responsibility.

Therefore, profit planning and control requires a **responsibility accounting system,** that is, one tailored to organizational responsibilities. Within this primary accounting structure, secondary classifications of costs, revenues, and other relevant financial data may be used to meet the needs of the enterprise. A responsibility accounting system can be designed and implemented regardless of the other features of the accounting system.

When the accounting system is established on a responsibility basis, the historical data provided become especially useful for planning and control purposes. Historical cost accounting has two main objectives with respect to financial data: (1) to determine revenues and expenses, including the cost of goods or services produced or purchased, and (2) to provide relevant revenue and expense data for planning and controlling costs. Traditionally, cost accounting has been focused more on determining the cost of products than on planning and control. As a result, the emphasis in account classifications has been, and in many firms continues to be, on a product-cost basis rather than on a responsibility basis. In responsibility accounting, this emphasis is reversed. Cost and revenue planning and control receive the primary emphasis. This concept does not imply that product costing will be less accurate. Costs initially accumulated for control purposes can be recast for product-costing purposes. However, costs initially accumulated for product-costing purposes cannot usually be recast efficiently for planning and control purposes. In sum, effective profit planning and control requires that the traditional accounting emphasis be reversed—the accounting system must be primarily oriented toward the planning and control needs of management. Most companies initiating a profit planning and control program find it necessary to analyze all aspects of the accounting system carefully, with a consequent reorganization of the system on a responsibility accounting basis.

EXHIBIT 2-7

Characteristics of a Typical Performance Report

Performance Report
For the Period January 1–March 31, 19XX
Responsible Organization Unit Southwestern Sales Region
Manager J. B. Doe

	MONTH OF MARCH			CUMULATIVE TO DATE		
ITEMS	ACTUAL RESULTS	PLANNED RESULTS	VARIATION (UNFAVOR-ABLE)	ACTUAL RESULTS	PLANNED RESULTS	VARIATION (UNFAVOR-ABLE)
Controllable items:						
Sales product A:						
Units	206	200	6			
Amount	$103,000	$100,000	$3,000			
Sales product B:						
Units	80	100	(20)			
Amount	$ 24,000	$ 30,000	($6,000)			
Total Sales ($)	$127,000	$130,000	($3,000)			
Region expenses:						
Travel expense	$ 16,000	$ 15,000	($1,000)			
Remaining expenses (detailed)	13,000	11,000	(2,000)			
Total expenses	$ 29,000	$ 26,000	($3,000)			
Region contribution (sales minus expenses)	$ 98,000	$104,000	($6,000)			

Comparisons between planned and actual results for control purposes are meaningless if the classifications of costs and revenues used in the profit plan and in the accounting system are not in harmony. A **chart of accounts** should be developed by responsibility centers and should be supplemented with standard instructions that prescribe in detail the authorized debits and credits to each type of account. This approach is a requisite to successful profit planning and control because the recording of an actual value in the wrong account affects two or more accounts, resulting in erroneous performance amounts in each account on the periodic performance reports for the respective responsibility centers.

Activity Costing

Responsibility accounting systems generally accumulate costs by department, and product-costing systems associate costs with units of product or service. Organizations also frequently find it useful to associate costs with activities. By decomposing an organization's production process into a discrete set of activities, and then associating costs with each of those activities, management is in a better position to determine the costs and benefits of continuing the activities. Moreover, by systematically identifying the activities throughout the organization, managers can identify redundant activities. Some managers have found, to their surprise, that the same activity was being done in a dozen different places in the company. An activity cost analysis can assist managers in eliminating redundant activities, eliminating activities that are not cost-benefit effective, and achieving greater coordination among the activities that remain.

The following excerpt from an article in *Management Accounting* describes how budgeting and activity analysis help JKL, Inc., a large New York advertising agency.

BUDGETING IN AN ADVERTISING AGENCY

Since devising the budgeting system JKL has become aware of which specific accounts are unprofitable and the reasons why. Since the budgeting and control system has been instituted, the agency has resigned several unprofitable accounts that otherwise would have gone unnoticed. Account managers and supervisors now feel responsible for the profitability of their accounts and carefully monitor actual hours used to make sure that they are being managed and run as efficiently as possible. For example, an account manager noticed a large amount of supervisory creative time was being spent on her account and decided to investigate further. It turned out that the supervisors were doing the actual creative work (rather than the creative department). She pointed this out to her superiors and a junior creative team was appointed to her account, saving a great deal of money.[6]

Zero-Base Budgeting

Associated with the concept of activity costing is zero-base budgeting. Under zero-based budgeting, every budget is constructed on the premise that every activity in the budget must be justified. Zero-base budgeting has been used by many organizations—both private organizations and governmental units. The concept of zero-base budgeting is described in the following excerpt from a *Management Accounting* article. This excerpt describes the use of zero-base budgeting by a public school district in suburban Rochester, New York.

ZERO-BASE BUDGETING IN A PUBLIC SCHOOL DISTRICT

Zero-base budgeting is not a magic formula, but an attitude, woven into a structured analytical process. As most administrators know, the usual approach to budgeting is to begin with the present level of operation and spending and then carefully justify the new programs or additional expenditures desired for next year. In zero-base budgeting there are no "givens." It starts with the basic premise that the budget for next year is zero—and that every expenditure, old and new, must be justified on the basis of its cost and benefit.

[6]William B. Mills, "Drawing Up a Budgeting System for an Ad Agency," *Management Accounting*, December, 1983, p. 52.

> That's the concept. But to ask a manager to start from nothing, invent a whole new way of operating, and then measure the benefit of everything he would do in relation to its cost would be mind-boggling at best and so impractical that it would likely never be done.
>
> So the discipline of zero-base budgeting takes a different approach—in fact, a reverse approach—to this problem of justifying everything. What it says is this: Begin with where you are and establish a business-as-usual budget for next year—the same way, and the same things you would do if you weren't concerned about constraints or total justification. Then start by asking, "What would happen if I didn't do this particular function at all?," and measure the impact of doing away with it completely. When you've done that, you have, in effect, backed into a cost/benefit analysis. Instead of justifying where you go from zero up, you start from where you are and evaluate what would happen if you went down. This comes out to be the truest form of cost/benefit analysis, for that function, in that place.
>
> The nature of this process is function oriented. You don't think in terms of a department, or a certain number of people in a certain place, but rather in terms of the functions being performed. In the case of a manufacturing application, for example, a production control department might do short-term and long-range planning, as well as quality control. You divide it up to say, suppose I didn't do any long-range production planning, what would that cost me? How much would I save? You would then measure the potential loss (in earnings from lost sales) against the amount you might save in immediate staff reduction. The other functions would be similarly analyzed. This process leads into the discipline of costs/benefit analysis in zero-base budgeting—begin where you are and start playing off alternatives.
>
> Virtually everything you do resolves to a selection among alternatives. In zero-base budgeting, the process of alternatives is more rigidly defined. Having measured the effect of eliminating a function, you must define what would happen if the function were reduced to a lower level of service. What would be saved? What would be the consequence of providing less or delayed service? Then you start all over by asking: Now, how could I provide these lower levels of service by doing things in a completely different way and at a lower cost? Thus, you are considering two types of alternatives simultaneously. It is the marriage of those two types into a defined system that is the essence of zero-based budgeting.[7]

Some organizations find that the concept starting from a zero point in budget construction is too unrealistic to be useful. Instead, they use a percentage-base budgeting approach, wherein some percentage of current expenditures is chosen as the base. For example, a 70 percent level is often chosen. Each organizational unit is then asked to provide budgetary information on the assumption that its operation will be funded at 70 percent of the preceding year's budget. The question to be addressed, then, is what activities would still be performed at a 70 percent level of funding. Detailed activity analysis is then conducted on the other activities that constitute the other 30 percent of the preceding year's budget. Are these activities needed? Are they cost-benefit effective? These are the relevant questions to be addressed.

[7] Arthur F. Brueningsen, "SCAT—A Process of Alternatives," *Management Accounting,* November, 1976, p. 56.

Application of the Exception Principle

The phases of the control process were discussed in Chapter 1. Control requires measurement of performance, and it must be approached in a systematic and consistent manner. Control in the broad sense can be attained in an enterprise by using a number of different approaches. The most important point is that control is attained through people and not "things." This means that there is no substitute for supervision of people and operations by competent managers who are cognizant of the behavioral implications of what they say and do.

A comprehensive profit planning and control program facilitates control in many ways; underlying these is the measurement of actual performance against planned objectives, goals, and standards and the reporting of that measurement in performance reports. This measurement and reporting extends to all areas of operations and to all responsibility centers in the enterprise. It involves reporting (1) actual results, (2) budgeted or planned results, and (3) the differences (performance variations) between the two. This type of reporting represents an effective application of the well-recognized management **exception principle.** The exception principle holds that the manager should concentrate primarily on the exceptional or unusual items that appear in daily, weekly, and monthly reports, thereby leaving sufficient managerial time for overall policy and planning considerations. It is the "out-of-line" items that need immediate managerial attention to determine the causes and to take corrective action. The items that are not out of line need not utilize extensive management time; however, they should trigger "rewards" in appropriate ways. To implement the exception principle, techniques and procedures must be adopted to call the manager's attention to the "out-of-control" items. Conventional accounting reports tend to present a mass of figures with no basis for calling attention to the unusual or exceptional items. Alternatively, **performance reports,** because they include a comparison of actual results with plans by areas of responsibility, emphasize in a relevant way performance variations. The out-of-line items stand out. It is with respect to these items that the busy executive should investigate, determine the causes, and take corrective action.[8]

A basic problem of control confronting managers from time to time involves the evaluation of performance information presented to them. Evaluation of an actual result must be based on some standard of performance, either specified or unspecified. For example, a performance report may show March actual sales of $103,000 for product A in the Southwestern sales region. The same report may show actual travel expense of $16,000. The problem facing the manager is whether these amounts represent favorable or unfavorable performance. The actual amounts, standing alone, shed little light on the issue. Some

[8]Thomas, *Readings in Cost Accounting,* Reading No. 28, "Exception Reports for Management Action," by Charles J. Bodenstab, p. 326.

standard or yardstick against which to measure the actual results is necessary if performance is to be evaluated.

The traditional accounting approach has been that of comparing current actual results with the actual results of some past period. For example, product A sales (Exhibit 2-7) for the preceding January were $90,000, and travel expenses were $20,000. Do these additional facts suggest satisfactory current performance in the Southwestern Region? The answer must be that there is still no adequate basis for evaluating performance. It may be that because of changes in conditions since last year, the prior sales and expense performances are not reliable standards. To extend the example, because of increased advertising, more salespeople, an expansion of territory, or changes in product prices or product lines, the product A sales goal was set at $100,000 for March 19XX. Or, in the case of travel expense changes in the region, the goal for travel expense was set at $15,000. In this case, sales performance was good and the travel expense performance was unsatisfactory. It is assumed that these latter amounts represent realistic goals. A comparison of actual results for the current period with the actual results of a prior period does not provide effective measurement of performance. Comparison with a reliable standard does provide a valid measurement. Comparison of current actual results with those of some past period may have value because trends are revealed; however, the comparison is generally inadequate for control purposes.

Comparison with the actual results of a prior period is insufficient for the following reasons: (1) conditions may have changed—reorganization, new products, new methods, price changes, volume differentials, technological improvements, increased labor efficiency; (2) accounting classifications may be different; and (3) performance in the prior period may have been unsatisfactory. On the other hand, assuming the planned goals are attainable and represent efficient performance in relation to the situation, a valid and significant measurement of actual performance is possible. The profit planning and control approach makes it possible for management to feel the pulse of the enterprise throughout the year and to know specifically where there is satisfactory or unsatisfactory progress toward the company's objectives and goals.

Progress or lack of progress toward goals must be recognized and evaluated throughout the year rather than at the end of the year, because it is then too late to take corrective action. Accordingly, performance reports for control purposes should be prepared and communicated at least on a monthly basis.

ORGANIZATIONAL ADAPTATION TO PPC   A profit planning and control program must rest upon a sound organizational structure for the enterprise and clear-cut lines of authority and responsibility. The purpose of organizational structure and the assignment of authority is to establish a framework within which enterprise objectives may be attained in a coordinated and effective way on a continuing basis. The scope and interrelationship of the responsibilities of each individual manager are specified.

To increase managerial and operational efficiency, practically all enterprises, except perhaps the very smallest ones, should be structurally disaggregated into organizational subunits. The manager of each subunit should be assigned specific authority and responsibility for the operational activities of that subunit. These subunits are often referred to as **decision centers** or **responsibility centers.** Although the latter term is widely used, the former is more descriptive of the primary focus that is most fundamental. A responsibility center (or decision center) can be defined as an organizational unit (or subunit) headed by a manager with specified authority and responsibility. Thus, the company as a whole is a responsibility center, as is each division, department, and sales district. Responsibility centers are further classified in respect to the extent of responsibility as follows:

1   **Cost center**—a responsibility center for which a manager is responsible for the controllable costs incurred in the subunit but is not responsible, in a financial sense, for profit or investment in the center. The lower-level and smaller-responsibility centers tend to be cost centers.

2   **Revenue center**—a responsibility center for which the manager is responsible for revenue. Sales districts are often designated as revenue centers.

3   **Profit center**—a responsibility center for which the manager is responsible for the revenues, costs, and profits of the center. Planning and control focuses on the center's profit.

4   **Investment center**—a responsibility center that goes one step further than a profit center. In an investment center, the manager is responsible for revenue, costs, profit, and the amount of resources invested in the assets used by the center. Planning and control focuses on the return on investment earned by the center.

Organizational subunits, whether cost, revenue, profit, or investment centers, are variously labeled as subsidiaries, divisions, departments, plants, business units, districts, and functions. It is through these responsibility centers that plans are implemented, objectives are attained, and control is implemented. A comprehensive profit planning and control program must be tailored to the organizational subunits and related structural characteristics of the enterprise. Thus, in better-managed companies we observe that within the specified time dimensions, the project plans, the strategic long-range plan, and the tactical short-range profit plan are structured first by organizational authorities and responsibilities, and second by product or service lines. In harmony with this frame of reference, the goals and plans of the several responsibility centers aggregate to the goals and plans for the enterprise as a whole. As a result, comprehensive profit plans normally are developed each year as follows:

1   Top management specifies entity objectives, goals, strategies, planning assumptions (premises), and guidelines that are communicated to the managers of the subunits.

2   The manager of each subunit, conforming to the broad guidelines, develops his or her own segment of the comprehensive profit plan. Typically, the first segment of the strategic and tactical profit plans that must be completed is the sales plan, because the activities of most companies depend on sales volume.

3 The manager of each subunit presents the subunit's profit plans to top management for critical review, evaluation, and suggested revisions when appropriate.

4 The plans of each subunit, as approved by higher management, are then consolidated into the comprehensive profit plan for the entire company.

Subsequent discussions in this book will emphasize the necessity of relating planning and control functions to the assigned authorities and responsibilities of the various subunits of an enterprise. From both conceptual and procedural points of view, the primary structure or classification of profit plans must be by organizational subdivisions or responsibility centers.

As a consequence of these requirements, an organization in the process of initiating a profit planning and control program should first consider its organizational structure and the related assignment of authorities and responsibilities. In most cases, it will be found that organizational adaptation and greater precision are necessary to place the operation on a sound footing for efficient implementation of the planning and control processes through comprehensive budgeting.

Responsibility accounting systems must often be adapted to specific organizational needs. As an illustration, the following excerpt from a *Management Accounting* article describes responsibility accounting for maintenance costs at

RESPONSIBILITY ACCOUNTING AT ARCO

Because of the type of set-up, AOGC realized it had to identify organizational centers and trace costs to individual managers responsible for making cost decisions at the Prudhoe Bay oil field. As a result, the company has implemented a responsibility accounting system that covers all its Prudhoe operations and provides the mechanism for control, reporting, budgeting and accountability of maintenance costs.

Before AOGC could develop the new system, it had to decide whether maintenance management or operations management was responsible for and had control over maintenance charges. From a practical standpoint, maintenance costs are difficult to control because the maintenance worker is not confined to a single cost center. Maintenance personnel may be required at various facilities at various times and therefore may charge time field-wide.

AOGC has fifteen maintenance shops, each representing a different area of expertise and potential source of charge to a facility. Whether to exercise control at the source (the maintenance shop) or at the terminus (the operations facility) became a major problem. Maintenance management argued validly that it controls dollars spent at facilities because it determines the number of people performing the work, the number of hours taken, how the work is done (repair or replace), and the overall efficiency of work performance. Operations argued effectively that it controls what maintenance is done and when. In reality, whether the work is unscheduled maintenance or preventive maintenance, the facility operating manager has the authority to determine how often he calls the maintenance person to his facility. Based on this fact and the knowledge that maintenance costs could be tracked accurately to the facility, AOGC elected to control costs at their terminus.[9]

[9]Patricia Anstine and Michael E. Scott, "ARCO Establishes Responsibility Accounting at Prudhoe Bay," *Management Accounting*, March 1980, pp. 13–20.

ARCO's oil operations at Prudhoe Bay, Alaska. These operations are conducted by the ARCO Oil and Gas Co. (AOGC).

Another example of adapting the responsibility accounting system to a company's organizational needs is given by the anecdote reported below. This incident, originally described by Raymond Villers, actually occurred.

RESPONSIBILITY ACCOUNTING AND CONTROL OF RUSH ORDER COSTS

The sales department manager would frequently request a rush order. The plant production scheduler would then argue that the rush order will disrupt production and cost a bundle. The manager would then reply by asking if the production scheduler wanted to take responsibility for losing the customer who had made the rush order. Naturally, the scheduler did not want to take this responsibility, and so the rush order was scheduled as requested. The result, however, was considerable ill feeling between the sales manager and production scheduler.

The solution, through responsibility accounting, was to determine the cost of rush orders and trace them back to the sales department. This procedure resulted in less frequent requests for rush orders, and the amiable acceptance of them by the plant production scheduler.[10]

Departments Versus Department Managers

In a responsibility accounting system, it is important to distinguish between departments and department managers. In evaluating the manager of a profit center, for example, only those costs and revenues that the manager controls or significantly influences should be used in the evaluation. However, in evaluating the economic viability of the profit center itself, all costs and revenues that are traceable to the center should be used in the evaluation.

In some cases, an effective manager may be in charge of a responsibility center that is not an economically viable investment. Conversely, even a poor manager can be made to appear effective when running an economically strong responsibility center. It is important, therefore, for the responsibility accounting system to distinguish between effective and ineffective managers and between strong and weak investments.

COORDINATION USING PPC   Some management authorities list coordination as a separate function of management; however, most view it as an effect that ensues when the managerial functions of planning, organizing, staffing, directing, and controlling are accomplished. **Coordination** is the synchronization of individual actions with the result that each subdivision of an entity effectively works toward the common objectives, with due regard for all other subdivisions and with unity of effort. Such a result is often referred to as **goal congru-**

---

[10]Raymond Villers, "Control and Freedom in a Decentralized Company," *Harvard Business Review* (32, 1954), p. 95. Copyright © 1954 by the president and fellows of Harvard College; all rights reserved. Reprinted by permission of *Harvard Business Review*.

ence. It means developing and maintaining the various activities within the enterprise in proper relationship to each other. This harmony of effort toward the enterprise objective is one of the central tasks of management because it involves a reconciliation of differences in effort, timing, policies, and allocation of resources. Frequently, a lack of coordination in an enterprise is apparent when an aggressive department head is permitted to expand the department out of proportion to others or to base major decisions on the specific needs of the department only, although the decisions may negatively affect other departments and alter their effectiveness. For example, there must be very close coordination between the sales and production departments. Sales should not plan to sell more than production can provide, and vice versa. There must be coordination at all vertical levels as well as horizontally.

How is coordination attained? Fundamentally, coordination is attained through effective performance of the management functions. However, certain of those functions have particular relevance in this respect. Coordination involves the interpersonal relationships of people in the work situation as they exchange views, technical expertise, gossip, and attitudes. When managers at all levels understand how their particular functions contribute to the overall enterprise objectives, a basic foundation for coordination is established. It is important that each member of management, from the top to the lowest level, knows well in advance what is planned and how, when, and by whom it is to be accomplished. Communication—downward, upward, and horizontally—is fundamental to coordination.

FORMAL VERSUS INFORMAL BUDGETS   This chapter gives a clear implication that certain phases of the planning and control functions should be formalized. A comprehensive profit planning and control program provides such formalization. The primary reasons for formalization are as follows:

1   The management process cannot be effectively accomplished in a completely random manner; planning and control should be logical, consistent, and systematic.
2   Because a large number of individuals are involved in the management process (both the supervisors and the supervised), the environment must be characterized by a reasonable degree of stability and consistency upon which people can rely from day to day.
3   Objectives, plans, and goals, if not written in terms of the probable future financial impacts on the enterprise, frequently turn out to be vague and uncommunicated "half-thoughts" and rumors of one or more individuals. Casual observation alone tells us that objectives, goals, policies, and procedures lack the necessary precision, consistency, understanding, and stability when "carried around in the head" of one individual or of diverse groups of managers and nonmanagers.
4   For effective communication and mutual understanding, formalization of certain objectives, goals, policies, and procedures is essential.
5   Formalization requires the establishment and observance of deadlines for decision making, planning, and control actions.
6   Formalization provides a logical basis for rational, significant, and consistent flexibility in implementing the planning and control processes.

Overformalization and inflexible administration, on the other hand, involve serious hazards of perhaps greater import than a lack of formalization. An unfavorable aspect that frequently derives from formal approaches is that the "written words and figures" are viewed inflexibly. Therefore, they may constrain the dynamics that are essential to all human endeavors. Management is not possible by rules alone. Many aspects of the management process cannot be implemented in a formal way. Informality has merit at all levels of management, and the executive should strive to attain an appropriate degree of balance between the two extremes. The essence of the concept of comprehensive profit planning and control is that **specified phases** of the management process can be formalized advantageously. However, application and implementation of written plans, policies, and procedures must take into account the salient features and unexpected events for each situation. A set of plans should not be allowed to "manage" the operation; rather the formal plans provide basic guidelines within which decisions are made. Moreover, as decisions are being made, plans must often be changed.

FLEXIBILITY IN APPLYING PPC   A profit planning and control program (or any other managerial tool) must not dominate a business. When implementing **plans,** there must be a forthright management "override" policy so that "straitjackets" are not imposed and all favorable opportunities are seized even though "they are not covered by the budget."

It is not uncommon for budgets to impose inflexibility on a business and act as a constraint on the decision-making freedom of managers and supervisors. However, a profit planning and control program administered in an enlightened way permits greater freedom at all management levels. This effect is possible because all levels of management are brought into the decision-making process when plans are developed. When the basic profit plan has been approved, upper management is then in a position to delegate more responsibility than would otherwise be possible. Also, the mere fact that an event or opportunity was not anticipated in the plans should have no bearing on whether the situation should be investigated and a decision made to replan. In such situations, the profit plan places management in the position of being able to assess, on a more objective basis, the soundness of a contemplated decision about unanticipated events. The profit planning and control approach anticipates exceptions, adjustments, and replanning as situations evolve. The prior profit plan provides a basis for evaluating the broader impact of the unanticipated events on the overall financial picture for the enterprise.

Similarly, in the area of **control**, flexibility is especially important. Expense and cost budgets must not be used and interpreted rigidly. The budget must not constrain rational decisions that should be made with respect to expenses merely because an expenditure was not anticipated. Also, variable expense budgets are frequently used to meet one of the problems of cost control arising from a change in circumstances. To illustrate, assume that the budget for Department X shows an expense allowance of $2,000 for labor and an expectation of 10,000 units of output (20 cents per unit). Now assume that unforeseen circumstances make it necessary for the department actually to produce 12,000 units of output and to incur direct labor costs of $2,350. Direct labor cost varies directly with output; therefore, a comparison of actual direct labor costs incurred in producing 12,000 units of output with a budget allowance for that cost based on 10,000 units of output would show an unfavorable and, more significantly, a meaningless variation of $350. Under variable budget procedures, the budget allowance would be adjusted to $2,400 (i.e., 12,000 × $.20) and a favorable variance of $50. would be reported. (The concept of variable budgeting is examined in Chapter 9.)

Throughout the following chapters, managerial flexibility to implement the results of the planning process is emphasized. Continuing emphasis is important because a budget should not be used as a straitjacket. The planning and control approach to management should not be used to constrain management in seizing opportunities, whether planned or not, that will enhance the economic well-being of the enterprise. The following excerpt from a *Management Accounting* article describes how 3M has managed to use its PPC system to enhance, rather than stifle, innovation.

ROLE OF FINANCIAL PLANNING AT 3M

The number of U.S. corporations that boast track records of perennial success and excellence has diminished in the last few years. The recent spate of megabucks mergers and acquisitions, decreasing productivity, economic downturns, and stiffer foreign competition have damaged companies' chances for sustained growth and profitability. A few exceptions, however, have survived these adversities and continue to achieve stellar performances. 3M, Minnesota Mining and Manufacturing Co., is a prime example.

In the top 50 of the Fortune 500, the $8 billion giant again made *Fortune* magazine's list of America's most admired corporations—this year rising to No. 2, just behind IBM. . . .

What is its formula for success? Chronicled along with 61 other high achievers in the 1982 best seller, *In Search of Excellence*, by Thomas J. Peters and Robert H. Waterman, Jr., then revisited in 1985's *A Passion for Excellence* by Peters and Nancy Austin, 3M is heralded as a model for product innovation and entrepreneurship. 3M also is a model for management accounting excellence.

Readers of the two books may have come away with a mental image of teams of 3M employees dashing through the hallways, spewing forth new product ideas to anyone who would listen, then plunging ahead with a frenzy of new product developments, all in a state of almost uncontrolled chaos. Highly charged creativity does abound in the St. Paul-headquartered corporation, but an underlying thread of good financial planning and tight cost control also permeates the entire organization. It extends from top management down through the center of every operating unit and every product and service created and is a vital part of everyday decision making.

New products are the lifeblood of 3M, and the company carefully nurtures its product champions, taking every step possible to see that its entrepreneurs have the best conditions under which to create. . . . At the same time, centralized legal, engineering, human resources, and finance departments keep the entrepreneurial spirits headed in the right direction.

Financial expertise, long recognized as one of 3M's greatest assets, is a major contributor to the corporation's success. 3M uses its financial control system to encourage rather than curtail innovation and creativity. Numbers are used to set goals and measure performance rather than to deny expenditures or punish unmet expectations.[11]

REALISTIC EXPECTATIONS IN PPC—A BEHAVIORAL PROBLEM

In profit planning and control, management must be realistic and avoid being either unduly conservative or irrationally optimistic. The care with which budget goals are set for such items as sales, production levels, costs, capital expenditures, cash flow, and productivity determines the usefulness of a profit planning and control program. For profit planning and control purposes, enterprise objectives and specific budget goals should represent **realistic expectations.** To be realistic, expectations must be related (1) to their specific time dimension and (2) to an assumed (projected) external and internal environment that will prevail during that time span. Within these two constraints, realistic expectations should assume a high level of overall efficiency; however, the objectives and goals should be attainable. Goals that are set so high that they are practically impossible to attain discourage serious efforts to reach them. Alternatively, goals set so low that they require no special effort will provide no motivation. Thus, enterprise objectives and specific budget goals, in order to constitute realistic expectations, must represent a real challenge to managers and to operational units. The top management of the enterprise has the direct responsibility for defining the level of challenge that should be represented by realistic expectations.

The development of realistic budget goals, and the efforts required to attain them, entail significant behavioral implications. Budget goals should be established on a participative basis and implemented in ways that provide positive reinforcement (i.e., positive motivation) rather than negative reinforcement. To accomplish this difficult task, management must consider consequences. For example, the attitudes of "can't do" and "won't do" must be dealt with. "Can't do" often means more attention needs to be given to employee training and facilities. "Won't do" usually means that the consequences of "doing it" should be reevaluated (positive rewards, challenges, pride, status, etc.). The objective is to provide maximum motivation to excel by the individual managers, the operational units, and the overall enterprise. The definition of realistic expectations in a given enterprise, therefore, should be related to many variables, such as size of the enterprise, characteristics of the managers, leadership characteristics, maturity of the enterprise, sophistication of the management (at all levels), nature of operations, and behavioral management. Fi-

---

[11]Kathy Williams, "The Magic of Management Accounting Excellence," *Management Accounting,* February 1986, pp. 21–27.

nally, this discussion of the definition of realistic expectations emphasizes the premise that managers at all levels will be better motivated in the long run if they are given realistic expectations as opposed to spurious expectations based on the premise that "high unattainable expectations are necessary for these kinds of people." For profit planning and control purposes, then, objectives should represent "expected actual," under the assumption that operations will be efficient under the expected conditions during the planning period.

Behavioral Impact of Budgets on People

Related to the issue of how to set budgetary expectations is the issue of how budgetary pressure affects people.[12] There is substantial evidence suggesting that supervisors often assume that budgets can be used as effective pressure devices to increase productivity. What supervisors often do not realize, however, is the behavioral effects of such budgetary pressure. One effect is that employees may consciously strive not to exceed budgeted performance in order to lessen the likelihood that the budgeted performance level will ultimately be set even higher. Moreover, employees often react to budgetary pressure by becoming tense, resentful, and suspicious of every new move management makes to increase productivity.

Another common reaction of people to budgetary pressure is to form informal groups. Such groups generally form gradually as employees realize that others also feel the budgetary pressure and that such pressure can be partially relieved by discussing it with others in a group. In some situations, such groups become very cohesive and serve as a springboard for bringing grievances to management on a number of issues.

Other human reactions to budgetary pressure include (1) supervisors trying to place the blame on others when production problems emerge, (2) staff-line strife, such as when supervisors place blame on the budget people or production-control personnel, (3) pressure that is allowed to build up with no healthy outlet, thereby reducing efficiency through distraction, nervousness, and so on.

A particularly damaging effect of budgetary pressure can result when people are continually made to feel as though they have failed in meeting the

[12]This section draws upon the seminal work of Chris Argyris, "Human Problems with Budgets," *Harvard Business Review*, January–February 1953, pp. 97–100; and *The Impact of Budgets on People* (New York: Controllership Foundation, 1952); as well as subsequent research by others: Edwin H. Caplan, "Behavioral Assumptions of Management Accounting," *Accounting Review*, July 1966; Don T. DeCoster and J. P. Fertakis, "Budget-Induced Pressure and Its Relationship to Supervisory Behavior," *Journal of Accounting Research*, Autumn 1968, p. 237–46; Anthony G. Hopwood, "An Empirical Study of the Role of Accounting Data in Performance Evaluation," *Empirical Research in Accounting: Selected Studies*, 1972, Supplement to *Journal of Accounting Research*, pp. 156–82; Michael Schiff and Arie Lewin, "The Impact of People on Budgets," *Accounting Review*, April 1970; Robert J. Swieringa and Robert H. Moncur, *Some Effects of Participative Budgeting on Managerial Behavior* (New York: National Association of Accountants, 1975); and Peter Brownell, "Participation in the Budgeting Process: When It Works and When It Doesn't," *Journal of Accounting Literature* (1, 1982), pp. 124–53.

budget. Such perceived failures often result in loss of interest in work, lower personal standards for achievement, loss of confidence, fear of new tasks or methods, lack of cooperation, and development of a critical attitude toward others.

In a study of sixteen manufacturing companies, Kenis[13] reported that budget goals that are "too tight" have negative effects on managers' job satisfaction, budgetary performance, and cost efficiency as compared with managers who reported having "about right" or "tight but attainable" budgetary standards. Moreover, "too tight" budgets caused significant job tension. Kenis's results are consistent with those of Hofstede,[14] Becker and Green,[15] and Dunbar.[16]

The implication of this discussion is not that budgets cause trouble, but rather that management should be sensitive to the behavioral implications of budgetary pressure when implementing a PPC program.

Padding the Budget—A Behavioral Problem

Participation in developing a profit plan may result in subtle (and often obvious) attempts to "pad" the budget. Here are some typcial views that help explain why padding the budget occurs:

1 Sales budget estimates are understated "to protect ourselves and exceeding the sales budget certainly can't be criticized."
2 Overestimating expenses "so we will have plenty of money and spending less than the budget looks good to the management."
3 Requesting more cash than needed "so that we won't have to ask for more and if we turn some back it will look good."

Padding of the budget is also referred to as **budgetary slack.**

Cyert and March[17] define budgetary slack as the difference between the total resources available to the firm and the total resources necessary to maintain the organizational coalition responsible for the budgetary slack. Schiff and Lewin[18] found that managers tend to consume budgetary slack to satisfy personal aspirations in "good years," and they tend to convert budgetary slack to profit in "bad years." Divisional management typically creates budgetary slack

[13]Izzettin Kenis, "Effects of Budgetary Goal Characteristics on Managerial Attitudes and Performance," *Accounting Review*, October 1979, pp. 707–21.

[14]G. H. Hofstede, *The Game of Budget Control* (The Netherlands: Koninklijke Van Gorcum and Comp. N.V. Assen, 1967).

[15]Selwyn Becker and David Green, "Budgeting and Employee Behavior," *Journal of Business*, October 1962, pp. 392–402.

[16]R. L. M. Dunbar, "Budgeting for Control," *Administrative Science Quarterly*, March 1971, pp. 88–96.

[17]Richard M. Cyert and James G. March, *The Behavioral Theory of the Firm* (Englewood Cliffs, N.J.: Prentice-Hall, 1963).

[18]Michael Schiff and Arie Lewin, "The Impact of People on Budgets," *Accounting Review*, April 1970.

by underestimating gross revenue, including discretionary increases in personnel requirements, establishing marketing and sales budgets with internal limits on money to be spent, using standard costs that do not reflect process improvements already available, and including discretionary special projects in the budget. Schiff and Lewin reported that in some cases, budgetary slack may account for as much as 20 to 25 percent of a division's budgeted operating expenses.

Budgetary slack often results from a logically circular phenomenon. Slack is built into a budget because the budget is typically cut in a higher-level review, and budgets are cut because slack has been built in.

A perceptive top management will develop effective approaches to minimize these somewhat natural tendencies toward padding budgets. The solution lies in budget education aimed at developing positive attitudes toward planning and control. Management should emphasize that **both** favorable and unfavorable variations will be carefully considered. All favorable and unfavorable variations due to padding or poor planning should be identified and discussed with each responsible person. Also, any broader problems created by poor planning should be emphasized. For example, a deliberately understated sales budget may have serious consequences in planning other functional activities. For example, production may be inadequate; the advertising program and distribution expense budgets may be adversely affected; the cash flow plans may be inadequate; and so on. Each responsible executive and supervisor must have guidance in preparing his or her own plans and estimates. Important ways to prevent padding of budgets are to specify a clear-cut process and to develop a formal approval policy. Starting with the lower levels of management and moving up in the management hierarchy, each budget must meet the tests of logic, realism, and identification of specific needs. Also, management must convince lower echelons that **additional budget changes** will be approved at any time, notwithstanding the budget as originally developed, should sufficient and compelling business reasons be evident. Lack of definite policies and failure by higher management to take sufficient time to evaluate such requests are usually prevalent where "padding" persists.

A related problem is the tendency of lower management to approve expenditures unwisely near the end of the budget period when there is an excess because "our budget allowance for the next period will be cut if we turn money back now." Again, the resolution of this type of problem is to be found in the area of enlightened management policies as well as flexibility, and in the attitudes of top management as perceived by the lower levels of management. Enterprise subunits should be strongly encouraged to save and turn back funds not needed while at the same time being assured, both by policy and by action, that subsequent budget allowances for their activity will not be adversely affected by this prior favorable action. Subsequent budget approvals should be evaluated on the basis of newly proposed programs and demonstrated needs rather than on the level of prior expenditures.

Budget-padding problems exist because of insufficient attention to policy making, communication, the budget approval process, and ineffective leadership. These problems are often identified with governmental budgeting, but there is no reason to assume that they do not exist in profit-making organizations. However, the problems are much more critical in the public sector because the approval bodies (legislatures) are not involved in the management process subsequent to approval.

Budget-padding problems can basically be resolved through effective and continuous budget education that focuses on enlightened management policies, flexibility in implementing the planning and control program, and a behavior management program. The budget education program must have as its objectives (1) communication of the policies and intentions of top management relative to the planning and control program, (2) development of positive attitudes wherein the individual manager identifies the success of the firm with his or her own personal success, and (3) instruction in the ways that the profit planning and control program can contribute to the effective performance of managerial tasks at each level in the enterprise.[19] The demonstrated competence of each manager to develop realistic plans and to avoid budget padding should be, as a company policy, an important criterion in evaluating the manager's performance.

Communication Is the Management Process: Behavioral Implications

Communication is a necessary activity in all facets of management. **Communication** can be broadly defined as an interchange of thought or information to bring about a mutual understanding between two or more parties. It may be accomplished by a combination of words, symbols, messages, and subtleties of understanding that come from working together, day in and day out, by two or more individuals. All communications involve a sender, a message, and a receiver. Communication may be thought of as the link that brings together the human elements in an enterprise. Managerial decisions and leadership are actuated by communication, the means by which behavior is affected, modified, and energized. Too often communication is taken for granted; consequently, information flows are inadequate. There must be three primary flows of information in an entity: downward, upward, and laterally in the organization.

Communication is a complex but necessary process that can be broken down into its basic elements, as shown in Exhibit 2-8. It involves significant and pervasive behavioral effects. In many organizations, ineffective communication is the root cause of many negative attitudes. Some of the main barriers to effective communication are the credibility of the sender, imprecise communication channels, unclear messages, inattention of the receiver, inappropriate

[19] See Andrew C. Stedry, *Budget Control and Cost Behavior* (Englewood Cliffs, N.J.: Prentice-Hall, 1960). Also see Thomas, *Readings in Cost Accounting,* Reading No. 10, "The Impact of People on Budgets," by Michael Schiff and Arie Y. Lewin, p. 133.

transmission means, message deficiencies, lack of basic communication skills, poor enterprise climate (e.g., fear), and reluctance to provide relevant information.

A profit planning and control program can be one of the more effective communication networks in an enterprise. Communication for effective planning and control requires that both the executive and the subordinate have the same understanding of responsibilities and goals. Profit plans, if developed through full participation and in harmony with assigned responsibilities, ensure a degree of understanding not otherwise possible. Full and open reporting in performance reports that focus on assigned responsibilities likewise enhances the degree of communication essential to sound management.

Throughout the remaining chapters of this book, considerable emphasis will be given to the potential impact that a comprehensive profit planning and control program can have on the communication process.

EXHIBIT 2-8
Elements of the Communication Process

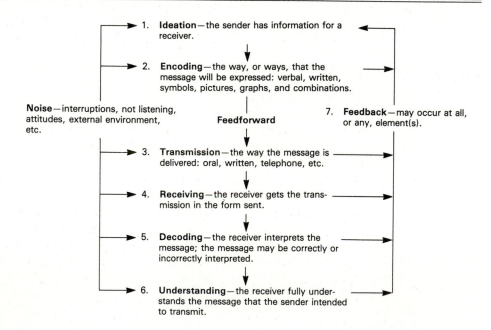

1. **Ideation**—the sender has information for a receiver.

2. **Encoding**—the way, or ways, that the message will be expressed: verbal, written, symbols, pictures, graphs, and combinations.

Noise—interruptions, not listening, attitudes, external environment, etc.

Feedforward

7. **Feedback**—may occur at all, or any, element(s).

3. **Transmission**—the way the message is delivered: oral, written, telephone, etc.

4. **Receiving**—the receiver gets the transmission in the form sent.

5. **Decoding**—the receiver interprets the message; the message may be correctly or incorrectly interpreted.

6. **Understanding**—the receiver fully understands the message that the sender intended to transmit.

ESTABLISHING THE FOUNDATION FOR PPC   In Chapters 1 and 2 the discussions have been general, although specific references have been made to certain aspects of profit planning and control programs. At this point it seems appropriate to summarize the steps that an enterprise should take to establish a sound foundation for initiating a profit planning and control program. These steps are as follows:

Step 1   There must be commitments by the top management to the broad concept of profit planning and control and a sophisticated understanding of its implications and operations.

Step 2   The characteristics of the enterprise and the environment in which it operates—including the controllable and noncontrollable variables—must be identified and evaluated so that relevant decisions may be made about the characteristics of a profit planning and control program that would be effective and practical.

Step 3   There should be an evaluation of the organizational structure and assignment of managerial responsibilities and implementation of changes deemed necessary for effective planning and control.

Step 4   There must be an evaluation and reorganization of the accounting system to ensure that it is tailored to the organizational responsibilities (responsibility accounting) so that it can provide data particularly useful for planning and control purposes.

Step 5   A policy determination must be made about the time dimensions to be used for profit planning and control purposes.

Step 6   A program of budget education should be developed to inform management at all levels about (a) the purposes of the program; (b) the manner in which it will operate, including the basic management policies and guidelines for its administration; (c) the responsibility of each level of management in the program; and (d) the ways in which the program can facilitate the performance of each manager's functions.

These six steps, if taken seriously at the outset, should pave the way for instituting a sound profit planning and control program.

In the following chapters, we will look at the various components of a comprehensive profit planning and control program. Specific examples of the major components will be given to serve as a basis for the discussion. In this manner, the discussion will be both conceptually sound and practical in application.

APPLICATION OF PPC TO VARIOUS TYPES OF ORGANIZATIONS   Some people say that comprehensive profit planning and control is applicable only to large and complex organizations. Also, a not unusual comment is that "comprehensive budgeting is a fine idea for most businesses, but ours is different," or "it is impossible to project our revenues and expenses," and so on. Sometimes specific industries are viewed as not amenable to profit planning and control. These views are common regarding nonmanufacturing enterprises—service companies, financial institutions, hospitals, certain retail businesses, construction companies, and real-estate enterprises. To the contrary, profit planning and control can be adapted to any organization (profit or nonprofit, service or manufacturing), regardless of size, special circumstances, or conditions. The fact that a company has peculiar circumstances or critical problems is frequently a good reason for the adoption of certain profit planning and control procedures. In respect to size, when operations are extensive enough to require more than one or two supervisory personnel, there may be a need for profit planning and control applications. The smallest company certainly has different needs in this respect than a large one. As with accounting, a single profit planning and control system that is appropriate for all enterprises cannot be designed. A profit planning and control system must be tailored to fit the particular enterprise, and it must be continually adapted as the enterprise and its environment change.

The discussions in this book apply to all types of businesses—large and small, manufacturing and nonmanufacturing. Specific references are made to these different types of enterprises in subsequent chapters.

SOME ARGUMENTS GIVEN FOR AND AGAINST PPC

The usefulness of comprehensive profit planning and control have been emphasized in the preceding discussions; however, it should not be assumed that the concept is foolproof or that it is free of problems. The following main arguments are usually given **against** profit planning and control:

1   It is difficult, if not impossible, to estimate revenues and expenses in our company realistically.
2   Our management has no interest in all the estimates and schedules. Our strictly informal system is better and works well.
3   It is not realistic to write out and distribute our goals, policies, and guidelines to all the supervisors.
4   Budgeting places too great a demand on management time, especially to revise budgets constantly. Too much paper work is required.
5   It takes away management flexibility.
6   It creates all kinds of behavioral problems.
7   It places the management in a straitjacket.
8   It adds a level of complexity that is not needed.
9   It is too costly, aside from management time.
10   The managers, supervisors, and other employees hate budgets.

The following main arguments are usually given **for** profit planning and control:

1   It forces early consideration of basic policies.
2   It requires adequate and sound organization structure; that is, there must be a definite assignment of responsibility for each function of the enterprise.
3   It compels all members of management, from the top down, to participate in the establishment of goals and plans.
4   It compels departmental managers to make plans in harmony with the plans of other departments and of the entire enterprise.
5   It requires that management put down in figures what is necessary for satisfactory performance.
6   It requires adequate and appropriate historical accounting data.
7   It compels management to plan for the most economical use of labor, material, and capital.
8   It instills at all levels of management the habit of timely, careful, and adequate consideration of the relevant factors before reaching important decisions.

9   It reduces cost by increasing the span of control because fewer supervisors are needed.

10 It frees executives from many day-to-day internal problems through predetermined policies and clear-cut authority relationships. It thereby provides more executive time for planning and creative thinking.

11 It tends to remove the cloud of uncertainty that exists in many organizations, especially among lower levels of management, relative to basic policies and enterprise objectives.

12 It pinpoints efficiency and inefficiency.

13 It promotes understanding among members of management of their co-workers' problems.

14 It forces management to give adequate attention to the effect of general business conditions.

15 It forces a periodic self-analysis of the company.

16 It aids in obtaining bank credit; banks commonly require a projection of future operations and cash flows to support large loans.

17 It checks progress or lack of progress toward the objectives of the enterprise.

18 It forces recognition and corrective action (including rewards).

19 It rewards high performance and seeks to correct unfavorable performance.

20 It forces management to consider expected future trends and conditions.

Aside from the arguments cited for and against PPC (some of them have little merit), the following critical features are always present:

1   **The Profit Plan Is Based on Estimates.** The advantages and disadvantages of a profit planning program depend to a large extent on the realism with which the basic estimates are made. For example, estimates must be based on all available facts and sound managerial judgment. Estimating sales and expenses cannot be an exact science; however, numerous statistical, mathematical, and other techniques that may be effectively applied to these problems can produce realistic results when tempered with sound reasoning and judgment. If there is conviction that such estimates can be made realistically, serious effort generally yields satisfactory results. Because the profit plan is based entirely on estimates and judgments, flexibility is essential in using and interpreting the results.

2   **A Profit Planning and Control Program Must Be Continually Adapted to Fit Changing Circumstances.** A comprehensive budget program cannot be started and perfected in a short time. Profit planning and control techniques must continually be adapted, not only for each particular enterprise but for changing conditions within the enterprise. Various techniques must be tried, improved, or discarded and replaced with others. In other words, a profit planning and control program must be dynamic in every sense of the word. It will usually take more than one year to attain a realistic program, and management must not expect too much during this period. Continuous budget education is necessary, especially during the formative period.

3   **Execution of a Profit Plan Will Not Occur Automatically.** Profit plans will be effective only if all responsible executives exert continuous and aggressive efforts toward their accomplishment. Responsibility center managers must accept responsibility for attaining or exceeding department goals specified in the profit plans. All levels of management must understand the program, must be convinced of its relevance to their function, and must participate in its implementation in an appropriate way.

4   **The Profit Plan Is Not a Substitute for Management.** Profit planning cannot substitute for enlightened management. It is a system that can aid in performing the management process. The budget manual of one prominent company states:

The profit plan should be regarded not as a master, but as a servant. It is one of the best tools yet devised for advancing the affairs of a company and the individuals in their various spheres of managerial activity. It is not assumed that any profit plan is perfect. The most important consideration is to make sure, by intelligent use of the profit plans, that all possible attainable benefits are derived from the plans as rendered and to replan when there are compelling business reasons.

CHAPTER SUMMARY   This chapter discussed the interrelationships between the management process and profit planning and control, with an emphasis on planning and control. It also described twelve fundamental concepts of PPC (see Exhibit 2-1).

A profit planning and control program helps the management perform its planning function by developing a strategic (long-range) profit plan and a tactical (short-range) profit plan. Both of these plans include monetary expectations (i.e., goals) for assets, liabilities, profits, and return on investment. The foundation for the strategic profit plan (usually extending three, five, or ten years into the future) includes the objectives, broad goals, planning premises, and strategies of the enterprise as developed by top management. The *tactical* (short-range) profit plan, can actually be viewed as the first year of the strategic profit plan. It is the detailed plan for the enterprise and for each of its responsibility centers.

A PPC program helps management perform its control function by providing realistic goals and standards that are implemented and are then compared with actual results to measure performance. Under PPC this performance measurement extends from the top to the lowest organizational level in the enterprise.

The chapter discussed some significant behavioral implications of PPC, with emphasis on developing positive reinforcement, improving motivation, developing goals, coping with the effects of budgetary pressure, resolving budget-padding problems, and using budgets for control (e.g., performance reports).

Comprehensive Demonstration Case

 *SUPERIOR COMPUTER
SERVICE AND SALES COMPANY*

This demonstration case continues the case study given in Chapter 1. You should reread that case before proceeding here.

Prior to giving the data (that Sparks had developed) to the bank, these data were shown to the consultant. After a brief discussion the consultant said, "This project should have some more work done on it to increase the probability that you will get the loan—and at a reasonable interest rate." Sparks said, "OK, what needs to be done?" The consultant answered, "If you want to go first class, a complete business plan would be the way to do it." After some discussion, Sparks said, "OK, let's go! Your fee sounds reasonable."

Working together, Sparks and the consultant developed the "Business Plan" shown below. Notice the following: (a) the change in company name that Sparks wanted, (b) a revision of the prior, overly optimistic projections, (c) the business plan, and (d) the cash-status projection (which includes repayment of the loan).

Superior Computer Service and Sales Company
Business Plan for Years 19D and 19E

COMPANY OBJECTIVES

1 To continue rendering our high-quality service on computers.
2 To immediately start giving the same high quality and prompt service on electric typewriters and photocopiers.
3 To adopt a progressive management approach and provide positive motivation to employees.
4 To install a simple, but effective, accounting system.

SPECIFIC GOALS

1 To earn a profit of at least 15 percent on revenue (income divided by revenue).
2 To increase service revenue at a 10 percent annual growth rate.
3 To generate sufficient cash each year to pay for operations, growth, and debt retirement.
4 To renovate the repair facilities to improve efficiency and make them more comfortable for employees.

STRATEGIES

1 To introduce a new line of service (electric typewriters and photocopiers) as a separate department.
2 To employ J. T. Smart on January 2, 19D. He is highly qualified to service photocopiers and typewriters. By the end of January, hire another service person.
3 Promote the new product:
   a Discuss the new service with current customers.
   b Direct mail to one thousand potential customers.
   c Call on about one hundred specially selected potential customers; use aggressive follow-up.
   d Advertise new and old services in local news media.
4 To set up a simple, but effective, accounting system. Hire an experienced accountant.

ORGANIZATION STRUCTURE

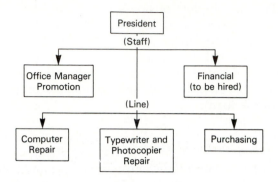

PROFIT PLAN (YEAR-END, DECEMBER 31)

	COMPUTERS	STRATEGIC PLAN	
	19D	19E	19F
Service revenues:			
Computers	$187,000	$230,000	$250,000
Typewriters and photocopiers	30,000	40,000	50,000
Total	217,000	270,000	300,000
Expenses*	184,000	225,000	244,000
Net income	$ 33,000	$ 45,000	$ 56,000

*Includes owner's salary and interest on loan.

	COMPUTERS	STRATEGIC PLAN	
	19D	19E	19F
Beginning cash balance	$ 20,000	$128,000	$ 35,000
Cash inflows:			
Operations (net)	28,000	47,000	52,000
Borrowing	300,000	-0-	-0-
Owner investment	-0-	-0-	28,000
Total cash available	348,000	175,000	115,000
Cash outflows:			
Payment on loan	100,000	100,000	100,000
Expansion of facilities			
and working capital	120,000	40,000	5,000
Owner withdrawals	-0-	-0-	-0-
Total cash expenditures	220,000	140,000	105,000
Ending cash balance	$128,000	$ 35,000	$ 10,000

NOTES

a   Historical data prepared by Sparks for years 19A–19C are attached.

b   The loan request was approved. Superior is required to submit quarterly financial reports to the bank.

Suggested References

CHAMBERLAIN, NEIL W., *The Firm: Micro-Economic Planning and Action* (a classic), New York: McGraw-Hill, 1962.

CHANDRA, GUYAN AND SURENDA SINGHVI, eds., *Budgeting for Profit*, Readings Nos. 1, 8, and 9. Oxford, Ohio: Planning Executives Institute, 1975.

GREENE, CHARLES N., EVERETT E. ADAM, JR., and RONALD J. EBERT, *Management for Effective Performance*, Chaps. 16 and 17. Englewood Cliffs, N.J.: Prentice-Hall, 1985.

RAPPAPORT, ALFRED, ed., *Information for Decision Making*, Readings Nos. 16, 17, and 18. Englewood Cliffs, N.J.: Prentice-Hall, 1982.

THOMAS, WILLIAM E., ed., *Readings in Cost Accounting, Budgeting and Control*, Readings Nos. 10, 21, and 28. Cincinnati: South-Western Publishing, 1983.

WILDAVSKY, AARON, *The Politics of the Budgetary Process*. Boston: Little, Brown, 1974.

Discussion Questions

1.   Briefly define comprehensive profit planning and control.

2.   This is a study question that requires you to identify the twelve fundamental concepts of profit planning and control given in the chapter. Match the descriptions with the key terms by entering capital letters in the appropriate spaces.

KEY TERMS		BRIEF DESCRIPTIONS
_____ (1)	Management process	A. Comparison of actual results with budget in performance reports
_____ (2)	Managerial commitment	B. Long-range profit plan
_____ (3)	Organizational structure	C. Develop historical accounting by responsibility centers
_____ (4)	Planning process	D. A management program to provide positive attitudes
_____ (5)	Control process	E. Development of objectives, goals, strategies, and standards
_____ (6)	Coordination	F. Includes planning, organizing, staffing, leading, and controlling

_____ (7) Communication channels	G. Specifies responsibility centers and the assignment of authorities and responsibilities
_____ (8) Strategic plan	H. Continuous feedforward, feedback, follow-up, and replanning—downward, upward, and laterally
_____ (9) Tactical plan	I. Significant management participation by all levels; acceptance of responsibilities
_____ (10) Responsibility accounting	J. Give primary managerial attention to "out-of-control" items
_____ (11) Exception principle	K. Continuous and consistent operation of all the management functions
_____ (12) Behavioral management	L. Short-range profit plan

3. Define feedforward, feedback, and replanning.

4. Explain and compare reference, wishful, and planned projections.

5. Explain the relationships among entity objectives, entity goals, and profit plans.

6. This is a study question. Match the primary participants with the related activities by entering appropriate letters in the spaces provided.

PPC ACTIVITY	PRIMARY PARTICIPANT
_____ (1) Develop the tactical profit plan	A. Middle managers
_____ (2) Develop entity objectives	B. President or board of directors
_____ (3) Develop the strategic profit plan	C. Operating managers
_____ (4) Develop entity goals, premises, and strategies	D. Top management group

7. It has been said that techniques, mathematical models, and simulations will not substitute for competent management. In light of this statement, explain the role of these tools in the management process.

8. What is meant by the term **time dimensions in PPC?** Distinguish between periodic and project plans.

9. What is the purpose of a planning calendar?

10. List and explain the four essential characteristics of a PPC performance report.

11. Define and justify a responsibility account system.

12. Explain the exception principle. Why is it important in PPC?

13. Distinguish between (a) cost centers, (b) profit centers, (c) revenue centers, and (d) investment centers.

14. Define coordination, and state how it can be improved by using PPC.

15. Why is flexibility in application of profit planning and control important?

16. Discuss the following statement: "Goals set for PPC purposes should be attainable and, at the same time, present a real challenge."

17. It has been said that "padding the budget invalidates the budget concept and little can be done about it." Explain the implications of this statement.

18. How can a PPC program enhance communication in an organization?

19. Why should management attention be devoted to favorable variances as well as unfavorable variances on performance reports?

20. Can profit planning and control be applied in small enterprises?

21. The planning function of management can be accomplished (1) with absolute formality at one extreme or (2) with complete informality at the other extreme. Explain the essence of these two extremes, and indicate what you think would be a rational approach in the typical medium-size business.

22. Elaborate on the following statement: "A meandering management is sure to be an inefficient management."

23. In respect to business management, someone has said "If you don't know where you are going, any old road will get you there." What are the implications of this statement?

CASE 2-1   *My secret budget!*

Price Department Store is a small business. During the past year the president, J. C. Price, gave each manager in the five sales departments a detailed sales plan (goal) and a selling expense budget. Price told the case writer: "My people do much, much better under a budget program if I give them sales budgets quite a bit in excess of what I really expect them to be able to do. Of course, they don't know what I really expect; therefore, the high budget goals that I give them keep the pressure on." The quarterly sales budgets are usually set at 15 percent above what Price really expects.

The case writer asked about the selling expense budgets: "Do you overstate them?" "Of course not, on most expenses, except their own salaries, I give them a tight budget—about 10 percent below—and for the same reason." "And how do they react to the quarterly performance reports?" was the case writer's query. Price's response was, "They usually say, 'I did my best.' Two managers did exceed by secret quarterly budgets on both sales and expenses, but no one fully met the budgets that I gave them."

REQUIRED

1. Do you agree with the president's viewpoint? Explain why.

2. What changes would you recommend? Explain the basis for your recommendations.

CASE 2-2   *A 10 percent cut in all expenses*

Daisy Manufacturers, Inc., produces and sells five products. Sales efforts encompass a ten-state area. The company is medium sized in relation to other companies in the industry. During the past four years, competition from foreign companies has increased. The company employs approximately five hundred people and has thirty-two departments and sales districts. During the past three years, the company has experienced a gradual, but significant, drop in profit. The company does not have a "profit planning and control program," although, as the executive vice-president stated: "We do an awful lot of planning and controlling."

Recently, the president sent a memorandum to all department and district managers that included the following directive: "Each department is expected to implement a 10 percent across-the-board cut, based on last year's results, in total expenses during the coming year. The quarterly financial statements will be evaluated to ascertain the effectiveness with which this directive is implemented."

REQUIRED

1. Evaluate the approach taken by the president to increase the company's profit.
2. Assuming some expenses were in fact too high, give some suggestions as to a general approach to increase profit.

CASE 2-3   *Which sales district performed the best?*

Town Sales company sells residential and industrial air-conditioning units in a twenty-county area in one of the midwestern states. The units are purchased from three different manufacturers and are sold directly to contractors and users. Company salespeople call on potential buyers; the territory is divided into five sales districts.

At the end of May 19B the following internal performance report, adhering to the format used in prior years, was distributed to the district managers:

Performance Sales Report
May 30, 19B

| | ACTUAL SALES | | | | VARIANCES* | |
| | | | YEAR TO DATE | | | |
DISTRICT	MAY 19A	MAY 19B	19A	19B	MONTH	YEAR TO DATE
1	$43,000	$47,000	$130,000	$135,000	$4,000	$5,000
2	56,000	57,000	165,000	164,000	1,000	1,000*

3	37,000	35,000	113,000	110,000	2,000*	3,000*
4	76,000	79,000	220,000	227,000	3,000	7,000
5†	62,000	60,000	190,000	191,000	2,000*	1,000

*Unfavorable.
†In operation three years.
Note: The accounting year ends December 31.

Sales Expense Report

	ACTUAL EXPENSES				VARIANCES*	
			YEAR TO DATE			
DISTRICT	MAY 19A	MAY 19B	19A	19B	MONTH	YEAR TO DATE
1	$ 4,500	$ 4,800	$ 15,000	$ 18,000	$ 300*	$3,000*
2	5,400	5,600	16,000	17,000	200*	1,000*
3	3,800	3,500	14,000	11,000	300	3,000
4	7,200	7,400	19,000	20,000	200*	1,000*
5	6,100	5,800	21,000	22,000	300	1,000*

*Unfavorable.

REQUIRED

1. Critique the above performance reports.
2. Now assume instead that Town prepared on a participative basis the following 19B tactical profit plan (simplified for case purposes).

	BUDGETED SALES		BUDGETED EXPENSES	
DISTRICT	MAY 19B	YEAR TO DATE	MAY 19B	YEAR TO DATE
1	$46,000	$133,000	$ 4,900	$ 17,000
2	60,000	170,000	5,700	18,000
3	32,000	105,000	3,200	10,000
4	82,000	230,000	7,000	18,000
5	60,000	190,000	5,700	23,000

Prepare a performance report that uses the information in the 19B profit plan. Also, give comments that emphasize favorable and unfavorable performance for the month of May 19B in terms of sales, expenses, and contribution margin (sales minus expenses) for each district.

CASE 2-4   *A busy bank controller!*

In an off-the-record discussion between the case writer and the president of the Ozarks Bank and Trust Company, the following statement was made: "Our budget system doesn't work too well for a number of reasons. For example, when the controller's department completes the annual budget, we sometimes ask for an evaluation of the impact of some alternative plans. We have to wait for four to five weeks. The controller blames it on the pileup of year-end accounting work. I have the feeling that all we get is the same set of figures as for the other alternatives except that they are reshuffled projections based on historical trends and ratios. It is my view that management needs better and more timely financial analyses on budgets from the controller than we are now getting. We want a budget completed by January 31."

REQUIRED

Evaluate the comments made by the president of the company.

3

The Profit Planning and Control Process

INTRODUCTION AND PURPOSE   The functions of management were discussed in Chapter 1, and the fundamentals of profit planning and control were discussed in Chapter 2. Chapter 3 will focus primarily on the **profit planning and control (PPC) process.** This application-oriented topic outlines the sequential phases that management must perform from the development of objectives for the business through control, corrective action, and replanning. The discussion will be related to profit-making enterprises, although PPC is applicable to other types of organizations. This chapter discusses PPC as a total planning and control package, rather than just selected parts of the PPC process.

Regardless of the type of endeavor, the management task is essentially the same, that is, to create and maintain an internal environment in which individuals working together as groups attain efficient performance in conformity with the broad objectives of the enterprise. The environment should motivate individuals to make their maximum contribution to the efforts of the group. Because economic, political, social, and technological factors operating in the external environment have a significant impact on all organizations, the management must understand them and try to harmonize the internal environment with them. Thus, the basic tasks of managing, planning, organizing, directing, and controlling are the same in business and nonbusiness enterprises.[1]

As you study this chapter, keep in mind that the management functions of planning and controlling are the primary focus of a PPC program. Most of the topics in this chapter will be discussed and illustrated in more detail in subsequent chapters.

Textbooks devoted primarily to the subject of management generally adopt one of two basic viewpoints:

1 Management by objectives (MBO)—this is a management viewpoint that emphasizes the planning function. Specification of enterprise objectives, goals, and plans is viewed

[1] A. Thompson Montgomery, *Management Accounting Information* (Reading, Mass.: Addison-Wesley, 1979), p. 79.

as the driving force that integrates financial resources, productive activities, and performance by people. It leads to the control function.

2   Management control systems (MCS)—this is a management viewpoint that emphasizes the control function. This viewpoint first specifies the necessity for, kinds of, and purposes of control. These are viewed as the imperatives that lead to planning, productive efficiency, and performance by people.[2]

Except for emphasis, both viewpoints are in conformity with the concept of PPC. Also, PPC is usually viewed by the authors of managerial accounting books as an important part of management accounting.[3]

THE PROFIT PLANNING AND CONTROL PROCESS   Exhibit 3-1 provides an overview of a typical **PPC process.** It necessarily integrates the planning, leading, and control functions of management (see Exhibit 1-1). A PPC program includes more than the traditional idea of a periodic or master budget. Rather, it encompasses the application of a number of related management concepts through a variety of approaches, techniques, and sequential steps. The term **comprehensive** means (1) the application of the broad concept of profit planning and control to all phases of operations in an enterprise and (2) the application of a total systems approach.

Consistent with the PPC process outlined in Exhibit 3-1, the typical **components** of a PPC program for a particular year are outlined in Exhibit 3-2. Notice the major components: (a) the Substantive Plan, (b) the Financial Plan, (c) Variable Expense Budgets, (d) Supplementary Data, and (e) Performance Reports. All of these components will be discussed and illustrated in subsequent chapters.

The **substantive plan** is represented by the broad objectives, strategies, specific plans, and programs of the organization, and by the concurrent commitment of management to long-range accomplishment of these objectives and plans. The substantive plan may be characterized as the "prose part" of the plan rather than the "numbers part" of the plan. It gives the foundation for the financial plan.

In contrast, the **financial plan** quantifies the planned financial results of implementing managerial objectives, planned strategies, plans, and policies. The financial plan then represents a translation into financial terms of objectives, goals, and strategies of management for specific periods of time.

With respect to these two basic plans, it is generally recognized that the substantive plan is often given inadequate attention. Alternatively, some companies perhaps give a disproportionate share of attention to the financial plan. The discussions in the first four chapters of this book attempt to place the substantive plan in perspective.

---

[2] Joseph A. Maciariello, *Management Control Systems* (Englewood Cliffs, N.J.: Prentice-Hall, 1984), Chap. 1; and Robert N. Anthony, John Dearden, and Norton M. Bedford, *Management Control Systems* (Homewood, Ill.: Richard D. Irwin, 1984), Chap. 1.

[3] Alfred Rappaport, ed., *Information for Decision Making, Readings in Cost and Managerial Accounting,* 3rd ed. (Englewood Cliffs, N.J.: Prentice-Hall, 1982), Reading No. 1, Charles T. Horngren, "Management Accounting: Where Are We?"

EXHIBIT 3-1

Overview of the PPC Process

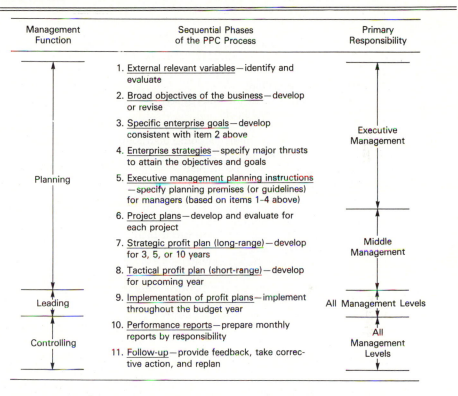

Management Function	Sequential Phases of the PPC Process	Primary Responsibility
Planning	1. External relevant variables—identify and evaluate	Executive Management
	2. Broad objectives of the business—develop or revise	
	3. Specific enterprise goals—develop consistent with item 2 above	
	4. Enterprise strategies—specify major thrusts to attain the objectives and goals	
	5. Executive management planning instructions—specify planning premises (or guidelines) for managers (based on items 1–4 above)	
	6. Project plans—develop and evaluate for each project	Middle Management
	7. Strategic profit plan (long-range)—develop for 3, 5, or 10 years	
	8. Tactical profit plan (short-range)—develop for upcoming year	
Leading	9. Implementation of profit plans—implement throughout the budget year	All Management Levels
Controlling	10. Performance reports—prepare monthly reports by responsibility	All Management Levels
	11. Follow-up—provide feedback, take corrective action, and replan	

The PPC process given in Exhibit 3-1 typically is repeated each budget year. Also, the components of a PPC program typically are restated for each budget year. For discussion purposes, we will assume that the strategic long-range profit plan covers a five-year time span and that the tactical short-range profit plan encompasses a twelve-month planning period. To visualize how the total systems approach as outlined might operate, assume that the formal PPC process (Exhibit 3-1) is **repeated on an annual basis.** Thus, all the basic steps in the planning phase would be reviewed and evaluated annually. The purpose is to update each component on the basis of managerial judgment and realistic performance expectations. In a particular year, some of the components, such as the broad objectives of the enterprise, may not be changed in any major respects, whereas other components may be completely revised for the upcoming year. In every case, however, we must anticipate that steps 3 through 8 would involve complete restatement each year.[4]

[4] The planning process should involve periodic, consistent, and in-depth replanning so that all aspects of operations are carefully re-examined and reevaluated. This prevents a budget planning approach that involves only justification of increases over the prior period. The concept of reevaluation and the necessity to justify all aspects of the plans periodically finds its strongest support in what has been called "zero-base budgeting." For a detailed discussion, see Peter A. Pyhrr, *Zero-Base Budgeting* (New York: John Wiley, 1973).

Next we will discuss the eleven steps in the PPC process (given in Exhibit 3-1) and relate them to the six PPC components (given in Exhibit 3-2).

EXHIBIT 3-2
Outline of the Components of a Typical PPC Program (for a Given Year)

A. **The Substantive Plan:**
   1. Broad objectives of the enterprise
   2. Specific enterprise goals
   3. Enterprise strategies
   4. Executive management planning instructions (planning premises)
B. **The Financial Plan:**
   1. Strategic long-range profit plan:
      a. Sales, cost, and profit projections
      b. Major projects and capital additions
      c. Cash flow and financing
      d. Personnel requirements
   2. Tactical short-range (annual) profit plan:
      a. Operating plan:
         Planned income statement:
         (1) Sales plan
         (2) Production (or merchandise purchases) plan
         (3) Administrative expense budget
         (4) Distribution expense budget
         (5) Appropriation-type budgets (e.g., research and development, promotion, advertising)
      b. Financial-position plan
         Planned balance sheet
         (1) Assets
         (2) Liabilities
         (3) Owners' equity
      c. Cash Flow Plan
C. **Variable Expense Budgets:**
   Output-expense formulas
D. **Supplementary Data:**
   (e.g., Cost-volume profit analyses, Ratio analyses)
E. **Performance Reports** (including any special reports)—each month-end and as needed.
F. **Follow-up, Corrective Action, and Replanning Reports**

Identification and Evaluation of External Variables

Chapter 1 briefly discussed the distinction between external and internal variables for an enterprise (see Exhibit 1-5). These variables exert major influences on an enterprise. The variable-identification phase of the PPC process focuses on (a) identifying and (b) evaluating the effects of the external variables. Identification also involves separate consideration of variables that are noncontrollable and those that are controllable. This means that management planning must focus on how to manipulate the controllable variables. Moreover, there must be managerial planning of how to work with the noncontrollable variables. That is, for both kinds of variables, how can management take advantage of potential favorable impacts and minimize potential unfavorable impacts on the enterprise? Exhibit 1-5 provided an example of one step in the evaluation of relevant variables. By **relevant variables** we mean those that will have a direct and significant impact on the enterprise. For a large business with a national market, the relevant variables would be broad in scope, whereas a small business would be concerned primarily with regional and local variables operating within the narrow environment of the enterprise. Analysis and evaluation of the environmental variables must be a continuing concern of management. This activity should involve all executive managers, who in turn should expect various staff groups to provide data and recommendations.

A particularly significant phase of this analysis includes an evaluation of the **present strength and weakness of the enterprise.** Planning must necessarily start with an objective and realistic understanding of the present status of products, services, markets, profits and returns on investments, cash flow, availability of capital, productive capabilities, and the competence of both management and nonmanagement personnel. This aspect of the planning process is usually difficult for most managements because deficiencies and inefficiencies are frequently difficult to identify and evaluate objectively by those directly involved. The comprehensive PPC approach is based on the expectation that these significant aspects of operations will be critically analyzed and evaluated periodically and in an orderly manner. In many companies, outside, independent assistance is almost essential to such an assessment. In this assessment and evaluation, present strengths and weaknesses should be classified between short-term and long-term potentials. For example, production capacity problems and the efficiency of certain groups of employees may be subject only to long-term resolution, whereas defective products may respond to short-term efforts. The better-managed companies have found that periodic (generally annual) assessment of strengths and weaknesses is a much more effective policy than one that states: "We will assess our strengths and weaknesses on a day-to-day basis as events are occurring."

This phase of the PPC process is fundamental in developing the substantive plan (see Exhibit 3-2). It is usually viewed as a special report used by the executive management and is not distributed to others.

Development of the Broad Objectives of the Enterprise

Development of the broad objectives of the enterprise is a responsibility of executive management. Based on a realistic evaluation of the relevant variables and an assessment of the strengths and weaknesses of the organization, executive management can specify or restate this phase of the PPC process.

The statement of broad objectives should express the mission, vision, and ethical character of the enterprise. Its purpose is to provide enterprise identity, continuity of purpose, and definition. One research study listed the purposes of the statement essentially as follows:

1   To define the purpose of the company (to state exactly why the company is in business).
2   To clarify the philosophy-character of the company (to state the moral and ethical principles that guide actions).
3   To create a particular "climate" within the business (to communicate the basic purposes and ethics of the company to all personnel in the company so that the employees may communicate them to customers and others outside the firm through their actions).
4   To set down a guide for managers so that the decisions they make will reflect the best interests of the business with fairness and justice to those concerned (to provide an overall guide to those in decision-making positions so that they can act independently, but within the framework of the firm's basic goals and principles).[5]

The statement of broad objectives normally should not specify quantitative goals. Rather, it should be a narrative expression of the purpose, objectives, and philosophical character of the business. It should represent the basic foundation or building block upon which to develop and positively reinforce pride in the company by management, other employees, owners, customers, and other enterprises that have commercial contacts with it. It should be designed for wide dissemination and should be "believable," which means that in the long run the company's actions must be in harmony with the statement.

The statement of broad objectives is the first part of the substantive plan of an organization (see Exhibit 3-2). A simplified example is given in the comprehensive case at the end of this chapter.

To illustrate the use of management by objectives (MBO) and the statement of enterprise objectives, we include below an excerpt from a *Management Accounting* article describing the budgeting process for the city of Charlotte, North Carolina.

BUDGETING BY OBJECTIVES IN THE CITY OF CHARLOTTE, NORTH CAROLINA

The objective of this article is to describe how the city of Charlotte, North Carolina, carries out its budgeting process while keeping its objectives and resources coordinated. . . .

Using this new approach, the city manager has been able to present a budget that enables the mayor and the city council to focus on objectives. The budget was guided by four primary objectives. These objectives were: (1) the property tax rate should not increase, (2) continued emphasis should be placed on making the best use of city employees and the present computer capability, (3) any budget increase should be held to a minimum, and (4) a balanced program of services should be presented.

---

[5] Adapted from Stewart Thompson, *Management Creeds and Philosophies*, Research Study No. 32 (New York: American Management Association), p. 9. Also see Alfred W. Schoennauer, *The Formulation and Implementation of Corporate Objectives and Strategies*, Research Series (Oxford, Ohio: Planning Executives Institute).

The services provided are broken down into six areas: (1) community development, (2) environmental health and protection, (3) protection of persons, and property, (4) transportation, (5) leisure-time opportunities, and (6) policy formulation and administration. Within each of these areas specific work objectives are determined, specific program changes are recommended to meet changing circumstances, resources are determined in terms of dollars and manpower, and recommendations are determined for city council action.

The transportation service area will be reviewed to illustrate how the individual service areas are presented in the budget. Each of the major service areas is handled in a similar manner.

The transportation budget starts with the overall objectives of the transportation service area and a recommendation of resources needed to meet the transportation objectives. The recommended resources are presented in terms of dollars and employment positions in a two year comparison. The overall objectives are stated in general terms. For instance, the overall objectives of the transportation program are stated as follows:

Plan and provide for the safe, convenient, economical and expeditious movement of people and goods, as desired and needed by residents and businesses in the Charlotte area. Furnish this capability through projects in new construction, capital improvement and maintenance which will facilitate a variety of transportation modes including automobiles, trucks, buses, airplanes and bicycles, and their associated traffic controls and facilities. Provide updated studies of feasible options for meeting immediate, short-term, and long-range transportation needs to guide the community and elected officials in making decisions that promote a highly usable, coordinated, effective, economical, and safe transportation network of facilities and services. Incorporate measures that demonstrate sensitivity and concern for potential impact on the environment and adjacent neighborhoods in all transportation undertakings.

The transportation budget is broken down into several areas such as airport, automotive services, traffic control, transportation planning and traffic engineering. Each of the areas such as traffic engineering is detailed in terms of general objectives, target clients, achievement and performance objectives, objective linkages, resources to meet the objectives, and recommended city council action.[6]

Development of Specific Goals for the Enterprise

The purpose of the "goals phase" of the PPC process is to bring the statement of broad objectives into sharper focus and to move from the realm of general information to more specific planning information. It provides both narrative and quantitative goals that are definite and measurable. These are specific goals that relate to the enterprise as a whole and to the major responsibility centers. These goals should be developed by executive management as the second component of the substantive plan for the upcoming budget year (see Ex-

---

[6] Charles H. Gibson, "Budgeting by Objectives: Charlotte's Experience," *Management Accounting,* January 1978, pp. 39 and 40.

hibit 3-2). Executive management should exercise leadership in this planning phase so that there will be a realistic and clearly articulated framework within which operations will be conducted toward common goals. Moreover, the specific goals provide a basis for performance measurement.

These broad, but specific, goals must be developed for both the strategic long-range plans and the tactical short-range plans. This statement of specific enterprise goals should define such operational goals as expansion or contraction of product and service lines, goegraphic areas, share of the market by major product service lines, growth trends, production goals, profit margins, return on investment, and cash flow. These specific goals in large measure are quantified and specified for each major subdivision of the enterprise. They are measurable for the areas of operation that are critical to long-run success of the enterprise. They must represent *realistic* goals as opposed to mere hopes or guesses. For an illustration, see the demonstration case at the end of this chapter.

Development and Evaluation of Company Strategies

Company strategies are the basic thrusts, ways, and tactics that will be used to attain planned objectives and goals. A particular strategy may be short-term or long-term. Here are some actual examples of basic strategies:

1 Increase long-term market penetration by using technology to develop new products and improve current products.
2 Emphasize product quality and price for the "top" of the market.
3 Expand marketing to all states in the USA. The company will not enter foreign markets in the foreseeable future.
4 Market with low price to expand volume (units).
5 Use both institutional and local advertising programs to build market share.
6 Improve employee morale and productivity by initiating a behavior management program.

The purpose of developing and disseminating enterprise strategies is to find the best alternatives for attaining the planned broad objectives and specific goals. Strategies focus on "how"; therefore, they outline a plan of action for the enterprise. Executive management must be creative and directly involved in the development of new strategies and in the adaptation of currently ongoing strategies in harmony with the relevant variables with which management must cope. In the development of basic strategies for the enterprise, executive management must focus on identification of the **critical areas** that influence the long-range success of the enterprise. Critical areas should be pinpointed through evaluation of relevant variables (Phase 1 discussed above). Notice that in Exhibit 3-2 it is shown as a component of the substantive plan.

Although strategy formulation is of continual concern to executive management, better-managed companies have found that **periodic reassessment** of the strategies is essential in light of a careful analysis of all relevant variables and their probable future impact on the enterprise. A statement of enterprise strategies for a particular year is shown in the comprehensive case at the end of the chapter.

Executive Management Planning Instructions

This phase involves **communication** of the substantive plan (Exhibit 3-2) to middle- and lower-management levels. It explains the broad objectives, enterprise goals, enterprise strategies, and any other executive management instruction needed to develop the strategic and tactical profit plans. It also is called the **statement of planning premises** or **the statement of planning guidelines.**

The executive planning instructions, issued by top management, communicate the planning foundation that is necessary for the participation of all levels of management in the development of the strategic and tactical profit plans for the upcoming budget year. Executive leadership is fundamental in developing and articulating this planning foundation, including the formulation of relevant strategies. Consequently, at this point in the planning process, the foundation has been established to articulate the broad and specific objectives of the enterprise and the strategies that facilitate their attainment. For example, both the executive in charge of the sales department and the manager of Plant 2 receive the planning premises and supporting procedural instruction for formulating, say, five-year and one-year sales plans in the one instance and profit plans for Plant 2 in the latter instance. Thus, we return to a fundamental principle stated in the preceding chapter; that is, communication is an essential part of the planning process.

Preparation and Evaluation of Project Plans

In Chapter 2 (Exhibit 2-6) we made a careful distinction between **periodic plans** and **project plans.** Recall that project plans encompass variable time horizons because each project has a unique time dimension. Project plans encompass such items as plans for improvement of present products, new and expanded physical facilities, entrance into new industries, exit from products and industries, new technology, and other major activities that can be separately identified for planning purposes. The nature of projects is such that they must be planned as separate units. In planning for a project, the time span considered must normally be the anticipated life span of the project. Projects approved must then be timed (or scheduled) into the strategic and tactical profit plans as diagramed in Exhibit 2-6. In addition to any ongoing projects, management should encourage on a continuing basis project proposals from any source within the enterprise. Consistent with this approach, during the formal planning cycle, management must evaluate and decide upon the plan status of each project **in process** and select any new projects to be initiated during time dimensions covered by the upcoming strategic and tactical profit plans. Although this phase was shown sequentially in Exhibit 3-1, we do not suggest in this instance—nor with respect to the other phases for that matter—that it is only a once-a-year management concern. However, preparation and evaluation of current and future project plans are essential on a formal basis as one of the profit planning phases outlined in Exhibit 3-1.

Development and Approval of Strategic and Tactical Profit Plans

When the managers of the various responsibility centers in the enterprise receive the Executive Management Planning Instructions and the Project Plans, they can begin intensive activities to develop their respective strategic and tactical profit plans. The strategic long-range plan and the tactical short-range profit plan are usually developed concurrently. It is possible (and not infrequent) that executive management or the chief financial executive will develop the strategic and tactical profit plans. This approach is seldom advisable because it denies full participation in the planning process by middle managers. Lack of participation can cause unfavorable behavioral effects. We will consider participative budgeting more extensively later in this chapter.

Assuming participatory planning and receipt of the Executive Management Instructions, the manager of each responsibility center will immediately initiate activities within his or her responsibility center to develop a strategic long-range profit plan (say, five years) and in harmony with the five-year plan, a tactical short-range profit plan (one year). Certain format and procedural instructions should be provided by a centralized source, normally the financial function, to establish the general format, amount of detail, and other relevant procedural and format requirements essential for aggregation of the plans of the responsibility centers into the overall profit plans. All of this activity must be coordinated among the centers in conformity with the organization structure. Exhibit 3-3 outlines the development of a typical short-term profit plan for a nonmanufacturing company.

As the two profit plans are being completed, the approval process must be initiated. This process involves approval, disapproval, or revision, based on either (a) action by executive management or (b) presentation and justification by the managers of the responsibility centers to the next higher level of authority. The latter approval process is often used because it entails numerous benefits. This approval process at its culmination would require that the manager of each major responsibility center be scheduled to present to executive management his or her plans and the underlying justifications. Each member of the executive management group would have been provided a copy of the center's plans to study before the final presentation. The manager of each major responsibility center should be given the opportunity to make a complete presentation of the plans and to use members of his or her staff and line people in this meeting. Following the presentation, an in-depth discussion on a give-

EXHIBIT 3-3

Development of a Typical Short-Tern (Tactical) Profit Plan for a Nonmanufacturing Company

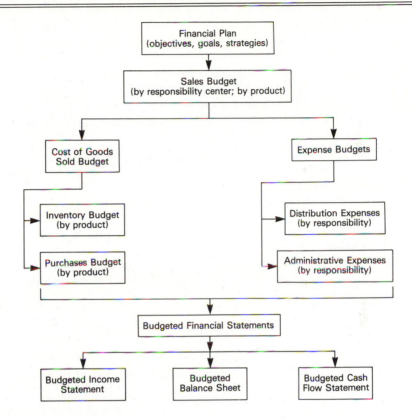

and-take basis should occur involving the members of the executive group and the manager of the responsibility center. The primary purposes of the presentation and related discussions are (1) to provide the manager of the responsibility center a full opportunity to "sell" his or her plans to executive management; (2) to provide the members of the executive committee an opportunity to discuss among themselves, and with the responsible manager, all relevant implications and assumptions implicit in the plans; and (3) to develop the best possible plan that the combined talents of the entire group, including the manager of the responsibility center, can devise. From these discussions some revision of the plans may occur or, alternatively, the plans may be considered sound in every major respect. Significantly, this approach enhances communication, coordination, and positive reinforcement. It is through this process that the basis for overall coordination of operational plans and efforts can be attained.

After the participatory approval process is completed for each major responsibility center and all relevant differences are resolved, the various plans and programs from the major responsibility centers are combined into the overall strategic and tactical profit plans for the enterprise as a whole. The process of combining the separate plans, each of which is presumably in harmony with the planning premises previously communicated by the executive management, is normally carried out as a centralized staff function under the supervision of the chief financial executive. Some companies use a staff member, the director of planning and control, or the budget director to coordinate these PPC activities.

When the two profit plans for the overall enterprise are completed, executive management should subject the entire planning package to a careful analysis and evaluation to determine whether the overall plans are the most realistic set that can be developed under the circumstances. When this point is reached, the two profit plans should be formally approved by the top executive and distributed to the appropriate managers. At this point we may note that, as a matter of security, only the top executives receive a complete copy of the profit plans.

The comprehensive case at the end of this chapter illustrates a partially completed strategic and tactical profit plan. Starting in Chapter 4, and continuing through later chapters, a detailed PPC case is given to supplement the discussion.

The use of long-term strategic planning and short-range tactical planning at Burroughs Corporation (now called UNISYS) is described in the following excerpt from a *Management Accounting* article.

LONG-RANGE AND SHORT-RANGE PLANNING AT BURROUGHS (UNISYS)

At Burroughs Corporation, we developed a manufacturing plant forecast to give our managers a comprehensive but consolidated view of future plant operations. The plant forecast is both a model and tool for management decisions. As a model, managers can use it to create, change, and delete data and assumptions. As a tool, it enables our managers to consolidate and integrate such key facts as personnel planning, cash flow, and investments into the corporate strategic planning process.

The manufacturing plant forecast used at Burroughs has improved management's ability to determine not only what impact changes in unit shipments, manpower mix, and capitalization decisions will have on future plant operations, but also how changes in product cost, cost reduction type capital projects, and improved operating performance will affect the net cost of operations. A disciplined, consistent, and standardized plant forecast is a priority at Burroughs, because of the company's major investment in development expense and product cost. Forty-five cents out of every dollar of corporate revenue is allocated for this area of operation.

The long-range forecast, the annual plan, and the quarterly and monthly outlook forecasts are prepared at various times of the year for management's review. Each plan has its own purpose and objective. The following departments provide information for the various forecasts.

☐   Development and Support Engineering: Expense levels, cost reductions, capital equipment;

- ☐ Industrial Engineering: Standards, productivity, production and facility capital equipment;
- ☐ Procurement: Material prices, lead time, contracts;
- ☐ Manufacturing: Inventory levels, production schedules;
- ☐ Product Assurance and Support: Qualification, receiving/inspection, scrap, rework, field support;
- ☐ Human Resources: Salary administration, benefits.

Burroughs' basic philosophy is: if you are going to measure the performance of a department or activity, then the department and individuals involved should supply the necessary input to assemble a good plan. As a result, management not only has as complete a financial forecast as possible, but a clear picture of the operational plans and controls that are currently in place is presented.

The purpose of the long-range plan forecast is to evaluate and determine what the future financial needs will be for an individual product or an entire program for the next three to five years. Based on information from product management, the forecast projects a product's anticipated financial performance and the impact it will have on existing corporate resources.

To be successful, a long-range plan must be able to achieve the following objectives:

1 Incorporate the engineering department's development and support expense for new products, features and cost reduction plans.
2 Review the plant capacity, personnel requirements in light of start-up products, and existing plant capitalization.
3 Identify future capital requirements for development departments, the manufacturing process, and support departments such as management information systems and the building structure.
4 Reflect changes in cash requirements for salaries, material, capital, etc.
5 Consider what impact inflation, fringe benefits, product cost and in overseas operations, the projected impact of exchange rates will have on the long-range profitability of the plant.

The annual forecast plan covers a two-year period and focuses on reviewing dynamic operational issues and marketing forecasts of current and soon-to-be-released products. The objectives of the plan are to:

1 Establish overhead rates based on fixed and variable types of expenses to be applied to various types of labor and material categories.
2 Determine transfer prices for equipment and services. Equipment is transferred to the books of the marketing organization that is responsible for marketing the product.
3 Issue budgets for operating departments.
4 Identify specific standard cost variances for material prices, material usage, labor efficiency and utilization, and time standard changes.
5 Detail manpower requirements by activity.
6 Calculate inventory levels and objectives.
7 Identify specific capital requirements and associated expense.
8 Prepare detailed plans for product introductions, cost profiles, and phase-out of replaced products.

> Quarterly forecasts and monthly outlooks are plans to monitor current performance against the annual plan and previously prepared operating forecast commitments. In these forecasts, greater emphasis is placed on analyzing cash flow, determining if the product cost improvements have been made, and if forecasted product shipments, expense control, labor productivity and recovery/improvement plans have been achieved. The goal is to keep management up-to-date on current developments in the event that immediate corrective action is necessary.[7]

Implementation of Profit Plans

Implementation of management plans that have been developed and approved in the planning process involves the management function of leading subordinates in attaining enterprise objectives and goals. Thus, effective management at all levels requires that enterprise objectives, goals, strategies, and policies be communicated and understood by subordinates. There are many facets involved in management leadership. However, a comprehensive profit planning and control program may aid substantially in performing this function. Plans, strategies, and policies developed through significant participation establish the foundation for effective communication. Preceding discussions emphasized that objectives and goals should be realistic and attainable; yet they should present a real challenge to the overall enterprise and to each responsibility center. The plans should have been developed with the managerial conviction that they are going to be met or exceeded in all major respects. If these principles are effective in the development process, the various executives and supervisors will have a clear understanding of their responsibilities and the expected level of performance.

Distribution of the profit plans within the enterprise was mentioned in a previous paragraph. It is desirable that the distribution of the profit plan include a "Statement of Planning Premises" from the top executive that emphasizes performance, challenge, and positive motivation. After distribution of the profit plans, a series of **profit plan conferences** should be scheduled. Under this plan, the chief executive officer should initially meet with the other top executives to discuss implementation and action in conformance with the objectives and goals specified in the profit plans. Similar conferences should be conducted until all major responsibility centers are reached. These conferences are intended to build profit consciousness, performance orientation, and aggressive, yet flexible, application of the plans to attain the objectives. These conferences also should cover the broader spectrum of the management process, including positive reinforcement and other behavioral issues. The conferences

[7] Dominic R. Janusky, "Plant Forecasting at Burroughs," *Management Accounting*, March 1985, pp. 59 and 60.

also should emphasize aggressive action and flexibility in implementing the plans and the control process. Special emphasis should be devoted to the manner in which unanticipated events and problems will be handled at various management levels. Profit plans cannot manage the business, and they must not constrain management in taking advantage of opportunities, even those not anticipated in the profit plans. Application of the management-by-exception principle and the principle of flexibility, both in respect to unforeseen events and opportunities and in the control process, should be emphasized.

An actual Statement of Planning Premises is shown in Exhibit 4-6 in the next chapter.

Use of Periodic Performance Reports

As profit plans are being implemented during the period of time specified in the tactical plan, periodic performance reports are needed. These performance reports are prepared by the accounting department on a monthly basis. Also, some special performance reports are prepared more often on an "as needed" basis. These performance reports (a) compare actual performance with planned performance and (b) show each difference as a favorable or unfavorable performance variation.

Performance reports were introduced in Chapter 1 under the heading "The Essence of Managerial Control." Also, Chapter 2 discussed performance reports under the heading "Management Control Using PPC." Exhibit 2-2 showed the format for a typical performance report. (It may be helpful to review those discussions.)

A clear distinction must be made between external and internal financial reports. Internal reports can be further classified as (a) statistical reports that give the basic quantitative internal statistics about the operations of the enterprise; (b) special managerial reports about nonrecurring and special problems; and (c) periodic performance reports. The latter reports focus on dynamic and continuous control tailored to the assigned managerial responsibilities. These reports are primarily repetitive, short-term reports developed for each of the **responsibility centers.** Short-term performance reporting is essential for effective control. For example, one important sales control approach compares actual sales with planned sales by areas of responsibility. Such a comparison at the end of the year would be of little or no value because it would be too late to take corrective action. On the other hand, daily, weekly, or even monthly sales reports may serve as a basis for effective and timely action. Actual performance statistics alone do not indicate high or low performance. Actual performance must be compared with **realistic goals** or **standards** in order to evaluate performance. For example, the concept of flexible expense budgets is used to provide realistic expense standards.

Use of Flexible Expense Budgets

The flexible expense budget is also referred to as the variable budget, sliding scale budget, expense control budget, and formula budget. The flexible budget concept applies only to **expenses.** It is completely separate from the profit plan, but it is used to complement it. Many companies do not use flexible budget procedures. Other companies integrate profit planning and flexible budget procedures.

Flexible budgets give realistic information about expenses that make it possible to compute budget amounts for various output volumes or rates of activity in each responsibility center. To do this, the flexible budget provides a **formula** for each expense in each responsibility center. The formula gives the relationship of each expense to **output** (volume of work) in the center. Each formula includes a constant expense factor and a variable expense rate.

In the case of a fixed expense, the variable rate is zero; in the case of a variable expense, the constant factor is zero; and in the case of a semivariable expense, there is a value for both the constant factor and the variable rate. To apply the concept in a department, then, each expense must be classified into one of three categories:

□ **Fixed expenses**—those that remain essentially constant in the short run, regardless of changes in output or volume of activity
□ **Variable expenses**—those that vary directly (in proportion) with changes in output
□ **Semivariable expenses**—those that are neither fixed nor variable but have both a fixed and a variable component

We can illustrate each category by assuming there are three types of expenses in Department 1, as shown below. Supervisory salaries of $10,000 per month is a fixed expense because it does not change due to different levels of output. Indirect material used in the manufacturing process is a variable expense with a variable rate of $1.50 per 100 direct labor hours of activity (that is, the measure of output). Indirect labor is a semivariable expense because it has both of the expense components—$450 per month fixed (the constant) plus $5.50 (the variable rate) per 100 direct labor hours. We will also assume that the **output** (work done or activity) in Department 1 can best be measured in terms of **direct labor hours worked.**

Department 1: Flexible Budget Expense Formulas

	EXPENSE FORMULA	
EXPENSE	FIXED AMOUNT (PER MONTH)	VARIABLE RATE (PER 100 DIRECT LABOR HOURS)
Supervisory salaries	$10,000	$ .00
Indirect materials	0	1.50
Indirect labor	450	5.50

Now assume that January has just ended and that the **actual accounting data** for the month are as follows.

Department 1: Actual Expense Data

Output (departmental activity)	2,000 direct labor hours
Supervisory salaries	$10,000
Indirect materials	$ 40
Indirect labor	$ 540

The flexible expense budget can be used to develop a realistic expense **performance report** for Department 1 at the end of January as follows.

Department 1: January Expense Performance Report

EXPENSE	COMPUTATION OF BUDGET EXPENSE GOAL	FLEXIBLE BUDGET GOAL	ACTUAL EXPENSE	EXPENSE VARIANCE
Supervisory salaries	$10,000 fixed plus zero variable	$10,000	$10,000	$ 0
Indirect materials	Zero fixed plus variable ($1.50 × 20)	30	40	(10)
Indirect labor	$450 fixed plus variable ($5.50 × 20)	560	540	20
Total		$10,590	$10,580	$10

Parentheses indicate unfavorable variances.

This example shows the relevance of the flexible budget approach in cost control. To illustrate the relevance, assume the **tactical profit plan** showed 1,500 hour of planned output. Thus, the three budget goals included in the original tac cal profit plan were (a) supervisory salaries, $10,000; (b) indirect materials, $1.50 × 15 = $22.50; and (c) indirect labor, $450 + ($5.50 × 15) = $532.50. Comparison of the actual expenses for January with these budget goals would have shown **unfavorable variances** of $17.50 for indirect materials and $7.50 for indirect labor, neither of which would be appropriate or fair to the supervisor of the department. The flexible budget goals overcome this differential-output problem.

Flexible expense budget formulas can be used in two phases of the PPC process. The above illustration showed how the formulas are used in **performance control reports.** They can also be used to develop expense amounts included in developing the **tactical profit plan.** If the flexible expense formulas are developed concurrently with the strategic and tactical profit plans, they are used to compute the budgeted expense amounts in the tactical profit plan. This is done by multiplying the planned output or activity of each responsibility center by the related variable expense rate for each center and then adding any fixed costs for the center.

The example above shows the complementary relationship between, or integration of, the tactical profit plan, the performance reports, and flexible expense budgets. It is occasionally said that the flexible budget technique represents a duplication. On the contrary, when these PPC techniques are properly understood and used, they complement each other. Flexible expense budgets are usually constructed early in the budget planning period because, as indicated, they provide cost data for the tactical profit plan. Flexible expense budgets and other supplementary analyses are discussed in detail in subsequent chapters.

Implementation of Follow-up

Follow-up is an important part of effective control. Because performance reports are based on assigned responsibilities, they are the basis for effective follow-up actions. It is important to distinguish between cause and effect. The performance variations are **effects** (the results); the management must determine the **underlying causes.** The identification of causes is primarily a responsibility of **line management.** Analysis to determine the underlying causes of both favorable and unfavorable performance variances should be given immediate priority. In the case of **unfavorable** performance variances, after identifying the basic causes, as opposed to the results, an alternative for corrective action must be selected. Then the corrective action must be implemented.

In the case of favorable performance variances, the underlying causes should also be identified. This case seldom requires corrective action. Rather, the underlying causes of favorable variances often provide valuable information for improving efficiency and for developing positive reinforcements to the less-successful operations and employees. This is called "transference of success."

Finally, there should be a special "follow-up of the prior follow-up actions." This step should be designed to (1) determine the effectiveness of prior corrective actions and (2) provide a basis for improving future planning and control procedures.

The primary objective of this brief discussion of the six major components of PPC (Exhibit 3-2) was to provide a "broad-brush picture" of a comprehensive profit planning and control program. It is important to have a broad perspective at this point so that the discussions of the application of PPC in the remaining chapters can be understood in proper relationship to the whole process. It is our conviction that the full potential of the various techniques, procedures, and approaches involved can be realized only if they are integrated into a coordinated, practical, and comprehensive system. All the concepts, techniques, and approaches described as parts of the system are widely discussed in the literature of management and accounting. However, very few attempts have been made to "package" them so that their interrelationships can be more clearly understood and their full potential realized in an enterprise. In this book they are packaged in the way that they are applied in well-managed companies.

TIMING OF THE PLANNING PROCESS—CONTINUOUS PROFIT PLANNING

Profit planning involves selection of defined periods of time for the strategic and tactical profit plans (often five years and one year, respectively). The annual planning phase for these budgets precedes the budget year. Replanning, to take into account feedback information, occurs throughout the budget year as needed. This timing pattern is appropriate for companies that can plan realistically one year in advance.

In contrast, some organizations experience conditions that make it inadvisable to plan very far into the future. Such organizations can use **continuous profit planning.** This approach requires frequent planning and replanning because of the dynamics of the environment or technology.

The procedure usually followed for tactical planning, when continuous profit planning is used, is to prepare an annual (or semiannual) profit plan, which is revised and replanned each month (or quarter) by progressively dropping the month (or quarter) just completed and adding another similar time period in the future. To illustrate the continuous approach, assume that prior to January a tactical profit plan is prepared extending, say, through June. At the end of January, the semiannual profit plan is replanned by dropping January and adding July, and at the same time the projections for February through June are revised when deemed appropriate. Thus, this approach results in a **continuous** semiannual profit plan for the business.

An example of an even more dynamic approach to profit planning and control is followed by a company widely recognized for its effective management. This company has used the concept of continuous profit planning and control for many years. An **annual** profit plan is prepared by each division of the company. These individual divisional plans are then combined and summarized into the overall profit plan. The annual profit plan is prepared in detail by month for the upcoming quarter and by quarter for the remaining nine months. Near the end of each quarter, the profit plan is extended another quarter by replanning the upcoming quarter (by month) and the following nine months (by quarter). Under this approach, management has monthly goals for the immediate quarter and quarterly goals for each of the three following quarters. In this particular business, there is a strategic long-range projection covering a period of ten years. This ten-year plan is restudied and replanned on a two-year cycle. The continuous approach eliminates the need for interim revision of tactical profit plans occasioned by unusual events and circumstances not previously anticipated. The important distinction of the continuous approach to profit planning is that management has detailed and continuous plans for a consistent period of time in the future, whereas under periodic profit planning, the short-range planning period runs out at the end of the year.

Factors such as selling seasons, length of the process or manufacturing time (or merchandise turnovers), seasonal cycles, natural business cycles for the industry, financial considerations, and other operating conditions may influence the length of the profit planning period.

With respect to the frequency of profit plan preparation and revision, well-managed companies that have had many years of experience with profit planning and control programs have found that replanning should be undertaken **formally and extensively at least on an annual basis.** Use of the continuous approach explicitly establishes the timing and frequency of the replanning process. Regarding the strategic long-range profit plan, some companies do not follow a pattern of annual revision, but rather the policy of "revising when circumstances have changed significantly." In our opinion, this latter policy is not sound. Instead, it is logical from the managerial point of view to adopt a policy of periodic revision of the long-range plan that normally should correspond with the formal planning activities for the tactical short-range plan.

From time to time all companies experience major unanticipated events, such as strikes or casualty losses (e.g., fires, floods, earthquakes), and replanning. When major events occur during the period covered by the short-range profit plan, a problem arises as to whether the plan should be revised for the remaining months of the budget period to take into account the effect of the major event. In the case of such a major event, unless it occurs near the end of the year, it would appear that complete revision of the tactical profit plan for the remainder of the year would be in order. In contrast, minor events and low performance normally should not cause revision of the basic profit plan. Frequent revision of profit plans to take into account minor events and inefficiencies tends to destroy the credibility of the plan and decrease the seriousness with which managers regard plans during their development and implementation.

LINE AND STAFF RESPONSIBILITIES RELATED TO PPC   The chief executive has ultimate responsibility for profit planning and control. However, there must be a concomitant assignment of responsibilities to line and staff executives. Each line executive must be assigned center responsibility for (1) operational decision inputs into the plan, (2) implementation, and (3) control. The profit planning and control program must be established upon a firm foundation of **line responsibility** and commitment to develop, implement, and attain the role of each center in the enterprise objectives and goals. We cannot overemphasize that a profit planning and control program should be viewed as an approach to assist managers in line positions in carrying out their basic responsibilities.

They should view the plans as their own, and they must assume full responsibility for attaining them.

In contrast, the staff responsibilities for a PPC program include (1) designing and improving the system (as opposed to making operational decision inputs), (2) supervising and coordinating the operation of the system, (3) providing expert technical assistance, analyses, and advice to the line managers, and (4) developing and distributing performance reports.

The chief financial officer should be assigned overall staff responsibility for the profit planning and control program. Normally the financial function includes a budget director, or director of planning and control, who should be assigned the staff supervisory responsibility. In view of the importance of an effective profit planning and control program, the position on the staff of the individual responsible for the program should be such that it will command attention and respect throughout the firm. It is advisable that the individual responsible for the profit planning and control function report directly to the chief financial officer or, in the absence of such a position, directly to the top executive. If there is a budget director as well as a chief financial officer, it seems preferable for the former to report to the latter, who in turn should report to the top executive. The positions implied for the chief financial officer and the budget director do not imply that they should have line authority in respect to planning inputs and control (except for their own responsibility center). Staff executives should not be assigned the responsibility for "enforcing the budget."

The typical staff duties of the budget director for a PPC program are as follows:

1   Advise the chief executive, appropriate top-management committees, and others on all aspects of the profit planning and control program.
2   Recommend the profit planning and control procedures and technical requirements for each component of the program.
3   Assume responsibility for organization of the program and the necessary time schedules to make it operative.
4   Provide overall technical supervision of the profit planning and control program.
5   Design and recommend essential forms, schedules, and reports relevant to the profit planning and control program.
6   Supervise the preparation and revision of the profit planning and control manual and other related materials for approval by the chief executive.
7   Furnish analyses of past and future costs, revenues, and so on, as requested by appropriate managers.
8   Translate certain preliminary policy decisions into their probable or alternative financial effect on future operations.
9   Prepare performance reports by responsibility center and by other relevant classifications.
10   Help analyze and interpret variances between actual and planned goals (staff basis only).
11   Perform specific clerical work associated with the profit planning and control program.

12 Supervise revision of both the profit plans and the profit planning and control program.

13 Perform various statistical analyses (upon request) that are related to the profit planning and control program.

14 Receive tentative plans and transmit them to appropriate executives for review and revision.

15 Organize, coordinate, and conduct appropriate training sessions and conferences related to the profit planning and control program.

16 Reproduce and distribute, in conformity with instructions of the chief executive, various components of the profit plans.

Most well-managed companies use an executive committee, or a comparable committee, in the profit planning and control process. This top-level committee should include the president and vice-presidents (including the chief financial executive). The chief executive often serves as chairperson of this committee for planning and control purposes. Fundamentally, this committee should have the responsibility for developing the substantive plan and for ascertaining that all aspects of the profit plans for the subunits are sound and, when combined into the overall comprehensive profit plan, for ensuring that they represent the best plans that can be developed under the circumstances. The direct responsibilities of this top-level committee are as follows:

1 Develop the substantive plan.

2 Receive and review profit plans from the major responsibility centers and make appropriate recommendations for their improvement.

3 Recommend decisions on major items incorporated into the profit plans where there may be conflict or lack of coordination among the functional subdivisions of the enterprise.

4 Recommend changes to improve the planning and control processes related to the profit planning and control program.

5 Receive and analyze periodic performance reports from the responsibility centers.

6 Consider various alternatives and make recommendations and decisions for corrective action.

7 Make recommendations for revision of the profit plans when conditions warrant.

8 Make recommendations for changes in profit planning and control program policies and procedures for greater effectiveness.

PPC POLICIES MANUAL   A **profit planning and control manual** is normally desirable to enhance communication, specify procedures, and provide reasonable stability in the operation of the system. A profit planning and control (or budget) manual should include the following:

1. A statement of objectives of the PPC program
2. Procedures to be followed in developing profit plans:
   a. Instructions and forms to be used
   b. Procedures for making planning decisions:
      —Operating executives
      —Staff executives
      —Top-management budget committee

3. A profit planning and control calendar that specifies completion dates for each part of the profit plan and for the submission of reports
4. Distribution instructions for profit plan schedules
5. Instructions and procedures with respect to performance reports
   a. Responsibility and procedures for preparation of reports:
      —Actual results
      —Budgeted data and variations
      —Analysis of variances
   b. Form, content of, and procedures for performance reports
   c. Distribution instructions for performance reports
6. Procedures for taking corrective action on variances:
   a. Unfavorable variances
   b. Favorable variances
7. Follow-up and replanning procedures

The following excerpt from a *Management Accounting* article describes the process used by Wisconsin Life Insurance Company in developing a budget manual.

DEVELOPMENT OF A BUDGET MANUAL
AT WISCONSIN LIFE INSURANCE COMPANY

Wisconsin Life Insurance Co. was growing—and growing fast. Although we were growing, the company had never had a budget manual. The area of budgeting had not been regarded as a priority. Managers drew up their budgets based on information filtered down to them, one at a time, piece by piece. As they were preparing their budget, some new information would come down from top management, here and there, and they would have to readjust their figures.

Then things began to change. Management recognized the need to have a systematic approach to budgeting, and a budget analyst was hired to create a budget manual that would be useful to line management as well as to each individual involved in the budget process.

As a first step, we decided to interview department heads, managers and supervisors who have some involvement with the budgeting process. We wanted to find out from these individuals what information they need; what are the most troublesome areas, when they work on their budgets? Are the available data, such as cost information on various expense items, adequate to enable them to do their budgeting? Or do they feel they have to contact various sources before they get an answer?

From these interviews, we learned that during the budget process department heads and their delegates usually do not have information readily on hand so they can use it. They have to contact different sources in order to obtain cost data. The most troublesome aspects from their standpoint have to do with budgeting for salary, travel/hotel/meal expenses, printing, paper costs, and office furniture and fixtures. In the absence of any agreed procedures, everyone tends to make an educated guess (sometimes referred to as a "guesstimate") regarding the costs involved. And the managers' guesses often are based on inaccurate or contradictory assumptions. . . .

In order for us to gain acceptance from users and have an effective budget system, we needed to create a budget manual that would provide easy-to-follow instructions on forms, a standard cost table for different kinds of expense to be used by everyone, and other user-oriented aids. A standard cost table on commonly used items (relating

> to travel, bureau and association dues, printing, office furniture price list, and so on) will provide for consistency and uniformity of approach throughout the organization.
>
> Our objective was to design a budget manual in which all needed information would be organized into one single document. The manual comprises two parts.
>
> Part 1 is the manual itself with sample forms and the instructions to go with each of the forms. Part 1 is supposed to remain constant from year to year, unless there is a significant change in procedures.
>
> Part 2 is what we term the "supplemental data." This supplemental package provides for several cost schedules that are to be used in connection with the budget cycle. These schedules, updated annually, include typical interstate travel costs, price lists of commonly used office furniture, equipment and supplies, paper costs, and other relevant costs.[8]

PLANNING PERSPECTIVES   The discussions in Chapters 2 and in this chapter emphasize the concepts and application of PPC to the management functions of planning, leading, and controlling. This relates to most enterprises, regardless of size and whether manufacturing or nonmanufacturing. One of the problems in long-range planning, in our opinion, has been confusion about its real nature and a tendency to pursue long-range planning on an informal, ad hoc basis.

Another problem is the failure to distinguish between strategic long-range planning and forecasting. Forecasting is a technical activity, usually assigned to technically trained staff specialists. Its purpose is to predict a probable outcome from a given set of circumstances for a specified period in the future. A forecast rests upon specified assumptions made by the forecaster. Forecasting often provides some of the basic data that are useful in the planning process. In contrast, planning, as we have outlined it in prior discussions, is a fundamental managerial activity (as opposed to a technical staff activity) that includes specific decisions about the objectives, goals, and strategies of the enterprise. It also requires preparation of strategic tactical profit plans.

Another common problem is partial planning. For example, some companies limit their long-range planning to a single key area such as captial additions. No attention is given to developing comprehensive plans that cover all facets of expected future operations. Concern with strategic planning for only one or a few of the key areas has tended to narrow the scope of the planning activity of management. The third type of problem relates to the definition of the term *long-range*. Some companies refer to their annual profit plan as long-range planning. In these cases, the substantive plan is often given inadequate attention.

Alternatively, many companies give attention only to the financial plan. The discussions in the first four chapters of this book place the substantive and financial plans in proper perspective.

---

[8] Chung Bothwell, "How to Improve Financial Planning with a Budget Manual," *Management Accounting*, December 1984, pp. 34 and 35.

SOME BEHAVIORAL IMPLICATIONS OF A PPC PROGRAM   Many companies, whether or not they use PPC, have a need to consider a behavior management program (see Chapter 1). The focus of such a program is to influence behavior or relationships with positive reinforcements (or motivations). The basic purpose is to attain **goal congruence** between the individual employees' goals and the goals of the enterprise. Individual goals include job satisfaction, financial rewards, recognition, career satisfaction, and security. Enterprise goals include profits, productivity, growth, product development, market share, public responsibility, and employee development. Employee and enterprise goals often involve conflicts. The burden of attaining goal congruence (i.e., minimization of goal conflicts) is a primary responsibility of the enterprise. These behavioral implications exist in all organizations.[9]

A PPC program can accentuate or ameliorate the behavioral problems in a company. PPC programs are effective in some companies and controversial in others. The key to effectiveness is the way that the management uses the PPC program. Often a PPC program will expose an already existing, and pervasive, set of behavioral problems in a company. This occurs because many behavioral problems are related to factors such as inadequate communication, job expectations, performance evaluations, rewards (both financial and nonfinancial), and relationships between supervisors and peers. One author emphasizes the wide range of factors shown in Exhibit 3-4.[10]

Nonparticipative planning, secrecy in how standards are set, authoritarian control procedures, excessive stress, uneven reward systems, and excessive emphasis on profits will generate increased negative motivation throughout a company. When such conditions prevail, employees (including middle- and lower-level managers) will adopt protective or defensive behavior tactics. These tactics include padding budgets, subtle attempts to "beat the system," decreases in product and service quality, absenteeism, lackadaisical attitudes, decrease in initiative, and covert information.

We cannot overemphasize the importance of human relations in profit planning and control. Many of the shortcomings attributed to budgeting programs can be directly identified with negative management attitudes and other behavioral problems. In the case of a weak or unsophisticated management, techniques such as PPC are frequently used as the "whipping boy." Obviously, a technique by itself can do nothing—the managers using it determine its value. It is the individual manager who makes the behavioral mistakes, exerts excessive pressure, establishes unrealistic standards, and is inflexible. A key function of the manager is to positively motivate people through enlightened leadership.

[9] William E. Thomas, ed., *Readings in Cost Accounting, Budgeting, and Control*, 6th ed. (Cincinnati: South-Western Publishing, 1983): Reading No. 7, Edwin H. Caplan, "Behavioral Assumptions of Management Accounting," and Reading No. 10, Michael Schiff and Arie Y. Lewin, "The Impact of People on Budgets."

[10] Gary Dessler, *Human Behavior, Improving Performance at Work* (Reston, Va.: Reston Publishing, 1980), p. 61.

EXHIBIT 3-4

Summary of Herzberg's Motivation-Hygiene Findings

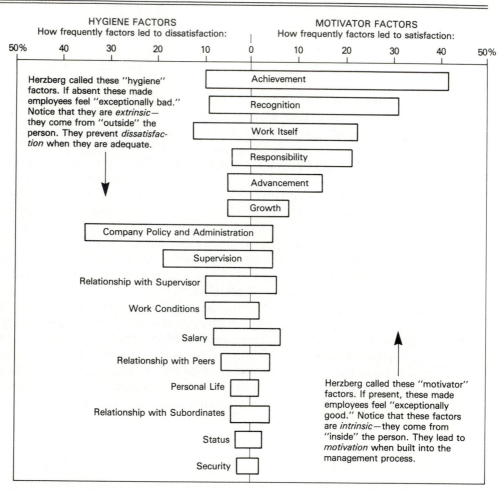

The behavioral implications of a profit planning and control program offer both opportunities and problems. In designing and administering a PPC program, the emphasis should be on maximizing positive reinforcement at all organizational levels. In considering the behavioral impacts, it may be helpful from time to time to distinguish between the viewpoint of the individual managers and that of the enterprise. They each have their own peculiarities, motivations, goals, and impacts. A common trait is to always blame the problems on someone else. Self-evaluation can solve many problems. Also, on certain issues, it is helpful to view the managers and nonmanagers separately because they have essentially different roles in the enterprise.

Management is a leadership or directive effort that sets objectives and goals and evaluates performance. PPC is a system designed to help management accomplish these responsibilities. Individual managers and other employees quickly identify the management approach used with the enterprise. The system, as they perceive it, will affect them positively or negatively. In the case of high negative motivations, they will become discouraged, resign, or often sabotage the system. They will even solicit help from others to sabotage or beat the system. Alternatively, if the system gains their favor, they will show enthusiasm, creativity, and productivity. Thus, the interface between the system and the managers at all levels is loaded with behavioral implications. This point suggests the importance of applying enlightened behavioral judgment in developing, administering, and improving the management system.

The behavioral conflicts between line and staff managers can be pervasive. The controller and budget director are staff personnel, and they are principally concerned with service. Staff personnel should not usurp line authority, nor give that impression. Staff personnel should not be directed to exercise authority over operating line personnel. The controller and budget director should not provide the decisional inputs to the profit plan because this is strictly a line function. Nor should the controller or budget director reprimand operating personnel for unfavorable results reflected on performance reports. The duties of the budget director were outlined above. Basically, the budget director should design and direct the budget program but should not provide decisional inputs or have responsibility for enforcing the budget. It is important to make a clear distinction between (1) enforcing the budget and (2) reporting actual results compared with budget goals. The controller and budget director are responsible for reporting to all levels of management the actual results of operations compared with the budget goals.

Corrective action resulting from either favorable or unfavorable results is strictly a line function. The controller or budget director should not be put in the position of approving budgets or taking line action concerning efficient or inefficient operating results outside the budget department. The controller and budget director should not be responsible for cost control. Rather, they may be properly charged to design an effective system of cost control. In the final analysis, line executives and supervisors should be charged with the direct responsibility for implementing cost control. A careful distinction between line and staff is essential to good management; the distinction must not only be drawn by top managment but there must also be assurance that the distinction is being followed throughout the company. The responsibilities for planning and control should be carefully specified in written instructions distributed to all managers. A company budget manual is important for disseminating general budget responsibilities and policies.

Participatory Budgeting

Participation of middle-level and lower-level managers in the budgeting process can have beneficial effects in at least two ways. First, the process of participation reduces information asymmetry in the organization, thereby enabling top management to gain insight into enviornmental and technological issues about which lower-level managers have specialized knowledge. Second, the process of participation may bring about a greater commitment by lower-level managers to carry out the budget plan and "meet the budget." Considerable study has been done in recent years on the process and impact of participatory budgeting. Brownell[11] has reviewed many of the studies' results, and we will summarize some of those findings below.

Brownell found that there are four classes of variables that moderate the impact of budgetary participation: cultural, organizational, interpersonal, and individual. The effects of these classes of variables are summarized in Exhibit 3-5.

EXHIBIT 3-5

Variables Moderating the Impact of Budgetary Participation

CULTURAL VARIABLES	
Nationality	In some cultures, participation is viewed as a norm of behavior, while in others it is viewed as a concession by management.
Legislative system, nationality	Some European economies are confronted with legislation concerning the participation of lower-level personnel.
Racial, religious	In some cultures, participation is structured around a cultural-group model (for example, the Israeli Kibbutz model).
ORGANIZATIONAL VARIABLES	
Environmental stability	Participation is an appropriate response to turbulent and dynamic environments.
Technology	Complex interdependencies among subunits in technologically sophisticated environments are better managed with participation.
Task uncertainty	High-information needs of uncertain task environments can be satisfied using a participatory approach.
Organizational structure	Large, decentralized organizations are better managed in a participative mode.

[11] Peter Brownell, "Participation in the Budgeting Process: When It Works and When It Doesn't," *Journal of Accounting Literature,* Spring 1982, pp. 124–53.

INTERPERSONAL VARIABLES

Task stress	In some organizations, participation is more effective in stressless situations, but less effective in stressful situations.
Group size	Participation is more effective in managing a small group than in managing a large group.
Intrinsic satisfaction of the task	Participation is more important when tasks are not intrinsically satisfying.
Congruence between task and individual	Where tasks are ambiguous, high need achievers prefer a participative style while low need achievers prefer more direction.

INDIVIDUAL VARIABLES

Personality (locus of control)	Participatory management is preferred by those who feel their destinies are under their own control; low participation is preferred by those who trust in luck or chance.
Personality (authoritarianism)	Highly authoritarian personalities prefer low participation, and vice versa.
External reference point	People who feel their experience offers a significant contribution prefer to participate; otherwise, low participation is preferred.
Perceived emphasis placed on accounting information	Managers who feel that their performance is judged relative to a budget prefer participation; otherwise, low participation is preferred.

Source: Peter Brownell, "Participation in the Budgeting Process: When It Works and When It Doesn't," *Journal of Accounting Literature,* Spring 1982, pp. 128, 134, and 140. This article also contains an extensive bibliography of the literature in this area.

Chendall[12] investigated the impact of personality combinations on the effectiveness of participative budgeting and found that the effects of participative budgeting on subordinates' satisfaction with their jobs and the budgets are influenced by the configuration of authoritarianism between the subordinate and the superior. Positive attitudes toward participation are stronger in dyads (i.e., pairs) consisting of subordinates and superiors who have the same levels of authoritarianism—either high or low. In a heterogeneous dyad, where the superior is authoritarian and the subordinate is nonauthoritarian, the superior prefers personal interactions based on power and authority. Also, the superior is likely to be more autocratic and less concerned with group approval. Low-authoritarian subordinates, who do not share these attitudes, often find that the personal exchanges forced by participation result in frustration and antago-

[12] Robert H. Chendall, "Authoritarianism and Participative Budgeting: A Dyadic Analysis," *Accounting Review,* April 1986, pp. 263–72.

nism. Conversely, when the subordinate is highly authoritarian, he or she expects guidance on the assignment of responsibilities and is likely to respond aggressively to a low-authoritarian superior who does not fulfill these expectations. On the other hand, when both actors in the budgeting exchange are lower authoritarians, participation will probably involve cooperation and trusting exchanges with the likelihood of enhanced subordinate satisfaction.

Merchant[13] studied the relationships of the corporate environment to types of budgeting processes and also to the outcomes of budgeting, such as managerial motivation, attitudes, and performance. He found that budgeting, as part of the corporate control strategy, is related to the corporate context. Larger firms tend to make relatively high use of more formal administrative controls, as opposed to interpersonal controls. In all the organizations studied, the more formal and elaborate budgeting processes are generally received well by the managers, and in larger firms they appear to be more positively linked with performance. In another study, Milani[14] found a significant positive association between the degree of budget participation and the attitudes of supervisors toward their jobs and the company.

Young[15] investigated the effects of risk aversion and budgetary participation on the existence of budgetary slack. He found that a subordinate who participates in the budgetary process tends to build slack (padding) into the budget; moreover, this slack is in part attributable to the subordinate's risk aversion. Brownell[16] reports the results of an empirical investigation in which the marketing and research and development units of a large firm were compared in terms of both the environmental conditions they face and the effects of their control system choices on managerial performance within the two functional areas. Limited support is provided for predicted environmental differences. R&D managers perceived their environment as more complex than that faced by their counterparts in marketing. Support was found for the hypothesis that budgetary participation would be more effective in R&D than in marketing. But the hypothesis that a heavy reliance on accounting information would be more appropriate in marketing than in R&D was not confirmed.

In summary, substantial research on budgetary participation, and the variables that moderate its effectiveness, suggest that the effectiveness of participation is highly dependent on the organization, its environment and technology, and the people who manage it. The use of participatory budgeting by the University Community Hospital in Tampa, Florida, is described in the following excerpt from a *Management Accounting* article.

---

[13] Kenneth Merchant, "The Design of the Corporate Budgeting System: Influences on Managerial Behavior and Performance," *Accounting Review*, October 1981, pp. 813–29.

[14] Kenneth Milani, "The Relationship of Participation in Budget Setting to Industrial Supervisor Performance and Attitudes: A Field Study," *Accounting Review*, April 1975, pp. 274–84.

[15] S. Mark Young, "Participative Budgeting: The Effects of Risk Aversion and Asymmetric Information on Budgetary Slack," *Journal of Accounting Research*, Autumn 1985, pp. 829–42.

[16] Peter Brownell, "Budgetary Systems and the Control of Functionally Differentiated Organizational Activities," *Journal of Accounting Research*, Autumn 1985, pp. 502–12.

PARTICIPATIVE BUDGETING IN A HOSPITAL

Because the department directors along with their first-line supervisors, vice presidents, the president, the finance committee and board of trustees have been involved in the budgetary process, the budget is felt to be owned by all of them as a total document. This feeling of ownership is particularly true in the case of the individual department director with reference to his specific portion of the budget. This commitment is taken seriously. Activities are monitored on a daily basis to ensure that prompt corrective action can be taken if necessary.

This daily monitoring is supplemented by a monthly budget report that compares the budgeted amounts agreed to by the department director with the actual amounts incurred. The hospital's experience has been that should adjustments be required during the year—be they an increase or decrease because of unforeseen increases or decreases in patient demand for services—that they be made without any reluctance because the total team is aware that one way to ensure continuing quality medical service is to conduct the financial affairs of the hospital in a professional and businesslike manner.

The degree of effectiveness of managers and first-line supervisors at our hospital—or any hospital, for that matter—depends upon many personality traits. One of the most important of these traits is the ability to be motivated by being involved. This trait is essential because the degree of decentralization typical in a hospital setting requires individuals to make timely quality decisions within the scope of established general guidelines. Furthermore, the various departments tend to be so diverse and complex that the department director is the "expert" who must relate to the vice president, a "generalist," in developing and executing a plan of operation. Therefore, the hospital setting is ideal for a high degree of participative budgeting given the diverse departments and individuals and groups of differing ranks.

The participative approach to budgeting has proven very successful at University Community Hospital. Our budget projections have proven to be extremely accurate because of a combination of good forecasting and willingness to cooperate in taking corrective action to overcome adverse variances. In fact, our overall projections have generally been so close to our actual experience that our finance committee of the board has jokingly suggested the budget was prepared after the fact. It would be difficult to envision our budget effort being accomplished in an effective manner without the participative approach.[17]

Budgeting and Motivation: An Expectancy Theory Perspective

The final topic to be addressed in this chapter is the role of budgeting in motivation.

Accounting theorists have used the **expectancy theory of motivation** to examine the behavioral impact of budgets. Under this theory of motivation, people select actions based on (1) the expectation that the action will result in particular outcomes and (2) the valences (or personal satisfaction) associated

---

[17] Marvin A. Feldbush, "Participative Budgeting in a Hospital Setting," *Management Accounting*, September 1981, pp. 43–46.

with the outcomes.[18] The expectancy model of motivation can be written as follows:[19]

$$M = IV_b + P_1\left(IV_a + \sum_{i=1}^{n} P_{2i} EV_i\right) \tag{1}$$

where

> M = Motivation to provide effort
>
> IV_a = Intrinsic valence (personal utility) as a result of successfully performing the task
>
> IV_b = Intrinsic valence (personal utility) resulting from behavior directed toward goal achievement
>
> EV_i = Extrinsic valence (personal utility) from the ith extrinsic reward, contingent on the task being completed
>
> P_1 = Expectancy that goal-directed behavior will result in the task being accomplished (range of P_1 is -1 to $+1$)
>
> P_{2i} = Expectancy that completion of the task will lead to the ith extrinsic reward (range of P_{2i} is -1 to $+1$)

Under expectancy theory, a person decides how much efforts to provide toward achieving a work goal by subjectively specifying the expectancy P_1 of accomplishing that goal given his or her effort. The person also estimates the expectancy P_2 that achievement of the work goal will result in attainment of various extrinsic rewards, such as promotion or pay raises. The individual determines values (valences) for the successful performance of the task, IV_a; the effort needed to complete the task, IV_b; and the extrinsic rewards to be obtained if the work goal is completed.

A superior can influence the variables in the subordinate employee's expectancy model by (1) specifying the extrinsic rewards, (2) changing the individual's expectancy that work-goal accomplishment will lead to those rewards, (3) modifying the subordinate employee's expectancy that effort will result in accomplishment of the task, (4) changing the subordinate employee's intrinsic value of goal accomplishment by striving to cause the subordinate employee to internalize the organization's goals, and (5) modifying the subordinate employee's valence for goal-directed effort.

Budgets are important communication vehicles in organizations. They provide one method through which a manager may communicate to a subordinate about the organization's objectives, the subordinate's role in reaching

---

[18] Expectancy theory was originally developed by J. W. Atkinson and V. H. Vroom. See J. W. Atkinson, "Toward Experimental Analysis of Human Motivation in Terms of Motives, Expectations and Incentives," in *Motives in Fantasy, Action and Society*, ed. J. W. Atkinson (New York: Van Nostrand, 1958); and V. H. Vroom, *Work and Motivation* (New York: John Wiley, 1964). Expectancy theory can be considered as a special case of expected utility theory. Applications of expectancy theory to accounting issues have been made by J. Ronen and L. Livingstone, "An Expectancy Theory Approach to the Motivational Impact of Budgets," *Accounting Review*, October 1975, pp. 671–85; K. Ferris, "A Test of the Expectancy Theory of Motivation in an Accounting Environment," *Accounting Review*, July 1977, pp. 605–15; H. Rockness, "Expectancy Theory in a Budgetary Setting: An Experimental Examination," *Accounting Review*, October 1977, pp. 893–903; and P. Brownell and M. McInnes, "Budgetary Participation, Motivation, and Managerial Performance," *Accounting Review*, October 1986, pp. 587–600.

[19] This version of the expectancy model was developed by R. J. House, "A Path-Goal Theory of Leader Effectiveness," *Administrative Science Quarterly*, September 1971, pp. 321–38. This formulation of the model was used by Ronen and Livingstone, "Expectancy Theory Approach to the Motivational Impact of Budgets," pp. 671–85, upon which the material presented here is based, and by Brownell and McInnes, "Budgetary Participation, Motivation, and Managerial Performance," pp. 587–600.

those objectives, and the conditions under which rewards will be earned by the subordinate. The budgeting process can significantly affect the subordinate's estimates of the variables in the expectancy model. Budgets reflect the expectations of management about the level of accomplishment that constitutes successful performance of a task. Moreover, budgets can be important inputs when the subordinate formulates the extrinsic valences, EV_i, associated with successful task accomplishment. The perceived difficulty in meeting a budget can affect a subordinate's expectancy that striving to meet the budget will be successful. Therefore, budget difficulty and the tightness of standards help a subordinate to formulate his or her P_1 expectancies. A budget can also provide structure to an otherwise unstructured task and assist in coordinating efforts toward goal achievement. This can affect a subordinate's value for IV_b, the intrinsic valence associated with goal-directed effort.

Some generally accepted tenets of responsibility accounting and budgeting may be interpreted in view of the expectancy model. (1) It is a commonly held view that budgets should be set at reasonably attainable levels. In light of the expectancy model, this means that P_1 will be low when standards are excessively tight or budgets are unrealistic. Subordinates may react to this by proving low effort levels because they do not view effort as being highly associated with goal accomplishment. (2) Participation by subordinates in the budgetary process is viewed by many, at least in some settings, as having beneficial effects on goal accomplishment. In view of the expectancy model, participation in the budgetary process may cause the subordinate to accept the organization's goal. This can increase the subordinate's value for IV_a, the intrinsic valence associated with successful performance of the task. (3) Management by exception is a managerial concept that is often used in budgeting and responsibility accounting systems. From the perspective of expectancy theory, nonreinforcement by management when budgetary goals are achieved may lead to a lowering of the subordinate's P_{2i} values, the expectancies that budgetary goal achievement will lead to extrinsic rewards. (4) It is a generally accepted tenet of responsibility accounting that a subordinate employee's performance should be judged on the basis of factors under the subordinate employee's control. From the viewpoint of the expectancy model, only those variables viewed as controllable by the subordinate will be associated with high values of P_1, the expectancy that the subordinate's effort will result in accomplishment of budgetary goals. Thus, several tenets of budgeting and responsibility accounting can be interpreted in light of the expectancy model of motivation.[20]

CHAPTER SUMMARY   The primary topic in this chapter was the PPC process. This process emphasizes the PPC phases related to planning, leading, and controlling (see Exhibit 3-1). Also, the components of a typical PPC program for a given year were discussed. The basic components are the (a) Substantive Plan,

---

[20] See Ronen and Livingstone, "Expectancy Theory Approach to the Motivational Impact of Budgets," pp. 671–85; and H. Bierman, T. Dyckman, and R. Hilton, *Cost Accounting: Concepts and Managerial Applications* (New York: Macmillan, 1990).

(b) Financial Plan, (c) Variable Expense Budgets, (d) Supplementary Data, (e) Performance Reports, and (f) Follow-up (see Exhibit 3-2). This chapter emphasized the PPC "total package," rather than selected parts.

Line and staff responsibilities and conflicts were discussed. Budget preparation and control were identified as primarily line responsibilities. Design and administrative operation of a PPC program were designated as primarily staff responsibilities.

The chapter discussed some critical behavioral implications of a PPC program. These behavioral effects may be either positive or negative. A basic task of top management is to attain goal congruence. That is, the main goals of the enterprise and the employees should be in harmony to the fullest extent possible. Enterprise goals include profits, productivity, growth, and employee development. Employee goals include job satisfaction, rewards, career opportunities, and recognition.

Comprehensive Demonstration Case

SUPERIOR COMPUTER SERVICE AND SALES COMPANY

This case continues the "Superior" case study started in Chapter 1 and continued in Chapter 2. You should review those two cases before proceeding. Notice that the case in Chapter 2 included a business plan through December 31, 19E, for Superior Computer Service and Sales Company. The purpose of this case is to give you an overview of the PPC process by using a highly simplified actual case.

The company continued its profitable growth through 19F. For example, the December 31, 19F, internal financial statements include the following:

	19F	
	ACTUAL	PLAN
Service revenues:		
Computer service	$280,000	$260,000
Typewriters and photocopiers	75,000	80,000
Total revenues	355,000	340,000
Expenses*	265,000	260,000
Net income	$ 90,000	$ 80,000

*Includes owner's salary and interest on the loan. Also, the principal was paid in full.

Because of the company's success since its organization, and particularly during the 19D–19F period, Sparks developed considerable interest in improving planning and control in the company. Also, the bank had recently approved a $500,000 line of credit for the company. During this time, some resources were used to design a "small, high-quality computer."

It is now January 1, 19G, and the tactical profit plan is complete for the 19G budget year. The three-year strategic profit plan is also complete (through

19I). Some of the summaries from the 19G PPC program, developed in the company, are given below. Notice that Superior Computer Service and Sales Company will start manufacturing and selling a small portable computer to "test the market." This activity will be financed with a $500,000 bank loan.

Summaries from the 19G profit plan (for instructional purposes only) are given below.

1. Evaluation of external variables:
   a. Population—Trade territory approximately 1 million; increasing about 3 percent per year.
   b. Industry sales—Estimated $750,000 in 19G; this rate probably will increase 10 percent over the next three years.
   c. Competition—Numerous small competitors; most have financial and product-quality problems. However, one competitor is significantly increasing its market share.
2. Objectives of the company:
   a. Increase share of market and expand into manufacturing and selling of a small computer.
   b. Serve customers with even better services and a new product.
   c. Improve quality of management at all levels.
   d. Make the company a more interesting place to work.
   e. Be a good social citizen in the community.
3. Specific goals for 19G, 19H, and 19I:
   a. Growth in service revenue of 8 percent per year.
   b. Return on owner's equity of 20 percent.
   c. Manufacturing the new computer—loss in 19G and 19H; profit in 19I.
4. Strategies to attain goals:
   a. Improve facilities to increase efficiency and improve working conditions for the employees.
   b. Increase resources and expertise in marketing. Enhance the advertising and direct-customer activities. Increase direct contacts with potential new customers.
   c. Revise technical training program for service personnel.
   d. Initiate a special program to introduce the new computer.
5. Strategic (long-term) Profit Plan (summary and partial only):

Budgeted (planned) Income Statement:

Items	19G	19H	19I
Service revenues	$383,000	$417,000	$446,000
Computer sales: Units	10	30	100
Amount	20,000	60,000	200,000
Total revenues	403,000	477,000	646,000
Expenses: Services	(287,000)	(317,000)	(345,000)
Computer	(70,000)	(90,000)	(140,000)
Net income:			
Services	96,000	100,000	101,000
Computer	(50,000)	(30,000)	60,000
Total	$ 46,000	$ 70,000	$161,000
Return on owner's equity (net income ÷ owner's equity)	11%	15%	23%

NOTE.   Not shown: Strategic balance sheets, capital additions plan, cash flow statements, and supporting schedules.

6. Tactical (short-term) Profit Plan (summary and partial only):

Budgeted (planned) Income Statement for 19G:

| | QUARTERS | | | | YEAR |
ITEMS	1	2	3	4	19G*
Service revenue:					
Computer service	$ 86,000	$ 72,000	$ 57,000	$ 72,000	$287,000
Typewriters and photo-					
copiers	26,000	25,000	18,000	27,000	96,000
Total service revenue	112,000	97,000	75,000	99,000	383,000
Computer sales	-0-	-0-	4,000	16,000	20,000
Total revenues†	112,000	97,000	79,000	115,000	403,000
Expenses:					
Computer service	64,000	58,000	52,000	58,000	232,000
Typewriters and photo-					
copiers	14,400	14,100	11,800	14,700	55,000
Total service expense	78,400	72,100	63,800	72,700	287,000
Computer expense					
(incl. CGS)	12,600	20,900	19,200	17,300	70,000
Total expenses†	91,000	93,000	83,000	90,000	357,000
Net income:					
Computer service	22,000	14,000	5,000	14,000	55,000
Typewriters and photo-					
copiers	11,600	10,900	6,200	12,300	41,000
Total service net income	33,600	24,900	11,200	26,300	96,000
Computers (loss)	(12,600)	(20,900)	(15,200)	(1,300)	(50,000)
Total net income	$ 21,000	$ 4,000	$ (4,000)	$ 25,000	$ 46,000

*Same as shown in the Strategic Plan.

†See attached schedule for:
    Revenues—classified by responsibility
    Expenses—classified by controllability and by assigned responsibility.

NOTES

(a)   Planned financial statements and supporting schedules are not shown. These are illustrated in subsequent chapters.

(b)   Prior to each quarter, the quarterly amounts are planned for each month, primarily for control purposes.

(c)   The seasonality of computer service is:

YEAR	1ST QTR.	2ND QTR.	3RD QTR.	4TH QTR.
$287,000	$86,000	$72,000	$57,000	$72,000
100%	30%	25%	20%	25%

(d)   Computer service expense was based on a flexible budget formula as follows:

Fixed expenses: $108,000 (i.e., $27,000 per quarter)	
Variable expenses: .43206 (of each sales $)	
First quarter:	
Fixed expenses	$27,000
Variable expenses (.43206 × $86,000)	37,000*
Total expenses	$64,000

*Rounded to the nearest thousand.

(e)   The flexible budget formula for typewriter and photocopier expense was: fixed, $6,000 per quarter, and variable, .32292 per sales dollar.

NOTE.   You should check the accuracy of the budgeted income statement given above.

Suggested References

ANTHONY, ROBERT N., JOHN DEARDEN, and NORTON M. BEDFORD, *Management Control Systems*, Chap. 1. Homewood, Ill.: Richard D. Irwin, 1984.

BROWNELL, PETER, "Participation in the Budgeting Process: When It Works and When It Doesn't," *Journal of Accounting Literature*, Spring 1982, pp. 124–53.

COLLINS, FRANK, PAUL MUNTER, and DON W. FINN, "The Budgeting Games People Play," *Accounting Review*, January 1987, pp. 29–49. Includes a comprehensive bibliography.

DESSLER, GARY, *Human Behavior, Improving Performance at Work*. Reston, Va.: Reston Publishing, 1980.

MACIARIELLO, JOSEPH A., *Management Control Systems*, Chap. 1. Englewood Cliffs, N.J.: Prentice-Hall, 1984.

SCHIFF, MICHAEL, and ARIE Y. LEWIN, *Behavioral Aspects of Accounting*. Englewood Cliffs, N.J.: Prentice-Hall, 1974.

THOMAS, WILLIAM E., ed., *Readings in Cost Accounting, Budgeting, and Control*, 6th ed., Cincinnati.: South-Western Publishing, 1983.

Discussion Questions

1.   Explain what is meant by MBO and MCS. Relate them to PPC.
2.   This is a study question. Match the phases of the PPC process with the brief descriptions by entering an appropriate letter in each blank space.

	DESCRIPTION	PPC PHASE
_____	(1) Develop short-range plans for the upcoming year.	A. External variables B. Broad objectives

_____ (2) Develop plans for each project.

_____ (3) Corrective action, and replanning based on periodic reports.

_____ (4) Major thrusts to attain objectives and goals.

_____ (5) Identify and evaluate important external factors.

_____ (6) Monthly comparative reports by assigned responsibilities.

_____ (7) Planning memo to middle and lower management; guidelines.

_____ (8) Develop, or revise, the philosophical tone and future expectations.

_____ (9) Leading to maximize attainment of plans.

_____ (10) Develop the long-range financial plan.

_____ (11) Broad but specific goals for the enterprise.

C. Broad but specific goals
D. Strategies
E. Executive management instructions
F. Project plans
G. Strategic plan
H. Tactical plan
I. Implementation
J. Performance reports
K. Follow-up

3. Explain and compare the (a) substantive plan and (b) financial plan.

4. This is a study question. Match the components of a typical PPC program for a given year with the brief descriptions by entering one letter in each blank space.

DESCRIPTION	COMPONENT
_____ (1) Special analyses such as cost-volume-profit and ratios	A. Substantive plan
_____ (2) Strategic long-range profit plan and tactical short-range profit plan	B. Financial plan
	C. Flexible expense budgets
_____ (3) Results in corrective action and replanning	D. Supplementary data
	E. Performance reports
_____ (4) Objectives, goals, and strategies	F. Follow-up reports
_____ (5) Periodic plan, actual, variances	
_____ (6) Output-expense relationships	

5. Outline one useful approach that a management could take to evaluate the relevant variables affecting the enterprise. (Also refer to Exhibit 1-5.)

6. Explain the nature and purpose of a statement of broad objectives for an enterprise.

7. What is the purpose of stating the specific goals of an enterprise and how should they relate to a statement of broad objectives?

8. Distinguish between enterprise goals and enterprise strategies. Why is the distinction necessary?

9. What is a statement of planning premises? What purpose does it serve?

10. In a general way, outline a participative approach for developing profit plans for a responsibility center in a medium-size firm (assume the responsibility center to be Plant 2).

11. Explain in general terms the concept of the flexible expense budget (refer to the demonstration case).

12. What should be the management policy about significant events that occur and were not anticipated in the profit plans?

13. Explain the concept of performance reports. What basic purpose do they serve?

14. Explain the implications of the following statement: "In using performance reports, it is important to distinguish between cause and effect."

15. Distinguish between the periodic budget approach and the continuous budget approach.

16. Differentiate between line and staff responsibilities with respect to a profit planning and control program.

17. What should be the role of the executive committee with respect to the profit planning and control program?

18. Why is a profit planning and control (or budget) manual usually desirable? What should it primarily include?

19. Distinguish between forecasting and planning.

20. Explain what is meant by goal congruence.

CASE 3-1   *A controller says no!*

The company president has asked you to make an independent evaluation of the operations of the Distribution Company, which is experiencing certain difficulties. You have concluded that a comprehensive profit planning and control program is advisable. In an executive meeting the company controller, a longtime employee, makes the following comments in your presence: "Oh, I realize that budgeting is perhaps all right in a few extremely large firms, but not ours. We have special problems, such as sales forecasting, because we have five different products distributed all over the U.S. In addition, you just can't tell what our expenses for the year are going to be. Besides, I don't have the time or help to prepare a budget. I probably couldn't make those salespeople follow it anyway." The other executives look at him in ways that you interpret to be possible agreement.

Narrate your reply exactly as you would give it to the president of the company.

CASE 3-2 *The two partners disagree*

For a number of years B. T. Krandall had sold a line of supplies used by hotels, motels, and similar establishments. At the age of forty-four, Krandall had managed to save a tidy amount, which was invested in common stocks. Krandall and B. B. Knox decided to open a small wholesale distribution company in another state where Knox resided. The Krandall-Knox partnership was formed to distribute a line of supplies similar to those sold by Krandall over the years. Krandall invested $50,000 and Knox invested $20,000. Three salespersons were employed initially. Krandall sold and worked directly with the salespersons to develop statewide distribution. Knox did the purchasing, shipping, and other administrative duties.

The company was successful, primarily because of Krandall's work with the sales force, as well as the fact that the chief competitor was an old "family" corporation. Krandall believed the competitor still operated "in the horse-and-buggy days," which was about right.

Within ten years Krandall-Knox had grown substantially. The data tabulated below show the growth at the end of the first, fifth, and tenth years:

	FIRST YEAR	FIFTH YEAR	TENTH YEAR
Home office employees	2	4	5
Sales force	3	10	22
General employees	0	1	3
Total assets	$ 60,000	$100,000	$135,000
Sales dollars	120,000	200,000	300,000
Partners' salaries	12,000	22,000	24,300
Income (after salaries)	18,000	24,000	27,000

In conformity with the partnership agreement, an annual audit was prepared by an independent CPA. After submission of the last audit report, the CPA handed Knox a separate memorandum. In it the CPA noted the profit trend related to total assets and sales and other data that "indicated some developing internal inefficiencies." The memorandum suggested that in view of the increasing size of the company, serious consideration be given to improving the accounting system and establishing a profit planning and control program. The memorandum stated that a PPC program could be particularly helpful in (1) setting prices, (2) increasing sales volume, (3) controlling expenses, and (4) managing inventory. The memorandum noted that inventory control appeared to be a growing problem in the firm.

Knox was impressed with the suggestions: "Krandall, I believe the CPA has something; why don't we get a program started right away? Our profit margin certainly is shrinking." "Well, I don't know. I'd have to oppose a budget if that is what they mean. The company I used to sell for had a budget and they were always hounding me on the expense budget and sales quota budget. I didn't need a budget. If I could have saved the time and worry, I could have sold even more," was Krandall's reply.

REQUIRED

Analyze the situation. Identify the primary problem or problems and provide recommendations with support.

CASE 3-3   *Which performance report should be used?*

Micro Corporation uses flexible expense budget procedures to control expenses. The flexible budget for Cost Center 23 is shown below.

Flexible Expense Budget
for the Year 19X, Cost Center No. 23

EXPENSES	FIXED ALLOWANCE PER MONTH	VARIABLE RATE PER 100 MACHINE HOURS
Supervisory salaries	$ 900	$ —
Indirect labor	200	.90
Maintenance parts	50	.05
Supplies used	—	.60
Power used	30	.10
Miscellaneous expenses	40	.12
Depreciation on machinery	100	—
Total	$1,320	$1.77

REQUIRED

a. The annual profit plan is being developed. It includes an estimate of the planned output of work for Cost Center 23. What amount for each expense should be included in the plan for Cost Center 23 (a) for the January output estimate of 20,000 direct machine hours? (b) for the annual output estimate of 260,000 direct machine hours? Show computations.

b. The profit plan was approved and January of the new year has ended. The accounting department reported the following for Cost Center 23 for January. Actual machine hours: 24,000. Actual expenses: supervisory salaries, $900; indirect labor $415; maintenance parts, $65; supplies used, $140; power used, $50; miscellaneous expenses, $70; and depreciation expense, $100. Using these data and the planned amounts developed in requirement a, prepare a performance report comparing actual expenses with budget allowances. Set up four amount columns: Actual expenses; Original Profit Plan amounts; Variations—amount; Variations—Percent of Budget.

c. Prepare another performance report comparing actual with flexible budget allowances adjusted to actual work done; 24,000 direct machine hours.

d. Which performance report should be used for Cost Center 23? Why?

CASE 3-4   Strategy—fixed and variable expenses

Simplex Corporation manufactures and sells two similar products—Super and Super D. The company has estimated that aside from overall volume increases, an increase in sales of one product would, on a unit basis, proportionately decrease the sales of the other product. However, neither product can be discontinued because they are mutually supportive. Management is considering three possible alternatives for strategic planning purposes: (1) push Super sales, (2) push Super D sales, or (3) push them equally. The following budget estimates have been prepared:

	SUPER	SUPER D
Unit sales price	$10.00	$13.00
Fixed overhead expense ($120,000 allocated on a 1:3 ratio)	1.00	3.00
Unit variable cost of goods sold	6.00	7.00
Sales commissions (20% of sales revenue)	2.00	2.60
Net profit per unit	$ 1.00	$ .40

REQUIRED

a. How many units of Super and Super D were used in computing the above budget estimates?

b. Prepare the above budget to show total dollars.

c. Based on the data given, what alternative should management select? Support your decision with figures and appropriate comments and a revised budget to support your analysis. Assume total unit sales remain the same as before.

CASE 3-5   Using a continuous budget plan

Compte Sales Company uses a continuous profit plan covering a six-month period. The plan is revised monthly. Summary profit plan data for one six-month period are shown below.

Compte Sales Company—Planned Income Statement (summary)
For the Period March–August 19X

	MARCH	APRIL	MAY	JUNE	JULY	AUGUST	TOTAL
Sales	$210,000	$216,000	$224,000	$208,000	$190,000	$180,000	$1,228,000
Cost of goods sold	84,000	86,000	90,000	83,000	76,000	72,000	491,000
Gross margin	126,000	130,000	134,000	125,000	114,000	108,000	737,000
Distribution expenses	52,000	53,000	55,000	51,000	49,000	47,000	307,000
Administrative expenses	26,000	27,000	27,000	25,000	24,000	24,000	153,000
Operating margin	48,000	50,000	52,000	49,000	41,000	37,000	277,000
Financial expenses	1,000	1,000	1,200	1,200	900	900	6,200
Income (before income tax)	47,000	49,000	50,800	47,800	40,100	36,100	270,800
Income taxes (40%)	18,800	19,600	20,320	19,120	16,040	14,440	108,320
Net income	$ 28,200	$ 29,400	$ 30,480	$ 28,680	$ 24,060	$ 21,660	$ 162,480

The month of March has just ended. Therefore, the March column will be dropped and a column for September will be added. In conformity with company planning procedures, the following decision inputs were developed by the management and given to the budget director:

1 Sales department's revised estimates: Sales—April, $220,000; May, $225,000; June, $210,000; July, $192,000; August, $182,000; September, $195,000. Distribution expense—a 2 percent increase; September estimate, $50,100.

2 Executive vice-president's estimates—administrative expenses for September, $25,000; no changes in prior months.

3 Treasurer's estimates—financial expenses for July through September, $1,100 per month.

4 Accounting department's estimates—cost of goods sold will increase in proportion to the increase in sales from the prior budget to the new budget, for each month; September CGS estimate, $78,000.

REQUIRED   (round to the nearest $10):

a. Prepare a revised profit plan following the concept of continuous budgeting. Include the new plans (estimates) and give appropriate comments about the estimates and an evaluation of the changes.

b. Prepare a separate narrative appraising the planning approach used by the company.

CASE 3-6   *An airline's controller prepares the budget*

Northeastern Airlines, Inc., operates a computer service in a four-state area. The president of the company told the case writer that the company had been budgeting for the last three years. The case writer learned of a particular sequence of events relating to the next budget year (same as the calendar year). Near the middle of October of last year, the president of the company telephoned the controller and asked, "Isn't it time to start thinking about the budget for next year?" Although there were many problems on the controller's desk, the controller agreed with the president. After hanging up the phone, the controller was thinking, "I wish I could figure some way to keep from being saddled with this forecasting job." On Monday, November 5, the controller assembled the key staff people to discuss the "budgets for next year," in anticipation of a telephone call from the president around the first of December.

As anticipated, the president called on December 3 and asked the controller to come in with "the summary budget statements for next year incorporating your recommendations." The next day the controller spent the entire morning with the president discussing the projected statements (an income statement detailed by quarter, a balance sheet for the end of the budget year, and a quarterly cash budget). In response to a question from the president, the controller stated that "these forecasts are a compilation of the best judgments of my staff on the projections of the trends of the actual results for the past year." The president expressed some definite ideas about an increase in sales revenue and profit that "must be included in the budget." Also, the president indicated that although union negotiations would probably cause an increase in some of the labor costs, expenses generally should be budgeted "tighter than last year." At lunch the same day, the president and the controller discussed these matters with the vice-president of sales and the vice-president of manufacturing. From these discussions, the controller concluded that some changes had to be made "to coincide with the president's wishes." The president told the controller to "plan another meeting on December 15 for a final wrapup of the budget for next year." The president expected the controller to have revised budget statements available for a discussion at a luncheon meeting on that date with the two vice-presidents.

As anticipated by the controller, that meeting resulted in approval of the revised budget statements. Copies of the budget were distributed to the four vice-presidents during the last week of December. Actual and budget are compared at the end of each quarter.

Northeastern Airlines, Inc., has a current revenue level of approximately ten million dollars and employs about three hundred people.

REQUIRED

Prepare a constructive, yet critical, assessment of the approach to budgeting used by Northeastern Airlines, Inc. Include your suggestions for change.

CASE 3-7   *I don't have much time left to supervise!*

Seton Manufacturing Company has been operating for many years as a manufacturer of products made from structural steel.

As a result of increased competition and a decrease in profits and return on investment during the past six years, the management decided to tighten up on operations. During the preceding year, the management had devoted considerable effort to improving supervisory skills and upgrading hourly paid workers. During this period, there were some layoffs. In such cases, the management evaluated employees carefully so that the less efficient would be laid off. The management felt that it had been successful in retaining the better employees. Considerable effort was also devoted to reducing costs. The accounting system was revised to implement responsibility accounting. An independent CPA had consistently recommended that a profit planning and control program be initiated.

Although competition remained strong and pressure on prices had been heavy during the past five years, the company had experienced a small annual increase in sales except for the last year when sales and production increased significantly. The company has approximately 225 regular employees. From time to time, 10 to 50 temporary employees are used.

During the past year, management initiated a profit planning program for the company. The president of the firm was convinced that such a program would be worthwhile. The president was strongly influenced by the discussions at a conference conducted by the American Management Association and felt that the program would improve management planning and control in the company. In addition, the president believed that an effective approach was needed to control expenses.

The profit planning and control program during the past year had exposed numerous problems. However, the president felt that this was to be expected during the first year. The budget director was a longtime employee and, not having had previous experience with a budget program, was also learning. Meetings were scheduled at the end of the year to review the budget procedures, progress, and related problems.

The factory manager and the budget director had recently met with the factory supervisors, excluding the foremen. The purpose of the meeting was "to critically examine our budget experience during the past year with a view to improving the procedures."

During the discussions, Sam Grant, one of the factory supervisors, commented: "I don't like this participation idea that we keep talking about. Last year I followed the instructions and let the foremen participate all over the place and it has given me nothing but big trouble. I used to have firm control over these people, but after this year I'm about ready to throw in the sponge."

"What's the problem?" asked Meg Johnston, the budget director.

"Well, it's like this," replied Sam. "First, I spend a lot of time telling these people that they are to draw up their own expense budgets; they were not too happy about it and I had a heck of a time getting them in on time. Then the budgets were all wrong and I had to change them. Then I had to spend a lot of time in cozy little chats trying to explain why they had to be changed. Finally, we got them in. Then the monthly performance reports began to arrive. Of course, the performance reports had all kinds of unfavorable expense numbers. You should hear the excuses and the complaints about the budgeted expenses. After I get through with all the conferences, which settled nothing, I don't have much time left to supervise. But more important, I feel that I have lost control over the foremen. They are giving me too much static and excuses now. I feel we should tell them what to do, how much to spend, and not encourage them to question everything. You need discipline and respect at this level, and the only way to get it is to be firm and rule with an iron hand. Otherwise we supervisors will lose our authority. I can tell by watching them whether they are doing a good job. Too much talk with the foremen is not good."

"But Sam," replied Fred Matson, the factory manager, "we let you participate in setting the expense budgets; don't you think that is working?"

"Well, the management will have to decide on that. I think supervisors have enough sense to know how to get along with their superiors. They realize you can't run an operation by mob rule."

After a few more comments, the meeting was adjourned for lunch.

REQUIRED

a. Identify at least three critical problems related to the PPC program.

b. For each problem, explain what the company should do.

CASE 3-8   *Some provocative comments in a bank setting*

The president of Cayuga Bank and Trust Company recently appointed a special committee to make recommendations to the executive committee about initiating a profit planning and control program in the company. The special committee spent considerable time investigating the advantages and disadvantages of such a program. The committee is now concentrating on the major problem areas related to such a program. Currently, the primary concerns of the committee are the motivational and behavioral implications.

In reviewing the literature, the committee was particularly interested in several sources that have commented about the effect of budgets on middle- and lower-level managers and supervisors. One source said that budgets were used by higher management in one company primarily as "pressure devices for continually increasing efficiency." The source concluded that in certain situations, budgets tend to generate negative motivations and decreasing efficiency.

Another source stated that in one company the "success of the budget people appeared to depend on their ability to find fault with the operating managers." Another source found that in most of the companies studied, "participation in budget development was believed to be very important." Still another source reported that "budgeting is more concerned with the concepts of human behavior than with the rules of accounting and, if good principles of human relationships are implemented, profit planning and control will be an effective management tool."

REQUIRED

Explain and evaluate each of the four quotations for the special committee.

CASE 3-9   *Competition decreases and creates a problem*

Supreme Corporation is a small company that manufactures three different models of a simple household item. The product is sold through independent wholesale outlets in a three-state area. Recently, a competitor appears to have dropped out of the market. The management of Supreme is interested in an evaluation of the effect on operations and profits because it believes that an increase in demand may be anticipated.

The management of the company has never used profit planning and control. Planning has been on an informal and nonsystematic basis. In discussing the new development with the board of directors (who meet quarterly), the president discussed in general terms the probable volume (in units) and unit prices due to the new situation. The board approved a resolution to have the company's CPA help with some analyses.

The actual income statement for the past year (simplified and with rounded amounts) showed the following:

Sales		$500,000
Cost and expenses:		
Direct materials	$110,000	
Direct labor	80,000	
Manufacturing expenses—fixed	20,000	
Manufacturing expenses—variable	40,000	
Administrative expenses	30,000	
Selling expenses	120,000	
Total		400,000
Net income		$100,000

Subsquently, in analyzing the situation (following certain procedures recommended by the CPA), the management developed the following estimates for the coming year:

1 Physical volume (i.e., units) of sales will increase by 20 percent.
2 Material prices will be increased by 15 percent.
3 Administrative expenses will increase *in total* by 10 percent.
4 Direct labor wage rates will increase by 20 percent.
5 Selling expenses will increase *in total* by 30 percent of dollar sales if sales prices are increased. If sales prices are not increased, these expenses will increase in total by 10 percent of dollar sales.
6 There will be a 10 percent reduction in the material content of each unit of finished goods.
7 Fixed manufacturing expenses of $20,000 will not change.

REQUIRED

a. Based on these estimates, management asked the controller to prepare two budgeted income statements as follows:

☐ Case A—The amount of income that would be earned assuming that selling prices are not changed.

☐ Case B—The amount of income that would be earned assuming that average selling prices are increased so that a 20 percent return is earned on estimated total assets of $655,000.

Use the following format:

		CASE A		CASE B	
		No change in selling price		To earn 20% on total assets	
	Past Year	Computations	Estimate Coming Year	Computations	Estimate Coming Year
Sales	$500,000				
Costs and expenses:					
Direct materials	110,000				
Direct labor	80,000				
Mfg. exp.—fixed	20,000				
Mfg. exp.—variable	40,000				
Administrative exp.	30,000				
Selling exp.	120,000				
Total	$400,000				
Income	$100,000				

Computations:

b. Evaluate the results of both case A and case B as to any limitations (or usefulness).
c. What additional analyses and approaches would you suggest that would be useful for management?

CASE 3-10   *A line versus staff conflict in a geophysical services company*

Technical Equipment Corporation (TEC) was organized in 1935 to sell geophysical services to oil-producing companies in the Southwest. Its expansion since that time, both in operations and in revenues, has been phenomenal. It now also manufactures equipment in related fields and sells to the U.S. government as well as to private operators. Sales for the next year are expected to reach $65 million. The company has manufacturing plants located in two large southwestern cities and has subsidiaries in nine foreign countries.

The company is alert to the latest management developments. Likewise, it is interested in new lines of business that it can enter profitably and methods to improve the current products and services.

The accompanying chart summarizes the organizational relationships within the firm. The company uses a responsibility accounting system and an effective comprehensive profit planning and control program. The management is considered to be both competent and aggressive.

The activities included in the Control and Finance Division (a staff group) are performed by five departments: Central Plant and Office Services; Secretary/Treasurer, who has responsibility for matters concerning corporate affairs and financial policy; Planning, which coordinates preparation of the annual (short-term) profit plan; Central Accounting, which is responsible for consolidation accounting and internal auditing; and Management Services, which prepares special reports and studies.

The six product divisions are profit centers, and each division head reports directly to top management. Staff department managers in the product divisions report to the division head and have only a functional relationship with their staff counterparts at the home-office level. TEC believes that the experience gained in specific product areas enables these staff individuals to develop their abilities to the fullest extent possible and thus justifies the possible extra cost resulting from some duplication of effort in performing staff functions.

There is no line of authority from the vice-president of control and finance, M. V. Watson, to the six product division controllers; each product division controller reports directly to the appropriate manager of the product division. Informal communication results from regular monthly meetings held by the vice-president of control and finance. The product controllers attend these meetings. At these meetings, profit planning and control problems are discussed. Each division controller can learn how the others are handling problems or can receive suggestions from them. These meetings are viewed by the top management as being especially useful.

Also, each product division controller prepares a monthly performance report for the division manager, a copy of which goes directly to the vice-president of control and finance. The latter officer is expected to review these performance reports and submit relevant comments to the executive vice-president, the product division head, or the product division controller, depending on the nature of the item. The vice-president of control and finance has been assigned overall responsibility for the reporting function (external financial reports and internal performance reports). A recent situation illustrates a problem of line-staff relationships.

In examining the monthly performance reports from the Measurements Equipment Division, Watson noticed that the inventory of manufactured parts of $200,000 had exceeded the planned level of $50,000 during a period of three months. Watson had been absent from the last two group meetings. Apparently the matter of the inventory variance had not been raised by Watson's assistant, who conducted the meetings when Watson was absent. Watson questioned Nolan, the Measurements Equipment Division controller, who had no specific information about the variance, stating that it was "nothing to be alarmed about." In view of the large amount of funds involved, Watson pursued the subject rather forcefully and told Nolan that it should have been investigated to determine the reasons for the variance. The following day, Watson received a telephone call from Sumner, head of the Measurements Equipment Division. Summer seemed annoyed and said, "Nolan felt that you were too hard on him. Incidentally, he reports to me, and the inventory is my responsibility." Nevertheless, Watson inquired about the unusual variance in inventory. Summer gave the distinct impression of not being aware of the variance and flatly stated that he did not know why it had happened. The telephone conversation ended with neither party indicating any further action.

Watson was very concerned about the matter because it would have a significant impact on cash flow and other financial factors. Consequently, Watson was certain that some action should be taken and therefore, discussed the situation in detail with Porter, the executive vice-president, who requested a complete explanation of the inventory variance in writing from Sumner.

REQUIRED

Be prepared to analyze the case and pinpoint the significant problems. How should these problems be resolved?

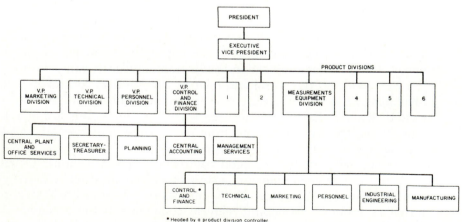

* Headed by a product division controller

Application
of Comprehensive Profit
Planning and Control

4

INTRODUCTION AND PURPOSE   Chapters 5 through 13 give a detailed discussion of the planning and control components of a PPC program. Therefore, it is important to have an overall view of the application of such a program and the interrelationships of those various components. The purpose of this chapter is to provide that application overview. To add realism and perspective, we use an actual case study, simplified for instructional purposes. The case, Superior Manufacturing Company, is used in the subsequent chapters for illustration. Generally, those aspects of the case relating to each chapter will be found at the end of that chapter. Because this is a comprehensive case, its continuity from chapter to chapter provides a learning vehicle. Therefore, you are urged to devote careful attention to the case and follow its continuity. The broad view of comprehensive planning and control will be evident throughout as you study the detailed techniques, approaches, and procedures.

In this chapter, we show a summary budget for each of the components of a comprehensive profit planning and control program shown in Exhibit 3-2. These components will be illustrated in the order listed there, and the same captions will be used.

Comprehensive Demonstration Case

SUPERIOR MANUFACTURING COMPANY:

BACKGROUND

Superior Manufacturing Company evolved from Superior Compu-Service started by H. T. Sparks on January 2, 19A (see page 22). During the years 19A, 19B, and 19C, the company was only a service firm. Starting in 19D, its name was changed to Superior Computer Service and Sales Company (see page 63).

121

The word Sales was used because the owner wanted to start selling some products related to the company's service operations. The company continued to grow during the years 19D through 19G. Starting in 19H the company began manufacturing and selling a small portable computer in addition to its service operations (see page 104). The company was more successful during the years 19H, 19I, and 19J than anticipated in its first strategic profit plan (see page 105).

During 19K, which was actually 1980, a large corporation purchased Superior Computer Service and Sales Company as a wholly owned subsidiary. Sparks received approximately $2 million in cash from the sale of the company, and he retained the legal right to use the name "Superior" if he were to start another computer company.

The next year, Sparks and four other investors bought all the outstanding shares of a different computer manufacturing company called Avon Company. The new owners changed the company name to Superior Manufacturing Company. It is now 1988, which for instructional convenience we will designate as 19X1. The year for which the budget is being prepared is 19X2. (From this point on, we will designate years in the comprehensive case numerically as 19X1, 19X2, etc.)

For the past four years, the company financial officer has prepared only a summarized annual budgeted income statement and balance sheet. During the January 19X1 meeting of the new board of directors, Sparks made a motion that the "company president establish a special management committee of five members to make an in-depth analysis of the application and potential of a comprehensive profit planning and control program for Superior."

The actual situation of Superior has been simplified in almost every respect. Sufficient size and detail is retained to provide an effective instructional approach and yet avoid excessive detail that would tend to obscure the important issues. For illustrative case purposes, Superior Manufacturing Company distributes two products (designated as products X and Y for instructional convenience) in three sales districts, and the manufacturing division includes three service and three producing departments.

Approximately six months after its appointment, the special committee made a complete report to the board of directors and the executive committee. The special committee strongly recommended early initiation of a comprehensive profit planning and control program. The committee also recommended that, prior to actual initiation, a careful study be made of the organizational structure of the company and the related responsibilities. The committee made a recommendation which was approved by the president. The organization chart for the company in Exhibit 4-1 shows the approved organizational and responsibility arrangements in the company. A detailed organizational manual that specifies responsibilities for each executive and manager was prepared, approved by the management, and distributed to various levels of management. Notice the various responsibility centers, the organization of the financial function, and the executive committee.

The special committee also recommended that "the accounting system be tailored to the organizational structure so that all costs, revenues, and other measurements reported through the accounting system will be accumulated and reported for internal purposes on a responsibility basis." Thus, the committee recommended what is called a responsibility accounting system. Accounting classifications were revised, and a formal accounting manual was prepared detailing the chart of accounts by responsibility. The manual also specified the type of accounting entries to be made in each account. The manual specified that standard costs for direct materials and labor should be used, and it stated the policies on indirect cost allocations and on the application of overhead to products produced, as well as many other details of the cost accounting system.

Similarly, the director of profit planning and control, which was a new position, prepared a detailed profit planning and control manual coordinated with the accounting manual. These three manuals (statements of general policies) were subsequently considered by the executive committee. After minor revisions, they were approved by the president and distributed as "standard company procedures," effective for the 19X2 budget year. Exhibit 4-2 summarizes selected information from the profit planning and control manual of Superior Manufacturing Company as finally approved and updated. It outlines the basic components of the comprehensive profit planning and control program in this company.

Time Periods of Superior's Profit Plans

The current year is 19X1, and the period planned is 19X2 and beyond. Therefore, the tactical short-range profit plan will cover the year 19X2, and the strategic long-range profit plan will cover the years 19X3–X7.

Evaluation of Relevant Variables and Strengths and Weaknesses Illustrated

During the early part of the current year, the president of Superior concluded that the executive committee had not adequately considered the controllable and noncontrollable variables affecting the company. Furthermore, there was no in-depth analysis of the company's strengths and weaknesses. To establish a basis for more emphasis on these factors in the planning process and to gain some expert assistance, the president engaged an outside consultant. The consultant's report was presented to the president on September 3. The report was comprehensive, and separate sections were devoted to two problems: (a) relevant variables and (b) strengths and weaknesses. With respect to the relevant variables, the consultant developed the matrix shown in Exhibit 1-5, which was supplemented with analyses and recommendations. The consultant recommended that more attention be given to the annual assessment of the noncontrollable variables and made specific recommendations with respect to planning for their impact on the company.

The consultant's report listed the company's primary strengths as (a) quality of the employees, (b) financial strength of the company, and (c) participative attitudes fostered by the management. The primary weaknesses listed were (a) lack of innovative and aggressive marketing strategies, (b) excessive returns of products sold because of quality, and (c) insufficient involvement in long-term social problems. After discussing the report, management decided to incorporate most of the recommendations into future planning.

EXHIBIT 4-1

Organization Chart, Superior Manufacturing Company, January 1, 19X2

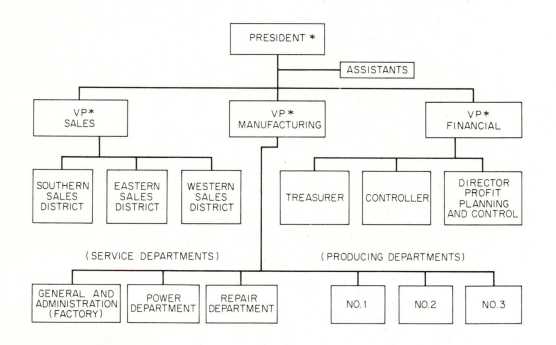

*On the executive committee.

EXHIBIT 4-2

Summary of the PPC Manual Superior Manufacturing Company Effective January 1, 19X2

1. Objectives of the profit planning and control program
2. Responsibilities and procedures for annual evaluation of the environmental variables affecting the future success of the company
3. Annual evaluation by the executive committee of the statement of broad objectives of the company

4. Top-management specification, on an annual basis, of the specific goals of the company:
   a. Growth objective
   b. Return-on-investment objective
   c. Social objectives
5. Development of basic strategies by executive management
6. Procedure for development of the profit plans:
   a. Distribution of planning premises
   b. Profit plans:
      (1) Strategic long-range profit plan—five-year time span, detailed by year; revised annually
      (2) Tactical short range profit plan—one-year time span, consistent with the annual period used for financial reporting purposes; detailed by quarter (each quarter is further disaggregated by month during the month preceding the beginning of each quarter)
      (3) Flexible expense budgets—prepared annually for factor expenses, distribution expenses, and administrative expenses
   c. Responsibilities for preparation of profit plans:
      (1) Overall responsibility—president (and executive committee)
      (2) Approval of planning premises—president (and executive committee)
      (3) Overall supervision of the budget program—financial executive and director of profit planning and control
      (4) Sales plan—vice-president, sales
      (5) Departmental expense budgets—manager of the respective departments (statistical analyses, cost analyses, and other services essential to the development of expense budgets, director of profit planning and control)
      (6) Profit plan consolidations and summaries—director of profit planning and control
      (7) Manufacturing budgets—vice-president, manufacturing
      (8) Cash flow and capital addition budgets—treasurer
   d. Initiation of departmental budgets—departmental manager:
      (1) Profit plans
      (2) Flexible expense budgets
   e. Profit plan approvals:
      (1) Initial approval by responsible manager concerned
      (2) Approval by next-higher manager
      (3) Presentation and discussion of profit plans with the executive committee
      (4) Final approval—president
7. Profit planning calendar (the strategic and tactical profit plans will be prepared concurrently):
   a. September 30—distribution of statement of planning premises
   b. October 1—start preparation of sales plan and departmental flexible expense budgets
   c. November 15—sales plan and flexible budgets completed
   d. December 1—production budget, materials budget, direct labor and factory overhead budgets completed
   e. December 7—proposed project budgets and tentative profit plans presented to the executive committee for analysis, suggestions, and evaluation
   f. December 12—final copy of revised profit plans and related proposals reviewed by the executive committee
   g. December 14—final approval of the profit plans by the president
   h. December 22—completion of reproduction of the profit plans
   i. December 30—distribution of the profit plans with covering letter prepared by the president

  j. Monthly budgets—by the end of March, June, and September, respectively, monthly breakdowns of quarterly budgets

  k. Expense control budgets—by the twenty-fifth of each month, the director of profit planning and control will submit to the various departmental managers budget expense estimates based on planned production for the upcoming month

  l. Monthly performance reports—the director of profit planning and control will distribute no later than the seventh of the following month the performance reports covering the preceding month (the actual data to be provided by the accounting department; budget amounts to be provided by the profit planning and control department)

Statement of Broad Objectives Illustrated

The statement of broad objectives of the company was completely rewritten to emphasize some of the consultant's major recommendations and to make it suitable for inclusion in the annual financial report to be distributed to shareholders. The final draft as revised by the executive committee and approved by the president is shown in Exhibit 4-3.

EXHIBIT 4-3

Statement of Broad Objectives, Superior Manufacturing Company, January 1, 19X2

The broad long-range objective of Superior Manufacturing Company is to create and maintain an enterprise environment that maximizes the interest and motivations of all its employees. This climate must be characterized by recognition of the personal long-range goals of its employees. The environment must be characterized by high ethical tone, honest and forthright actions, high standards of performance, and realistic and fair rewards for that competence. To accomplish these goals requires fair evaluation of the performance of individuals, particularly those in management positions. Appropriate attention to the well-being and working conditions of the employees and realistic compensation for performance require that the company operate on a profitable basis both in the short run and the long run, and that it earn a reasonable rate of return on the funds invested in the business.

Another broad objective of the company is to increase sales by expanding into new products and new geographical areas. This growth objective of the company, in turn, entails expansion of the number of employees, facilities, and financial resources. Specifically, the company's growth objective is to expand at a rate faster than the industry in which it operates.

Another broad objective is to develop an expanding number of customers who have confidence in the products distributed by the company and trust in the actions and basic honesty of all the company representatives and of the company overall. To accomplish this broad objective, we aim to manufacture and distribute only quality products and to maintain a high level of excellence in the manufacture of those products. Our pricing policy will be competitive when related to quality and dependability. We want our customers to be proud of the products they acquire from us because we realize that our present customers should be our best "salespersons."

Superior Manufacturing Company is a corporation owned by approximately three thousand shareholders; therefore, another broad objective is to earn a reasonable rate of return on the owner's investment and to build a larger and more dynamic company for them. We aim to speak candidly with our stockholders in matters of broad company policy and financial performance.

Another broad objective is to fill the role of a responsible corporate citizen in the broader community. This role entails responsible participation in community affairs and in the promotion of broad programs aimed at improving the social and economic well-being of the broader citizenry. Consistent with our profit objectives, the company will engage in programs to train and use individuals from all walks of life with particular emphasis on the disadvantaged. In these matters, the basic guidelines will be the long-range impact on the broader community and on the long-range affairs of the company.

A final broad objective of the company is to operate with a positive and dynamic philosophy of management, which is vital to a competitive and growing company. In accomplishing this objective, long-range efforts will be planned and implemented to continuously and consistently increase the expertise of the management at all levels and to take full advantage of the latest techniques and innovations as they are developed. In carrying out this objective, the management is committed to give long-range objectives priority over short-range results and to institute a management development program that will assure an adequate supply of competent young managers from within the company so that the long-range success of the company is assured. In fulfilling this role, the management is committed to an enlightened approach to the behavioral problems in industry and to full managerial participation by those found competent. A behavior management program will be initiated during 19X2.

The President

Statement of Specific Goals Illustrated

Consistent with the statement of broad objectives, the executive committee developed the statement of specific goals for the company shown in Exhibit 4-4.[1]

EXHIBIT 4-4

Statement of Specific Goals, Superior Manufacturing Company, January 1, 19X2

1. Growth objective—a 4 percent annual growth in sales volume for the next five years; the growth for 19X2 should approximate 3 percent and for the following year approximate 4 percent, and it should then exceed 4 percent in subsequent years of the five-year plan. The relevant factors influencing this growth plan are the following:
   a. Product Z will be introduced at the beginning of 19X3.
   b. Two years hence, start entry into the Asian market.
   c. An intensive market training program will be initiated during 19X2.
   d. Product pricing policies will not be changed.
   e. Aggressive and sophisticated sales efforts will be appropriately funded.

[1] William E. Thomas, ed., *Readings in Cost Accounting, Budgeting and Control* (Cincinnati: South-Western Publishing, 1983), Readings Nos. 6 and 12.

2. Return on total investment objective for the company—24 percent pretax; the actual return on investment for the current year will be approximately 22 percent. This return-on-investment objective should be realistic if
   a. The sales plan is accomplished
   b. Cost control objectives are realistically planned and attained
   c. Investment in assets is realistically planned and controlled
3. Profit margin objectives are as follows:
   a. Company overall pretax 15 percent.
   b. Direct district operating profit margin: Southern, 21 percent; Eastern, 23 percent; Western, 23 percent.
4. Cash flow objective—to internally generate sufficient cash for debt payments and for current operations.
5. Research objective—to undertake and complete analysis and evaluation of product X to improve its applications. To experiment with and test the relevance of certain suggestions received from customers about products X and Y. To continue active research to develop new products. To plan an increase in the research budget of approximately 5 percent over the preceding year (see actual data attached).
6. Factory productivity objective—to plan a realistic increase in productivity (efficiency in factory operations); this increase would be reflected in the plans through increased quality control, better expense control, and lower unit costs, particularly for factory overhead and labor costs. Plans should also be included to improve the technology of the plant and to expand the application of our computer resources.
7. The profit plan will include initiation of a formal behavioral management program and revitalization of the performance evaluation system, with particular attention to evaluation of managerial competence at all levels.
8. Cost control objective—the plans should include a commitment to improve cost control at all levels of management and to relate expenditures to output (productivity). Flexible expense budgets will be used in the control of expenses. The emphasis will not be on reducing expenses; rather the emphasis will be on improving the ratio between expenses and output. Profit plans should include expense estimates based only on real needs justified by programs. The attention of all managers and supervisors is called to the company policy on expense control; that is, flexibility will be the focus of management's attention so that when unanticipated events arise, additional funds will be made available for essential needs even though not budgeted. Similarly, when needs decrease and there are excess budget allowances, the unused funds will be used for other needs consistent with the judgment of the management concerned. Unspent funds of this nature will not reflect unfavorably on future budget requests of the related responsibility center.

Statement of Basic Strategies Illustrated

In harmony with the evaluation of relevant variables, the broad enterprise objectives, and the specific goals, top management developed basic strategies for the coming year, as summarized in Exhibit 4-5.

EXHIBIT 4-5

Statement of Basic Strategies, Superior Manufacturing Company, January 1, 19X2

1. To increase market penetration and to stay in front of the competition in all marketing areas. The following strategies to attain this goal will be aggressively pursued:
   a. Establish product research (new product development and improvement of

present products) on a long-range budget basis. To this end, we will commit an increasing share of funds that become available for the next five years to research.

b. During 19X3, introduce in all market areas the new product (product Z) that has shown considerable promise in the three market tests completed to date. Special promotional efforts will be planned and funded.

c. Increase the quality of our products by
   (1) Increased technological efficiency in our plants
   (2) Increased competence of selected factory employees (and factory supervisors)
   (3) Improvement of quality control techniques

d. Revitalize the training program for our marketing specialists, giving special emphasis to aggressive sales efforts on a sophisticated level in order to appeal to preferred customers.

2. Except for short-term needs, to finance all expansion of company operations from internally generated cash.

3. To increase our product efficiency aggressively by
   a. Upgrading productive personnel through
      (1) Careful evaluation and improvement of quality control
      (2) Identification of weaknesses in individual performance and correction of these through training and positive approaches on a sound behavioral basis
      (3) Improvement of selectivity in initial employment
      (4) Maintenance of machinery in top operating condition
   b. Using the latest technological advances for productive facilities, including expansion of our computer applications in the factory

4. To increase management sophistication of all levels by expanding our executive development program. During the coming year, we will develop a formal plan for raising the competence of our younger managers. To provide a sufficient and ready supply of competent individuals for the higher-management positions.

5. To increase our return on investment in conformity with the broad objectives, we will
   a. Increase market penetration as specified in item 1 above
   b. Improve expense control at all levels, and relate cost and other expenditures to output (productivity)
   c. Continue our present pricing strategy

Planning Premises Illustrated

Each year, the formal planning activities at the lower levels of management are initiated by means of a "planning premises memo" distributed by the president to the manager of each major responsibility center. Attached to the memo are the relevant guidelines and instructions developed by the executive committee and approved by the president. The planning premises memo is shown in Exhibit 4-6.

EXHIBIT 4-6

Planning Premises Memorandum for 19X2, Superior Manufacturing Company, September 25, 19X1

To all vice-presidents and division managers:

The purposes of this letter and the attachments are (a) to initiate the formal planning activities in each of your responsibility centers for the next planning period (19X2 and beyond) and (b) to provide goals, guidelines, and planning procedures that we will use to develop the 19X2 profit plans. There are no changes in the policies set forth in the profit planning and control manual. For your convenience, our planning calendar is attached. Notice that it has been slightly revised to fit the 19X2 calendar. In conformity with our standard procedure manuals and assigned responsibilities, the project plans, the five-year strategic profit plan, and the annual tactical plan will be developed.

You can take justifiable pride in the accomplishments of our company over its life span, particularly in recent years. The interest, enthusiasm, and understanding about the new comprehensive profit planning and control program that have been exhibited by all levels of management are commendable. At the outset, I want to encourage each of you, collectively and individually, to continue making constructive suggestions to increase the operational efficiency of our company, the sophistication of our management, and the effectiveness of our management programs.

Last year our annual sales volume reached record levels, and in my judgment our operational efficiencies also established new peaks. It is well to take satisfaction with our accomplishments in the past, but it is important that we focus our energies and attention on the future. In this context, the guidelines provided in this letter represent the collective judgments of your executive committee and of myself. They are intended to provide a basis for greater accomplishments in the future; accomplishments that, in the long run, will be to the advantage of all employees individually and collectively.

The executive committee has just completed an in-depth assessment of the company in view of our long-term expectations. As a result of that assessment, we have concluded that increased emphasis should be given to marketing strategies, consistent product quality, and certain programs that serve broad societal needs. This increased emphasis has been incorporated into the guidelines attached to this letter. A copy of the statement of broad objectives of the company is attached. Notice that it has been significantly revised from the one for this past year.

Attached to this letter for your guidance are the following separate items:

1   Statement of broad objectives.

2   Statement of specific goals.

3   Summary of basic strategies.

4   Historical data (relating to the industry and our company for the past several years). The data presented were selected by the financial vice-president on the basis of their relevance to your planning problems. Additional data desired may be obtained readily upon request.

5   Economic statistics (including economic projections and a relevant commentary that may be useful to you in making certain planning decisions for your responsibility center). These data were developed by the economic analysts and from selected sources. If additional data are required, you should contact the financial vice-president.

6   Planning calendar.

7   Instructions prepared by the director of profit planning and control about schedule format and related matters essential to aggregating your planning results into the overall company plans. Please contact the director if there are any procedural, format, or budget administration questions.

In preparing plans for your responsibility center, the following underlying assumptions should be used:

a   The industry is expected to continue its expansion at about 3 percent per year. Our sales growth will continue to exceed the industry rate.

b   General business conditions are expected to continue at the present growth rate during the next five years. A slight decrease in business conditions is expected during the last half of 19X2 (refer to the economic analysis attached).

c   No major economic, social, or military catastrophe is anticipated.

To provide additional guidance and to discuss your specific problems, within the next two weeks I will schedule several meetings with the vice-presidents and other senior members of the management group. Following these discussions, each vice-president will schedule planning conferences with his or her key managers, at which time the policies with respect to the profit planning and control program will be discussed. In addition, these guidelines and their application should be discussed with your supervising manager to establish a basis for significant participation in the planning process.

It is essential that we adhere to the planning calendar and that we exert our best efforts to develop realistic programs and plans, then to evaluate them in dollars so that we may have a realistic plan of the probable financial results for 19X2 and beyond.

We should remember that planning is a major management responsibility. Therefore, we should expect to spend the effort required to develop realistic plans. In the process, each member of the executive committee, including myself, will be available for advice, suggestions, and tentative evaluations. Each member of management is urged to work closely with the financial executive who has staff responsibility for overall supervision of the operation of the profit planning and control program. In this connection, however, I want to make it clear, as does the financial vice-president, that the financial division will serve only in a staff capacity to provide advice and assistance.

The line executives and managers are directly responsible for the decision inputs. The profit plan, when completed, must be viewed as the plans and commitments of the operating management and not of the staff.

I am confident that we will develop an excellent profit plan and that we will meet or exceed its goals by the end of the planning period. Your cooperation and constructive efforts will ensure the attainment of this objective.

The President

Project Planning Illustrated

The company has been using project planning for major projects. For example, the new product Z has been set up as a project plan. Project plans will be developed to cover the estimated life span of the effort. Each year all project plans will be updated. Ideas for new projects (including improvements in current operations) will be encouraged at all levels of management. The company has developed a set of procedures to ensure that all ideas and suggestions are given careful attention and evaluation. Under these procedures, a project number is assigned to each suggestion, and if the project is approved, it is incorporated into the strategic and tactical profit plans (see Exhibit 2-6).

Exhibit 4-7 contains a suggestion that has been processed through the various evaluations and has survived for inclusion in the five-year and one-year profit plans. The exhibit indicates the evaluation and approval processes, as well as instructions for including the project in periodic profit plans. The capital additions budget subsequently illustrated includes this project. Notice that this project was suggested several years earlier and tentatively approved for inclusion in the 19X2 profit plans.

Strategic and Tactical Profit Plans Illustrated

Superior Manufacturing Company annually prepares two periodic profit plans—a strategic long-range profit plan encompassing a time horizon of five years beyond the upcoming year (for the period 19X3–19X7) and a tactical short-range profit plan encompassing twelve months that correspond with the upcoming budget period (calendar year 19X2). First, we will illustrate some parts of the long-range profit plan followed by illustrations from the short-range profit plan.

STRATEGIC LONG-TERM PROFIT PLAN   The strategic long-term plan for Superior Manufacturing Company is in conformity with the broad objectives of the enterprise, the specific objectives, and the long-range strategies illustrated above. The long-range plan is broad and shows summary data. Part of the long-range plan is more or less informal as represented by tentative commitments made by the executive committee in its planning sessions. The formal portion of the long-range plan includes the following basic components detailed by each year: income statement, balance sheet, cash flow projection, capital expenditures plan, personnel requirements, research plans, and a long-range market penetration plan. Thus, the long-range plan covers all the key areas of anticipated activity: sales, expenses, research and development, capital expenditures, cash, profit, and return on investment. The income statement component of the long-range plan for Superior Manufacturing Company is shown in Exhibit 4-8.

Notice in Exhibit 4-8 that although sales are shown as a total amount for each year, there is a supporting plan that provides more detail about the various products, distribution expenses, and planned promotional efforts. Another important feature is the classification of expenses into two components: variable and fixed cost (discussed in detail in subsequent chapters). The planning of three important ratios—that is, two profitability indices, profit margin and return on investment, and the growth trend—are reflected in sales dollars.

TACTICAL SHORT-TERM PROFIT PLAN   To provide a broad view of a complete short-range profit plan, selected summary profit plans for the Superior Manufacturing Company are shown in this section. The plans shown here are primarily annual results; the details by months, responsibility, and products will be discussed and illustrated at the end of subsequent chapters. The annual

EXHIBIT 4-7

Project Proposal Summary, Superior Manufacturing Company

THE SUPERIOR MANUFACTURING COMPANY

PROJECT PROPOSAL SUMMARY

PROJECT NO. ___*1 - 101*___   DATE *Jan. 15, 19X2*

DIVISION OR DEPARTMENT *Company*

ORIGINATED BY *A. B. Commerce*   TITLE *Vice President*

EVALUATIONS: (File Code *20*)

	Date Completed	Supervisor	Recommendation
			Proceed with technical
Policy	*8-1-84*	*Hudson*	*and economic evaluations*
Technical	*7-1-85*	*Hammer*	*Favorable*
Economic	*9-1-85*	*Donley*	*Cost #120,000 (est.)*

APPROVALS:

Tentative Approval by Executive Committee *Jan. 1, 19X0*
Approval by President for Inclusion in Profit Plan Dated: *Include in 19X2*
    plans for construction to start in 19X3.
Project Authorization (AFE) Date _____

REVIEWS subsequent to Approval for Inclusion in Profit Plan:

(1) _____
(2) _____
(3) _____

PROJECT SUMMARY:

DESIGNATION: *new building - for expansion of Mfg. facilities*
    (see file 20-1-101-9)
ESTIMATED STARTING DATE *Jan. 19X3* ESTIMATED COMPLETION DATE *Sept. 19X3*
PRIORITY *a-5*
COST ESTIMATES (Cash Flow): TOTAL $ *120,000*
    BY YEAR: Yr 1 *$120,000* Yr 2 _____ Yr 3 _____ Yr 4 _____ Yr 5 _____
        Balance _____
RETURN ON INVESTMENT ANALYSIS *17% (DCF) See file 20-1-101-9*

COMMENTS _____
_____

summaries and discussions given in this chapter include only those details essential (1) to provide a general understanding of the annual profit plan and (2) to provide an overall view of the comprehensive short-range profit plan. You should review the organizational chart and the statements of broad objectives, the specific goals, the strategies, and the planning premises memo as background before studying these schedules. Notice how the tactical profit plan dovetails with the strategic long-range profit plan.

You should particularly notice that the budgets and subbudgets illustrated here and in subsequent chapters are segmented as follows:

1 By organizational responsibility. We have emphasized that participation is valuable in the planning process and that control can be exercised effectively only through assigned responsibilities. Consequently, the profit planning and control program must be tailored, first and foremost, to the organizational structure and the related responsibilities. This frame of reference is included in almost all the schedules included in the short-range profit plan and also in the periodic performance reports prepared and distributed throughout the year to all levels of management.

EXHIBIT 4-8

Strategic Long-Term Profit Plan (partial), Superior Manufacturing Company, Five-Year Plan—Income Statement (In Thousand Dollars)

	ACTUAL		PROJECTED					
	19X0	19X1	19X2	19X3	19X4	19X5	19X6	19X7
Sales	$5,691	$5,963	$6,100	$7,000	$7,400	$8,000	$8,800	$9,500
Variable costs	3,700	3,870	3,940	4,650	4,880	5,350	5,890	6,360
Marginal income	1,991	2,093	2,160	2,350	2,520	2,650	2,910	3,140
Fixed costs	1,100	1,160	1,310	1,400	1,430	1,470	1,580	1,680
Miscellaneous items	(15)	10	(20)	(50)	(20)	(30)	(16)	(20)
Net before taxes	906	923	870	1,000	1,110	1,210	1,346	1,480
Estimated taxes	270	325	260	490	540	590	650	700
Net income	$ 636	$ 598	$ 610	$ 510	$ 570	$ 620	$ 696	$ 780
Ratios:								
Profit margin								
—pretax	15.9	15.5	14.3	14.3	15.0	15.1	15.3	15.6
Return on invest-								
ment—pretax	28.0	27.6	17.4	29.6	30.0	30.0	31.0	31.0
Sales trend	93.3	97.8	100.0	114.7	121.3	131.1	144.3	155.7

Note: Since this strategic profit plan is being prepared during August 19X1, the "Actual" column for 19X1 consists of seven months of actual data and projected data for the remaining five months of 19X1.

2 By interim periods. Superior Manufacturing Company segments the tactical profit plan for the first quarter of the annual period on a monthly basis; estimates for subsequent quarters are subsequently categorized by monthly periods during the year. Segmentation on a time basis is especially significant because, to be relevant, many goals must be immediate goals. For example, an annual sales quota would not motivate salespersons as much as a series of monthly, or even daily, sales quotas. The strategic profit plan is categorized by years.

3 By product-cost classifications. The tactical profit plan must be structured to meet the data needs for unit product cost, project cost, and other cost constructions that are not necessarily based on organizational responsibilities or uniform time periods.

Some of the budget schedules illustrated in this and subsequent chapters are designed to show the approach used to develop them. This format is used only for instructional purposes. For the final profit plans, some of these instructional schedules should be redesigned to increase their readability, and some of them may well be omitted from the actual profit plan distributed within the company.

To facilitate understanding, we will differentiate the various subbudgets by schedule number in contrast with other presentations in the text that are designated as exhibits. The discussion below gives an overview of selected budget schedules for Superior Manufacturing Company. At this time, you should concentrate on (1) the decisional input sources for the information shown in the various budgets (plans), (2) the flow of information from one phase to the next, and (3) the format of the schedules showing responsibility, time horizons, and product classifications.

TACTICAL SALES PLAN ILLUSTRATED After the planning premises have been received, development of the sales plan is the next step in preparing the profit plans for Superior Manufacturing Company. The strategic and tactical sales plans have three distinct parts: (1) the planned volume of sales at the planned sales price per unit for each product; (2) the sales promotional plan (advertising and other promotional costs); and (3) the sales (or distribution) expense plan (salesperson's remuneration and other order-getting and order-filling expenses). Superior Manufacturing Company sells two products (designated X and Y) in three sales districts (designated Southern, Eastern, and Western). The sales plan is the direct responsibility of the sales vice-president. A tentative sales plan is presented to the executive committee by the sales vice-president after revision in conformity with the judgments of the executive committee.

The annual sales budget summary (as approved) for the company for the planning year ending December 31, 19X2, is shown in Schedule 1. For instructional purposes, a reference heading "Ref." is used to provide a line and a column to indicate sources of data. When the source is from a prior schedule, its schedule number is used. When the data come from a basic input source, such as a decision-making authority, the word "Input" is used. Notice that the basic inputs used to develop this schedule are (1) the planned unit sales price—a decision of top management, and (2) the planned number of units to be sold (assuming the planned sales price and the planned promotional and other sales efforts). The other components of the sales plan will be illustrated in Chapter 5.

SCHEDULE 1. Superior Manufacturing Company

Tactical Sales Plan Summary—Volume and Dollars
By District, By Product
For the Year Ending December 31, 19X2

RESPONSIBILITY		TOTALS	PRODUCT X		PRODUCT Y	
			UNITS	AMOUNT	UNITS	AMOUNT
	Ref.		(Input)		(Input)	
Southern Sales District		$2,120,000	340,000	$1,700,000	210,000	$ 420,000
X—$5.00; Y—$2.00*	(Input)					
Eastern Sales District		2,907,000	500,000	2,550,000	170,000	357,000
X—$5.10; Y—$2.10*	(Input)					
Western Sales District		1,068,000	160,000	816,000	120,000	252,000
X—$5.10; Y—$2.10*	(Input)					
Total		$6,095,000	1,000,000	$5,066,000	500,000	$1,029,000

*Average unit sales price planned. (See Schedule 21 for details.)

If Superior were a merchandising business, it would develop a sales plan in the way described above. A service business would also proceed in this fashion, with the product columns replaced by the major categories of services provided.

PRODUCTION PLAN ILLUSTRATED   When the sales plan is completed, the next step in building the short-range profit plan for Superior Manufacturing Company is to develop a production plan. The production plan involves determining the number of units of each product that must be manufactured to meet planned sales and maintain the planned inventory levels of finished goods. Planning production requirements necessitates another decisional input, that is, the management decision about inventory levels of finished goods that are to be planned. Thus, the production budget summary shown in Schedule 2 was developed using planned sales from Schedule 1, the beginning inventories of finished goods, and the ending inventory levels of finished goods. At this time we will not discuss inventory policy except to assume that the ending inventories shown in Schedule 2 are consistent with Superior's inventory policy.

Production planning and scheduling are factory functions involving determination of the amount of goods to produce and production timing; therefore, the production plan is the primary responsibility of the manufacturing vice-president. Product X is processed through all three factory production departments, and product Y is processed through production departments 1 and 3 only.

Notice in the next several paragraphs that the production plan provides the basic foundation for planning direct material, direct labor, and manufacturing overhead costs.

SCHEDULE 2. Superior Manufacturing Company

Production Budget Summary*
By Product Units
For the Year Ending December 31, 19X2

		PRODUCTS (UNITS)	
		X	Y
	Ref.		
Units required to meet sales budget	1	1,000,000	500,000
Add planned finished goods ending inventory, December 31, 19X2	(Input)	200,000	120,000
Total units required		1,200,000	620,000
Less finished goods beginning inventory, January 1, 19X2	(Given)	240,000	100,000
Planned production for 19X2		960,000	520,000

*See Schedules 22 and 23 for details.

DIRECT MATERIALS AND PARTS BUDGET ILLUSTRATED   Direct materials, as a manufacturing cost, is represented by the materials and parts used directly in manufacturing finished goods. The direct materials and parts budget shows the estimated amount of materials and parts required to produce the number of units of finished goods planned in the production budget. It does not show dollar amounts. The basic input is the number of units of each type of material and part required to manufacture each unit of finished goods. Thus, preparation of the direct materials and parts budget requires a careful study of the products to determine unit usage rates. The unit usage rates are multiplied by the planned number of units of finished goods to be produced to compute the total units of materials and parts required.

The direct materials and parts budget summary in units for Superior Manufacturing Company is shown in Schedule 3. Notice that the company uses three direct materials designated as A, B, and C. Computations underlying this schedule are shown in a later chapter (Schedules 24 and 25).

PURCHASES BUDGET ILLUSTRATED   The direct materials and parts budget provides the purchasing manager with data needed to develop a purchase plan. This requires a decisional input, that is, the management policy regarding the level of materials and parts inventories to be maintained. Using the materials and parts budget and the inventory policy, the **number of units** of each type of each item that must be **purchased** to support the production plans can be planned as shown in Schedule 4, the purchases budget summary. Finally, another decisional input is required—the **planned unit purchase price** for each type of material and part. With this additional input, the total cost of planned purchases for each material and part can be computed.

SCHEDULE 3. Superior Manufacturing Company

Direct Materials Budget Summary in Units*
By Material, By Product, By Department
For the Year Ending December 31, 19X2

| | | DIRECT MATERIAL (UNITS REQUIRED FOR PRODUCTION) | | |
RESPONSIBILITY		A	B	C
	Ref.			
By product:	24			
X	&	960,000	1,920,000	1,920,000
Y	25	520,000	520,000	
Total		1,480,000	2,440,000	1,920,000
By department:				
No. 1		1,480,000		
No. 2			1,920,000	
No. 3			520,000	1,920,000
Total		1,480,000	2,440,000	1,920,000

*See Schedules 24 and 25 for details.

SCHEDULE 4. Superior Manufacturing Company

Purchases Budget Summary*
For the Year Ending December 31, 19X2

| | | DIRECT MATERIALS | | |
		A	B	C
	Ref.			
Units required for production	3	1,480,000	2,440,000	1,920,000
Add desired ending inventory Dec. 31, 19X2	(Input)	245,000	370,000	450,000
Total units required		1,725,000	2,810,000	2,370,000
Less beginning inventory, Jan. 1, 19X2	(Given)	220,000	360,000	460,000
Units to be purchased		1,505,000	2,450,000	1,910,000
Planned unit purchase price	(Input)	$.30	$.20	$.25
Total cost of purchases		$ 451,500	$ 490,000	$ 477,500

*See Schedules 26, 27, and 28 in subsequent chapters for details.

The purchases budget is a **direct responsibility of the purchasing manager**. This manager works under direct supervision of the manufacturing vice-president. It is a direct responsibility of the purchasing manager to be knowledgeable about the market for the items that must be purchased. Therefore, it is the responsibility of the purchasing manager to plan the unit costs for use in the purchases budget.

Notice in the purchases budget summary that both units of material and dollar costs are specified. This schedule is one of the building blocks for both the planned income statement and the cash flow plan, which are discussed subsequently.

DIRECT LABOR BUDGET ILLUSTRATED   Direct labor is defined as those labor costs directly identifiable with the production of specific units of finished goods. The production plan (Schedule 2) provides the underlying data for planning the direct labor requirements. The direct labor budget requires two additional decisional inputs: (a) the standard direct labor hours per unit of each unit of finished goods and (b) the average hourly wage rates planned. This budget must show the planned direct labor hours and cost by organizational responsibility and by product. The **manufacturing vice-president is directly responsible** for developing the direct labor budget. The three production department managers and the standards-measurement group cooperatively develop the decisional inputs (that is, the standard times and wage rates) for this budget. The direct labor budget summary for Superior Manufacturing Company is shown in Schedule 5.

If this were a merchandising or service company, it would not have a direct labor budget. Labor would be budgeted as an operating expense along with the other major expenses incurred in operating the business.

SCHEDULE 5. Superior Manufacturing Company

Direct Labor Budget Summary
By Product, By Department
For the Year Ending December 31, 19X2

		UNITS TO BE PRODUCED	STANDARD LABOR HOURS	TOTAL STANDARD HOURS	AVERAGE WAGE RATE	DIRECT LABOR COST
	Ref.	2	(Input)		(Input)	
By product:						
X		960,000	1.0	960,000	$1.50	$1,440,000
Y		520,000	.4	208,000	1.50	312,000
Total				1,168,000		$1,752,000
By department (responsibility):						
1*				488,000	$2.00	$ 976,000
2*				192,000	1.50	288,000
3*				488,000	1.00	488,000
Total				1,168,000		$1,752,000

*Computation shown in Schedules 30 and 31.

BUILDING SERVICES BUDGET ILLUSTRATED   Before illustrating the planning of manufacturing overhead costs, we must consider the building services budget because Superior Manufacturing Company uses one building for the three major home-office functions of administration, production, and sales. Concurrent with the profit planning activities as illustrated for the sales vice-president and the manufacturing vice-president, the building supervisor must prepare a building services budget. This budget, shown in Schedule 6, is an expense projection based on expected building use. The **building supervisor is directly responsible for this budget** and must work in cooperation with the other managers to develop some of the estimates. For example, building services salaries are based on top-management decisions; depreciation expense is basically an accounting determination; and insurance and taxes would reflect managerial policies and externally determined rates. Superior Manufacturing Company allocates building costs to the three major functions on the basis of floor space occupied; the planned allocation is shown on Schedule 6.

The building services budget for a merchandising or services firm would be similar to that shown in Schedule 6.

SCHEDULE 6. Superior Manufacturing Company

Building Services Budget Summary*
For the Year Ending December 31, 19X2

	TOTAL YEAR
Supervisory salaries	$ 24,000
Repairs and maintenance	18,000
Depreciation	60,000
Insurance	3,600
Taxes	2,400
Wages	27,000
Heat	13,000
Water	2,000
Total	$150,000
Building services cost allocation: (on basis of floor space)	
Selling (20%)	$ 30,000
Administrative (20%)	30,000
Factory (60%)	90,000
Total	$150,000

*See Schedule 34 for details.

MANUFACTURING OVERHEAD BUDGET ILLUSTRATED   Recall that Superior Manufacturing Company has three producing departments and three service departments in the factory. Therefore, factory overhead (expense) budgets for **each** of these six departments must be prepared by the manufacturing vice-president. In turn, the vice-president establishes a policy that requires each department supervisor to develop his or her proposed factory overhead budget.

The production budget shows the planned production for each product manufactured; therefore, it provides the underlying foundation for planning factory overhead costs. The production budget provides a basis for projecting the **planned volume of work or activity** for each producing department. In turn, the planned activities of each producing department provide a basis for estimation of the volume of work or activity that can be expected in each of the three factory **service departments.** The general factory overhead department is the administrative center for the factory; the power department produces electricity for use by the production departments; and the repair department repairs machinery and other facilities used by the three producing departments.

The departmental factory overhead budgets for each of the six factory departments, as approved by the vice-president of manufacturing, are summarized in Schedule 7. Notice that all expenses are planned by responsibility (that is, by department). The expense accounts listed for each department are also used in the responsibility accounting system. The costs are based on work or volume of activity based on either (a) direct estimates by the managers or (b) departmental flexible budget formulas.

The building services allocation ($90,000 from Schedule 6) is included in Schedule 7 as a total. It is not reallocated to the six departments individually. This treatment reflects the fact that the departmental supervisors do not exercise control over either building services cost or the allocation of its cost. Control of building services cost is the direct responsibility of the building superintendent.

An overhead budget similar to that shown in Schedule 7 would also be developed by a merchandising firm or a service firm.

INVENTORY BUDGET ILLUSTRATED.   At this point, the managers have planned the costs for the factory; information is now available to develop the planned dollar values of the inventories for (1) raw materials, (2) work in process, and (3) finished goods. Copies of the production, direct materials, purchases, direct labor, and factory overhead budgets are given to the director of planning and control. The staff uses these figures to compute and assemble data for the budgeted inventory levels (units and dollars) and cost of goods sold. To compute these two budgets **no additional decisional inputs** are needed, with the exception of the **inventory cost flow method** to be used. Superior Manufacturing Company management uses the first-in, first-out cost flow policy for all inventories.

The budget of beginning and ending inventories is shown in Schedule 8. The related cost of goods sold budget summary is shown in Schedule 9. The details are illustrated in subsequent chapters.

DISTRIBUTION AND PROMOTIONAL EXPENSE BUDGETS ILLUSTRATED.   The overall sales plan for Superior Manufacturing Company includes three components: (1) planned sales volume (Schedule 1), (2) planned promotional expenses, and (3) other planned distribution expenses. Distribution and promotional expenses in this company are combined into one budget, which shows separate budgets for each of the three sales districts and for home-office sale activities

SCHEDULE 7. Superior Manufacturing Company

Manufacturing Overhead—Budget Summary*
By Department for the Year Ending December 31, 19X2

| | | RESPONSIBILITY | | | | | | |
| | | PRODUCING DEPARTMENTS | | | SERVICE DEPARTMENTS | | | |
ACCOUNT	Ref. (Inputs)	NO. 1	NO. 2	NO. 3	GENERAL FACTORY OVERHEAD	POWER DEPT.	REPAIR DEPT.	TOTAL ALL DEPTS.
Supervisory salaries		$120,000	$22,440	$ 35,040	$ 96,000	$ 36,000	$ 3,600	$313,080
Indirect labor	"	145,800	3,648	44,248				193,696
Maintenance parts	"	10,920	624	4,240		6,800		22,584
Fuel	"					24,000		24,000
Supplies used	"	32,240	1,440	14,600			1,360	49,640
Travel and entertainment	"				7,040			7,040
Telephone and telegraph	"				7,856			7,856
Depreciation	"	7,320	768	4,392	1,560	5,400	120	19,560
Insurance	"	1,200	120	600	240	840	36	3,036
Taxes	"	1,800	240	720	360	960	84	4,164
Stationery and office supplies	"				3,744			3,744
Wages	"					36,000	4,800	40,800
Total		$319,280	$29,280	$103,840	$116,800	$110,000	$10,000	$689,200
Building services cost allocation	6							90,000
Total factory overhead								$779,200

*See Schedules 33 and 34 for details.

SCHEDULE 8. Superior Manufacturing Company

Budget of Beginning and Ending Inventories*
For the Year Ending December 31, 19X2
(Input—FIFO Method)

INVENTORY	Ref.	BEGINNING INVENTORY UNITS 2 & 4	UNITS	TOTAL VALUE	ENDING INVENTORY UNITS 2 & 4	UNITS	TOTAL VALUE
Raw materials:							
Material A		220,000	$ .30	$ 66,000	245,000	$ .30	$ 73,500
Material B		360,000	.20	72,000	370,000	.20	74,000
Material C		460,000	.26	119,600	450,000	.25	112,500
Total				$257,600			$260,000
Work in process		10,000	1.38	$ 13,800	10,000	1.38	$ 13,800
(Prod. Y—Dept. 3)							
Finished goods:							
Product X		240,000	3.36	$806,400	200,000	3.36	$672,000
Product Y		100,000	1.38	138,000	120,000	1.38	165,600
Total				$944,400			$837,600

*See Schedules 27 and 60.

SCHEDULE 9. Superior Manufacturing Company

Cost of Goods Sold Budget Summary*
For the Year Ending December 31, 19X2

	Ref.		ANNUAL
Direct raw materials used:			
Beginning inventory, Jan. 1, 19X2	8	$ 257,600	
Purchases of raw materials	4	1,419,000	
Total		$1,676,600	
Less ending inventory, Dec. 31, 19X2	8	260,000	
Cost of raw materials used			$1,416,600
Direct labor	5		1,752,000
Manufacturing expenses	7		779,200
Total charges to manufacturing			3,947,800
Add beginning work in process inventory	8		13,800
			3,961,600
Less ending work in process inventory	8		13,800
Total cost of goods manufactured			3,947,800
Add beginning finished goods inventory	8		944,400
			4,892,200
Less ending inventory of finished goods	8		837,600
Cost of goods sold			$4,054,600

*See Schedule 61 for details.

SCHEDULE 10. Superior Manufacturing Company

Distribution Expense Budget Summary*
For the Year Ending December 31, 19X2

ACCOUNT	GENERAL SALES OVERHEAD	SALES DISTRICT SOUTHERN	EASTERN	WESTERN	TOTAL
	Ref.				
Supervisory salaries	(Input) $144,000	$ 72,000	$ 96,000	$ 36,000	$348,000
Travel and entertainment	" 38,907	25,279	30,812	11,641	106,639
Telephone and telegraph	" 15,861	9,379	14,828	4,915	44,983
Depreciation—office equipment	" 600				600
Stationery and office supplies	" 11,049				11,049
Auto expense	" 25,913				25,913
Commissions	"	84,800	116,280	42,720	243,800
Freight and express	"	19,198	19,471	7,844	46,513
Advertising	" 60,000	24,000	36,000	12,000	132,000
Total	$296,330	$234,656	$313,391	$115,120	$959,497
Building services cost allocation	6				30,000
Total distribution expense					$989,497

*See Schedule 42 for details.

(by responsibility). The sales vice-president, in conformity with the basic planning policies of the company, requested each district sales supervisor to submit expense plans consistent with the volume of planned sales in each district. Home-office selling expenses were planned by the vice-president's assistants. These four distribution (i.e., selling) expense budgets, as approved by the vice-president of sales, are shown in Schedule 10. The building services allocation ($30,000 from Schedule 6) is shown in Schedule 10.

The cost estimates were based on the volume of activity shown in the sales budget by using either (a) judgment or (b) variable expense formulas for each sales district. The promotional (advertising) amounts were based on the specific goals and strategies provided in the planning premises memorandum.

ADMINISTRATIVE EXPENSE BUDGET ILLUSTRATED   The three general administrative departments are administrative, accounting (including the director of profit planning), and treasurer. The head of each of these departments submitted an expense budget for consideration and approval by the financial vice-president. These three expense budgets are shown in Schedule 11. The budget of "other income and expenses" for the company was prepared by the financial vice-president as shown in Schedule 12.

BUDGETED INCOME STATEMENT ILLUSTRATED   Copies of the sales, factory cost, and expense budgets are given to the director of planning because they are needed to prepare the planned income statement. The financial staff estimated

SCHEDULE 11. Superior Manufacturing Company

Administrative Expense Budget Summary*
For the Year Ending December 31, 19X2

ACCOUNT	Ref.	DEPARTMENTS AMINIS-TRATIVE	ACCOUNT-ING	TREAS-URER	TOTAL
Supervisory salaries	(Input)	$60,000	$48,000	$36,000	$144,000
Travel and entertaining	"	9,000	1,200	1,200	11,400
Telephone and telegraph	"	9,114	1,210	3,158	13,482
Depreciation—office equipment	"	600	2,400	1,200	4,200
Insurance	"	240	240	480	960
Taxes	"	240	360	120	720
Stationery and office supplies	"	122	610	1,829	2,561
Lawyers' retainer fee	"	1,800			1,800
Loss on bad debts	"			12,190	12,190
Audit fees	"	2,400			2,400
Total		$83,516	$54,020	$56,177	$193,713
Building services cost allocation					30,000
Total Administrative Expense					$223,713

*See Schedule 44 for details.

SCHEDULE 12. Superior Manufacturing Company

Budget of Other Income and Expenses
For the Year Ending December 31, 19X2

	Ref.		ANNUAL
Other incomes:			
Interest income (on building fund)	(Input)	$ 500	
Miscellaneous incomes	"	37,120	
Total			$37,620
Other expenses:			
Interest expense			3,750
Net (other income)			$33,870

income taxes and completed the budgeted income statement shown in Schedule 13. Notice that the budgeted profit margin of 14.13 percent is close to the 15 percent objective specified in the statement of goals (Exhibit 4-4). The president decided that the planned dividend amount was $12,000. Using the budgeted net income and the planned dividend, the financial staff prepared the budgeted statement of retained earnings shown in Schedule 14.

SCHEDULE 13. Superior Manufacturing Company

Budgeted Income Statement*
For the Year Ending December 31, 19X2

	Ref.	AMOUNT	PERCENT OF SALES
Sales	1	$6,095,000	100.00
Cost of goods sold	9	4,054,600	66.52
Gross margin on sales		$2,040,400	33.48
Less:			
Distribution expenses	10	989,497	16.23
Administrative expenses	11	223,713	3.67
Total		$1,213,210	19.90
Operating income		$ 827,190	13.57
Add net of other income and expense	12	33,870	.56
Net income before federal income taxes		$ 861,060	14.13
Federal income taxes	(Input)	258,318	4.24
Net income		$ 602,742	9.89

*See Schedules 64, 65, and 66 for details.

SCHEDULE 14. Superior Manufacturing Company

Statement of Budgeted Retained Earnings
For the Year Ending December 31, 19X2

	Ref.	
Balance, retained earnings, Jan. 1, 19X2	(Given)	$ 522,770
Add net income budgeted	13	602,742
Total		$1,125,512
Less budgeted dividends	(Input)	12,000
Balance, retained earnings, Dec. 31, 19X2		$1,113,512

CAPITAL ADDITIONS BUDGET ILLUSTRATED The capital additions budget includes such items as planned extensions of plant, new buildings, extraordinary repairs that are to be capitalized, building programs, and machinery acquisitions. The budget of capital additions included in the tactical short-range profit plan is only that specific part of the strategic long-range capital additions plan that will materialize during the budget year. The budget of capital additions included in the annual profit plan for Superior Manufacturing Company was prepared by the financial vice-president and the staff. However, the **decisional** inputs to this budget were initiated and decided upon by the line executives and then approved by the executive committee and the president. Notice that each item included in the capital additions budget is a **project plan,** such as the one shown in Exhibit 14-7. The capital additions budget summary for Superior

SCHEDULE 15. Superior Manufacturing Company

Capital Additions Budget Summary*
For the Year Ending December 31, 19X2

ITEMS	ESTIMATED STARTING DATE	ESTIMATED COMPLETION DATE	ESTIMATED COST	YEAR BUDGETED FOR	
				19X2	19X3
New building	Jan. 19X3	Sept. 19X3	$120,000		$120,000
Machinery—Dept. 1	July 19X3	Sept. 19X3	10,000		10,000
Repair tools	Jan. 19X2	Jan. 31, 19X2	200	$ 200	
Power motor	Dec. 19X2	Dec. 31, 19X2	8,500	8,500	
Total			$138,700	$ 8,700	$130,000
Assets funded:					
New building				20,000	
Total cash required in 19X2 for capital additions				$28,700	

Depreciation data:
  Repair tools—5-year life, no scrap value.
  Power motor—10-year life, no scrap value.
*See Schedules 46 and 47 for details.

Manufacturing Company is shown in Schedule 15. Notice that the 19X2 cash requirement for capital additions is shown.

CASH FLOW BUDGET ILLUSTRATED The cash flow budget shows the planned sources and uses of cash during the budget year. The profit plan schedules prepared and illustrated thus far, with certain adjustments, provide the information needed to develop the cash flow budget. The **financial vice-president** is directly responsible for developing the cash flow budget. The cash flow budget for Superior Manufacturing Company is shown in Schedule 16. In this budget, the cash disbursements for expenses are not the same as the same expense totals shown in the expense budgets because there are certain noncash expenses, such as depreciation expense, accrued expenses, and bad debt expense. These accrual-basis (i.e., noncash) amounts are shown in the income statement, but they do not require cash currently. Schedule 16, which is a summary for the year, does not give the adjustments and computations necessary to convert planned revenues and planned expenses on an accrual basis to a cash flow basis. These adjustments and computations are discussed in a subsequent chapter.

BUDGETED BALANCE SHEET ILLUSTRATED The projected balance sheet reports the effect of the plan of operations on the assets, liabilities, and capital of the company. The budgeted balance sheet is prepared by the budget director from plans shown in other components of the profit plan. The annual planned balance sheet for Superior Manufacturing Company is shown in Schedule 17. Detailed computations are shown in subsequent chapters.

SCHEDULE 16. Superior Manufacturing Company

Cash Flow Budget Summary*
For the Year Ending December 31, 19X2

	Ref.		
Beginning cash balance, Jan. 1, 19X2	(Given)		$ 54,000
Budgeted cash sources:			
Collections of accounts receivable[†]		$6,095,886	
Other income	12	37,120	
Proceeds of short-term notes payable	(Input)	100,000	
Total budgeted receipts			6,233,006
Total			$6,287,006
Budgeted cash uses:			
Raw material purchases—accounts payable[†]		$1,429,140	
Direct labor	5	1,752,000	
Factory overhead costs[†]		612,800	
Distribution expenses[†]		958,897	
Administrative expenses[†]		173,243	
Building services[†]		84,000	
Capital additions	15	28,700	
Notes payable	(input)	250,000	
Dividends	14	12,000	
Accrued and deferred items	(input)	359,710	
Total budgeted disbursements			5,660,490
Ending cash balance, Dec. 31, 19X2			$ 626,516

*See Schedules 50, 54, and 57 for details.
[†]Computations illustrated in subsequent chapters.

Final Approval of the Strategic and Tactical Profit Plans

The strategic long-range profit plan and the tactical short-range profit plan for Superior Manufacturing Company, as illustrated in this chapter, are assembled under the supervision of the director of planning and control. When their consolidation is completed, the two plans are reproduced and distributed to the members of the executive committee about one week prior to the final planning session. When the executive committee and the president are satisfied that the best plans possible under the circumstances have been developed, the plans are approved by the president and returned to the financial vice-president for distribution in accordance with company policy. Each vice-president receives a complete copy of the profit plans; other managers receive components that are relevant to their particular functional responsibilities.

The next important step involves the leading function of management. That is, leadership is needed to implement the profit plans and to administer control to ensure the attainment of the broad objectives and specific goals explicitly included in the two profit plans. This step requires aggressive and continuous effort by top management, and then by all managers, to meet or surpass the goals in each responsibility center.

SCHEDULE 17. Superior Manufacturing Company

Budgeted Balance Sheet
As of December 31, 19X2

ASSETS			
Current assets:	Ref.		
Cash	16		$ 626,516
Accounts receivable*		$ 156,114	
Less: Allowance for doubtful			
accounts*		$ 18,190	137,924
Raw material inventory	8		260,000
Work in process inventory	8		13,800
Finished goods inventory	8		837,600
Prepaid insurance			17,724
Supplies inventory*			5,200
Total current assets			$1,898,764
Funds:			
Building fund*			40,500
Operational (fixed) assets:			
Land			25,000
Building		1,800,000	
Less: Accumulated depreciation		420,000	1,380,000
Machinery and equipment		288,700	
Less: Accumulated depreciation		107,740	180,960
Total operational assets			1,585,960
Total assets			$3,525,224
LIABILITIES AND STOCKHOLDERS' EQUITY			
Current liabilities:			
Accounts payable*		$ 41,960	
Audit fee payable	(Input)	2,400	
Property taxes payable*		7,284	
Accrued interest payable*		1,750	
Federal income tax payable	(Input)	258,318	
Total current liabilities			$ 311,712
Long-term liabilities:			
Long-term notes payable	(Input)		50,000
Total liabilities			$ 361,712
Stockholders' equity:			
Common stock	(Given)	2,000,000	
Contributed capital in			
excess of par	(Given)	50,000	2,050,000
Retained earnings	14		1,113,512
Total stockholders' equity			3,163,512
Total liabilities and			
stockholders' equity			$3,525,224

*Computations explained in subsequent chapters.

Flexible Expense Budget Illustrated

Performance reports of expenses can be developed using one of two approaches as follows:

1 **Fixed budget comparison**—Actual results are compared with the planned expenses shown in the **tactical profit plan** to compute performance variances.
2 **Flexible budget comparison**—Actual results are compared with flexible budget formulas applied to actual output or activity to compute performance variances.

Superior Manufacturing Company uses flexible expense budgets for factory overhead, distribution expenses, and administrative expenses.

For example, during the early part of the 19X2 budget process, the company prepared the Flexible Expense Budget for the Manufacturing Departments shown in Schedule 18 (partial). Notice the fixed and variable components for each expense. The **activity or output** in Department 1 is measured in direct labor hours.

Flexible budgets (formulas) are used in a PPC program for two different purposes:

1 Preparation of the tactical profit plan—to compute planned expense amounts in each responsibility center. This means that the flexible budget formulas for each center must be developed early in the budget development period.

SCHEDULE 18. Superior Manufacturing Company

Flexible Expense Budget—Manufacturing Department (partial)*
For the Year Ending December 31, 19X2

	PRODUCING DEPARTMENTS			
	DEPT. 1		DEPT. 2	DEPT. 3
EXPENSE	FIXED ALLOWANCE PER MONTH REGARDLESS OF VOLUME OF WORK	VARIABLE AMOUNT PER 100 DIRECT LABOR HOURS WORKED		
Supervisory salaries	$10,000	—		
Indirect labor	3,000	$22.50		
Maintenance parts	300	1.50		
Supplies used	450	5.50		
Depreciation (output basis)	—	1.50		
Insurance	100	—		
Taxes	150	—		
Total	$14,000	$31.00		

*Refer to Schedule 33. Determination of the amounts is discussed in Chapter 10.

2 Preparation of periodic performance reports—to compute budget expense amounts adjusted to actual output or activity in each responsibility center. The actual expense amounts are compared with the adjusted budget amounts to compute the expense performance variances.

COMPUTATION OF BUDGETED EXPENSES FOR THE TACTICAL PROFIT PLAN   The flexible budget formulas (Schedule 18) are multiplied by the planned levels of activity to compute the budgeted expenses. For example, refer to the profit plan summary of manufacturing overhead given in Schedule 7. The 19X2 planned expenses for Producing Department 1 were computed as follows:

Producing Department No. 1—Computation of 19X2 Expense Budget
(Output or Activity Measured in Direct Labor Hours)

ACCOUNT	COMPUTATION BASED ON FLEXIBLE BUDGET (SCH. 18) AND DIRECT LABOR HOURS (SCH. 5)	BUDGETED AMOUNT
Supervisory salaries	($10,000 × 12) plus ($0 × 4880)	$120,000
Indirect labor	($3,000 × 12) plus ($22.50 × 4880)	145,800
Maintenance parts	($300 × 12) plus ($1.50 × 4880)	10,920
Supplies used	($450 × 12) plus ($5.50 × 4880)	32,240
Depreciation	($0 × 12) plus ($1.50 × 4880)	7,320
Insurance	($100 × 12) plus ($0 × 4880)	1,200
Taxes	($150 × 12) plus ($0 × 4880)	1,800
Total	($14,000 × 12) plus ($31.00 × 4880)	$319,280

Notice that the level of output or activity in Department 1 is measured in direct labor hours (488,000), which is shown in the direct labor budget. Schedule 7, the manufacturing overhead budget summary in the tactical plan, shows the $319,280 computed above.

PERFORMANCE REPORTS WITH FLEXIBLE EXPENSE BUDGETS ILLUSTRATED   The extent to which the planned objectives are being attained, exceeded, or not attained during the budget period is reported to all levels of management using internal performance reports. Periodic performance reports are prepared for each responsibility center and are distributed monthly to all levels of management. As with the profit plans, distribution of the total package of performance reports is limited to the vice-presidents; other managers receive the performance reports that are relevant to their particular responsibility centers.

To illustrate the approach used by Superior Manufacturing Company, two separate performance reports are shown in Schedules 19 and 20. Schedule 19 is a performance report on **sales performance,** and Schedule 20 is a performance report on **factory overhead.** In these performance reports, notice two distinct features: (1) reporting by responsibility centers and (2) comparison of

SCHEDULE 19. Superior Manufacturing Company

Sales Performance Report by District and by Product
January 19X2

RESPONSIBILITY	ACTUAL SALES JANUARY		PLANNED SALES		VARIANCES FAVORABLE—UNFAVORABLE*		
	UNITS	AMOUNT	UNITS	AMOUNT	UNITS	AMOUNT	% OF BUDGET
Ref.							
Southern District:							
Product X	34,000	$170,000	30,000	$150,000	4,000	$20,000	13
Product Y	14,000	28,000	15,000	30,000	1,000*	2,000*	7*
Total		$198,000		$180,000		$18,000	10
Eastern District:							
Product X[b]	38,000	$190,000	40,000	$204,000	2,000*	$14,000*	7*
Product Y	10,000	21,000	11,000	23,100	1,000*	2,100*	9*
Total		$211,000		$227,100		$16,100*	7*
Western District:							
Product X	16,000	$ 81,600	15,000	$ 76,500	1,000	$ 5,100	7
Product Y	9,000	18,900	8,000	$ 16,800	1,000	2,100	13
Total		$100,500		$ 93,300		$ 7,200	8
Grand total		$509,500		$500,400		$ 9,100[a]	2
Summary by product:							
Product X	88,000	$441,600	85,000	$430,500	3,000	$11,100	3
Product Y	33,000	67,900	34,000	69,900	1,000*	2,000*	3*
Total		$509,500		$500,400		$ 9,100[a]	2

[a]Variation due to:

(1) Variation in Units	$12,900
(2) Variation in Sales Price	$ 3,800*
Total	$ 9,100

[b]Authorized price reduction in this district to $5.00 per unit, in effect for entire month.

Comments:
1. Southern District failure to meet forecast for product Y should be investigated.
2. Eastern District needs immediate attention.
3. Western District should be commended—investigate possibility of technical or managerial assistance to other districts.

actual results with planned goals and the resultant performance variations, both in dollars and percentages of budget. The variations column calls attention to the exceptional items.

In Schedule 20, the "budget" column is headed "Flexible Budget Adjusted to Actual Volume." This heading suggests use of the flexible budget approach to control expenses. Budget amounts for expenses are based on *actual output* of the department rather than on the output originally planned for that department. Thus, in Schedule 20 the amounts in the column "Flexible Budget Adjusted to Actual Volume" were computed by adding to the fixed cost amount

SCHEDULE 20. Superior Manufacturing Company

Performance Report on Manufacturing Overhead, by Departments
January 19X2
PART 1—Departmental Report of Manufacturing Expenses (Overhead)

| | | | BUDGET CONTROL REPORT | |
| | | | VARIANCES INDICATING STATUS OF CONTROL: FAVORABLE —UNFAVORABLE* | |
RESPONSIBILITY	COST REPORT MONTH ACTUAL	FLEXIBLE BUDGET ADJUSTED TO ACTUAL VOLUME	AMOUNT	% OF BUDGET
Producing Dept. No. 1:[a]				
(Actual Volume 35,000 DLH)				
Supervisory salaries[†]	$10,000	$10,000		
Indirect labor	10,550	10,875	$325	3
Maintenance parts	1,500	825	675*[b]	82*
Supplies used	2,200	2,375	175	7
Depreciation[†]	525	525		
Insurance[†]	100	100		
Taxes[†]	150	150		
Total	$25,025	$24,850	$175*	1*
Producing Dept. No. 2:				
(Actual Volume 13,800 DLH)				
Supervisory salaries[†]	$ 1,870	$ 1,870		
Indirect labor	240	262	$ 22	8
Maintenance parts	60	48	12*	25*
Supplies used	80	109	29	27
Depreciation[†]	55	55		
Insurance[†]	10	10		
Taxes[†]	20	20		
Total	$ 2,335	$ 2,374	$ 39	2
Producing Dept. No. 3:				
(Actual Volume 36,200 DLH)				
Supervisory salaries[†]	$ 2,920	$ 2,920		
Indirect labor	3,600	3,370	$230*	7*
Maintenance parts	370	331	39*	12*
Supplies used	1,170	1,105	65*	6*
Depreciation[†]	326	326		
Insurance[†]	50	50		
Taxes[†]	60	60		
Total	$ 8,496	$ 8,162	$334*	4*

[†]These items are noncontrollable within the department.

[a]The amounts for producing Department 1 were computed using the flexible budget formulas given in Schedule 18.

[b]Due to breakdown of machine resulting from incorrect adjustments.

the variable amount. The variable amount was computed by multiplying 350 direct labor hours (actual output measured in terms of actual hours worked) by the flexible budget rates shown in the flexible budget for Department 1, Schedule 18. For example, the indirect labor amount of $10,875 was computed as follows:

$$\$3,000 + (\$22.50 \times 350) = \$10,875$$

Some companies compute this budget amount on the basis of standard productive hours rather than actual productive hours. Generally the former is preferable. This is discussed in a subsequent chapter.

APPLICATION OF PROFIT PLANNING AND CONTROL IN NONMANUFACTURING ENTERPRISES   The discussion in this chapter has emphasized the application of PPC in manufacturing companies. This section discusses the application of PPC in nonmanufacturing enterprises. For instructional convenience, we will focus on wholesale and retail companies. Instead of converting materials and component parts into finished goods, which are then sold, wholesale and retail (i.e., merchandising) enterprises purchase goods and then resell them in essentially the same form. Also, nonmanufacturing companies often sell services, sometimes related to the goods they sell and sometimes services only. Service companies include such enterprises as banks, insurance companies, airlines, hotels, and restaurants. A wholesale or retail company would not develop budgets for production, raw materials and parts, direct labor, and manufacturing (or factory) overhead. Instead, such an enterprise would develop what is commonly called a **merchandising budget.** It includes planned sales, inventory, and purchases.

Although budgeting in manufacturing enterprises has received more attention in business literature, comprehensive budgeting has been used more in retailing than in manufacturing situations. The reasons are that there tend to be more competitors and the operating margin (that is, profit as a percentage of sales) in merchandising businesses is typically very low. While it is not unusual for a manufacturing business to make a 10 percent profit on net sales, a 2 to 3 percent profit on net sales is considered good in many retail businesses. Also, the purchasing function is particularly critical because (a) many lines of merchandise (such as styled clothing) must be ordered far in advance of delivery and (b) a multitude of different items are typically sold in a retail company (such as grocery, drug, and department stores). Another reason is that, historically, the financial control function in retail companies (particularly in department stores) has been emphasized more than in manufacturing companies.

Comprehensive profit planning and control in wholesale, retail, and service enterprises rests upon the same foundation as in manufacturing companies: (1) development of objectives, goals, and strategies, (2) preparation of a strategic long-term plan, (3) preparation of a tactical short-term plan, (4) continuous leadership to attain the goals and plans, and (5) a dynamic control system that uses performance reports for all responsibility centers. The topics discussed in Chapters 1 through 3 have equivalent application in nonmanufacturing enterprises. Moreover, in this chapter, Exhibits 4-1 through 4-9 have equivalent application in nonmanufacturing companies.

As in manufacturing companies, the controller or budget director should be assigned the responsibility for supervising and designing the PPC program. The decisional inputs to the profit plan should be provided by the managers of the responsibility centers on a participative basis. A well-defined organizational structure is as essential to effective profit planning and control in nonmanufacturing enterprises as it is in manufacturing companies, and for the same reasons. The organization chart given in Exhibit 4-9 shows how department stores are typically organized.

Many retail companies set up their tactical budgets on a six months' basis with a breakdown by months within the period. The budget periods frequently are February through July and August through January, because this represents the two major merchandising seasons: spring-summer and fall-winter. Where practicable, the budget should be for a twelve-month period, with a breakdown by months.

This discussion of the application of comprehensive PPC in nonmanufacturing enterprises is continued in subsequent chapters.

EXHIBIT 4-9

Simplified Organization Chart of a Department Store (Buying and Selling Functions Integrated)

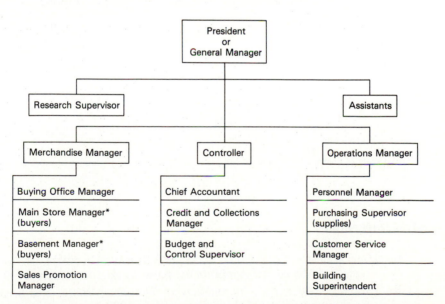

*These are often further disaggregated by product lines (e.g., ladies' furnishings, men's furnishings, sporting goods, and electronic equipment).

CHAPTER SUMMARY This chapter gave an overview of the application of PPC in a typical case. The entire chapter discussed and illustrated the budget components in the comprehensive case, Superior Manufacturing Company. Summary budget schedules were used in this chapter. Subsequent chapters will discuss the various topics and the comprehensive case in greater detail. Development of the PPC plan for 19X2 is summarized in Exhibit 4-10.

EXHIBIT 4-10
Superior Manufacturing Company, Summary of PPC Planning

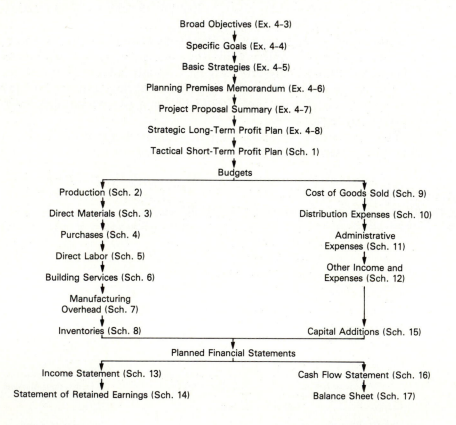

Suggested References

BIERMAN, HAROLD, THOMAS DYCKMAN, and RONALD HILTON, *Cost Accounting: Concepts and Managerial Applications.* New York: Macmillan, 1990.

RAPPAPORT, ALFRED, ed., *Information for Decision Making,* Readings 16 and 17. Englewood Cliffs, N. J.: Prentice-Hall, 1982.

Discussion Questions

1. What do you consider to have been the significant steps taken by Superior Manufacturing Company preliminary to initiating the profit planning and control program?

2. Relate the "president's profit planning memo" to the statement of broad objectives, the evaluation of relevant variables, and strategy formulation.

3. Superior Manufacturing Company uses project planning and periodic planning. How do these two planning activities interrelate in the examples given in the chapter?

4. Throughout the chapter, various budgets and subbudgets for Superior Manufacturing Company are illustrated. What are the three primary segmentations explicitly included in each one?

5. The production plan (budget) provides the foundation for certain other subbudgets. Identify each of them.

6. How does Superior Manufacturing Company use flexible expense budgets?

CASE 4-1   *A long-range planning department*

The following excerpt was taken from a company brochure, "Tradition and Tomorrow," produced by Tennessee Gas Transmission Company:

Long Range Planning

Planning has always been essential to the long-term success for any enterprise, and especially so in today's competitive business environment.

Our Long Range Planning Department, accordingly, offers you a unique opportunity to build a broad experience base in a very short time, through multiple assignments involving daily interface with all Tennessee Gas Transmission functions.

You'll perform economic analyses, recommend strategies, and develop appropriate plans that ensure our continued success. The pace is fast and the assignments demanding, but the rewards include rapid personal development and the satisfaction of impacting the way we deal with the critical issues facing the company and the industry.

The Development Program in Long Range Planning includes the opportunity to work in three key areas:

☐ Long Range Planning—Your first assignment usually begins with participation in a gas industry analysis, from which you'll gain extensive insight into the business. You'll also review TGT's industry competition, study investment opportunities and ascertain the potential effect of legislation and regulatory rulings important to the company. This experience will prepare you for participation in the development of the company's five-year plan, the management tool and benchmark against which company performance is measured.

☐ Economic Analysis—Assignments within this group include detailed economic studies of all the components of gas supply projects and contracts, the projection of gas supply costs, evaluations of financing required for, and marketability of, gas supplies, and examination of the financial feasibility of proposed pipeline projects.

☐ Strategy—A key responsibility of this section is the investigation and evaluation of potential new business opportunities for the company. The group also recommends the strategies for achieving success in our business plans and monitors the effectiveness of those strategies, thus helping management seize the opportunities evolving rapidly in our changing marketplace.

Qualifications: The wide array of assignments in Long Range Planning requires aggressive individuals with outstanding academic records, coupled with strong oral and written communication skills. The qualified candidate will have an MBA degree, with an undergraduate degree in engineering, mathematics, business or economics. Strong analytical skills, creativity, and business acumen are essential.

REQUIRED—BE PREPARED TO DISCUSS THE FOLLOWING:

a. Does this excerpt relate to tactical or to strategic planning? Explain.

b. Does this excerpt conflict with the participation concept of planning? Explain.

c. Do you agree with this excerpt from the behavioral (motivation) view? Explain.

CASE 4-2   *Role of a controller*

Niagara Company is a medium-size manufacturer whose products are sold throughout the northeastern United States. The company is organized into five separate divisions (as profit centers) along product lines; there are five major product lines. In an interview with the case writer, the financial vice-president outlined company procedures used for developing profit plans each year.

During the last quarter of each calendar year, the company prepares an annual profit plan and a three-year profit plan. The manager of each profit center is responsible for developing these two plans for each division. The controller outlined the planning procedures as follows: "On September 1, each division manager receives a brief statement of planning guidelines from top management. Basically, these guidelines specify that the division managers must follow the format for budget schedules designed by my people and that, on the average, there must be a 6 percent increase in sales each year (we are rather inflexible on this from year to year) and that there must be an improvement in the return on investment. Also, major strategies are reviewed. These profit plans must be completed by October 15 and submitted to me for review and evaluation. Around November 1, we schedule a meeting with the top management of each division, at which time the manager presents the plans. Plans are carefully evaluated by the top-management group. Subsequent to that meeting, each manager has ten days to review the plans and return them to my office for another review and evaluation. We then send them to the president of the company, who approves them and returns them to me for distribution. The approved plans are distributed back to the divisions shortly after Christmas.

"The vice-president of engineering is responsible for preparing a research and development plan and a capital additions budget. This is done by working closely with the division managers. Although each division is responsible for preparing its own sales plan, each must work closely with the company sales vice-president, and also with the manufacturing vice-president. The manufacturing division is set up as a cost center. Products are transferred to the sales divisions at actual production cost. Of course, my people work directly with the division manager to help translate their programs into dollars. I work directly with the president and the other members of top management in analyzing the plans, developing possible alternatives, and working out problems revealed by the plans of the division managers. It is not unusual for me to return a tentative profit plan to a divisional manager prior to its submission to the top-management group for critical analysis. I do this to help the divisional manager prepare the best possible plan prior to being questioned by the other members of top management."

REQUIRED

Critically evaluate the role of the controller in the planning process.

CASE 4-3   *Let's reorganize the old budget system!*

Easter Company is a wholesale grocer within a ten-county marketing area. It has six warehouses, each located in a different city and varying in size with the population of the immediately surrounding area. The company uses a centralized budget system, which was designed about twenty years ago by the company accountant. Practically all the "budget work" has been done by this individual (and assistants) in the accounting department. Annual budgets are prepared and distributed to six warehouse managers in the company. Monthly reports provided to each manager compare budgeted revenues and costs with actual revenues and costs on a monthly and a cumulative basis. A summary budget report has been prepared for the company president. It includes the reports of each of the six warehouses and general administration.

Recently, the company accountant retired and a replacement was employed. The replacement has been given the title of financial vice-president. The new financial vice-president has a college degree in accounting and finance and has had three years' experience with a national accounting firm. At the time of employment, it was agreed that "the financial function will be reorganized and modernized so that the management will have access to the latest approaches and techniques for improving the company's profitability."

The new financial vice-president has listed a number of ideas to be considered for implementation in the near future. The list includes the following: (1) initiate management participation in planning, (2) emphasize financial data that are useful for internal management purposes, (3) emphasize control, (4) introduce responsibility accounting, (5) do not include cost allocations on performance reports, (6) implement project planning, (7) implement periodic planning—time dimensions, and (8) delegate responsibility for planning decision inputs.

REQUIRED

Evaluate the situation facing the new financial vice-president. Briefly explain the essence of each item on the list prepared by this financial vice-president. Explain generally how each might be applied in this particular company.

CASE 4-4 *Should the president of an insurance company be fired?*

Fidelity Insurance Company has been operating for eight years. During this period, profits fluctuated considerably and were never particularly good. Within the last two years, two wholly owned subsidiary corporations were formed.

The members of the board of directors were particularly disturbed by the profit situation and the evidence of inadequate planning and control. Therefore, they engaged a consultant to make a study of the company and to make specific recommendations for correcting the problems. The consultant submitted a comprehensive report to the board including specific recommendations. The recommendations included specific proposals relating to organization structure and policy formulation. In addition, a revision of the accounting system was recommended to facilitate accounting and reporting by responsibility.

Excerpts from the consultant's recommendations for a planning and control program follow.

General

Management planning and control are essential to the success of business operations. The more complex and decentralized operations become, the greater the need for a program designed to aid operating management in performing these functions.

Profit planning and control involve the development of a plan of operations by those directly responsible for the management of the major units of the company. This requires the formal expression of the plans in financial terms; formal approval of the plans by the policy-making body; and finally, dynamic control to ensure conformance with the approved plans except to the extent that the original plans are revised by the approving authority. Control requires monthly performance reports covering each major unit, showing (1) plan (budget), (2) actual, and (3) differences or variances. We recommend that a copy of the monthly performance report be given to each member of the board of directors.

Application to Fidelity Corporation and Subsidiaries

The concept of profit planning and control should be applied to the operations of Fidelity Corporation and the two subsidiary corporations:

1. Fidelity Corporation
   a. The board of directors should initially establish broad objectives and goals and lay down broad operational policies relative to the major units of the company.
   b. The president of Fidelity should develop a statement of planning guidelines for the company.
   c. The president should distribute the planning guidelines to the managers of the subunits with a time schedule for responses.
   d. Each manager (item c above) should develop a plan of operations for each specific subunit. Each plan should specify:
      (1) Time covered (one year/five years)
      (2) Planned revenues
      (3) Planned expenses
      (4) Planned expenditures for capital additions
      (5) Cash requirements
      (6) Other major items

      Items (2) through (6) should be planned by month, and the long-range plan should be planned by year.

      The plans thus developed should be presented to the president, whose responsibility it is to ensure that they are in conformance with the guidelines set forth by the board of directors. The president is responsible for the soundness of the final plans.
   e. The president's office should consolidate these several plans into an overall coordinated plan for presentation to the board of directors. This should be accomplished prior to the beginning of the budget year.
   f. The board of directors should evaluate the plan and give final approval after making any changes deemed advisable.
   g. The president should be allowed to assume full responsibility within the general framework of the approved plans. Also, the president should be assigned responsibility for ensuring that operations (including all expenditures) conform to the plan to the fullest extent possible. Major revisions in the plan during the year should be brought before the board for prior approval.
   h. Records should be maintained so that monthly performance reports for each responsibility area can be developed for management. These reports should be prepared as follows:

CONTROLLABLE ITEMS	MONTH			YEAR TO DATE		
	PLAN	ACTUAL	VARIANCE	PLAN	ACTUAL	VARIANCE
Wages, etc.	$2,000	$2,100	($100)	$6,000	$5,800	$200

   The board should evaluate performance and keep in touch with operations through the president and by means of the performance reports.
2. Subsidiaries
   a. The president of Fidelity should prescribe broad policies, major operational decisions, and planning guidelines for the subsidiaries.

b. The subsidiaries should follow the planning and control approach outlined above. Authority (and hence budget control) should be as follows: functional supervisors to general managers to Fidelity president to Fidelity board of directors.

At the next meeting of the board of directors, the consultant's report was discussed. The members appeared to be favorable to the report. Near the end of the discussion, the president made the following comments: "I'm afraid this budget will put me in a straitjacket. Conditions around this area are just too dynamic for such precision—every day new problems arise that could not possibly have been anticipated in the budget. We just can't plan ahead like this—there would be so many necessary changes that it would be a waste of time. We've got to meet these problems as they arise. Further, if I took all the time needed to develop a budget, I wouldn't have time to do much else. I know Bowers and Brown pretty well, and I don't think either of them would take to it at all; they like action—not paper work. Their operations are just starting, and we have to feel our way along there too. If you ask them, you will find that paper work will not solve any control problems that they may have."

REQUIRED

a. Be prepared to discuss and evaluate the recommendations relating to profit planning and control.

b. Consider the points raised by the president. What would you suggest about them?

c. What reasonable alternatives should the board consider? Comment on each.

CASE 4-5   *Develop a tactical profit plan*

TIM Manufacturing Company produces seat covers for automobiles. There are two models: Custom and Standard. The covers are sold in two states, Texas and Arizona. Three materials are used, designated as A, B, C. There are two producing departments—Cutting and Finishing. The following profit plan estimates have been made for the coming year, 19X7.

1 Sales plan—Custom 10,000 in Texas, 4,000 in Arizona; Standard 30,000 in Texas, 10,000 in Arizona. Sales prices to retailers—Custom $15; Standard $12.

2 Inventories (FIFO):

INVENTORY	BEGINNING		ENDING	
	UNITS	UNIT COST	UNITS	UNIT COST
Raw material:				
A	500	$ 1.25	1,000	$ 1.25
B	2,000	.50	2,000	.50
C	3,000	.40	2,000	.40
Work in process	—		—	
Finished goods:				
Custom	200	11.00	200	12.00
Standard	400	7.00	300	8.00

3 Raw material requirements—Each unit of Custom produced requires one unit of material A and two units of B. Standard requires two units of B and two units of C.

4 Estimated cost of material—Material A, $1.25; B, $.50; C, $.40.

5 Estimated unit direct labor cost—Custom, $3.00 in Cutting and $4.50 in Finishing. Standard, $2.50 in each department.

6 Overhead budgets have been prepared that show the following unit overhead rates:

DEPARTMENT	CUSTOM	STANDARD
Cutting	$1.00	$.50
Finishing	1.25	.70

7 Expenses: Distribution $70,000   (including noncash items $10,000)
                        Administrative   50,000   (including noncash items $5,000)
                        Net of other expenses
                            over other incomes   2,825
                        Federal income tax average rate 30%

OTHER DATA:

8 Beginning balance in retained earnings, $125,000.

9 Planned dividends to be paid during year, $30,000.

10 Planned cash receipts:

Cash sales	$475,000
Accounts receivable collections	225,000
Other incomes	175
Proceeds of bank loan	10,000
Sale of treasury stock	15,000

11 Planned cash payments (in addition to those previously indicated):

Accounts payable (assume all raw materials are purchased on account)	$105,000
Capital additions	40,000
Accrued and deferred items (no unpaid wages)	15,000
Other expenses	3,000
Estimated income taxes to be paid during the year	20,000
Payment on long-term note	50,000

12 Beginning cash balance, $60,000.

13 Noncash items in the overhead budget amounted to $10,380.

REQUIRED

Prepare the following budgets using the decisional inputs provided above. Design the budgets to provide the essential data in easily understood form. Use the schedule numbers and titles listed below.

BUDGET SCHEDULE NUMBER	TITLE
1	Sales plan summary—by product, by district. (*Hint:* Total sales, $690,000.)
2	Production plan summary—by product units only.
3	Direct materials plan summary (in units)—by product, by raw material.
4	Purchases planned beginning summary—by material. (*Hint:* Total cost of purchases, $103,545.)
5	Cost of raw materials required for production—by product, by material.
6	Schedule of the three kinds of beginning and ending inventories. (*Hint:* Finished goods ending inventory, $7,850.)
7	Direct labor plan summary—by product, by department.
8	Overhead plan summary—by product, by department. (*Hint:* Multiply the units to be manufactured by the appropriate overhead rates given. Total overhead cost for standard is $47,880.)
9	Cost of goods manufactured and sold summary (for both products combined). (*Hint:* Total CGS planned is $487,400.)
10	Complete the following schedule:

Planned Income Statement for the Year Ending December 31, 19—

ITEM	REF.	AMOUNTS	% OF SALES
Sales	1	$690,000	100.0
Cost of goods sold			
Gross margin			
Less: Distribution expenses	Input	$70,000 10.1%	
Administrative expenses			
Operating margin			
Less: Net of other expenses and income			
Net income before income tax			
Income tax			
Net income		$55,842	8.1

11   Complete the following schedule:

Planned Cash Budget For the Year Ending December 31, 19 —

ITEM	REF.		AMOUNT
Beginning cash balance	Input		$ 60,000
Budget cash sources: Cash sales	Input	$475,000	
Collections on accounts receivable			
Other income			
Sale of treasury stock			
Proceeds of bank loan			
Total budgeted sources			725,175
Total cash available			
Budgeted cash uses: Accounts payable	Input	$105,000	
Accrued and deferred items			
Other expenses			
Income taxes			
Direct labor			
Overhead			
Dividends			
Distribution expenses			
Advertising expenses			
Payment on long-term note			
Capital additions			
Total budgeted uses			
Ending cash balance planned			$ 43,675

CASE 4-6   *Develop a tactical profit plan to earn $100,000*

BAT, Inc., produces high-quality batteries. To simplify the case assume there are two products: auto batteries and boat batteries. The batteries are sold only to retail outlets in two regions—Southwest and Southeast. Assume the company is organized into the following responsibility centers:

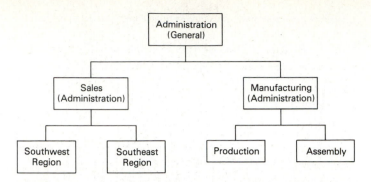

The company executives are developing the annual profit plan on a responsibility basis. The executives have assessed the relevant variables, agreed on the broad company objectives and basic strategies, and completed the five-year, long-range plan on a tentative basis. The following relevant data (decisional inputs) for the annual profit plan have been assembled:

1 Sale prices to retail outlets: Auto batteries, $30; Boat batteries, $35.

2 Average raw material costs (per unit of raw material): Material A, $1; Material B, $2.

3 Average direct labor rates (per hour): Production, $4; Assembly, $3.

4 Product specification:

BATTERIES	UNITS OF RAW MATERIAL REQUIRED PER UNIT OF PRODUCT		DIRECT LABOR HOURS REQUIRED PER UNIT OF PRODUCT	
	PRODUCTION MAT—A	ASSEMBLY MAT—B	PRODUCTION	ASSEMBLY
Auto	6	1	$1\frac{1}{2}$	1
Boat	7	$1\frac{1}{2}$	$1\frac{1}{2}$	1

5 Planned sales (in units):

BATTERIES	SOUTHWEST	SOUTHEAST
Auto	20,000	19,500
Boat	4,200	5,000

6 Inventory levels planned (in units):

ITEM	BEGINNING	ENDING
Auto batteries	3,000	3,500
Boat batteries	1,200	1,000
Raw Mat—A	2,100	1,100
Raw Mat—B	1,500	2,000

Note: Assume no change in work in process inventory. The company uses LIFO cost.

7 Planned costs by responsibility center (excluding raw materials and direct labor):

COST	ADMINISTRATION	MANUFACTURING PRODUCTION	ASSEMBLY
* Salaries (supervision)	$33,450	$ 62,415	$16,510
Indirect labor		7,350	4,900
Electricity		4,410	2,940
*#Insurance	300	900	600
*#Depreciation	600	15,000	3,000
*#Taxes	2,400	1,200	900
* Maintenance		30,000	3,000
Maintenance		3,675	2,450
Total	$36,750	$124,950	$34,300

* Fixed costs: others are variable costs.
#Noncash items.

8 Administration (general) and distribution marketing expenses are planned to be $265,900. This amount includes $30,000 noncash items.

9 The beginning cash balance was $33,000; the company policy is to maintain a $30,000 minimum cash balance. Purchases of raw materials are on a strict cash basis because of favorable cash discounts. The planned beginning accounts receivable balance is $60,000. At year-end, accounts receivable is expected to be 5 percent of annual sales. Cash also will be paid for capital expenditures, $50,000; notes payable, $75,000; and dividends, $20,000. Money can be borrowed in multiples of $1,000 at 10 percent annual interest. Assume a minimum of six-month loans and borrowings and repayments at the beginning of quarters only.

10 The annual income tax rate is 50 percent (to simplify the calculations).

REQUIRED

Prepare the following subbudgets for the annual profit plan using the decision inputs given above. Design the budgets to provide the essential data needed for communication to the various managers. Use the schedule letters and titles given below.

SCHEDULE	TITLE
(a)	Sales plan summary—by product, by responsibility (sales district). (*Hint:* Total sales, $1,507,000.)
(b)	Production plan summary—in units by product.
(c)	Direct materials planned usage (units only)—by raw material, by product.
(d)	Purchases budget summary—by raw material units and dollars. (*Hint:* Total cost of purchases, $410,000.)
(e)	Planned inventory levels (units and dollars)—by raw material (units, unit cost, and total cost), by finished goods (after completing Schedule j).
(f)	Cost of raw material required for production (summary)—by responsibility, by product, by raw material as follows:

		BY RESPONSIBILITY AND MATERIAL		
BY PRODUCT	REF.	PRODUCTION (RAW MAT. A)	ASSEMBLY (RAW MAT. B)	TOTAL COST*

Hint: Grand total, $410,000

(g)   Cost of direct labor required for production (summary)—by responsibility, by product, by material similar to Schedule f. (*Hint:* Total cost of labor, $441,000.)

(h)   Manufacturing overhead costs applied to products (summary)—by product, by department. The manufacturing overhead rates, based on direct labor hours, are: production, $2.00; assembly, $1.00. (*Hint:* Multiply these rates by planned direct labor hours by department. Total, $196,000.)

(i)   Planned cost of goods manufactured (summary)—by product (costs, by product). (*Hint:* Auto batteries, $21; boat batteries, $22 each.)

(j)   Complete the following schedule:

Planned Income Statement (Summary)—by Product

ITEM	REF.	AUTO BATTERIES	BOAT BATTERIES	TOTAL
Sales	(a)			$1,507,000
Cost of goods sold		$829,500		
Gross margin			$110,400	
Administration and distribution expenses	Input	x	x	265,900
Net income (pretax)		x	x	
Income tax		x	x	
Net income planned		x	x	$ 100,000

(k)   Complete the following schedule:

Planned Cash Sources and Uses

ITEM	REF.	AMOUNTS		
Balance at beginning	Input			$ 33,000
Planned cash source: Sales: Prior accounts receivable				
Sales during year	(a)			
Total			$1,567,000	
Amount estimated not collected at year-end				
Cash inflow from sales				
Total cash available				
Planned cash uses: Direct materials				

Direct labor				
Manufacturing overhead: Administration				
Production				
Assembly				
Administrative and distribution				
Income taxes				
Total used for operating expenses			1,538,000	
Capital additions				
Note payable				
Dividends				
Total cash uses				1,503,000
Planned cash balance (prior to any financing)				$ 21,650

CASE 4-7   *Should the company use flexible expense budgets?*

G and M Company manufactures six lines of products that are processed through five production departments in the factory. There are three service departments in addition to the production departments. The company has been budgeting for three years and is in the process of updating its system, including reorganization of the internal reports.

The management has decided that monthly performance reports for each responsibility center will be distributed that will give the information classified by the nature of the expenditure and by the responsibility unit where the decision or action occurred. Dollar budget amounts will be compared with actual performance, and the resulting variances will be expressed in dollars and as a percentage of budget for each expense. The controller has been developing account codes and formats for the performance reports.

An issue yet to be resolved is whether to apply the concept of a fixed budget or the concept of a flexible budget in the performance reports for expenses. Sales are highly seasonal for this company, and it is not economical to stock finished goods inventory in sufficient quantity to permit a stable level of production from month to month. To illustrate the problem, Producing Department 1 is used. The output (amount of work) of this department is measured in direct machine hours (each of the six products passes through this particular department). The tactical short-range profit plan shows an expected productive departmental output for January of the budget year of 20,000 direct machine hours. At this level of output, supervisory salaries were budgeted at $8,000; indirect materials at $3,000; and indirect labor at $10,000. There were a number of expenses incurred in this department; however, these three are sufficient for case purposes.

At the end of January, the accounting department reported that Producing Department 1 actually operated at 22,000 direct machine hours and incurred the following expenses: supervisory salaries, $8,000; indirect materials, $3,500; and indirect labor, $11,200.

In considering the flexible budget concept, it was tentatively decided that supervisory salaries represent a fixed cost that should be budgeted at $8,000 per month; indirect materials were considered to be a variable cost amounting to $.15 per direct machine hour; and direct labor was a semivariable cost with a fixed monthly amount of $4,000 plus a variable rate of $.30 per direct machine hour.

REQUIRED

a. Explain the concept of a fixed budget versus a flexible budget as applied in controlling costs.

b. Explain why the output of Department 1 was not measured in units of goods produced during the period.

c. Prepare a simplified performance report for Department 1 using the fixed budget concept.

d. Prepare a performance report using the flexible budget concept.

e. For this particular department, which concept do you think is preferable from the control point of view? Explain the basis for your choice.

Planning and Controlling Revenues: Sales and Services

5

INTRODUCTION AND PURPOSE   The preceding chapter gave an overview of a comprehensive profit plan. The initiating management decisions in developing the plan were the statements of broad objectives, specific goals, basic strategies, and planning premises. Following those activities and decisions, the strategic (long-range) and tactical (short-range) profit plans are developed. These profit plans are based on a structured planning process that includes a series of sequential steps. The end result is called a comprehensive profit plan.

The purpose of this chapter is to discuss the sales planning process and the characteristics of a comprehensive sales plan. Also, the related management responsibilities, approaches, forecasting techniques, and uses of a sales plan are discussed. The comprehensive demonstration case—Superior Manufacturing Company—will be continued to illustrate a tactical sales plan.

COMPREHENSIVE SALES PLANNING   The sales planning process is a necessary part of PPC because (a) it provides for the basic management decisions about marketing, and (b) based on those decisions, it is an organized approach for developing a comprehensive sales plan. If the sales plan is not realistic, most if not all of the other parts of the overall profit plan also are not realistic. Therefore, if the management believes that a realistic sales plan cannot be developed, there is little justification for PPC. Despite the views of a particular management, such a conclusion may be an implicit admission of incompetence. Simply, if it is really impossible to assess the future revenue potential of a business, there would be little incentive for investment in the business initially or for continuation of it except for purely speculative ventures that most managers and investors prefer to avoid.

A comprehensive sales plan includes two separate, but related, plans—the strategic and the tactical sales plans. A comprehensive sales plan incorporates such management decisions as objectives, goals, strategies, and premises. These translate into planning decisions about planned volume (units or jobs) of goods and services, prices, promotion, and selling efforts.

The primary purposes of a sales plan are (a) to reduce uncertainty about future revenues, (b) to incorporate management judgments and decisions into the planning process (e.g., in the marketing plans), (c) to provide necessary information for developing other elements of a comprehensive profit plan, and (d) to facilitate management's control of sales activities.

SALES PLANNING COMPARED WITH FORECASTING   Sales planning and forecasting often are confused. Although related, they have distinctly different purposes. A *forecast* is not a plan; rather it is a statement and/or a quantified assessment of future conditions about a particular subject (e.g., sales revenue) based on one or more explicit assumptions. A forecast should always state the assumptions upon which it is based. A forecast should be viewed as only one input into the development of a sales plan. The management of a company may accept, modify, or reject the forecast. In contrast, a *sales plan* incorporates management decisions that are based on the forecast, other inputs, and management judgments about such related items as sales volume, prices, sales efforts, production, and financing.

A sales forecast is converted to a sales plan when management has brought to bear management judgment, planned strategies, commitments of resources, and the managerial commitment to aggressive actions to attain the sale goals. In contrast, sales forecasting is a technical staff function. For example, Tennessee Gas Transmission in its 1986 brochure, "Tradition and Tomorrow," stated:

> Market Planning & Analysis—As an analyst in this department, you'll prepare, using sophisticated computer modelling tools, 6- to 18-month forecasts based on the latest market information and trends; perform long-term gas market research based on economic and competitive analyses; and develop in-depth reports for national and state agencies and TGT senior management.

It is important to make a distinction between the sales forecast and the sales plan primarily because the internal technical staff should not be expected—or permitted—to make the fundamental management decisions and judgments implicit in every sales plan. Moreover, the influence of management actions on sales potentials is difficult to quantify for sales forecasting. Therefore, the elements of management experience and judgment must mold the sales plan. Another reason for identifying sales forecasting as only one step in sales planning is that sales forecasts are conditional. They normally must be prepared prior to management decisions or plans in such areas as plant expansion, price changes, promotional programs, production scheduling, expansion or contraction of marketing activities, and other resource commitments. The initial forecasts—and there should usually be more than one to indicate probable sales under various alternative assumptions—are an important source of information in the development of managerial strategies and resources commitments.

The confusion between forecasting and planning was emphasized by one author as follows:

> When the leader of an organization says that he would like a forecast, what he often means is that he wants a plan. He wants to make something happen, and he uses this plan as a target for people in his organization.[1]

STRATEGIC AND TACTICAL SALES PLANS COMPARED

In harmony with a comprehensive profit plan, both strategic long-term and tactical short-term sales plans must be developed. Thus, the usual case is a five- or ten-year strategic sales plan and a one-year tactical sales plan. Many sales and product decisions commit a large amount of resources involving a life span of many years. Basic strategies and major decisions that involve commitments of resources and long life spans are difficult to stop.

Sometimes it may be helpful to view the development of the long-range and short-range sales plans as separate activities. However, they must be integrated because the short-range sales plan should dovetail with the strategic long-range plan in all major respects.

STRATEGIC SALES PLAN   As a practical approach, a company may schedule completion of the strategic long-term sales plan as one of the first steps in the overall planning process. For example, a company operating on a calendar year may complete a long-term sales plan, at least in tentative form, by the end of July because this gives sufficient lead time for interim considerations essential to development of next year's comprehensive short-term profit plan during the latter part of the preceding calendar year. Long-term sales plans are usually developed as annual amounts. The long-term sales plan uses broad groupings of products (product lines) with separate consideration of major and new products and services. Long-term sales plans usually involve in depth analyses of future market potentials, which may be built up from a basic foundation such

---

[1] J. Scott Armstrong, *Long-Range Forecasting, from Crystal Ball to Computer* (New York: John Wiley, 1978), p. 5.

as population changes, state of the economy, industry projections, and finally company objectives. Long-term managerial strategies would affect such areas as long-term pricing policy, development of new products and innovations of present products, new directions in marketing efforts, expansion or changes in distribution channels, and cost patterns. The influence of managerial strategy decisions is explicitly brought to bear on the long-term sales plan primarily on a judgmental basis.

TACTICAL SALES PLAN   A common approach used for short time horizons in a company is to plan sales for twelve months into the future, detailing the plan initially by quarters and by months for the first quarter. At the end of each

EXHIBIT 5-1

Strategic and Tactical Sales Plans—Summarized and Graphed

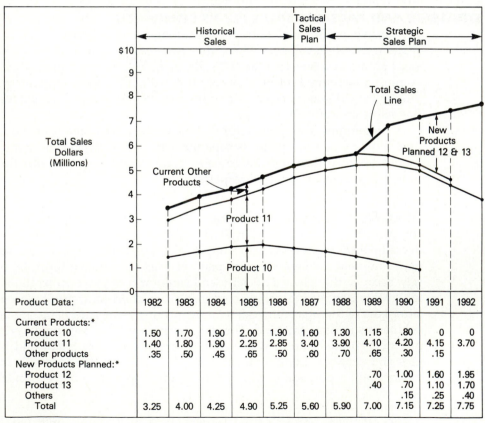

Product Data:	1982	1983	1984	1985	1986	1987	1988	1989	1990	1991	1992
Current Products:*											
Product 10	1.50	1.70	1.90	2.00	1.90	1.60	1.30	1.15	.80	0	0
Product 11	1.40	1.80	1.90	2.25	2.85	3.40	3.90	4.10	4.20	4.15	3.70
Other products	.35	.50	.45	.65	.50	.60	.70	.65	.30	.15	
New Products Planned:*											
Product 12								.70	1.00	1.60	1.95
Product 13								.40	.70	1.10	1.70
Others									.15	.25	.40
Total	3.25	4.00	4.25	4.90	5.25	5.60	5.90	7.00	7.15	7.25	7.75

*Million dollars.

month or quarter throughout the year, the sales plan is restudied and revised by adding a period in the future and by dropping the period just ended. Thus, tactical sales plans are usually subject to review and revision on a quarterly basis. The short-term sales plan includes a detailed plan for each major product and for groupings of minor products. Short-term sales plans are usually developed in terms of physical units (or jobs) and in sales and/or service dollars. Short-term sales plans must also be structured by marketing responsibility (e.g., by sales districts) for planning and control purposes. Short-term sales plans may involve the application of technical analyses; however, managerial judgment plays a large part in their determination.

The amount of detail in a tactical sales plan is a function of the company's environment and characteristics. A short-range sales plan should include considerable detail, whereas a long-range plan should be in broad terms. To establish policy about detail in the short-range sales plan, the main question is use of the results. First, the major consideration is to provide detail by responsibility for planning and control purposes. Second, the short-range sales plan must provide detail needed for completing the profit plan components by other functional managers. That is, the production managers will need sufficient detail for planning production levels and plant capacity needs; the financial manager will need sufficient detail for assessing and planning cash flows, unit product costs, inventory needs, and so on. Third, the amount of detail also depends on the type of industry, size of the firm, availability of resources, and use of the results by management.

The relationships between the strategic and tactical sales plans are shown in Exhibit 5-1.

COMPONENTS OF COMPREHENSIVE SALES PLANNING   A comprehensive sales plan should satisfy the requirements of, and be consistent with, the overall comprehensive PPC program. The components of comprehensive sales planning are listed in Exhibit 5-2.

EXHIBIT 5-2
Components of Comprehensive Sales Planning

A Components of the foundation for comprehensive sales planning (see Exhibits 3-1, 3-2, and 3-3):

COMPONENT	ILLUSTRATION
1. External variables identified and evaluated	Exhibit 1-5

COMPONENT	ILLUSTRATION
2. Broad enterprise objectives and goals formulated	Exhibits 4-3 and 4-4
3. Strategies for the company developed	Exhibit 4-5
4. Planning premises specified	Exhibit 4-6

B   Components of a comprehensive sales plan:

COMPONENT	STRATEGIC PLAN	TACTICAL PLAN
1. Management policies and assumptions	Broad and general	Detailed and specific for the year
2. Marketing plan (sales and services revenues)	Annual amounts; major groups	Detailed; by product and responsibility
3. Advertising and promotion plan	General; by year	Detailed and specific for the year
4. Distribution (selling) expense plan	Total fixed and total variable expenses; by year	Fixed and variable expenses; by month and by responsibility

DEVELOPING A COMPREHENSIVE SALES PLAN   Starting with the *foundation* of a comprehensive sales plan (Exhibit 5-2), a basic question is, How should a company proceed to prepare a comprehensive sales plan? The components of the plan listed in Exhibit 5-2 provide guidance that can be generalized for discussion purposes as follows:

Step 1   Develop management guidelines specific to sales planning including the sales planning process and planning responsibilities.

Step 2   Prepare one (or more) sales (market) forecasts consistent with specified forecasting guidelines including assumptions.

Step 3   Assemble all the other data that will be relevant in developing a comprehensive sales plan.

Step 4   Based on steps 1, 2, and 3 above, apply management evaluation and judgment to develop a comprehensive sales plan.

Step 5   Secure managerial commitment to attain the goals specified in the comprehensive sales plan.

Next, we will discuss each of the above steps. However, we emphasize that these steps must be revised and implemented in various ways depending on the characteristics of the business and the expertise of the management.

Step 1—Develop Management Guidelines for Sales Planning

All management participants in the sales planning process should be provided with specific management guidelines to be followed in sales planning. Fundamentally, these guidelines should specify sales planning responsibilities. The purpose of these guidelines is to attain coordination and uniformity in the sales planning process. The guidelines should emphasize enterprise objectives, goals, and sales strategies. The guidelines also should direct attention to such areas as product emphasis, general pricing policies, major market thrusts, marketing strategies, and competitive position.

Step 2—Prepare Sales Forecasts

One or more sales forecasts should be prepared. Each separate forecast should use different assumptions, which should be clearly explained in the forecast. The management guidelines (step 1 above) should provide the broad assumptions. The forecasts should include strategic and tactical forecasts that are consistent with the time dimensions used in the comprehensive profit plans. A prominent source explained the purpose of a forecast as follows:[2]

> The notion that planning and forecasting are different functions deserves special mention here. Forecasting is generally used to predict (describe) what will happen (for example, to sales demand, cash flows, or employment levels) given a set of circumstances (assumptions). Planning, on the other hand, involves the use of forecasts to help make good decisions about the most attractive alternatives for the organization. Thus a forecast seeks to describe what will happen, whereas a plan is based on the notion that by taking certain action now the decision maker can affect subsequent events in a given situation, and thus influence the final results in the direction desired. For example, if a forecast shows that demand will fall in the next year, management may want to prepare a plan of action that will compensate for or reverse the predicted drop in demand. Generally speaking, forecasting and forecasts are inputs to the planning process.

Forecasting methods are broadly classified as (a) quantitative, (b) technological, and (c) judgmental. These forecasting methods include time-series smoothing, decomposition for time series, advanced time series, simple regression, multiple regression, and modeling. Numerous books are devoted wholly to these forecasting topics.[3]

---

[2] Steven C. Wheelwright and Spyros Makridakis, *Forecasting Methods for Management* (New York: John Wiley, 1985), p. 25. Forecasting is a broad and complex topic. It is outside the scope of this textbook. We highly recommend this reference because of its management emphasis and its technical and practical features.

[3] Source cited in Armstrong, *Long-Range Forecasting;* and John J. McAuley, *Economic Forecasting for Business Concepts and Applications* (Englewood Cliffs, N.J.: Prentice-Hall, 1986).

Step 3—Assemble Other Relevant Data

In addition to steps 1 and 2, all other information relevant to developing a realistic sales plan should be collected and evaluated. This information should relate to both constraints and opportunities. The primary constraints that should be evaluated are:

1 Manufacturing capacity
2 Sources of raw materials and supplies, or goods for resale
3 Availability of key people and a labor force
4 Capital availability
5 Availability of alternative distribution channels

These five factors require evaluation and coordination among the heads of the various functional areas in developing a realistic sales plan.

Capacity to produce is crucial; its evaluation involves the plant superintendent and others concerned about capital additions. There is no point in planning a greater quantity of sales than can be produced, nor is it usually advisable to operate a plant above its economic capacity. Alternatively, there may be excess productive capacity and idle facilities that are costly. The capital additions budget is directly related to the sales plan because new capacity, rearrangement, extraordinary repairs, and expansion frequently need special consideration. The sales plan often necessitates a complete evaluation of plant capacity.

Sources of raw materials, supplies, and goods for resale should be evaluated. Questions about quantity, sales prices, quality, and delivery schedules must be resolved.

Availability of personnel can be a critical factor in determining the amount of goods that can be produced and sold. This factor may apply to all classes of personnel and especially to highly skilled employees. This issue poses a problem for the director of personnel about recruitment and training programs, especially if significant increases in sales and production are planned. The cost of training personnel is often a decisive factor. Also, a significantly reduced sales volume can create serious personnel problems.

The adequacy of cash for capital additions and working capital is also critical when planning sales. This is a problem for the company treasurer because it entails the problem of financing the production, capital additions, and sales effort implicit in the sales plan. Liquidity is important because cash must be available when needed for capital additions, research, payrolls, raw materials, inventories, expenses, liabilities, and dividends. Sales may not provide sufficient ready cash if credit sales are high and collections are slow.

Opportunities are seldom given adequate attention during the sales planning process. Sales planning opportunities include redesign of old products and introduction of new products, changes in sales territories, pricing innovations (e.g., customer bonuses), attractive packaging, advertising innovation, and new marketing strategies. In all instances, the effects of expected competitors should be evaluated.

Step 4—Develop the Strategic and Tactical Sales Plans

Using the information provided in steps 1, 2, and 3, the management develops a comprehensive sales plan. To do this, the planning process must be structured to maximize (a) motivation of the sales force and (b) realism in the sales plan. This process should recognize the importance of management goals—both strategic and tactical. For both the behavioral motivation and judgmental imperatives, the process should involve participation by the sales managers from the bottom up to the fullest extent possible. When it is feasible, salespersons who deal directly with customers should participate because they are often able to obtain relevant information from the customers about their future purchasing plans and competitive pressures. This means that all participants should be provided information relevant to their participative role that was generated in steps 1, 2, and 3. Extensive participation by middle- and lower-level managers is more appropriate and useful in developing the tactical (short-term) sales plan than in developing the strategic (long-term) sales plan. The latter should primarily involve top-management participation.

An important part of a participative approach to develop a tactical sales plan is the opportunity to present, explain, defend, and respond to questions about a proposed sales plan for each major participating group. One scenario would be for the manager of each sales region, in conformity with a pre-planned schedule, to present a recommended regional sales plan to a sales planning group headed by the top sales executives. The give and take in such sessions, if unbiased and depersonalized, is invaluable in making sound managerial judgments. Later, the top sales executive would make a similar presentation of the proposed company sales plan to the top executive committee. The latter committee would then, after any changes, recommend it to the president for approval.

The process of developing a realistic sales plan should be unique to each company because of the company's characteristics—its products, its distribution channels, and the competence of its marketing group. Four different participative approaches widely used are characterized as follows:

a Sales force composite (maximum participation)
b Sales division managers composite (participation limited to managers only)
c Executive decision (participation limited to top management)
d Statistical approaches (technical specialists plus limited participation)

SALES FORCE COMPOSITE This approach emphasizes the judgments and expertise of the sales force because it provides for a series of evaluations and approvals. A high level of participation, from the bottom up, is emphasized. The approach is limited primarily to tactical short-term sales planning. It can be outlined as follows:

1 The home sales office provides district sales offices with a record of previous sales and any new or revised managerial policies that are relevant to the sales districts in making sales estimates for the planning period. Usually, the historical sales data are listed on a standard form that provides space to record the estimated sales.

2 Salespersons are requested to fill in their estimates based on the historical data and their knowledge of the particular territory and customers. Salespersons are usually asked to base their estimates on current economic conditions. When a salesperson provides dollar estimates as well as units, the current selling prices are usually applied.

3 Estimates made by the salespersons are reviewed by the district sales manager. The form previously mentioned provides space for revision of each salesperson's estimates by the district manager. The two estimates are transmitted by each district sales manager to the top sales executive by a specified date.

4 The various district estimates are reviewed and revised by the top sales executives. Significant revisions should be discussed with the district sales managers concerned. The top sales executives may also convert the quantity estimates to dollar estimates by applying unit selling prices consistent with revised managerial pricing polices. The sales executives, working in cooperation with the company economist or with others who have responsibility for appraising the general economic outlook, adjust the sales estimate for this factor. Because general economic conditions can affect the sales potential markedly, serious consideration must be given to this important factor in developing the sales plan.

5 The tentative sales plan is then presented to the executive committee and to the president for consideration and tentative approval. At this level, the results of steps 2 and 3 are considered and may result in revision. The deliberations at this level should be primarily concerned about the soundness of the unit and dollar estimates and may result in (a) tentative approval, (b) tentative approval with certain changes, or (c) instructions for a complete or partial reconsideration of the sales potential. The sales plan is also judged by whether it is within the capacities of the company.

6 After tentative approval, copies of the tentative sales plan are distributed to the managers of other functional subdivisions so that other planning activities can be started. As the overall profit plan is developed, it may be necessary to reconsider the tentative sales plan in some respects. This balancing of considerations, and the resulting revisions in the profit plan as it is being developed, should provide a realistic plan of operations for the company.

7 The final sales plan is distributed through the sales function. It is then the basis for sales quotas and day-to-day planning in sales activities. In this approach, the promotion, advertising, and distribution expense components are concurrently developed during the process, as outlined above for the total marketing plan.

This approach has many variations. It is used more frequently by small companies and by those having a small number of products. The principal advantages are that (a) estimates are made by the individuals closest to the customer, and (b) it is approved initially by those who have the responsibility for achieving the sales goals. The disadvantages are that (a) salespersons may be too optimistic or, conversely, turn in low estimates for self-protection, and (b) inadequate attention may be given to the broad causal variables. The participants may not give sufficient attention to the latter problem and thus improperly evaluate the market potential. These disadvantages can be largely overcome through budget education and motivation.

SALES DIVISION MANAGERS COMPOSITE   This approach emphasizes the responsibilities of the district or product sales managers rather than the individual salespersons. The approach is commonly used for short-term sales planning. It operates in a manner almost identical with that outlined above for the sales force composite approach except that the initial sales estimates are prepared by the sales managers rather than by the salespersons. The method is widely used by companies of all sizes.

A variation of this approach is based on an informal survey of the principal customers of the company. Under this approach, sales are estimated on the basis of reports prepared by special company representatives who contact customers for the primary purpose of evaluating their future needs. From the sales forecasts available, and the information gathered by the special representatives and interpreted through their personal observation and judgments, an initial sales estimate for each geographical sales division (or product) is developed. These estimates are then adjusted to take into account basic information that the higher sales managers have about such factors as expected economic conditions, population trends, purchasing power, and other conditions that may affect the market. In addition, consideration should be given to sales of the last year or two and to stock holdover on the part of customer outlets. This method is useful in situations where the number of customers is limited.

EXECUTIVE DECISION   Some companies find it inappropriate to send representatives into the field or to ask the sales force to make initial sales estimates. This is especially so when salespersons are not trained to perform this function or when the market situation is complex. Therefore, it is not uncommon for sales planning to be essentially completed by the higher managers. This approach has numerous procedural variations.

Perhaps the simplest variation, often used by medium to small businesses, is the *jury of executive opinion method.* In its simplest form, it represents the combined judgments, or opinions, of the top executives within the company. Although it may represent a wide range of specialized experience and knowledge, unless supplemented with historical data, a technical sales forecast, and an evaluation of the effects of causal variables, the resulting estimates must be viewed as guesses, more or less educated.

Small companies often use simple procedures, starting with an analysis of historical sales data by product and territory as a basis for planning sales. The initial sales estimate is then made as a staff function. The results are then adjusted by the top sales executive for such factors as expected economic conditions, management sales policies, and desired growth objectives. Next, the tentative sales estimates are given to the managers of the respective district (or product) sales offices for consideration, review, and suggested revision. Using this practical approach, many companies have been able to develop a realistic sales plan.

The executive opinion method is used frequently because it is simple, direct, and economical.

STATISTICAL APPROACHES A forecasting method is sometimes adapted for direct use as the initial step in developing a sales plan. Use of any statistical method for this narrow purpose requires a technically trained person. For example, in one medium-size, highly decentralized company, each autonomous plant manager is required to develop (1) a five-year profit plan for the plant and (2) a comprehensive one-year profit plan including a marketing plan and all other related plans for the plant. As the initial step, the economic research staff develops projections of approximately ten different indexes relating to various economic indicators (causal variables), such as gross national product, housing starts, regional bank deposits, and a projection of probable sales by the plant. These forecasts are given to each plant manager. Each plant manager may decide to use one or more of them (or none) in developing the profit plans for the plant. Starting with the statistical forecast of sales, the plant managers develop their own profit plan. Approval is by the president of the company.

Most managers are not familiar with the theoretical aspects of forecasting and its limitations because they do not have the inclination or time to investigate it in depth. Yet many companies have a forecasting function because it can help them cope with an increasingly uncertain environment. Management planning involves uncertainty, and reliable forecasts can help reduce the uncertainty in planning.[4]

Step 5—Secure Managerial Commitment to Attain the Goals in the Comprehensive Sales Plan

Top management must be fully committed to attaining the sales goals that are specified in the approved sales plan. This commitment requires full communication to the sales managers of the goals, approved marketing plan, and strategies by sales responsibilities. The commitment must be strong and ever present in day-to-day operations.

CONSIDERATION OF ALTERNATIVES IN DEVELOPING A REALISTIC SALES PLAN

Developing a realistic sales plan involves consideration of numerous policies and related alternatives and a final choice by executive management among many possible courses of action. Important decisions must be made about such issues as new products, discontinuance of present products, pricing, expansion or contraction of sales areas, size of sales force, new distribution channels, distribution cost limitations, and advertising and other promotional policies. A realistic sales plan includes a complex set of interrelated management decisions.

[4] Adapted from Wheelwright and Makridakis, *Forecasting Methods for Management.*

In addition to advertising expense, selling expense, and marketing plans, a completed sales plan encompasses work programs and organization for sales effort and a host of other coordinative understandings necessary for efficient and aggressive efforts to maximize sales revenue at minimum cost. Many combinations of emphasis are possible. This suggests the importance in sales planning of applying sophisticated approaches to the fullest extent possible and use of computers for data processing and analyses. It also implies numerous subjective judgments and decisions by management. The sophisticated analyses, techniques, and approaches provide more relevant information than otherwise upon which these managerial judgments and decisions are made under conditions of uncertainty. To the extent that the sophisticated approaches shed additional light on the probable outcomes of different alternatives, they contribute to the quality of management's decisions by reducing uncertainty.

For illustrative purposes, we will consider two pervasive sales planning problems: (a) price-cost-volume alternatives and (b) product-line alternatives.

Price-Cost-Volume Considerations in Sales Planning

Price-cost-volume strategy is a vital part of sales planning. In a competitive market, price and sales volume are mutually interdependent. Because sales volume and price are so closely tied together, a complicated problem is posed for the management of almost every company. Thus, two related basic relationships involving the sales plan must be considered: (1) estimation of the demand curve, that is, the extent to which sales volume varies at different offering prices; and (2) the unit cost curve, which varies with the level of productive output. This price-cost-volume relationship has a significant impact on the managerial strategy that should be adopted.

There is an obvious, but frequently overlooked, contrasting relationship that should be analyzed in depth in the development of pricing strategy. An increase in sales price with no resultant change in volume is reflected dollar for dollar in pretax profits. Alternatively, an increase in sales volume with no increase in sales price is reflected in pretax profit only by the difference between sales dollars per unit and variable cost per unit of product. To illustrate—Simple Trading Company sells one product. The tentative 19X2 budgeted income statement shows the following (dollars in thousands):

> Sales: 5,000 units at $2 (000) per unit
> Costs: Fixed $4,000 (000), which will remain constant
>   during the year

The members of the executive committee have tentatively concluded that this budget does not meet the company's profit objective. At their last meeting, they briefly discussed two competing alternatives: A—increase price by 10 percent, or B—increase volume (units) by 10 percent. Which alternative should be recommended? An analysis is shown in Exhibit 5-3 with a third alternative added.

EXHIBIT 5-3

Price-Cost-Volume Analysis in Sales Planning
Simple Trading Company ($000)

ITEMS		TENTATIVE BUDGET		ALTERNATIVE A (10% PRICE INCREASE)		ALTERNATIVE B (10% VOLUME INCREASE)		ALTERNATIVE C (10% PRICE INCREASE; 5% VOLUME INCREASE)
Volume (units)		5,000		5,000		5,500		5,250
Revenue	($2.00)	$10,000	($2.20)	$11,000	($2.00)	$11,000	($2.20)	$11,550
Variable costs	($1.00)	5,000	($1.00)	5,000	($1.00)	5,500	($1.00)	5,250
Contribution margin		5,000		6,000		5,500		6,300
Fixed costs		4,000		4,000		4,000		4,100
Profits		$1,000		$2,000		$1,500		$2,200

Recommendation based solely on the analysis in Exhibit 5-3: Alternative C because it

1 Increases price 10 percent and the small volume increase (5 percent) increases profit and cash inflow
2 Increases volume 5 percent by improving efficiency and marketing efforts
3 Increases fixed costs by $100 to provide cash to fund new marketing efforts

   Now, disregard the above alternatives and assume that a foreign business made an offer of $1.50 cash per unit to be delivered during 19X2. Should this offer be accepted (based on the tentative budget)? Capacity to deliver would not be a problem. The analysis of this offer is shown in Exhibit 5-4.

EXHIBIT 5-4

Pricing for a Noncompetitive Customer, Simple Trading Company

ITEM		TENTATIVE BUDGET		NEW CUSTOMER		TOTAL MARKET
Volume (units)		5,000		1,000		6,000
Revenue	($2.00)	$10,000	($1.50)	$1,500		$11,500
Variable costs	($1.00)	5,000	($1.00)	1,000	($1.00)	6,000
Contribution margin		5,000		500		5,500
Fixed costs		4,000		-0-		4,000
Profit		$ 1,000		$ 500		$ 1,500

Note: Any sales price per unit that is above the variable cost per unit of $1.50 will increase profit by $1.50.

Recommendation: Accept the order subject to the following:

   The proposal and the related analysis are based on the premise that (1) the present market will carry all the fixed costs, and (2) the new contract will have no impact on volume and price in the present market. Clearly, if the assumptions were valid, both in the short run and long run, the pricing strategy would be appropriate; otherwise, it would not be an economically viable strategy.

Product-Line Considerations in Sales Planning

Determination of the number and variety of products that a company will plan to sell is crucial in the development of a sales plan. Both the strategic and tactical sales plans must include tentative decisions about new product lines to be introduced, old product lines to be dropped, innovations, and product mix.

Product mix refers to the volume relationship among two or more products. For example, assume that 1,000 units of product R and 2,000 units of product S were sold and that the sales plan for the coming year calls for 1,200 units of product R and 1,800 of S. The total product units is 3,000 in each case; therefore, a change in sales mix is planned for next year. The products with the highest contribution margin per unit should be pushed to the extent that is realistic. (See Exhibits 5-3 and 5-4.)

Assuming the long-range sales plan includes changes in product lines, with broad specification as to the timing of such changes, those changes anticipated for the coming year (the period for which the short-range sales plan is being developed) must be brought into sharp focus through management decisions and be included in the short-range plan. To develop the annual sales plan, top management must make decisions about product-line development and marketing activities. Policies must respond to such issues as the following: Which products will be pushed? When will the new product be available for shipment? Which products will be dropped and when? What quality and style changes will be made? What about "loss leaders"? These policy decisions about both the long-term and short-term sales plans will usually have a major effect on plans in other areas of the company, such as plant capacity, financing, territorial expansion, and research.

A primary objective in sales planning should be to maximize profits in the long run rather than the short run. For example, certain short-run decisions may increase immediate profits but adversely affect profits in the long run. Thus, we see that if care is not exercised, short-run decisions may be in conflict with long-term objectives.

As an indication of the importance of product-line decisions, recent surveys focusing on why businesses failed reveal that one primary cause is failure of management to keep up with competitors in product development, improvement, and design.[5]

CONTROL OF SALES AND RELATED EXPENSES   The development of, and top-management commitment to, a realistic sales plan provides the foundation for effective control of sales efforts and distribution expenses. We have emphasized that the several components of the sales plan should specify management responsibilities because this is the basis for effective control.

---

[5] The concepts referred to in this section are discussed in detail in Chapters 10 and 14.

Control in the sales function should be viewed as a comprehensive activity encompassing sales volume, sales revenue, promotion costs, and distribution expenses. Effective control requires that both sales volume and distribution expenses be viewed as one problem rather than as two separate and diverse issues. The sales plan gives the goals that are to be attained by the sales function. The top marketing executive has overall responsibility for control of the sales activities. Normally, sales quotas for salespersons should be consistent with the sales plan, although in some cases there may be temporary reasons for developing quotas for individual salespersons that are somewhat in excess of or, in other cases, somewhat below realistic expectations. However, in such cases the sales goals, expense budgets, and other objectives included in the sales plan should be realistic expectations. Control in the sales function, as in all other functions, is attained by management actions.

The sales goals (volume and dollar revenue), promotion plans (planned expenditures), and distribution activities (distribution expenses) are basic goals. These are relatively broad goals, which suggest the need for numerous short-term and specific standards as part of the total control effort of the management. Examples of specific standards that may be used for sales control purposes are

1   Number of calls per period per salesperson
2   Number of new qualified prospects
3   Number of new customers
4   Dollars of direct selling expenses per salesperson
5   Selling expenses as a percentage of sales dollars
6   Average size of orders
7   Number of orders not honored
8   Number of orders per call made
9   Dollar sales quotas per salesperson per period

Effective control of selling activities also requires periodic performance reports by responsibility that include both sales and expenses. Performance reports should normally be prepared and distributed on a monthly basis. However, certain critical sales activities (e.g., sales made) and problems may require weekly or even daily performance reports. Performance reports for the marketing function should be prepared by the financial executive's staff and distributed soon after the end of the period.

The performance report should be comprehensive for each responsibility center. For example, a sales district performance report should show (1) performance in generating sales revenue, (2) performance in controlling district distribution expenses, and (3) performance of other related activities under the direct control of the district sales manager. The performance report should compare actual results with planned results and report the variances. Normally, the report should show both the period just ended and cumulative to date. Performance reports should be consistent with the pyramiding principle. That is, the performance reports for the lowest level of management should report specific revenues and expenses by detailed classifications (products in the case of sales and nature in the case of expenses). For each higher level of management, the pyramiding effect requires summary performance reports that show totals by responsibility center. This type of performance report is illustrated in the comprehensive demonstration case, Superior Manufacturing Company (see Chapter 15).

Planning and controlling distribution expenses are discussed in Chapter 9.

PLANNING SALES IN A NONMANUFACTURING COMPANY   The preceding

chapters discussed the general application of PPC to **nonmanufacturing companies.** This chapter has discussed sales planning in manufacturing companies. This section focuses on sales planning in nonmanufacturing companies. The prior discussions in general apply to nonmanufacturing companies; however, there is a basic difference between these two types of enterprises that influences the application of sales planning. Typically a nonmanufacturing enterprise (e.g., wholesale and retail) purchases and sells a number of dissimilar products that vary in major ways, such as usage, size, weight, price, style, and service required (think of a large department or grocery store). Because of this diversity in characteristics of items sold, planning focuses more on dollars than on units.

The Merchandise Budget

The term **merchandise budget** is used in nonmanufacturing companies. It usually includes planning of sales, inventory, markdowns, employee discounts, stock shortages, purchases, and gross margins. The sales plan is the first merchandise budget in a merchandising company. Two different approaches are used to plan sales, depending on the characteristics of the company. The two approaches are:

1 **Unit-price approach.** First the units to be sold and the unit sales price for each product are planned. This is identical with the approach discussed earlier in this chapter for manufacturing enterprises. This method is practical when (a) the number of product lines is small, and (b) the selling price is relatively high. For example, this approach usually would be practical for an automobile dealer (except for the parts operation).

2 **Sales-dollar approach.** This approach plans sales in dollars only for each sales department. Sales departments often are organized in retail enterprises by product lines (e. g., women's clothes, men's clothes, sporting goods, shoes). This approach is used when (a) the number of product lines is large, and (b) the selling prices across product lines vary significantly. In these cases it often is impractical to plan units and individual prices for all items (think of a grocery store).

Large and integrated retail businesses often use both methods because they have sales departments that meet the criteria for one approach and other departments that meet the criteria for the other approach.

Regardless of the two approaches, wholesale and retail companies often develop independent sales **projections** using the different methods discussed in the prior sections of this chapter. Two common projections are:

1 Projection of total company sales dollars.
2 Projection of total sales by sales departments that are aggregated to develop total projected company sales.

Typically, one of these independent projections is made at the staff level. Concurrently, a sales **plan** is developed on a participative basis (judgmental) by the department managers. This plan is then compared with the projection to flush out the reasons for any significant differences. The final result of these activities is used as the sales plan to be implemented. In planning sales in a merchandising company a number of factors should be given consideration, such as:

1. External environment
   a. General business conditions that may affect the company during the coming period.
   b. Local business conditions expected to prevail.
   c. The trend of population in the marketing area.
   d. Probable inflation or deflation.
   e. Expected changes in the competitive situation.
   f. Fashion or technological movements expected.
2. Internal environment
   a. Changes in promotional policies.
   b. Changes in location and space.
   c. Changes in personnel policies.
   d. Changes in physical arrangement and merchandise layout.
   e. Changes in price policy.
   f. Changes in credit policy.

Sales Planning Illustrated for a Department Store

For illustrative purposes we will consider Ready Department Store. The company developed the sales plan shown in Exhibit 5-5. Exhibit 5-6 shows the same sales plan detailed by departments and months. Notice the detailed amounts and the related percents. This case is continued in Chapter 7 (planning purchases and inventories).

EXHIBIT 5-5

Sales Plan Summary (By Months), Ready Department Store

MONTH	PLANNED NET SALES BY MONTH (ROUNDED)	SALES PERCENTAGES BY MONTH
February	$ 90,000	15.25%
March	95,000	16.10
April	102,000	17.29
May	112,000	18.98
June	110,000	18.65
July	81,000	13.73
Total	$590,000	100.00%

EXHIBIT 5-6

Detailed Sales Plan, Amounts and Percents (By Departments and Months), Ready Department Store

SALES DEPARTMENT	FEBRUARY		MARCH		APRIL		MAY		JUNE		JULY		TOTAL SALES	
	%	AMOUNT	%	AMOUNT	%	AMOUNT	%	AMOUNT	%	AMOUNT	%	AMOUNT	%	AMOUNT
Women's Coats and Suits	9	$ 8,100	7	$ 6,650	5	$ 5,100	5	$ 5,600	4	$ 4,400	4	$ 3,240	6	$ 33,090
Women's Dresses	33	29,700	35	33,250	40	40,800	38	42,560	39	42,900	40	32,400	38	221,610
Men's Furnishings	18	16,200	20	19,000	21	21,420	19	21,280	20	22,000	18	14,580	19	114,480
Draperies, Curtains, Etc.	12	10,800	15	14,250	15	15,300	12	13,440	13	14,300	10	8,100	13	76,190
Others	28	25,200	23	21,850	19	19,380	26	29,120	24	26,400	28	22,680	24	144,630
Total Sales	100	$90,000	100	$95,000	100	$102,000	100	$112,000	100	$110,000	100	$81,000	100	$590,000
Total—%		15.25		16.10		17.29		18.98		18.65		13.73		100.00

CHAPTER SUMMARY This chapter discussed a comprehensive sales plan in the context of a comprehensive profit plan. A comprehensive sales plan includes interrelated strategic (long-term) and tactical (short-term) sales plans. Comprehensive sales planning includes the following components: management guidelines, sales forecasts and other relevant information, and plans for marketing, advertising, and distribution expenses. The chapter discussed five typical steps used to develop a comprehensive sales plan. Sales forecasts are often used in planning sales. However, a sales forecast is not a sales plan. Rather, it is a statement (usually quantified) that contains an assessment about future conditions regarding a particular subject (e.g., sales) based on explicit assumptions. In contrast, a sales plan is developed by management to be used as a goal commitment for the business.

Sales forecasts are only one of many data inputs that are used to develop a sales plan. For example, an especially important input is the combined estimates developed by the various managers on a participative basis.

Comprehensive Demonstration Case

 *SUPERIOR MANUFACTURING COMPANY*

Superior Manufacturing Company uses a strategic long-term profit plan that is replanned each year. This plan was shown in Chapter 4, Exhibit 4-8. Notice in the exhibit that 19X2 planned sales are $6,100,000 (i.e., $6,095,000 rounded). Also, Chapter 4, Schedule 1, shows Superior's "Tactical Sales Plan Summary." Notice that in this schedule planned sales are $6,095,000 for 19X2. Superior develops a more-detailed tactical sales plan in Schedule 21; notice that it shows total 19X2 planned sales of $6,095,000. This detailed sales plan gives a three-way classification of sales: (a) by sales district (i.e., by responsibility), (b) by product (i.e., X and Y), and (c) by time period (i.e., quarters and by months for the first quarter).

To develop Superior's comprehensive sales plan, a small forecasting group prepares strategic and tactical sales forecasts (by product). Based on these forecasts, other relevant information, and managerial judgment, the strategic profit plan is extended for an additional year (and the oldest year is dropped).

The tactical sales plan is developed on a participative basis. During September of the current year, the director of profit planning and control obtains from the accounting department historical sales data for each district for the past twelve months. The historical sales data are classified by months, quarters, and products. These data are entered on **special forms,** which are given to the sales district managers by September 15. These forms are returned to the top marketing manager by October 15, with the recommended sales plans entered thereon by the sales district managers. The plans include recommendations of the district managers about sales volume, sales price, district advertising and promotion programs and costs, number of salespersons, and

SCHEDULE 21. Superior Manufacturing Company

Marketing Plan (Detailed)
By Product, Time, and District
For the Year Ending December 31, 19X2

	Ref. (Input)	TOTALS UNITS (INPUT)	TOTALS AMOUNT	SOUTHERN DISTRICT UNITS (INPUT) $5.00 PER UNIT	SOUTHERN DISTRICT AMOUNT	EASTERN DISTRICT UNITS (INPUT) $5.10 PER UNIT	EASTERN DISTRICT AMOUNT	WESTERN DISTRICT UNITS (INPUT) $5.10 PER UNIT	WESTERN DISTRICT AMOUNT
PRODUCT X:									
January		85,000	$ 430,500	30,000	$ 150,000	40,000	$ 204,000	15,000	$ 76,500
February		90,000	455,500	35,000	175,000	45,000	229,500	10,000	51,000
March		95,000	481,500	30,000	150,000	50,000	255,000	15,000	76,500
Total 1st Quarter		270,000	$1,367,500	95,000	$ 475,000	135,000	$ 688,500	40,000	$ 204,000
2nd Quarter		260,000	1,317,000	90,000	450,000	135,000	688,500	35,000	178,500
3rd Quarter		190,000	962,500	65,000	325,000	90,000	459,000	35,000	178,500
4th Quarter		280,000	1,419,000	90,000	450,000	140,000	714,000	50,000	255,000
Total X		1,000,000	$5,066,000	340,000	$1,700,000	500,000	$2,550,000	160,000	$ 816,000

	(Input)	TOTALS UNITS (INPUT)	TOTALS AMOUNT	SOUTHERN DISTRICT UNITS (INPUT) $2.00 PER UNIT	SOUTHERN DISTRICT AMOUNT	EASTERN DISTRICT UNITS (INPUT) $2.10 PER UNIT	EASTERN DISTRICT AMOUNT	WESTERN DISTRICT UNITS (INPUT) $2.10 PER UNIT	WESTERN DISTRICT AMOUNT
PRODUCT Y:									
January		34,000	$ 69,900	15,000	$ 30,000	11,000	$ 23,100	8,000	$ 16,800
February		41,000	84,500	16,000	32,000	14,000	29,400	11,000	23,100
March		45,000	92,600	19,000	38,000	15,000	31,500	11,000	23,100
Total 1st Quarter		120,000	$ 247,000	50,000	$ 100,000	40,000	$ 84,000	30,000	$ 63,000
2nd Quarter		135,000	278,000	55,000	110,000	45,000	94,500	35,000	73,500
3rd Quarter		95,000	195,500	40,000	80,000	35,000	73,500	20,000	42,000
4th Quarter		150,000	308,500	65,000	130,000	50,000	105,000	35,000	73,500
Total Y		500,000	$1,029,000	210,000	$ 420,000	170,000	$ 357,000	120,000	$ 252,000
Total X and Y			$6,095,000		$2,120,000		$2,907,000		$1,068,000

distribution expenses. The top marketing manager reviews the district estimates in depth and compares them with the sales forecast developed by the forecasting group. The top marketing manager, working directly with the various district managers and the central forecasting group, develops a tentative sales plan. This plan is given to the president by November 1. Shortly thereafter, a meeting of the executive committee is called. At that time, the top marketing manager explains the sales plan and the underlying assumptions; shortly thereafter (and after any judgmental changes are made) the plan is tentatively approved for incorporation into other budgets and the planned income statement.

Notice the time classifications in Schedule 21. Quarters other than the first one are planned by months during the last month of the preceding quarter.

For instructional purposes, Superior's schedules are designed to show computations and buildup. Notice that the summary schedule is frequently given after the detailed schedules. This indicates that it is frequently necessary to complete the detailed schedule prior to the summary. The design of profit plan schedules is an important responsibility of the director of profit planning and control. There is no standard design suited to all purposes; the schedules must be especially designed to fit the needs and characteristics of each company. Some of the schedules shown for Superior Manufacturing Company are indicative of effective formats; others include the detailed computations for instructional purposes.

Suggested References

ARMSTRONG, J. SCOTT, *Long-Range Forecasting, from Crystal Ball to Computer*. New York: John Wiley, 1978.

BALLS, DALE G., and LARRY C. PEPPERS, *Business Fluctuations, Forecasting Techniques and Applications*. Englewood Cliffs, N.J.: Prentice-Hall, 1982.

MCAULEY, JOHN J., *Economic Forecasting for Business Concepts and Applications*. Englewood Cliffs, N.J.: Prentice-Hall, 1986.

WHEELWRIGHT, STEVEN C., and SPYROS MAKRIDAKIS, *Forecasting Methods for Management*. New York: John Wiley, 1985.

SALES EXECUTIVE CLUB OF NEW YORK, *Sales Forecasting: Timesaving and Profit-making Strategies That Work*. Glenview, Ill.: Scott, Foresman, 1984.

Discussion Questions

1. What is a comprehensive sales plan? What are its primary purposes?
2. Distinguish between a sales forecast and a sales plan.
3. Why is it important that a clear-cut distinction be made between a sales forecast and a sales plan?
4. Explain the tactical sales plan and describe how it is related to the overall profit planning and control program.

5. What is the relationship of the long-range sales plan to the sales plan that is included in the annual profit plan?

6. With which of the following statements do you agree? Why?
   a. The objective in sales planning is to guess what actual sales will be and then to compare actual sales with planned sales to determine whether the plan was realistic.
   b. The objective in sales planning is to establish sales goals, to make a commitment to accomplish them, and then to compare actual sales with planned sales to determine whether the sales effort was effective.

7. Distinguish between a strategic sales plan and a tactical sales plan.

8. Below are listed the components of comprehensive sales planning. To the right, use a check mark to classify each one as either "foundation" or "sales plan."

COMPONENT	FOUNDATION	SALES PLAN
(1) Planning premises	_____	_____
(2) Marketing plan	_____	_____
(3) Advertising and promotion plan	_____	_____
(4) External variables	_____	_____
(5) Management policies	_____	_____
(6) Strategies	_____	_____
(7) Distribution expense plan	_____	_____
(8) Broad company objectives	_____	_____

9. The five steps in developing a comprehensive sales plan, in random order, are (a) prepare a sales forecast, (b) ensure management commitment, (c) assemble other relevant data, (d) develop management guidelines, (e) develop the tactical and strategic profit plans. Arrange the letters (a) through (e) to show a rational order of application.

10. Match the methods of developing a sales plan with the descriptions by entering an appropriate letter in each blank.

BRIEF DESCRIPTION	METHOD
_____ (1) Use of sales force technical analyses; requires technically trained people	A. Sales force composite
	B. Supervisors composite
	C. Executive decision
	D. Statistical approaches
_____ (2) A jury of the judgments of persons in the top central offices	
_____ (3) Bottoms-up emphasis; high level of participation	
_____ (4) The judgments of the sales managers dominate	

11.   Data for the 19X2 tactical profit plan of WH Company:

ITEM	PRODUCT T	PRODUCT S
Sales price	$ 10	$ 20
Units	4,000	3,000
Variable costs	$24,000	$45,000
Fixed costs	(unallocated)	$20,000

REQUIRED (SHOW COMPUTATIONS)

1. Prepare the 19X2 planned income statement for WH Company.
2. Which product should be pushed during the year? Why?

12.   Hurd Company sells one product in a regional market (five New England states). The 19X2 planned income statement showed the following:

Sales planned	$900,000
Profit plan	100,000
Fixed costs planned	?
Variable costs planned	$60 per unit
Number of units	10,000

A foreign company has submitted a cash proposal for 2,000 units "at the lowest price."

REQUIRED

1. Prepare the 19X2 planned income statement (before the proposal). Show computations.
2. Explain any pricing alternatives. What price would you recommend? Explain why.

13.   What are the principal features of control when using a comprehensive sales plan?

14.   What should be the relationship between the sales plan and sales quotas for salespersons?

15.   Refer to the demonstration case, Superior Manufacturing Company, to answer the following questions about product X only:
(a)   Schedule 21: Total sales, $_____; units_____.
(b)   Schedule 1 (Chapter 4): Total sales, $_____; units_____.
(c)   Exhibit 4-8: Total sales, $_____; units_____.
Explain any discrepancies or omissions.

16.   There are two primary aspects of department store budgeting that distinguish it from manufacturing situations; briefly explain these two distinguishing features.

17.   Define the term **merchandise budget.**

CASE 5-1   *Planning decisions given; now prepare a tactical sales plan*

Toni Company sells two products—FUN and MORFUN. These products are distributed in two sales regions—Eastern and Western. The following data have been developed for the 19X2 budget year:

1   Gross sales:

	PRODUCT FUN (UNITS)		PRODUCT MORFUN (UNITS)	
	EASTERN DISTRICT	WESTERN DISTRICT	EASTERN DISTRICT	WESTERN DISTRICT
January	2,000	3,000	3,000	4,000
February	2,200	3,400	3,300	4,500
March	2,300	3,400	3,500	4,600
2nd Quarter	6,600	9,000	8,000	10,000
3rd Quarter	7,000	9,900	8,500	10,300
4th Quarter	5,000	7,000	6,000	8,000
Total, Year	25,100	35,700	32,300	41,400

2   Sales prices planned:
FUN—Eastern, $3.30; Western, $3.40.
MORFUN—Eastern, $4.30; Western, $4.40.

3   It is estimated that sales returns and allowances will be as follows:
FUN—One percent of gross sales.
MORFUN—One and one-half percent of gross sales.

4   District expenses planned (summarized for case purposes):

	FIXED PER MONTH		VARIABLE PER $100 GROSS SALES DOLLARS	
EXPENSE	EASTERN	WESTERN	EASTERN	WESTERN
Distribution (selling)	$1,000	$1,500	$4.00	$4.00
Advertising and promotion	2,000	2,200	0	0

REQUIRED

1.   Give the four components of the tactical sales plan for this company.

2.   Based on the above data, answer the following questions:
    a.   What pricing policy has been set by management?
    b.   What amount of gross sales dollars is planned for FUN in the Eastern district and for MORFUN in the Western district?

3.   Complete the following schedules:

SCHEDULE 1

Detailed Marketing Plan
By District, Product, and Time Period
For the year ending December 31, 19X2

TIME	EASTERN DISTRICT				WESTERN DISTRICT				YEAR		
	FUN (@ $3.30)		MORFUN (@ $4.30)		FUN (@ $3.40)		MORFUN (@ $4.40)		UNITS		TOTAL AMOUNT
	UNITS	AMOUNT	UNITS	AMOUNT	UNITS	AMOUNT	UNITS	AMOUNT	FUN	MORFUN	
Jan.	2,000	$ 6,600									$47,300
Feb.	2,200	7,260									
Mar.	2,300	7,590									
Total Qtrs.											
1	6,500	21,450									
2	6,600	21,780									
3	7,000	23,100									
4	5,000	16,500									
Year	25,100	$82,830									
Less: returns and allowances		828									
Net sales		$82,002									

SCHEDULE 2

Marketing Plan Summary
By Gross Sales and Units, by Sales District (responsibility)

| TIME | GROSS SALES DOLLARS | | | UNITS OF PRODUCT | |
	EASTERN	WESTERN	TOTAL	EASTERN	WESTERN
Jan.	$ 19,500				
Feb.	21,450				
Mar.	22,640				
Total Qtrs:					
1	63,590				
2	56,180				
3	59,650				
4	42,300				
Year	$221,720				

SCHEDULE 3

Promotion Plan Expenses
By Responsibility

| TIME PERIOD | BY RESPONSIBILITY | | YEAR TOTAL |
	EASTERN	WESTERN	
Jan.	$2,000	$2,200	$4,200
Feb.			
Mar.			
Total Qtrs:			
1			
2			
3			
4			
Year			

SCHEDULE 4

Distribution Expense Plan
By Responsibility (show computations)

TIME PERIOD	BY RESPONSIBILITY (DISTRICTS)					
	EASTERN			WESTERN		
	FIXED	VARIABLE	TOTAL	FIXED	VARIABLE	TOTAL
Jan. Feb. Mar.	$ 1,000 + ($4 × 195.0) = $ 1,780			$ 1,500 + ($4 × 278.0) = $ 2,612		
Total Qtrs: 1 2 3 4						
Year	$12,000 +	$2,217.2	= $20,869	$18,000 +	$3,035.4	= $30,141

4. Complete the following schedule to compute total profit of the two combined districts (exclusive of home-office expenses):

Sales revenue .... $

Less expenses:
    Cost of goods sold $266,993
    Promotion ....
    Distribution ....
    Total expenses ....
Total Profit of Districts .... $

CASE 5-2   A young and effective regional sales manager disagrees with the company president

Fuial Sales Company is a wholesale distributor in a two-state region. The company has been moderately successful and has been operating for ten years. During the past year, the company president became concerned about profits. As a result, the president decided to start a budget program. The first profit plan is being developed, and a sales plan is being considered.

At a recent meeting of the sales managers, attended by the president and vice-president of sales, an aggressive sales and expanded promotion program was worked out. The discussion of expenses was lively because considerable pressure was being exerted by the president and the vice-president to minimize selling expenses. Near the end of the discussion, a young and effective regional sales manager stated: "Well, we've squeezed a lot of money out of the regional sales expenses, but it seems to me that we have used most of the savings by increasing home-office expenses. If I interpret correctly, the reason for the only increase in my expense is a new district-allocated home office expense."

REQUIRED

Assess the statement by the regional sales manager including its implications, and provide appropriate recommendations.

CASE 5-3   Resolving a disagreement about the marketing plan: Which sales price to use?

The executives of Richard Sales Company are considering pricing policies for the sales plan currently being developed. One particular problem is the current selling price of the main product, $10.50 per unit.

The sales department executive believes that the price should be reduced to $10.00. The other executives believe that this decrease in price would not be offset by increased volume as is claimed. They favor keeping the price at $10.50. As a result of the discussions about the various alternatives, a complete study has been made. The following data were developed:

1   Sales price-volume market data:

ASSUMED SELLING PRICE	ESTIMATED MARKET AT GIVEN PRICE (UNITS)
$10.00	12,000
10.20	11,500
10.40	11,300
10.50	11,000
10.60	10,600
10.80	9,500
11.00	9,000

2   Total fixed expenses, $35,000 (this cost will be constant at all the volumes listed above)

3   Estimated variable expenses per unit of product, $6.00

REQUIRED

1. You are the staff person who developed the above data. You are to present it to the executive committee and then respond to any questions. Prepare a volume-price analysis that indicates which alternative should be selected. Prepare the analysis in a form suitable for advance submission to the executive committee. Supplement it with appropriate comments and/or graphs. (Hint: Draw a graph with revenues and expenses on the vertical scale, and volume in units on the horizontal scale, to add to the effectiveness of the presentation. Give your recommendations with support.)

2. Indicate some approaches that you may have used to develop the price-volume data.

CASE 5-4 *Recommend a "classy" approach for developing a comprehensive sales plan*

Classy Boat Company manufactures pleasure boats, which are sold on a nationwide basis and have been profitable. Classy boats (made in three different sizes) are known for their style and performance. Annual sales for the past two years averaged $10 million. The company has used a centrally developed annual budget for the past five years. The budget is prepared by the controller and is then given to the president of the company. During the preparation period, the controller obtains from the regional managers, by telephone, "the best estimate" of how many total boats will be sold during the upcoming budget year. The controller apportions this total to each of the three different boat sizes based on sales during the preceding year.

Because of the variances between budgeted and actual sales of the three-size lines, the president is concerned about the approach used in developing the sales plan. The annual sales plan has been subdivided by quarters and is not revised during the year. The controller has suggested that a technical person be hired to prepare, as he stated, "a series of forecasts for the company on a continuing basis." The president's response was, "I am reluctant to add another employee just to play with numbers all year. I am not interested in spending more of my time on the budget. However, we need monthly budget data on sales and profits. Also, the sales managers should do a better job with their estimates." The controller was inwardly surprised by the president's sudden interest. Consequently, the controller decided to recommend (a) a monthly sales plan and (b) identification of each expense as either fixed or variable.

To illustrate these ideas, the controller, using actual data of the preceding year for Sales Region No. 1, developed the following income statement format:

Sales (4th quarter only):	
Size A (6 × $20,500)	$123,000
Size B (4 × $18,000)	72,000
Size C (7 × $15,000)	105,000
Total sales revenue	300,000
Cost of goods sold: (fixed, $60,000)	(156,000)
Administrative expenses (fixed, $8,000)	(10,000)
Distribution expenses (fixed, $60,000)	(68,000)
Profit contribution, Region 1	$66,000

REQUIRED

1. Outline your recommended comprehensive PPC program for this $50 million company.

2. Present a complete recommended proposal for preparing an annual comprehensive sales plan for Classy Boat Company.

3. Give a format that you would recommend for the planned income statement.

CASE 5-5   *Developing a comprehensive and realistic sales plan: Does the president lose or save the day?*

Diamond Company is one of approximately fifteen companies in its industry. It is below the average-size company in the industry. The sales volume last year was approximately $15 million. The company has never used a budget. However, for many years it has set monthly sales quotas for its sales force. The sales quotas are set and distributed each month about one week before the quota month starts. For example, by January 25, the salespersons will have received their February sales quotas. The sales quotas are developed in the office of the vice-president of sales. About fifteen days after each month-end, each salesperson receives a "quota report" for the preceding month, which compares actual sales dollars with quota sales dollars. A modest dollar bonus is given at year-end to salespersons who exceeded their total quotas for the year. The amount of the bonus depends on the percentage of the quota excess. About 80 percent of the sales force receive an annual bonus. The sales quotas are set in terms of total sales dollars, although the company manufactures and sells five different, but related, products. The company has previously had a geographical advantage because all of its competitors were located in distant regions of the country. This advantage was because of regional identity and transportation. Two years ago, however, one longtime competitor started operations in Diamond's territory.

Diamond Company is a corporation, and all of its capital stock is owned by family members of the original founder. A son of the founder is now president of the company. Some of the other family members occupy important positions in the company.

During the past three years, the percentage increase in total sales and profits has been lower. If this trend is not reversed, sales dollars will decrease the next year. The president of the company is concerned about these trends and (as he said) "decided to make a determined effort to reverse the situation." This focus on the sales trends only is complicated because the vice-president of sales is a brother of the president. The president said that to ameliorate this family problem, "We must take a hard look at all operations of the company including some of the longtime management practices used in the company." The top managers agreed collectively that some outside consultant evaluations and recommendations should be obtained. This case focuses only on what was done in the sales division.

A consulting firm was selected, and it agreed to provide "a comprehensive evaluation, with recommendations, of the company's management practices." One significant recommendation was that a planning and control system should be initiated. One phase of this recommendation stated that "the sales function should be reorganized and made more competitive with competitors." The consultants' report also emphasized the importance of realistic sales planning and control.

The president decided that the company did not have the expertise to plan and control sales effectively as recommended by the consultants. The vice-president of sales also believed that "the company probably needs some help here." Therefore, the president decided to establish an economic analysis and sales forecasting group. "Through a mutual friend," the president said, he had "learned of a very bright young man who had just completed a master's degree at a large university. His areas of concentration at the university were economics and quantitative methods." Shortly after this young man's employment and upon his recommendation, another individual was hired. She had received a bachelor's degree with a concentration in marketing from the same university. These two individuals and a secretary constituted the new group. Upon instructions from the president, the group immediately plunged into the process of developing "a five-year, long-range sales forecast and a one-year sales forecast; the latter to be developed in detail."

The two experts attacked this project with considerable zeal. The first step taken was to obtain, from the accounting department, sales by product for the past ten years, detailed by month. Because the company sold five different products, a significant amount of historical data was available. However, the data showed only dollar sales by product, by month. After some experimentation with statistical techniques, the forecasters decided to use total company sales for extrapolation purposes. Well-known statistical techniques were used to measure the seasonality in the series. Next, the cyclical component was isolated by using an economic indicator with business cycle movements that seemed "relevant to the company situation." A trend was then fitted to the data. The trend was projected for the five-year long-term forecast, and the seasonal for the next twelve months. The cyclical component was likewise projected for the five-year period, and on this basis a one-year monthly forecast and a five-year sales forecast were developed. Next, the forecasting group decided to develop a sales forecast in a different way and compare the results. Population estimates for the area covered by the sales efforts were developed for the five-year period. A projection of the general economic conditions was then developed. In turn, a projection of total industry sales was developed. The industry projection was based in large measure on industry statistics and projected data that were obtained from the industry association. Next, percentages of the industry sales were projected by year so that application of these percentages to the industry forecast would provide the company sales forecast. The two approaches provided substantially different results. However, the forecasters felt that the background that they had gained put them in a position to make reasonable judgments so that a realistic sales forecast could be developed.

During the time that the forecasting activities were being conducted, there was very little communication with the vice-president of sales because he did not evidence much interest in the group. Sometimes the group would call on the president for a decision, such as when they requested the purchase of a computer and a printer, which was approved by the president. At the end of approximately three months, the forecasters informed the president that they had completed a one-year sales forecast by month and a five-year, long-range sales forecast. A copy of their forecasts was given to the president. The next day the president's secretary called their secretary to tell them that the president had scheduled a meeting of the vice-presidents, at which time he wanted "the sales forecasts presented, explained, and all questions resolved." The meeting was scheduled within one week; therefore, the forecasters were quite concerned about the best approach for presenting it (but they have their own spreadsheets and graphs).

REQUIRED

1. Evaluate the appropriateness of the attitudes and actual roles in the new approach to sales planning by the (a) president, (b) vice-president of sales, and (c) economic and forecasting group, including explanatory comments.

2. Given what has happened to date and that the president will not change the scheduled meeting time or agenda, give your recommendations.

CASE 5-6   *A bargain price poses a critical planning decision!*

HAC Company manufactures combination heating and air-conditioning units. The outside condensing component is purchased from an outside supplier as needed in manufacturing. This component is also sold separately by HAC Company as replacements, with the HAC label on each component.

In addition to selling the line to various trade outlets in a three-state area, the company manufactures the combination unit for X Company, which operates in another region of the country and sells these units under a different trade name. The combination unit manufactured by HAC Company is recognized as one of the better units produced anywhere. On units sold in the three-state area, HAC has a freight advantage over the other competitors because their manufacturing plants are located outside the three-state area.

HAC Company has been successful; that is, the sales have been showing a gradual and consistent increase in the three-state area. Orders from the other company have increased from year to year during the past five years at a rate approximately twice that of the HAC units in its three-state area. In 19X2, sales to X Company amounted to 20 percent of the total volume produced by HAC.

HAC Company is currently involved in developing its profit plan for 19X3. It has an effective profit planning and control program. The annual sales plan has been realistic each year for the past five years except for one year when actual sales were 15 percent below plan.

The 19X3 tentative budget includes planned sales to X Company of 2,000 units (which will be one-fourth of HAC's production) at $6,000 per unit. The sale price to regular customers in HAC's three-state area is $7,200.

Recently HAC received a tentative cash offer of $6,200 per unit for 500 units of the regular product during 19X3. This offer came from a company that is outside HAC's area, but it would compete in X Company's sales areas. This offer has caused HAC to reconsider the arrangement with X Company. HAC's 19X3 tentative budget includes the X Company agreement as follows:

Sales to X Company (2,000 units)	$12,000,000
Variable costs to manufacture (2,000 units)	(7,200,000)
Fixed costs (one-fourth of the total fixed costs planned for all of HAC's operations)	(5,000,000)
Profit (loss) on the contract	$ 200,000

RECOMMENDATION: Discontinue the sales to X Company or increase the price to $6,500.

REQUIRED

1. Prepare three analyses related to the sales of X Company: (a) profit analysis of the contract itself, (b) profit analysis of the company without the contract, and (c) profit analysis of the company with the contract.

2. Identify and explain the major issues that the executive committee should consider about the special sales agreement with X Company and the new tentative offer.

CASE 5-7   *Big trouble with performance reports in the sales function!*

Atlanta Wholesale Company distributes products on a national scale. The company has been in operation for approximately twenty years and has been successful. The management has used a budget program for a number of years. Currently, the budget program is being revised to include the latest approaches and techniques, increased use of computer facilities, and attainment of a higher level of management participation. The financial and sales executives have been working to develop an improved system of performance reporting for the sales division.

The approach used for performance reporting has been unchanged for a number of years. Essentially, the approach involves a monthly performance report wherein actual sales and actual expenses by sales district are compared with the budgeted sales goals and expense objectives included in the annual profit plan. The emphasis in the performance reports has been on product lines. In discussing these matters, the sales executive stated: "My people always get real mad when the performance reports come out because they believe that the variances for expenses are unfair, particularly when their sales are above quotas for the period. At the same time, I have been concerned about the fact that unfavorable expense variances tend to show up when a sales force fails to meet its sales goals. Do you think we can do something about these problems, because it is a continuing negative motivation?" The financial executive promised that he would work on the problem and, within the next few days, have a "definite approach to suggest."

On the following Monday, the financial executive sent Schedules 1 and 2 to the marketing executive with a handwritten note stating: "Bob, let's get together tomorrow and discuss the ideas explicitly illustrated in the two schedules attached. I have designed these illustrations to suggest a much better approach to develop the expense allowances in the sales division. I have used the Western sales district as an example, and I have also used hypothetical figures (simplified) to illustrate the concepts. Notice the fixed and variable expense classifications and the manning requirements. These are essentially new concepts for us that I think we should discuss with a view to their immediate application to your problems. In Schedule 2, I have sketched a revised summary performance report for your division and have carried forward the hypothetical figures from the Western sales district. I will be interested in your reaction to these suggestions and to your judgment as to whether the concepts can be applied on a practical basis throughout your division. Incidentally, this is similar to the approach that I suggested earlier for the purchasing department, and they have reacted favorably. How about ten o'clock tomorrow in your office?"

SCHEDULE 1. Atlanta Wholesale Company

Sales Plan—Budget of District Costs

Responsibility Center: Western Sales District   Period: 19X9
Supervisor: A. B. Combs   Approvals:

EXPENSE CLASSIFICATION	CONSTANT (PER MONTH)	VARIABLE RATE (PER $100 SALES)
Variable expenses:		
Sales commissions		$5.00
Travel and entertainment		3.00
Telephone and telegraph		.40
Miscellaneous		.10
Fixed expenses:		
Supervisory salaries	$24,000	
Utilities	300	
Rent	800	
Miscellaneous	200	
Total	$25,300	$8.50
Manning requirements:		
Supervisors	3	
Salespersons	12	
Secretaries	2	
Total employees	17	

SCHEDULE 2. Atlanta Wholesale Company

Performance Report—By Responsibility Center

Responsibility Center: Sales Division (Summary)   Period: Feb. 19X9

Supervisor: R. M. Bacon   Reviews:

CURRENT MONTH		RESPONSIBILITY (SEE DISTRICT REPORTS FOR DETAILS)	YEAR TO DATE	
ACTUAL	PERFORMANCE VARIANCE*		ACTUAL	PERFORMANCE VARIANCE*
		Sales Revenue: Eastern District Mid District		
$310,000†	$10,000	Western District	$640,000	$8,000
		Totals District Expenses: Eastern District Mid District		
53,850	2,200*	Western District Home-Office Costs Manning: Eastern District Mid District	107,050	2,050*
17	0	Western District Home Office	17	0

*Unfavorable.

†Actual for February: Sales, $330,000; expenses, $53,200 (the prior month).

REQUIRED

1. Explain the basis for the problems identified by the sales executive. What concept did the financial executive recommend and illustrate in Schedule 1? Explain the primary concepts illustrated in Schedule 1.

2. Explain the basic concepts that the financial officer illustrated in Schedule 2.

3. Show how the "current month" and "year to date" variations were computed in Schedule 2.

CASE 5-8   *A more-profitable sales plan poses some difficult planning problems*

The executives of Slick Manufacturing Company are in the process of developing the annual profit plan for the coming year 19X2. A meeting of the executive committee is scheduled for next Monday at 9:00 A.M. This is the third meeting about the profit plan. The following revised 19X2 profit plan (summarized) is to be discussed:

Sales (product X, $200,000 + product Y, $315,000)..............$515,000
Cost of goods sold...
Administrative expenses..
Distribution expenses...
Profit...

The significant increase in the sales plan raised a number of new problems, such as plant capacity. The Monday meeting will consider these problems. Additional data about the above profit plan related to these new problems are as follows:

1   The above marketing plan ($515,000) includes a significant increase in sales volume. Also, the long-range plan includes a 12 percent increase in sales in 19X3 and a 7 percent increase in 19X4. The president believes these plans are realistic, assuming the other problems can be ironed out.

2   The treasurer has prepared a tentative cash budget at the planned sales volume (excluding capital additions requirements), which indicates a cash deficit during the third and fourth quarter of 19X2. The projected deficit is $60,000 in September.

3   The manufacturing division has estimated the current plant capacity for economic operation as 450,000 direct machine hours (DMH) of output.

4   The personnel manager is concerned about the vice-president's estimate because additional highly skilled workers in manufacturing would be required to meet the production requirements of the sales plan. The personnel manager believes that people can be hired, but that the wage demands will likely be above what is currently paid the skilled employees in the same categories.

5   The purchasing manager anticipates no difficulty in obtaining the required quantity and quality of raw materials and supplies. In fact, there may be a slight cost saving due to increased volume.

6   The sales division manager recommended the following 19X2 planned sales prices: product X, $2.00; product Y, $2.25.

7   The company has established a line of credit for $100,000. The treasurer believes it would be difficult to increase this amount. The company has 10,000 shares of unissued common stock; the current market price is $9.50 per share. Two years ago, the board of directors voted not to sell the shares at that time.

8   The industrial engineers have developed the following planned machine hours per unit of product: product X, 1 1/4; product Y, 2 1/2.

9   A survey of plant capacity estimated that additions to plant capacity can be made as follows at the cost indicated:

Increase in Capacity

DMH	ESTIMATED COST
25,000	$ 40,000
50,000	70,000
100,000	110,000
150,000	150,000

REQUIRED

1. Prepare an analysis of plant capacity needed to meet the requirements of the 19X2 plan.
2. Extend your analysis of plant capacity to include 19X3 and 19X4. Give your recommended increase in plant capacity, if any.
3. Assume a decision is made to add capital additions (plant capacity expansion) that would require $110,000 cash. Compute the cash shortage after the capital additions, and give two or more possible sources of cash.
4. Comment on the availability of personnel. Also, comment on any other considerations related to the problems caused by the marketing plan.

CASE 5-9   Developing a complete marketing plan*

Swift Department Store is currently developing the budget for the period August through January. The budget is detailed by months. Planned net sales for the six months total $900,000 (before deductions); distributed 13 percent to Jewelry, 43 percent to Men's Furnishings, 41 percent to Women's and Misses' Coats and Dresses, and 3 percent to Miscellaneous. Distribution of sales targets by months are as follows:

		SALES DEPARTMENTS		
MONTH	JEWELRY	MEN'S FURNISHINGS	WOMEN'S AND MISSES' COATS AND DRESSES	MISCELLANEOUS
August	8.0%	8.2%	14.4%	12.1%
September	9.8	8.3	20.8	16.3
October	11.3	9.1	18.9	15.7
November	18.5	20.7	16.7	18.2
December	45.3	47.4	13.7	27.3
January	7.1	6.3	15.5	10.4

The above data were developed by the VP Sales working with all of the sales managers. A separate independent forecast of sales supports these plans.

REQUIRED

1. Prepare a sales budget summary by department.
2. Prepare a detailed sales budget by department and by month.

CASE 5-10   Projecting versus planning sales for a retail business

You are preparing the sales budget for the fall season for the Avis Department Store. The following projected data are available:

*Continued in Chapter 7 for the inventory and purchases budgets.

Actual sales for the same period last year	$400,000
Expected decrease in consumer prices	2%
Expected decrease in number of transactions	1%

Planned distribution of sales, by sales departments:

DEPT.	PROJECTED
X	40%
Y	50
Z	10

By sales department, by months:

	SALES DEPARTMENT		
MONTH	X	Y	Z
August	15%	13%	10%
September	17	18	12
October	18	12	12
November	16	14	18
December	24	30	27
January	10	13	21

REQUIRED

1. Prepare a sales budget summary and a detailed sales budget.

2. Evaluate the approach used by the company to plan sales.

Planning and Controlling Production: Work-in-Process and Finished-Goods Inventories

6

INTRODUCTION AND PURPOSE   In developing a comprehensive profit plan, the requirements of the sales plan must be translated into the supporting activities of the other major functions. In the case of a service company, the sales plan must be converted to service capability requirements; for a retail or wholesale enterprise, the sales plan must be translated into merchandise purchases requirements; and for a manufacturing enterprise, the sales plan must be converted to production (manufacturing) requirements. This and the next three chapters focus on a manufacturing enterprise; therefore, they discuss the **manufacturing plan,** or budget. This plan includes subbudgets for the following: production, finished-goods and work-in-process inventories, and manufacturing overhead. Many of the concepts of inventory planning, although illustrated in a manufacturing context, are also applicable to nonmanufacturing settings.

OVERVIEW OF PRODUCTION PLANNING   The marketing plan specifies the planned volume of each product (or groups of similar products) for each time period throughout the planning period. The next step in a manufacturing enterprise is to develop a **production plan.** This entails the development of policies about efficient production levels, use of productive facilities, and inventory levels (finished-goods and work-in-process inventory). The quantities specified in the marketing plan, adjusted to conform to production and inventory policies, give the volume of goods that must be manufactured by product and by interim time period. Thus, the production budget can be represented in this way: Sales volume ± Finished goods inventory change = Production requirements. Exhibit 6-1 graphically shows the flow of planning activities from sales through the manufacturing plan.

EXHIBIT 6-1

Planning Manufacturing Operations

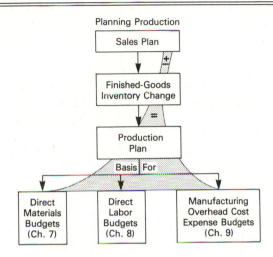

In addition to the manufacturing plan, there is a need for budgets that plan costs in the nonmanufacturing functions of product promotion, selling, and administration. These budgets are discussed in Chapter 9.

The relationships among the various steps in the budgeting process are shown in Exhibit 6-2. These steps will be discussed in this and the next three chapters.

Responsibility for Production Planning

The completed marketing plan should be given to the manufacturing executive who is responsible for translating it into a production program consistent with managerial policies and subject to certain constraints. Planning, scheduling, and dispatching of the actual production throughout the year are functions of the production department; therefore, it is essential that responsibility for the planning and control of these functions be performed by the production managers. These managers have firsthand knowledge of the plant and personnel capacities, availability of materials, and production process. Although responsibility rests directly upon the production managers, top-management policies must be considered in such matters as inventory levels, stability of production, and capital additions (plant capacity). An efficient and coordinated production plan requires the careful attention of executive management, particularly where there is multiplant production requiring the determination of both time and place of production.

EXHIBIT 6-2

Budgeting Process (Sales Through Production Planning) for a Manufacturing Company

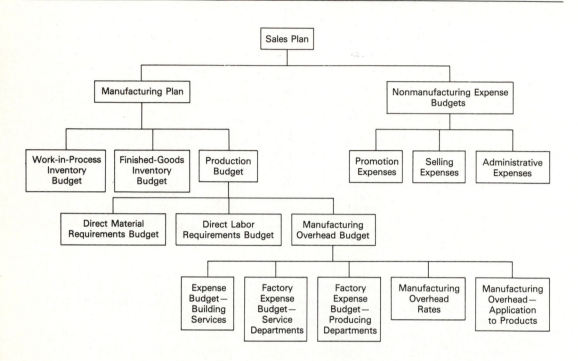

With respect to production planning, the managers must plan an optimum coordination between sales, inventory, and production levels. An efficient and coordinated production plan is necessary for economical manufacturing. Lower production costs usually result from standardization of products and from stable production levels. Sales managers are usually aggressive in requesting new products and changes in the old products. There may be pressure from both sales and manufacturing for high inventory levels. Therefore, there must be coordination between sales plans, production plans, and inventory policies. The production budget and inventory policies provide the basis for obtaining this coordination. Later in this chapter, we will discuss some recent developments in production and inventory scheduling systems known as **material requirements planning (MRP)** systems and **just-in-time (JIT)** manufacturing systems.

PRODUCTION BUDGET   The production budget specifies the planned quantity of goods to be manufactured during the budget period. To develop the production budget, the first step is to establish policies for inventory levels. The next step is to plan the total quantity of each product that is to be manufactured during the budget period. The third step is to schedule this production by interim periods.[1] A complete production plan should show budget data classified by (a) products to be manufactured, (b) interim time periods, and (c) activities of each responsibility center in the manufacturing process.

The production budget is the initial step in budgeting manufacturing operations. In addition to the production budget, three other principal budgets are relevant to manufacturing: (1) the direct material and purchased components budget, which specifies the planned material and components requirements; (2) the labor budget, which shows the planned quantity and cost of direct labor; and (3) the manufacturing expense or factory overhead budget, which includes the plans for all factory costs other than direct material and direct labor. These three budgets are discussed in Chapters 7, 8, and 9, respectively.

To plan production effectively, the manufacturing manager must develop information about the manufacturing operations necessary for each product. The manager should develop information about the uses and output capacities of each manufacturing department. The managers must provide historical data about production quantities, costs, and the availability of resources. The director of profit planning and control should provide staff assistance when needed.

When the production plan has been completed by the production manager, it should be given to the executive committee for evaluation and then to the president for tentative approval prior to its use as a basis for developing the direct materials, direct labor, and factory overhead budgets.

General Considerations in Planning Production and Inventory Levels

The production plan does not aim to set the precise amounts and timing of actual production during the budget period. Rather, the production plan represents the implications of planned sales volume for planned production volume as a basis for planning the various aspects of the manufacturing function—plant capacity requirements, direct material and component requirements, timing of purchases, direct labor requirements and costs, and factory overhead.

The production budget should be developed in terms of quantities of physical units of finished goods. Therefore, when it is possible to plan sales volume by units as well as by dollar amounts, production budgeting is simplified.

To develop the production plan, manufacturing executives must resolve the problem of coordinating sales, inventories, and production so that the lowest possible overall cost results. The importance of coordination of production planning cannot be overemphasized, because it affects so many decisions relat-

---

[1] This chapter presumes a manufacturing situation, but similar concepts are used to plan inventory levels used in nonmanufacturing companies. The production budget is the manufacturing equivalent of the merchandise budget in wholesale and retail establishments.

ing to cost, capital commitments, employees, and so on. Decisions required to develop the production plan include the following:

1   Total production requirements (by product) for the budget period
2   Inventory policies about levels of finished goods, work in process, and the cost of carrying inventory
3   Plant capacity policies, such as the limits of permissible departures from a stable production level throughout the year
4   Adequacy of manufacturing facilities (expansion or contraction of plant capacity)
5   Availability of direct materials, purchased components, and labor
6   Length of the processing time
7   Economic lots or runs
8   Timing of production throughout the budget period, by product and by responsibility centers

The approach used by a particular company should depend upon its size and the characteristics of its manufacturing processes. This chapter focuses on two complex issues: (1) planning and controlling inventories and (2) planning and controlling production. It is outside the scope of this book to discuss the many approaches that are in books devoted entirely to these problems. Those approaches vary from crude rule-of-thumb methods to very sophisticated approaches involving linear programming, other mathematical models, and computer techniques.[2] The remainder of this chapter will discuss some of the principal budget issues posed by these problems.

Time Dimensions of Production Planning

Planned levels of production are important long-range and short-range issues. To develop a long-range plan (say, five years in the future), broad estimates of production levels are necessary to plan plant capacity requirements (involving capital additions), factory cost structures, personnel requirements, and cash flows. For long-range planning purposes, only major increases or decreases in inventories need to be taken into account.

Developing a tactical short-range profit plan requires a different approach because of the need for greater precision and detail. The short-range production plan should be in harmony with the time dimensions used in the short-range profit plan. Thus, the common pattern should be an annual production plan detailed by products and by months or quarters. Also, the production activities should be planned by responsibility centers within the manufacturing division.

[2] Elwood S. Buffa, *Production-Inventory Systems, Planning and Control,* 3rd ed. (Homewood, Ill: Richard D. Irwin, 1979); and Franklin G. Moore and Ronald Jablonski, *Production Control,* 3rd ed. (New York: McGraw-Hill, 1969).

Developing the Production Plan

Production managers must translate the quantities in the sales budget into unit production requirements for the budget period for each product while considering management inventory policies. For example, if the inventory policies have been determined and if they specify an ending inventory of finished goods of 1,500 units, the annual production requirements for Baker Manufacturing Company for product K can be computed as follows:

	UNITS OF PRODUCT K
Required for sales (from sales plan)	14,200
Add planned ending inventory level of finished goods (based on management policy)	1,500
Total required	15,700
Less beginning inventory of finished goods	2,000
Planned production for year	13,700

Because the production plan is developed prior to the end of the current year, the beginning inventory for the budget period must be estimated. The estimate is based on the status of the inventory at the date the budget is being prepared, and it is adjusted for planned operations for the balance of the current year. Normally, there will be little difficulty in estimating this inventory within reasonable limits.

When the budgeted production for the budget period has been determined, the next problem is prorating this production by interim periods during the budget year. Interim production must be planned to (1) provide sufficient goods to meet interim sales requirements, (2) keep interim inventory levels within policy constraints, and (3) manufacture the goods as economically as possible. These three objectives may not always be in complete harmony. For example, assuming seasonal sales, it is possible to maintain a stable production level only if inventories are allowed to fluctuate inversely with sales. On the other hand, a stable inventory level is possible only if production is allowed to fluctuate directly with sales. From the point of view of economic operations, it is generally desirable to keep both inventories and production stable, a situation that is impossible given seasonal sales. Thus, an efficient production plan should represent the optimum coordination between sales requirements, essential inventory levels, and stable production levels.

To illustrate the problem of attaining optimal coordination among planned sales, inventory policies, and production, we will continue the above illustration for Baker Manufacturing Company. Assume the following plans and policies.

1. Marketing plan:

	SALES PLAN (UNITS)		SALES PLAN (UNITS)
January	1,500	July	700
February	1,600	August	600
March	1,600	September	900
April	1,400	October	1,100
May	1,200	November	1,200
June	1,000	December	1,400
		Annual Total	14,200

2. Additional budget data:
   a. Inventory at beginning of year, 2,000 units
   b. Inventory planned for end of budget year, 1,500 units

QUERY: How should the annual production volume of the 13,700 units (i.e., 14,200 − 2,000 + 1,500) be scheduled throughout the year? Notice the problem of reducing inventory by 500 units.

With a highly seasonal sales volume, one of three basic patterns of production-inventory levels can be budgeted in this case:

1 Give precedence to production stability. Establish a stable production policy and thereby cause inventory to fluctuate inversely with the seasonal sales pattern. This alternative is shown in Exhibit 6-3 as Proposal A and graphed in Exhibit 6-4.

2 Give precedence to inventory stability. Establish a stable inventory policy and thereby cause production levels to fluctuate directly with the seasonal sales pattern. This alternative is shown in Exhibit 6-3 as Proposal B and graphed in Exhibit 6-5.

3 Give neither inventory nor production precedence. Establish inventory and production policies so that reasonable flexibility is allowed in both inventory and production. In other words, try to develop the optimal coordination (in terms of the effect on profits) among sales, inventory, and production. One possible alternative is shown in Exhibit 6-3 as Proposal C and graphed in Exhibit 6-6. In this case, it is assumed that management specified the following management policies: (a) do not allow production to vary more than 15 percent above or below the yearly average, (b) observe a maximum inventory of 1,600 units and a minimum inventory of 1,400 units, and (c) plan for vacations during July, August, and September.

Exhibit 6-3 shows two factors that complicate production timing: (1) highly seasonal sales and (2) a 25 percent reduction during the year in physical inventory. Proposal A causes the inventory to fluctuate from a low of 500 units to a high of 1,700 units, but it provides a relatively stable production level. Proposal B causes a stable inventory level of 1,500 units. Proposal B shows an immediate reduction to a standard inventory level of 1,500 units; however, this procedure causes production to fluctuate with sales from a low of 600 units to a high of 1,500 units. Considering both inventory and production policies as stated, and the additional factor of vacations during July, August, and the first part of September, a workable balance is suggested in Proposal C, although management policies need to be slightly violated.

EXHIBIT 6-3

Production and Finished-Goods Inventory Budgets

PROPOSAL A—Policy, Stable Production Level

	YEAR	JAN.	FEB.	MAR.	APR.	MAY	JUNE	JULY	AUG.	SEPT.	OCT.	NOV.	DEC.
Planned sales	14,200	1,500	1,600	1,600	1,400	1,200	1,000	700	600	900	1,100	1,200	1,400
Add ending inventory	1,500	1,700	1,300	900	600	500	600	1,000	1,500	1,700	1,700	1,700	1,500
Total	15,700	3,200	2,900	2,500	2,000	1,700	1,600	1,700	2,100	2,600	2,800	2,900	2,900
Less beginning inventory	2,000	2,000	1,700	1,300	900	600	500	600	1,000	1,500	1,700	1,700	1,700
Planned production	13,700	1,200	1,200	1,200	1,100	1,100	1,100	1,100	1,100	1,100	1,100	1,200	1,200

PROPOSAL B—Policy, Stable Inventory Level

	YEAR	JAN.	FEB.	MAR.	APR.	MAY	JUNE	JULY	AUG.	SEPT.	OCT.	NOV.	DEC.
Planned sales	14,200	1,500	1,600	1,600	1,400	1,200	1,000	700	600	900	1,100	1,200	1,400
Add ending inventory	1,500	1,900	1,800	1,700	1,600	1,500	1,500	1,500	1,500	1,500	1,500	1,500	1,500
Total	15,700	3,400	3,400	3,300	3,000	2,700	2,500	2,200	2,100	2,400	2,600	2,700	2,900
Less beginning inventory	2,000	2,000	1,900	1,800	1,700	1,600	1,500	1,500	1,500	1,500	1,500	1,500	1,500
Planned production	13,700	1,400	1,500	1,500	1,300	1,100	1,000	700	600	900	1,100	1,200	1,400

PROPOSAL C—Policy, Flexible Production and Inventory Levels

	YEAR	JAN.	FEB.	MAR.	APR.	MAY	JUNE	JULY	AUG.	SEPT.	OCT.	NOV.	DEC.
Planned sales	14,200	1,500	1,600	1,600	1,400	1,200	1,000	700	600	900	1,100	1,200	1,400
Add ending inventory	1,500	1,700	1,300	1,100	1,100	1,300	1,500	1,500	1,600	1,600	1,700	1,700	1,500
Total	15,700	3,200	2,900	2,700	2,500	2,500	2,500	2,200	2,200	2,500	2,800	2,900	2,900
Less beginning inventory	2,000	2,000	1,700	1,300	1,100	1,100	1,300	1,500	1,500	1,600	1,600	1,700	1,700
Planned production	13,700	1,200	1,200	1,400	1,400	1,400	1,200	700	700	900	1,200	1,200	1,200

EXHIBIT 6-4

Sales, Production, and Inventory Budgets—Proposal A—Policy, Stable Production Level

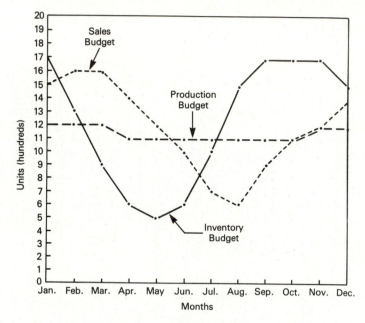

EXHIBIT 6-5

Sales, Production, and Inventory Budgets—Proposal B—Policy, Stable Inventory Level

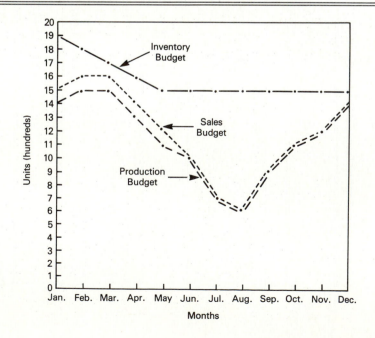

EXHIBIT 6-6

Sales, Production, and Inventory Budgets—Proposal C—Policy, Flexible Production and Inventory Levels

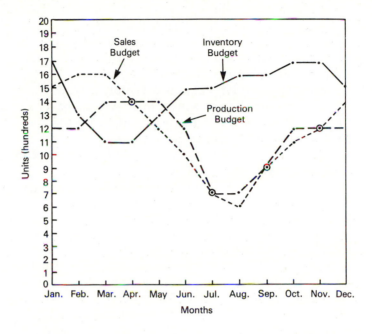

This illustration shows that careful analysis is necessary to plan the optimal coordination between sales, production, and inventory. Graphs are an important way to show the related aspects of this coordination problem. In view of the significance and complexity of these types of problems, sophisticated approaches using mathematical models and computers are especially helpful.

Developing Inventory Policies

In most businesses, inventories represent a relatively high investment and may have a significant impact on the major functions of the enterprise and its profit. Each of the related functions causes different, and frequently inconsistent, inventory demands, such as the following:

- **Sales**—large inventories of finished goods are needed to meet market needs readily.
- **Production**—large inventories of raw materials and purchased components are needed to ensure availability for manufacturing activities. Also, a flexible inventory policy for finished goods is needed to facilitate the attainment of stable production levels.
- **Purchasing**—large purchases minimize unit cost and overall purchasing expenses; therefore, a flexible inventory policy for materials and purchased components is desirable.
- **Finance**—low inventory levels minimize investment requirements (cash) and reduce inventory carrying costs (storage, obsolescence, risks, etc.).

The objectives of inventory policies should be (1) to plan the optimal level of inventory investment, and (2) through control, to reasonably maintain these optimal levels. Inventory levels should be maintained between two extremes: an excessive level causing excessive carrying costs, risks, and investment, and an inadequate level to meet sales and production demands promptly (high stockout cost). An important consideration when planning and controlling inventories is that they must absorb the difference in stock between sales volume and production (or purchase) levels.

Management often neglects inventory planning and control. As a result, to compensate for an excess inventory level, management suddenly may have to reduce selling prices of the goods to an undesirable level. This action becomes necessary to liquidate the inventory rapidly in order to generate cash to meet immediate demands by creditors. Often this action is also accompanied by a drastic reduction in production.

In an actual case, a company applied for a sizable bank loan to obtain cash for current operations. The bank's investigations revealed that the company had excessive inventories and no inventory control policies. The management had said that "no one in the company would allow any appreciable overstocking." Yet an analysis of average withdrawals from inventory showed that there was about an eighteen years' supply of several slow-moving items. With respect to these items, the manufacturing department, thinking only of the trouble and cost of setup time, had produced large quantities without considering the relative turnover of the items. It was simply a case of not having control of inventories. This problem applies to inventories of supplies, materials and components, work in process, and finished goods. To develop production requirements, consideration must be given to the finished-goods and work-in-process inventories. It is impossible to develop a realistic production plan without definite inventory policies. One of the principal advantages of production planning is that it forces advance consideration of the inventory problem.

Inventory policies should include (1) the establishment of inventory standards, such as maximum and minimum levels or target turnover rates, and (2) the application of techniques and methods that will ensure conformity with planned inventory standards. Budgeting requires that inventory policies be established and provides for reporting variances of actual inventory levels from standard levels from month to month.

To determine inventory policies for finished goods, management should consider these factors:

1. Quantities (in units) needed to meet sales requirements. Resolving this problem entails consideration of the sales budget and seasonality of demand. The sales department executives should be directly involved in this problem.
2. Perishability of items.
3. Length of the production period.
4. Storage facilities.
5. Adequacy of capital to finance inventory production some time in advance of sales.
6. Distribution time requirements.

7. Cost of holding inventory. Frequently there are numerous and significant costs connected with stocking large quantities of goods. The principal holding costs involved are labor, insurance, taxes, rent, depreciation, transportation, and handling.
8. Protection against direct material and component shortages.
9. Protection against labor shortages.
10. Protection against materials and parts price increases.
11. Risks involved in inventory:
    a. Price declines
    b. Obsolescence of stock
    c. Casualty loss and theft
    d. Lack of demand
    e. Customer return policies

Some of these factors counteract one another; the point is that an optimal inventory policy reflects a balance among these factors.

It is desirable to express the inventory policies relative to finished goods as precisely as possible. To state inventory policy as "our plans are to keep inventory at the minimum" is inadequate. In contrast, inventory standards should be expressed—by product or by lines—in terms such as the following:

METHOD	EXAMPLE OF POLICY EXPRESSION
1. Months' supply	For product X—Three months' supply based on moving three months average of budgeted requirements
	For product Y—Two months' supply based on average annual issues budgeted for the year
2. Maximum limit	For product X—Inventory not to exceed 5,000 units
3. Maximum and minimum limits	For product X—Maximum 5,000 units; minimum 3,000 units
4. Specific amount	For product X—Double the sales of the past month
	For product Y—Equal to the sales budgeted for the following month
5. Inventory turnover rates	For product X—Turnover rate to be six annualized (six turnovers per year)
	For product Y—Turnover rate to be two on a monthly basis (two turnovers per month)

To illustrate, some actual inventory policy statements are given below:

☐ CASE A—The sales budget specified 1,200,000 units of product A. After careful consideration of the significant factors affecting inventory requirements, the management specified a standard inventory level of two months' supply based on an annual average. The two months' supply would be 200,000 units (1,200,000 × 2/12). Although simple and direct, such a policy is rigid; consequently, it might be unrealistic if sales are highly seasonal.

❑ CASE B—The inventory policy for product B is to maintain a two months' supply for the beginning inventory based on a three-month moving average of planned sales. This approach provides a fluctuating inventory level consistent with seasonal sales demands, as is demonstrated below:

MONTH	BUDGETED UNITS TO BE SOLD DURING MONTH	THREE MONTHS' MOVING AVERAGE	BEGINNING INVENTORY (TWO MONTHS' SUPPLY)
December (actual preceding year)	82,000		
January ⎤	85,000	85,667*	171,334
February ⎬ budget year	90,000	90,000	180,000
March ⎟	95,000		
Etc. ⎦			

*(82,000 + 85,000 + 90,000) ÷ 3 = 85,667 × 2 = 171,334.

❑ CASE C—The inventory policy for product C is to set the inventory amount to reflect a turnover of three times per year. The sales plan was 150,000 units of product C. The inventory level for each interim period would be 150,000÷3=50,000. Notice that this approach yields a stable inventory level.

❑ CASE D—Management decided that the inventory policy for product D would be based on a turnover of four, annualized (that is, a three-months' supply). The budgeted sales for the first three months was as shown below. A standard inventory, in units, related to sales trend is readily computed as illustrated. Notice that the inventory level parallels the variation in sales volume:

MONTH	BUDGETED SALES (UNITS)		INDICATED INITIAL INVENTORY (UNITS)
January	12,000	× 3 =	36,000
February	11,000	× 3 =	33,000
March	14,500	× 3 =	43,500

Regardless of the approach used to specify the inventory policy, it is essential that (1) definite inventory policies be established and kept current, (2) responsibility for inventory planning and control be assigned to specified individuals, (3) procedures be developed for accounting for inventories, and (4) a reporting system be designed to inform management of the status of inventory control.

Later in this chapter, we will discuss a relatively recent development in inventory management known as *just-in-time (JIT)* inventory management.

Setting Production Policies

Seasonal sales are typical in most companies. Yet production efficiency is usually enhanced by relatively stable production levels. In many companies where sales of the primary product are seasonal, production levels are stabilized by developing new products that can be stored or that have inverse seasonal patterns. Inventory-fluctuation provides a tempting method of leveling production, yet as previously discussed, certain pitfalls should be considered. Stabilization of production is desirable for a number of compelling reasons and generally results in significant reductions of costs and improvements in operations. The advantages of stable production levels can be outlined as follows:

1. Stability of employment, resulting in:
   a. Improved morale and hence greater worker efficiency
   b. Less labor turnover
   c. Attraction of better employees
   d. Reduction of expense for training new employees
2. Economics in purchasing raw materials and components as a result of
   a. Availability
   b. Volume discounts
   c. Simplified storage problems
   d. Smaller capital requirements
   e. Reduced inventory risk
3. Better utilization of plant facilities, which tends to
   a. Reduce the capacity required to meet peak seasons
   b. Avoid idle capacity

One potential hazard of significant ups and downs in production is the effect on personnel. Periodic layoffs and subsequent efforts to hire employees tends to lower morale and may discourage competent employees. Such a policy is counter to an important objective of management, which is to provide reasonable job security. The introduction of profit planning and control, with the consequent planning of production and inventories, can help resolve this major problem.

Adequacy of Manufacturing Facilities

Developing an efficient production plan requires consideration of the adequacy of manufacturing facilities. Sufficient capacity must be maintained to produce the planned volume of goods and to meet peak loads during the planning period. The production capacity of individual departments, processes, and machines should be assessed and coordinated in the production budget to avoid production bottlenecks and idle capacity.

Plant and department capacities for each responsibility center should be analyzed by production managers in terms of potential or maximum plant capacity and normal or practical capacity. **Maximum capacity** may be thought of as the "theoretical" engineering capacity, whereas **practical capacity** is somewhat less, representing the level at which the plant or department can operate most efficiently. Idle or excess plant capacity is the difference between the actual operating rate of activity and practical capacity. **Breakeven capacity** is the rate of activity at which the sales value of the goods produced is equal to the cost of producing and selling those goods. It is important that top management be informed about maximum capacity, practical capacity, operating capacity, and breakeven capacity of the plant. Usually capacities are expressed as percentages of maximum capacity.

Plant and responsibility center capacities can be measured in one of several ways. If there is only one product or several almost identical products, capacity should be measured in physical units of output. In other circumstances, capacity must be measured in terms of some common denominator of output, such as direct labor hours, direct machine hours, dollar sales of goods produced, dollar cost of goods produced, and total weight.

Production planning is directly related to the capital expenditures budget with respect to (1) plant additions required, (2) extraordinary repairs and rearrangements, and (3) retirement or disposal of excess plant capacity. If plant equipment appears to be inadequate, management must make plans to obtain the additional capacity or revise the production and sales requirements. In planning capital expenditures (i.e., capital additions), management must consider the time required to obtain and ready the additions to productive capacity. This problem poses the related problem of financing. Care must be exercised lest expensive plant additions are planned to meet short-term peak demands only to remain idle for considerable periods of time thereafter. The capital expenditures budget is discussed in Chapter 11.

Availability of Raw Materials and Labor

In some cases, the production plan can be significantly influenced by the availability of the required raw materials, components, and labor. Raw material availability may be affected by such factors as prices, perishability, economies in purchasing, and quality considerations. For example, canning plants usually have to schedule production when the raw materials are in season. Even in cases where the raw materials can be stored, there is the problem of weighing the advantages of stable production against the problems and costs incident to warehousing large inventories. The availability of skilled labor, and the time and cost to train employees, are important variables that should be considered in planning production.

Length of the Production Period

The production budget illustrated on page 217 shows the number of units that must be completed to meet the sales plan and inventory requirements. A direct conversion from the sales budget to the production budget, as illustrated there, is appropriate if the manufacturing time is relatively short. In situations where production requires several weeks or months, it is necessary to prepare additional plans indicating the timing of the units to be started and the timing of the units to be completed. For example, if processing requires approximately four months, the plan of units to be started must be moved forward at least four months ahead of the dates shown in the production budget for **units to be completed.** In addition, if the product consists of many component parts that are manufactured by the company, it is necessary to prepare a separate **component parts production budget** that shows the timing of (1) parts to be started and (2) parts to be completed. The schedules indicating starting and completion dates provide essential data for the purchasing department in planning raw materials purchases. **Materials requirements planning (MRP)** systems constitute one type of approach used to resolve the production planning problem. MRP concepts are discussed later in the chapter.

Another factor influencing production planning is the work-in-process inventory. If no significant fluctuation is planned in this inventory during the year, there will be no significant effect on production. Therefore, in this case, inventory fluctuation can be ignored in production planning. However, should significant changes be planned in the work-in-process inventory, the changes must be taken into account in production planning. Two approaches are used to resolve this problem, depending on the circumstances. In cases where the processing time is short, a change in work-in-process inventory can be incorporated into the usual production budget format as follows:

Units required for sales	100,000
Add ending inventory of finished goods	20,000
Total	120,000
Less beginning inventory of finished goods	15,000
Units to be completed for finished goods	105,000
Add equivalent units in ending work-in-process inventory*	5,000
Total	110,000
Less equivalent units in beginning work-in-process inventory	6,000
Equivalent units to be manufactured	104,000

*Equivalent units represent the units produced, both completed and partially completed, in a given period. For example, if a department with no beginning inventory completed 1,000 units and had on hand an ending inventory of 200 units estimated to be one-half completed, the equivalent units produced would be [1,000 + (200 × 1/2)] = 1,100.

When the manufacturing time is long enough to require the preparation of schedules of units to be started and units to be completed, the adjustment for changes in work-in-process inventories can be made in these schedules rather than only in the schedule of units to be completed, as illustrated above. In situations where processing time is short, it may be more practical to adjust production starting times to delivery times through flexibility in the work-in-process and finished-goods inventories. The principal difficulty involved in using inventories for this purpose is that a large amount of working capital could inadvertently become tied up in such inventories.

MATERIAL REQUIREMENTS PLANNING (MRP)   In modern production operations, production is usually coordinated throughout the various production stages. **Material requirements planning,** or **MRP,** is a technique for coordinating production in multistage production environments with many parts, materials, subassemblies, components, and finished products. An MRP system begins with a **master schedule** for the end products needed. It then backs up through the production process to determine when and how much of each material, part, or subassembly will be required. Because the requirements for parts and materials are determined from the production schedule of the finished product, these inputs have interdependent demands.[3]

Most MRP systems are complicated and require highly sophisticated computer programs to control the flow of parts and materials through the production process. MRP systems often are integrally related to the production budgeting process. Cost break-downs for materials and labor are necessary ingredients in both the MRP and budgeting systems. Moreover, the scheduling of materials, parts, and labor requirements in the MRP system becomes the basis for budgeting these inputs in the profit planning and control system. In some cases, the software for the MRP system and the software for the budgeting system are integrally related.

Two primary data files are used in an MRP system: an **inventory item master** file and a **product structure** file. The inventory master file lists all the material and parts items in inventory. This file contains a variety of technological and cost accounting data about each part or material item. The product structure file contains the details for the production of all items produced—both subassemblies and end products. The following excerpt from an article in *Management Accounting* describes how an MRP system can be used to facilitate the development of product costs for budgeting and other purposes.

This brief exposure to MRP concepts is intended to emphasize the integral relationship between the budgeting process and the production planning

The *product structure* is a file which provides the part numbers of the component parts of each manufactured item. The relationships of all parts to each other is organized into a tier of inventory items in a hierarchy rising from simple raw materials to manufactured component parts, then to subassemblies and complex final assemblies. The system is integrated by software called a "Bill of Materials" processor. The product structure allows one to call out or retrieve a bill of material for any item.

[3] John McClain and L. Joseph Thomas, *Operations Management,* 2nd ed. (Englewood Cliffs, N.J.: Prentice-Hall, 1985), p. 360.

> If the cost elements are provided, a detailed, costed bill of material can be generated. . . . By updating costs of the basic component parts, such as raw materials and purchased and manufactured parts, costs of all of the more complex upper-level assemblies can then be updated through a process called a *cost explosion* defined as level-by-level cost retrievals of all bills of material.
>
> With such sophisticated systems available, the revision of product costs is a relatively simple step-by-step process, usually performed annually. Now new costs of purchased raw materials and component parts can be developed. Labor and overhead rates also can be updated for manufactured parts and assembled components; these rates are calculated through the use of operations routings, which define each step in the manufacture or assembly of a part or finished product. When these basic costs are developed and the cost files are updated, the cost explosion process is used for updating the costs of the entire *inventory item master.*[4]

process. Further details of MRP and other sophisticated production planning systems are beyond the scope of this book.[5]

JUST-IN-TIME (JIT) PRODUCTION

The **just-in-time (JIT)** approach to production planning is a recent trend in manufacturing. The main characteristics of modern production environments on which JIT is based are as follows:

1 It is inefficient and costly to hold large inventories of safety stock for raw materials, subassemblies, or finished products. Therefore, these safety stocks should be minimized.

2 Setup times for production can be minimized through the use of robotics and process improvement studies. Therefore, frequent production setups may not be inefficient.

3 Very high quality of subassemblies and final products must be achieved in order to reduce the need for safety stocks, as mentioned in item 1 above.

In light of these considerations, many companies have adopted an approach to manufacturing called just-in-time production. JIT is a production concept in which virtually nothing is purchased or manufactured until just before it is needed. The concepts were originally made famous by Toyota[6] and have resulted in huge cost savings for a variety of companies, such as Honeywell, Ingersoll-Rand, and A. P. Parts.[7]

The use of the JIT approach to manufacturing or the use of an MRP production planning system does not change either the importance of, or the procedures used, in production budgeting as related to a comprehensive PPC system. It is, however, essential that the budgeting process reflect the implications (1) for lower inventory levels and more frequent purchasing implicit in the JIT approach, and (2) the production sequencing implications of an MRP environment.

[4] B. Bowers, "Product Costing in the MRP Environment," *Management Accounting*, December 1982, pp. 24 and 25.

[5] See McClain and Thomas, *Operations Management*.

[6] Y. Monden, "What Makes the Toyota Production System Really Tick?" *Industrial Engineering* (Vol. 13, No. 1).

[7] J. Swartley-Loush, "Just-in-Time: Is It Right for You?" *Production Engineering*, June 1985, pp. 61–64.

THE PRODUCTION BUDGET AS A PLANNING, COORDINATING, AND CONTROL

TOOL   The production budget contributes to planning, coordination, and control. The fact that a detailed production plan is developed and based on a realistic sales plan means that management has analyzed and made specific its plans about the production planning function and related problems. Developing a detailed production budget forces planning decisions about production plans, material and component requirements, labor requirements, plant capacity, capital additions, and inventory policies. Production planning tends to expose weaknesses and sources of future problems that can be avoided by timely management decisions.

Just as significant is the coordination that results from effective production planning. The production plan must be coordinated with plans related to financing, capital additions, product development, and sales. A critical problem in all manufacturing situations is that of coordinating the operations of the sales and production departments effectively. The sales executive should be acutely aware of production problems, and the production executive must be aware of sales developments. It may be desirable to revise the sales plan to emphasize those products that the factory can readily and efficiently produce. The translation of sales demands into production effort can be complex, and if not resolved on a sound basis, may be the cause of considerable inefficiency in the company. Such inefficiencies can usually be attributed to a lack of timely planning and to an indefinite assignment of responsibilities.

The production plan, as finally approved, should be viewed as a master production plan to be executed by the production department. It should not be used inflexibly but rather as a guide to the actual, detailed production planning and scheduling carried on by the production department on a day-to-day or week-to-week basis. It should not be viewed as an order to proceed with production; actual production should be ordered by the production planning and scheduling department on a current basis that reflects the actual sales trends as they evolve during the budget period. The production plan may be considered the framework within which current production orders are issued. Variations in actual sales and in other conditions may call for departures from the original production plan.

The production budget is the primary basis for planning raw material and component requirements, labor needs, capital additions, cash requirements, and factory costs. Therefore, the production plan becomes the foundation for factory planning in general. It gives the factory executives sound data on which to base operational decisions.

An adequate production control system is essential to managerial control of costs, quality, and quantities. The principal procedures involved in production control are the following:

1   Materials control
2   Analysis of production processes by responsibility centers in the production division
3   Routing production

4 Scheduling production
5 Dispatching production
6 Follow-up

In addition to daily and weekly controls of production volume and the level of the finished-goods inventory, the status of these two factors should be reported on the *monthly performance report* wherein actual results are compared with plans and standards.

Quantitative Methods in Planning and Controlling Production

In planning and controlling production (and the related inventories), linear-programming and inventory models have a broad application, which should be fully intergrated with a comprehensive profit planning and control program. Some of these mathematical approaches are relatively simple, whereas others are highly sophisticated involving complex mathematical models and requiring a wide range of computer capability. Inventory models quantify the effects of relevant variables underlying policy decisions.[8] They can be designed for cost minimization or other specified managerial objectives. Production models likewise vary from relatively simple to highly sophisticated mathematical and computer approaches. Models have been developed for resolving such production programs as attainment of optimal coordination in production between sales and inventories; determination of economic production runs; allocation of productive capacity to products; product mix; and cost minimization in the manufacturing processes. This book cannot treat these topics in detail. However, other sources for more detailed discussion are listed as "Suggested References" at the end of the chapter.

CHAPTER SUMMARY   The production plan is an important tool of planning, coordination, and control. By expressing the manufacturing budget as a planning tool, it establishes the foundation for planning all aspects of such factory operations as raw material needs, factory labor needs, supervisory needs, factory overhead, plant capacity, and factory service activities. The coordination between sales plans, inventory policies, and production requirements comes into focus and is resolved in the production plan. It is also an important factor in the overall coordination of such functional activities as cash flow planning, financing, research and development, engineering, and capital additions. It establishes the basis for control of production, inventories, production costs, and labor in the factory.

---

[8] One common inventory model, the *economic-order-quantity* (EOQ) model, is discussed in Chapter 7.

Comprehensive Demonstration Case

   *SUPERIOR MANUFACTURING COMPANY*

It is impractical to illustrate all the factors affecting the production budget. It is assumed that Superior Manufacturing Company's inventory policy calls for a three months' supply of finished goods and that production will be kept essentially stable. Manufacturing conditions are such that variations of approximately 15 percent in production levels are possible without seriously affecting the number of permanent employees and other cost-incurring variables.

The manufacturing vice-president, in consultation with the other manufacturing managers and, in particular, with the production manager, prepares the production plan to meet the sales requirements. This production plan and the resulting inventory plans were given to the executive committee and have been tentatively approved by the president. The annual production plan for Superior Manufacturing Company was shown in Chapter 4 (Schedule 2).

The detailed production plan, by product and by interim time periods, for Superior Manufacturing Company is shown in Schedule 22. Notice that production is budgeted by month for the first quarter and by quarter for the remainder of the year, as was illustrated for the sales plan in Chapter 5 (Schedule 21). Schedule 22 is supplemented by a schedule of production activities for each cost center (not illustrated).

SCHEDULE 22. Superior Manufacturing Company

Production Plan (Detailed)
By Product, by Time
For the Year Ending December 31, 19X2

REF.	REQUIRED FOR SALES 21	ADD ENDING INVENTORY OF FINISHED GOODS	TOTAL REQUIRED	LESS BEGINNING INVENTORY OF FINISHED GOODS	UNITS TO BE COMPLETED
Product X					
January	85,000	225,000	310,000	240,000	70,000
February	90,000	215,000	305,000	225,000	80,000
March	95,000	200,000	295,000	215,000	80,000
Total 1st Quarter	270,000	200,000	470,000	240,000	230,000
2nd Quarter	260,000	180,000	440,000	200,000	240,000
3rd Quarter	190,000	220,000	410,000	180,000	230,000
4th Quarter	280,000	200,000	480,000	220,000	260,000
Total	1,000,000	200,000	1,200,000	240,000	960,000

Product Y					
January	34,000	100,000	134,000	100,000	34,000
February	41,000	95,000	136,000	100,000	36,000
March	45,000	88,000	133,000	95,000	38,000
Total 1st Quarter	120,000	88,000	208,000	100,000	108,000
2nd Quarter	135,000	93,000	228,000	88,000	140,000
3rd Quarter	95,000	125,000	220,000	93,000	127,000
4th Quarter	150,000	120,000	270,000	125,000	145,000
Total	500,000	120,000	620,000	100,000	520,000

See Schedule 2 for Summary.

Notice in Schedule 22 that the work-in-process inventory was ignored. This omission was possible because it was assumed that this inventory level will remain unchanged during the budget year. Assume work-in-process inventories to be as follows throughout the year:

> Product X: Zero
> Product Y: 10,000 units

Because the finished-goods inventory, in units, is developed concurrently with the production plan, it is appropriate at this time to prepare the budget of finished-goods inventories illustrated in Schedule 23. Notice that provision is made for unit costs and total costs that can be entered later when the budgeted cost of manufacturing is determined (see Schedule 63, Chapter 13).

SCHEDULE 23. Superior Manufacturing Company

Finished-Goods Inventory Budget
For the Year Ending December 31, 19X2

19X2: REF.	TOTAL COST ALL PRODUCTS	PRODUCT X			PRODUCT Y		
		UNITS	UNIT COST	TOTAL COST	UNITS	UNIT COST	TOTAL COST
January 1	$	240,000	$	$	100,000	$	$
January 31		225,000			100,000		
February 29		215,000			95,000		
March 31		200,000			88,000		
End of 2nd Qtr.		180,000			93,000		
End of 3rd Qtr.		220,000			125,000		
End of 4th Qtr.		200,000			120,000		

Suggested References

BIERMAN, HAROLD, JR., THOMAS DYCKMAN, and RONALD HILTON, *Cost Accounting: Concepts and Managerial Applications.* New York; Macmillan, 1990.

MCCLAIN, JOHN, and L. JOSEPH THOMAS, *Operations Management*, 2nd ed. Englewood Cliffs, N.J.: Prentice-Hall, 1985.

MONDEN, Y. "What Makes the Toyota Production System Really Tick?" *Industrial Engineering*, (Vol. 13, No. 1).

SEGHUND, R., and S. IBARRECHE, "Just in Time: The Accounting Implications," *Management Accounting*, August, 1984, pp. 43–45.

SWARTLEY-LOUSH, J., "Just-in-Time: Is It Right for You?" *Production Engineering*, June 1985, pp. 61–64.

Discussion Questions

1. Define *production budget*, and explain why this budget is a necessary step in developing the profit plan.
2. What other budgets are closely related to the production budget?
3. Who should be responsible for development of the production plan? Explain.
4. What is the relationship of the work-in-process and finished-goods inventories to the production plan?
5. What is the primary objective in developing the production plan?
6. What is meant by inventory policies? What are the primary problems in developing realistic inventory policies related to the production plan?
7. Why is it usually desirable to maintain a stable production level?
8. What is an MRP system, and how is it related to production budgeting in a PPC program?
9. What is meant by JIT? What are its implications for the budgeting process in a PPC program?
10. In what ways are manufacturing facilities related to the production plan?
11. Discuss the relationship between the production budget and the availability of raw materials, components, and labor.
12. What basis should be used to determine the detailed breakdown (disaggregation) of the production plan?
13. Outline the planning, coordination, and control aspects of the production plan.

CASE 6-1   *How to develop and use a production plan*

Corona Manufacturers has been in operation for approximately twenty years. The company manufactures two primary products that are distributed in five geographical sales regions covering the entire United States. Manufacturing operations are conducted in three producing departments, and there are two service departments in the factory. Top management is represented by the chief executive officer, an executive vice-president, and vice-presidents for each function—sales, manufacturing, and finance. The company employs approximately two hundred individuals, and annual sales last year were approximately $30 million.

To manufacture the two products, three raw materials are used. The products are processed through each of the producing departments. Product A incurs a relatively high proportion of direct labor cost and a lower proportion of direct material cost. In contrast, product B requires a high number of direct machine hours and large amounts of direct materials. Production time for product A is approximately twice that for product B. Raw materials are relatively cheap and there is high machine utilization; therefore, product B is less costly per unit and more profitable per unit than product A. However, the sales mix ratio is approximately three to one in favor of product A. The two products are not substitutable because they are used for different purposes and are purchased by different customers.

Although the company has been reasonably successful and has grown steadily, profits and return on investment for the past three years have leveled off. Because of the recent retirement of some long-term managers (including the chief executive officer), changes in certain management approaches were made during the past year. The new chief executive officer, R. M. May, had been the financial vice-president and had eight years' experience with the company. The changes involved manufacturing operations and the hiring and training of personnel. May formed an executive committee comprised of the chief executive and all the vice-presidents (a first for the company). During the past year, May decided to implement a profit planning and control program that includes a five-year, long-range plan and a one-year, short-range profit plan. The first long-range plan has been completed, and the executives are now establishing procedures for developing the short-range profit plan. The long-range plan is disaggregated for each year of the five-year span. May decided that the annual profit plan will be developed by quarter with the first quarter detailed by month; subsequent quarters will be detailed prior to the beginning of each quarter. Consistent with decisions already made, the marketing vice-president has completed a sales plan, and it has been tentatively approved by the executive committee. The sales plan encompasses the promotion plan, a distribution plan, and a marketing plan. The last plan specifies the planned quantities and dollars of revenue by product.

The manufacturing vice-president is currently developing aproaches to set up the production plan and will subsequently develop the production plan for inclusion in the annual profit plan.

REQUIRED   You are to respond to the following factors being considered by the manufacturing vice-president:

1. Classifications of planned data that should be incorporated into the annual production plan
2. Assigned management responsibilities for developing the annual production plan (including the necessary procedures)
3. Underlying data and basic policies essential for developing the annual production plan
4. Use of the completed production plan

CASE 6-2   *Prepare a production plan: What problems are encountered?*

Midwest Plastics Company has been engaged in profit planning for several years. The president stated (with justification) that inventory control and production planning had not been satisfactory. This was due primarily to poorly planned production and inventory budgets.

You are to make a detailed analysis and recommendation on the problem for the 19B profit plan currently being prepared. Your analysis and recommendations will be presented to the executive committee.

Despite seasonality, the sales department has been successful in developing a realistic sales plan on a monthly basis for each year. The following sales data are available for 19B.

1   Sales plan summary for 19B:

MONTH	UNITS	MONTH	UNITS	MONTH	UNITS
January	36,000	May	32,000	September	26,000
February	38,000	June	26,000	October	30,000
March	38,000	July	22,000	November	36,000
April	36,000	August	20,000	December	40,000

2   The January 1, 19B, finished-goods inventory is 96,000 units.
3   The work-in-process inventory will remain constant.
4   The actual annual sales for 19A, including the December estimate, were 350,000 units.
5   The average finished-goods inventory for 19A was 70,000 units.

REQUIRED

1. Prepare the annual production budget, assuming the policy of management is to budget the finished-goods ending inventory at a standard amount based on the 19A historical sales to inventory turnover ratio.

2. Prepare a schedule that shows monthly sales, production, and inventory levels assuming (1) a stable inventory, (2) stable production, and (3) your recommended inventory-production levels. In developing your recommendations, assume the following policies have been established:

    (a) The president has set a policy that a maximum inventory of 85,000 units and a minimum of 75,000 units should be used except in unusual circumstances.

    (b) A stable level of production is strongly preferred except that during vacation season (July and August) production can be reduced by 25 percent. Also, a 7.5 percent variation in production above and below the average level is acceptable.

3. What are the primary problems facing the company in planning production? Give your broad recommendations.

CASE 6-3   *Evaluate inventory and production plans*

Thomas Manufacturing Company produces soil pipe, sewer pipe, fittings, joints, and other related items in many sizes and of several different materials. Most of the finished goods are stored outside between date of completion and date of shipment to customers.

Production problems are critical, particularly because of high setup costs for production. For example, to produce soil pipe, considerable rearrangement in the factory is necessary and special molds must be taken out of storage and prepared for use. As a result of the high setup costs, big runs are usually made to keep unit costs competitive.

Inventory storage costs are low (estimated by the management to be about $10 per unit per year), and deterioration is not a problem. Obsolescence is considered to be a relatively minor factor in terms of two or three years. The company finances the inventory locally. Other than fixed factory overhead, production costs for material and labor tend to vary directly with the number of units produced.

The company has just started a budget program. The tentative sales plan and other data are as follows:

a Sales budget for 19E:

| | | | | INTERIM PERIODS FOR 19D AND 19E | | | | | |
| | | | | 1st QUARTER | | | QUARTER | | |
	19A	19B	19C	JAN.	FEB.	MAR.	2ND	3RD	4TH
Soil pipe									
Actual	11,000	12,000	15,000	1,500	1,200	1,000	3,000	4,000	4,500
Budget, next year (19E)				1,500	1,500	1,200	3,500	4,000	4,500

	19A	19B	19C	1st QUARTER JAN.	FEB.	MAR.	QUARTER 2ND	3RD	4TH
Sewer pipe									
Actual	8,000	8,000	9,000	1,000	1,100	1,100	4,000	2,500	1,500
Budget, next year (19E)				1,200	1,200	1,200	4,800	3,000	1,500
Fittings									
Actual	15,000	16,000	23,000	2,400	2,200	2,000	6,500	6,500	6,000
Budget, next year (19E)				2,600	2,600	2,200	7,500	7,000	5,500
Joints									
Actual	4,000	4,500	4,800	700	700	800	2,200	2,300	1,900
Budget, next year (19E)				800	800	800	2,300	2,400	2,000

The header spans: "INTERIM PERIODS FOR 19D AND 19E" over the last six columns, with "1st QUARTER" over JAN./FEB./MAR. and "QUARTER" over 2ND/3RD/4TH.

b Other data:

	PLANNED FOR 19E				
PRODUCT	INVENTORY JAN. 1, 19E (UNITS)	AVERAGE UNIT COST[a]	AVERAGE (LOT) PRODUCTION[b] (UNITS)	AVERAGE SETUP COST	AVERAGE PRODUCTION AND SETUP TIME PER LOT (DAYS)[c]
Soil pipe	21,000	$8.50	30,000	$15,000	70
Sewer pipe	34,000	6.00	40,000	20,000	90
Fittings	22,000	1.50	25,000	10,000	70
Joints	4,000	4.50	10,000	8,000	20

[a] Includes setup costs based on average (lot) production.
[b] Estimated to be the economic production lot.
[c] Based on 250 working days per year.

REQUIRED

1. Assess the inventory position on January 1, 19E, to determine whether it is excessive in terms of months' supply.

2. Assess the production plans to determine whether planned production is adequate in terms of months' supply.

3. Assess the planned ending inventory position to determine whether it is excessive.

4. Assess the overall plans as reflected in your assessments in requirements 1, 2, and 3.

5. Indicate relevant approaches and factors that management should consider in resolving its production and inventory planning problems.

CASE 6-4 *What should be done about an overinvestment in inventory?*

For some time, Hot Metal Works has been experiencing a critical shortage of cash to meet payrolls and to pay for raw materials. During July of the current year (19D), the situation became critical. A request was made to the bank for a $200,000 loan. The company was unable to give the bank audited financial statements. The bank refused to consider the loan until a CPA was called in to conduct an examination of the current financial condition of the company and to report to them. The company agreed to this condition. The CPA developed the data shown below (as well as other relevant data) about the finished-goods inventory.

There are unusually high setup costs on products E and G. Product C has a relatively long processing period (twenty-three days). The unfavorable inventory situation occurred because the production manager consistently overproduced on each order received from sales to save setup costs. The manager had no knowledge of any inventory policies or levels. Also, the sales division does not maintain a formal record of inventory levels. Most of the products were stored outside in the yard.

PRODUCT	UNITS ON HAND	CURRENT AVERAGE UNIT COST	NUMBER OF UNITS SOLD 19 A	19 B	19 C
A	12	$18	15	12	8
B	100	9	150	170	180
C	21,000	4	2,000	1,900	1,600
D	6,000	7	8,000	8,000	8,000
E	79,000	5	4,000	4,200	4,500
F	48,000	6	8,000	7,800	7,500
G	34,000	8	2,000	1,800	1,500
H	—	32	100	150	175
I	900	21	1,500	1,700	2,000
J	10,000	10	14,000	16,000	18,000

REQUIRED

1. Estimate the company's overinvestment in inventory. At the conclusion of the audit, assume that the CPA concluded that there were no valid reasons why any item should be stocked in excess of a two-years' supply.

2. Give your recommendations about the inventory and production. Explain the basis for your recommendations.

CASE 6-5   *Can you prepare a production budget summary and a monthly production budget?*

Atlantic Fabrication Company manufactures three products. The planning budget is being developed for the coming year. The annual sales plan prepared by the sales division showed the following: product 1, 100,000 units; product 2, 150,000 units; and product 3, 80,000 units.

Sales are seasonal; for example, the sales plan showed the following sales by month for product 1:

MONTH	UNITS	MONTH	UNITS
Jan.	10,500	July	5,200
Feb.	10,300	Aug.	5,000
Mar.	9,400	Sept.	7,500
Apr.	8,500	Oct.	8,800
May	8,000	Nov.	9,500
June	7,000	Dec.	10,300

The following inventory levels have been tentatively planned:

	FINISHED GOODS		WORK IN PROCESS			
	BEGINNING	ENDING	BEGINNING		ENDING	
PRODUCT	UNITS	UNITS	UNITS	PERCENT COMPLETE	UNITS	PERCENT COMPLETE
1	1,000	12,000	0	—	0	—
2	10,000	8,000	2,000	100	2,000	100
3	5,000	5,000	2,000	50	6,000	50

REQUIRED

1. Prepare the annual production budget summary for the company by product.
2. What policies would you suggest relative to monthly inventory and production levels for the company for product 1? Give support for your recommendations.
3. Prepare a production budget by month for product 1 in conformity with your recommendation in requirement 2.

CASE 6-6   Simplified ways to compute inventory levels

Staley Company executives are trying to establish inventory policies as part of the development of a budget program. Several alternatives have been discussed concerning inventory levels, among them the moving-average method and an average-withdrawal method. The sales plan shows the following data for the main product:

DATE	UNITS
December (preceding year)	800,000
January	780,000
February	780,000
March	810,000
April	830,000
May	820,000
June	800,000
July	700,000
August	600,000
September	650,000
October	700,000
November	780,000
December	820,000
January (following year)	810,000

REQUIRED

1. Use a three-month moving average to compute the inventory level by month; a one and one-half months' supply is specified by the inventory policy.

2. Compute the inventory level by month assuming inventory policy requires that average withdrawals for the fourteen periods be determined and that a one and one-half months' average supply be planned.

3. Compute the beginning inventory level by month assuming the inventory policy is to start each month with an inventory equivalent to one-fourth of the sales planned for that month.

4. Assess each approach.

Planning and Controlling Purchases and Materials Usage: Manufacturing and Nonmanufacturing

7

INTRODUCTION AND PURPOSE   A comprehensive profit planning and control program includes planning and controlling raw materials and components used in the manufacturing of finished products. This phase of productive activity involves another coordination problem similar to the one discussed in Chapter 6. In this case, the coordination to be planned and controlled is among (1) production requirements for materials and component parts, (2) raw material and parts inventory levels, and (3) purchases of raw materials. When the required quantities of each product to be manufactured are specified in the production plan, the next step in planning the manufacturing program involves consideration of the various production requirements and costs—direct materials and component parts, direct labor, and factory overhead. This chapter discusses planning and controlling direct material and parts costs.

THE RAW MATERIALS AND COMPONENT PARTS BUDGET   To ensure that the appropriate amounts of raw materials and component parts will be on hand at the time required and to plan for the costs of such materials and parts, the tactical short-term profit plan should include (1) a detailed budget that specifies the quantity and cost of such materials and parts, and (2) a related budget of materials and parts purchases. Planning raw materials and parts usually requires the following four subbudgets:

1 **Materials and Parts Budget.** This budget specifies the planned quantities of each raw material and part required for planned production. It should specify quantities of each raw material and part by time, product, and responsibility center.

2 **Materials and Parts Purchases Budget.** The materials and parts budget specifies the quantities and timing of each raw material and component part needed; therefore, a plan for purchases must be developed. The purchases and parts budget specifies the planned quantities of materials and parts to be purchased, the estimated cost, and the required delivery dates.

240

3   **Materials and Parts Inventory Budget.** This budget specifies the planned levels of raw material and parts inventory in terms of quantities and cost. The difference in units between the requirements as specified in the materials budget (item 1) and the purchases budget (item 2) is shown as planned increases or decreases in the materials and parts inventory budget.

4   **Cost of Materials and Parts Used Budget.** This budget specifies the planned cost of the materials and parts (item 1) that will be used in the productive process. Notice that this budget cannot be completed until the planned cost of purchases (item 2) is developed.

The four separate subbudgets listed above are directly related. Collectively, they can be viewed as the materials and purchases budget. In simple situations, all four may be combined; items 1 and 4 are frequently combined. In more complex situations, separate budgets, as defined above, are essential—especially when the related budget data must be developed sequentially.

In designing each of these materials and parts budgets, two basic objectives, in addition to planning, are overriding:

1   **Control.** Raw material and part costs are subject to direct control at the point of usage; therefore, the related activities and costs should be budgeted in terms of responsibility centers, and by interim time periods.

2   **Product Costing.** Direct material and part costs are included in manufacturing costs (product costs); therefore, they must be identified by product.

Because of these two basic objectives, direct materials and component parts should be budgeted: by type of raw material and part, by responsibility centers, by interim periods, and by type of finished product. These multiple classifications tend to complicate the budgeting format used.

Next, we discuss each of the four subbudgets defined above. The basic issues, techniques, approaches, and decisions discussed in Chapter 6 that relate to optimal coordination among sales, inventory levels, and production also apply here. The same factors must be considered; the same approaches and techniques are applicable; and essentially the same types of decisions must be made.

The Materials and Parts Budget

Materials used in a factory are traditionally classified as **direct** or **indirect.** Parts are usually classified only as direct. **Direct material** is generally defined to include all materials and parts that are an integral part of the finished product and can be directly identified with (traced to) the unit costs of the finished products. Direct material cost is usually a **variable cost**—that is, a cost that varies in **proportion** to changes in productive output or volume. **Indirect** material is generally defined as material used in the manufacturing process, but the costs of which are not directly traceable to each product. A related indirect cost, frequently referred to as factory supplies, consists of items used in a general way, such as grease, lubricating oils, and other maintenance supplies.

The materials budget includes only the quantities (not cost) of direct materials, factory supplies, and indirect materials that are included in the manufacturing or factory overhead budget. The budgeted quantities of each raw material and part needed for each finished product must be specified in the materials and parts budget by interim periods (months and quarters) and by responsibility centers. The product, interim period, and responsibility center classifications should follow the pattern used in the sales and production plans. The manufacturing managers should be responsible for developing the data included in the materials and parts budget. The principal purposes in developing detailed raw material and parts requirements for planned production are to provide data for developing the four budgets listed above.

The basic (estimated) inputs required to develop the direct materials and parts budget are (1) volume of output planned (from the production plan) and (2) standard usage rates by type of raw material and part for each finished product. Material usage rates are applied to the production data (from the production plan) to develop the materials and parts budget. In many manufacturing situations, it is not difficult to determine standard unit usage rates for unit raw materials and parts used in each department per unit of finished product. For example, to manufacture such items as furniture, clothing, mechanical equipment, appliances, and liquids, definite and easily determinable quantities of parts and raw material are required. In many cases, precise measurement of the quantity of raw material is essential to the desired quality of the resulting output. Unit usage rates can be derived (1) during initial development of the product, (2) from engineering studies, or (3) from past consumption records and bills of materials. Where specific unit usage rates cannot be developed in this way, planning of raw material and parts requirements may be a critical budget problem.

Two indirect approaches to developing usage requirements are sometimes used. One indirect approach is to develop some method of estimating total raw material quantities required for production through the use of adjusted historical ratios such as the ratio of material quantity usage to direct machine hours. The other indirect approach involves the development of a relationship (usually expressed as a ratio or percentage) between material cost in dollars and some other variable that can be projected with some degree of confidence. For example, some companies plan raw material cost as a percentage of direct labor cost. The latter approach is usually less desirable because the relationship between labor cost and materials cost is usually tenuous. In either indirect approach the manager responsible for preparing the raw material budget must usually apply a ratio. The following relationships have been used.

1   The ratio of the quantity of each kind of material or part to the physical volume of production. This ratio, for the past few months or year, can be calculated from historical records and adjusted for changed conditions.

2   The ratio of the materials and parts used to some measure of production such as direct labor hours or direct machine hours.

3   The ratio of material cost to direct labor cost.

When a standard cost system is used for accounting purposes, standard material and part usage rates are already available and should be used for profit planning and control purposes. However, should the standard-cost usage rates be unrealistic (that is, too tight or too loose), material and part usage variances from the standard cost must be budgeted. In planning the materials and parts budget, realistic allowance must be made for normal spoilage, waste, and scrap.

The materials budget for Superior Manufacturing Company is shown in Schedules 24 and 25 at the end of this chapter.

The Materials and Parts Purchases and Inventory Budgets

Careful planning of purchases can result in significant cost savings in many enterprises. If realistic estimates of material and part requirements are specified in the materials and parts budget by interim periods, the purchasing manager can effectively plan the purchasing activities. The purchasing manager should be assigned the direct responsibility for preparing a detailed plan of purchases.

The purchases budget specifies (1) the quantities of each type of material and part to be purchased, (2) the timing of those purchases, and (3) the estimated cost of material and part purchases (per purchased unit and in total). Thus, the purchases budget differs from the materials and parts budget in two primary ways. First, these budgets usually specify different quantities of each type of material and part. This difference in quantities results from the planned changes in materials and parts inventory levels. Second, the materials and parts budget specifies only quantities, whereas the purchases budget specifies both quantities and dollar costs. The purchases budget is directly concerned with the timing of actual receipt of materials and parts rather than with timing of purchase orders or usage. The purchasing manager must order materials and parts so that delivery dates will correspond to the materials and parts inventory levels and usage requirements in the production process.

To develop the purchases budget the purchasing manager is responsible for the following:

1 Adhering to management policies about materials and parts inventory levels.
2 Determining the number of units and the timing of each type of material and part to be purchased.
3 Estimating the unit cost of each type of material and part to be purchased.

Materials and Parts Inventory Policies

The quantity differential planned between the materials and parts budget and the purchases budget is accounted for by the change in materials and parts inventory levels. As with the finished-goods inventory budget, with respect to sales and production, the materials and parts inventory budget provides a cushion between material and parts requirements and purchases. If material and parts requirements are seasonal, a stable material and parts inventory level means that purchases must exactly parallel factory material and parts requirements. Yet, in the same case, purchases can be at a uniform level only if inventory is allowed to absorb variations in material and parts requirements. The optimal purchasing plan will generally be between these two extremes. The timing of purchases will depend on inventory policies. The primary considerations in setting inventory policies for materials and parts are

1 Timing and quantity of manufacturing needs
2 Economies in purchasing through quantity discounts
3 Availability of materials and parts
4 Lead time (order and delivery)
5 Perishability of materials and parts
6 Storage facilities needed
7 Capital requirements to finance inventory
8 Costs of storage
9 Expected changes in the cost of materials and parts
10 Protection against shortages
11 Risks involved in inventories
12 Opportunity costs (inadequate inventory)

   Like finished-goods inventory policies, raw material and parts inventory policies are intended to minimize the sum of two classes of costs: the cost of carrying the inventory and the cost of not carrying enough. Reference to the inventory discussions in the preceding chapter will indicate that some of the costs influencing inventory policy determinations are not reflected directly in the accounting reports. For example, interest on the money invested in materials and parts inventory must normally be measured separately; yet it is a real production cost.
   Management policy with respect to purchases and inventory should be specified. The two basic timing factors are (1) how much to purchase at a time (2) when to purchase.

ECONOMIC ORDER QUANTITY (EOQ) MODEL   A well-known approach to computing the economic order quantity (EOQ) uses the following formula:

$$EOQ = \sqrt{\frac{2AO}{C}}$$

where

> A = Annual quantity used in units
> O = Average annual cost of placing an order
> C = Annual carrying cost of carrying one unit in inventory for one year (e.g., storage, insurance, return on investment in inventory)

To illustrate the application of the EOQ model, consider the following data:

Annual usage planned (in units)	5,400
Cost to place an order	$10.00
Annual carrying cost per unit in inventory	$ 1.20

Computation:

$$EOQ= \sqrt{\frac{(2)(5,400)(\$10)}{(\$1.20)}}= \sqrt{\frac{\$108,000}{\$1.20}}= \sqrt{90,000}=300 \text{ units}$$

Based on the data given, the economic order quantity is 300 units; at this value, cost is minimized. Notice that as A or O gets larger or as C gets smaller, the EOQ increases. This item would be ordered, on the average, eighteen times per year (5,400 ÷ 300=18).

The time when a purchase is made is called the **reorder point.** The re-order point is reached when the inventory level is equal to the quantity needed to sustain production for a period equal to the time to reorder and receive the replenishments. Often, it is also desirable to include a safety stock to accommodate unusual fluctuations in usage and replenishment time (for example, if there is a two-week replenishment time and fifteen-day provision for unusual fluctuations). In the example above, the reorder point would be determined as follows:

	UNITS
Average monthly usage planned (5,400 ÷ 12)	450
Two-week replenishment provision (450 ÷ 2)	225
Add safety stock provision	225
Reorder point (reorder when inventory level reaches this level)	450

Other approaches to this problem require turnover ratios, monthly supply data, days of cost of goods sold in inventory, and specifications of minimum and maximum limitations. The approaches suggested in the preceding chapter for planning and controlling finished-goods inventories are also appropriate.

JUST-IN-TIME PURCHASING   A recent development in materials and parts inventory control is called just-in-time (JIT) purchasing and manufacturing. Its primary objective is to minimize inventory levels and the resulting costs. In this approach, materials and parts are not purchased until needed for production, thereby minimizing inventory holding costs. In such an approach, it is critical to anticipate exactly when the materials and parts will be needed for production so that the acquisition can be reflected in the materials and parts budget for PPC purposes. See the preceding chapter for additional discussion of the JIT approach.[1]

Estimating Unit Costs for Materials and Parts

The purchasing manager is responsible for estimating the unit cost of each raw material and part. Purchasing managers may be reluctant to make such cost estimates because they recognize that there may be many significant factors, external to the company, that will affect raw material and part prices. Nevertheless, failure to develop realistic estimates may have far-reaching effects throughout the company. For example, in situations where materials and/or parts are a significant component of the cost of the finished product, materials and parts costs are important in planning sales prices, financing policies, and cost control, all of which must be concerned with future rather than historical material and parts costs. Executive management should insist that the purchasing manager assess probable future trends in material and parts costs. This assessment should include detailed price studies based on such factors as the expected general economic conditions, industry prospects, demand for the material and parts, and related market conditions. In short, the purchasing manager has a planning responsibility not too different from that faced by the sales manager when the latter develops the sales plan.

The planned cost of materials and parts should be the estimated invoice price, less any purchase discounts, plus freight and handling charges incident to delivery of the goods. It is frequently impractical to identify transportation costs with specific materials and parts; therefore, the planned purchase price is often the net cost of raw materials and transportation, and handling costs are separately planned and budgeted. Purchase contracts may provide some unit cost data. Historical costs, as indicated by the cost records, may provide a basis for estimating some unit costs. In many cases, fluctuating material and parts unit prices must be planned for the budget period. Many materials have prices that tend to vary seasonally, thereby necessitating the budgeting of varying unit purchasing costs.

When an MRP (material requirements planning) system is used, the cost of raw materials and parts is recorded in the **cost explosion** that details the materials and parts required for every phase of production. See the preceding chapter for further discussion.[2]

---

[1] See J. Swartley-Loush, "Just-in-Time: Is It Right for You?" *Production Engineering*, June 1985, pp. 61–64; and R. Seglund and S. Ibarreche, "Just-in-Time: The Accounting Implications," *Management Accounting*, August 1984, pp. 43–45.

[2] See John McClain and L. Joseph Thomas, *Operations Management* (Englewood Cliffs, N.J.: Prentice-Hall, 1985), for a discussion of MRP systems.

Planning Material and Parts Costs for Large Numbers of Products

Many companies have hundreds of products. Rather than budget material costs in detail for each product, some companies select representative products in each of several product classes. The material and parts costs for these products are budgeted in detail, and then the results are applied to the remainder of the products in the class. The following excerpt from an article in *Management Accounting* describes how this approach is used by Chesebrough-Ponds, Inc.

BUDGETING WITH REPRESENTATIVE PRODUCTS AT CHESEBROUGH-PONDS, INC.

In 1980 we began automation of our established cost of sales projection system within the Health and Beauty Products division of Chesebrough-Ponds, Inc. This system projects an expected product cost for future accounting periods. Several key products are used to represent the division's most cost-impactive items. These products are broken down to their most detailed elements (material packaging parts, raw ingredients for formulas, direct labor and overhead) and each element is projected outward for four quarters of the upcoming operating year.

Our system does not employ sophisticated techniques beyond what is required to choose a representative sample of products. Each selected product acts as the model for its respective product line and the quarter by quarter changes in total cost are used for all products within the line. The steps involved in the overall process are:

1   The annual sales forecast in evaluated on product line basis to highlight where the major activity will take place in the upcoming year.

2   Sample products are selected for detailed cost projection. The resulting increases or decreases in these samples are applied to their respective product lines.

3   An evaluation is made of the results to ensure that the proper attention is given to all product lines.

The projection system does not end once it has delivered cost data for the sample. A monitoring exercise is carried out for the entire operating year. At the end of each quarter the actual performance of the sample is measured against its original projection. Any large deviations can be investigated for the effect they may have on the parent product line. Also at this time, new projections are made. The system projects on a rolling four quarter basis while the prior quarter is dropped and a future quarter is picked up.[3]

The Cost of Materials and Parts Used Budget

The quantity of materials and parts required for planned production is specified in the materials and parts budget, and unit material and parts costs are specified in the purchases budget. Thus, quantity and unit cost data are

---

[3] Dwight Worrell, "Cost of Sales: A Budgeting Priority," *Management Accounting*, August 1983, p. 67.

available to develop the budgeted cost of materials and parts that will be used. If the purchases budget anticipates a constant unit cost for a material or part during the planning period, multiplication of units by the unit cost yields the budgeted material or parts cost. Alternatively, when a changing unit price is planned for materials and parts, the budget of the cost of materials and parts used and the related inventory budget must be developed using a selected inventory flow such as FIFO, LIFO, moving average, or weighted average. FIFO is usually preferred because of its internal consistency. A specially designed spreadsheet is often used to facilitate the computation. Development of the four materials budgets are illustrated at the end of the chapter for Superior Manufacturing Company.

PLANNING, COORDINATION, AND CONTROL ASPECTS OF RAW MATERIALS AND PARTS BUDGETING

Formulation of detailed plans for materials and parts requirements, inventories, and purchases is an important part of the planning function of top management. Planning and control of materials and parts costs are frequently critical because the cost of production and the efficiency with which operation can be conducted on a day-to-day basis depend to a large degree on the smooth flow of materials and parts (at a reasonable cost) to the various subdivisions of the factory. Materials and parts **planning** improves coordination of effort by pinpointing responsibilities; careful thought is required to anticipate and iron out difficulties that otherwise might not become apparent until after actual operations start, resulting in delays, mixups, and consequent high costs. Materials and parts planning avoids the accumulation of excess inventories and inventory shortages, both of which can be extremely costly. Materials and parts budgeting forces the manufacturing and purchasing executives to anticipate significant problems and to make decisions when they should be made rather than when they have to be made. Given purchases planning, the purchasing department has definite objectives rather than the generalized goal "to buy what is needed." Definite purchasing plans should permit better organization and more efficiency in purchasing department operations, with consequent cost reduction and improved cash flow planning.

Coordination of raw materials and parts requirements, inventory levels, and purchasing is an important factor in efficient operations. Material and part costs and inventories may have major effect on profits, working capital, and cash position. Buying on the spur of the moment almost always results in excess costs—if the invoice cost is not excessive, related clerical, handling, freight, and administrative costs are almost certain to be. Quality is also frequently sacrificed when hasty purchases become necessary to avoid production stoppages. Planned purchasing results in better coordinated efforts in the purchasing and warehousing functions, with consequent reductions in these overhead costs.

In carrying out the purchasing responsibilities, the purchasing manager must continuously develop and maintain dependable sources of supply. The manager should be knowledgeable about the various suppliers' potentials and limitations. Alternative sources of supply must be encouraged and developed to cope with such problems as acquiring new sources when other suppliers fail to deliver, securing improved quality, and obtaining lower prices. The purchasing manager has the direct responsibility for knowing the current price situation and the probable future changes. All these responsibilities are best met when the purchasing manager can operate with definite policies and with realistic plans of future needs.

Control of materials and parts is facilitated in several ways by materials and parts budgeting. Having set definitive inventory policies and standards, management has taken the first step in inventory control. Reports comparing actual inventory levels with standard inventory levels, and actual unit material and part costs with the budgeted unit costs, facilitate **management by exception.** The purchases budget, approved by top management, constitutes approval for purchasing certain qualities and quantities of materials and parts at the planned cost. Taking into account significant variations of actual production requirements from the budget, the purchasing executive can proceed with the primary responsibility for purchasing materials and parts as planned. The purchasing manager will need to go to higher management only when unusual circumstances arise. For example, should an opportunity arise to purchase an unusually large quantity of material at a favorable price, the proposal would be submitted to higher management. The question, having been placed before top management, would also be considered by other managers, such as the finance executive and storage personnel, because their operations would be affected by the decision. Careful consideration of all factors affected by the special purchase action, rather than one based on the single factor of a lower unit price, would generally result in a better decision. It might be that problems in financing, warehousing, or other inventory risk factors offset the single advantage of a lower unit price. If materials and parts requirements are not known, as in cases where there is no profit plan, control of this type would be lacking and a large purchase at low prices might prove more costly because of warehousing, deterioration, obsolescence, inventory overstocking, and inadequate financing.

Internal performance reports on at least a monthly basis should be used to show by responsibility (1) material and part price variances, (2) material and part usage variances (including spoilage, waste, and abnormal scrap), and (3) inventory level variances from standards. To illustrate, the **two basic responsibilities** for materials and parts—purchasing and usage—may be included in monthly internal performance reports as follows:

1 Purchasing Function—the Purchasing Manager's Responsibility for Prices, Quantities Purchased, and Inventory Levels.

The internal report structure can vary considerably. The following simplified example suggests the key features.

☐ Assumption 1—January purchases budget for material A:

Units to be purchased	12,000
Planned unit cost	$1.20

☐ Assumption 2—Actual purchases during January:

Units	11,500
Actual unit cost	$1.26

The January performance report on the **purchasing function** should include the following:

Performance Report

DEPARTMENT	PURCHASING		MANAGER	B. M. KING	

	MONTH OF JANUARY, 19A				
				VARIANCE	
CONTROLLABLE ITEMS	MONTH ACTUAL	MONTH PLANNED	AMOUNT	PERCENT	
Material A:					
Units Purchased	11,500	12,000	500*	4*	
Unit Price	$1.26	$1.20	$ .06*	5*	
Cost	$14,490	$13,800†	$690.00	5*	
Inventory Turnover Ratio	2.7	2.5	0.2	8	
Part 102 (etc.)					
Department Expenses:					
(Detailed)					
Etc.					

* Unfavorable variance.
† Planned cost is actual units multiplied by the standard price (11,500 × $1.20 = $13,800).

This performance report shows the purchasing manager's responsibility for (1) quantities purchased versus planned purchases, (2) purchase price variance, (3) status of inventory turnover, and (4) control of purchasing department expenses. In some industries, purchasing performance also is measured by the quality of the items purchased. For example, a meat processor or a refinery will have high or low product quality depending on whether the materials used in production are inferior or not.

2   User Function—the Production Department Supervisor's Responsibility for Material and Part Usage.

Actual material and part usage by product, compared with standard material and part usage for the month and cumulative to date, should be reported in the performance reports for the responsibility center Department X as shown below.

☐ Assumption 1—Profit plan data for Manufacturing Department:

Units of product W to be manufactured in January	2,200
Units of material A required for each unit of product	2
Unit cost planned for material A (per prior example)	$1.20

☐ Assumption 2—Actual results in Producing Department X for January:

Units of product manufactured	2,000
Units of material A used	4,300
Price paid during January for each unit of Material A (per prior example)	$1.26

The January performance report on Producing Department X should be similar to this:

Performance Report

DEPT. PRODUCING DEPT. X		DEPT. MANAGER T. M. MOORE		
		MONTH OF JANUARY, 19A		
DEPARTMENTAL			VARIANCE	
CONTROLLABLE COSTS	ACTUAL	PLANNED	AMOUNT	PERCENT
Departmental Output	2,000	2,200	200*	9*
Material A:				
Units	4,300	4,000	300*	8*
Cost	$5,160	$4,800	$360*	8*
Etc.				
Direct labor				
Etc.				
Departmental overhead				
Etc.				

*Unfavorable.

Notice that the "actual" cost ($5,160) is based on the standard price per unit of $1.20 (as opposed to the actual price of $1.26), so that the departmental manager will not be accountable for the price variance because it is a responsibility of the purchasing manager. Notice also that the "Planned" column for Material A is based on actual output, that is 2,000 units

(2,000 × 2 × $1.20=$4,800). We must not compare an actual expenditure ($5,160 in this case) incurred in manufacturing 2,000 units with a budget amount based on the original planned volume of 2,200 units. Such a report would compare unlike items, and the resulting performance variance would not be appropriate. Performance reports and the analysis of cost variances are discussed more extensively in Chapters 15 and 16.

PLANNING INVENTORY LEVELS AND PURCHASING IN A NONMANUFACTUR-ING ENTERPRISE

Chapter 5 discussed sales planning in a nonmanufacturing enterprise. This section focuses on planning inventory levels and purchases for nonmanufacturing enterprises. After completion of the sales plan (see Exhibits 5-5 and 5-6 for Ready Department Store), three other plans (i.e., budgets) must be developed:

1 Inventory plan—the amount of merchandise that should be on hand at the beginning of the month (often abbreviated as BOM stock levels).

2 Purchases plan at retail prices—the amount of merchandise that should be purchased each month. This plan also shows the ending inventory (abbreviated as EOM stock levels).

3 Purchases at planned cost—the expenditures required to pay for the planned purchases of merchandise.

A distinctive feature of planning inventory levels and purchasing is that the plans are first developed in terms of **retail prices.** Next, there is a conversion from retail price to purchase cost. This means that since sales are planned at retail prices, the BOM stock levels are planned at retail. Because the BOM inventory for one month is the EOM inventory for the preceding month, planning focuses on sales and the BOM stock (inventory) level each month. Planning and controlling inventory levels are continuing and critical problems. When sales and stock requirements have been projected, purchase requirements can be computed as a residual quantity.

The principal factors to be considered in determining beginning-of-month (BOM) stock levels have been stated as follows:

1 Basic stock requirements, that is, the investment necessary to maintain adequate assortments of those items for which the demand is relatively stable.

2 Promotional merchandise needed to reach planned volume for the month.

3 Policy of the department: Is it to be a dominant policy so far as competition is concerned?

4 What is the relation of stock to sales? Does this relation ensure maximum turnover and at the same time afford complete stocks?

5 Outlook for prices.

PLANNING INVENTORY LEVELS

Retail and wholesale companies must plan the amount of inventory stock that should be on hand at the beginning of the month. BOM plus the planned inflow of goods during the month must be adequate to support planned sales. However, inventory must be kept at levels that minimize the risk of losses through style or seasonal changes, obsolescence, and excess capital tied up in inventory. The coordination of sales needs, purchases, and stock levels requires sound judgment in addition to analytical and computerized approaches. Nonmanufacturing companies often use **stock-sales ratios** to plan suitable stock levels. Two methods of computing the stock-sales ratio are as follows:

1 At retail price:

$$\frac{\text{Average inventory at retail}}{\text{Net sales}} = \text{Stock-sales ratio at retail}$$

2 At cost price:

$$\frac{\text{Average inventory at cost}}{\text{Cost of sales}} = \text{Stock-sales ratio at cost}$$

Usually, wholesale and retail companies base the computation on retail rather than on cost. Trade publications provide useful information on past industry averages for the stock-sales ratio.

To illustrate application of the BOM stock-sales ratio by Ready Department Store, assume that a BOM stock-sales of 2 for February is planned for the Women's Coats and Suits Department (Exhibit 5-6). Because planned sales for February are $8,100, the BOM planned stock level at the beginning of February would be $16,200 at retail. The planned February BOM for each department can be computed as shown in Exhibit 7-1. Stock levels and stock-sales ratios should be developed separately for each department and each type of merchandise.

PLANNING PURCHASES   The following formula is usually applied to compute the planned purchases **at retail value:**

Planned purchases (at retail value) = Planned net sales + Planned reductions
                                        + Planned EOM stock
                                        − Planned BOM stock

The logic of the formula is that purchases must be equivalent to sales, plus or minus changes in the inventory of goods on hand, assuming all goods are priced at retail. In addition, enough goods must be purchased to include all reductions in goods.

EXHIBIT 7-1

Computation of BOM Inventory Stock Levels
(By Department, for February only)
Ready Department Store

DEPARTMENT	PLANNED BOM STOCK SALES RATIO		PLANNED NET SALES (FEB.) (FROM EXHIBIT 5-6)		PLANNED FEB. BOM STOCK (AT RETAIL)
Women's Coats and Suits	2	×	$ 8,100	=	$ 16,200
Women's Dresses	3	×	29,700	=	89,100
Men's Furnishings	2.5	×	16,200	=	40,500
Draperies, Curtains, etc.	1.5	×	10,800	=	16,200
Other	3.5	×	25,200	=	88,200
Total	2.78 (average)		$90,000	=	$250,200

Reductions include (1) markdowns, (2) discounts given to employees, (3) discounts given to certain types of customers such as clergymen, and (4) inventory shortages due to theft and other causes. The formula can be further clarified by the following illustration:

ITEMS—PRICED AT RETAIL	CASE A	CASE B	CASE C
Planned sales	$10,000	$10,000	$10,000
Add planned reductions	—	1,000	1,000
Total	10,000	11,000	11,000
Add planned inventory (EOM stock)	—	—	5,000
Total	10,000	11,000	16,000
Less planned beginning inventory (BOM)	—	—	4,000
Purchase required at retail value	$10,000	$11,000	$12,000

The formula can be applied to a stock classification, to a department, or to an entire store. The planned purchases (priced at retail value) for February for the planned net sales shown in Exhibit 5-6 can be computed as shown in Exhibits 7-1 and 7-2. The reductions are not included in the sales budget; however, they must be included in purchases because goods lost or stolen must have been purchased.

Exhibit 7-2 shows **planned purchases computed at retail prices** only. However, the purchases must be planned **at cost.** This requires a **conversion** from retail prices to cost prices as shown in Exhibit 7-3. The last column shows the purchases budget at cost. The conversion of purchases at retail price to purchases at cost is made by multiplying the retail amount by the **cost multiplier,** which is the complement of the planned **initial markup** percentage on sales price (see the next section of the chapter).

EXHIBIT 7-2

Computation of Planned Purchases at Retail Price

(by Department, for February only)

Ready Department Store

	1	2	3	4	5
DEPARTMENT	PLANNED NET SALES (EXHIBIT 5-6)	PLANNED REDUCTIONS (GIVEN)	PLANNED EOM STOCK FOR FEB.* (GIVEN)	PLANNED BOM STOCK FOR FEB. (EXHIBIT 7-1)	PLANNED FEB PURCHASES (1 + 2 + 3 − 4)
Women's Coats and Suits	$ 8,100	$ 500	$ 16,200	$ 16,200	$ 8,600
Women's Dresses	29,700	2,000	87,100	89,100	29,700
Men's Furnishings	16,200	1,000	41,500	40,500	18,200
Draperies, Curtains, etc.	10,800	800	17,000	16,200	12,400
Other	25,200	1,200	86,000	88,200	24,200
Total	$90,000	$5,500	$247,800	$250,200	$93,100

*The EOM inventory each month (e.g., February) is the BOM inventory for the following month (e.g., March).

EXHIBIT 7-3

Conversion of Planned Purchases from Retail Prices to Cost Prices

(By Department, for February only)

Ready Department Store

DEPARTMENT	PLANNED PURCHASES (EXHIBIT 7-2) (AT RETAIL)	PLANNED INITIAL MARKUP ON SALES PRICE	COST MULTIPLIER	FEBRUARY PLANNED PURCHASES* (AT COST)
Women's Coats and Suit	$ 8,600	60%	40%	$ 3,440
Women's Dresses	29,700	70%	30%	8,910
Men's Furnishings	18,200	50%	50%	9,100
Draperies, Curtains, etc.	12,400	40%	60%	7,440
Other	24,200	50%	50%	12,100
Total	$93,100			$40,990

*The illustrative data were developed for only one month (February); the procedure would be identical for each month.

The planned purchases, at cost, are incorporated into the other budgets, such as the cash budget, in a manner similar to that illustrated for manufacturing costs in manufacturing companies.

Markup and Cost Multipliers Used in Retail Companies

The term **markup** refers to the difference between the cost and selling price of a commodity. Markup is variously expressed as a dollar amount or as a percentage of either (1) cost or (2) retail price. For example, if 100 items that cost $60 (total) were marked to sell for $100, the markup would be $40, or $.40 per unit. The markup as a **percentage** could be expressed in either of the following ways:

1   On cost $$\frac{\$40}{\$60} = 66\tfrac{2}{3}\%$$

2   On retail price $$\frac{\$40}{\$100} = 40\%$$

In nonmanufacturing enterprises, the distinction between **initial** markup and **maintained** or **realized** markup is important. This distinction is used for pricing, budgeting, and accounting purposes. **Initial markup** is the difference between the cost and the original or first retail price placed on goods. The initial markup amount in the above example was $40, or $.40 per unit. **Maintained markup** is the difference between cost and the actual sales price. If, in the example above, the 100 items were marked down from $100 to $90 and then sold, the maintained markup (also called the gross margin) would be $30, or $.30 per unit. The example can be summarized in this way:

	INITIAL MARKUP	MAINTAINED MARKUP (GROSS MARGIN)
Sales (100 units)	$100	$90
Cost of sales	60	60
Initial markup	$ 40 (40% on sales)	
Maintained markup		$30 (33 1/3% on sales)

The difference between initial markup and maintained markup is due to the effect of additional markups and reductions, which includes markdowns, discounts, and stock shortages.

In planning, careful consideration must be given to developing (1) the planned initial markup and (2) the planned maintained markup. The procedure can be illustrated by the following example:

Planned net sales	$5,000
Planned reductions	400
Total goods required at retail (before reductions)	$5,400
Planned maintained markup on net sales, 60%; that is, $5,000 × 60% =	$3,000

Question. What should be the planned initial markup on the goods required ($5,400 in this instance) to attain the 60 percent maintained markup planned ($3,000 in this instance)?

Response. The initial markup must be equal to the maintained markup of $3,000 plus the reductions of $400. Therefore, the initial markup percentage (on retail) must be[4]

$$\$3,400 \div \$5,400 = 62.9629\% \text{ on retail (or 170\% on cost)}$$

Verification:

Sales (gross retail value)	$5,400
Reductions	400
Net sales	5,000
Cost of goods sold $5,400 × (1.0 − .629629)	2,000
Maintained gross margin	$3,000
Maintained markup: $3,000 ÷ $5,000 = 60%	

MARKUP CONVERSION Although markups are usually based on retail price, when the goods arrive a markup on cost must be applied to attain the desired markup on retail. For example, an item that costs $.60 each must be marked up

---

[4] A shortcut approach that can be demonstrated algebraically for computing the required initial markup is

$$\frac{60\% + 8\%*}{100\% + 8\%} = 62.9629\%$$

$$*(\$400 \div \$5,000 = 8\%)$$

Also see the next section for conversion of the 62.9629% on retail to 170% on cost.

$66\frac{2}{3}$ percent **on cost** to sell at a price that will give 40 percent **on the retail price,** namely:

□   Case A—Markup based on cost price:

1. Cost	$.60	
2. Sales price ($.60 × $166\frac{2}{3}$%)		$1.00
3. Markup on cost ($.60 × $66\frac{2}{3}$%)		$.40

□   Case B—Markup based on sales price:

1. Sales price		$1.00
2. Markup on retail price ($1.00 × 40%)		$.40
3. Cost ($1.00 × 60%)	$.60	

Tables giving equated markup figures may be available, or they can be computed using an algebraic formula. However, a simple procedure can be used to convert from markup on retail to markup on cost, or vice versa. Notice the relationship between the two columns below:

	EQUATED MARKUP	
	MARKUP BASED ON RETAIL (RETAIL FRACTION ALWAYS SMALLER)	MARKUP BASED ON COST (COST FRACTION ALWAYS LARGER)
$\frac{1}{3}$ on retail	$\frac{1}{3}$ ($33\frac{1}{3}$%)	$\frac{1}{2}$ (50%)
40% on retail	$\frac{40}{100}$ (40%)	$\frac{40}{60}$ ($66\frac{2}{3}$%)
30% on retail	$\frac{30}{100}$ (30%)	$\frac{30}{70}$ (42.8%)
50% on retail	$\frac{50}{100}$ (50%)	$\frac{50}{50}$ (100%)

Conversion from the retail fraction to the cost fraction merely involves carrying over the numerator and taking the difference between the retail numerator and denominator for the cost denominator. Converting from the cost fraction to the retail fraction can be accomplished with the reverse procedure: The retail denominator is the sum of the cost numerator and denominator. The method is easily remembered when it is realized that the cost fraction must always be a larger fraction than the retail fraction.

Open-to-Buy Planning

Open-to-buy is a term generally used in nonmanufacturing enterprises to refer to that amount that a buyer can spend for goods during a specified time period. For example, if the cost of planned purchases for a particular department for the month is $2,000, open-to-buy is $2,000 before any purchases are made. If by the fifteenth the buyer has spent $1,200, the open-to-buy is $800.

Control of purchases is frequently attained by using open-to-buy reports. Computation of open-to-buy throughout a specific period can be a function of several factors. For example, assume the following data for Women's Coats and Suits (from Exhibit 7-2):

	AT RETAIL
Planned sales for February	$ 8,100
BOM inventory	16,200
Planned EOM inventory	16,200
Planned reductions for the month	500
Actual sales to date (February 20)	5,000
Actual reductions to date	300
Merchandise received to date (at retail)	6,000
Planned initial markup 40 percent on retail (i.e., $66\frac{2}{3}\%$ on cost)	

The open-to-buy at February 20 can be computed as follows:

NEEDED STOCK

Planned EOM inventory		$16,200
Planned sales for remainder of February:		
Planned sales for February	$ 8,100	
Less actual sales to February 20	5,000	3,100
Planned reductions for remainder of February		
Planned reductions for February	500	
Less actual reductions to February 20	300	200
Total stock needed		$19,500

AVAILABLE STOCK

Stock on hand at February 20			
BOM inventory	$16,200		
Goods received to February 20	6,000	$22,200	
Less:			
Actual reductions to February 20	300		
Actual sales to February 20	5,000	5,300	$16,900
Stock on order for February delivery			2,000
Total			$18,900
Open-to-buy at retail (on February 20)			600
Cost multiplier (100% − 40%)			60%
Open-to-buy at cost (on February 20)			$ 360

If available stock were in excess of needed stock, the department would be "overbought."

Up to this point we have discussed the primary issues involved in developing the **merchandise budget.** Its development has been illustrated (for Ready Department Store) as follows:

PLAN	EXHIBIT NUMBER	BASIC MANAGEMENT (DECISIONAL) INPUTS
Sales Plan by Month	5-5	1. Projection of total company sales—dollars
		2. Projected seasonal sales cycle—percentages
Sales Plan by Department	5-6	3. Projected departmental share of total sales by month—percentages
Inventory Plan (BOM)	7-1	4. Planned BOM stock/sales—ratios
Purchases Budget (at retail)	7-2	5. Planned reductions by department—dollars or percentage
Purchases Budget (at cost)	7-3	6. Planned initial markups on retail—percentages

Planning the expenses in nonmanufacturing enterprises is discussed in Chapters 9 and 10.

CHAPTER SUMMARY   A comprehensive profit planning and control program includes planning and controlling the raw materials and component parts used in the production process. To implement this planning and control objective, budgets are prepared for materials and parts needs, materials and parts purchases, and desired inventory levels. In developing these budgets, recognition must be given to management's production and procurement strategies. For example, in companies where material requirements planning (MRP) systems or just-in-time (JIT) purchasing strategies are used, the materials and parts budgets must reflect these approaches to conducting operations.

To control material and part costs, the internal performance reports, prepared at least on a monthly basis, can be used to identify usage and price variances and variations between actual and planned inventory levels.

Nonmanufacturing enterprises also make use of materials budgets. Service companies, such as airlines, budget for fuel, in-flight food, and repair parts. Retail enterprises develop detailed budgets for purchasing and inventorying merchandise. Nonprofit organizations also make heavy use of materials budgeting. In hospitals, for example, budgets for medication, linen, and housekeeping supplies are important in controlling costs.

Comprehensive Demonstration Case

SUPERIOR MANUFACTURING COMPANY

This section illustrates the four budgets discussed in this chapter. They are used for planning materials and parts by Superior Manufacturing Company. Refer to the sales plan illustrated Chapter 5, Schedule 21, and the production plan at the end of Chapter 6, Schedule 22, to review the continuity in planning.

Superior Manufacturing Company uses three raw materials—A, B, and C—in producing the two products X and Y. The flow of these two products through the factory is shown in Exhibit 7-4. Notice that product X passes through the three producing departments, whereas product Y passes through producing departments 1 and 3 only.

Exhibit 7-4 gives the following standard material usage rates per unit of finished goods:

	UNITS OF RAW MATERIAL REQUIRED FOR EACH UNIT OF PRODUCT		
PRODUCT:	MATERIAL A	MATERIAL B	MATERIAL C
X	1 (in Dept. 1)	2 (in Dept. 2)	2 (in Dept. 3)
Y	1 (in Dept. 1)	1 (in Dept. 3)	

EXHIBIT 7-4

Raw Material and Product Flows, Superior Manufacturing Company

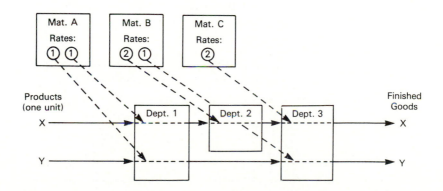

Materials planning by Superior Manufacturing Company includes four subbudgets and nine schedules as follows:

A. *Materials and Parts Budget:*
   Sch. 24—Units of raw material required by products and by time periods
   Sch. 25—Units of raw material required by products and by responsibility centers (e.g., departments)
   Sch. 3—Materials and parts budget summary
B. *Materials and Parts Purchases Budget:*
   Sch. 26—Purchases budget, detailed
   Sch. 4—Purchases budget, summary
C. *Materials and Parts Inventory Budget:*
   Sch. 27—Raw materials inventory budget
   Sch. 8— Schedule of beginning and ending inventories
D. *Cost of Materials and Parts Used Budget:*
   Sch. 28—Cost of materials used for production, detailed
   Sch. 29—Cost of materials used for production, summary

MATERIALS AND PARTS BUDGET The quantities (units) shown in the three schedules (24, 25, and 3) were computed by multiplying the production requirements from the production budget by the raw material usage rates given in Exhibit 7-4. The usage rate are included in these schedules for instructional purposes. The classification of raw material by department in Schedule 25 is significant because control of raw material usage is the responsibility of managers of the responsibility centers. Classification by products in Schedule 24 is important primarily for product-costing purposes.

The materials budget shows both the quantities and the timing of raw materials needed by the factory for specific production. The timing of raw material needs is important in developing the purchases budget and in actual purchasing activities.

PURCHASES AND INVENTORY BUDGETS The purchasing manager provided the following decisional inputs for the budget:

Unit Raw Material Price (Net of Purchase Discount)
For the Year Ending December 31, 19X2

RAW MATERIAL	UNIT PRICE
A	$.30
B	.20
C	.25

Beginning Inventories (January 1, 19X2)

RAW MATERIAL	UNITS	UNIT PRICE
A	220,000	$.30
B	360,000	.20
C	460,000	.26

Notice that for material C there is a different unit price for the beginning inventory and purchases; therefore, it is necessary to know the inventory flow method used by the cost accounting department. For raw materials, Superior Manufacturing Company uses first-in, first-out (FIFO). The actual beginning inventory of raw materials will not be known when the purchases budget is prepared. The inventory given above represents either (1) values taken from the previous budget or (2) estimates of actual ending inventory levels (for December 31, 19X1), based on actual levels and prices at the budget preparation date, adjusted for changes expected during the remainder of the current year.

Based on the input data above, and additional quantity data from the materials budget, the purchases budget was constructed as illustrated in Schedule 26. Purchases are shown in units and dollars by type of raw material and by interim periods.

The purchases budget illustrated is a spreadsheet rather than an appropriate format for inclusion in the formal profit plan. Notice that computation of the purchases budget requires that the interim raw material inventory levels be determined. The purchases budget, as illustrated, does not indicate dollar valuations. Although the schedule could be designed to show this information, it is usually preferable to set up separate inventory valuation schedules. The raw material inventory budget for Superior Manufacturing Company, showing inventory quantities and valuations by type of raw material by component time periods, is shown in Schedule 27.

COST OF MATERIALS AND PARTS USED BUDGET   The final step in planning raw materials is to prepare a budget schedule indicating the cost of raw materials used for production. This procedure is detailed for Superior Manufacturing Company in Schedule 28. The units agree with the materials budget and the dollar unit cost from the purchases budget. The schedule is designed primarily to show the cost of materials used by time period for each type of finished product. This schedule is used to prepare the total budgeted cost of manufacturing each product for each time period throughout the budget year (as shown in Chapter 13, Schedule 58). The estimated cost of materials used is summarized in Schedule 29.

SCHEDULE 24. Superior Manufacturing Company

Materials Budget—Unit Requirements for Raw Materials
By Material, Product, and Time Periods
For the Year Ending December 31, 19X2

REF.	PRODUCT X PRODUCTION PLANNED 22	UNIT USAGE (GIVEN)	RAW MATERIAL REQUIRED (UNITS)	PRODUCT Y PRODUCTION PLANNED 22	UNIT USAGE (GIVEN)	RAW MATERIAL REQUIRED (UNITS)	TOTAL RAW MATERIAL REQUIRED (UNITS)
Material A							
January	70,000	1	70,000	34,000	1	34,000	104,000
February	80,000	1	80,000	36,000	1	36,000	116,000
March	80,000	1	80,000	38,000	1	38,000	118,000
Total First Quarter	230,000	1	230,000	108,000	1	108,000	338,000
Second Quarter	240,000	1	240,000	140,000	1	140,000	380,000
Third Quarter	230,000	1	230,000	127,000	1	127,000	357,000
Fourth Quarter	260,000	1	260,000	145,000	1	145,000	405,000
Total	960,000	1	960,000	520,000	1	520,000	1,480,000
Material B							
January	70,000	2	140,000	34,000	1	34,000	174,000
February	80,000	2	160,000	36,000	1	36,000	196,000
March	80,000	2	160,000	38,000	1	38,000	198,000
Total First Quarter	230,000	2	460,000	108,000	1	108,000	568,000
Second Quarter	240,000	2	480,000	140,000	1	140,000	620,000
Third Quarter	230,000	2	460,000	127,000	1	127,000	587,000
Fourth Quarter	260,000	2	520,000	145,000	1	145,000	665,000
Total	960,000	2	1,920,000	520,000	1	520,000	2,440,000
Material C							
January	70,000	2	140,000				140,000
February	80,000	2	160,000				160,000
March	80,000	2	160,000				160,000
Total First Quarter	230,000	2	460,000				460,000
Second Quarter	240,000	2	480,000				480,000
Third Quarter	230,000	2	460,000				460,000
Fourth Quarter	260,000	2	520,000				520,000
Total	960,000	2	1,920,000				1,920,000

SCHEDULE 25. Superior Manufacturing Company

Materials Budget—Unit Requirements for Raw Materials*
By Product, Department and Time
For the Year Ending December 31, 19X2

	STANDARD MATERIAL RATES	REF.	RAW MATERIAL UNIT REQUIREMENTS							
			JAN.	FEB.	MARCH	1ST QTR.	2ND QTR.	3RD QTR.	4TH QTR.	TOTALS
		(GIVEN)								
Product X										
Scheduled Production in Units		22	70,000	80,000	80,000	230,000	240,000	230,000	260,000	960,000
Raw Material Requirements										
A used in Department 1	1		70,000	80,000	80,000	230,000	240,000	230,000	260,000	960,000
B used in Department 2	2		140,000	160,000	160,000	460,000	480,000	460,000	520,000	1,920,000
C used in Department 3	2		140,000	160,000	160,000	460,000	480,000	460,000	520,000	1,920,000
Product Y										
Scheduled Production in Units		22	34,000	36,000	38,000	108,000	140,000	127,000	145,000	520,000
Raw Material Requirements										
A used in Department 1	1		34,000	36,000	38,000	108,000	140,000	127,000	145,000	520,000
B used in Department 3	1		34,000	36,000	38,000	108,000	140,000	127,000	145,000	520,000
Total Material Requirements										
Department 1 Material A			104,000	116,000	118,000	338,000	380,000	357,000	405,000	1,480,000
Department 2 Material B			140,000	160,000	160,000	460,000	480,000	460,000	520,000	1,920,000
Department 3 Material B			34,000	36,000	38,000	108,000	140,000	127,000	145,000	520,000
Department 3 Material C			140,000	160,000	160,000	460,000	480,000	460,000	520,000	1,920,000

*See Schedule 3 for summary.

SCHEDULE 26. Superior Manufacturing Company

Purchases Budget
For the Year Ending December 31, 19X2

	REF.	UNITS REQUIRED FOR PROD.	ADD ENDING INVENTORY	TOTAL UNITS REQUIRED	LESS BEGINNING INVENTORY	PURCHASES UNITS	PURCHASES UNIT COST	TOTAL COST
		24	(GIVEN)		(GIVEN)		(GIVEN)	
Raw Material A								
January		104,000	208,000	312,000	220,000	92,000	$0.30	$ 27,600
February		116,000	232,000	348,000	208,000	140,000		42,000
March		118,000	240,000	358,000	232,000	126,000		37,800
1st Quarter		338,000	240,000	578,000	220,000	358,000		107,400
2nd Quarter		380,000	260,000	640,000	240,000	400,000		120,000
3rd Quarter		357,000	227,000	584,000	260,000	324,000		97,200
4th Quarter		405,000	245,000	650,000	227,000	423,000		126,900
Total		1,480,000	245,000	1,725,000	220,000	1,505,000		$ 451,500
Raw Material B								
January		174,000	350,000	524,000	360,000	164,000	$0.20	$ 32,800
February		196,000	380,000	576,000	350,000	226,000		45,200
March		198,000	400,000	598,000	380,000	218,000		43,600
1st Quarter		568,000	400,000	968,000	360,000	608,000		121,600
2nd Quarter		620,000	420,000	1,040,000	400,000	640,000		128,000
3rd Quarter		587,000	400,000	987,000	420,000	567,000		113,400
4th Quarter		665,000	370,000	1,035,000	400,000	635,000		127,000
Total		2,440,000	370,000	2,810,000	360,000	2,450,000		$ 490,000
Raw Material C								
January		140,000	470,000	610,000	460,000	150,000	$0.25	$ 37,500
February		160,000	480,000	640,000	470,000	170,000		42,500
March		160,000	470,000	630,000	480,000	150,000		37,500
1st Quarter		460,000	470,000	930,000	460,000	470,000		117,500
2nd Quarter		480,000	490,000	970,000	470,000	500,000		125,000
3rd Quarter		460,000	475,000	935,000	490,000	445,000		111,250
4th Quarter		520,000	450,000	970,000	475,000	495,000		123,750
Total		1,920,000	450,000	2,370,000	460,000	1,910,000		$ 477,500
								$1,419,000

SCHEDULE 27. Superior Manufacturing Company

Raw Material Inventory Budget
In Units and Dollars
For the Year Ending December 31, 19X2

	REF.	MATERIAL A ($.30 PER UNIT)		MATERIAL B ($.20 PER UNIT)		MATERIAL C (SEE FOOTNOTES)		TOTAL MATERIALS INVENTORY
		UNITS	AMOUNT	UNITS	AMOUNT	UNITS	AMOUNT	
		26		26		26		
Beginning Inventories								
January		220,000	$66,000	360,000	$72,000	460,000	$119,600[a]	$257,600
February		208,000	62,400	350,000	70,000	470,000	120,700[b]	253,100
March		232,000	69,600	380,000	76,000	480,000	121,600[c]	267,200
2nd Quarter		240,000	72,000	400,000	80,000	470,000	117,500[d]	269,500
3rd Quarter		260,000	78,000	420,000	84,000	490,000	122,500	284,500
4th Quarter		227,000	68,100	400,000	80,000	475,000	118,750	266,850
Ending Inventory		245,000	73,500	370,000	74,000	450,000	112,500	260,000

[a] $.26 per unit.
[b] 320,000 units at $.26; 150,000 units at $.25.
[c] 160,000 units at $.26; 320,000 units at $.25.
[d] All other units at $.25.

SCHEDULE 28. Superior Manufacturing Company

Estimated Cost of Materials Used for Production—Detailed
For the Year Ending December 31, 19X2

PERIOD AND MATERIAL	REF.	PRODUCT X UNITS REQUIRED 25	PRODUCT X UNIT PRICE (GIVEN)	PRODUCT X AMOUNT	PRODUCT Y UNITS REQUIRED 25	PRODUCT Y UNIT PRICE (GIVEN)	PRODUCT Y AMOUNT	TOTALS UNITS 25	TOTALS AMOUNT
January									
A		70,000	$.30	$ 21,000	34,000	$.30	$ 10,200	104,000	$ 31,200
B		140,000	.20	28,000	34,000	.20	6,800	174,000	34,800
C		140,000	.26	36,400				140,000	36,400
Total				$ 85,400			$ 17,000		$ 102,400
February									
A		80,000	$.30	$ 24,000	36,000	$.30	$ 10,800	116,000	$ 34,800
B		160,000	.20	32,000	36,000	.20	7,200	196,000	39,200
C		160,000	.26	41,600				160,000	$ 41,600
Total				$ 97,600			$ 18,000		$ 115,600
March									
A		80,000	$.30	$ 24,000	38,000	$.30	$ 11,400	118,000	$ 35,400
B		160,000	.20	32,000	38,000	.20	7,600	198,000	39,600
C		160,000	.26	41,600				160,000	41,600
Total				$ 97,600			$ 19,000		$ 116,600
1st Quarter									
A		230,000	$.30	$ 69,000	108,000	$.30	$ 32,400	338,000	$ 101,400
B		460,000	.20	92,000	108,000	.20	21,600	568,000	113,600
C		460,000	.26	119,600				460,000	119,600
Total				$ 280,600			$ 54,000		$ 334,600
2nd Quarter									
A		240,000	$.30	$ 72,000	140,000	$.30	$ 42,000	380,000	$ 114,000
B		480,000	.20	96,000	140,000	.20	28,000	620,000	124,000
C		480,000	.25	120,000				480,000	120,000
Total				$ 288,000			$ 70,000		$ 358,000
3rd Quarter									
A		230,000	$.30	$ 69,000	127,000	$.30	$ 38,100	357,000	$ 107,100
B		460,000	.20	92,000	127,000	.20	25,400	587,000	117,400
C		460,000	.25	115,000				460,000	115,000
Total				$ 276,000			$ 63,500		$ 339,500
4th Quarter									
A		260,000	$.30	$ 78,000	145,000	$.30	$ 43,500	405,000	$ 121,500
B		520,000	.20	104,000	145,000	.20	29,000	665,000	133,000
C		520,000	.25	130,000				520,000	130,000
Total				$ 312,000			$ 72,500		$ 384,500
Total for Year				$1,156,600			$260,000		$1,416,600

SCHEDULE 29. Superior Manufacturing Company

Estimated Cost of Materials Used for Production—Summary
For the Year Ending December 31, 19X2

	REF.	TOTALS			PRODUCT X			PRODUCT Y		
		UNITS 3	AMOUNT		UNITS 3	PRICE (GIVEN)	AMOUNT	UNITS 3	PRICE (GIVEN)	AMOUNT
Materials										
A		1,480,000	$ 444,000		960,000	$.30	$ 288,000	520,000	$.30	$156,000
B		2,440,000	$ 488,000		1,920,000	.20	384,000	520,000	.20	104,000
C		1,920,000	484,600		1,920,000	*	484,600			
	28		$1,416,600				$1,156,600			$260,000

*460,000 units @$.26; balance @$.25

Suggested References

McClain, John and L. Joseph Thomas, *Operations Management.* Englewood Cliffs, N.J.: Prentice-Hall, 1985.

Seglund, R., and S. Ibarreche, "Just-in-Time: The Accounting Implications," *Management Accounting,* August 1984 pp. 43–45.

Swartley-Loush, J. "Just-in-Time: Is It Right for You?" *Production Engineering,* June 1985, pp. 61–64.

Discussion Questions

1. Which principal budgets are usually needed in planning for materials and parts? Briefly explain each.
2. Identify who should be responsible for developing each of the several budgets related to planning materials and parts.
3. Distinguish between direct materials and parts, indirect materials, and supplies. How does this classification affect profit planning and control?
4. Why is it important to plan materials and parts quantity requirements?
5. What are the main approaches used to develop materials and parts usage rates?
6. What is the relationship between the materials and parts budget, the purchases budget, and the materials and parts inventory budget?
7. In establishing inventory policies, what overriding factors should management consider?
8. Explain the concepts of economic order quantity and the reorder point.
9. Who should be assigned the responsibility for providing the data input about materials and parts unit costs? How should these estimates generally be developed?
10. To control materials and parts, there are two basic responsibilities. List the two responsibilities, and explain the profit planning and control approach to resolving each.
11. How are "representative products" used in budgeting materials and parts when there are large numbers of products?
12. Assume the following budget data are available for a particular department of X Department Store: sales, $70,000; EOM stock, $120,000; planned reductions, $3,000; BOM stock, $140,000; planned initial markup on sales price, 40 percent. Compute the amount of goods that should be purchased (1) at retail value and (2) at cost. Explain the logic of the formula that you utilize.
13. Define reductions. Why must they be considered in computing purchases?
14. Distinguish between (a) initial markup and (b) maintained markup.
15. An item that cost $70 is marked to sell for $100. What is the markup (a) on retail and (b) on cost?

CASE 7-1   *Planning for special problems related to raw materials*

Sunbelt Processors, Inc., a medium-size manufacturer, distributes its products nationwide. The company produces three products that are sold through wholesale channels to other manufacturers. The products sold reflect a moderate seasonality; however, the seasons tend to offset each other so that company production is essentially stable during the year. The company is initiating a profit planning and control program. Top management has decided to use a long-range plan extending four years into the future beyond the upcoming year. This long-term plan will be reevaluated annually. An annual profit plan for the upcoming year is currently being developed. In view of the relative stability of production, the plan will be disaggregated by month for the entire year during its initial preparation.

In analyzing the use of each raw material and the purchasing activities of the past year, the case writer noted the following:

(a) Manufacturing operations occur in seven processing departments. There are also three service departments in the factory. In manufacturing the three products, twelve different raw materials are used in varying quantities; however, no single product requires all twelve of the raw materials. One raw material that is used primarily in one of the products is also used as "indirect materials" in four of the processing departments. Indirect material usage of this raw material approximates one-third of the total volume purchased. It is unrealistic to try to identify the usage of this particular raw material with the several products; therefore, it is classified as an indirect material (with the exception of the one product mentioned).

(b) Several of the raw material suppliers give quantity discounts. That is, when a purchase order exceeds a certain stated level, a quantity discount (5 percent) is given to the purchaser. During the past year, approximately two-thirds of the purchases of these particular raw materials involved orders large enough to qualify for the quantity discount.

(c) Some of the raw materials are purchased at a relatively uniform level throughout the year. However, some of the other raw materials are purchased on a highly seasonal basis. The seasonality is primarily the result of availability of those raw materials. They tend to have a lower unit cost when the supply is high. In some cases, perishability creates high storage costs.

(d) One raw material, purchased in large quantities, is obtained from one supplier only. Other suppliers in the market are at some distance, which causes a relatively high freight differential cost.

(e) The length of time between the date of an order and the delivery date of the raw material varies widely across the twelve raw materials. For example, the shortest delivery time on one raw material is approximately five days, and the longest time is thirty-eight days. The average delivery time for all raw materials is approximately fifteen days.

(f) Some raw materials have a high unit cost (highest, $21), whereas others have a relatively low unit cost (lowest, $1.20).

(g) Usage rates vary widely for the twelve raw materials. For example, the raw material that has the highest utilization requires approximately twelve times the amount of raw material that has the lowest utilization.

Procedures for planning raw materials are under consideration by the management. The sales plan and the production plan have been tentatively agreed upon as being realistic. The production plan gives the number of units of each of the three products to be produced each month throughout the budget year.

REQUIRED

1. Describe the approach that you would recommend for planning raw materials in this company. You should include recommendations about the subbudgets required, basic classifications of data, and responsibilities for budget inputs.

2. Give recommendations, with support, for the planning approach that should be used for each of the special problems associated with the raw materials activity mentioned above.

CASE 7-2 *Prepare a planning schedule for raw materials; prepare a purchases budget*

Nile Company is a medium-size manufacturer of several lines of products that are sold to other manufacturers. The company uses three raw materials, designated materials X, Y, and Z. Raw materials constitute the largest item of cost in the manufacturing process. The profit planning and control program has been in operation one year and is being improved and adapted to new problems as they arise. An annual profit plan is developed and disaggregated by month for the year, and the long-range plan has a three-year time horizon. The manufacturing activities are in five producing departments. There are four service departments. Production is under the general supervision of the factory manager; the purchasing manager and the supervisors of the nine departments in the factory report to the factory executive (VP).

According to the factory executive, "the control of raw materials in this company has not been effective in the profit planning and control program." To concentrate on this problem, this case is limited to one producing department (Department 1), one raw material (raw material X), and one finished product (product B). The following standards have been tentatively established for the annual profit plan:

a. Planned production of product B:

TIME PERIOD	UNITS
January	10,000
February	12,000
March	14,000
2nd Quarter	42,000
3rd Quarter	35,000
4th Quarter	30,000

b. Usage rates for raw materials:

PRODUCT AND RAW MATERIAL	STANDARD USAGE RATE
Product B:	
Material X	3
Etc.	

c. Planned purchase price per unit of raw material:

PERIOD	UNIT COST FOR MATERIAL X
January	$5.00
February	5.50
March	5.50
2nd Quarter	6.00
3rd Quarter	6.00
4th Quarter	5.00

d. The inventory policy specifies that the beginning inventory for raw material X for each month shall be equal to one-half the planned monthly withdrawals for that period. Economic lot quantities and reorder points have been computed.

e. The first month of the year covered by the annual profit plan (January) has just ended, and the performance reports covering January are being prepared. The budget manager and the factory manager are redesigning the performance report structure for raw materials because the prior performance reports have not been useful.

f. Actual results for January:
   (1) Production of product B—10,500 units
   (2) Units of raw material X purchased—30,000
   (3) Unit price paid for raw material X—$5.20
   (4) Units of raw material X used—31,610

REQUIRED

1. Prepare a planning schedule that shows the "required units of raw material X for product B." This planning budget should be viewed as one part of the annual profit plan; specifically, it should be part of the materials budget.

2. Prepare the purchases budget through March for raw material X.

3. Design your recommended performance reports that will show the effectiveness with which raw materials were controlled during January. Use the data in the case to give the appropriate amounts in your recommended performance reports.

4. Explain and justify your recommendations about the performance reports that you developed in requirement 3.

CASE 7-3   *Materials budget and economic order size*

Bacon Manufacturing Company uses a special dry-cell battery as a component part in its manufacturing process. Four batteries are used for each unit of finished product. The annual profit plan is disaggregated by quarters. The production plan specified the following output: 1st Quarter, 31,500; 2nd Quarter, 32,750; 3rd Quarter, 16,750; and 4th Quarter, 19,000.

The replenishment time for this part averages seven days, and unusual demands from the factory and variations in replenishment time suggest the need for a three-day safety stock. Average cost to place an order is $11.00, and the carrying cost is estimated to be $.03 per unit in inventory. Throughout each quarter, production is relatively stable. Unit purchase price planned is $.30.

REQUIRED

1. Prepare the materials budget.
2. Calculate the reorder point and safety stock.
3. Calculate the economic lot size.

CASE 7-4   Should the company make or buy a component part?

Stoner Company uses three different component parts (materials) in manufacturing its primary product. Stoner manufactures two of the parts (designated parts 2 and 3) and purchases one (designated part 1) from outside suppliers. The company is currently developing the annual profit plan. Sales are highly seasonal. Part 2 cannot be acquired from outsiders; however, part 3 can be purchased. The three parts have critical specifications. The annual profit plan provided data for the following computations:

ITEM	PART 3 UNIT COST (AT 12,000 UNITS)
Material (direct)	$1.40
Labor (direct)	2.20
Fixed overhead allocated	.40
Annual machinery rental (special machines used only for component 3)	.50
Variable factory overhead	1.00
Average storage cost per year	.40
Total	$5.90
Average inventory level, 500 units	

In view of the $5.90 unit cost, the purchasing manager contacted outside suppliers and found one that would sign a one-year contract to deliver "12,000 top-quality units as needed during the year at $5.20 per unit." Serious consideration is being given to this alternative.

REQUIRED

1. Should Stoner make or buy part 3?
2. Explain the relevant factors influencing your decision.

CASE 7-5   *Making some tough decisions about raw materials*

Barker Company uses two major raw materials in manufacturing one primary product. The company is developing the purchases and materials budgets. For the past three years, the company developed a sales plan and has recently decided to extend budgeting to all phases of operations.

This case focuses on budgeting raw materials. The following budget data for 19A have been developed.

	MATERIAL T			MATERIAL U		
	UNITS REQUIRED FOR PRODUCTION (BUDGETED)	DAYS RE-QUIRED FOR DELIVERY (AVER-AGE)	UNIT PRICE LAST YEAR	UNITS REQUIRED FOR PRODUCTION (BUDGETED)	DAYS RE-QUIRED FOR DELIVERY (AVER-AGE)	UNIT PRICE LAST YEAR
19A						
January	3,500	14	$8.50	12,250	8	$3.00
February	4,000	14	8.50	14,000	7	3.10
March	4,500	18	9.20	15,750	6	3.10
2nd Quarter	14,000	18	9.30	49,000	6	3.20
3rd Quarter	11,000	10	8.60	38,500	5	3.30
4th Quarter	8,000	7	8.10	28,000	5	3.50
19B						
January	3,300	14	—	12,000	8	—

The purchasing manager is currently developing the purchases budget. Five problems exist about which the purchasing manager has asked for your advice; they are as follows:

(a) In view of the increasing price of material U and a consequent increase in the sales price of the finished product, it has been proposed that a lower quality of material be used. It is estimated that this step would reduce the unit cost of material U by 15 percent.

(b) The purchasing manager believes that an average price for the year should be used for planning purposes because "it is only a guess anyway. I have no control over the price." The chief accountant believes that the price for each interim period should be used because "we use FIFO in accounting for raw materials, and an average price would produce meaningless variations, particularly in view of the fluctuating price of the raw materials."

(c) The freight charge is a problem—should the unit price be budgeted before or after the freight charge? Experience has shown that freight charges on material T average about 5 percent of the cost, whereas freight charges on material U average about 10 percent. The problem is complicated by the fact that the freight charges are paid upon delivery of the materials, whereas the materials are paid for at the end of the discount period.

(d) The cash discounts allowed on material T average 3 percent, whereas there are no cash discounts allowed on material U. During the past year, Barker received discounts on approximately half the purchases of material T. The purchasing manager is concerned about the approach to use for planning cash discounts.

(e) The management has determined that the beginning inventory of material T each period should be equal to the projected usage for the period, and for raw material U, half the projected usage. They are now concerned about the safety stock level for each raw material.

REQUIRED

1. What are your recommendations with respect to each of these problems? Justify your recommendations.

2. Apply the inventory policy already established and your recommended safety stock levels and other data to develop a schedule for product T that shows for each period only the following: (1) units to be purchased and (2) order dates.

CASE 7-6   *Format and prepare budgets for materials, purchases, inventory, and production cost*

Upstate Products Company manufactures two products, S and P. There are two manufacturing departments. Product P is processed through both departments, whereas product S is processed through Department 1 only. Raw material A is used in Department 1 for both products, and raw material B is used in Department 2 only. A profit plan is prepared on an annual basis. To simplify the case for instructional purposes, data are given for only one quarter. Budget estimates developed to date include the following:

(a) Production budget (units)

PRODUCT	JANUARY	FEBRUARY	MARCH
S	5,000	6,000	7,000
P	8,000	9,000	10,000

(b) Estimated beginning inventories:

Material A— 70,000 units at $3.00 per unit
Material B—120,000 units at $2.20 per unit

(c)   Budget material prices (for purchases):

Material A—$3.00
Material B—$2.00

(d)   Raw material requirements for finished goods:

PRODUCT	MATERIAL A	MATERIAL B
S	5	0
P	6	7

(e)   Ending raw material inventories planned:

Material A—January and February, 70,000; March, 80,000
Material B—To remain constant at 120,000

REQUIRED

Prepare appropriate quarterly profit plan budgets as follows:

1. Materials, by product, and material, by time
2. Purchases, by material and time
3. Raw materials inventory, by material and time (use FIFO)
4. Cost of raw materials used, by department, product, material, and time period

Be prepared to justify your particular formats.

CASE 7-7   *Prepare the purchases budget, and compute BOM, EOM, and markups*

This case from Swift Department Store is a continuation from Chapter 5, Case 5-9. All the data given here are the same as those in Case 5-9. Additional data are as follows:

a   Planned BOM stock ratios for August are: Jewelry, 3.9; Men's Furnishings, 4.8; Women's and Misses' Coats and Dresses, 2.0; and Miscellaneous, 3.1

b   Planned reductions for August are: Jewelry, $700; Men's Furnishings, $2,500; Women's and Misses' Dresses, $3,600; and Miscellaneous, $100

c   Planned BOM stock ratios for September are: Jewelry, 3.6; Men's Furnishings, 4.6; Women's and Misses' Coats and Dresses, 2.0; and Miscellaneous, 3.0

d   Planned initial markups on retail are: Jewelry, 45 percent; Men's Furnishings, 40 percent; Women's and Misses' Coats and Dresses, 40 percent; and Miscellaneous, 50 percent

e Planned sales for August 19XX, from the sales budget developed in Case 5-9, requirement 2 (before deductions):

	PLANNED SALES	
DEPARTMENT	AUGUST	SEPTEMBER*
Jewelry	$ 9,360	$ 11,446
Men's Furnishings	31,734	32,121
Women's & Misses Coats and Dresses	53,136	76,752
Miscellaneous	3,267	4,401
Total	$97,497	$124,720

*Needed to compute August EOM.

REQUIRED

1. Compute the planned August BOM stock levels for each department.
2. Prepare the budget schedule for August purchases at retail and cost. This can be one or two schedules, as you prefer.
3. Compute the budgeted maintained markup by department (per budget).
4. Prepare a list of managerial "decisional inputs" to the above plans identified by requirements.

CASE 7-8   *At issue—initial markup and maintained markup*

Budget goals for Department A (Men's Furnishings) for the period are as follows (assume no inventory change):

Planned sales	$10,000
Planned markdowns	100
Planned discounts	400
Planned stock shortage	200

REQUIRED

1. Compute the planned initial markup percentage that should be planned to attain a planned gross margin of 55 percent on sales.
2. Compute the resulting planned gross margin percentage assuming a planned initial markup of 60 percent.

CASE 7-9   *What is the company's open-to-buy status?*

The following data are for Department X and Y of Tex Department Store. The planning period is March 1 through March 15.

ITEMS	DEPARTMENT X	DEPARTMENT Y
Planned sales for the month	$25,000	$ 7,000
Actual sales to date	11,000	3,700
BOM inventory	55,000	18,000
EOM inventory	58,000	17,000
Merchandise received to date	16,000	4,500
Merchandise ordered for March delivery	6,000	2,500
Planned reductions	2,000	400
Actual reductions to date	800	300
Planned initial markup	30%	35%

REQUIRED

Compute the open-to-buy amount as of March 15 for each department.

Planning and Controlling Direct Labor Costs

8

INTRODUCTION AND PURPOSE In some companies, labor costs are greater than all other costs combined. Even when this is not the case, effective planning and systematic control of labor costs are essential. Planning and controlling labor costs involve major and complex problem areas: (1) personnel needs, (2) recruitment, (3) training, (4) job description and evaluation, (5) performance measurement, (6) union negotiations, and (7) wage and salary administration. Each of these problems may dominate in various situations. A comprehensive profit planning and control program should incorporate appropriate approaches applicable to each problem area. A profit planning and control program cannot resolve special personnel problems, but it directs careful consideration to them and aids in placing them in perspective. Effective planning and control of long-term and short-term labor costs will benefit both the company and its employees.

Labor costs include all expenditures for employees: top executives, middle-management personnel, staff officers, supervisors, and skilled and unskilled employees. To plan and control labor costs effectively, the different types of labor costs must be separately considered. This chapter discusses only one type of labor cost, **direct labor.**

Labor generally is classified as direct or indirect. Direct labor costs include the wages paid to employees who work directly on specific productive output. As with direct material costs, labor costs that can be directly traced to specific production are defined as direct. Indirect labor involves all other labor costs, such as supervisory salaries and wages paid to toolmakers, repair personnel, storekeepers, and custodians. Direct material and direct labor costs are frequently referred to collectively as the prime costs of product.

The direct labor budget includes the planned direct labor requirements necessary to produce the types and quantities of outputs planned in the production budget. Although some companies prepare a labor budget that includes both direct and indirect labor, it is usually preferable to prepare a separate direct labor budget and to include indirect labor in the factory overhead budgets. This procedure is consistent with the usual cost accounting treatment of indirect labor costs as a component of manufacturing overhead.[1] Also, overtime and premium pay related to direct labor should be budgeted as separate costs.

The primary reasons for using a separate direct labor budget are to provide planning data about the amount of direct labor required, number of direct labor employees needed, labor cost of each product unit, and cash flow requirements. Another purpose of the direct labor budget is to establish a basis for control of direct labor.

The responsibility for preparing the direct labor budget should be assigned to the executive responsible for the manufacturing function. The cost accounting and personnel departments provide support and supplementary information. When the direct labor budget is completed by the manufacturing managers, it should be given to the budget manager for review and next submitted to the executive committee. When the direct labor budget is tentatively approved, it becomes part of the profit plan.

The direct labor budget can be presented in several ways. Separate budgets are usually developed for direct labor hours and direct labor costs, as is illustrated in the Superior Manufacturing Company case.

APPROACHES USED IN PLANNING DIRECT LABOR COSTS   For the annual profit plan, the direct labor budget should be developed by responsibility centers, interim periods, and products. Classification by organizational responsibility and by interim periods is essential for control purposes; classification by product is necessary for planning the cost of producing each product.

The approach used to develop the direct labor budget depends primarily on the (1) method of wage payment, (2) type of production processes involved, (3) availability of standard labor times, and (4) adequacy of the cost accounting records relating to direct labor costs.

Basically, three approaches are used to develop the direct labor budget:

1   Estimate the standard direct labor hours required for each unit of each product; then estimate the average wage rates by department, cost center, or operation. Multiply the

---

[1] Overtime and premium costs are those costs above the regular direct labor hour rate. For example, if one direct labor employee whose hourly rate was $6 worked one hour overtime at time and one-half, the overtime cost would be $3; the $6 is still considered as direct labor cost.

Overtime should be included in the direct labor budget as follows: Extra *standard* hours at the average wage rate should be included in the direct labor budgets. Overtime premium is computed by multiplying the overtime hours worked by the overtime bonus (in the case of doubletime, it is the same rate as the regular labor rate). Overtime premium should be budgeted and accounted for. There are two different situations:

   a.   If directly related to a specific product by necessity (not by choice), the overtime premium should be included in the cost of the product and related to the departments in which it is incurred.

   b.   If the overtime premium cannot be related to a specific product (e.g., because the scheduling of production is random), it should be included in manufacturing overhead. (See Chapter 9.)

standard time per unit of product by the average hourly wage rate, giving the direct labor cost per unit of output for the department, cost center, or operation. Multiply the units of output planned for the department, cost center, or operation by the unit direct labor cost rate to obtain the total direct labor cost by product.

2   Estimate ratios of direct labor cost to some measure of output that can be planned realistically.

3   Develop personnel tables by enumerating personnel requirements (including costs) for direct labor in each responsibility center.

Some companies develop personnel tables to aid in planning and controlling overall employee costs. Under this approach, the manager of each responsibility center must prepare a detailed personnel table listing each position classified by type of job and wage rate. One such classification is direct labor. Under this classification, the exact amount of employee time for each type of work planned is identified with the responsibility center.

Planning Direct Labor Hours

Internal conditions will determine whether it is feasible to relate planned production in a producing department to direct labor hours (productive hours). Similarly, internal factors may indicate the most practical approach to use for planning direct labor hours.

An important function of industrial engineers is to develop standard labor times for various operations and products. In some producing departments, reliable labor time standards can be developed. In some cases, it is impractical to estimate direct labor time except in terms of averages based on experience. Four approaches commonly used in planning standard labor times are the following:

1   **Time and Motion Studies.** These studies are usually made by industrial engineers. They analyze the operations required on a product (by cost centers). By observation (and by actual timing with a stopwatch), a standard time for each specific operation is determined. The industrial engineer must decide (frequently along with the union) whether the fastest, slowest, or average employee time should be used. Nevertheless, time and motion studies can provide reliable information about the labor time needed to perform each specific operation. The results of time and motion studies can provide basic input data for developing the direct labor hours needed to meet planned production. When supervised by competent industrial engineers, time and motion studies generally represent the best approach to the planning of standard labor time.

2   **Standard Costs.** If a standard cost accounting system is used, careful analyses of direct labor hour requirements per unit of production will generally have been made. In such cases, the standard labor time per unit of product used in the cost system can be used to derive labor hour requirements. Frequently such standards are rather exacting and require that budgeted variations from standard hours be included in the annual profit plan (discussed in Chapter 17).

3   **Direct Estimate by Supervisors.** Some companies ask the manager of each productive operation to estimate the direct labor hours required for the planned output. In making

such estimates, the manager must rely on (1) judgment, (2) recent past performance of the department, (3) assistance from the next level of management, and (4) technical staff personnel.

4 **Statistical Estimates by a Staff Group.** Cost accounting records of past performance usually provide useful information for converting production requirements to direct labor hours. This approach is frequently used for producing departments that process several products simultaneously. The historical ratio of direct labor hours to some measure of physical output is computed and then adjusted for planned changes in the responsibility center. The accuracy of this method depends on the reliability of the cost records and the uniformity of the production process from period to period. However, it is questionable because past inefficiencies will often be projected into the future. Even though some other method of estimating direct labor hours is used, historical ratios of direct labor hours to productive output are frequently good checks on the accuracy of other methods used. Some companies use several approaches to estimate direct labor hours. A particular method applicable in one productive department or cost center may not be applicable in another.

To illustrate one of the four approaches, assume two primary products are processed through four producing departments. We will concentrate on one product and one department. The production budget specified 1,000 completed units of product A in the first month of the planning period (January). In Department 1 this product goes through four different operations (designated 2, 3, 5, and 6), each one involving direct labor time. The industrial engineers, using time and motion studies, developed the following standard times for each operation in the department:

	DEPARTMENT 1					
	STANDARD DIRECT LABOR HOURS PER OPERATION					
OPERATION	1	2	3	4	5	6
Time (hours)	1.00	1.50	0.60	0.40	1.75	2.25

Total planned direct labor hours is 6,100, computed as follows:

January 19A, Product A

OPERATION	COMPUTATION	DIRECT LABOR HOURS
2	1,000 × 1.50 =	1,500
3	1,000 × 0.60 =	600
5	1,000 × 1.75 =	1,750
6	1,000 × 2.25 =	2,250
Total	1,000 × 6.10 =	6,100

Use of Learning Curves

One concept that is sometimes used in planning labor costs is the **learning curve.** Considerable experience indicates that in some manufacturing settings, there is a constant percentage reduction in the average direct labor input time per unit of product as the cumulative output doubles. Exhibit 8-1 provides illustrative data using an 80 percent learning curve.[2]

EXHIBIT 8-1

Example of an 80% Learning Curve

(a) NUMBER OF UNITS	(b) AVERAGE DIRECT LABOR HOURS	(a) × (b) TOTAL DIRECT LABOR HOURS
1	125	125
2	$125 \times .8 = 100$	200
4	$125 \times .8^2 = 80$	320
8	$125 \times .8^3 = 64$	512
16	$125 \times .8^4 = 51.2$	819.20
32	$125 \times .8^5 = 40.96$	1,310.72

The first unit of production requires 125 hours. The average time required for the first two units is 80 percent of that time, or 100 hours. Thus, the first two units require 200 total hours. When cumulative output doubles again, from two units to four units, the average time required for the first four units is 80 percent of that required for the first two units, or 80 hours. The first four units require 320 total hours. This reduction continues, reducing labor time per unit

EXHIBIT 8-2

Graph of an 80% Learning Curve

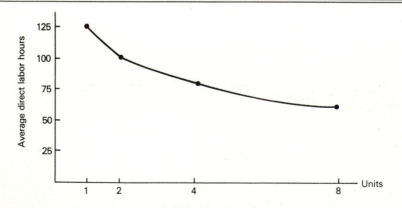

as learning occurs and as output increases. The learning effect is shown graphically in Exhibit 8-2.

Learning curves have been used extensively in industries such as aircraft, shipbuilding, and home appliances. The learning curve concept is especially applicable in industries when labor cost is a large component of total production costs and the production operation is complex. In such production operations, the learning curve should be considered when planning labor costs across several years, as in the strategic, long-range budget. Also, each period's tactical, short-term budget will reflect labor costs that are consistent with the position on the learning curve for that particular time period.

The learning curve concept has also been applied by some companies to all production costs, rather than just labor costs. When applied to all production costs, the learning curve is called the "experience curve."[3]

Planning Wage Rates

If it is possible to relate planned production to direct labor hours and to plan wage rates realistically for each productive department, computation of planned direct labor cost involves multiplying planned labor hours by planned wage rates. Within a particular company, there may be one or more productive departments where this direct approach is feasible.

Determination of average direct labor wage rates in a productive department or cost center frequently may not be a serious problem. The preferred approach is to plan such rates by enumerating the direct labor employees in the department or operation and their expected individual wage rates, and then compute an average. For example, a company may perform the analysis as follows:

	PLANNED WAGE RATE*	NUMBER OF DIRECT LABOR EMPLOYEES†	WEIGHTED AMOUNT	AVERAGE WAGE RATE
Operation 1:				
Group A	$4.00	4	$ 16.00	
Group B	6.00	16	96.00	
		20	$112.00	$5.60
Operation 2:				
Etc.				

*Throughout this chapter, the wage rates are simplified for instructional purposes.
†Full-time equivalents.

[3] For further information on learning and experience curves, see Bierman, Dyckman, and Hilton, *Cost Accounting: Concepts and Managerial Applications*; Robert S. Kaplan, *Advanced Management Accounting* (Englewood Cliffs, N.J.: Prentice-Hall, 1982); and Robert Magee, *Advanced Managerial Accounting* (New York: Harper & Row, 1986).

A less-reliable approach involves computing the historical ratio between wages paid and direct labor hours worked in the department. The historical ratio is then adjusted for conditions that have changed or are expected to change. Average wage rates based on historical data are useful for future planning only to the extent that there is consistency in operations and in the hours worked at different wage rates. For example, assume the following historical data:

EMPLOYEE GROUP	DIRECT LABOR HOURS	AVERAGE WAGE RATE	LABOR COST
A	2,000	$4.00	$ 8,000
B	3,000	6.00	18,000
Total	5,000	$5.20	$26,000

An average wage rate based on the data given above is $5.20. However, if the budgeted hours for each employee were 2,500, with no change in wage rates, the average rate would be $5.00 rather than $5.20. The difference indicates the distortion that can occur in average rates if the ratio of hours worked to different individual wage rates changes.

In some cases, the size of the department, the diversity of its work, and the variations in its hourly wages may be of such significance that the department, or the responsibility center, should be subdivided into cost centers. Separate estimated direct labor hours and average wage rates would then be planned for each cost center.

If a standard cost system is used in the cost accounting department, the standard wage rates developed for that purpose can be used for budgeting purposes. It may be desirable, however, to budget certain wage rate variances between standard allowances and planned budget allowances (discussed in Chapter 17).

The preceding discussion emphasizes two planning inputs—hours and wage rates—necessary to develop the direct labor budget. This approach has definite advantages. However, practical considerations may make this approach impractical. The alternative approach is to estimate total direct labor cost. This method involves making an estimate of total direct cost and then allocating it to (1) units of production or (2) some other measure of output, such as machine hours, direct material cost, or processing time.

If a straight piece-rate system of compensating labor is used, the labor cost per unit of production is known. The piece-rate system bases the compensation on the quantity produced. Various bonus systems of wage payments complicate the planning of direct labor costs. In such cases, ratios are generally used.

STRUCTURE OF THE DIRECT LABOR BUDGET   The direct labor budget must be in harmony with the structure of the annual profit plan. Therefore, it should show planned direct labor hours and cost by responsibility, by time (month or quarter), and by product. When standard labor times and average wage rates are developed on a sound foundation of realistic policies and plans, development of the direct labor budget poses few problems. It is usually preferable to develop a separate direct labor budget for each department that encompasses two subbudgets, one specifying hours only and the other specifying direct labor costs. These characteristics of the direct labor budget are illustrated for Superior Manufacturing Company at the end of this chapter.

Uses of the Direct Labor Budget

Effective planning of direct labor hours and costs has the following advantages for a company:

1   The personnel function can be more efficiently performed because a basis is provided for effective planning, recruitment, training, and use of personnel.
2   The finance function can be more effectively performed because labor is often one of the largest demands on cash during the year. Knowing the direct labor cost estimate enables the finance officer to plan the cash requirements for interim periods.
3   The budgeted cost of manufacturing each product (unit costs and total cost) may be an important factor in several areas of decision making, such as pricing policy and union negotiations.
4   The control of direct labor costs is significantly enhanced.

CONTROL OF DIRECT LABOR COSTS   Control of direct labor costs is often a major problem for management. Effective control of direct labor depends on competent supervision, direct observation, and performance reports. However, there is a definite need for standards by which the supervisor may gauge performance. Planning the work flow and arrangement of supplies and equipment have definite effects on direct labor costs. The two primary elements of control of direct labor costs are (1) day-to-day attention to such costs and (2) performance reporting and evaluation of results.

The direct labor standards in the direct labor budget are compared with actual results and are often reported in daily performance reports to supervisors. For example, one company, where direct labor costs were high, instituted a daily report on direct labor costs for each supervisor. By 9:00 A.M. daily, each supervisor had a report on the direct labor performance for the preceding day. The report showed (1) actual hours worked, (2) standard hours for the actual output, and (3) variances in hours. Such information may be expressed in terms of time only or in terms of both time and dollar costs, depending on the control elements that are vested in the supervisors. For effective control, budget amounts may need to be revised to reflect events that have a major impact on labor costs beyond the control of the immediate supervisor. Examples are changes in labor contracts, modifications of plant, and rearrangements of work flow and production operations.

With respect to monthly reporting and control of direct labor, the internal **monthly performance report** should include actual direct labor data compared with planned labor hours and costs (adjusted to actual output), by responsibility. These reports are essential for management assessment of the effectiveness of control. They spur management actions directed toward higher operational efficiency. The performance reports on direct labor may be (1) separate reports or (2) included in the regular departmental performance report. To illustrate performance reporting, return to the example in Chapter 7 for Department X (page 251). Assume the annual profit plan specified the following January data for Department X:

Planning data:	
Units of product to be manufactured in January	2,200
Standard labor hours per unit required in Department X	2
Average direct labor wage rate per hour in Department X	$5.00
Actual results for January:	
Units of product manufactured in January	2,000
Actual direct labor hours incurred during January	4,250
Actual direct labor cost incurred during January	$21,800

The January performance report for Department X should reflect the following with respect to direct labor:

Performance Report

DEPT. PRODUCTION DEPT. X   DEPT. MANAGER TIMOTHY WILLIAMS

MONTH JANUARY 19A

DEPARTMENTAL CONTROLLABLE COSTS	MONTH ACTUAL	MONTH PLANNED	VARIANCE AMOUNT	VARIANCE PERCENT
Departmental output (units)	2,000	2,200	200*	9*†
Material and parts: (illustrated in Chapter 7)				
Direct labor:				
Hours	4,250	4,000‡	250*	6*
Average wage rate	$5.13	$5.00	$.13*	3*
Cost	$21,800.00	$20,000.00	$1,800.00	9*
Departmental overhead: Etc.				

*Unfavorable.
†200 ÷ 2,200 = 9% (rounded).
‡Standard labor hours, per unit; 2 times actual units produced, 2000.

Variations computed by comparing actual direct labor costs with the standard allowance may be due to (1) labor usage (labor efficiency variance) or (2) labor wage rates (wage rate variance). The above performance report shows the following:

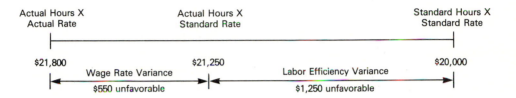

Labor usage is controllable at the supervisor's level. Even so, unfavorable labor variances may be due to defective materials, defective tools, mechanical failures, or other circumstances beyond the supervisor's immediate control. In addition, the wage rates are often determined in management-union negotiations. However, the wage rate variance is frequently controllable at the supervisor's level. To illustrate, a supervisor may cause a wage rate variance by using workers with higher wage rates than the rate specified for a particular operation. In any event, a supervisor should comment on each significant variance—about its cause and how it will be corrected. Consistent reporting of wage rate variances (favorable or unfavorable) calls into question the validity of the standards being used.

CHAPTER SUMMARY   Effective planning and control of labor costs are essential ingredients in an overall program of profit planning and control. Labor costs include all expenditures for employees, from top executives down to unskilled laborers. Direct labor costs include the wages paid to employees who work directly on the company's product, while indirect labor costs refer to the costs of other employees who do not work directly on the product. In budgeting direct labor costs, it is necessary to estimate both the quantity of labor that will be required and the rate that will be paid per hour for the various classes of labor. Time and motion studies and learning curves are among the techniques used to estimate the quantity of labor that will be required in the production process.

It is also important for service and retail companies to budget labor costs. Labor accounts for a very large portion of expenditures in banks, restaurants, hotels, hospitals, and transportation companies. The classification **direct labor** is not generally used by such companies, and labor costs are usually referred to as an **operating expense.**

Comprehensive Demonstration Case

 *SUPERIOR MANUFACTURING COMPANY*

Superior Manufacturing Company uses direct labor in each producing department. The planned quantity of direct labor hours used per unit, by department, and by product is as follows:

	DIRECT LABOR HOURS PER UNIT OF PRODUCT	
DEPARTMENT	PRODUCT X	PRODUCT Y
1	.4	.2
2	.2	—
3	.4	.2

The following average wage rates for direct labor have been tentatively approved for planning purposes:

DEPARTMENT	AVERAGE HOURLY WAGE RATES*
1	$2.00
2	1.50
3	1.00

*Simplified for instructional purposes.

Superior Manufacturing Company develops two subbudgets for direct labor: one that emphasizes direct labor cost and one that gives labor hours only. The first one is shown in Schedule 30. To develop this budget, "units to be produced" were taken from the production budget (Schedule 22, Chapter 6) and extended using the divisional input data given above. For clarity, computations are shown on the schedule. Notice that the classification of labor cost is by product, time period, and organizational responsibility (department). These classifications are consistent with the overall profit plan, as shown in all prior budget schedules prepared for Superior Manufacturing Company.

The direct labor budget in hours only is shown in Schedule 31. These hours agree with those shown in Schedule 30. However, the company has found it useful to prepare a separate budget schedule that specifies hours only. These data are needed in subsequent budget schedules of manufacturing overhead. For purposes of convenience, payroll deductions have been disregarded.

SCHEDULE 30. Superior Manufacturing Company

Direct Labor Budget—Cost by Product, Department, and Time
For the Year Ending December 31, 19X2

PERIOD AND DEPARTMENT	TOTAL LABOR COST REF.	PRODUCT X UNITS TO BE PRODUCED 22	STANDARD HOURS (INPUT)	TOTAL STANDARD PRODUCTIVE HOURS	WAGE RATE PER HOUR (INPUT)	AMOUNT	PRODUCT Y UNITS TO BE PRODUCED 22	STANDARD HOURS (INPUT)	TOTAL STANDARD PRODUCTIVE HOURS	WAGE RATE PER HOUR (INPUT)	AMOUNT
January											
Dept. 1	$ 69,600	70,000	.4	28,000	$2.00	$ 56,000	34,000	.2	6,800	$2.00	$ 13,600
Dept. 2	21,000	70,000	.2	14,000	1.50	21,000					
Dept. 3	34,800	70,000	.4	28,000	1.00	28,000	34,000	.2	6,800	1.00	6,800
Total	$ 125,400			70,000		$ 105,000			13,600		$ 20,400
February											
Dept. 1	$ 78,400	80,000	.4	32,000	$2.00	$ 64,000	36,000	.2	7,200	$2.00	$ 14,400
Dept. 2	24,000	80,000	.2	16,000	1.50	24,000					
Dept. 3	39,200	80,000	.4	32,000	1.00	32,000	36,000	.2	7,200	1.00	7,200
Total	$ 141,600			80,000		$ 120,000			14,400		$ 21,600
March											
Dept. 1	$ 79,200	80,000	.4	32,000	$2.00	$ 64,000	38,000	.2	7,600	$2.00	$ 15,200
Dept. 2	24,000	80,000	.2	16,000	1.50	24,000					
Dept. 3	39,600	80,000	.4	32,000	1.00	32,000	38,000	.2	7,600	1.00	7,600
Total	$ 142,800			80,000		$ 120,000			15,200		$ 22,800
1st Quarter											
Dept. 1	$ 227,200	230,000	.4	92,000	$2.00	$ 184,000	108,000	.2	21,600	$2.00	$ 43,200
Dept. 2	69,000	230,000	.2	46,000	1.50	69,000					
Dept. 3	113,600	230,000	.4	92,000	1.00	92,000	108,000	.2	21,600	1.00	21,600
Total	$ 409,800			230,000		$ 345,000			43,200		$ 64,800

SCHEDULE 30. (Continued)

PERIOD AND DEPARTMENT	TOTAL LABOR COST	PRODUCT X UNITS TO BE PRODUCED	STAND-ARD HOURS	TOTAL STANDARD PRODUCTIVE HOURS	WAGE RATE PER HOUR	AMOUNT	PRODUCT Y UNITS TO BE PRODUCED	STAND-ARD HOURS	TOTAL STANDARD PRODUCTIVE HOURS	WAGE RATE PER HOUR	AMOUNT
	REF.	22	(INPUT)		(INPUT)		22	(INPUT)		(INPUT)	
2nd Quarter											
Dept. 1	$ 248,000	240,000	.4	96,000	$2.00	$ 192,000	140,000	.2	28,000	$2.00	$ 56,000
Dept. 2	72,000	240,000	.2	48,000	1.50	72,000					
Dept. 3	124,000	240,000	.4	96,000	1.00	96,000	140,000	.2	28,000	1.00	28,000
Total	$ 444,000			240,000		$ 360,000			56,000		$ 84,000
3rd Quarter											
Dept. 1	$ 234,800	230,000	.4	92,000	$2.00	$ 184,000	127,000	.2	25,400	$2.00	$ 50,800
Dept. 2	69,000	230,000	.2	46,000	1.50	69,000					
Dept. 3	117,400	230,000	.4	92,000	1.00	92,000	127,000	.2	25,400	1.00	25,400
Total	$ 421,200			230,000		$ 345,000			50,800		$ 76,200
4th Quarter											
Dept. 1	$ 266,000	260,000	.4	104,000	$2.00	$ 208,000	145,000	.2	29,000	$2.00	$ 58,000
Dept. 2	78,000	260,000	.2	52,000	1.50	78,000					
Dept. 3	133,000	260,000	.4	104,000	1.00	104,000	145,000	.2	29,000	1.00	29,000
Total	$ 477,000			260,000		$ 390,000			58,000		$ 87,000
Total for Year	$1,752,000			960,000		$1,440,000			208,000		$312,000

SCHEDULE 31. Superior Manufacturing Company

Budgeted Direct Labor Hours by Product, Department, and Time
For the Year Ending December 31, 19X2

PERIOD	TOTAL	DEPARTMENT 1			DEPARTMENT 2			DEPARTMENT 3		
		PRODUCT X	PRODUCT Y	TOTAL	PRODUCT X	PRODUCT Y	TOTAL	PRODUCT X	PRODUCT Y	TOTAL
REF.		30	30		30			30	30	
January	83,600	28,000	6,800	34,800	14,000	—	14,000	28,000	6,800	34,800
February	94,400	32,000	7,200	39,200	16,000	—	16,000	32,000	7,200	39,200
March	95,200	32,000	7,600	39,600	16,000	—	16,000	32,000	7,600	39,600
Total 1st Quarter	273,200	92,000	21,600	113,600	46,000	—	46,000	92,000	21,600	113,600
2nd Quarter	296,000	96,000	28,000	124,000	48,000	—	48,000	96,000	28,000	124,000
3rd Quarter	280,800	92,000	25,400	117,400	46,000	—	46,000	92,000	25,400	117,400
4th Quarter	318,000	104,000	29,000	133,000	52,000	—	52,000	104,000	29,000	133,000
Total for Year	1,168,000	384,000	104,000	488,000	192,000	—	192,000	384,000	104,000	488,000

293

Suggested References

BIERMAN, HAROLD, JR., THOMAS DYCKMAN, and RONALD HILTON, *Cost Accounting: Concepts and Managerial Applications.* New York: Macmillan, 1990.

BUMP, E. A., "Effects of Learning on Cost Projections," *Management Accounting,* May 1974.

KAPLAN, ROBERT S., *Advanced Management Accounting,* Englewood Cliffs, N.J.: Prentice-Hall, 1982.

MAGEE, ROBERT, *Advanced Managerial Accounting,* New York: Harper & Row, 1986.

"The Tri-Star's Trail of Red Ink," *Business Week,* July 28, 1980, p. 88.

Discussion Questions

1. Define direct labor budget, and relate this budget to the annual profit plan.
2. Who should be responsible for developing the direct labor budget?
3. What are the primary purposes of the direct labor budget?
4. What are the primary approaches used to develop the direct labor budget?
5. How should direct labor hours usually be estimated?
6. What is meant by a "learning curve," and how is it used in budgeting for direct labor?
7. How should estimated average wage rates usually be developed?
8. Is direct labor normally a fixed cost, a variable cost, or a semivariable cost? Explain.
9. How should direct labor be classified in the direct labor budget? Explain.
10. How can budgeting direct labor contribute to managerial planning and control?
11. What are the basic approaches used to control direct labor?

CASE 8-1   *Design labor schedules and estimate direct labor hours*

Idaho Metals Company manufactures special metal parts that are sold in a seven-state region. Two regular products, A and B, are produced throughout the year. A small constant inventory of these two products is maintained at all times. Also, the company does special jobs (contracts) for regular customers. These special jobs are limited by the manufacturing capabilities of the company. They are accepted primarily as a service to the regular customers, and the work is quite profitable. These jobs usually have a flexible delivery date and can be used as fill-in work. The major problem of the special jobs is storage space "on the floor" because regular production must move around them. The company manufactures the "highest quality obtainable." Therefore, regular customers remain for years and have a close relationship with the company.

There are three service departments and six production departments in the factory; each has a manager. One production department, No. 3, is subdivided into two cost centers. The company uses standards to account for direct materials and direct labor. The top manufacturing manager has a two-person standards group that keeps the standards up to date. Operations are planned on a six-month cycle detailed by month. Certain planned inputs for the upcoming six-month period are summarized below for the six production departments.

Product A passes through all six of the producing departments; product B passes through all producing departments except cost center 3B. Special jobs normally require the equivalent of 10 percent of the total work scheduled in each department on products A and B combined, except in Milling and Grinding where they require 5 percent.

Department Operating Plans Summarized (Planned)*

	DEPARTMENT	MINUTES TO PERFORM THE OPERATION	AVERAGE DIRECT LABOR RATES PER HOUR
1	Preparation	30	$3.00
2	Cutting and Shipping	40	3.30
3A	Cost Center A—Drilling	10	2.00
3B	Cost Center B—Tapping	20	2.20
4	Milling and Grinding	50	4.00
5	Assembly	30	3.00
6	Inspection	15	Two salaries of $700 each per month

*Includes the special jobs.

REQUIRED

1. Design schedules (top captions and side captions) for the direct labor budget. There is a need in the company for separate schedules for (a) hours only and (b) cost.

2. Prepare a direct labor budget for the first month (January) that includes both hours and cost. The sales plan calls for 900 units of product A, 600 units of product B, and the "normal" quantity of special jobs. Show classifications for product and department.

CASE 8-2   *Evaluate the company's approach to budgeting labor; make recommendations on some critical decisions*

Benson Machine Company has approximately 145 employees. Benson operates a machine shop. Two regular products are manufactured that are sold to distributors. In addition, the company accepts jobs to manufacture items according to specifications furnished by the customer. These items vary from small, simply constructed bearings to complex subassemblies. Orders vary from ten units to several thousand, with frequent repeat orders.

The company has been budgeting for the past two years. The budget year starts January 1. It is now December 16 and the budget for the upcoming year is being completed. Although direct labor is controlled primarily by using labor standards and by close supervision at all times, a direct labor budget is prepared so that income, cash, and certain other budgets can be developed.

The direct labor budget is developed by relating labor costs to sales dollars. Computations for the profit plan being developed are as follows:

DEPARTMENT	DIRECT LABOR COST DURING PAST 12 MONTHS	DOLLAR SALES DURING PAST 12 MONTHS	HISTORICAL RATIO	PROJECTED RATIO
1	$13,500	$200,000	6.75	6
2	4,500	200,000	2.25	2
3	8,400	200,000	4.20	4
4	11,600	200,000	5.80	5
5	15,700	200,000	7.85	7
6	17,800	200,000	8.90	8
	$71,500		35.75	32

		DIRECT LABOR BUDGET						
QUARTER	PLANNED SALES	DEPT. 1 RATIO 6	DEPT. 2 RATIO 2	DEPT. 3 RATIO 4	DEPT. 4 RATIO 5	DEPT. 5 RATIO 7	DEPT. 6 RATIO 8	TOTAL RATIO 32
1	$ 50,000	$ 3,000	$ 1,000	$ 2,000	$ 2,500	$ 3,500	$ 4,000	$16,000
2	56,000							17,920
3	60,000	Etc.	Etc.	Etc.	Etc.	Etc.	Etc.	19,200
4	59,000							18,880
Year	$225,000	$13,500	$ 4,500	$ 9,000	$11,250	$15,750	$18,000	$72,000

Some producing departments are forced to work overtime. Although there is some seasonality in the overtime, unusually large orders with tight delivery dates may come in at any time. The union contract requires that time and one-half be paid for overtime up to ten hours per week. Above this time, the pay is double time. During the past two years, considerable discussion has taken place in the budget meetings as to how overtime should be included in the budget. The practice so far has been to "sort of average it in by increasing the average wage rates." The executive responsible for operations said that the "inaccuracy of the direct labor budget has been due primarily to this overtime approach; if we didn't have this problem we could budget direct labor with some assurance."

The top management also is concerned about the upcoming union contract negotiations. Because the company has not had to consider this problem since adoption of the budget program, the problem of budgeting overtime has not been considered. The union contract expires at the end of February of the coming year. Preliminary discussions have been held with the union representatives. The union has presented a proposal that calls for a 15 percent increase in average hourly pay. The management has taken the position that the economic outlook does not justify a wage increase. Top management feels that competition is stronger than ever; price resistance is very stiff; and any attempt to raise prices, as would be necessary in the face of a wage increase, would cause serious loss of business. The company would have to lay off workers. In a closed meeting on December 10 of the current year, top management tentatively decided that it would be willing to sign a new contract with a wage rate increase of 5 percent.

There is disagreement in the executive committee regarding whether a wage increase should be included in the direct labor budget for the upcoming year. Two members of the committee said, "We don't want to develop another budget at the end of February."

REQUIRED

Evaluate the approach used by the company to develop the direct labor budget. Present recommendations that appear appropriate, including overtime and the union demands.

CASE 8-3   *Compute the planned direct labor hours and direct labor costs*

Pocono Corporation produces products X, Y, and Z. All three products are processed through process 1; Y and Z through process 2; and Z through process 3. The company prepares a semiannual profit plan. Profit plan data developed to date are as follows:

1   Production budget (units):

TIME	X	Y	Z
July	5,000	3,000	21,000
August	7,000	6,000	26,000
September	10,000	8,000	30,000
4th Quarter	25,000	18,000	75,000

2   Indirect labor cost plans:

TIME	PROCESS 1	PROCESS 2	PROCESS 3
July	$35,000	$20,000	$15,000
August	37,000	21,000	16,000
September	38,000	24,000	18,000
4th Quarter	98,000	62,000	48,000

3 Direct labor standard hours planned per unit of product:

PRODUCT	PROCESS 1	PROCESS 2	PROCESS 3
X	1 1/2	—	—
Y	1 1/2	3	—
Z	1 1/2	2	5

4 Average wage rates planned:

Process 1	$2.00
Process 2	2.20
Process 3	1.80

REQUIRED Pocono develops two direct labor budgets designated as follows: (1) planned direct labor hours and (2) planned direct labor cost.

1. Compute the following amounts that would be shown on the schedule for "planned direct labor hours." Show computations.
   a. Direct labor hours during July for process 2, by product
   b. Total direct labor hours for the six-month period for process 2, by product
2. Compute the following amounts that would be shown on the schedule for "planned direct labor cost." Show computations.
   a. Direct labor cost during July for process 2, by product
   b. Direct labor cost for the six-month period, by process and by product

CASE 8-4 *Prepare direct labor hour and cost budgets*

Cayuga Chemicals, Inc., produces two products, AX and BX. The products are processed through two departments, 1 and 2. The following planning budget data have been developed:

1 From the production plan (units):

TIME	AX	BX
January	5,000	14,000
February	4,000	12,000
March	6,000	15,000
2nd Quarter	18,000	50,000
3rd Quarter	22,000	60,000
4th Quarter	16,000	45,000

2 Standard labor times developed by the industrial engineers (hours per unit of finished product):

	HOURS PER UNIT	
PRODUCT	DEPARTMENT 1	DEPARTMENT 2
AX	4	3
BX	2	5

3 Average wage rates to be budgeted (simplified):

Department 1	$2.10
Department 2	1.90

REQUIRED

Prepare the following direct labor budgets by time, department, and product: (1) direct labor hours; (2) direct labor cost.

CASE 8-5   *Design a departmental performance report*

Roth Company manufactures four different products that are variously processed through seven producing departments. Direct labor is used in each of the departments. A comprehensive profit planning and control program is currently being developed. The first annual profit plan was recently completed. The following data were taken from the direct labor budget:

		JANUARY		FEBRUARY
	PRODUCTION PLAN UNITS	PLANNED DIRECT LABOR HOURS	PLANNED DIRECT LABOR COST	ETC.
Department 1:				
Product X	5,000	9,000	$36,000	
Product Y	8,000	17,600	52,800	
Department 2:				
Etc.				

The first month (January) of operations under the annual profit plan has just ended; the controller's department has provided the following actual data for January:

	UNITS PRODUCED	DIRECT LABOR HOURS	DIRECT LABOR COST
Department 1			
Product X	5,400	10,000	$41,500
Product Y	7,800	17,000	49,300

The format of the departmental performance reports is under consideration. Tom Collins, the manager of Department 1, has expressed a keen interest in both the format and the "figures" that will be reflected in the performance reports.

REQUIRED

Design a departmental performance report that incorporates all features that you consider relevant and useful in this company. Prepare a sample report format for Department 1. Use the above data on direct labor to illustrate your format recommendations. Be prepared to justify your recommendations.

CASE 8-6   *Prepare a performance report*

Carolina Fabricators, Inc., prepares an annual profit plan detailed by month. At the end of each month, performance reports are prepared for management that compare actual costs with budget standards. At the end of March, the following data are available:

1   Actual direct labor costs:

MONTH	DEPT. A	DEPT. B	DEPT. C
January	$53,000	$53,000	$67,000
February	44,000	47,000	62,200
March	40,000	44,000	48,800

2   Direct labor information included in the profit plan:

MONTH	DEPT. A HOURS	DEPT. A AMOUNT	DEPT. B HOURS	DEPT. B AMOUNT	DEPT. C HOURS	DEPT. C AMOUNT
January	30,000	$60,000	27,000	$56,700	28,000	$61,600
February	24,000	48,000	23,000	48,300	27,000	59,400
March	23,000	46,000	23,000	48,300	20,000	44,000

3 Actual units produced:

MONTH	DEPT. A	DEPT. B	DEPT. C
January	13,000	8,500	30,000
February	11,000	7,500	28,000
March	10,000	7,000	22,000

4 Standard labor hours per unit of product:

Dept. A	2
Dept. B	3
Dept. C	1

5 Average wage rates planned:

Dept. A	$2.00
Dept. B	2.10
Dept. C	2.20

6 Actual direct labor hours:

MONTH	DEPT. A	DEPT. B	DEPT. C
January	28,000	29,500	39,500
February	19,000	20,000	19,500
March	20,000	20,500	21,000

REQUIRED

Prepare a performance report showing the status of direct labor control for March and the year to date. Be prepared to justify your approach.

Planning and Controlling Expenses: Manufacturing Overhead, Product Quality Costs, and Distribution and Administrative Expenses

9

INTRODUCTION AND PURPOSE   Managers should view expense planning and control as necessary to maintain reasonable expense levels to support the objectives and planned programs of the enterprise. Expense planning should not focus on decreasing expenses, but rather on better utilization of limited resources. Viewed in this light, expense planning and control may cause either decreased or increased expenditures. Expense planning and control should focus on the relationship between expenditures and the benefits derived from those expenditures. The desired benefits should be viewed as goals, and sufficient resources must be planned to support the operating activities essential for their accomplishment.

Some companies cut expenses without considering the effects on benefits. Others do not commit sufficient resources to the maintenance of assets such as equipment and buildings. Inevitably, such short-range decisions, although temporarily reducing expenses, soon cause even higher costs because of breakdowns, inefficient machines, frustrated employees, faulty machine tolerances, major repair costs, and shortened asset lives. Cost control should be firmly tied to (1) future goals and planned operations and (2) organizational responsibilities. The essence of expense control is the concept of a **standard.** A standard is the amount that an expense should be under a given set of conditions (such as work programs, products, management policies, and environmental variables).

This chapter primarily discusses the problems of planning and controlling the three broad categories of expenses: manufacturing overhead; distribution expenses; and general administrative expenses. This chapter also emphasizes cost planning for the tactical short-range profit plan. The next chapter focuses on the analysis and control of expenses.[1]

After a discussion of certain cost concepts, this chapter is subdivided as follows:

1   Manufacturing expense (factory overhead)
2   Product quality expenses
3   Distribution or selling expenses
4   General administrative expenses
5   Financial and other expenses

COST VERSUS EXPENSE   Two terms, **cost** and **expense,** are often used in the same sense. For financial accounting purposes, **cost** is defined as an expenditure that is entirely recorded as an asset and becomes an expense when it is "used up" in the future. Thus, a cost account is an asset account (e.g., inventory). **Expense** is defined as an expenditure that is currently consumed or a cost that has been "used up." For management accounting purposes, these terms are not rigidly defined; they are used to mean "sometimes an asset and sometimes an expense."

Classification of Costs by Responsibility

Because control is exercised through responsibilities, it is necessary that costs be planned by organizational responsibility centers. The chart of accounts used by the accounting department and the design of the expense budgets should be tailored to organizational responsibilities.

Cost allocations essential for financial accounting purposes (such as for product costing) are inappropriate for control purposes. The basis used for the allocation of an expense is usually arbitrary, and the resulting amount allocated is not controllable by the organizational unit to which it is assigned. In concept, then, we emphasize that cost allocation is generally inconsistent with control objectives.

Cost Behavior

Knowlege of cost behavior—that is, the response of a cost to different volumes of output—is essential in cost planning and control. Cost behavior can be viewed from the vantage point of the entire enterprise (as in cost-volume-profit analysis) or in the context of a specific responsibility center (as is necessary in planning and controlling costs). Cost behavior poses a practical question: as the output (level of activity) in a responsibility center increases or decreases, what happens (or should happen) to each expense incurred in that center?

---

[1] Throughout these discussions, the two terms **cost** and **expense** are used interchangeably.

When expenses (or costs) are viewed in relation to changes in output, three distinct expense categories emerge (see Chapter 10):

1 **Fixed expenses**—Those expenses that are constant in total, from month to month, regardless of fluctuations in output or volume of work done. Because any expense can change, this concept must be applied (a) to a realistic or relevant range of output and (b) in relation to a given set of conditions (management policies, time constraints, and characteristics of the operation). Examples of fixed expenses are salaries, property taxes, insurance, and depreciation (straight-line).

2 **Variable expenses**—Those expenses that change in total, directly with changes in output or volume of work done. The output must be measured in terms of some activity base, such as units completed, direct labor hours, sales dollars, or number of service calls, depending on the activities in the responsibility center. Examples of variable costs in a factory are direct materials, direct labor, and power usage.

3 **Semivariable expenses**—Those expenses that are neither fixed nor variable because they possess some characteristics of both. As output changes, semivariable expenses change in the same direction but not in proportion to the change in output.

Determination of the relationship of expenses to output or volume is necessary to apply techniques such as flexible expense budgets, cost-volume-profit analysis, marginal cost analysis, direct costing, and differential cost analysis. Each of these techniques is discussed in subsequent chapters. The next chapter discusses fixed and variable expense analyses and certain applications in cost planning and control.

Controllable and Noncontrollable Expenses

Closely related to expense classification by responsibility is the differentiation between controllable and noncontrollable expenses. Controllable expenses are those that are subject to the authority and responsibility of a specific manager. Care must be exercised because the classification of an expense item as controllable or noncontrollable must be made within a specific framework of responsibility and time. For example, the expenses of a particular responsibility center usually include some expenses, such as supervisory salaries, that are not ordinarily controllable within the responsibility center, but rather at higher levels of management. Within the responsibility center such an expense may be classified as noncontrollable. But when viewed in terms of larger organizational segments, or for the enterprise as a whole, salaries are controllable. Similarly, expenses such as depreciation usually are not controllable within the short run but are controllable in the long run. In the case of depreciation, management decisions about capital additions determine the subsequent depreciation expense amount. In the final analysis, all expenses are controllable, depending on responsibility and timing.

The concept of controllability is useful for expense control if cost classifications are related to responsibility centers. Each expense in a responsibility center should be clearly identified as either controllable or noncontrollable within that particular center. To apply this concept, it may occasionally be advisable to establish two accounts for a particular type of expense in a responsibility center. For example, salaries can be separated into two accounts, Salaries—Controllable, and Salaries—Noncontrollable, and budgeted accordingly.

Some companies include in the monthly performance report for each responsibility center only those expenses that are controllable within the center. Other companies include all the expenses of the center, but they clearly identify the controllable and noncontrollable expenses. For either method, it is important that all expenses be included on some performance report and identified as the responsibility of a specified manager. An expense classified as noncontrollable on a responsibility center performance report should be included as controllable on the performance report for a higher level of responsibility.

Notice that the expense classifications—controllable and fixed, and noncontrollable and variable—are not synonymous. In the short run, fixed expenses usually are not subject to the same degree of control as are variable expenses. Practically all variable expenses, by their nature, are controllable in the short run. On the other hand, depreciation on an output basis, for example, is a variable expense that is noncontrollable in the short run. Conversely, certain salaries are controllable in the short run, although they are fixed expenses.

Cost Reduction and Cost Control

In view of the imprecision of cost terminology, it is useful to make a distinction between two related concepts, cost reduction and cost control. Cost (or expense) reduction programs are directed toward specific efforts to reduce costs by improving methods, work arrangements, and products. To illustrate, a company reported a significant reduction in the manufacturing costs of a small screen designed to cover an air intake by simply reducing the number of cross wires (without reducing the utility) that needed to be "turned at the ends" as shown below. Another company, as a result of a cost reduction program, replaced all old-style water faucets with others that automatically turn off when released. The cost reduction was substantial.

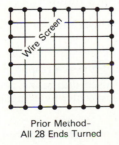

Prior Method–
All 28 Ends Turned

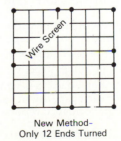

New Method–
Only 12 Ends Turned

Cost Reduction Example

In a broad sense, cost control includes cost reduction. In a narrower sense, cost control may be thought of as managerial efforts to attain cost goals within a particular operational environment. Management should attack costs in several ways, such as cost reduction programs, cost planning, and continuous attention to cost-incurring decisions. Separate attention to the concepts of cost reduction and cost control is often advisable.

PLANNING EXPENSES   When developing the tactical profit plan, the expenses for each responsibility center should be carefully assessed. In harmony with the concept of participation, expense planning should involve all levels of management. Participation is essential in developing realistic expense budgets for each responsibility center. In planning expenses for a responsibility center, the output or activity for that center must be planned. For example, to develop an expense plan for the power department, the expected demands for power first must be planned. An expenditure plan for research and development must be related to the type and extent of research activities planned. Thus, we see that all expense planning should be based on planned outputs.

With respect to formal development of the tactical short-term profit plan, we should expect to develop a separate expense budget for each responsibility center. We have already discussed the development of direct material and direct labor budgets on this basis. To develop the manufacturing plans to be incorporated into the short-term profit plan, the following budget sequence is typical:

1   **Direct Material and Labor Cost Budgets**—Developed immediately after the production budget is completed and tentatively approved.
2   **Manufacturing or Factory Overhead Budgets**—Developed immediately after the production budget, as tentatively approved, has been converted to expected output (however measured) for each producing and service department in the factory.
3   **Distribution Expense Budgets**—Developed concurrently with the sales plan because they are mutually dependent.
4   **Administrative Expense Budgets**—Developed immediately after the approved sales plan (and perhaps the production budget) has been converted to planned activity for each administrative department involved.

Detailed expense budgets for each responsibility center should be included in the short-term profit plan for a number of reasons, principally these:

1   So that the effects of various planned revenues and related expenses can be aggregated in a planned income statement.
2   So that the cash outflow required for costs and expenses can be realistically planned.
3   So that an initial objective can be provided for each responsibility center.
4   So that a standard can be provided and used during the period covered by the profit plan for each expense in each responsibility center for comparison with actual expenses on the performance reports.

These four reasons suggest the importance of the careful planning of expenses and use of the resulting plans for further planning, control, and evaluation.

Planning Manufacturing or Factory Overhead

After the production plan has been completed, expense budgets should be developed for each responsibility center in the organization. These expense budgets should be detailed by interim time periods (months or quarters) for the three categories: direct materials, direct labor, and manufacturing overhead. After the production plan is completed, these cost budgets normally are developed simultaneously and are then consolidated into a budget appropriately labeled the **planned cost of goods manufactured.** This budget requires that all manufacturing costs be identified, **either directly or by allocation,** with each product.

Manufacturing overhead is that part of total production cost not directly identifiable with (traceable to) specific products or jobs. Manufacturing overhead consists of (1) indirect material, (2) indirect labor (including salaries), and (3) all other miscellaneous factory expenses; such as taxes, insurance, depreciation, supplies, utilities, and repairs.

Manufacturing overhead includes many dissimilar expenses; therefore, it causes problems in the allocation of these costs to products. Since there are many different types of expenses, control responsibility is often widely diffused. For example, such items as depreciation, taxes, and insurance are usually not subject to direct control by factory managers, but rather by higher-level management.

There are two distinct types of responsibility centers (e.g., departments) in most manufacturing companies: producing and service. Producing centers are those manufacturing departments that work directly on the products manufactured. Service departments do not work on the products directly, but rather they furnish service to the producing departments and to other service departments. Typical service departments in a factory are the maintenance or repair department, power department, purchases department, production planning department, time and motion study department, and general factory administration. Responsibility for the operation of each department should be classified separately in the chart of accounts used by the cost accounting department. Finally, the expenses of each department should be planned and controlled separately.

For both budgeting and cost accounting purposes, manufacturing overhead involves the following two problems:

1 Control of manufacturing or factory overhead
2 Allocation of manufacturing or factory overhead to products manufactured (product costing)

These two problems require different solutions. Frequently they are viewed as one problem, with a consequent limitation on the usefulness of the solution. The difference between the two problems is critical with respect to the allocation of service department and other indirect factory overhead costs to the producing departments.

CONTROL OF MANUFACTURING OVERHEAD We have emphasized that expense control requires identification of expense controllability with each responsibility center manager. This means that noncontrollable costs should not be identified as a responsibility of the manager of the center. Thus, to control manufacturing overhead, "clean" expenses must be considered, that is, direct expenses only, exclusive of any allocated expenses. For example, Producing Department 1 uses a large amount of power generated by the power department. In recording actual expenses and budgeting expenses, and in reporting for control purposes, the expenses of the power department should be identified with the manager of the power department only. In contrast, the expenses of Producing Department 1 should be identified with the manager of Producing Department 1, exclusive of any allocation of actual power costs. The manager of the power department is responsible for the costs of the services provided. The manager of the using department has no control over those costs. What the manager of the producing department does control is the **amount of services (power) used,** rather than the cost of the service. Therefore, the performance report of Producing Department 1 should show the quantity of power used compared with the quantity of power that should have been used in producing the goods completed. In summary, it is preferable that service usage be controlled on the basis of units of service rather than on the basis of dollar cost of service. If it is desirable to use dollar cost, then the using department should be charged at standard rates rather than at actual rates.

PRODUCT COSTING To plan the cost of goods manufactured by product, it is necessary that all indirect factory overhead costs be allocated to production. In the example cited above, the costs of power used by Producing Department 1 must be allocated to the output of the producing department to compute the total cost of production in Producing Department 1. The two objectives, cost control and product costing, are resolved by using a separate approach for each objective. Costs are accumulated and reported for control purposes prior to allocation; product costing then follows by using allocation procedures.

For the short-term profit plan, the overall manufacturing expense budget includes a budget of expense for each department in the factory following the expense classifications used in the cost accounting department. The reliability with which the expense plans can be made depends on (1) the reliability of the accounting records and (2) the seriousness of management's attitude toward expense planning. As with most of the subbudgets, it is desirable to have estimates of manufacturing expense prepared by the manufacturing managers. Thus, the manager of each responsibility center should assist in preparing the expense budgets.

Selecting the Activity Base

A primary problem in planning and controlling expenses is the selection of an appropriate measure of output or activity for each responsibility center. The measure of output or activity selected is called the **activity base,** or output factor, or simply the "output." If a department produces only one output or provides only one service, the activity base of that department is best measured in terms of the particular product or service. Alternatively, in the case of a department that simultaneously produces multiple kinds of output or provides multiple kinds of services, the measurement of output is complex. The outputs of different products or services cannot be combined into a single sum. Therefore, the problem is to select a common or equivalent measure that can be identified with each product or service so that aggregate output can be expressed as a single amount for certain purposes. For example, a producing department that manufactures several products simultaneously might use direct machine hours as the activity base. The following measures of output (activity base) for the two basic types of factory departments are frequently used:

1   Producing departments:
  a.   Units of output (if only one kind of output)
  b.   Direct labor hours
  c.   Direct machine hours
  d.   Direct labor dollars
  e.   Raw material units consumed
  f.   Process time
2   Service departments:
  a.   Repair and maintenance—direct repair hours
  b.   Power department—kilowatt hours delivered
  c.   Purchases department—net purchase dollars
  d.   General factory administration—total direct labor hours or number of employees in the factory

The selection of an appropriate activity base for each department is a responsibility of the factory manager in cooperation with the controller and the budget manager.

DEVELOPING FACTORY OVERHEAD BUDGETS   The development of the various components of the factory overhead budget involves several steps that can best be communicated by illustration. Therefore, the next few paragraphs focus on a hypothetical illustration (1) to develop departmental overhead budgets and (2) to compute the planned cost of goods manufactured. Assume that the production plan, materials, and direct labor budgets have been completed for Hypothetical Company. The approved production plan specifies the following annual data:

PRODUCT	UNITS TO BE PRODUCED
A	7,000 gallons
B	4,000 pounds

Now we have the problem of developing factory overhead expense budgets for each department. The company has two producing departments (No. 1

and No. 2) and one service department (repair and maintenance). Department 1 works only on product A; Department 2 works on both products. The activity bases are as follows:

DEPARTMENT	ACTIVITY BASE
1	Units of product A
2	Direct machine hours (DMH)
Repair and maintenance	Direct repair hours (DRH)

The first step in developing the departmental overhead expense budgets is to translate the requirements specified in the production plan into output or activity in each department. The following two decisional inputs have been developed for this purpose:

1 Standard direct machine hours per unit in Department 2: for product A—4; for product B—3

2 Standard repair hours: for Department 1—.20 DRH (direct repair hours) for each unit of product A; for Department 2—.07 DRH for each direct machine hour

These data make it possible to compute the output or activity planned for each department as follows:

DEPARTMENT	COMPUTATIONS	PLANNED DEPARTMENTAL OUTPUT OR ACTIVITY ACTIVITY BASE	QUANTITY
1	Taken directly from the production plan	Units of product A	7,000
2	Product A: 7,000 × 4 DMH = 28,000		
	Product B: 4,000 × 3 DMH = 12,000	DMH	40,000
Repair and maintenance	Dept. 1: 7,000 × .20 = 1,400		
	Dept. 2: 40,000 × .07 = 2,800	DRH	4,200

Now that each department manager knows the planned output or activity for each department, each manager is in a position to plan departmental overhead expenses. The expense budgets are detailed by month for each expense. However, for this illustration we will use only the following annual totals:

DEPARTMENT	PLANNED OUTPUT OR ACTIVITY	DECISIONAL INPUTS BY DEPARTMENT MANAGER PLANNED OVERHEAD EXPENSE
1	7,000 units of A	$26,000
2	40,000 DMH	16,000
Repair and maintenance	4,200 DRH	6,000

The three departmental overhead budgets summarized immediately above were developed by the department managers and were approved by higher management. The budget data will be used for three primary purposes: (1) to develop the planned cost of goods manufactured; (2) to estimate cash outflows; and (3) for control during the upcoming year (that is, for cost goals and performance reports). Only the first use will be illustrated at this time. The other uses are discussed in later chapters.

PLANNED COST OF GOODS MANUFACTURED   The total factory overhead must be allocated to the two products manufactured. **Predetermined overhead rates** must be developed for each of the two **producing** departments to accomplish this purpose. The planned service department expenses must be **allocated** to the two producing departments. The budgeted overhead rates for the two producing departments can be computed as follows:

	PRODUCTION DEPARTMENTS	
	1	2
Producing department overhead planned (per above)	$26,000	$16,000
Allocation of repair and maintenance cost on the basis of planned service usage (DRH):		
$\frac{1,400}{4,200} \times \$6,000$	2,000	
$\frac{2,800}{4,200} \times \$6,000$		4,000
Total overhead allocated to products	$28,000	$20,000
Planned output (activity base):		
Dept. 1—units of product A	7,000	
Dept. 2—direct machine hours		40,000
Overhead rates:		
Dept. 1—per unit of product A ($28,000 ÷ 7,000)	$ 4.00	
Dept. 2—per direct machine hour ($20,000 ÷ 40,000)		$ .50

Using these overhead rates, we can develop the planned cost of goods manufactured. The planned output of each product (expressed in terms of the activity base) is multiplied by the predetermined overhead rates. The computations are as follows:

	PRODUCT A—7,000 UNITS		PRODUCT B—4,000 UNITS	
COMPUTATIONS	TOTAL COST	UNIT COST	TOTAL COST	UNIT COST
Direct material costs (planned)	$ 70,000	$10.00	$60,000	$15.00
Direct labor costs (planned)	35,000	5.00	14,000	3.50
Total direct costs	105,000		74,000	
Factory overhead costs applied:				
Product A:				
Dept. 1, 7,000 units × $4.00 = $28,000				
Dept. 2, 7,000 units × 4 DMH × $.50 = $14,000	42,000	6.00		
Product B:				
Dept. 2, 4,000 units × 3 DMH × $.50			6,000	1.50
Planned cost of goods manufactured	$147,000	$21.00	$80,000	$20.00

Application of these procedures in a more complex situation is illustrated for Superior Manufacturing Company at the end of this chapter.

PRODUCT QUALITY COSTING   The importance of maintaining high quality in manufactured products has been made more apparent in recent years by the pressures of foreign competition and new production methods, such as the just-in-time approach (see Chapter 6). As product quality is given greater importance, the opportunity costs because of low-quality products, or alternatively the opportunity gains of high-quality products, loom even larger. For this reason, some companies are spending increased amounts to improve the quality of their products. These companies have also started to explicitly account for, budget, and control costs actually incurred to enhance product quality. The following excerpt from a *Management Accounting* article describes the various types of product quality costs.

Given the increasing importance of quality costs, such costs should be measured, carefully monitored, and planned as realistically as possible.

PRODUCT QUALITY COSTS

The quality costs discussed here deal with costs associated with **quality of conformance** as opposed to costs associated with **quality of design.** Quality of design refers to variations in products which have the same functional use.[2] For example, a Cadillac and a Chevrolet automobile may be used for the same function, transportation, but their design qualities are different. For this type of quality, higher quality generally means higher costs. The same relationship, however, does not exist when cost associated with quality of conformance is considered.

---

[2] J. M. Juran and F. M. Gyrna, *Quality Planning and Analysis*, (New York: McGraw-Hill, 1971).

Quality of conformance refers to the degree with which the final product meets its specifications. In other words, quality of conformance refers to the product's fitness for use. If products are sold and they do not meet the consumers' expectations, the company will incur costs because the consumer is unhappy with the product's performance. These costs are one kind of quality costs that will be reduced if higher quality products are produced. Thus, higher quality may mean lower total costs when quality of conformance is considered. Accountants, therefore, should be aware of the costs associated with quality of conformance and how they can be of assistance to management.

The costs associated with quality of conformance generally can be classified into four types: **prevention costs, appraisal costs, internal failure costs,** and **external failure costs.**[3] The prevention and appraisal costs occur because a lack of quality of conformance can exist. The internal and external failure costs occur because a lack of quality of conformance does exist.

Prevention costs are the costs associated with designing, implementing, and maintaining the quality system. These costs include engineering quality control systems, quality planning by various departments, and quality training programs.

Appraisal costs are the costs incurred to ensure that materials and products meet quality standards. These costs include inspection of raw materials, laboratory tests, quality audits, and field testing.

Internal failure costs are the costs associated with materials and products that fail to meet quality standards and result in manufacturing losses. They include the cost of scrap, repair, and rework of defective products identified before they are shipped to consumers.

External failure costs are the costs incurred because inferior quality products are shipped to consumers. They include the costs of handling complaints, warranty replacement, repairs of returned products, and so forth (emphasis added.)[4]

PLANNING DISTRIBUTION (SELLING) EXPENSES

Distribution expenses include all costs related to selling, distribution, and delivery of products to customers. In many companies, this cost is a significant percentage of total expenses. Careful planning of such expenses affects the profit potential of the firm.

The two primary aspects of planning distribution expenses are as follows:

1 **Planning and Coordination**—In the development of the tactical profit plan, it is essential that a favorable "economic" balance be achieved between sales effort (expense) and sales results (revenue).

2 **Control of Distribution Expenses**—Aside from planning considerations, it is important that serious effort be given to controlling distribution expenses. Control is especially important, since (a) distribution expenses are frequently a significant portion of total expense, and (b) both sales management and sales personnel tend to view such expenses lightly, in some cases extravagantly, such as entertainment expenditures. Distribution expense control involves the same principles of control as manufacturing overhead. Control must be built around the concepts of (a) responsibility centers and (b) expense objectives.

[3] Quality Cost–Cost Effectiveness Committee, *Quality Costs—What and How* (American Society for Quality Control, 1971).

[4] H. P. Roth and W. J. Morse, "Let's Help Measure and Report Quality Costs," *Management Accounting*, August 1983, p. 50.

Fundamentally, the top marketing executive has the direct responsibility for planning the **optimum economic balance** (for profit potential) between (1) the sales budget, (2) the advertising budget, and (3) the distribution expense budget. Therefore, profit planning and control views sales, advertising, and distribution expenses as one basic problem rather than as three separate problems. This view is logical because of the interrelationships between them. The sales budget rests solidly upon the promotional program. The amount of expenditures to get a given amount of sales revenue is limited. The practice of some companies of starting with a sales goal, then budgeting a fixed percentage of those revenues for sales overhead, another fixed percentage for direct marketing expenses, and still another fixed percentage for advertising, is not a positive management approach to a serious planning problem. In contrast, the sales executives in well-managed companies, working as a group, develop the marketing, promotional, and distribution expense plans simultaneously. Next, the expenditures essential to carry out the promotional, marketing, and distribution phases are planned. These expense estimates then become an important part of the input data for the profit plan. Although practice varies, these decisional inputs are separately included in (1) the promotion and advertising plan and (2) the budget of selling expenses.

Distribution expenses include two major types: (1) home-office expenses and (2) field expenses. From the planning and control point of view, these expenses must be planned by responsibility center. In some cases, this might be by sales district; in other cases, by products. In all cases, the planning structure should follow the basis on which the sales efforts are organized. The concepts of controllable versus noncontrollable costs, fixed versus variable costs, and itemization by types of expenditure discussed in the first part of the chapter should be used in planning and controlling distribution expenses.

PREPARING DISTRIBUTION (SELLING) EXPENSE BUDGETS   Distribution expenses are not product costs and are not allocated to specific products. A separate distribution expense plan should be developed for each responsibility center in the distribution function. Typically, this would encompass "home-office" centers and "field" centers. The top marketing executive has the overall responsibility for developing the distribution expense plans or budgets. Following the principle of participation, the manager of each responsibility center should be assigned direct responsibility for that department's distribution expense plan. Thus, the promotion manager should be responsible for developing the promotion plan, and the field sales managers should be responsible for developing both their marketing plans (see Chapter 5) and their distribution expense budgets. The distribution expense budgets should separately identify controllable and noncontrollable expenses, and these budgets should be detailed by interim time period. The distribution expense budgets prepared by the sales managers should be based on a planned volume of activity or output. Usually the preferable activity base (that is, the method of measuring output or activity) for the various responsibility centers in the distribution function is sales dollars.

When developing the expense budgets for each responsibility center, the managers should conform to the broad guidelines (planning premises) established by top management, planned marketing programs, and their own judgment. The distribution expense budgets should be submitted by the managers of the responsibility centers to the next level of management for evaluation, approval, and consolidation. The final approval of expense plans is the responsibility of the top management.

As in planning and controlling expenses in other functional areas, there are a number of special problems in planning distribution expenses. It would be impractical to attempt to treat comprehensively, or even list, all of these problem areas. One example of such a problem that does not fit neatly into general budget procedures is travel expenses incurred by salespersons. Many companies report that they plan and control these expenses by computing them as a function of sales (either quantity or dollar sales). That is, they assume this particular expense should increase as sales increase, and vice versa. Conversely, some sales executives say that certain distribution expenses should be planned to vary inversely with sales. As sales fall off, more effort and travel may be essential to reverse the sales trend. This particular problem, as with other special problems, must be analyzed, planned, and controlled separately. Other special problems in planning distribution costs relate to freight, entertainment, warehousing, returned goods, and special allowances.

Development of a promotion and advertising plan is a complex endeavor that should involve most of the marketing managers. This is one reason why companies often have an advertising manager. The advertising plan can vary from international to local advertising on a small scale. Although comprehensive treatment of this topic is outside the scope of this book, we might note some aspects of the problem. Certain types of advertising expenditures are best planned and controlled on the basis of definite appropriations for specific time periods. Market research and advertising expenditures are typical examples. Top management should require that such activities be specifically planned and that the attendant expenditures be carefully estimated. When such plans are approved by top management, they may constitute appropriations of a specific amount necessary for the execution of each plan. Control is achieved through continuous reporting of actual progress and expenditures compared with the plans.

Various approaches are used to determine the promotion and advertising appropriation. The more commonly used approaches can be characterized as (a) arbitrary appropriation, (b) all available funds, (c) competitive parity, (d) percentage of sales, (e) fixed sum per unit, (f) previous year's profits, (g) return on investment, and (h) the task method.

The promotion and advertising budget should be the direct responsibility of the advertising manager. The detailed promotion budget should be presented to the budget committee along with the sales budget. These two plans should be approved or disapproved as a unit. In this way, the budget department receives the detailed and approved promotion budget for incorporation into the overall profit plan.

For analytical purposes, expenditure plans given in an appropriation budget should be viewed as fixed expenses. The total amount of the expense for the period is determined by management policy. Notice in the Superior Manufacturing Company case given at the end of this chapter that such expenses are shown as fixed. In the accounting department, promotion and advertising expenses, after having been budgeted for the year, may be accrued on a monthly basis by a debit to an advertising clearing account. Actual expenditures are then debited to the latter account. In such cases, the related budget procedures should be consistent. Distribution expense budgets are illustrated at the end of the chapter for Superior Manufacturing Company.

PLANNING ADMINISTRATIVE EXPENSES   Administrative expenses include those expenses other than manufacturing and distribution. They are incurred in the responsibility centers that provide supervision of and service to all functions of the enterprise, rather than in the performance of any one function. Because a large portion of administrative expenses are fixed rather than variable, the notion persists that they cannot be controlled. Aside from certain top-management salaries, most administrative expenses are determined by management decisions. It is common to find administrative expenses "top heavy" when measured by the volume of business done. In recent years, some informed observers have expressed the opinion that a developing characteristic of industry in the United States is the relative high cost of administration. These expenses, along with labor costs, have frequently made it difficult to price products competitively in the international market. General administrative expenses are close to top management; therefore, there is strong tendency to overlook their magnitude and effect on profits. Each administrative expense should be directly identified with a responsibility center, and the center manager should be responsible for planning and controlling the expense. This fundamental of expense control is especially important for administrative costs because there is often a failure to pinpoint responsibility for expenses of a general nature. For this and other reasons, many companies have found it helpful to apply the fixed–variable expense concept to administrative expenses. In such cases, the variable expenses are usually related to total sales dollars. This approach tends to emphasize that when volume drops, some of these expenses should decrease also, or else the profit potential is lowered.

Central administration in any company, except very small ones, is carried on in several special responsibility centers, such as central administration, the controller's department, the treasurer's department, the personnel department, and central staff. Thus, the overall administrative expense budget includes several departmental budgets. The manager of each of these responsibility centers should be assigned the primary responsibility for planning and controlling operations, including the requisite expenses that are subject to control. The administrative expense budgets for each responsibility center, after preparation by the respective managers, should be subject to approval by higher management in the same manner as was discussed for all other budgets.

It is advisable to base budgeted administrative expenses on specific plans and programs. Past experience, adjusted for anticipated changes in management policy and general economic conditions, is helpful. Because most administrative expenses are fixed, an analysis of the historical record will often provide a sound basis for budgeting them.

The concept of flexible expense budgets (see Chapter 10) has not been widely accepted for controlling administrative expenses, but there is seldom any practical reason for not applying the concept to these expenses. The fact that most of the administrative expenses are fixed simplifies the application of flexible budgets.

HEADCOUNT FORECASTING   In the nonmanufacturing functions of a business (such as general administration, R&D, marketing, and product engineering), the most significant expense usually is salaries. Some companies have developed formal procedures for projecting and controlling such expenses. These methods are known as **headcount forecast algorithms.** The methods used by Intel Corporation, described in the following excerpt from a *Management Accounting* article, are typical.

HEADCOUNT FORECASTING AT INTEL CORPORATION

How do you control indirect costs in a dynamic environment? Intel Corporation's answer is an indirect headcount (cost) algorithm. The headcount algorithm is a systematic method that helps managers evaluate requests for additional staffing of indirect product specialists or "heads," and at the same time control indirect costs and improve productivity. **Intel managers found it especially helpful when considering the reallocation of resources among rapidly expanding or contracting product groups.**

The concept of using algorithms to control costs is not new. Management accountants use similar algorithms to control variable expenses. For example, the flexible budget algorithm typically adjusts the allowance for variable indiret costs based upon some measure of manufacturing activity. Control is enhanced when actual costs are compared with the flexible budget allowance for the level of volume actually experienced. As the operations become more capital intensive and indirect fixed costs become a larger segment of the total expenses, controls that focus on variable indirect costs are no longer adequate.

At Intel, a major component of indirect costs is salaries for marketing and other product support groups. Traditionally, such cost pools have been considered fixed costs. However, the headcount algorithm treats these costs essentially as step-variable costs and attempts to establish target spending levels as a function of multiple volume measures and other significant characteristics of each product group.

As the company became more capital intensive, indirect expenses began to represent a larger segment of total expenses and the company decided it was time to exercise more control over the staffing of nonproduction areas of the company's operations. Top management became committed to the development of a method to forecast manpower needs. Before deciding on the basic algorithm approach, management considered and rejected other models. Regression analysis and time series analysis were ruled out because of a lack of historical data and a rapidly changing future environment.

The headcount algorithm was selected because it is simple, understandable, and at the same time realistic. Managers are able to use it to effectively measure productivity in the nonproduction areas including consumer marketing and technical marketing engineering, and product engineering.

The basic approach to forecasting algorithms is a weighted average of forecasted indicators divided by their targets:

$$\text{Headcount Forecast} = \sum_{i=1}^{N} \frac{\text{Weight } i \times \text{Forecast Indicator } i}{\text{Indicator Target}}$$

At Intel the indicators, targets, and weights were determined from in-depth interviews with customer marketing engineers (CME) and technical marketing engineers (TME), as well as with product engineers (PE). During these interviews the engineers identified several predictors for manpower needs including: sales revenue, volume, product maturity and development, and market segment.

For example, the CMEs agreed that for their area of operation the major indicators for headcount were revenue, new products, and total products. These items were then incorporated into the algorithm. Further analysis revealed that the most important of these three indicators was revenue; new products and total products were of less but equal importance.[5]

[5] Michael Gilchrist, Diane D. Pattison, and Ronald J. Kudla, "Controlling Indirect Costs with Head-count Forecast Algorithms," *Management Accounting*, August 1985, pp. 47–48.

Comprehensive Demonstration Case

 *SUPERIOR MANUFACTURING COMPANY*

Manufacturing Overhead Expense Budgets Illustrated

Recall that the factory division of Superior Manufacturing Company (Exhibit 4-1) has three service departments (general and administrative, power, and repair) and three production departments (designated 1, 2, and 3). The marketing function includes three sales districts and the home office. There are four general administrative departments (administrative, accounting, treasurer, and building services). Since there are fourteen different departments, fourteen responsibility center expense budgets must be prepared. First, we will illustrate the building services and factory expense budgets.

Management selected the following activity bases for the factory departments:

DEPARTMENT	ACTIVITY BASE (OUTPUT)
Producing	Departmental direct labor hours (DLH)
General and administration—	
factory	Total direct labor hours
Power	Kilowatt hours
Repair	Direct repair hours (DRH)

The company owns a building that houses all divisions of the company.
The occupancy by the three divisions is as follows:

OCCUPANCY	FLOOR SPACE
Factory	60%
Sales	20%
General and administration	20%
Total	100%

Occupancy expense is allocated to the three divisions by using the above
floor-space percentages. The building superintendent provided the building
services budget shown in Schedule 32.

The next step is to translate the production budget (Schedule 22, Chapter 6) into output or activity generated for each department in the factory.
Since direct labor hours is the activity base for the three production departments, the direct labor budget (Schedule 28, Chapter 7, and Schedule 31,
Chapter 8) provides the planned activity base data. The managers of the power
and repair departments translated the production budget into the following
planned outputs for their respective departments:

Planned Outputs for the Service Departments

POWER DEPARTMENT		REPAIR DEPARTMENT	
	KILOWATT HOURS (000)		DIRECT REPAIR HOURS
January	1,450	January	290
February	1,600	February	330
March	1,600	March	320
Second Quarter	5,100	Second Quarter	1,000
Third Quarter	4,800	Third Quarter	970
Fourth Quarter	5,450	Fourth Quarter	1,090
Total	20,000	Total	4,000

SCHEDULE 32. Superior Manufacturing Company

Expense Budget—Building Services Cost
For the Year Ending December 31, 19X2

EXPENSE	REF	ANNUAL TOTAL	1ST QUARTER			QUARTERS			
			JANUARY	FEBRUARY	MARCH	1ST	2ND	3RD	4TH
		(INPUT)	(INPUT)	(INPUT)	(INPUT)	(INPUT)	(INPUT)	(INPUT)	(INPUT)
*Supervisory salaries		$ 24,000	$ 2,000	$ 2,000	$ 2,000	$ 6,000	$ 6,000	$ 6,000	$ 6,000
Repairs and maintenance		18,000	1,500	1,500	1,500	4,500	4,500	4,500	4,500
*Depreciation		60,000	5,000	5,000	5,000	15,000	15,000	15,000	15,000
*Insurance		3,600	300	300	300	900	900	900	900
*Taxes		2,400	200	200	200	600	600	600	600
Wages		26,800	2,250	2,150	2,150	6,550	6,750	6,750	6,750
Heat and light		13,200	1,800	1,000	900	3,700	2,000	2,750	4,750
Water		2,000	150	150	170	470	630	500	400
Total		$150,000	$13,200	$12,300	$12,220	$37,720	$36,380	$37,000	$38,900
Building services cost allocation:									
Factory 60%		$ 90,000	$ 7,920	$ 7,380	$ 7,332	$22,632	$21,828	$22,200	$23,340
Sales 20%		30,000	2,640	2,460	2,444	7,544	7,276	7,400	7,780
Administrative 20%		30,000	2,640	2,460	2,444	7,544	7,276	7,400	7,780
Total 100%		$150,000	$13,200	$12,300	$12,220	$37,720	$36,380	$37,000	$38,900

*Noncontrollable in this department.

The manager of each of the six factory departments, on the basis of the planned volume of work as translated from the production plan, developed tentative expense budgets for their respective centers. In developing these expense budgets, they were assisted by their immediate supervisors, staff from the manufacturing manager's office, and personnel from the office of the director of profit planning and control. The tentative expense budgets were carefully reviewed by higher management. After all agreed-upon changes were made, the factory expense budgets were approved as shown in Schedules 33 and 34. Notice that the expense budgets show (1) planned output and (2) expense goals for each expense within the department. Notice also that noncontrollable expenses are separately identified.

The next step in completing the overall manufacturing budget involves the allocation of planned factory overhead costs to each of the products being manufactured (X and Y). Recall that direct material and direct labor costs were identified with each product in Schedules 28 and 31, Chapters 7 and 8. The company uses predetermined overhead rates to allocate factory expenses to products. The computation of an overhead rate for each of the three production departments is shown in Schedule 35. Notice that the total annual expense was taken from the six factory overhead expense budgets and entered on this schedule as direct department costs. Next, the building services cost and the three service department costs were allocated to the three production departments so that these three rates "carry" all the factory overhead for product-cost allocations. Allocations were based on the following data:

DEPARTMENT	FACTORY OCCUPANCY (%*)	GENERAL AND ADM. FACTORY OVERHEAD (%)	POWER DEPT.— KILOWATT HRS. (000)	REPAIR DEPT.—DIRECT REPAIR HRS.
Power	10.000	10		
Repair	5.000	10	500	
Producing 1	36.890†	50	10,000	1,600
2	18.312	10	5,000	800
3	28.798	20	4,500	1,600
Total	100.000%	100%	20,000	4,000

*The 60% allocated to the factory is reallocated to the factory departments on this basis.

†Carrying percentages to three decimal places is done here to make the overhead rates come out even (for instructional convenience only).

The total costs of each production department (direct plus service department allocations) were divided by the planned total direct labor hours (output) to compute the three **planned overhead rates (per DLH).**[6]

The next step in developing product cost is to use these overhead rates to apply planned overhead to each product. Since the factory overhead rates were based on direct labor hours (that is, the activity base) and the direct labor budget (Schedule 31, Chapter 8) specifies direct labor hours by product, we can allocate overhead to the two products by multiplying the respective overhead rates by the planned hours. This allocation is shown in Schedule 36, "Manufacturing Expenses Applied by Product." Notice that the total overhead expenses planned ($779,200, shown in Schedule 34) agrees with the total applied amount shown in Schedule 36.

The use of predetermined overhead rates to allocate factory overhead, which includes both fixed and variable expenses, results in a stable charge during the year to each unit of product for this particular element of cost. Because the departmental expense budgets show planned costs as they are expected to accrue, while the application of overhead through the rates will track the seasonal pattern of planned production, a **budgeted over/under applied** factory overhead for interim periods must be planned during the year. This effect is shown in Schedule 37, "Budgeted Overhead Over/Under Applied." Notice, however, that at year-end the total overhead planned and the total overhead applied are equal.

All budgeted factory expenses for Superior Manufacturing Company are identified with the various types of finished goods in the following budget schedules:

EXPENSE COST	SCHEDULE
Direct materials	28
Direct labor	30
Manufacturing expenses	36

The planned cost of goods manufactured, which aggregates these three costs, will be shown in Chapter 13 (Schedule 58).

[6] When it is possible to identify separately the fixed and variable components of expense in each departmental overhead budget, overhead rates can be computed separately for the fixed and variable components in each department. This feature is particularly relevant for (1) variance analyses, (2) direct costing, and (3) breakeven analyses. (These topics are discussed in Chapters 14, 16, and 17.) Also, it is generally agreed that a more theoretically correct and useful allocation is possible if fixed and variable costs are allocated separately and on different bases. Generally, fixed service department expenses should be allocated on the basis of capacity to use services, whereas variable expenses should be allocated on the basis of expected actual use of services.
Notice that the overhead rates are based on planned actual volume for the year. Generally speaking, there are three levels at which overhead rates may be set. Authorities are not in agreement about the preferable rate. You are referred to books on cost accounting for further study. The three levels are (1) budgeted output for the year, (2) practical plant capacity, and (3) the average or normal output for several years.

SCHEDULE 33. Superior Manufacturing Company

Factory Expense Budgets
(Service Departments)
For the Year Ending December 31, 19X2

EXPENSE	REF.	ANNUAL TOTAL	FIRST QUARTER			QUARTERS		
			JANUARY	FEBRUARY	MARCH	SECOND	THIRD	FOURTH
General and Administrative								
Factory Overhead:								
Volume—Total DLH	31	1,168,000	83,600	94,400	95,200	296,000	280,800	318,000
*Supervisory Salaries	(Input)	$ 96,000	$ 8,000	$ 8,000	$ 8,000	$ 24,000	$ 24,000	$ 24,000
Travel and entertainment	"	7,040	518	572	576	1,780	1,704	1,890
Telephone	"	7,586	627	649	650	1,972	1,942	2,016
*Depreciation	"	1,560	130	130	130	390	390	390
*Insurance	"	240	20	20	20	60	60	60
*Taxes	"	360	30	30	30	90	90	90
Stationery and office supplies	"	3,744	271	303	306	948	902	1,014
Total		$ 116,800	$ 9,596	$ 9,704	$ 9,712	$ 29,240	$ 29,088	$ 29,460
Power Department:								
Volume—Kilowatt Hours (000's)	"	20,000	1,450	1,600	1,600	5,100	4,800	5,450
*Supervisory salaries	"	$ 36,000	$ 3,000	$ 3,000	$ 3,000	$ 9,000	$ 9,000	$ 9,000
Maintenance	"	6,800	506	548	548	1,728	1,644	1,826
Fuel	"	24,000	1,740	1,920	1,920	6,120	5,760	6,540
*Depreciation	"	5,400	450	450	450	1,350	1,350	1,350
*Insurance	"	840	70	70	70	210	210	210
*Taxes	"	960	80	80	80	240	240	240
Wages	"	36,000	3,000	3,000	3,000	9,000	9,000	9,000
Total		$ 110,000	$ 8,846	$ 9,068	$ 9,068	$ 27,648	$ 27,204	$ 28,166
Repair Department:								
Volume—Repair Hours	(Input)	4,000	290	330	320	1,000	970	1,090
*Supervisory salaries	"	$ 3,600	$ 300	$ 300	$ 300	$ 900	$ 900	$ 900
Supplies used	"	1,360	99	112	109	340	330	370
*Depreciation	"	120	10	10	10	30	30	30
*Insurance	"	36	3	3	3	9	9	9
*Taxes	"	84	7	7	7	21	21	21
Wages	"	4,800	400	400	400	1,200	1,200	1,200
Total		$ 10,000	$ 819	$ 832	$ 829	$ 2,500	$ 2,490	$ 2,530

*Noncontrollable in this department.

SCHEDULE 34. Superior Manufacturing Company

Factory Expense Budgets
(Production Departments)
For the Year Ending December 31, 19X2

EXPENSE	REF.	ANNUAL TOTAL	FIRST QUARTER			QUARTERS		
			JANUARY	FEBRUARY	MARCH	SECOND	THIRD	FOURTH
Production Department 1								
Volume—DLH	31	488,000	34,800	39,200	39,600	124,000	117,400	133,000
*Supervisory salaries	(Input)	$120,000	$10,000	$10,000	$10,000	$ 30,000	$ 30,000	$ 30,000
Indirect labor	"	145,800	10,830	11,820	11,910	36,900	35,415	38,925
Maintenance parts	"	10,920	822	888	894	2,760	2,661	2,895
Supplies used	"	32,240	2,364	2,606	2,628	8,170	7,807	8,665
*Depreciation	"	7,320	522	588	594	1,860	1,761	1,995
*Insurance	"	1,200	100	100	100	300	300	300
*Taxes	"	1,800	150	150	150	450	450	450
Total		$319,280	$24,788	$26,152	$26,276	$ 80,440	$ 78,394	$ 83,230
Production Department 2								
Volume—DLH	31	192,000	14,000	16,000	16,000	48,000	46,000	52,000
*Supervisory salaries	(Input)	$ 22,440	$ 1,870	$ 1,870	$ 1,870	$ 5,610	$ 5,610	$ 5,610
Indirect labor	"	3,648	266	304	304	912	874	988
Maintenance parts	"	624	48	52	52	156	152	164
Supplies used	"	1,440	110	120	120	360	350	380
*Depreciation	"	768	56	64	64	192	184	208
*Insurance	"	120	10	10	10	30	30	30
*Taxes	"	240	20	20	20	60	60	60
Total		$ 29,280	$ 2,380	$ 2,440	$ 2,440	$ 7,320	$ 7,260	$ 7,440

SCHEDULE 34. (Continued)

EXPENSE	REF.	ANNUAL TOTAL	FIRST QUARTER			QUARTERS		
			JANUARY	FEBRUARY	MARCH	SECOND	THIRD	FOURTH
Production Department 3								
Volume—DLH	31	488,000	34,800	39,200	39,600	124,000	117,400	133,000
*Supervisory salaries	(Input)	$ 35,040	$ 2,920	$ 2,920	$ 2,920	$ 8,760	$ 8,760	$ 8,760
Indirect labor	"	44,248	3,271	3,583	3,612	11,204	10,735	11,843
Maintenance parts	"	4,240	324	346	348	1,070	1,037	1,115
Supplies used	"	14,600	1,070	1,180	1,190	3,700	3,535	3,925
*Depreciation	"	4,392	313	353	356	1,116	1,057	1,197
*Insurance	"	600	50	50	50	150	150	150
*Taxes	"	720	60	60	60	180	180	180
Total		$103,840	$ 8,008	$ 8,492	$ 8,536	$ 26,180	$ 25,454	$ 27,170
Summary:								
*Building services cost (from Sch. 32)		$ 90,000	$ 7,920	$ 7,380	$ 7,332	$ 21,828	$ 22,200	$ 23,340
Service departments		236,800	19,261	19,604	19,609	59,388	58,782	60,156
Production departments		452,400	35,176	37,084	37,252	113,940	111,108	117,840
Total		$779,200	$62,357	$64,068	$64,193	$195,156	$192,090	$201,336

*Noncontrollable in this department.

SCHEDULE 35. Superior Manufacturing Company

Computation of Planned Overhead Rates
For the Year Ending December 31, 19X2

ALLOCATION	TOTAL	SERVICE DEPARTMENTS			PRODUCTION DEPARTMENTS		
		GEN. ADM.	POWER	REPAIR	1	2	3
Direct Dept. Costs (Schedules 33 and 34)	$689,200	$116,800	$110,000	$10,000	$319,280	$29,280	$103,840
*Allocations:							
1. Building Services (Schedule 32)	90,000		9,000	4,500	33,201	16,481	26,818
2. General and Administrative		$116,800	11,680	11,680	58,400	11,680	23,360
3. Power Department			$130,680	3,267	65,340	32,670	29,403
4. Repair Department				$29,447	11,779	5,889	11,779
Total	$779,200				$488,000	$96,000	$195,200
Direct labor hours (Schedule 31)					488,000	192,000	488,000
Overhead rates (per DLH)					$1.00	$ .50	$ .40

Standard service charges:

Power: $\frac{\$130,680}{20,000}$ = $6.53 per 1,000 kilowatt hours

Repair: $\frac{\$29,447}{4,000}$ = $7.36 per direct repair hour

*Distribution basis (page 321):
1. Relative floor space
2. Selected percentages
3. Planned kilowatt hours
4. Planned direct repair hours

SCHEDULE 36. Superior Manufacturing Company

Manufacturing Expenses Applied by Product
For the Year Ending December 31, 19X2

	REF.	TOTALS	FIRST QUARTER			QUARTERS			
			JANUARY	FEBRUARY	MARCH	FIRST	SECOND	THIRD	FOURTH
Product X									
Department 1									
Direct labor hours	31	384,000	28,000	32,000	32,000	92,000	96,000	92,000	104,000
Rate	35	× $1.00	$1.00	$1.00	$1.00	$1.00	$1.00	$1.00	$1.00
Amount		$384,000	$28,000	$32,000	$32,000	$ 92,000	$ 96,000	$ 92,000	$104,000
Department 2									
Direct labor hours	31	192,000	14,000	16,000	16,000	46,000	48,000	46,000	52,000
Rate	35	× $ .50	$ .50	$ .50	$ .50	$ .50	$ .50	$ .50	$ .50
Amount		$ 96,000	$ 7,000	$ 8,000	$ 8,000	$ 23,000	$ 24,000	$ 23,000	$ 26,000
Department 3									
Direct labor hours	31	384,000	28,000	32,000	32,000	92,000	96,000	92,000	104,000
Rate	35	× $ .40	$ .40	$ .40	$ .40	$ .40	$ .40	$ .40	$ .40
Amount		$153,600	$11,200	$12,800	$12,800	$ 36,800	$ 38,400	$ 36,800	$ 41,600
Total product X		$633,600	$46,200	$52,800	$52,800	$151,800	$158,400	$151,800	$171,600
Product Y									
Department 1									
Direct labor hours	31	104,000	6,800	7,200	7,600	21,600	28,000	25,400	29,000
Rate	35	× $1.00	$1.00	$1.00	$1.00	$1.00	$1.00	$1.00	$1.00
Amount		$104,000	$ 6,800	$ 7,200	$ 7,600	$ 21,600	$ 28,000	$ 25,400	$ 29,000
Department 3									
Direct labor hours	31	104,000	6,800	7,200	7,600	21,600	28,000	25,400	29,000
Rate	35	× $ .40	$ .40	$ .40	$ .40	$ .40	$ .40	$ .40	$ .40
Amount		$ 41,600	$ 2,720	$ 2,880	$ 3,040	$ 8,640	$ 11,200	$ 10,160	$ 11,600
Total product Y		$145,600	$ 9,520	$10,080	$10,640	$ 30,240	$ 39,200	$ 35,560	$ 40,600
Total all products		$779,200	$55,720	$62,880	$63,440	$182,040	$197,600	$187,360	$212,200

SCHEDULE 37. Superior Manufacturing Company

Budgeted Overhead Over/Under Applied*
For the Year Ending December 31, 19X2

| | | | ALL DEPARTMENTS | | |
	REF.	PLANNED ACCRUALS	TOTAL APPLIED	OVER	UNDER	CUMULATIVE
	REF.	33 & 34	36			
Time periods:						
January		$ 62,357	$ 55,720		$ 6,637	$ 6,637
February		64,068	62,880		1,188	7,825
March		64,193	63,440		753	8,578
First Quarter		190,618	182,040		8,578	8,578
Second Quarter		195,156	197,600	$ 2,444		
Third Quarter		192,090	187,360		4,730	10,864
Fourth Quarter		201,336	212,200	10,864		
Annual total		$779,200	$779,200	$13,308	$13,308	

*Although not illustrated here, it is frequently advisable to compute the application of fixed and variable overhead separately and maintain this segregation in cost of goods manufactured, sold, and in inventories. This segregation can be accomplished in the accounts or as a separate analysis and is useful as a basis for certain managerial decisions.

Selling Expense Budgets Illustrated

Recall that the sales division of Superior Manufacturing Company (Exhibit 4-1) has three sales districts (Southern, Eastern, and Western) and one general department (general sales overhead, that is, home sales office).

The promotion plan developed by the advertising manager is summarized in Schedule 38. Notice that one-twelfth of the annual allowance is shown in the expense budgets as a monthly fixed expense because it represents an annual appropriation.

SCHEDULE 38. Superior Manufacturing Company

Promotion Plan Summary
For the Year Ending December 31, 19X2

DEPARTMENT	ANNUAL APPROPRIATION
Home Office	$ 60,000
Southern District	24,000
Eastern District	36,000
Western District	12,000
Total	$132,000

The manager of each sales district and the home sales office developed a tentative expense budget, which was given to higher management for evaluation and approval. Notice that the **activity base** (measure of output) in each expense budget is **sales dollars.** The activity-base output for each department is shown in the sales plan (Schedule 21, Chapter 5). The distribution expense budgets are shown in Schedule 39.

ADMINISTRATIVE EXPENSE BUDGETS ILLUSTRATED   The organization chart for the company shows three administrative departments (administrative, accounting, and treasurer). The **activity base** for these departments selected by the management is **total** sales dollars as shown in the sales budget (Schedule 21, Chapter 5). Based on the planned output or activity, the departmental managers developed their expense budgets, which were approved by higher management. These expense budgets are shown in Schedule 40.

The director of profit planning and control consolidates the fourteen expense budgets illustrated into the overall profit plan, as will be shown in Chapter 13.

PLANNING EXPENSES IN NONMANUFACTURING ENTERPRISES   A nonmanufacturing enterprise should develop expense budgets for company administrative expenses and distribution expenses by responsibility centers, as discussed above for manufacturing enterprises.

Similar to that described for manufacturing companies, each manager who has cost-incurring responsibilities should actively participate in planning the expenses for the particular responsibility center. Expenses should be classified as fixed or variable. Flexible expense budgets similar to those discussed in Chapter 10 should be used. A problem in flexible budgeting is selection of appropriate measures of responsibility center activities. In nonmanufacturing companies, net sales dollars is appropriate for some centers while the number of transactions may be more appropriate for others.

To evaluate and adjust expense budgets developed by participating managers, a computation such as the following can be used:

Planned February sales (Exhibit 5-6)	$90,000
Planned cost of sales, at cost (Exhibit 7-3)	40,990*
Planned gross margin (maintained markup)	49,010
Necessary profit margin (3% of net sales)	2,700
Budget expense limitation	$46,310

*No inventory change in February.

When the expense budgets are approved, they are incorporated into the profit plan and provide essential data for budgeting cash, and the like, in the manner previously discussed and illustrated.

SCHEDULE 39. Superior Manufacturing Company

Selling Expense Budgets
For the Year Ending December 31, 19X2
Activity Base—Sales Dollars

EXPENSE	REF.	ANNUAL TOTAL	FIRST QUARTER			QUARTERS			
			JANUARY	FEBRUARY	MARCH	FIRST	SECOND	THIRD	FOURTH
General Sales Overhead									
*Supervisory salaries	(Input)	$144,000	$12,000	$12,000	$12,000	$ 36,000	$ 36,000	$ 36,000	$ 36,000
Travel and entertainment	"	38,907	3,208	3,389	3,545	10,142	10,053	8,052	10,660
Telephone	"	15,861	1,314	1,353	1,387	4,054	4,035	3,607	4,165
*Depreciation—office equipment	"	600	50	50	50	150	150	150	150
Stationery and office supplies	"	11,049	909	968	1,019	2,896	2,868	2,221	3,064
Auto expense	"	25,913	2,132	2,275	2,397	6,804	6,734	5,165	7,210
Advertising	"	60,000	5,000	5,000	5,000	15,000	15,000	15,000	15,000
Total		$296,330	$24,613	$25,035	$25,398	$ 75,046	$ 74,840	$ 70,195	$ 76,249
Southern Sales District									
*Supervisory salaries	"	$ 72,000	$ 6,000	$ 6,000	$ 6,000	$ 18,000	$ 18,000	$ 18,000	$ 18,000
Travel and entertainment	"	25,279	2,129	2,314	2,184	6,627	6,525	5,466	6,661
Telephone and telegraph	"	9,379	789	847	806	2,442	2,410	2,075	2,452
Commissions	"	84,800	7,200	8,280	7,520	23,000	22,400	16,200	23,200
Freight and express	"	19,198	1,628	1,857	1,696	5,181	5,054	3,738	5,225
Advertising	"	24,000	2,000	2,000	2,000	6,000	6,000	6,000	6,000
Total		$234,656	$19,746	$21,298	$20,206	$ 61,250	$ 60,389	$ 51,479	$ 61,538

SCHEDULE 39. (Continued)

EXPENSE	REF.	ANNUAL TOTAL	FIRST QUARTER			QUARTERS			
			JANUARY	FEBRUARY	MARCH	FIRST	SECOND	THIRD	FOURTH
Eastern Sales District									
*Supervisory salaries	(Input)	$ 96,000	$ 8,000	$ 8,000	$ 8,000	$ 24,000	$ 24,000	$ 24,000	$ 24,000
Travel and entertainment	"	30,812	2,470	2,675	2,852	7,997	8,065	6,454	8,296
Telephone	"	14,828	1,198	1,277	1,346	3,821	3,848	3,221	3,938
Commissions	"	116,280	9,084	10,356	11,460	30,900	31,320	21,300	32,760
Freight and express	"	19,471	1,530	1,724	1,893	5,147	5,213	3,679	5,432
Advertising	"	36,000	3,000	3,000	3,000	9,000	9,000	9,000	9,000
Total		$313,391	$25,282	$27,032	$28,551	$ 80,865	$ 81,446	$ 67,654	$ 83,426
Western Sales District									
*Supervisory sales	"	$ 36,000	$ 3,000	$ 3,000	$ 3,000	$ 9,000	$ 9,000	$ 9,000	$ 9,000
Travel and entertainment	"	11,641	1,001	865	1,045	2,911	2,804	2,580	3,346
Telephone and telegraph	"	4,915	421	371	437	1,229	1,190	1,109	1,387
Commissions	"	42,720	3,732	2,964	3,984	10,680	10,080	8,820	13,140
Freight and express	"	7,844	674	583	704	1,961	1,890	1,740	2,253
Advertising	"	12,000	1,000	1,000	1,000	3,000	3,000	3,000	3,000
Total		$115,120	$ 9,828	$ 8,783	$10,170	$ 28,781	$ 27,964	$ 26,249	$ 32,126
Summary Total									
Total all departments		$959,497	$79,469	$82,148	$84,325	$245,942	$244,639	$215,577	$253,339
*Add building services cost		30,000	2,640	2,460	2,444	7,544	7,276	7,400	7,780
Total company		$989,497	$82,109	$84,608	$86,769	$253,486	$251,915	$222,977	$261,119

*Noncontrollable in this department.

SCHEDULE 40. Superior Manufacturing Company

Administrative Expense Budgets
For the Year Ending December 31, 19X2
Activity Base—Total Sales Dollars

	REF.	ANNUAL TOTAL	FIRST QUARTER			QUARTERS			
			JANUARY	FEBRUARY	MARCH	FIRST	SECOND	THIRD	FOURTH
Administrative Department									
*Supervisory salaries	(Input)	$ 60,000	$ 5,000	$ 5,000	$ 5,000	$15,000	$15,000	$15,000	$15,000
Travel and entertainment	"	9,000	750	750	750	2,250	2,250	2,250	2,250
Telephone	"	9,114	750	798	839	2,387	2,364	1,840	2,523
*Depreciation	"	600	50	50	50	150	150	150	150
*Insurance	"	240	20	20	20	60	60	60	60
*Taxes	"	240	20	20	20	60	60	60	60
Stationery and office supplies	"	122	10	11	12	33	32	23	34
Lawyer retainer fee	"	1,800	150	150	150	450	450	450	450
Audit fee	"	2,400	200	200	200	600	600	600	600
Total		$ 83,516	$ 6,950	$ 6,999	$ 7,041	$20,990	$20,966	$20,433	$21,127
Accounting Department									
*Supervisory salaries	"	$ 48,000	$ 4,000	$ 4,000	$ 4,000	$12,000	$12,000	$12,000	$12,000
Travel and entertainment	"	1,200	100	100	100	300	300	300	300
Telephone and telegraph	"	1,210	100	104	107	311	310	266	323
*Depreciation	"	2,400	200	200	200	600	600	600	600
*Insurance	"	240	20	20	20	60	60	60	60
*Taxes	"	360	30	30	30	90	90	90	90
Stationery and office supplies	"	610	50	54	57	161	160	116	173
Total		$ 54,020	$ 4,500	$ 4,508	$ 4,514	$13,522	$13,520	$13,432	$13,546

332

SCHEDULE 40. (Continued)

	REF.	ANNUAL TOTAL	FIRST QUARTER			QUARTERS			
			JANUARY	FEBRUARY	MARCH	FIRST	SECOND	THIRD	FOURTH
Treasurer Department									
*Supervisory salaries	(Input)	$ 36,000	$ 3,000	$ 3,000	$ 3,000	$ 9,000	$ 9,000	$ 9,000	$ 9,000
Travel and entertainment	"	1,200	100	100	100	300	300	300	300
Telephone	"	3,158	260	276	290	826	818	643	871
*Depreciation	"	1,200	100	100	100	300	300	300	300
*Insurance	"	480	40	40	40	120	120	120	120
*Taxes	"	120	10	10	10	30	30	30	30
Stationery and office supplies	"	1,829	151	162	172	485	479	347	518
Loss on bad debts	"	12,190	1,001	1,080	1,148	3,229	3,190	2,316	3,455
Total		$ 56,177	$ 4,662	$ 4,768	$ 4,860	$14,290	$14,237	$13,056	$14,594
Summary									
Total all departments		$193,713	$16,112	$16,275	$16,415	$48,802	$48,723	$46,921	$49,267
*Building services cost		30,000	2,640	2,460	2,444	7,544	7,276	7,400	7,780
Total company		$223,713	$18,752	$18,735	$18,859	$56,346	$55,999	$54,321	$57,047

*Noncontrollable within the department.

CHAPTER SUMMARY This chapter discussed the problems of planning and controlling three broad categories of expense: factory or manufacturing overhead, distribution expenses, and general administrative expenses. To accomplish these planning and control objectives, expenses should be classified by responsibility, designated as controllable or noncontrollable, and estimated with respect to their cost behavior pattern.

It is important to be aware of the distinction between cost reduction and cost control. **Cost control** refers to managerial efforts to attain cost goals, while **cost reduction** implies that existing cost levels must be reduced. **Product quality costing** refers to the efforts of some companies to systematically identify the costs that are incurred to maintain an acceptable level of product quality. **Quality of conformance** refers to the degree to which the final product adheres to its specifications. The costs associated with quality of conformance include prevention costs, appraisal costs, internal failure costs, and external failure costs. Headcount forecasting is a method used by some firms to predict indirect labor costs such as general administration, research and development, marketing, and product engineering.

Nonmanufacturing companies use similar techniques to plan and control expenses. For example, airlines must plan and control the costs of indirect labor, aircraft repair, scheduling, ticketing and customer service, and advertising.

Suggested References

BIERMAN, HAROLD, JR., THOMAS DYCKMAN, and RONALD HILTON, *Cost Accounting: Concepts and Managerial Applications*. New York: Macmillan, 1990.

CLARK, J., "Costing for Quality at Celanese," *Management Accounting*, March 1985, pp. 42–46.

HORNGREN, C. T., and G. FOSTER, *Cost Accounting: A Managerial Emphasis*. Englewood Cliffs N.J.: Prentice-Hall, 1987.

KAPLAN, R. S., "Measuring Manufacturing Performance: A New Challenge for Managerial Accounting Research," *Accounting Review*, October 1983, pp. 686–705.

ROTH, H. P., and W. J. MORSE, "Let's Help Measure and Report Quality Costs," *Management Accounting*, August 1983, pp. 50–53.

Discussion Questions

1. What are the primary reasons for, and focus of, planning expenses?
2. Why is it especially important to classify expenses in terms of organizational responsibility?
3. Explain the classification of expenses related to changes in output or activity.
4. Distinguish between controllable and noncontrollable costs.

5. Distinguish between expense control and expense reduction.

6. Which primary classifications of expenses should be incorporated into the annual profit plan?

7. What are the unique problems related to planning manufacturing expenses or factory overhead?

8. Explain the problem of cost allocation as related to (1) product costing and (2) cost control.

9. What is meant by the activity base? Explain its significance.

10. What are the primary types of product quality costs?

11. What is a headcount forecast algorithm?

12. What is the relationship between the marketing plan, sales budget, and distribution expenses?

13. "Promotion and advertising expenses are usually best planned and controlled on the basis of definite appropriations." Explain this statement.

14. Who should be responsible for preparing expense budgets? Explain.

CASE 9-1   *Make extensive recommendations about expense control*

Ervin Manufacturing Company produces a line of electric heaters that are distributed nationwide through hardware and similar wholesale outlets. The heaters are designed primarily for heating small areas and are portable. Both 110- and 220-volt heaters are manufactured, and the lines include fourteen different models of varying sizes, styles, and prices. The heaters are manufactured in a central plant. Ervin sells directly to approximately forty different wholesale outlets, which in turn sell the heaters to retail outlets. Annual sales during the past year approximated $38 million. The organization of the company is summarized below. The company has been operating for approximately thirty years.

The company employs a traditional cost accounting system (historical absorption basis), and quarterly financial statements are prepared for internal management purposes. There are approximately two hundred stockholders. A summarized (and unaudited) financial statement is mailed to the stockholders annually. During the past three years, the company lagged the industry average in both profits and growth. The organization chart shows two changes that were made during the past year by the new president employed from outside the company: (1) the sales division was reorganized and the six sales regions were established (prior to this reorganization all sales supervision was direct from the home office); (2) the financial division was organized (prior to the reorganization the functions were performed separately by a treasurer and chief accountant, who were designated as staff assistants). Each division is headed by a vice-president, including the newly employed financial vice-president. The president and the financial vice-president are designing and implementing a comprehensive profit planning and control program. The president stated that a decision had been made to "adopt a responsibility accounting system and to use standard costs in the factory division." The president favors "bottom-up" planning and control and appears to fully realize that due to past precedent, it will be difficult to implement in the short run in this company. At a recent meeting of the executive committee (president and the three vice-presidents), the president stated that "each division manager will be responsible for planning and controlling all aspects of his or her function."

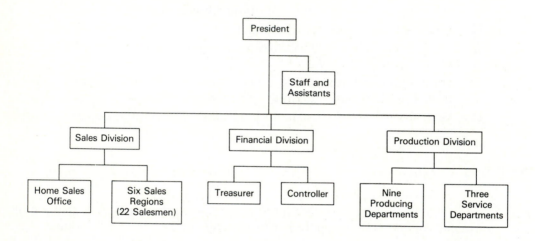

This case focuses on the approaches that should be used in planning and controlling expenses throughout the company.

REQUIRED

1. You are to consider all aspects of planning and controlling expenses in the company and give your recommendations. You should consider such factors as organizational responsibility, accounting approaches, expense classifications, planning expenses, approval of budgets, performance reports, and corrective action. Justify all the recommendations that you make.

2. Assume that a supervisor of profit planning and control will be hired. Where should this supervisor be placed in the organization structure? What should the supervisor's responsibilities be in respect to planning and controlling expenses?

CASE 9-2   *Develop an overhead accounting system*

Barden Manufacturing Company is a medium-size company that produces two primary products sold in the automotive parts industry. There is a single plant, and manufacturing operations entail a particularly high investment in machinery. Consequently, manufacturing overhead is a significant cost; this case focuses on this cost. The plant is managed by Sam Collins, the manufacturing manager. The plant includes two service and two producing departments (actually there are more departments, but these four are representative for case purposes). Product X is processed through both producing departments, whereas product Y is processed only through the first department. The two producing departments are designated as 1 and 2, and the two service departments as 3 and 4 for convenience. Direct material and direct labor costs are incurred in both producing departments. During the past year, the company initiated a profit planning and control program. The controller stated that efforts were continuing "to perfect the program and to coordinate it with the cost accounting system." In past years, the cost accounting system was kept as simple as possible. Actual material, labor, and factory overhead costs were accumulated for each month and then allocated to the two products at the end of each month. The management has decided to use standard (i.e., budgeted) rates for factory overhead.

Management is currently preparing the annual profit plan. The sales plan has been tentatively approved. Based on the sales plan and the inventory policies (for products X and Y), the following production plan has been developed by the manufacturing manager and staff:

PRODUCT	ANNUAL	JANUARY	FEBRUARY	MARCH	REMAINING MONTHS
X	12,500	1,000	800	1,100	9,600
Y	20,000	1,800	1,400	2,300	14,500

The manufacturing manager, in cooperation with the controller's department, developed the following measures of output:

DEPARTMENT	ACTIVITY BASE
1 Producing	Direct machine hours
2 Producing	Units of product
3 Factory administrative	Number of employees in factory
4 Maintenance	Direct repair hours

The following standards have been established for planning purposes for the budget year:

a Direct machine hours per unit of product in Dept. 1: X—4; Y—5
b Direct repair hours: Dept. 1—4 for each 100 direct machine hours; Dept. 2—.16 for each unit of product
c Excerpt from staffing table (number of employees planned): Dept. 1—40; Dept. 2—25; Dept. 3—10; Dept. 4—5
d Totals from department overhead budgets for the budget year: Dept. 1—$764,000; Dept. 2—$330,500; Dept. 3—$70,000; Dept. 4—$123,000

REQUIRED

1. Do you agree with the "activity base" selected for each department? Explain.
2. Translate the production budget into "annual activity" for each of the four departments.
3. Compute the standard overhead rates for each producing department. The allocations of service department overhead will be on the basis of activities determined in requirement 2.
4. Develop the planned cost of goods manufactured for the year by product. Planned costs: direct material—product X $62,500; product Y, $80,000; direct labor—product X, $37,500; product Y, $40,000.
5. Describe one approach the company may have used to develop the department overhead budget amounts given in requirement 4 above.

CASE 9-3   *Overhead rates; statement of cost of goods manufactured; performance report*

Carter Manufacturing Company produces two products (designated X and Y). The manufacturing division consists of two producing departments (designated 1 and 2) and two service departments (designated 3 and 4). The company uses a historical (absorption) cost system except that predetermined (budgeted) overhead rates are used in the producing departments to allocate factory overhead to the products. The rate for Department 1 is based on direct machine hours (DMH), and the rate for Department 2 is based on direct labor hours (DLH). In applying overhead during the year, the budgeted overhead rates are multiplied by actual hours. The following budget and actual data are available:

1. Annual profit plan data:
   a. Factory overhead budgeted for the year: Dept. 1, $85,000; Dept. 2, $72,500; Dept. 3, $20,000; Dept. 4, $15,000. Machine operators' salaries are treated as an overhead cost.
   b. Budgeted units to be produced: product X, 50,000; product Y, 30,000.
   c. Budgeted material cost per unit of product (all used in Dept. 1): product X, $4.00; product Y, $5.00. No material is added in Dept. 2.
   d. Budgeted time required for production: direct machine hours in Dept. 1 for each unit of finished goods—product X, $1\frac{1}{2}$; Product Y, 1. Direct labor hours in Dept. 2 for each unit of finished goods—product X, 2; product Y, $2\frac{1}{2}$.
   e. Average wage rates budgeted in Dept. 2: product X, $2.40; product Y, $2.50.
   f. Allocation of service department cost to producing departments:
      Dept. 3—allocate $\frac{1}{2}$ to Dept. 1 and $\frac{1}{2}$ to Dept. 2
      Dept. 4—allocate $\frac{2}{3}$ to Dept. 1 and $\frac{1}{3}$ to Dept. 2
2. January actual data:
   a. Units actually produced in January—product X, 4,000; product Y, 3,000.
   b. Actual direct machine hours in Dept. 1—product X, 6,100; product Y, 4,150.
   c. Actual costs incurred:

DEPT.	FACTORY OVERHEAD	DIRECT MATERIAL	DIRECT LABOR HOURS	DIRECT LABOR AMOUNT
1	$7,700	X $16,300 Y 15,200		
2	6,800		X 8,200 Y 7,400	$19,730 18,400
3	2,000			
4	1,600			

REQUIRED

1. Compute the budgeted overhead rate for each producing department; show your computations.
2. Use the actual data for direct materials and direct labor and the budgeted overhead rates computed in requirement 1 to prepare a statement of "Cost of Goods Manufactured—January Actual."
3. Prepare a performance report for January that will reflect the status of cost control for each item of cost by department. Since the company does not develop monthly cost budgets, it uses one-twelfth of the annual budget amount for factory overhead as the monthly budget goal. Explain any concerns that you have about the performance report.

CASE 9-4   *Criticize an expense budget and a performance report*

The January performance report for Department 21 (given below) was received by the manager of the department, Martin Gaines, on the twelfth of February. Gaines quickly noticed that all the variances were "unfavorable—and wrong!" The company has been budgeting expenses for the past three years. Monthly performance reports are prepared for each responsibility center. The manager of each responsibility center is expected to discuss the center's report in detail with the factory manager and to work out approaches to correct unfavorable variances. The Department 21 expense budget from the annual profit plan is also shown below.

The discussion with Jim Fowler, the factory manager, started like this: "Martin, I'm glad you came in. We need to discuss your performance report." "Well, Jim, that's not what I came in to talk about. I'm all tied up with the special milling machine. It's not working right, and we need to fly in some parts as well as a specialist to help us—can you approve it now? I would like to defer discussing that report until next week (February 26) when we have plenty of time. If you ask me, something needs to be done about those performance reports anyway." "OK, Martin."

The factory expense budgets shown in the annual profit plan (given below) were initially prepared in the controller's department and then submitted to the factory manager for "evaluation and return." The factory manager in turn referred them to the departmental managers for comment. Subsequently, they were approved by the factory manager as shown below.

DEPARTMENT 21: January Performance Report

	ACTUAL	BUDGET	VARIANCE
Output (units)	13,000	11,000	2,000
Direct material	$20,000	$19,500	$ 500
Direct labor	32,700	32,500	200
Departmental overhead:			
Salaries	2,500	2,500	
Indirect labor	4,950	4,350	500
Supplies	3,850	3,200	650
Overtime	1,100	1,000	200
Miscellaneous	670	550	120
Power (standard charge)	1,090	1,040	50
Total	$66,860	$64,640	$2,220

DEPARTMENT 21: Expense Budget from the Annual Profit Plan

	ANNUAL	JANUARY	FEBRUARY
Output (units)	120,000	11,000	9,000
Direct material	$180,000	$16,500	$13,500
Direct labor	300,000	27,500	22,500
Departmental overhead:			
Salaries	30,000	2,500	2,500
Indirect labor	48,000	4,350	3,650
Supplies	36,000	3,200	2,800
Overtime	12,000	1,000	1,000
Miscellaneous	6,000	550	450
Power	9,600	880	720
Total	$621,600	$56,480	$46,120

REQUIRED

1. Do you agree with the approach used to develop the expense budgets for the annual profit plan? Explain.

2. Critically examine all aspects of the performance report. Do you find any basis for Gaines's criticisms? Explain. Give your recommendations for improvement.

CASE 9-5 *Analyze budget amounts and recommend how to start a PPC program*

Value Food Processing Company employs approximately 375 people and distributes its products in a three-state area. The company has never prepared a budget. To support an increased line of credit, the bank has requested the management to furnish a budgeted income statement, a cash flow statement, and a balance sheet covering the next six months. The sales and production budgets have been tentatively approved by the management. No substantial change in inventories is planned.

The sales manager developed the following budget of sales and distribution expenses:

| | ACTUAL PAST SIX MONTHS | | PROPOSED |
	AMOUNT	PERCENT	BUDGET
Sales revenue	$6,800,000		$7,956,000
Sales expenses:			
Salaries	181,600	15.0	212,400
Commission	340,000	28.1	397,800
Promotion	160,600	13.3	188,300
Travel	275,400	22.8	322,800
Entertainment	40,300	3.3	46,700
Freight	179,200	14.8	209,500
Depreciation, taxes, and insurance			
on autos	17,500	1.4	19,800
Miscellaneous	15,400	1.3	18,400
Total	$1,210,000		$1,415,700

The production manager developed the following budget of factory costs:

	ACTUAL PAST SIX MONTHS	PROPOSED BUDGET
Direct material	$2,924,000	$3,500,000
Direct labor	1,571,000	1,880,472
Factory overhead:		
Salaries	253,800	253,800
Wages	204,200	224,620
Supplies	87,500	102,375
Utilities	135,100	135,100
Depreciation, taxes, and insurance		
on autos	165,200	165,200
Services	58,400	64,240
Miscellaneous	68,200	79,794
	972,400	1,015,129
Total	$5,467,400	$6,395,601

The president said, "From now on we will continue to budget operations each year in this manner."

REQUIRED

1. Give an analysis that shows how the distribution and factory budget amounts were derived.

2. Assess the budget amounts and approach used. Give your basic recommendations for starting a profit planning and control program in Value Company.

10

Flexible Expense Budgets: Concepts, Development, and Application

INTRODUCTION AND PURPOSE   The preceding chapter discussed the planning of expenses for inclusion in the short-term (tactical) profit plan. This chapter discusses the concept of flexible expense budgets. The focus will be on both planned expenses and the control of expenses. The flexible budget concept is complementary to the tactical profit plan. Flexible budgets for expenses have two functions: (1) to provide expense plans for the tactical profit plan and (2) to provide expense plans adjusted to actual output, for comparison with actual expenses in periodic performance reports.

This chapter discusses and illustrates the theory, construction, and application of flexible budgets for expenses in a comprehensive profit planning and control program.

Flexible budgets directly relate only to expenses (and costs). Flexible budgets are also called variable, dynamic, activity, and output-adjusted expense budgets. The term **flexible budgets** is used in this book because it focuses on fixed, variable, and semivariable expenses—not just variable expenses.

CONCEPTS OF FLEXIBLE EXPENSE BUDGETS   The fundamental concept of flexible budgets for expenses is that all expenses are incurred because of (a) the passage of time, (b) output or productive activity, or (c) a combination of time and output or activity. If this premise is reasonable in a business (or any other entity), the expenses can be given mathematical formulations from which expense plans can be computed for planning and control. Application of this concept means that

1 Expenses must be identified as to their fixed and variable components when related to output or productive activity.

2 Expenses must be reasonably related to output or productive activity.

3 Output or productive activity must be reliably measurable.

4 Flexible budget formulas for each expense must be for a specified time period and for a specified relevant range of output or productive activity.

5 For planning and control purposes, flexible budget formulas must be developed for each expense in each responsibility center in an enterprise.

RELATIONSHIP OF EXPENSES TO OUTPUT OR PRODUCTIVE ACTIVITY The foundation underlying flexible budgets for expenses (and costs) is the concept of expense variability. This concept focuses on the effect on expenses (and costs) of the passage of time and output or productive activity.

Throughout this chapter, we use **expense** to include **costs** because flexible budgets relate to both of these terms. Technically, costs are expenditures that are capitalized as assets and later become expenses when the related goods and services are used or the manufactured goods are sold. Also, we use the terms **activities** and **activity base** to include output and productive activities.

Any attempt to set budget amounts for expenses related to actual output or activity in a responsibility center requires data about the effect of output or activity on expenses. The point is, As output or activity increases or decreases in a responsibility center, what should be the behavior of each expense incurred in that center? Some "fixed" expenses, such as monthly salaries, are not influenced by changes in output or activity. Also, some "variable" expenses, such as direct raw materials used in production, fluctuate proportionally with changes in output or activity. Then there are "mixed" expenses that change but not in direct proportion to changes in volume or activity. The primary objective of the flexible budget approach is to show how, and to what extent, each expense in a responsibility center is changed by the amount of work done in that center.

Flexible budget formulas are developed that specify for each expense a fixed (or constant) amount and a variable rate per unit of activity. The variable rate specifies the relationship between the expense and the related output or productive activity. For example, Exhibit 10-1 shows a flexible expense budget for one responsibility center. Notice the five flexible budget formulas:

EXPENSE	FIXED AMOUNT (PER MONTH)	VARIABLE RATE (PER UNIT OF ACTIVITY)
Direct material	$ -0-	$10.00
Direct labor	-0-	8.00
Salaries	6,000	-0-
Supplies	-0-	1.00
Indirect labor	4,000	2.00

If 10,000 units of output or activity are planned for a particular month, the planned amount of indirect labor would be: $4,000 + ($2 \times 10,000) = $24,000$.

EXHIBIT 10-1

Flexible Budget—Hypo Company, Department 22, Year 19X

	Supervisor	John Ware
	Base Units of output	Component part X-17
	Relevant range for use	9,000 to 12,000 units inclusive

CONTROLLABLE EXPENSES	COST BEHAVIOR*	FIXED AMOUNT PER MONTH	VARIABLE RATE PER UNIT OF OUTPUT
Direct material	V	$ 0	$10.00
Direct labor	V	0	8.00
Department overhead:			
Salaries	F	6,000	0
Supplies	V	0	1.00
Indirect labor	SV	4,000	2.00
Total		$10,000	$21.00

*V—Variable
 F—Fixed
SV—Semivariable

Because some expenses are part fixed and part variable, expenses are classified into three categories:

1 Fixed expenses
2 Variable expenses
3 Semivariable expenses

To classify expenses and costs on this basis, it is essential that each category be clearly defined. Throughout accounting and budgeting literature, these classes of expense have been variously labeled and defined. We have selected the above terminology for discussion purposes.

Fixed Expenses Defined

Fixed expenses are those that do not vary with output or productive activity. They accrue primarily with the passage of time, that is, they are time expenses. They remain constant in amount for a given short-term period within a relevant range of activity (discussed later). Fixed expenses are caused by the holding of assets and the other factors of production in a state of "readiness to produce"; therefore, they are frequently called capacity costs. Fixed expenses are of two principal types. First, executive management decisions establish commitments to certain fixed expenses. Examples of such expenses are depreciation, taxes, and insurance. Second, some fixed expenses are set by management discretion on a short-term basis. Salaries, advertising expenditures, and research expenditures fall into this category. They may fluctuate by reason of changes in the basic structure of the business, operating methods, and discretionary changes in management policy. The following list explains the characteristics of fixed expenses that a company should consider in establishing a practical definition.

1   **Relationship to Output Activity**—Fixed expenses result from the capacity to produce or to perform some activity. They may be influenced by factors other than the passage of time, but not by output or the performance of activity.

2   **Relevant Range**—Fixed expenses must be related to a relevant range of activity. Few, if any, expenses would remain constant over the wide range of output or activity from zero to full capacity. The fixed expenses at one range of activity will normally be different at other ranges because increases or decreases in capacity may change fixed expenses. Therefore, in the definition and classification of expenses it is essential that a relevant range of activity be specified. The relevant range of activity sets up definite limitations on the validity of the flexible budget formulas.

3   **Time Costs**—Because fixed expenses primarily accrue with the passage of time, the amount of a fixed expense must also be related to a specified period of time. For budget purposes, fixed expenses should be related to the annual accounting period and expressed as a constant amount per month.

4   **Management Regulated**—Estimates of many fixed expenses imply that certain management policy decisions have been made. Many fixed expenses are dependent on specific management decisions. They may change only if these decisions change. For example, in budgeting salaries, managerial policies on salary levels must be known or anticipated to set the fixed amount.

5   **Fixed in Total but Variable per Unit**—A fixed expense is constant in the total amount each period; however, when viewed in terms of units of output, it has a variable effect on unit cost. These different effects frequently cause confusion. Assume fixed costs of $9,600 within a relevant range of 800 to 1,200 units. If 1,200 units are produced, the fixed cost per unit is $8.00; however, if 1,000 are produced, the fixed cost per unit is $9.60. The total cost remains constant at $9,600 regardless of the quantity produced, whereas the unit cost changes inversely with volume.

6   **Practical Application**—Practical considerations do not require an expense to be absolutely fixed. In application, a fixed expense is one that is constant for all practical purposes.

Controllability of fixed expenses is sometimes incorrectly viewed. All fixed expenses are controllable over the life span of the company. Some, but not all, fixed expenses are subject to short-run management control. Numerous fixed expenses are determined annually by the discretionary management policies. Depreciation expense in a short time period is subject to very little control. Control was "exercised" when the asset was acquired and when the depreciation rate was set.

The characteristics of two kinds of fixed expenses are shown in Exhibit 10-2. Case I illustrates an unusual fixed expense that appears to remain constant over the wide range of acitivty from zero to full capacity. Case II shows a more typical fixed expense, which is constant within specified relevant ranges of activity. In both cases, the expense should be included in the variable budget as a fixed expense at $3,000 per period.

EXHIBIT 10-2

Fixed Expenses Illustrated

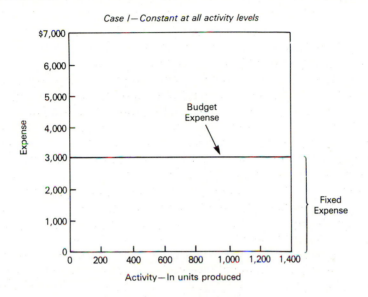

Case I — Constant at all activity levels

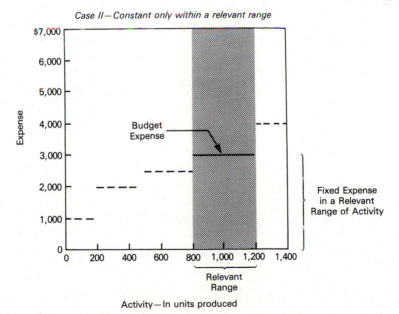

Case II — Constant only within a relevant range

Variable Expenses Defined

Variable expenses (and costs) vary in direct proportion to changes in output or activity in a responsibility center. Variable expenses are activity based because they are incurred as a direct result of output, productive activity, or work done. They would not exist were it not for the performance of some activity. A variable expense is necessarily zero at zero activity. Variable expenses increase or decrease directly with changes in output; therefore, if output is doubled, the variable expense is doubled; or if output decreases by 10 percent, the expense decreases by 10 percent. The following list explains the primary characteristics a company should consider in establishing a practical definition of variable expenses:

1   **Proportionally Related to Activity**—Variable expenses vary in proportion to output or productive activity rather than with the passage of time. Because they vary in direct proportion to changes in output or activity, they are constant on a per-unit basis when related to some measure of activity.

2   **Relevant Range**—Variable expenses must be related to activity within a relevant range of operations. Outside this normal range, the pattern of variable expenses will usually change.

3   **Activity Costs**—Because variable expenses fluctuate in proportion to changes in output or activity, it is important that a reliable measure of activity be selected. For example, in a producing department working on several different products simultaneously, units of the several products would not be additive. Therefore, some common measure of work done, such as machine hours or direct labor hours, must be used. The measure of output or activity selected is generally referred to as the activity base.

4   **Management Regulated**—Most variable expenses can be affected by the discretionary decisions of management. For example, the management of a factory may decide to use a less-expensive raw material than that currently used, thereby reducing the amount of variable cost, although the cost is still variable but at a different rate.

5   **Variable in Total but Fixed per Unit**—A variable expense or cost is variable when related to output; however, when viewed as a unit cost it is a constant. Assume a variable cost of $4,000. If 800 units are produced, the variable cost per unit is $5.00. However, if 1,200 units (a 50 percent increase) are produced, the variable cost would be $6,000 (a 50 percent increase); the variable cost per unit remains $5.00.

6   **Practical Considerations**—A variable expense need not be absolutely variable in application. Many so-called curved expenses can be classified as variable when the curve is approximately straight within a narrow relevant range.

For all practical purposes, variable expenses are controllable at some responsibility level.

The characteristics of different kinds of variable expenses are shown in Exhibit 10-3. Case I shows two variable expenses that seem to vary directly with volume from zero to full capacity activity. Both expenses should be shown as variable in the flexible budget: A at $5.00 and B at $2.00 per unit. Case II illustrates a type of variable expense that varies with output or activity within ranges of activity; however, the rate changes as activities move to other relevant ranges. For relevant range C, this expense should be shown in the flexible budget at $2.00 per unit.

EXHIBIT 10-3

Variable Expenses Illustrated

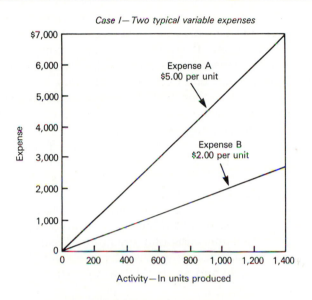

Case I— Two typical variable expenses

Expense A
$5.00 per unit

Expense B
$2.00 per unit

Activity— In units produced

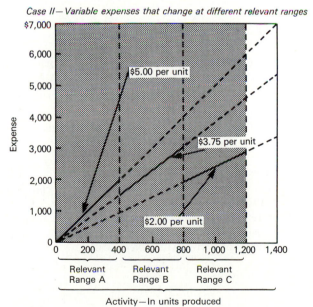

Case II— Variable expenses that change at different relevant ranges

$5.00 per unit

$3.75 per unit

$2.00 per unit

Relevant
Range A

Relevant
Range B

Relevant
Range C

Activity— In units produced

Semivariable Expenses Defined

Semivariable or semifixed expenses and costs increase or decrease as output or activity increases or decreases, but not in proportion to changes in the activity base. Under this definition, semivariable expenses have some of the characteristics of both fixed and variable costs. The variability of semivariable expenses is caused by the combined effect of (a) passage of time, (b) activity or output, and (c) discretionary management decisions. Semivariable expenses frequently represent a significant portion of company expenses.

The characteristics of four kinds of semivariable expenses are shown in Exhibit 10-4. Case I shows a typical semivariable expense with straightline characteristics for a fixed component and a variable component. This expense would be included in the flexible budget as follows: fixed amount per period, $2,000; variable rate per unit produced, $2.86. Case II illustrates a step expense, having both fixed and variable characteristics; it also shows the application of a straightline assumption for flexible budget purposes. Whether or not this straightline assumption can be used depends on the significance of the steps in the relevant range. Cases III and IV illustrate curved expenses. Complex cost characteristics and the application of a straightline assumption for budget purposes are shown. For practical purposes, step and curved expenses are usually classified as semivariable and are budgeted on a straightline basis within the relevant range.

Analysis of Variable and Semivariable Expenses

The critical problem in developing flexible budget formulas for each responsibility center in a business is determination of the (a) fixed component and (b) variable rate for each expense or cost account. This problem is often difficult to resolve for semivariable expenses.

The analysis of variable and semivariable expenses to determine the fixed and variable components requires the following:

1 Precise definition of expenses (discussed above).
2 Careful selection of an activity base for each responsibility center that realistically measures the output or productive activity.
3 Identification of the relevant range of output or productive activity.
4 Selection of appropriate methods to analyze expenses to separately identify the fixed and variable components of semivariable expenses.

We will now discuss items 2, 3, and 4.

Selection of the Activity Base

One activity base must be selected for each responsibility center. Fixed expenses are time related and, for flexible budget purposes, are related to a short

EXHIBIT 10-4

Semivariable Expenses Illustrated

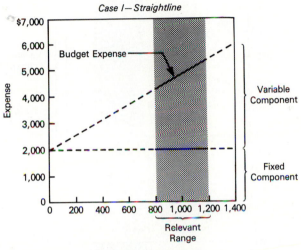

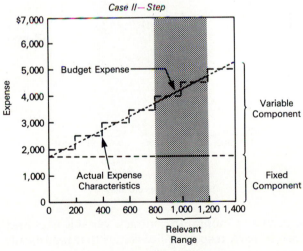

EXHIBIT 10-4   *(cont.)*

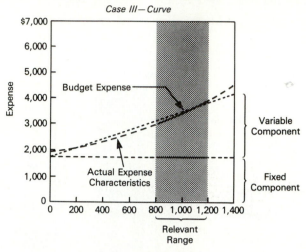

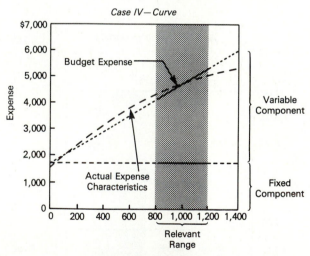

time span such as a month. In contrast, variable expenses must be related to an activity base in each responsibility center that realistically measures the output or productive activity of the center. In the simple case of a responsibility center that produces one kind of output, variable expenses can be related to units produced as the activity base. For example, if the power department produces only kilowatt hours of electricity, power department variable expenses can be related to kilowatt hours because this activity base would realistically measure the output of the department. However, in the case of a department producing more than one type of output, such as two or more dissimilar products, some equivalent measure of the different outputs must be selected as the activity base. For example, one department may use direct labor hours, another department may use direct machine hours, and repair department may use direct repair hours as their respective activity bases. The activity base selected must be the one that most realistically measures the overall activity of the responsibility center.

Several criteria for selecting a measure of output or activity base should be considered:

1   The activity base should measure fluctuations in the output that cause the expenses to vary.
2   The activity base should be affected as little as possible by factors other than output.
3   The activity base should be easily understood.
4   The activity should be reliably measurable and cost-effective.

The selection of an activity base for each service department is often a special problem. Activity bases used in the producing departments should not necessarily be used in the service departments. When service departments, such as the power and repair departments, have reliable measures of activity, these measures should be used. Certain service departments, such as administration, clerical, time and motion, and personnel, generally do not have reliable units of measurement. In such cases, it might be necessary to measure activity in terms of the sales volume, the overall production of the plant, or the output of producing departments that are most frequently served.

Cost variability analyses are frequently meaningless because an unreliable activity base is used, thereby showing low correlation between cost and activity. Another problem in many cost centers is that the activity base gradually tends to become inappropriate. For example, the installation of additional or new machinery in a factory cost center may necessitate a change from direct labor hours to direct machine hours as the activity base.

Selection of an appropriate activity base for each responsibility center is also essential in planning expenses (see Chapter 9), even if flexible expense budgets are not used in the company.

Identifying the Relevant Range of Activity

We have said that the relevant-range concept is important in planning and controlling expenses in a responsibility center. The relevant range relates to a responsibility center. There are not separate relevant ranges for each expense in the center. As a practical matter, the relevant range—on a monthly basis—should approximate the monthly high (maximum limit) and monthly low (minimum limit) of output or activity. The narrower the relevant range, the greater the reliability of the budget estimates.

METHODS OF DETERMINING COST VARIABILITY   Look again at the flexible budget shown in Exhibit 10-1 and consider the approaches that might have been used to develop the fixed amounts and the variable rates shown there. The fixed, variable, and semivariable categories used are in conformity with the definitions given above. In Exhibit 10-1, the activity base was units of output because Department 22 produces only one product. The next step was, by using analyses, estimates, and judgments, to determine the variability of each expense incurred in the responsibility center. Determination of variability yields the two components of each expense: (1) the fixed or constant amount per period and (2) the variable rate per unit of the activity base. A "pure" fixed expense has a constant component amount and a zero value for the variable component. A "true" variable expense has a zero value for the fixed component and a constant rate per unit of activity. A semivariable expense has both a constant amount and a rate for the variable component.

Determination of the variability of each expense item in a responsibility center is the most critical problem in the development of flexible expense budgets. Numerous methods have been developed for resolving this difficulty. The purpose of this section is to explain and illustrate the primary methods that are normally used. Most of these methods involve an analysis of historical expenses, which is only one input for estimating the variability of future costs.

The classification of expenses by variability should begin with a careful study of each expense in the responsibility center under consideration. The purpose of this study is to identify those expenses that contain only "pure" fixed or variable components. When the fixed and variable expenses are separately identified, the remaining accounts can be viewed as semivariable. Each expense account determined to be semivariable must be analyzed to identify its fixed and variable components. The methods discussed in this section are based on the assumption that semivariable expenses can be analyzed and that their fixed and variable components can be reliably estimated. These estimates (i.e., the flexible budget formulas) involve two steps: (1) analysis of each expense followed by (2) managerial judgment to move from the analyzed "historical figures" to realistic flexible budget formula amounts.

Now we will return to Exhibit 10-1, Department 22. A study of the expense accounts and other data, such as material and labor standards, showed that direct material and direct labor are "pure" variable expenses; material usage varies up and down proportionately with output (i.e., units produced), and direct labor likewise is incurred only as production proceeds. The variable rates for these two expenses included in the budget for Department 22 were computed from material and labor standards as follows:

Direct material: Planned cost per unit of raw material, $2.50
                    Planned usage—four units of raw material for each unit of output
                    Computed variable rate per unit of output: $2.50 × 4 = $\underline{\underline{\$10}}$

Direct labor: Planned average wage rate in the department, $4.00
                     Planned labor usage—two direct labor hours for each unit of output
                     Computed variable rate per unit of output: $4 \times 2 = \underline{\underline{\$8}}

Continuing for Department 22, it was clear that salaries are a "true" fixed cost. Management policies on the number of salaried persons and the amount of their monthly salaries provided a fixed amount (per month) of $6,000. The management also determined that supplies used is a variable expense. Having made these determinations, the remaining expense, indirect labor, was classified as semivariable.[1]

This scenario for Department 22 brings us to the point in time when the semivariable expenses must be analyzed to determine their fixed and variable components. The analytical methods used for this purpose can be classified under three broad categories:

1 Direct estimate method
2 Budgeted high and low point method
3 Correlation method

Several applications of each method are discussed and illustrated next. In these discussions, we will be concerned about future expenses rather than historical expenses. In discussing each method, we will assume that a suitable activity base has been selected. Although the technical aspects of each method will be given primary consideration, remember that management judgment is necessary for their application. Also, no particular method of cost analysis is appropriate for all situations, or for all responsibility centers, or each expense. Typically, a company should use several of the methods discussed below for different responsibility centers or different expenses.

Direct Estimate Method

The direct estimate method involves special techniques of cost analysis used only in special cases. Basically, a direct estimate implies a concentrated attack upon particular expenses. We will discuss two variations of the direct estimate method: (1) industrial engineering studies and (2) direct analysis of historical data coupled with interpretation of related managerial policies.

---

[1] In Exhibit 10-1, we included direct material and direct labor costs in the flexible budgets, which is appropriate. However, in subsequent illustrations and discussions, these two costs are not included in the flexible budget. The latter approach may be used because these two costs normally are separately planned and controlled, as illustrated in Chapters 7 and 8. In those chapters, these two costs were viewed as true variable costs and the performance reports illustrated there used adjusted budget amounts for comparison purposes.

Industrial Engineering Studies

Many companies rely heavily on industrial engineers for cost data, including the variability of certain costs. Because engineers are directly involved in the design of products, plant layout, production problems, and the related costs, they are in a particularly favorable position to provide certain cost data for budget purposes. Engineering studies based on analysis and direct observation of processes and operations frequently provide the most reliable variability estimates of certain costs and expenses. Industrial engineering studies can provide such data as rates of material consumption, labor requirements, power usage, and waste and spoilage allowances.

Engineering studies are necessary when historical expense data are not available, but even when such data are available, engineering studies are preferable in many situations. In such cases, analysis of historical data can also be used to check the reasonableness of engineering estimates. Conversely, when estimates are based primarily on an analysis of historical expense data, engineering studies should be made periodically to check the analysis of past experience.

In Exhibit 10-1, we assumed that the direct material and direct labor usage standards in Department 22 were developed by using industrial engineering studies.

Direct Analysis of Historical Data and Management Policies

Usually when the direct analysis approach is used, a direct judgmental estimate of the variability of an expense is made by means of (1) an inspection of the historical activity of the expense, (2) an interpretation of relevant management policies, and (3) an evaluation of the nature and cause of the expense. Statistical procedures are not used.

The estimate developed is one of two types:

1   An estimate of what the expense should be at certain specified activity levels within the relevant range. This procedure provides information for a table format of flexible budget (discussed later; see Exhibit 10-9).
2   An estimate of the fixed and variable components of the expense. This procedure provides data for a formula format of flexible budget (see Exhibit 10-1).

The steps involved in a direct estimate of the variability of a particular expense in a responsibility center can be summarized as follows:

1   Selection of the activity base for the center
2   Identification of the relevant range—the maximum and minimum limits of normal volume expectancy
3   Determination of the various levels within the relevant range for which allowances are to be developed if a table type of budget is used
4   Estimation of cost variability by direct analysis, inspection, and judgment

The direct estimate approach is usually inappropriate for overall use in a company; however, it can be useful in certain responsibility centers or for an individual expense that requires special attention by the management.

The direct estimate method generally is used when:

1   The expense is not amenable to formalized methods. For example, terminal payments to employees would ordinarily have to be estimated on a direct basis after the employee turnover experience and management policies are taken into account.

2   A new responsibility center is established for which there is no historical experience.

3   A new or nonroutine activity is contemplated that would increase expenses—for example, rearrangement of factory equipment.

4   New machines or additional machines are installed, making historical expenses inapplicable.

5   Management decisions are anticipated that will significantly alter the pattern of expense variability.

6   Changes in methods of operations are made that significantly alter the patterns of expense variability.

7   Situations exist where direct observation of processes and operations may provide a basis for reliable expense estimates.

8   A check on the reliability of estimates developed by other methods is desired.

We can logically assume that the salary fixed component of $6,000 shown in Exhibit 10-1 was developed by using direct analysis of historical data coupled with management policies with respect to salary levels for the planning period.

Budgeted High and Low Point Method

The budgeted high and low point method is based on the concept of developing two expense budget allowances at two different assumed levels of activity for certain expenses in a responsibility center. The fixed and variable components of each expense are computed by using an arithmetical interpolation between the two budgets, assuming straightline relationships. This method can be outlined as follows:

1   Select the activity base for the responsibility center.

2   Identify the relevant range for the responsibility center, that is, the minimum and maximum levels within which departmental output will fluctuate during the year.

3   Develop an expense budget for each expense at (a) the maximum level and (b) the minimum level, that is, two expense budgets.

4   Interpolate between the two budgets to determine the fixed and variable components of each expense as follows:
   a.   Subtract the minimum volume from the maximum volume.
   b.   Subtract the minimum expense from the maximum expense.
   c.   Divide the difference in expense by the difference in volume to derive the variable rate.

d. Compute the fixed component by subtracting the variable component portion (variable rate multiplied by the maximum or minimum volume) from the maximum or minimum expense estimate; the difference is the fixed component.

To illustrate, assume that indirect labor is being analyzed and that the activity base is units of output as in Exhibit 10-1. Let us see how the $4,000 fixed component and the $2 variable rate for indirect labor in that illustration might have been determined. We will illustrate the above steps as follows:

1   Activity base for Department 22—units of output
2   Relevant range—maximum, 12,000 units; minimum, 9,000 units
3   The manager of Department 22 with the assistance of his supervisor and various staff members, developed the following expense budgets for indirect labor:

At maximum level (12,000 units)	$28,000
At minimum level (9,000 units)	22,000

4   Interpolation to compute the fixed and variable components of indirect labor:
   a.   To compute the variable rate:

	BUDGETED EXPENSE		ACTIVITY (UNITS)
At maximum	$28,000		12,000
At minimum	22,000		9,000
Difference	$ 6,000	÷	3,000 = $2 variable rate per unit

   b.   To compute the fixed component (amount per period):

	AT MAXIMUM LEVEL	(OR)	AT MINIMUM LEVEL
Total expense	$28,000		$22,000
Less variable component	(12,000 × $2) 24,000	(9,000 × $2)	18,000
Difference—fixed component	$ 4,000		$ 4,000

Thus, the flexible budget would reflect the results as shown in Exhibit 10-1: fixed per month, $4,000; and variable rate per unit of output, $2. The arithmetical computation illustrated is simply a straightline interpolation between the maximum and minimum values. The critical aspects of this method are the validity of the two budget estimates and whether the cost can be realistically assumed to be straightline in relationship to output. This method is often used because (a) it is based on budget estimates (rather than historical data directly), and (b) it provides for effective participation by the supervisor of the responsibility center.

Correlation Methods

Correlation methods are widely used in the analysis of expenses and costs. These methods analyze historical expense data in relation to historical output or activity data to determine how costs have varied with output in the past, which is, in turn, the basis for estimating how costs should vary with output or activity in the future. Because correlation techniques use historical data, a critical problem arises when changes in accounting classifications, operations, methods of manufacturing, management policies, and other such changes tend to make historical data nonrepresentative of future expectations.

Correlation techniques use monthly historical data for analytical purposes. Monthly data for the past twelve to eighteen months are preferable because that generally avoids major distortion. Correlation methods, in general, involve the following steps:

1 An analysis of the relationship between expense and output or activity as indicated by historical data provided by the accounting records. This analysis shows how the expense varied with output or activity in the past.

2 Following this analysis, a judgmental expense estimate is made of how the expense should vary with output in the future, taking into account new conditions that are expected to develop during the budget year, such as changes in management policies, general economic conditions, and methods of operation.

3 The expense estimates are given to (a) the supervisors of the responsibility centers for their recommendations and (b) next level of management for approval.

4 The revised fixed amounts and variable rates are formalized in the flexible expense budget that is approved by top management.

The correlation methods discussed here assume linear relationships; however, some companies use curvilinear regression, such as the logarithmic and reciprocal regression relationships. Two correlation methods are discussed in this chapter:

1 Graphical method—scatter graphs

2 Regression analysis—method of least squares

Graphical Method

The graphical method uses "scatter graphs" to determine visually the fixed and variable components of an expense. The analysis involves the preparation of a graph with historical expense data plotted on the vertical scale (Y axis) and output or activity data (however measured) on the horizontal scale (X axis). After the historical data are plotted on the graph, a visual trend line is drawn through the plotted points. The trend line is positioned through the points to show the relationship between the two variables—expense and activity. The point at which the trend line intersects the vertical scale (at zero activity) indicates the fixed component of the expense, and the slope of the trend line represents the variable component.

Historical data to illustrate the method are given in Exhibit 10-5 for Indirect Material in Department Z. The activity base is direct machine hours. Based on the data, a scatter graph was constructed and a straight trend line was drawn visually through the plotted points, as shown in Exhibit 10-6.

The numbers on the graph identify the plotted points with the months.

The fixed and variable components of the expense—Indirect Materials—indicated by the trend line are then determined in this manner:

Monthly fixed component (point at which the trend line intersects the Y axis)	$200

Variable component (interpolate between any two points on the trend line)

Expense at 40,000 DMH	$800
Expense at Zero DMH	200
Cost increase spread over 40,000 DMH	$600

Variable rate or slope of trend line ($600 ÷ 40,000) = $ .015 per DMH

The computations can be checked as follows:

Fixed cost at 50,000 DMH	$200
Variable cost at 50,000 DMH (× $ .015)	750
Total—(trend line intersection at 50,000 DMH)	$950

The resulting flexible budget amounts would be as shown below **assuming** a judgmental adjustment down of 10 percent in the fixed component. The adjustment down represents a **judgment** on the part of management about what the cost **should be** as opposed to **what it was.**

	EXPENSE FORMULA	
ACCOUNT	FIXED PER MONTH	VARIABLE RATE PER DMH
Indirect material	$180	$ .015

Graphical analysis is relatively simple and provides a visual and readily comprehensible picture of the expense activity relationship. It is difficult to assess such relationships in a listing of historical data (as in Exhibit 10-5). Graphical analysis is frequently used as a preliminary study to gain insights about additional analyses that may be needed. Its primary weakness is lack of objectivity in drawing the trend line; except by chance, no two individuals would draw exactly the same trend line through the points. However, the margin of error usually is minor for the purposes intended. This method can be applied to individual expenses, groups of expenses, departmental expenses, and companywide expenses.

EXHIBIT 10-5

Department Z—Historical Cost and Activity
Expense—Indirect Material; Activity Base—Direct Machine Hours

| | | HISTORICAL DATA | |
| | | DIRECT | INDIRECT |
MONTH	POINTS ON CHART	MACHINE HOURS	MATERIAL EXPENSE
January	(1)	44,000	$ 875
February	(2)	41,000	850
March	(3)	45,000	875
April	(4)	43,000	850
May	(5)	36,000	750
June	(6)	22,000	550
July	(7)	23,000	500
August	(8)	15,000	450
September	(9)	30,000	600
October	(10)	38,000	700
November	(11)	41,000	800
December	(12)	44,000	850
Total		422,000	$8,650

EXHIBIT 10-6

Graphical Method for Expense Analysis*

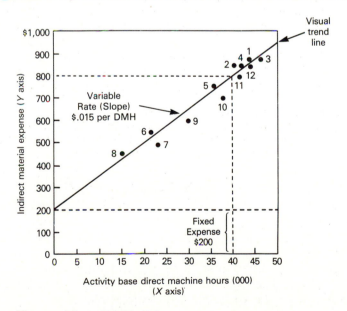

*Source of data—Exhibit 10-5

Graphical analysis is one of the more useful, yet simple, analytical tools available to the budget analyst. Through use and experimentation, cost accountants and budget experts have found it invaluable. The relationship of expense to output is only one of the many applications of graphical analysis to analyze expense and cost relationships. However, graphical representation of costs related to time periods, traditionally used by accountants, has limited significance other than to show timing trends as opposed to expense-activity relationships.

Regression Analysis Using the Method of Least Squares

In the analysis of historical cost and output data, the statistical method of least squares can be used to compute the trend line. The method can be adapted for curved costs; however, the straightline adaptation is usually adequate for describing the underlying expense-activity relationship for budgeting purposes.

The method of least squares is a mathematical approach used to compute a unique regression line through a given series of specified data points, such as those plotted in Exhibit 10-6. The computed trend line will be the only one where the sum of the deviations of the points from the trend line is zero, and the sum of the squares of the deviations will be less than the sum of the squares from any other straight line; thus, it is a unique trend line. The method is purely objective because the same trend line will always be developed from the same data, whereas the graphical method trend line's position and slope are subject to the analyst's judgment.

Fitting a unique mathematical trend line for an expense using the method of least squares involves the use of two sets of data—monthly expense data and the activity base data. These two variables are usually identified in this way:

1 Independent variable (X variable)—The independent variable is the one that can be observed. It is the activity base.

2 Dependent variable (Y variable)—The dependent variable is the one that changes or is thought to change with changes in the other (that is, the independent) variable—this is the expense that is to be estimated.

In the mathematical definition of a trend line that expresses the relationship between the two variables, the equation for a straight line can be expressed as $Y = a + bX$, where Y represents the dependent variable, a denotes the constant factor, b designates the slope of the trend line, and X represents the independent variable. Simply, a expresses the position of the trend line and b the slope of the trend line. Therefore, b expresses the effect on Y (the dependent variable) of any change in X (the independent variable). The regression equation can be shown graphically, as in Exhibit 10-7.

EXHIBIT 10-7

Graphic Explanation of the Regression Equation

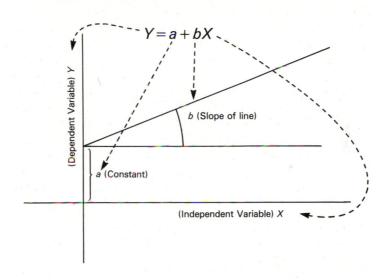

The illustration suggests that the approach is adaptable to the analysis of expense to determine its variability or relationship to activity changes. Here, too, we are seeking an expression of the underlying relationship between two variables: expense and activity. Specifically, we want to know the effect on expense of changes in output or activity. Applying the least squares technique to the problem at hand, the equation can be adapted as follows:

$Y = a + b X$

Let the dependent variable Y
(plotted on vertical axis) represent TOTAL EXPENSE . . . .

Let a (constant value)
represent the FIXED COMPONENT OF EXPENSE . . . .

Let b (slope of trend line)
represent the VARIABLE COMPONENT (RATE) OF EXPENSE . . . .

Let the independent variable X
(plotted on horizontal axis) represent OUTPUT OR ACTIVITY . . . .

The a value represents the fixed expense per month, and the b value represents the variable expense rate per direct machine hour in the flexible budgets as illustrated for indirect material in Department Z. Therefore, the problem is to develop these respective values. We are analyzing historical cost and activity data to determine these values (a and b) that are expressive of cost variability. The a and b values can be computed by using the following equations.

(Note: N represents the number of pairs of data points for X and Y; Σ denotes summation.)[2]

$$a = \frac{\Sigma X^2 \, \Sigma Y - \Sigma X \, \Sigma XY}{N \Sigma X^2 - (\Sigma X)^2}$$

$$b = \frac{N \Sigma XY - \Sigma X \, \Sigma Y}{N \Sigma X^2 - (\Sigma X)^2}$$

The equations above require computations best accomplished on a spreadsheet. To illustrate, a least squares spreadsheet is shown in Exhibit 10-8. The Exhibit 10-5 data about Indirect Material for Department Z are used to illustrate the spreadsheet. We illustrate a manually prepared analysis for instructional purposes only. Software can be bought, or is easy to develop, that will compute regression values quickly and correctly when used with mainframe or personal computers. Also, some pocket calculators are programmed to make regression calculations.

To compute a value:

$$a = \frac{\Sigma X^2 \, \Sigma Y - \Sigma X \, \Sigma XY}{N \Sigma X^2 - (\Sigma X)^2}$$

$$= \frac{(15,986)(\$8,650) - (422)(\$321,425)}{(12)(15,986) - (422)^2} = \underline{\underline{\$191.85}}$$

To compute b value:

$$b = \frac{N \Sigma XY - \Sigma X \, \Sigma Y}{N \Sigma X^2 - (\Sigma X)^2}$$

$$= \frac{(12)(\$321,425) - (422)(\$8,650)}{(12)(15,986) - (422)^2}$$

$$= \underline{\underline{\$ .01504}} \text{ per direct machine hour}$$

($15.04 per thousand DMH)

Resulting equation:

$$Y = a + bX$$

$$Y = \$191.85 + \$.01504X$$

$$\qquad\quad \uparrow \qquad\qquad\quad \uparrow$$

$$\qquad\;\; \text{Fixed} \qquad\quad \text{Variable}$$

$$\qquad \text{Component} \quad\;\; \text{Component}$$

---

[2] The equations for computing a and b can be rearranged in several different ways.

EXHIBIT 10-8

Method of Least Squares Spreadsheet

N	MONTH	DIRECT MACHINE HOURS (000) X	INDIRECT MATERIAL EXPENSE Y	XY	X²
			HISTORICAL DATA		
1.	January	44	$ 875	$ 38,500	1,936
2.	February	41	850	34,850	1,681
3.	March	45	875	39,375	2,025
4.	April	43	850	36,550	1,849
5.	May	36	750	27,000	1,296
6.	June	22	550	12,100	484
7.	July	23	500	11,500	529
8.	August	15	450	6,750	225
9.	September	30	600	18,000	900
10.	October	38	700	26,600	1,444
11.	November	41	800	32,800	1,681
12.	December	44	850	37,400	1,936
	Summations (Σ)	422	$8,650	$321,425	15,986

The analysis in Exhibit 10-8 shows the fixed and variable components of indirect material for the period covered by the historical data. The next step in developing the flexible budget is to adjust the completed values for conditions or changes anticipated for the future that did not previously exist. For example, assume it is decided that the computed fixed component is satisfactory but the variable component should be reduced to $.145 per unit. The flexible budget for Department Z would include the following:

	EXPENSE FORMULA	
EXPENSES	FIXED PER MONTH	VARIABLE RATE PER 100 DIRECT MACHINE HOURS
Indirect material	$192.00*	$1.45*

*Practical considerations suggest that the fixed component be rounded to the nearest dollar and larger amounts to the nearest tens or hundreds of dollars. Likewise where the number of direct hours is large in a department, the variable rate should be expressed in terms of the nearest tens, hundreds, or perhaps thousands of hours. Rounding on variable rates must be done carefully, especially where the base is large, because the effect of a minor rounding when applied to a large number of hours might be substantial.

The method of least squares is particularly useful and objective for analyzing historical data. It is important to realize, however, that the results are often misleadingly precise; therefore, they must be tempered with experience and management judgment. The underlying mathematical assumptions must be understood. If used properly, this approach to determine expense variability is effective.

NEGATIVE VALUES IN EXPENSE ANALYSES A negative fixed amount or a negative variable rate can be computed when the correlation methods are used. Negative values are unrealistic. They are caused by inappropriate historical expense or activity data. Inappropriate data are caused by such factors as an expense out of control, nonlinear expenses, incorrect accounting, nonrepresentative data, incorrect activity base, discretionary expense decisions, inappropriate relevant range, nonrecurring events, and external influences.

When historical expenses are analyzed, the expense and activity data should be carefully studied prior to formal analysis. Any months showing unusual or nonrepresentative conditions should not be included in the analysis. For example, assume that during March of the past year the company participated in an annual trade show at considerable expense, which was recorded in a recurring expense account. The additional expenditures for the trade show should be excluded from any analysis of expense variability. They should be budgeted separately.

Negative results persisting after adjustments of the data indicate the need for further analysis to determine exactly why the expense data are random. The causative factors should be identified so that the item can be given special consideration.

A direct estimate method should be used in such cases because negative values should not be used in budget expense formulas.

FLEXIBLE BUDGET FORMATS Flexible expense budgets can be formatted in several ways:

1 Table format
2 Formula format
3 Graphical format

TABLE FORMAT This format shows budget expenses for several different levels of output or activity within the relevant range. This format of expressing flexible budgets is frequently used for instructional purposes; however, the formula format appears to be more widely used in actual practice. The table format is shown in Exhibit 10-9. Notice that the activity base is direct machine hours and that budget amounts are given for four different activity levels within the relevant range. The fixed and variable components of each expense are not indicated. This budget format makes it possible to accommodate irregular step and curved expenses without the straightline assumption.

EXHIBIT 10-9

Flexible Budget—Table Format*

ACTIVITY—MACHINE HRS.	350,000	400,000	450,000	500,000
PERCENT	70	80	90	100
Foremen salaries	$12,000	$12,000	$12,000	$12,000
Indirect labor	14,000	16,000	18,000	20,000
Miscellaneous expenses	24,000	27,000	31,000	34,000
Total	$50,000	$55,000	$61,000	$66,000

*Relevant range, 350,000 to 500,000 direct machine hours.

Notice that in Exhibit 10-9 foremen salaries are a fixed expense, indirect labor is a variable expense, and miscellaneous expenses are a step expense.

When the table format is used, a problem often arises when budget amounts are needed for some activity level between two activity levels for which budget amounts are provided. Two approaches to this problem are used:

1 Use the budget amount nearest to the needed activity level. For example, if the budget for 460,000 direct machine hours were needed, the expense at 450,000 direct machine hours would be used.

2 Determine the needed budget amount by straightline interpolation. The budget amount for 460,000 direct machine hours would be computed as follows:

EXPENSE	BUDGET AMOUNT AT 450,000 HOURS	ADD INTERPOLATED INCREASE	BUDGET AMOUNT AT 460,000 HOURS
Foremen salaries	$12,000	(Constant—no interpolation necessary)	$12,000
Indirect labor	18,000	$(\$20,000 - \$18,000) \times \left(\dfrac{460,000 - 450,000}{500,000 - 450,000} \right)$	18,400
Miscellaneous expenses	31,000	$(\$34,000 - \$31,000) \times \left(\dfrac{460,000 - 450,000}{500,000 - 450,000} \right)$	31,600
Total	$61,000	$(\$66,000 - \$61,000) \times \left(\dfrac{460,000 - 450,000}{500,000 - 450,000} \right)$	$62,000

To determine the budget amounts at 460,000 hours, the amount at 450,000 hours must be increased by one-fifth of the difference (10,000 hours represents one-fifth of the increase to the next activity level).

FORMULA FORMAT This format provides a formula for each expense account in each responsibility center. The formula gives the fixed amount and the variable rate. This is more compact and generally more useful because the components of each expense are given. The formula format uses straightline relationships. However, steps within the relevant range can be specified by a footnote, as shown in Exhibit 10-10.[3]

EXHIBIT 10-10

Flexible Budget—Formula Format*

EXPENSE	FIXED PER MONTH	VARIABLE RATE PER 100 DIRECT MACHINE HOURS
Foremen salaries	$12,000	
Indirect labor		$ 4.00
Miscellaneous expenses	4,000**	6.00
Total	$16,000	$10.00

*Relevant range—350,000 to 500,000 direct machine hours.
**Step—Decrease to $3,000 at 400,000 (or less) machine hours.

GRAPHICAL FORMAT This format is sometimes used for step or nonlinear expenses, as shown in Exhibits 10-3 and 10-4. Budget amounts are read directly from the graph. This method is sometimes useful when step or nonlinear expenses are not to be used on a straightline relationship basis.

CAN THE CONCEPT OF EXPENSE VARIABILITY BE REALISTICALLY APPLIED?

There is some skepticism about the classification of expenses in relation to output or activity changes. It is generally recognized that some expenses are fixed and others are variable, but there is some doubt as to whether some of the semivariable expenses can be split accurately into their fixed and variable components. Also, there is doubt about the straightline assumptions that are used. Proponents of the concept of expense variability respond to these arguments as follows:

1 Although expenses in the past have varied erratically, such behavior should not be viewed as normative for the future. Many expenses may have been erratic because of poor control, waste, inefficiency, faulty accounting, and unwise management decisions.

2 Many expenses are subject to discretionary management policies. The fact that policies were changed during the period under analysis may have caused erratic expense variations. These "policy variations" can be isolated and should be taken into consideration in estimating expense variability for the future.

3 Past expenses that have been erratic will generally "shape up" when budgeted and controlled. Exhibit 10-11 shows this effect in an actual case.

4 Actual costs that are dissimilar should be classified separately in the accounting system. For example, certain indirect labor costs may vary in proportion to output; however, management policy may require that any indirect-labor employee laid off will be paid

[3] The formula type of flexible budget also was shown in Exhibit 10-1; throughout the chapter, only the formula type of flexible budget is used.

two weeks' severance pay. This severance pay should not be classified as a normal indirect labor expense, but as a special expense. Mixing the two different expenses in one account would tend to destroy the pattern of variability for each account.

5 Flexible budget procedures do not necessarily require the use of straightline relationships for all expenses.

6 Certain expenses in all companies will be influenced by special factors, some external and some internal, which may require special consideration for planning purposes. The number of such expenses is much lower than is commonly supposed.

7 Perfect linearity is not required for practical considerations. Approximate linearity usually is sufficiently accurate if sound management decisions and control persist.

8 Industry surveys reveal numerous cases where expense variability related to activity levels of output or activity is identified on a practical and useful basis.

9 The type of operations engaged in by the company determines the extent to which expense-activity relationships may be resolved.

In recent years, some companies have experienced considerable technology changes. Some of these changes, such as more automation, cause higher fixed costs and lower variable costs. Also, some technology changes require employees with significantly increased skills. As a consequence, such companies will try to stockpile rather than lay off employees with the key skills by using them temporarily in other jobs.

EXHIBIT 10-11

Typical Improvement in Expense Variability Following Implementation of Budget Control

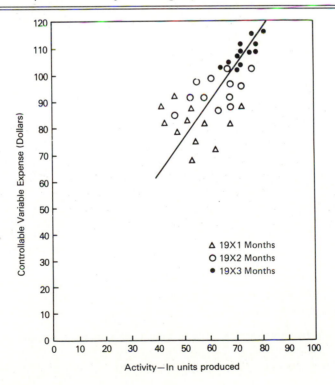

Participation by Managers in Developing Flexible Budgets

The technical aspect of flexible budgets may make it difficult in a particular case to attain satisfactory participation of the responsibility center managers where the concept is applied. Direct estimates, even though developed by industrial engineering studies, should be discussed with the responsibility center managers who must use them. The development of the flexible budget formulas, even when performed at staff level, should provide a basis for participation by the affected responsibility center managers. The statistical approaches use historical data and require technical competence; thus, the analytical efforts involved are generally performed at the staff level. In this situation, participation is best attained, prior to approval, by either (1) submitting the proposed flexible budget formulas to the respective responsibility center managers for their evaluation and recommendations or (2) submitting the expense schedules for the annual profit plan (which were derived from the flexible budget formulas) to the responsibility center managers for evaluation and recommendations. In view of the importance of satisfactory participation in the planning process, effective ways to implement it should be used when the flexible expense budget formulas are being developed.

USES OF FLEXIBLE BUDGETS   The primary purpose of flexible budgets is to enhance expense control. Therefore, we can identify three specific uses of flexible budgets:

1   To facilitate preparation of the expense budgets for the responsibility centers for inclusion in the tactical profit plan.

2   To provide expense goals for the managers of responsibility centers during the period covered by profit plan.

3   To provide budget expense amounts adjusted to actual activity for comparison purposes (against actual expenses) in the monthly performance reports.

Flexible expense budgets can be applied in all the functions in a company—manufacturing, selling, and administrative—although they are more frequently used in the responsibility centers in the manufacturing function. They are especially appropriate in responsibility centers where (1) operations tend to be repetitive, (2) there are numerous heterogeneous expenses, and (3) output or activity can be realistically measured.

To place the three uses of flexible expense budgets in perspective, understand that the development of flexible budget formulas normally occurs early in the planning cycle. For example, a realistic policy would be to set the target completion date for flexible budgets as "prior to completion of the sales plan." Because flexible budget formulas do not relate to a specific level of output but to a relevant range, the analytical work essential to their development can usually proceed independently of the other phases of the tactical planning cycle.

PREPARING THE EXPENSE BUDGETS FOR THE TACTICAL PROFIT PLAN   When the flexible budget formulas are completed early in the tactical planning cycle, they can be used directly in preparing the expense budgets that are to be included in the annual profit plan. To illustrate this particular use, we refer to Exhibit 10-1, which shows the flexible budget formulas for Department 22. Now assume that the planned activity for the department has been developed as follows: Year 19X—120,000 units; January—9,000 units; February—11,000 units; etc. With these two sets of data, we can clerically develop the expense budget for the department that would be included in the annual profit plan; this is shown in Exhibit 10-12. Examine that illustration and the computations of each expense. If the flexible budget formula is not available, the expenses included in Exhibit 10-12 would have to be estimated in a more time-consuming manner, as discussed in Chapter 9.

EXHIBIT 10-12

Profit Plan Expense Budget for Department 22—Annual Profit Plan for 19X

CONTROLLABLE EXPENSES	ANNUAL 19X	JANUARY	FEBRUARY	ETC.
Output planned (units)	120,000	9,000	11,000	
Direct material	$1,200,000	$ 90,000	$110,000	
Direct labor	960,000	72,000	88,000	
Department overhead:				
Salaries	72,000	6,000	6,000	
Supplies	120,000	9,000	11,000	
Indirect labor*	288,000	22,000	26,000	
Total	$2,640,000	$199,000	$241,000	

*Clerical computations (refer to Exhibit 10-1):
Annual—($4,000 × 12) + ($2 × 120,000) = $288,000
January—$4,000 + ($2 × 9,000) = $22,000
February—$4,000 + ($2 × 11,000) = $26,000

PROVIDE EXPENSE GOALS   We will now return to Department 22, Exhibit 10-1, to illustrate the second use of flexible budgets. First, assume that we are ready to start February 19X operations. Notice in Exhibit 10-12 that the planned output for February was 11,000 units. If that planned output is still valid, the expense goals included in the annual profit plan would serve as the expense targets for the manager of Department 22 throughout February. Instead, now assume that for various reasons the management has just decided that 12,000 units should be produced in February. In this latter case, the expense estimates in the annual profit plan (based on 11,000 units of output) would be inappropriate; the manager of Department 22 needs new expense amounts at 12,000 units. With the flexible budget formulas available (Exhibit 10-1), we can compute new expense targets as shown in Exhibit 10-13. These up-to-date expense goals should be used by the manager of Department 22 throughout February.

TO PREPARE THE MONTHLY PERFORMANCE REPORTS   This use focuses on performance measurement after the actual expenses have been incurred. Periodic performance reports for each responsibility center should be comprehensive along the lines discussed and illustrated in the preceding chapters. They

EXHIBIT 10-13

Department 22—Revised Output for February 19X; 12,000 Units

CONTROLLABLE EXPENSES	COMPUTATIONS	EXPENSE TARGETS
Direct material	$ 10 × 12,000	$120,000
Direct labor	$ 8 × 12,000	96,000
Department Overhead:		
Salaries		6,000
Supplies	$ 1 × 12,000	12,000
Indirect labor	$ 4,000 + ($ 2 × 12,000)	28,000
Total	$10,000 + ($21 × 12,000)	$262,000

Note to Department Manager: This projection is based on the output scheduled for your department during February and puts you in a position to control these expenses during the month in an effort to meet or better your expense control goals.

should encompass all controllable items and should compare actual performance with planned performance. With respect to expenses included on the performance report, one of two basic comparisons can be used:

1 **Fixed or Static Budget Comparisons.** This approach is used when the flexible budget concept is not applied. In this situation, actual expenses are compared with the original budget amounts shown in the annual profit plan. This approach is appropriate in situations where actual output attained is essentially the same as originally specified in the annual profit plan. However, when actual output differs significantly from the original plans, the comparison is inappropriate. The designation "fixed or static budget comparisons" implies that there is no need for adjusted budget amounts; the original budget amounts are used. Fixed or static budget comparisons for expense control are seldom appropriate in a responsibility center because (a) actual output is often significantly different from that shown in the original profit plan and (b) usually variable and semivariable expenses are incurred in the responsibility centers. If only fixed expenses are incurred in a responsibility center, a need for flexible budget procedures would not exist.

2 **Flexible Budget Comparisons.** This approach is used when the flexible budget concept is applied in the responsibility center. In this situation, actual expenses incurred are compared with flexible budget amounts adjusted to the actual output attained.

To illustrate use of a flexible budget for performance reporting, refer again to Exhibit 10-1, Department 22, and assume that at the end of February that actual output attained was 11,500 units. Comparison of actual costs with the original profit plan (Exhibit 10-12) would be inappropriate because that plan anticipated 11,000 units of output. The expense target values shown in Exhibit 10-13 likewise are inappropriate because they anticipated an output of 12,000 units. Thus, we must compute adjusted expense amounts based on actual output of 11,500 units for comparison with the actual expenses incurred. The performance report would appear as shown in Exhibit 10-14.

The more complex the operations, the greater the problem of expense control. In complex circumstances, expenses can be effectively controlled only through planning, continuous effort, and a well-designed system of control. Expense control is a line responsibility, not a staff function. A control system does not and cannot control expense. Instead it gives the managers of the responsibility centers a tool of control—a tool that can be made effective by those managers. The responsibility center managers will view expense control seriously if top management exhibits an active interest in it. Investigations have shown that lower levels of management tend to view expense control in the same light as their supervising managers. If top management is lackadaisical and inconsistent about expenses, the lower-level managers will be likewise. Merely talking about expense control and "riding" some supervisor on occasion will not contribute to effective expense control. Intelligent, organized, and consistent effort is crucial in performing this vital managerial function effectively.

EXHIBIT 10-14

Performance Report, Department 22

Department 22		Date February 19X	
Supervisor John Ware			
CONTROLLABLE EXPENSES	ACTUAL 11,500 UNITS	BUDGET ADJUSTED TO 11,500 UNITS	VARIANCE (UNFAVORABLE)
Direct material	$116,000	$115,000	($1,000)
Direct labor	91,500	92,000	500
Department overhead:			
Salaries	6,000	6,000	0
Supplies	12,100	11,500	(600)
Indirect labor	28,300	27,000	(1,300)
Total	$253,900	$251,500	($2,400)

The essentials of an effective expense control system can be outlined as follows:

1 Top management should provide active and consistent support to the control system.
2 Expense control should be clearly identified as a line responsibility.
3 The control system should be designed to fit the peculiarities of the situation.
4 Realistic expense standards (budget amounts) should be developed for use as a basis for measuring performance.
5 There should be short-term periodic performance reporting.
6 Expense standards should be related to actual output.
7 The control system and the performance reports generated should be simple and understandable to all levels of management.
8 Expense control is effective prior to cost incurrence rather than after expense incurrence. Therefore, expense standards should be used for control in two ways:
   a. To control expenses before incurrence.
   b. To measure the effectiveness with which expenses were controlled.
9 Expense control should be applied to expenses prior to their allocation.
10 Effective follow-up procedures should be used to correct inefficiencies.

A properly designed and operated budget program will include an effective expense control system. Expense responsibility will have been defined, and expense standards established. The fact that the responsibility center managers are brought into the entire planning and control processes will in itself tend to generate enthusiasm and expense consciousness.

Comprehensive Demonstration Case Continued

 *SUPERIOR MANUFACTURING COMPANY*

Recall that Superior Manufacturing Company has fourteen departments—six factory, four sales, and four general administration departments (including building services). At the end of Chapter 9, the expense budgets for each of these departments were illustrated. They were designed for incorporation into the annual profit plan. For instructional reasons, it was assumed in that chapter that flexible expense budgets were not used. However, we now assume that the company uses flexible expense budgets in all departments except building services. Flexible budgets for each of these thirteen responsibility centers are shown below in Schedules 41 through 44. These budget formulas were applied to the planned activity (output) in each department to develop the original expense schedules included in the annual profit plan (Chapter 9: Schedules 33, 34, 39, and 40). For example, the January 19X2 column for "General and Administrative Factory Overhead" in Schedule 33 was based on total direct labor hours in the factory that were taken from the direct labor budget (Schedule 31, page 293). The budget expense amounts were computed by applying the direct labor hours to the flexible expense budget formulas (Schedule 41). The original expense amounts for "General and Administrative Factory Overhead" (given in Schedule 33) were computed as follows for 19X2:

EXPENSE	REF.	FIXED PER MONTH 41		JANUARY DLH (00) 31		VARIABLE RATE 41		JANUARY BUDGET
Salaries		$8,000	plus	836	×	$ .00	equals	$8,000
Travel and entertainment		100	"	836	×	.50	"	518
Telephone		460	"	836	×	.20	"	627
Depreciation		130	"	836	×	.00	"	130
Insurance		20	"	836	×	.00	"	20
Taxes		30	"	836	×	.00	"	30
Stationery and office supplies		20	"	836	×	.30	"	271
Total		$8,760	"	836	×	$1.00	"	$9,596

SCHEDULE 41. Superior Manufacturing Company

Flexible Budget—Manufacturing Division
(Service Departments)
For the Year Ending December 31, 19X2

| | SERVICE DEPARTMENTS | | | | | |
| | GENERAL AND ADMINISTRATIVE | | POWER | | REPAIR | |
EXPENSE	FIXED PER MONTH	VARIABLE PER 100 TOTAL DLH	FIXED PER MONTH	VARIABLE PER 1000 KILOWATT HOURS	FIXED PER MONTH	VARIABLE PER DIRECT REPAIR HOUR
*Supervisory salaries	$8,000		$3,000		$300	
Maintenance			100	$ .28		
Fuel				1.20		
Supplies used						$.34
Travel and entertainment	100	$ .50				
Telephone	460	.20				
*Depreciation (time basis)	130		450		10	
*Insurance	20		70		3	
*Taxes	30		80		7	
Stationery and office supplies	20	.30				
Wages			3,000		400	
Total	$8,760	$1.00	$6,700	$1.48	$720	$.34

*Noncontrollable in these responsibility centers.

SCHEDULE 42. Superior Manufacturing Company

Flexible Budget—Manufacturing Division
(Production Departments)
For the Year Ending December 31, 19X2

| | PRODUCTION DEPARTMENTS | | | | | |
| | DEPARTMENT 1 | | DEPARTMENT 2 | | DEPARTMENT 3 | |
EXPENSE	FIXED PER MONTH	VARIABLE PER 100 DEPT. DLH	FIXED PER MONTH	VARIABLE PER 100 DEPT. DLH	FIXED PER MONTH	VARIABLE PER 100 DEPT. DLH
*Supervisory salaries	$10,000		$1,870		$2,920	
Indirect labor	3,000	$22.50		$1.90	800	$ 7.10
Maintenance parts	300	1.50	20	.20	150	.50
Supplies used	450	5.50	40	.50	200	2.50
*Depreciation (output basis)		1.50		.40		.90
*Insurance	100		10		50	
*Taxes	150		20		60	
Total	$14,000	$31.00	$1,960	$3.00	$4,180	$11.00

*Noncontrollable in these responsibility centers.

SCHEDULE 43. Superior Manufacturing Company

Flexible Budget—Sales Division
For the Year Ending December 31, 19X2

EXPENSE	SOUTHERN		EASTERN		WESTERN		GENERAL SALES OVERHEAD	
	FIXED PER MONTH	VARIABLE PER $100 NET DIST. SALES	FIXED PER MONTH	VARIABLE PER $100 NET DIST. SALES	FIXED PER MONTH	VARIABLE PER $100 NET DIST. SALES	FIXED PER MONTH	VARIABLE PER $100 NET TOTAL SALES
*Supervisory salaries	$6,000		$ 8,000		$3,000		$12,000	
Travel and entertainment	900	$ .683	1,010	$ .643	340	$ .708	916	$ .458
Telephone	400	.216	630	.250	180	.258	824	.098
*Depreciation—office equipment							50	
Stationery and office supplies							169	.148
Auto expense							336	.359
Commissions		4.00		4.00		4.00		
Freight and express	100	.849	140	.612	230	.476		
Advertising	2,000		3,000		1,000		5,000	
Total	$9,400	$5.748	$12,780	$5.505	$4,750	$5.442	$19,295	$1.063

*Noncontrollable in these responsibility centers.

SCHEDULE 44. Superior Manufacturing Company

Flexible Budget—Administrative Division
For the Year Ending December 31, 19X2

EXPENSE	ADMINISTRATIVE FIXED PER MONTH	ADMINISTRATIVE VARIABLE PER $100 NET SALES	ACCOUNTING FIXED PER MONTH	ACCOUNTING VARIABLE PER $100 NET SALES	TREASURERS' FIXED PER MONTH	TREASURERS' VARIABLE PER $100 NET SALES
*Supervisory salaries	$5,000		$4,000		$3,000	
Travel and entertainment	750		100		100	
Telephone	150	$ .120	50	$ .01	60	$ .04
*Depreciation	50		200		100	
*Insurance	20		20		40	
*Taxes	20		30		10	
Stationery and office supplies		.002		.01		.03
Lawyer retainer fee	150					
Loss on bad debts						.20
Audit fee	200					
Total	$6,340	$ .122	$4,400	$ .02	$3,310	$ .27

*Noncontrollable in these responsibility centers.

To develop the flexible budget formulas for the thirteen departments, Superior uses various approaches for analyzing expense variability. We will illustrate one of these approaches which was used for "General Sales Overhead." The method of least squares was used to analyze the expenses in this particular department. Since the flexible budget formulas are developed during the first part of October, historical expense and sales data used in the analysis include the twelve months prior to October 1, 19X2. These historical data were provided by the accounting records. Schedule 45 shows the method of a least squares spreadsheet.

Based on the method of least squares analysis, management judgment, and direct analysis, the following flexible budget formulas were developed for "General Sales Overhead" (shown in Schedule 43):

1 Supervisory salaries, $12,000 per month (management anticipates no change during 19X2).

2 Travel and entertainment—expense data as shown on the spreadsheet Schedule 45 (Y).

3 Telephone—expense data as shown on the spreadsheet (Y).

4 Depreciation—office equipment, $50 per month (no change per depreciation schedule).

5 Stationery and office supplies—expense data as shown on the spreadsheet (Y).

6 Auto expense—expense data as shown on the spreadsheet (Y).

7 Advertising—budget from the advertising budget (Schedule 38). Total net sales for company as shown on the spreadsheet (X).

SCHEDULE 45. Superior Manufacturing Company

Least Squares Spreadsheet
General Sales Overhead
(Analysis for 19X2 Flexible Budget)

MONTHS	REF.	NET SALES (000) X (GIVEN)	X²	TRAVEL AND ENTERTAINMENT Y (GIVEN)	XY	TELEPHONE Y (GIVEN)	XY	STATIONERY AND OFFICE SUPPLIES Y (GIVEN)	XY	AUTO EXPENSE Y (GIVEN)	XY
19X0											
October		$ 490	$ 240,100	$ 3,300	$ 1,617,000	$ 1,300	$ 637,000	$ 900	$ 441,000	$ 2,200	$ 1,078,000
November		520	270,400	3,400	1,768,000	1,400	728,000	910	473,200	2,250	1,170,000
December		560	313,600	3,420	1,915,200	1,350	756,000	1,020	571,200	2,300	1,288,000
19X1											
January		560	313,600	3,500	1,960,000	1,380	772,800	1,000	560,000	2,300	1,288,000
February		510	260,100	3,200	1,632,000	1,290	657,900	950	484,500	2,150	1,096,500
March		440	193,600	2,950	1,298,000	1,290	567,600	830	365,200	1,950	858,000
April		390	152,100	2,700	1,053,000	1,200	468,000	750	292,500	1,650	643,500
May		350	122,500	2,400	840,000	1,170	409,500	700	245,000	1,550	542,500
June		410	168,100	2,830	1,160,300	1,190	487,900	760	311,600	1,850	758,500
July		500	250,000	3,250	1,625,000	1,350	675,000	870	435,000	2,150	1,075,000
August		520	270,400	3,300	1,716,000	1,320	686,400	900	468,000	2,200	1,114,000
September		600	360,000	3,550	2,130,000	1,400	840,000	1,070	642,000	2,450	1,470,000
Summations (Σ)		$5,850	$2,914,500	$37,800	$18,714,500	$15,640	$7,686,100	$10,660	$5,289,200	$25,000	$12,412,000

To compute a and b values: $a = \dfrac{\Sigma X^2 \Sigma Y - \Sigma X \Sigma XY}{N \Sigma X^2 - (\Sigma X)^2}$ $b = \dfrac{N \Sigma XY - \Sigma X \Sigma Y}{N \Sigma X^2 - (\Sigma X)^2}$

Travel and entertainment:

$$a = \frac{(2,914,500)(37,800) - (5,850)(18,714,500)}{(12)(2,914,500) - (5,850)^2} = \frac{688,275,000}{751,500} = \$916. \quad \text{Fixed per month}$$

$$b = \frac{(12)(18,714,500) - (5,850)(37,800)}{(12)(2,914,500) - (5,850)^2} = \frac{3,444,000}{751,500} = \$ \ .458 \quad \text{Variable per \$100 net sales}$$

*Telephone:
$= \$824.$ Fixed per month
$= \$ \ .098$ Variable per $100 net sales

*Stationery and office supplies:
$= \$169.$ Fixed per month
$= \$ \ .148$ Variable per $100 net sales

*Auto expense:
$= \$336.$ Fixed per month
$= \$ \ .359$ Variable per $100 net sales

*Computed in the same manner.

It is important to realize that although these flexible budget formulas were used directly as computed for instructional purposes, they should have been tempered with judgment, taking into account new conditions such as revised operations, differing management policies, and changes in the general economic outlook.

OVERVIEW OF THE CONCEPT OF EXPENSE VARIABILITY   Our focus in this chapter has been on a concept that has wide applicability in (1) profit planning, (2) management decision making, and (3) accounting. The concept is cost variability, which is the basic foundation for (1) flexible expense budgets, (2) breakeven analyses, (3) marginal cost analyses, (4) direct costing, and (5) variance analyses. These applications of the concept of cost variability, which are appropriate for both manufacturing and nonmanufacturing enterprises, are discussed in succeeding chapters.

Suggested References

BIERMAN, HAROLD, JR., THOMAS DYCKMAN, and RONALD HILTON, *Cost Accounting: Concepts and Managerial Applications.* New York: Macmillan, 1990.

CHANDRA, GYAN, and SURENDRA SINGHVI, eds., "Difficulties in Flexible Budgeting," in *Budgeting for Profit.* New York: Planning Executives Institute, Research Series 1975, 126.)

GARDNER, FRED V., *Variable Budget Control* (an early classic). New York: McGraw Hill, 1940.

HORNGREN, CHARLES T., and GEORGE FOSTER, *Cost Accounting.* Englewood Cliffs, N.J.: Prentice-Hall, 1984.

MACIARIELLO, JOSEPH A., *Management Control Systems,* Chap. 12. Englewood Cliffs, N.J.: Prentice-Hall, 1984.

MONTGOMERY, A. THOMPSON, *Management Accounting Information,* Chap. 12. Reading, Mass.: Addison-Wesley, 1979.

MOWEN, MARYANNE M., *Accounting for Costs as Fixed and Variable,* p. 75. Montvale, N.J.: National Association of Accountants, 1986.

Discussion Questions

1. Define the term flexible budget. Explain the basic concept that underlies flexible budgets.
2. How are flexible budgets used?
3. Define fixed, variable, and semivariable expenses.
4. Distinguish between controllable and noncontrollable expenses. Are fixed expenses, variable expenses, and semivariable expenses controllable? Explain.

5. What is meant by the relevant range of activity? How is it related to the classification of expenses as fixed or variable?

6. Explain the relationship of total fixed costs and total variable costs to cost per unit.

7. What is meant by the activity base? Why is it important that the activity base be carefully selected?

8. What are "stepped" and "curved" expenses? How are they usually analyzed for flexible budget purposes?

9. In developing a flexible budget, why is the analysis of semivariable expenses especially critical?

10. Three different approaches are used to analyze semivariable expenses to determine expense variability. Identify and explain each approach.

11. Explain adaptation of the equation $Y = a + bX$ to the problem of determining variability.

12. Identify the three formats used for flexible budgets and state when each would be preferable.

13. Prepare a flexible budget (formula format) based on the following graph:

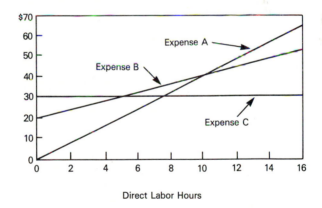

Direct Labor Hours

What is the activity base?

14. Prepare a flexible expense budget (formula format) based on the following data (X = Direct machine hours):

Expense A:	$Y = \$60 + \$3X$	
Expense B:	*DMH*	*Budget*
	100	$200
	120	240
Expense C:	At 150 DMH, budget $380 (constant $50)	

15. The flexible budget for Responsibility Center X was as follows:

EXPENSE	FIXED PER PERIOD	VARIABLE PER MACHINE HOUR
A	$140	$ -0-
B	-0-	5.00
C	130	4.00

The annual profit plan starts January 1. It is now April 20. Compute the following budget amounts for each expense and in total:

(1) The March amounts in the annual profit plan assuming 1,000 planned machine hours.
(2) The March expense goal assuming the management now plans 1,200 machine hours.
(3) The March performance report shows 1,100 actual machine hours.

CASE 10-1   *Can you prepare a flexible budget?*

The manager of the repair and maintenance department of Airport Auto Rental, Inc., in response to a request, submitted the following budget estimates for the department that will be used to prepare the budget for the coming budget year. Three representative expenses are used for case purposes.

CONTROLLABLE EXPENSES	PLANNED EXPENSE AT 6,000 DIRECT REPAIR HOURS	PLANNED EXPENSE AT 9,000 DIRECT REPAIR HOURS
Employee salaries	$3,000	$3,000
Indirect repair materials	4,020	6,030
Miscellaneous costs	1,320	1,680
Etc.		

REQUIRED

1. What is the activity base and the relevant range? Explain.
2. Prepare a table-format flexible budget for the department (use increments of 1,000 direct repair hours).
3. Prepare a formula format expense budget for the department.
4. Prepare a graphical format flexible budget for the department.
5. What would be the budget amount at 8,500 direct repair hours?
6. Which flexible budget format would you recommend for this department? Why?

CASE 10-2   *A subtle way to introduce change by a new management*

The stock of Robin Tool Company, a manufacturer of small, specialized tools, was closely held by three members of the Robin family—one brother, Samuel, and two married sisters. Samuel had been president of the company since the death of the senior Robin in 1966. The recent death of Samuel, resulting from a heart attack, came as a shock to the other officers of the company, all of whom had been hired by the senior Robin. Samuel Robin's stock passed to his wife and three daughters, none of whom were affiliated with the company. These events resulted in the employment of a new president from the outside. The new president, Richard E. Johnson, brought in two former associates, who were given the positions (newly created) of executive vice-president (R. C. Conklin) and controller (A. J. Mohle).

During the first year, the new officers completed an extensive internal reorganization. Simultaneously, the controller revised the accounting system to emphasize control by adapting it to the new organization structure. The other officers accepted these changes. The acceptance was due to three principal factors: (1) competence of new officers, (2) company loyalties existing among the former employees, and (3) recognition that the company had gradually become less competitive in the industry during the past six years.

Subsequent to the revision of the accounting system, immediate steps were taken to institute a system of sales planning that tied in with the newly adopted quota system whereby monthly quotas would be developed for each salesperson.

With historical expense data for two years, classified in accordance with the new system of accounts now available, controller Mohle felt that the next major step should be to develop a complete budget program including effective expense control procedures.

During a conference of supervisors called by Mohle and the plant manager to discuss problems of expense control, R. V. Mellon, the manager of Production Department 3, stated: "I have had no experience with expense budgets, but a friend of mine who works for another plant in the city warned me about how they work in that company. He is asked to prepare a detailed annual expense budget for his department. When the monthly reports come out, his actual expenses are compared with one-twelfth of the annual budget. Frankly, he says it causes a lot of trouble and is of no use as far as he is concerned. He is trying to get rid of it."

After some discussion in the meeting, someone suggested that monthly expense budgets for each department might be prepared during each preceding month. Controller Mohle pointed out that although this procedure might be useful, planning expenses only one month in advance would not satisfy the planning needs of the management. Another suggestion was to have each department manager develop an annual department expense budget detailed by month. Another plant manager said, "We cannot guess expenses for December twelve months in advance for a number of reasons. Perhaps the most important reason is that we have no idea as to how much work we will be doing in December. We get production orders about ten days in advance now. I cannot see how guessing expenses will help control them." Another supervisor interjected, "In my department, expenses are determined by the work we do more than anything else. I would hate to see my June expenses (when production usually is at the top) set up against the same budget as my August expenses (when production usually is at the bottom)."

Mellon, who had evidenced an understanding of the need for some new expense control procedures, suggested that the company "might establish percentages or rates for each expense in each department so that the budget expense amounts would be doubled in a month when output was doubled compared with another month."

Mohle, who participated on an advisory basis, had indirectly guided the discussions. At this point, be suggested that the company experiment with "flexible expense budgets" and explained that this would require:

1 Identification of the controllable and noncontrollable expenses in each department.
2 Specification of how the output of each department should be measured.
3 Identification of the fixed and variable expenses in each department.
4 Agreement on flexible budget amounts and rates that would relate each expense to the measure of department output.
5 Monthly performance reports for the manager of each department that would compare actual expenses with budget amounts adjusted to actual output—the flexible budgets would make this possible.

After discussing these ideas, the meeting closed with this comment by Mellon: "But many of my expenses, such as indirect labor, are neither fixed nor variable." Spears, another department manager, stated: "It appears to me that tying budget allowances to direct labor hours would encourage supervisors to incur more direct labor hours, which in itself adds to expenses, so that budget allowances would be higher."

Another meeting was scheduled for the following day. In preparation for the next meeting, Controller Mohle decided to use Department 3 expenses and production (output) as a basis for discussion of the flexible budget concept.

Production Department 3 had a high ratio of machines to manpower. Practically all the different types of tools manufactured pass through Department 3; therefore, it appeared to Mohle that overall productive output in the department was best measured in direct machine hours (DMH). The accounting department used DMH as a basis for allocating departmental overhead to production cost.

Inspection of the actual controllable expenses in the department for the past year indicated that a few expenses, such as depreciation and salaries, were fairly constant from month to month, although DMH varied considerably from month to month during the same period. A few expenses, such as direct material used and direct labor, clearly varied with output. However, most of the expenses appeared to vary in some degree, although not directly, with productive activity. Indirect labor was typical of the latter type of expense, as indicated by the following historical data provided by the accounting department (simplified for instructional purposes):

MONTH (NUMBERED FOR CONVENIENCE)	DEPARTMENT NO. 3	
	DMHs (000)	INDIRECT LABOR EXPENSE
1	170	1650
2	160	1470
3	160	1480
4	150	1450
5	150	1460
6	140	1450
7	130	1420
8	120	1200
9	130	1440
10	150	1490
11	160	1490
12	170	1500

To prepare for the meeting, Mohle constructed a graph with actual indirect labor (vertical scale) compared with productive activity (horizontal scale). He planned to focus the discussion on three questions: (1) How did actual indirect labor expense in Department 3 change last year in regard to productive activity?; (2) What should be the planned relation of indirect labor expense to planned production activity?; and (3) How should the department's expenses be shown on the monthly performance reports?

REQUIRED

1. Give and briefly explain three fundamental requirements of effective expense control.

2. Construct a graph of actual indirect labor. Be prepared to give an explanation of the analysis and its application in the analysis of indirect labor expense.

3. What would you recommend as the flexible budget for indirect labor assuming a management decision to increase fixed expense 5 percent and decrease variable expense 10 percent?

4. What budget variance should be reported to January of the coming year, assuming actual expense of $1,670 and production output of 180,000 DMH?

5. How should the following individuals be involved in setting the constant and variable values for Department 3: Mohle, Mellon, Mellon's next superior, executive committee, and president?

6. How would you answer Spears's comment about DLHs?

CASE 10-3 *Prepare and use your flexible budget*

Your company is developing a flexible budget for Production Department 1, which is a large department containing a number of similar machines. The activity base selected is direct machine hours. Because of the diverse nature of expenses in the department, several approaches are used in developing the fixed and variable components of each expense. The analyses have been completed with the results indicated below.

a. Supervisory salaries last year amounted to $239,984; the management has decided to plan a 10 percent increase for the upcoming year.

b. Least squares analyses of monthly expense data for the past nine months provided the following results (the variable rate given is $ per DMH):
(1) Depreciation $\quad Y = \$9,600 + \quad 0X$
(2) Indirect Materials $Y = 500 \quad + \$.08X$
(3) Power expense $\quad Y = 0 \quad + \$.02X$

The management has reviewed these results and has decided that indirect materials should be decreased 10 percent and power expense increased 5 percent.

c. Property taxes last year were $1,067; it is estimated that there will be a $12\frac{1}{2}$ percent increase in taxes for the coming year.

d. Indirect supplies are estimated to be $2,000 at a monthly volume of 100,000 DMH; the management and the industrial engineers agreed that this expense should be 60 percent variable and 40 percent fixed.

e. Indirect wages have been estimated to be $42,000 at 100,000 DMH and $36,000 at 80,000 DMH.

f. Maintenance has been estimated as follows:

At maximum output	$20,000
At minimum output	17,000

g. The method of least squares analysis on a monthly basis indicates that miscellaneous expenses should be: fixed, $1,500; variable, $.005 per DMH. The economist estimates that a general price increase of 8 percent will occur that will affect this expense; however, management decided that the variable portion is 10 percent too high now (at present prices).

REQUIRED

1. Prepare the flexible budget with the amounts you would recommend for inclusion therein. Make the budget complete in every detail and provide explanatory comments if needed. The relevant range is 80,000 to 100,000 DMH. Use the formula format and show the variable rates per 100 DMH.

2. Compute budget amounts for January of the budget year, assuming planned direct machine hours of 90,000 for January.

CASE 10-4   *Multiple uses of a flexible budget*

Production Department 9 is one of sixteen departments in the factory; it is involved in the production of all the five products manufactured. The department is highly mechanized, and as a result the output is measured in direct machine hours. Flexible budgets are used throughout the factory for planning and controlling expenses. This case focuses on the application of flexible budgets in Department 9. The following data covering a time span of approximately six months were taken from the various budgets, accounting records, and performance reports (only representative items and amounts are used for case purposes):

1   On September 14, 19X, the following flexible budget was approved for the department. It will be used throughout the 19Y operating year. This budget was developed through the cooperative efforts of the department manager, the next-higher manager and staff members from the budget department.

19Y Flexible—Production Department 9

CONTROLLABLE EXPENSES	FIXED AMOUNT PER MONTH	VARIABLE RATE PER DIRECT MACHINE HOUR
Employee salaries	$2,800	$ 0
Indirect wages	5,000	.04
Indirect materials	0	.09
Etc.		
Total	$7,800	$.13

2   On November 3, 19X, the sales plan and the production budget were completed. To continue preparation of the annual profit plan, which was detailed by month, the production budget was translated into planned activity for each of the factory departments. The planned activity for Production Department 9 was:

	FOR THE TWELVE MONTHS ENDING DECEMBER 31, 19Y				
	YEAR	JANUARY	FEBRUARY	MARCH	ETC.
Planned output in direct machine hours	310,000	20,000	24,000	30,000	236,000

3   On February 26, 19Y, the manager of Production Department 9 was informed that planned output for March had been revised to 33,000 direct machine hours. The manager expressed doubt as to whether this level of work could be attained.

4   At the end of March 19Y, the accounting records showed the following actual data for the month for the department:

Actual output in direct machine hours..................	32,000
Actual controllable expenses incurred:	
Employee salaries..	$ 2,900
Indirect wages	6,580
Indirect materials...	2,830
Etc.	

REQUIRED   The requirements illustrate several uses of the flexible budget during the period September 19X through March 19Y.

1. What activity base is used in this department? What is the relevant range in the department? Explain.

2. The budgeted high-low point method was used to develop the flexible budget for the department. Explain and illustrate essentially how this method was applied in this case.

3. Explain and illustrate with complete schedules how the flexible budget could be used at each of the following dates:
   a. November 3, 19X, or shortly thereafter
   b. February 26, 19Y, or shortly thereafter
   c. March 31, 19Y, or shortly thereafter

CASE 10-5   *Twenty-one flexible budgets!*

Mann Manufacturing Company, a medium-size company on the West Coast, has been in business for twenty-four years. The company operates two manufacturing plants that produce six products distributed throughout the United States. The six product lines are "backyard items" and are sold to wholesale distributors who, in turn, distribute them to retail outlets. Sales are highly seasonal.

This case focuses on the two manufacturing plants. Each plant is operated as a separate profit center under the direction of two plant managers. For case purposes, the plants are designated as Plant A and Plant B. The sales function is centralized. Therefore, the two plant managers have no sales responsibility. Plant output is billed to the sales division at a transfer price set by top management. Each plant manufactures different products, and each plant manager has responsibility for product improvement, meeting sales delivery requirements, production planning, inventory control, cost control, quality, profit planning, and other plant activities.

Due to the diverse products manufactured, the measures of overall plant output are: Plant A—standard direct labor hours; Plant B—standard prime cost of products completed. Direct labor in Plant A is a significant element of cost, and labor standards have been used for about five years. These labor standards were developed by using engineering analyses, and they specify the number of direct labor hours required for each production operation in the factory. Average wage rates for each production operation are used for planning and control purposes. These average wage rates are historical averages adjusted by managerial judgment. Plant B expected costs for direct material and direct labor are planned for each product annually. In view of the similarity of the products, these standards are considered to be realistic.

Plant A is organized into nine separate departments: three administrative, two factory service, and four production departments. Plant B is organized into thirteen separate departments: two administrative, four factory service, and seven production departments. The corporate offices are located at Plant B; they include the central sales division headed by a marketing vice-president; the financial division headed by a financial vice-president (the controller and the treasurer are in this division); and the production division headed by a production vice-president (the two plant managers report directly to this vice-president). At each plant, there is a "financial group" of three employees including a plant controller. These financial groups report directly, on a line basis, to the respective plant managers; however, they have functional responsibility to the financial vice-president.

For the past four years, the company has developed an annual profit plan and a three-year long-range plan. These plans are developed annually; the annual planning cycle extends from September 1 through December. The accounting period (and the profit plans) agrees with the calendar year. The annual profit plan is subdivided on a monthly basis when initially developed. Each plant manager is responsible for developing the annual profit plan for the respective plant and is expected to be ready to present these plans for consideration to top management by November 15 of each year.

Monthly performance reports are distributed to each responsibility center in the company. These performance reports are prepared on the central computer by the company controller and are distributed by the tenth of the following month. These performance reports show "actual, month, and cumulative to date" and "variances, month, and cumulative to date." Because of continuing complaints about the "expense variances" from operating managers in both plants, the management of the company is seriously thinking about adopting flexible budget procedures for all responsibility centers in the company.

REQUIRED

1. Should the company start using flexible budgets? Explain the basis for your recommendation.
2. If flexible budgets are to be used, give your recommendations about such major issues as organization, management participation, format, developing flexible budgets, measurement of outputs, and uses of flexible budget data.

CASE 10-6   *Can you "eyeball" a trend line?*

The historical data given below were taken from the cost records of Speedy Printing Company.

DEPARTMENT X	DIRECT LABOR HOURS	EXPENSES			
MONTH	(THOUSANDS)	INDIRECT LABOR	SALARIES	MAINTE- NANCE	MISCELL- ANEOUS
1	8.0	$750	$300	$620	$170
2	9.0	820	300	680	180
3	9.5	850	300	685	195
4	8.1	760	300	625	175
5	7.0	690	300	600	140
6	6.8	675	300	590	125
7	6.0	610	300	520	110
8	6.1	600	300	512	100
9	6.7	660	300	585	120
10	7.2	700	300	610	150
11	8.0	740	300	690	165
12	9.8	880	300	685	200

DEPARTMENT Y	DIRECT MACHINE HOURS	EXPENSES	
MONTH		MAINTENANCE	SUPPLIES USED
1	19,000	$250	$475
2	18,000	230	450
3	18,000	240	440
4	17,000	225	430
5	17,000	210	420
6	16,000	200	410
7	14,000	190	360
8	14,000	200	350
9	17,000	230	425
10	19,000	240	480
11	20,000	260	510
12	21,000	280	515

REQUIRED

DEPARTMENT X

1. Prepare a graphic analysis of the above historical data; relate each expense to the activity base.

2. Using the graphs developed in requirement 1, prepare a formula format flexible budget for Department X. Assume no changes because of management judgment.

3. Prepare a schedule that shows the budget at 7,000 and 9,000 direct labor hours.

DEPARTMENT Y

4. Analyze each expense by using the method of least squares. You can do this manu-

ally by using a pocket calculator or a computer. (Hint: Summation of X^2 is 3,726 DMH.)

5. What is the flexible budget formula for each expense?

CASE 10-7   *A challenge—can you spot the deficiencies? But more important, can you develop ways to correct them?*

Olds Manufacturing Company produces three different but related products that are distributed nationally through established wholesale channels. The company is weak in accounting planning and control. For fifteen years the company has had a budget program, but apparently it has never been "modernized." As a result, it has had little impact on the management process. The accounting period ends December 31. Recently the longtime controller retired, and a relatively young CPA with industrial experience in a dynamic company was hired to take his place. Upon arrival, the new controller was given the "monthly budget report." The following excerpt from it, relating to Production Department 13 only, was selected for case purposes. The department produces only one item—a component part that is used in each of the three products. After reviewing the report, the new controller concluded that (1) it was misleading, (2) it was conceptually deficient, and (3) the unit cost amounts shown were deceptive.

Olds Manufacturing Company

Production Department 13
Monthly Budget Report—March 19XX

	ACTUAL	BUDGET	DIFFERENCE
Costs:			
Raw material	$14,500	$16,000	$1,500
Direct labor	21,500	22,000	500
Overhead:			
Supervision*	5,300	5,000	300
Indirect labor	3,900	4,000	100
Repairs	1,400	1,400	—
Power	2,600	3,000	400
Supplies used	950	1,000	50
Depreciation*	7,000	7,000	—
Taxes*	400	400	—
Insurance*	200	200	—
Allocated costs*	18,000	20,000	2,000
Total	$75,750	$80,000	$4,250
Unit cost	$4.21	$4.00	

*For case purposes, assume that these are fixed costs and that the remaining are variable costs.

REQUIRED

1. Identify and explain the basis for the new controller's three conclusions.

2. List and briefly explain your recommendations for improving the report to enhance it for control purposes.

3. Redraft the report to conform with your recommendations in requirement 2. Show your underlying computations.

CASE 10-8 *An oil company needs your expert help!*

Texmo Service Company performs services for the oil industry. Texmo, a medium-size company, has been in operation since 1958. The company operates in the United States and Canada.

Operations at the field level are under the supervision of division managers who are usually engineers. The typical division covers an extensive territory. The size of a division depends on the geographical concentration of oil exploration and production activities.

For example, one state is divided into three divisions, whereas another division covers two states. The amount and type of equipment used in a division depend on the amount of activity and the characteristics of that activity. For example, a district involved in only production requires different services than a district involved in only exploration.

Monthly activities are reported in terms of the (1) number of jobs (i.e., services) by type, (2) total revenue by type of job, and (3) average revenue per average job. Expenses are reported by division and by type of job.

Prior to the beginning of each semiannual period, each division manager is required to prepare a budget. Exhibit 1 shows a typical budget for the first month (January) of the semiannual budget. At the end of each month, a performance report is prepared for each division comparing the budget (as revised by higher management) with the actual results as shown in Exhibit 2.

While discussing this procedure, one division manager commented: "The operating report is not fair as far as I am concerned. For example, in January my jobs were 10 percent above budget, which is a good thing, but my expenses show unfavorable variances, and although both types of jobs earned more per job, the average per job went down $18. On the other hand, if my Type X jobs are down by 20 percent, my Type X expense allowance is cut 20 percent. Can't we do something about this?"

REQUIRED

1. Critically evaluate the approach and format used in the operating report.

2. Recast the performance report to reflect your recommendations. Assume the following are realistic amounts:

EXPENSE	FIXED PER MONTH	VARIABLE RATE PER JOB
Type X expenses	$2,000	$150
Type Y expenses	3,000	156
Division overhead	3,200	20

EXHIBIT 1. Texmo Service Company
Six-Month Budget, January to June 19B

DIVISION: 5 INVESTMENT DIVISION: $17,050					MANAGER: C. E. DAVIS APPROVED: DEC. 10, 19A		
PARTICULARS	JAN.	FEB.	MAR.	APR.	MAY	JUNE	TOTAL
Revenues:							
Type X jobs—No.	10						
$ Amount	8,000	(January only is shown for instructional purposes)					
Type Y jobs—No.	30						
$ Amount	14,000						
Total jobs —No.	40						
$ Amount	22,000						
Av. per job	550						
Expenses:							
Type X jobs (Itemized—$)	3,500						
Type Y jobs (Itemized—$)	7,680						
Division overhead (Itemized—$)	4,000						
Total expenses	15,180						
Division net revenue	6,820						
Percent of total revenue	31%						

EXHIBIT 2. Texmo Service Company
Operating Report, dated January 31, 19B

DIVISION: 5				MANAGER: C. E. DAVIS CUMULATIVE _____ MONTHS TO DATE _____		
	MONTH OF JAN. 19B			CUMULATIVE TO DATE		
PARTICULARS	ACTUAL	BUDGET	VARIATIONS	ACTUAL	BUDGET	VARIATIONS
Revenues:						
Type X jobs—No.	8	10	2*	(Not applicable for first month)		
$ Amount	6,580	8,000	1,420*			
Type Y jobs—No.	36	30	6*			
$ Amount	16,920	14,000	2,920			
Total jobs —No.	44	40	4			
$ Amount	23,500	22,000	1,500			
Av. per job	534	550	16*			
Expenses:						
Type X jobs (Itemized—$)	3,300	2,800	500*			
Type Y jobs (Itemized—$)	8,450	7,680	770*			
Division overhead (Itemized—$)	4,050	4,000	50*			
Total expenses	15,800	14,480	1,320*			
Division net revenue	7,700	7,520	180			
Percent of total revenue	33%	34%	12%*			

*Unfavorable.

Planning and Controlling
11 Capital Expenditures

INTRODUCTION AND PURPOSE   The preceding chapters discussed the characteristics and development of a comprehensive profit plan. This chapter continues those discussions by focusing on another important element, capital expenditures, often called capital budgeting. Capital budgeting is the process of planning and controlling the strategic (long-term) and tactical (short-term) expenditures for expansion and contraction of investments in operating (fixed) assets.

The purpose of this chapter is to discuss and illustrate the importance of, and the approaches used to develop, a capital expenditures budget, its components, and its role in planning and controlling. This chapter also focuses on the capital expenditures budget process, the decisions about what projects should be initiated, and the timing problems. The comprehensive demonstration case—Superior Manufacturing Company—is continued to illustrate a tactical capital expenditures budget.

CAPITAL EXPENDITURES DEFINED   A capital expenditure is the use of funds (e.g., cash) to obtain operational assets that will (a) help earn future revenues or (b) reduce future costs. Capital expenditures include such fixed (i.e., operational) assets as property, plant, equipment, major renovations, and patents.[1] Typically, capital expenditure projects involve large amounts of cash, other resources, and debt that are tied up for relatively long periods of time.

Capital expenditures are investments because they require the commitment of resources today to receive higher economic benefits (i.e., profits) in the future. Capital expenditures become expenses in the future as their related goods and services are being used to earn higher future profits from future rev-

[1] The term **capital** is used in the context of capital expenditures and capital budgets to mean the "long-term, and more or less permanent, commitments of current and future cash for long-term assets, often called capital assets." The terms **capital expenditures budget** and **capital additions budget** are used interchangeably.

394

enues or to achieve future cost savings. The related future expenses, such as depreciation expense, are identified with the future periods when the capital additions are used for their intended purposes. Therefore, capital expenditures involve two planning and controlling phases: (1) investments and (b) expenses.

A major issue in planning capital expenditures is the problem of ensuring that a company has the **capacity** to produce, acquire, or be able to deliver the goods and services that will be needed to meet its sales and services plans (see Chapter 5).[2] A major issue in controlling the actual expenditure of funds is the problem of ensuring that the actual expenditures are consistent with the plans and that funds are available when the expenditures are incurred (see Chapter 12).

CHARACTERISTICS OF A CAPITAL EXPENDITURES BUDGET   The capital expenditure budget (or plan) is an important part of a comprehensive profit plan.[3] It is directly related to a company's operating assets, especially land, equipment, and other operational assets and cash. Capital expenditures are usually classified in a capital expenditures budget as follows:

a Major capital additions projects—these projects usually require large commitments of funds for operational assets that have lives that extend over a long period of time. They tend to be unique, nonrecurring projects that represent new directions and major steps, and technological improvements. Examples are acquisition of land, new buildings, and extensive renovations, improvements, and maintenance. Each major project is assigned a special designation.

b Minor or small capital expenditures—these are small, low-cost, recurring, and ordinary capital expenditures. Examples are recurring replacements and maintenance of operational assets, and the purchase of special tools and attachments that contribute to future revenues or cost savings. Minor capital expenditures are usually grouped together as a single monthly amount (i.e., appropriation) for capital budgeting purposes. Minor capital expenditures should not include the usual ordinary and ongoing repairs and maintenance. These expenditures should be included in expense budgets.

The above classification of capital expenditures means that the capital expenditures budget has a strong project orientation because most projects incur large amounts of funds and time.

Another primary characteristic of a capital expenditures budget is its time dimension. In Chapter 2, Exhibit 2-6 emphasized the time dimensions of profit planning and control. The time dimensions of a capital expenditures budget must be consistent with the comprehensive profit plan. This means that a capital expenditures budget must include (a) a strategic (long-term) capital expenditures budget and (b) a tactical (short-term) capital expenditures budget.

[2] Charles N. Greene, Everett E. Adam, Jr., Ronald J. Ebert, *Management for Effective Performance* (Englewood Cliffs, N.J., Prentice-Hall, 1985), p. 632.
[3] The capital expenditures budget is variously referred to as the capital additions budget, plant and equipment budget, construction budget, capital outlay budget, investment budget, or plant additions budget.

PROJECT ORIENTATION IN THE CAPITAL EXPENDITURES BUDGET Because of the long time span and major resource commitments, major capital expenditures typically are budgeted as separate projects. Each project is unique to a specific asset or group of assets (i.e., investment), the amount and sources of its funding, and its timing (both construction or acquisition time and subsequent use or service time). Major projects are usually named and numbered. Typically, they are **separately** analyzed, planned, approved or rejected, completed (if approved), and controlled. Therefore, the capital expenditures budget is primarily composed of a series of identified projects related to specific time dimensions.

Importance of Project-Related Information

A capital expenditure is important to the ongoing operations of the entity. Also, the information used in the analysis and evaluation of alternative projects is important. The data used must be reliable, accurate, and relevant because management may use these data to reach a decision on the capital expenditures budget. Yet, this is often one of the major weaknesses of the capital expenditure process. Data elements can be categorized as a matrix:

	EXTERNAL	INTERNAL
Financial	• Market and Economic Trends	• Cash Outflows • Cash Inflows
Nonfinancial	• Government Regulation • Technological Advancements	• Operating Volumes • Productivity Impact

One of the most important elements from a capital expenditures budget perspective involves cash outflows and inflows:

1 Cash outflows: These include the cost of the project in terms of cash outlays at various times during the life of a project. Provision should be made for probable government regulations and the latest applicable technological advances. Provision should also be made for the residual value of old equipment, tax losses incurred from disposition, and so on. Provision should be made for the cost of borrowing necessary funds.

2 Cash inflows: The expected cash revenues, net of cash operating expenses by time period, must be carefully planned. The analysis of cash inflow must be very carefully planned because estimates often are "too optimistic or too pessimistic."

TIME DIMENSIONS IN THE CAPITAL EXPENDITURES BUDGET Because of the strategic and tactical time dimensions in a comprehensive profit plan and the significance of capital expenditure projects, the capital expenditures budget includes three time dimensions: (1) a time dimension required by a particular

project that extends the farthest into the future, (2) a time dimension in conformity with the strategic long-range profit plan, and (3) a time dimension consistent with the short-range profit plan. Typically, the capital expenditures budget
extends beyond the long-term profit plan because of the long-term nature of
some capital additions. These time dimensions in relation to projects are illustrated for a typical case in Exhibit 11-1. Notice that the strategic profit plan has
a time dimension of five years, the tactical profit plan is one year, and the capital expenditures plan spans fourteen years. The spans of the separate projects
are: A, eight and one-half years; B, four years; C, eight years; D, five years; E,
eight years; and F, eight years.

Exhibit 11-2 shows a typical summary of a strategic long-term capital expenditures budget. Notice that it separately identifies the **major projects** and
gives the project designations, planned initiation dates, funds committed, and
timing of the related cash payments.

The minor, or small, capital expenditures (often called undesignated capital expenditures) cannot, or need not, be planned in detail far in advance. Capital additions of this type typically include purchases of relatively low cost furniture and tools, minor renovations, and **recurring** repairs. These **minor** capital
expenditures are usually shown as single or blanket amounts in the strategic
capital expenditures budget. Notice the "undesignated" category in Exhibit 11-2.

EXHIBIT 11-1

Time Dimension and Project Components of a Typical Capital Expenditures Budget

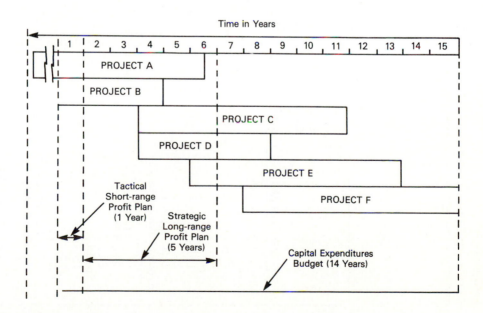

EXHIBIT 11-2
A Long-Range Capital Expenditures Budget

398

XYZ Company—Long-Range Plan

Summary Capital Expenditures Budget by Project and Years

For the Period January 1, 19C Through 19G

(Expressed in Thousands of Dollars—Only Representative Amounts Shown)

DESCRIPTION OF PROJECTS	REFERENCE FOR DETAIL	BUDGETED		AMOUNT AUTHORIZED TO JAN. 1, 19C	AMOUNT SUBJECT TO AUTHORIZATION	AMOUNT SPENT TO JAN. 1, 19C	UNEXPENDED BALANCE OF APPROPRIATION	YEAR OF EXPENDITURE—CASH REQUIREMENTS					
		INITIAL DATE	TOTAL AMOUNT					19C	19D	19E	19F	19G	SUBSEQUENT YEARS
Approved major projects													
Regular:													
Project A	A-1	19A	$1,000	$800	$ 200	$700	$100	$150	$ 75	$ 50	$ 25		
Etc.													
Special:													
Project E	E-1	19B	500	200	300	180	20	220	70	30			
Etc.													
Total Approved													
Budgeted major projects—19C*													
Regular:													
Project G	G-1	19C			11			11					
Project H	H-1	19C	800		800			100	150	250	200	75	25
Etc.													
Special:													
Project M	M-1												
Etc.													
Undesignated†													
Total budgeted—19C		19C	270					50	50	50	60	60	
Grand total													
For Information:													
Future projects under study:													
Project X	X-1	19D	1,700		1,700				200	350	500	400	250
Etc.													

*Detailed in 19C profit plan.

†To take care of low-cost and frequent capital additions; see annual profit plan for 19C departmental appropriations.

The tactical short-term capital expenditures budget show the details of the major projects only for one year. However, the annual "appropriation" for the minor capital expenditures often cannot be planned in detail. Therefore, the usual approach for the minor capital expenditures is to use an undesignated amount as a blanket appropriation detailed by **responsibility centers,** rather than by projects.

A tactical (annual) capital expenditures budget for the comprehensive case—Superior Manufacturing Company—is shown in Schedule 46 at the end of this chapter.

BENEFITS OF A CAPITAL EXPENDITURES BUDGET

BENEFITS OF A CAPITAL EXPENDITURES BUDGET   A capital expenditures budget provides many benefits from the management planning and controlling vantage points. The capital expenditures budget enables executive management to plan the amount of resources that should be invested in capital additions to satisfy customer demands, meet competitive demands, and ensure growth. The budget process for capital additions is essential for management to avoid (a) idle operating capacity, (b) excess capacity, and (c) investments in capacity that will earn less than an adequate return on the funds invested.

The development of a strategic (long-term) and a tactical (short-term) capital expenditures budget is also beneficial because it requires sound **capital expenditures decisions** by management. By using this process, management can develop and carefully evaluate alternative capital expenditures. Very often management must ration its capital requirements among the various acceptable alternatives. It is not simply a matter of how much the enterprise can afford (in cash), but how much in terms of personnel, effort, and supervisors can be given to new projects versus ongoing operations. The capital expenditures budget also focuses the attention of executive management on cash flows, a crucial and often neglected problem. Finally, the capital expenditures budget increases coordination among responsibility centers because capital additions decisions often affect the entire company, although not in the same way for all units of the organization. In some cases, several projects will be mutually exclusive and will be "either/or" decisions that management must make. In other cases, several projects will be mutually dependent. Therefore, the several projects must be packaged together. Relationships between projects such as these require careful coordination among the various responsibility centers.

RESPONSIBILITIES FOR DEVELOPING THE CAPITAL EXPENDITURES BUDGET

The top executive, working with the other members of executive management, has the primary responsibility for the capital additions budget. However, the primary responsibility for projects and other proposals should include divisional and departmental managers. Policies and procedures should be established to encourage ideas and proposals for capital additions from sources within and even outside the company.

For **major** capital expenditures, procedures should be established to ensure appropriate analysis and evaluation. Many companies report that they must guard against a tendency to disregard a proposal that, on the surface, may not appear to have much potential but may actually be economically sound based on careful analysis. Procedures should require the originator to submit a proposal in writing including (1) a description of the proposal, (2) reasons for the recommendations, (3) sources of relevant data, (4) advantages and disadvantages of the proposal, and (5) recommended starting and completion dates. On the basis of an analysis along these lines, top management may decide to drop the proposal or to proceed with future analysis and planning on a designated **project** basis.

Budget requests for **minor** (i.e., low-cost and repetitive) capital expenditures should come from the managers of the responsibility centers because they should be primarily responsible for estimates of the needs for their particular operation and their subsequent control.

An executive, such as the financial executive or chief engineer, should be primarily responsible for **coordinating** the development of the capital expenditures budgets.

The Capital Expenditures Budget Process

Because capital expenditures involve the long-term commitment of large amounts of resources, decisions concerning them have a significant, long-term effect on the economic health of a company. This fact suggests the need for careful analysis and planning on the part of top management. An ill-advised decision about capital expenditures frequently cannot be reversed before it seriously affects the financial health of the company. Inadequate management attention to a capital addition may result in overinvestment or underinvestment and a consequent deterioration of a company's competitive position in the industry. A prudent management should not undertake a capital addition unless (a) it is necessary for continued operations, or (b) it is probable that it will yield a return at least equal to the long-term objective for return on investment. Because of the importance of sound capital expenditure decisions, the management should design a systematic process to develop the long-term and short-term capital expenditures budget.

The primary phases of a yearly budget process for planning and controlling capital expenditures are summarized in Exhibit 11-3.

Capital Expenditure Decisions—Evaluation of Projects and Proposals

The preceding discussions about the capital expenditures budgets—strategic and tactical—emphasized their importance and the related management responsibilities. The crucial capital expenditure decisions are the choices of man-

EXHIBIT 11-3

A Process for Planning and Controlling Capital Expenditures

PHASE	COMPONENT (ACTIVITY)
1	Identify and generate capital additions projects and other needs—this activity should be continuous in most cases.
2	Develop and refine capital additions proposal—collection of relevant data about each proposal, including any related alternatives.
3	Analyze and evaluate all capital additions, proposals, and alternatives. Emphasis should be given to the validity of the underlying financial and operational data.
4	Make capital expenditure decisions to accept the best alternatives and the assignment of project designations to selected alternatives.
5	Develop the capital expenditures budget: (a) Strategic plan—Replan and extend the long-term plan by dropping the past year and adding one year into the future. (b) Tactical plan—Develop a detailed annual capital expenditures budget, by responsibility center and by time, that is consistent with the comprehensive profit plan.
6	Establish control of capital expenditures during the budget year by using periodic and special performance reports by responsibility centers.
7	Conduct postcompletion audits and follow-up evaluations of the actual results from capital expenditures in periods after completion.

agement from the competing capital expenditures alternatives (e.g., projects). Such decisions must focus on two overriding problems:

a Investment decisions—selecting the best alternatives based on their economic worth to the company—called **investment worth.**

b Financing decisions—determining the amounts and sources of funds needed to pay for the selected alternatives. This cash constraint may necessarily limit the projects and proposals that can be initiated.

Capital expenditures involve two kinds of assets: (a) depreciable assets, such as buildings and equipment, and (b) nondepreciable assets, such as land. Capital expenditures that involve depreciable assets are much more common. The total cash returns on these two kinds of capital additions are significantly different:

a Depreciable assets usually have no, or a small, residual value at the end of their useful lives. Therefore, the total expected cash returns must include both return of the investment cost (i.e., the principal) plus interest on the investment.

b Nondepreciable assets usually leave the investment intact at the end of the investment period. Therefore, the total expected cash returns usually include interest only.

Financing decisions about rationing scarce resources among capital expenditures are significant; therefore, the financial executive must use a systematic approach in planning the financing of the company's capital expenditures.[4]

Capital budget decisions about the alternatives should usually be based on an objective evaluation of the **investment worth** of each alternative. Basically, investment worth is profit divided by investment. Traditionally, companies measure investment worth by using two basic approaches: (1) discounted cash flow models and (2) shortcut estimates (e.g., payback). Regardless of which of the two approaches is used, practical constraints such as the following may be overriding in certain cases:

1 **Urgency**—The urgency of the operational requirements may preclude extensive analyses, searches for sources of supply, and others. For example, a machine breaks down, it is beyond practical repair, operations are at a standstill, and urgency dictates that the machine that can be delivered first must be selected. This is sometimes called the emergency persuasion method and often there is no analysis or formal planning.

2 **Repairs**—Availability of spare parts and maintenance experts may be controlling. In some cases, this is an important factor that rules out foreign equipment as a practical alternative. For example, some companies do not purchase certain foreign-made equipment or machines because of the repair problems encountered outside major population areas.

3 **Credit**—Some suppliers provide generous credit terms versus a local bank, as the only other source of loans with an interest rate may be high.

4 **Noneconomic**—Local suppliers, political and social considerations, and other noneconomic persuasions and preferences.

METHODS OF MEASURING THE ECONOMIC VALUE OF A CAPITAL EXPENDITURE
Numerous methods of measuring the economic value (also called investment worth) of an investment are described in management accounting and finance books and articles. To meet the objectives of this book, we will discuss the four most widely used methods of measuring economic value:

DISCOUNTED CASH FLOW (DCF) METHODS:

1 Net present value
2 Internal rate of return

SHORTCUT AND SIMPLE METHODS:

1 Payback
2 Accounting rate of return

[4] This is a financing problem, which is a responsibility of the financial executive. We do not discuss this topic because books on finance are available that describe it in detail.

Discounted Cash Flow Methods to Measure Economic Value

Because a capital expenditure is for an asset, the essence of capital additions decisions is that the **investment worth** (or economic value) of a proposed capital addition should be measured like any other investment. That is, the investment worth should be measured as the rate of return (interest rate) that will be earned on the investment. The rate of return earned should be computed on a cash flow basis (rather than on the accrual accounting basis). This means that the cash outflows (i.e., cah payments) for an investment should be related to the cash inflows (i.e., cash receipts) from that investment. Conceptually, if the amounts and timing of the cash outflows and cash inflows related to an investment are the same, the rate of return (i.e., interest rate) is zero. Of course, in practice, the cash inflows from an investment must usually be more than the cash outflows, which means that interest is earned. Therefore, measurement of the investment worth of a capital expenditures should explicitly include interest, which is the time value of money. This is because any rational investor would rather have a dollar today than at any future date.

The discounted cash flow methods explicitly recognize the effects of the time value of money and in that way measure economic value or investment worth as a true interest rate. The basic concept is that investment cost is a cash outflow at **present value,** and the related cash inflows necessarily are **future values.** These future cash inflows must be discounted to their present values so that they can be appropriately subtracted, added, and compared with investment cost. The true rate of interest for any investment is the rate that will discount the future net cash inflows to a sum that exactly equals the investment cost. Discounting a future amount to the present involves the concept of **present value.**

Prior to discussing the two discounted cash flow (DCF) methods of measuring investments, we will discuss the concept of *present value* and then relate it to our specific problem of evaluating the investment worth of a proposed capital expenditure. Present value involves two different types of future amounts: (a) the present value of a single future amount and (b) the present value of a series of equal future amounts (called an annuity).

PRESENT VALUE OF A SINGLE FUTURE AMOUNT   The present value concept can be illustrated simply: What is the present value of $1,000 to be received one year hence ($n = 1$), assuming an interest rate of 10 percent ($i = 10\%$)? The present value can be computed as follows:

$$PV = F\left(\frac{1}{1 + i}\right)^{n}$$

where

PV = Present value
F = Future sum of money
i = Interest rate per period
n = Number of periods

Substituting ($n = 1; i = 10\%$):

$$PV = \$1,000\left(\frac{1}{1 + .10}\right)^1$$

$$= \$\ 909.09$$

Proof:

Present value	$ 909.09
Interest ($909.09 × .10)	90.91
Value one year hence	$1,000.00

Instead of making the computation shown above, we can refer to a "Present Value of $1" table (Table A, Exhibit 11-4) and obtain the **present value factor** for 10 percent for one year. Because such tables are based on $1, this factor (0.909) is multiplied by the $1,000 to compute the same present value, $909.09, computed above. Similarly, we can determine the present value of $4,500 to be received three years hence at an interest rate of 6 percent. Reading from the table (the 6 percent column, the line for three years), we find the factor 0.840. The present value is ($4,500 × 0.840) = $3,780. The following schedule shows that this computation is correct.

YEAR (n)	PRINCIPAL INVESTED AT BEGINNING OF YEAR	ADD EARNINGS (6% × COL. 1)	PRINCIPAL PLUS EARNINGS INVESTED AT END OF YEAR
1	$3,780	$226	$4,006
2	4,006	240	4,246
3	4,246	254*	4,500
Total		$720	

*Rounded to come out even because the table was limited to three places.

This case can be diagrammed as follows:

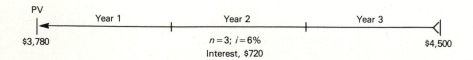

EXHIBIT 11–4

Present Value Tables

TABLE A.   Present Value of $1 (Symbol p); Based on a $1 Single Future Amount

YEARS (n)— AT YEAR-END	1%	2%	4%	6%	8%	10%	12%	14%	15%	16%	18%	20%	22%	24%	25%
1	0.990	0.980	0.962	0.943	0.926	0.909	0.893	0.877	0.870	0.862	0.847	0.833	0.820	0.806	0.800
2	0.980	0.961	0.925	0.890	0.857	0.826	0.797	0.769	0.756	0.743	0.718	0.694	0.672	0.650	0.640
3	0.971	0.942	0.889	0.840	0.794	0.751	0.712	0.675	0.658	0.641	0.609	0.579	0.551	0.524	0.512
4	0.961	0.924	0.855	0.792	0.735	0.683	0.636	0.592	0.572	0.552	0.516	0.482	0.451	0.423	0.410
5	0.951	0.906	0.822	0.747	0.681	0.621	0.567	0.519	0.497	0.476	0.437	0.402	0.370	0.341	0.328
6	0.942	0.888	0.790	0.705	0.630	0.564	0.507	0.456	0.432	0.410	0.370	0.335	0.303	0.275	0.262
7	0.933	0.871	0.760	0.665	0.583	0.513	0.452	0.400	0.376	0.354	0.314	0.279	0.249	0.222	0.210
8	0.923	0.853	0.731	0.627	0.540	0.467	0.404	0.351	0.327	0.305	0.266	0.233	0.204	0.179	0.168
9	0.914	0.837	0.703	0.592	0.500	0.424	0.361	0.308	0.284	0.263	0.225	0.194	0.167	0.144	0.134
10	0.905	0.820	0.676	0.558	0.463	0.386	0.322	0.270	0.247	0.227	0.191	0.162	0.137	0.116	0.107
11	0.896	0.804	0.650	0.527	0.429	0.350	0.287	0.237	0.125	0.195	0.162	0.135	0.112	0.094	0.086
12	0.887	0.788	0.625	0.497	0.397	0.319	0.257	0.208	0.187	0.168	0.137	0.112	0.092	0.076	0.069
13	0.879	0.773	0.601	0.469	0.368	0.290	0.229	0.182	0.163	0.145	0.116	0.093	0.075	0.061	0.055
14	0.870	0.758	0.577	0.442	0.340	0.263	0.205	0.160	0.141	0.125	0.099	0.078	0.062	0.049	0.044
15	0.861	0.743	0.555	0.417	0.315	0.239	0.183	0.140	0.123	0.108	0.084	0.065	0.051	0.040	0.035

TABLE B. Present Value of an Ordinary Annuity of $1; Received at Each Year-end for n Years (Symbol P)

YEARS (n)— AT YEAR-END	1%	2%	4%	6%	8%	10%	12%	14%	15%	16%	18%	20%	22%	24%	25%
1	0.990	0.980	0.962	0.943	0.926	0.909	0.893	0.877	0.870	0.862	0.847	0.833	0.820	0.806	0.800
2	1.970	1.942	1.886	1.833	1.783	1.736	1.690	1.647	1.626	1.605	1.566	1.528	1.492	1.457	1.440
3	2.941	2.884	2.775	2.673	2.577	2.487	2.402	2.322	2.283	2.246	2.174	2.106	2.042	1.981	1.952
4	3.902	3.808	3.630	3.465	3.312	3.170	3.037	2.914	2.855	2.798	2.690	2.589	2.494	2.404	2.362
5	4.853	4.713	4.452	4.212	3.993	3.791	3.605	3.433	3.352	3.274	3.127	2.991	2.864	2.745	2.689
6	5.795	5.601	5.242	4.917	4.623	4.355	4.111	3.889	3.784	3.685	3.498	3.326	3.167	3.020	2.951
7	6.728	6.472	6.002	5.582	5.206	4.868	4.564	4.288	4.160	4.039	3.812	3.605	3.416	3.242	3.161
8	7.652	7.325	6.733	6.210	5.747	5.335	4.968	4.639	4.487	4.344	4.078	3.837	3.619	3.421	3.329
9	8.566	8.162	7.435	6.802	6.247	5.759	5.328	4.946	4.772	4.607	4.303	4.031	3.786	3.566	3.463
10	9.471	8.983	8.111	7.360	6.710	6.145	5.650	5.216	5.019	4.833	4.494	4.192	3.923	3.682	3.571
11	10.368	9.787	8.760	7.887	7.139	6.495	5.988	5.453	5.234	5.029	4.656	4.327	4.035	3.776	3.656
12	11.255	10.575	9.385	8.384	7.536	6.814	6.194	5.660	5.421	5.197	4.793	4.439	4.127	3.851	3.725
13	12.134	11.343	9.986	8.853	7.904	7.103	6.424	5.842	5.583	5.342	4.910	4.533	4.203	3.912	3.780
14	13.004	12.106	10.563	9.295	8.244	7.367	6.628	6.002	5.724	5.468	5.008	4.611	4.265	3.962	3.824
15	13.865	12.849	11.118	9.712	8.559	7.606	6.811	6.142	5.847	5.575	5.092	4.675	4.315	4.001	3.859

PRESENT VALUE OF MORE THAN ONE FUTURE AMOUNT, ORDINARY ANNUITY   A somewhat different present value situation occurs when there are several future cash inflows from an investment. The typical case of an investment (e.g., capital expenditures) involves a series of periodic future cash inflows. Computing the present value in such cases often involves the application of an ordinary annuity. The characteristics of an ordinary annuity are equal future amounts, equal interest periods, and a constant rate of interest, and the future amounts are at the end of each interest period.[5] If any of these characteristics are not effective, present value of $1 amounts must be used.

The following case is presented to illustrate an ordinary annuity: What is the present value of three $1,000 payments, one to be received at the end of each of the next three years (n), assuming an interest rate (i) of 6 percent? Stated differently, what would you have to pay as a lump sum at the beginning of year 1 for an annuity contract that pays you in return $1,000 at the end of each of three years, at an interest rate of 6 percent? The situation can be presented graphically as follows:

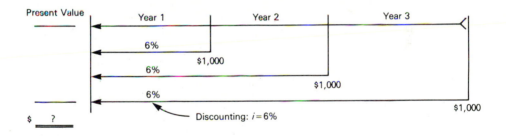

The cost of the annuity contract (present value of the future inflows) can be computed by a formula. However, if the table "Present Value of an Ordinary Annuity of $1; Received Annually at Each Year-end for n Years" (Table B, Exhibit 11-4) is available, the computation is quite simple. From the table, we obtain the discount factor of 2.673 (6 percent column, line for three years). The

---

[5] Annuity tables can be based on several assumptions, namely, that the cash flow occurs (1) at year-end, (2) in uniform monthly installments, or (3) continuously during the year. For purposes of illustration herein, tables under the first assumption are used, although the second and third assumptions are often more representative of actual conditions.

If the future amounts are at the beginning of the interest period, an annuity-due value must be used. Annuity-due values can be computed by multiplying any ordinary annuity value by $1 + i$.

present value can be directly computed: $(2.673 \times \$1,000) = \$2,673$. The computation can be verified as follows:

YEAR	PRINCIPAL INVESTED AT BEGINING OF YEAR a	INVESTED AT BEGINNING (6% × COL. a) b	ANNUITY PAYMENTS AT YEAR-END c	BALANCE INVESTED AT YEAR-END a + b − c
1	$2,673	$160	$1,000	$1,833
2	1,833	110	1,000	943
3	943	57	1,000	-0-
Total interest		$327		

Note: The answer in this illustration is $2,673. Notice that we could have made three PV of $1 computations with the same total: PV $1,000 for 1 year plus PV $1,000 for 2 years plus PV $1,000 for 3 years = $2,673.

CASH FLOW CONSIDERATIONS   The discounted cash flow methods use only net cash flows to measure an investment in capital additions. The net cash outflow used includes the cash cost plus any direct cash payments, such as freight, and less any cash deductions, such as a cash discount for early payment. The net periodic cash inflows from a depreciable asset should exclude all **noncash** expenses, such as depreciation expense (because it is a noncash expense). The tax effect of depreciation expense should be included as a cash flow. Corporations, but not sole proprietorships and partnerships, are subject to income tax. However, depreciation expense does reduce income tax payments and, as a result, reduces cash outflow. This effect is called the "depreciation income tax shield." To illustrate:

	DEPRECIATION EXPENSE	
	NONE	$10,000
Cash revenues	$200,000	$200,000
Cash operating expenses (excluding depreciation expense if any)	140,000	140,000
Net cash inflow before income tax	60,000	60,000
Less: Income tax at 30%:		
No depreciation expense ($60,000 × 30%)	18,000*	
Depreciation expense ($60,000 − $10,000) × 30%)		15,000*
Net cash inflow including income tax	$ 42,000	$ 45,000

*Notice that the income tax shield was $3,000 even though depreciation expense of $10,000 was a noncash expense; nevertheless it increased net cash inflow by $3,000 (i.e., $10,000 × 30%).

The cash inflows for a project usually come from revenues and/or a cost saving. *A cost saving is equivalent to a revenue* because it increases profits.

Cash outflows usually occur at the beginning of a project, and cash inflows typically occur during the life of a project. Typical cash flows are as follows:

- **Cash inflows:**
  Revenues from the project
  Cost savings from the project
  Reductions of current assets
  Increases in current liabilities
  Residual (salvage) value on project assets at the end of their useful life
- **Cash outflows:**
  Initial investment (including directly related payments)
  Repairs and maintenance
  Operating costs of the project
  Increases in current assets
  Reduction in current liabilities

Often capital expenditure projects do not produce **measurable** revenues. Therefore, the economic value or investment worth of such projects is measured in terms of cost savings. For competing projects, the project that produces the largest net cash-cost saving is to be preferred (absent any other compelling factors) because it will produce higher profits than the other projects.

We will now return to the primary problem of computing the economic value or investment worth of a proposed capital expenditure using the two DCF methods—net present value and internal rate of return.

Net Present Value Method Used to Rank Investments

The DCF net present value method compares the present value of the net cash inflows with the present value of the initial net cash cost of a capital expenditure project; the dollar difference between these two present value amounts is called **net present value.** The **net** cash inflows (i.e., cash inflows minus cash outflows) are discounted to present value by using a "target" or minimum rate of return (i.e., an interest rate).[6] Therefore, this method requires determination of three items for a project—initial cash outflow, future net cash inflows, and a target rate of return.

If the computed dollar difference between the initial net cash investment (the present value cash paid for the investment) and the computed present value of the net cash inflows from the investment is favorable (i.e., positive) to the net cash inflows, the project will earn more than the target rate of return. If the difference is not favorable to the net cash inflows, the project will not earn the target rate of return. When ranking competing projects, the one with the highest net present value (in dollars) is ranked first (absent any other compelling factors). The present value method is illustrated in Exhibit 11-5. Notice

---

[6] The minimum rate is also called the target rate, required rate, discount rate, and cutoff rate.

EXHIBIT 11-5

Net Present Value Method Used to Rank Investments

Case Data for Machines A and B

	MACHINE A	MACHINE B
Useful life (no residual value) (n)	10 years	12 years
Net initial cash cost (outflow)	$11,000	$15,000
Average annual net cash inflow*	2,750	2,750
Target rate of return (i)	15%	15%

Graphical Analysis—Machine A

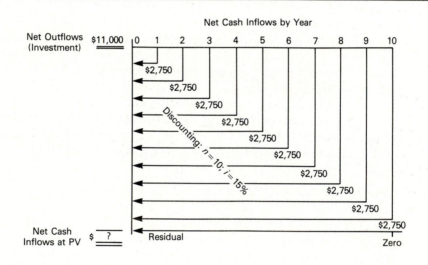

Computation of Net Present Value

	CASH	PV FACTOR—TABLE B	PRESENT VALUES MACHINE A	PRESENT VALUES MACHINE B
Machine A:				
Net cash inflow per year	$ 2,750	$n = 10; i = 15\%$-5.019	$13,802	
Net cash outflow—investment	11,000	(already at PV)	11,000	
Machine B:				
Net cash inflow per year	2,750	$n = 12; i = 15\%$-5.421		$14,907
Net cash outflow—investment	15,000	(already at PV)		15,000
Difference—net PV (unfavorable)			$ 2,802†	$ (93)

*At year-end.
†Preferable over Machine B by $2,895.

that Machine A would be ranked over Machine B because its net present value is much higher. Machine B will not earn the targeted rate of return of 15 percent.

EQUAL NET CASH INFLOWS   In Exhibit 11-5, the inflows were *equal each year,* which means that this is an annuity. Therefore, we used Exhibit 11-4. Table B, "Present Value of an Ordinary Annuity of $1; Received at Each Year-end for *n* Years." The PV factor from the table at 15 percent for ten years was 5.019. The present value of the ten equal annual revenues (cash inflows) of $2,750 multiplied by the table factor gave a present value of $13,802. Residual value was zero. A residual value must be present-costed for the entire life of the project because this cash inflow (sale of the old asset) is at the end. A cash trade-in value is handled like a residual value. The $2,802 favorable difference between the present value of the cash inflows and the cash outflow for the investment in Machine A indicates that this proposal will return substantially more than the 15 percent target rate set by the management. On the basis of **investment worth,** it appears to be a desirable investment. In contrast, Machine B shows a negative net present value of $93. It is an unacceptable investment in addition to being ranked below Machine A.

UNEQUAL NET CASH INFLOWS   If the net periodic cash inflows are unequal, the annuity table values (Exhibit 11-4, Table B) cannot be used as shown in Exhibit 11-5. Instead, each net periodic cash inflow must be separately discounted by using the present value of $1 (Exhibit 11-4, Table B).

Internal Rate-of-Return Method Used to Rank Investments

The net present value method discussed above uses a target or minimum rate of return (i.e., interest rate) determined by top management; therefore, it does not compute the **true** rate of return for a project. In contrast, the internal rate-of-return method[7] does not use a target or minimum rate. Instead it computes the true rate of return, which is a more complex computation.

The internal rate of return (i.e., the true interest rate) is the rate that will discount all the future net cash inflows so that their discounted sum (i.e., total present value) will exactly equal the initial outflows (i.e., cash cost) of the investment in the project.

The internal rate of return on a project cannot be computed directly. Computation of the internal rate involves two cases:

1   The net cash inflows are equal each period.
2   The net cash inflows are unequal for two or more periods.

---

[7] The internal rate-of-return method is also called the time-adjusted rate-of-return method and the time rate-of-return method.

EQUAL NET CASH INFLOWS When the net cash inflows are equal each period, the internal rate of return can easily be computed by using the three-step

EXHIBIT 11-6

Internal Rate-of-Return Method with Equal Periodic Net Cash Inflows

Case Data for Machines A and B

	MACHINE A	MACHINE B
Useful life (no residual value) (*n*)	10 years	12 years
Net initial cash investment cost (outflow)	$11,000	$15,000
Average annual net cash inflow	2,750	2,750
Internal rate of return—to be computed (*i*)		

Computation of Internal Rate of Return ($n = 12$; $i = $?):

Step 1 Compute the annuity factor that can be found in the PV table (Exhibit 11-4, Table B):

Formula:

$$\frac{\text{Net initial cash cost}}{\text{Average annual net cash inflow}} = \text{Table factor of the internal rate of return}$$

Computation:

Machine A: $\dfrac{\$11,000}{\$\ 2,750} = 4.0$ for 10 years   Machine B: $\dfrac{\$15,000}{\$\ 2,750} = 5.455$ for 12 years

Step 2 For Machine A, use Table B, "Present Value of an Ordinary Annuity of $1; Received Annually at Each Year-end for *n* Years" (on the line "10 years") and find the discount factor closest to 4.0—in this case, the 4.0 between 20 percent (4.192) and 22 percent (3.923). From this we can deduce that the true rate of return is approximately 21 percent. Similarly, the true rate for Machine B is approximately 15 percent.

Step 3 For more precision, use straight-line interpolation between 20 percent and 22 percent as follows for Machine A:

$$22\% - 3.923 \quad\rbrace\ .077$$
$$?\ -\ 4.000 \quad\rbrace\ .269$$
$$20\% - 4.192$$

$$\frac{.077}{.269} \times 2\% = .572\%$$

$$22\% - .572\% = 21.428\% \text{ true rate of return}$$

approach shown in Exhibit 11-6. The case data are the same as those given in Exhibit 11-5. Notice in Exhibit 11-6 that Machine A, with a true rate of return of approximately 21 percent, would be ranked before Machine B because its true rate is approximately 15 percent.

UNEQUAL NET CASH INFLOWS   When the cash flows are unequal, an annuity table cannot be used to determine the internal rate of return. In this case, therefore, we must (a) use present values of $1 (Exhibit 11-4, Table A) and (b) use a trial-and-error approach. An example of this case is given in Exhibit 11-7. This exhibit gives the case data a graphical analysis and the trial-and-error computations. The separate discounting must be as follows: $5,050 discount for one period; $4,550 discount for two periods; $4,050 discount for three periods; and so on—that is, each annual cash inflow must be discounted separately. In this situation, we must **estimate** the internal rate by inspection and then test it. Let us assume that we estimate that the rate will be 15 percent.[8] We will test at that rate; if it misses the mark, we will test again and so on until the true rate is pinpointed.

Our first trial demonstrated that the 15 percent rate was too high because the sum of the discounted cash inflows was below $15,000; the second trial demonstrated that 14 percent was also too high. The third trial at 12 percent equates the investment cost of $15,000 with the sum of the present values of the earnings for the five years; therefore, the internal rate of return for the proposal is 12 percent.[9]

EXHIBIT 11-7

Internal Rate-of-Return Method with Unequal Periodic Net Cash Inflows

Case Data for Machine X

Net initial cash cost (outflow), $15,000; useful life 5 years; no residual value. Average annual net cash inflows by year:

Year 1	$5,050	Year 4	$3,550
Year 2	4,550	Year 5	3,050
Year 3	4,050	Total	$20,250

[8] Numerous suggestions have been made for making a "ballpark" estimate. Although none of them are particularly useful in all cases, one that is simple and in many cases helpful is as follows:

$$\frac{\text{Average periodic cash flow} - \text{Depreciation}}{\text{Average investment}} = \frac{(\$20,250 \div 5) - \$3,000}{\$15,000 \div 2} = 14\%$$

[9] The computations are more complex when items such as residual value, multiple investment dates, partial disinvestment, and cost savings (rather than earnings) are involved.

Graphical Analysis of the Cash Flows and PV Analysis

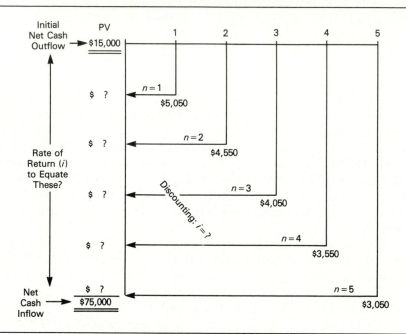

Trial-and-error Computation to find the Internal Rate of Return: Initial Machine Cost, $15,000

YEAR	EARNINGS (CASH INFLOW ESTIMATED)	FIRST TRIAL @15% DISCOUNT FACTOR FROM TABLE A	PRESENT VALUE	SECOND TRIAL @14% DISCOUNT FACTOR FROM TABLE A	PRESENT VALUE	THIRD TRIAL @12% DISCOUNT FACTOR FROM TABLE A	PRESENT VALUE
1	$ 5,050	.870	$ 4,394*	.877	$ 4,429	.893	$ 4,510
2	4,550	.756	3,440	.769	3,499	.797	3,626
3	4,050	.658	2,665	.675	2,734	.712	2,884
4	3,550	.572	2,031	.592	2,102	.636	2,258
5	3,050	.497	1,516	.519	1,583	.567	1,729
Total	$20,250		$14,046		$14,347		$15,007 = $15,000 cash cost

*$5,050 = × .870 = $4,394, etc.

	15% is too high	14% is too high	12% is the true rate

Evaluation of Discounted Cash Flow Methods

The two discounted cash flow methods of computing the economic value (or investment worth) of investments are conceptually superior to other methods because they are based on the time value of money and they presume the full recovery of the investment.

The **net present value method** has the following advantages: (a) it computes the true interest rate, (b) it is easy to apply because it does not use a trial-and-error approach, and (c) it is easy to adapt for risk (by using different interest rates for the later years of a project). It has the following disadvantages: (a) the target or minimum rate is difficult to determine, (b) it does not provide the true rate of return on the investment, and (c) it assumes that all net cash inflows from an investment are immediately reinvested at the target rate selected for discounting.

Selection of the minimum rate of return (item a above) is a critical problem because it will affect the results in subtle as well as obvious ways. Generally viewed, the minimum desired rate of return should not be less than the **cost of capital** to the enterprise.

The reinvestment assumption (item c above) is critical when projects that are being ranked have different lives. In such cases, if the reinvestment assumption is not met (either above or below the target rate), the ranking is suspect. For example, if a project with a shorter life has a target rate of 10 percent but has an internal rate of return less than that rate, it is overstated; or if its internal rate of return is more than 10 percent, it is understated. Most managers view this as a conceptual issue, but not a practical problem.

The **internal rate of return method** has the following advantages: (a) it avoids the necessity of selecting a target or minimum rate of return for discounting, (b) the true rate of return on an investment is computed, (c) it bases preferences on the true rate of return (rather than on a dollar difference called net present value), and (d) it does not have the reinvestment burden described above for the net present value method. Its primary disadvantages are (a) it is complex when the periodic net cash flows are unequal, and (b) it is difficult to use for risk and sensitivity analyses.

Shortcut and Simple Methods to Measure the Economic Value of Investments

Next we discuss two methods of measuring investment worth that are often described as providing simple, practical, and ballpark answers. One method—payback—is probably used alone, or with a DCF method, the most often because it focuses primarily on early cash inflows.

THE PAYBACK METHOD   The payback method computes the payback period, which is the number of **years** that it takes to recoup a cash investment from the annual net cash inflows from the investment. Therefore, the formula is

$$\text{Payback period in years} = \frac{\text{Net cash investment}}{\text{Annual net cash inflow, or net cash cost savings}}$$

Examples:

Machine A (10-year life)—net cash cost, $24,000; annual net cash inflow, $4,000

$$\text{Payback period} = \frac{\$24,000}{\$4,000} = 6 \text{ years}$$

Machine B (10-year life)—net cash cost, $19,000; annual net cash inflow, $3,800

$$\text{Payback period} = \frac{\$19,000}{\$\ 3,800} = 5 \text{ years}$$

Conclusion: Based only on the payback computations, Machine B is preferable because the cash investment will be fully recovered one year earlier than for Machine B.

EVALUATION   The payback method is probably used more than any other method because (a) it is easy to compute and does not require extensive data, (b) it is based on cash flows rather than accrual-basis amounts, (c) it measures comparative investment worth accurate enough for some cases and decision makers, (d) it can screen comparative results to eliminate the worst alternatives, and (e) it emphasizes those alternatives that have a faster cash return.

The payback method has several major defects: (a) it does not measure profitability of an investment, such as 10 percent per year; (b) it does not consider the time value of money, that is, interest, because early and later dollars are not differentiated; and (c) it breaks down when the alternative investments have significantly different useful lives. For example, if Machine A had a twenty-year life compared with the ten-year life of Machine B, the former would be a much better investment.

When the annual net cash inflows are not the same each year, the above formula must be applied by accumulating each year's net cash inflows until the sum equals the investment cost.

The payback method is used when (a) quick information or an estimate about investment worth is desired, (b) precision is not crucial, (c) a large number of proposals are to be screened on a preliminary basis, (d) cash and credit are difficult to get, and (e) the risk is high or the future potentials beyond the payout period are difficult to assess.

THE AVERAGE RETURN ON TOTAL INVESTMENT METHOD   The average return on total investment method is one variation of what sometimes is called the accounting rate-of-return method. One of these variations is based only on accrual-based revenues and cash cost, which is not a cash-basis analysis. However, we will discuss a variation called the **average cash return on total cash**

investment. We prefer it to the other shortcut because it it a cash-basis analysis. The formula used is

$$\frac{\text{Average cash return}}{\text{on total cash investment}} = \frac{\text{Average annual net cash inflow}}{\text{Cash outflow (cost) of the investment}}$$

Substituting the illustrative data given in Exhibit 11-5:

MACHINE A

$$\frac{\$\ 2{,}750}{\$11{,}000} = 25\% \text{ average return}$$

MACHINE B

$$\frac{\$\ 2{,}750}{\$15{,}000} = 18\% \text{ average return}$$

The average cash return on the total cash investment has two advantages: (a) it is simple to compute, and (b) it is based only on cash flows. However, it has two disadvantages: (a) it completely disregards the time value of money, and (b) it uses average net cash inflows for both equal and unequal annual net cash inflows. As a consequence, it has little relevance even in simple situations.[10]

THE ROLE OF JUDGMENT   When using the results of the various methods of measuring investment worth discussed in this chapter, the role of **managerial judgment** should not be overlooked. Because all the evaluations are based on **estimates** of future potentials, the results are no better than those estimates. In large measure, the estimates are subjective. Also, there may be some factors related to a proposal that cannot be quantified. For example, the effect of a particular proposal on employee morale or an emergency capital addition may significantly affect output or product quality. Also, some factors cannot be expressed in figures. Therefore, nonquantitive factors may necessarily be overriding in the decision to make a particular capital expenditure. An understanding of the assumptions that underlie the computations in each method is essential. In decision making, the management must guard against accepting a quantitive expression as being infallible and thus be lulled into a false sense of confidence. The role of management judgment still looms large despite the precise mathematical results obtained from the various methods of measuring investment worth.

[10] A variation of this method uses average investment (i.e., cash cost ÷ 2) as the denominator to recognize the impact of depreciation on the carrying value of the asset. This does not add to the relevance of the answer; the computed rate of return is double the rate shown in the illustration.

CONTROLLING CAPITAL EXPENDITURES   Planning capital expenditures sets the stage for control. The importance of control of capital expenditures cannot be overemphasized. Control is not solely, nor even primarily, downward pressure on expenditures. Control must rest upon sound management planning that restricts expenditures to economically justifiable additions yet guards against stagnation in the maintenance, replacement, and acquisition of capital assets.

Control of capital expenditures is best understood and implemented if the distinction between major projects and minor expenditures is maintained (see page 395). Major capital expenditures involve large amounts of funds for single projects, and their economic feasibility normally relates to management strategies. On the other hand, minor capital expenditures relate to ongoing operations involving almost all the operating managers.

Controlling Major Capital Expenditures

Inclusion of major capital expenditure projects in the tactical profit plan means that top management has decided to proceed with the project at a specific time. This inclusion, however, should not constitute orders to proceed unilaterally. A system of control that reports to executive management the progress, cost, and status of capital additions throughout the year is essential.

The first element of current control involves authorization to start a project, including the appropriation of funds, even though the project was included in the annual profit plan. For major capital additions projects, top management should reserve the responsibility for this final go-ahead authorization, which may consist of formal or informal notification, depending on the internal situation. The usual practice is to give final approval of major capital additions on a **request for capital expenditure** form. Exhibit 11-8 shows a typical format.

The second element of current control of major capital expenditures is accumulating data on costs, work progress, and cumulative expenditures on each project in process. As soon as a major capital project is authorized and initiated, cost records should be set up by project number. This record should provide for accumulation of costs by project, by responsibilty, and for supplementary information about the progress.

The third element of current control is a periodic **capital expenditure status report** that shows for each project such items as the following:

□   **Costs:**
Amount budgeted
Expenditures to date
Outstanding commitments
Amount unexpended per budget
Estimated cost to complete project
Indicated overexpenditure or underexpenditure

EXHIBIT 11-8

Authorization For Capital Expenditure

AFE No. _____

Division _____ Plant _____ Date _____

Responsible Manager _____ Recommended starting date _____

This authorization request for a capital expenditure is made because of a (an):

_____ Output increase
_____ Cost reduction
_____ Change in product
_____ Other—explain

_____ Major repair
_____ Change in production process or line
_____ Change to enhance quality control
_____

Project designation _____

Description and explanation of the underlying reasons (use additional pages if needed):

Summary of estimated costs and return:

Estimated cash cost:
Materials $ _____
Labor   _____
Purchase cost of item
  (or components)   _____
Other costs (explain)   _____
Total cash costs   _____
Contingency amount, _____ %   _____
        Total $ _____

Return on investment (DCF)   _____ %
Payback period   _____ Yrs.

Estimated useful life   _____ Yrs.

Residual value $ _____

Time to construct (or
  purchase)   _____ Mos.

Brief explanation:

Financial executives analysis:
Cash flow estimate: Realistic _____ ;   Too high _____ ;   Too low _____
Income tax implications, summarized: _____
_____.

Financing implications, summarized: _____
_____.

Approvals and authorization:

	DATE		
	APPROVAL	DISAPPROVAL	REASONS
Requested by			
Department manager	_____	_____	_____
Executive committee	_____	_____	_____
President	_____	_____	_____
Board of directors	_____	_____	_____

□ **Progress report:**
  Date started
  Data originally scheduled for completion
  Estimated days needed to complete project
  Estimated date of completion
  Percentage completed to date (in terms of time)
  Percentage completed to date (in terms of cost)
□ **Comments for top management:**
  Quality of work
  Unexpected circumstances

The final element of control is management decision making to correct deficiencies and to ensure effective implementation adequacy of the corrective actions.

Controlling Minor or Small Capital Expenditures

These capital expenditures are usually provided for in a "blanket" appropriation for each responsibility center. The center managers should be given the authority (perhaps with an overview constraint) to issue final authorization within the budget total for specific center expenditures as needed. For example, the authority to approve these minor or small expenditures within the budget appropriation limit can be delegated along the following lines:

AMOUNT	APPROVAL REQUIRED
Up to $1,000	Center manager
$1,001 to $3,000	Plant manager
$3,001 to $10,000	Vice-president in charge of manufacturing
Over $10,000	President

Control of these capital expenditures can be attained by using an authorization procedure similar to the above. The actual expenditures should be accumulated by the responsibility center. Then the actual expenditures are compared with plan allowances in the periodic capital expenditures status report, or this can be included in the regular monthly performance report for each responsibility center. The report should show actual and planned expenditures, and variances.

POSTCOMPLETION AUDITS OF MAJOR CAPITAL EXPENDITURE PROJECTS

The final element of control of major capital expenditure projects is a postcompletion audit (see Exhibit 11-3). The purpose of a postcompletion audit is to assess the extent to which the originally approved project and its final completion were in harmony. This audit is intended to provide management information about how realistic (in terms of investment worth) the planning phase was and why any deficiencies occurred. This information is essential to improve planning, decisions, and major capital expenditures in the future.

After a major project is completed, the cost records should be completed and the total cost recorded in the accounts as an asset. Underexpenditures on one project should not be offset against the budget excess of other projects without the formal approval of top management; otherwise, control may be lost. A final report on the completed project should be prepared for top management. Follow-up includes final inspections and related reports.

The criterion for selecting projects for this type of audit is generally the total funds expended. However, often the decision is made based on the type of expenditure, specific management request, or time frame since a project was put into service.

Deferred postcompletion audits should be done several years after a major project is completed. These special audits (often called economic analyses) of certain projects should be made at various periods subsequent to completion to determine whether the project is producing the results anticipated in the analysis that supported the original management decision to undertake the project. The advantages of a postcompletion audit can be summarized as follows:

1 The audits indicate the importance given by management to valid estimates in the capital expenditures process.
2 The audit of completed projects may allow for corrections of similar errors in current projects while corrections are still possible.
3 It provides a signal to those persons assembling data estimates that they must be careful, holding them responsible for incorrect data, etc.
4 It provides management with a means to verify the strengths and weaknesses in the organization's capital expenditures budget procedures.

Comprehensive Demonstration Case

 *SUPERIOR MANUFACTURING COMPANY*

The executive management of Superior Manufacturing Company develops a long-term capital expenditures plan that is revised annually. The long-term plan is not illustrated herein (it is structured by projects). The annual capital expenditures budget in Schedule 46 shows the 19X2 segment. In this company, the major capital expenditure projects that are included are defined as "any capital expenditure $100 (simplified for case purposes only) or over." Because of this definition, minor or small capital expenditures are not material in amount; therefore, they are incorporated into the planning of repair costs and are included in the departmental expense budgets. Notice in Schedule 46 that (a) the major capital expenditures for 19X2 are shown in detail, and (b) the 19X3 items in the long-term capital expenditures budget are listed. Also, this short-term budget (for 19X2) shows the planned payments of cash during 19X2 and depreciation information. Cash information is shown because it will be needed to prepare the cash budget (Chapter 12).

Schedule 47—budgeted depreciation—is shown here because it must include depreciation on the new (19X2) capital additions. Data from this schedule will be used to prepare the planned financial statements (see Chapter 13). For instructional purposes, we suggest that you refer to the flexible expense budgets for Superior (Schedules 41, 42, and 43 in Chapter 10) and notice the minor repairs planned.

CHAPTER SUMMARY   This chapter discussed the capital expenditures budget. Capital expenditures are planned and controlled in the same way for both manufacturing and nonmanufacturing enterprises. Capital expenditures are for (a) major capital additions such as land, buildings, major improvements, and maintenance, and (b) minor or small capital expenditures that should initially be recorded as assets because they help generate future revenues. The capital expenditures budget includes a strategic plan and a tactical plan for (a) the major capital expenditures projects and (b) a blanket appropriation for the minor or small expenditures.

A process for planning and controlling capital expenditures is given in Exhibit 11-3. The primary problems in developing a capital expenditures budget are (a) the identification, analysis, and evaluation of all relevant capital expenditure alternatives, and (b) based on investment worth, selection of the best alternatives. This chapter discussed approaches to measure investment worth: (a) discounted cash flows (present value) and (b) shortcut and simple methods. The discounted cash flow methods are preferable because they explicitly use the time value of money (i.e., interest).

The chapter also emphasized the control of capital expenditures by using performance reports by responsibility centers and projects. Postcompletion audits also were discussed as a way to improve the capital budgeting decisions and process.

SCHEDULE 46. Superior Manufacturing Company

Annual Capital Expenditures Budget
For the Year Ending December 31, 19X2

ITEM	ESTIMATED STARTING DATE	ESTIMATED COMPLETION DATE	ESTIMATED COST	ANNUAL TOTAL	19X2 BUDGET—DATE OF CASH PAYMENTS						
					FIRST QUARTER			QUARTERS			
					JAN.	FEB.	MARCH	FIRST	SECOND	THIRD	FOURTH
Major items for 19X2:											
Repair tools	19X2	19X2	$ 200	$ 200	$200	$	$	$200	$	$	$
Power motor	19X2	19X2	8,500	8,500							8,500
Total			$ 8,700	$ 8,700	$200			$200			$ 8,500
Assets funded:											
New building				20,000							20,000
Cash required by time period				$ 28,700	$200			$200			$28,500
Information about items tentatively planned for 19X3:											
New building	19X3	19X3	$120,000	$120,000							
Machinery—Dept. 1	19X3	19X3	10,000	10,000							

	ESTIMATED	
	DEPRECIABLE LIFE	SCRAP VALUE
Depreciation information:		
19X2:		
Repair tools	5 years	—
Power motor (Power Dept.)	10 years	—
19X3:		
New building	Undecided	—
Machinery—Dept. 1	Undecided	—

NOTE: Low-cost and recurring capital expenditures are not shown in this schedule, only because they are not material in amount. They are directly incorporated into the departmental expense budgets as repair and maintenance expenses.

SCHEDULE 47. Superior Manufacturing Company

Schedule of Budgeted Depreciation
For the Year Ending December 31, 19X2

ITEM	DEPRECIATION RATE	ASSET BALANCE 1/1/X2 (INPUT)	ASSETS ACQUIRED 19X2	ASSET BALANCE 12/31/X2	ACCUMULATED DEPRECIATION BALANCE 1/1/X2 (INPUT)	DEPRECIATION CHARGED 19X2	ACCUMULATED DEPRECIATION BALANCE 12/31/X2	JAN.	FEB.	MARCH	SECOND	THIRD	FOURTH
								FIRST QUARTER			QUARTERS		
Building	30 yrs.	$1,800,000	—	$1,800,000	$360,000	$60,000	$420,000	$5,000	$5,000	$5,000	$15,000	$15,000	$15,000
General purpose tools	5 yrs	7,800		7,800	4,680	1,560	6,240	130	130	130	390	390	390
Power machinery	10 yrs.	54,000	$8,500	62,500	21,600	5,400	27,000	450	450	450	1,350	1,350	1,350
Repair tools	5 yrs.	400	200	600	200	120	320	10	10	10	30	30	30
Machinery—Dept. 1	$.015*	100,000		100,000	20,000	7,320	27,320	522	588	594	1,860	1,761	1,995
Machinery—Dept. 2	.004*	20,000		20,000	12,000	768	12,768	56	64	64	192	184	208
Machinery—Dept. 3	.009*	72,000		72,000	13,500	4,392	17,892	313	353	356	1,116	1,057	1,197
Sales office equipment	8 yrs.	4,800		4,800	2,400	600	3,000	50	50	50	150	150	150
Accounting office equipment	5 yrs.	12,000		12,000	6,000	2,400	8,400	200	200	200	600	600	600
Treasurer's office equipment	5 yrs.	6,000		6,000	2,000	1,200	3,200	100	100	100	300	300	300
Administrative office equipment	5 yrs.	3,000		3,000	1,000	600	1,600	50	50	50	150	150	150
Subtotals		$ 280,000	$8,700	$ 288,700	$ 83,380	$24,360	$107,740	$1,881	$1,995	$2,004	$ 6,138	$ 5,972	$ 6,370
Grand total		$2,080,000	$8,700	$2,088,700	$443,380	$84,360	$527,740	$6,881	$6,995	$7,004	$21,138	$20,972	$21,370
Depreciation expense analysis by function:													
Manufacturing						$19,560		$1,481	$1,595	$1,604	$ 4,938	$ 4,772	$ 5,170
Selling						600		50	50	50	150	150	150
Administration						4,200		350	350	350	1,050	1,050	1,050
Total						$24,360		$1,881	$1,995	$2,004	$ 6,138	$ 5,972	$ 6,370

*Per direct labor hour.

Suggested References

BIERMAN, HAROLD JR., THOMAS DYCKMAN, and RONALD HILTON, *Cost Accounting: Concepts and Managerial Applications*. New York: Macmillan, 1990.

BIERMAN, HAROLD, JR., and SEYMOUR SMIDT, *The Capital Budgeting Decision*. New York: Macmillan, 1984.

BLOCHER, E., and C. STICKNEY, "Duration and Risk Assessments in Capital Budgeting," *Accounting Review*, January 1979, pp. 180–88.

GARRISON, RAY H., *Managerial Accounting*, Chaps. 14 and 15. Plano, Tex.: Business Publications, 1985.

GREENE, CHARLES N., EVERETT J. ADAM, JR., and RONALD J. EBERT, *Management for Effective Performance*, Chap. 20. Englewood Cliffs, N.J.: Prentice-Hall, 1985.

HORNGREN, CHARLES T., and GEORGE FOSTER, *Cost Accounting, A Management Emphasis*, Chaps. 19 and 20. Englewood Cliffs, N.J.: Prentice-Hall, 1987.

LARKER, D. F., "The Perceived Importance of Selected Information Characteristics for Strategic Capital Budgeting Decisions." *Accounting Review*, July 1981, pp. 519–38.

RAPPAPORT, ALFRED, ed., *Readings in Managerial Accounting*, Reading Nos., 19, 20, 21, 22, and 23. Englewood Cliffs, N.J.: Prentice-Hall, 1982.

THOMAS, WILLIAM E., ed., *Readings in Cost Accounting Budgeting and Control*, Reading Nos. 13–16. Cincinnati: South-Western Publishing, 1983.

Discussion Questions

1. Define capital expenditures.
2. Describe the primary characteristics of a capital expenditures budget.
3. Distinguish between major and minor capital expenditures.
4. Explain five benefits of a capital expenditures budget.
5. Below is a scrambled list of the planning and controlling process for capital expenditures. To the left, number them in a logical completion sequence:

   _____ (a) Conduct postcompletion audits
   _____ (b) Develop strategic and tactical capital budgets
   _____ (c) Identify capital addition projects and other needs
   _____ (d) Make capital expenditure decisions that accept the best alternatives
   _____ (e) Establish control of capital additions; performance reports
   _____ (f) Analyze and evaluate all promising alternatives
   _____ (g) Develop capital addition proposals

6. Explain what is meant by economic value or investment worth, and relate it to the planning and control of capital expenditures.
7. Explain the basic commonality and the basic difference between the net present value method and the internal rate-of-return method.

8. If a project will generate an average annual net cash flow of $60,000 for five years, and it had a cash cost of $200,000, assuming a target rate of 6 percent, its net present value would be $————.

9. If a project that cost $66,240 (cash) will produce a $20,000 net cash inflow at each year-end for four years, its internal rate of return is ————%.

10. Explain the difference between a "present value of $1" and a "present value of an ordinary annuity of $1." Give an example, assuming $n = 10$, $i = 10\%$, and a principal amount of $150. Why are your computed values different?

11. Explain and evaluate the payback method of evaluating proposed capital expenditures. Give an example that shows a ten-year payback period.

12. Define and evaluate the average cash return on total cash investment.

13. Explain and evaluate the discounted cash flow methods of evaluating proposed capital expenditures.

14. In applying the discounted cash flow methods, explain why depreciation is not considered a cost.

15. Explain what is meant by "postcompletion audits."

CASE 11-1 *Recommend how this company should plan and control capital expenditures*

Airparts Manufacturing Company has been a rapidly growing manufacturer of parts for the aircraft industry. It manufactures approximately fifteen different parts that are sold directly to users. The parts are similar; however, they are manufactured to specifications provided by the purchaser. Orders are by formal contracts for large numbers of each part to be delivered over a specified period of time. Airparts uses a number of different machines and related equipment in the manufacturing function. Frequent changes in parts manufactured and new models require numerous changes and adaptations in the manufacturing departments. Consequently, there are numerous capital expenditures of relatively small cost; however, the total amount each year is significant. No major capital expenditure projects have been planned nor undertaken during the past six years.

The company is organized into three major divisions: sales, production, and finance, and each division is managed by a vice-president. The production division has separate departments for administration, engineering, production planning and scheduling, and purchasing. Also, there are three plants. Each plant (1) has three service departments and nine producing departments; (2) is operated as a "profit center," although sales are the responsibility of the sales division; and (3) has a controller who reports to the plant manager and, functionally, to the financial vice-president. The company uses an up-to-date cost accounting system for the plants. During the past three years, each plant developed an annual profit plan by using a sales plan devised by the vice-president of sales. The plants use a "bottoms-up approach" to develop expense budgets. The plant budgets are combined by the executive committee to develop the overall profit plan. A five-year broad plan is developed and revised each year by the executive committee. The accounting and calendar year coincide.

The five-year plan is developed during April–June, and the planning cycle for the annual profit plan extends from September 1 through December 20 of each year. The executive committee, comprised of the president, executive vice-president, and the three functional vice-presidents, exercises the overall budgetary evaluation. The president has final approval authority for all budgets. The financial function is subdivided into four departments: accounting; planning and control; internal auditing; and treasurer.

During the past two years, the customers have indicated some concern about the product quality of Airparts output. Questions have been raised about the lag in new and technologically advanced manufacturing equipment used by Airparts. Reflecting these customers concerns, top management is seriously considering three major capital expenditure projects: (1) technologically renovating Plant 1 (oldest plant); (2) building a new plant that will produce a new line of products; and (3) replacing four identical machines (essential to operations and very expensive) in Plant 2. With respect to the machines, two competing suppliers have made tentative, although quite different, proposals. The competing machines are different—they have different cost and operating characteristics—however, either kind will meet the department's needs. They are major improvements over the old machines. They will produce at a faster rate and will attain higher tolerances. In terms of urgency, the management has tentatively ranked the three expenditures in inverse order to the listing above.

Upon inquiry, the case writer was told that the five-year plan includes "a single line for capital expenditures and no particular procedures are used to develop and evaluate long-range needs. We just include a dollar judgment provided by the vice-president of production. In recent years, there have been no major capital expenditures such as the three now under consideration. The annual profit plan includes a single figure for each plant called 'small capital additions.' These amounts are provided by the vice-president of production. The plant managers are instructed not to exceed these budgeted amounts."

In response to a question by the case writer, the president said, "I feel that we have not yet come up with appropriate budgetary approaches to cope with the problems that are evolving in the area of capital expenditures."

REQUIRED

1. Give a general evaluation with emphasis on the capital expenditures budget. Provide recommendations about the types of such budgets, capital expenditures, and time dimension.

2. Recommend a capital budgeting process for this company. For each phase, give specific activities and identify the related responsibilities.

3. Give your detailed recommendations for handling major capital additions.

4. Give your recommendation for planning the small, low-cost, recurring capital expenditures.

5. Give your recommendations for control of (a) major projects and (b) small, low-cost capital expenditures.

CASE 11-2 *Measuring investment worth; stable cash flows*

The management of Davy-Jones Manufacturing Company is purchasing a machine required for a special operation. It is considering two competing machines. The following data have been developed to provide a basis for selecting one alternative over the other.

	MACHINE A	MACHINE B
Cost of machine (cash)	$120,000	$120,000
Estimated life, in years (straightline)	8	15
Estimated average annual earnings (including depreciation but before deducting income taxes)	$ 24,000	$ 16,800
Residual value	0	0
Income tax rate—30%		
Target rate of return—15%		

REQUIRED

1. Compute the average annual net cash inflow for each machine. Assume depreciation is the only noncash expense.

2. Compute the following measures of economic value or investment worth: (a) DCF, net present value method, (b) DCF, internal rate-of-return method, (c) payback method, and (d) average cash return on total cash invested.

3. Prepare a tabulation to compare and evaluate the results. Which machine should be selected? Explain why.

CASE 11-3 *Measuring investment worth for three alternatives; stable cash inflows*

The management of Walker Company has to replace an old machine and is considering the purchase of a new machine that incorporates the latest technology. Three competing manufacturers have machines that would satisfy the management's specifications. Data collected to date on each of the three competing machines are as follows:

	MACHINE A	MACHINE B	MACHINE C
Cash price	$12,000	$14,600	$20,000
Cash trade-in value of old machine (fully depreciated)	$ 1,000	$ 1,100	$ 1,200
Estimated useful life (years)	5	5	5
Estimated cash residual (scrap) value	$ 1,000	$ 1,500	$ 2,000
Average annual earnings before deducting depreciation and income taxes*	$ 4,500	$ 5,400	$ 8,100

*Depreciation is the only noncash expense related to these amounts.

The management has asked you to prepare an analysis of investment worth and to provide a ranking of the three machines on this basis. The company has always used payback and average return on total assets for these purposes. The company uses straightline depreciation for income tax purposes; the average income tax rate is 30 percent. The target rate of return is 15 percent.

REQUIRED

1. Compute the average annual net cash inflow for each machine. Treat the residual value as a reduction in the cost of the asset. (Hint: the amount for Machine C is $6,678.)

2. Compute the following measures of economic value or investment worth: (a) DCF, net present value method, (b) payback method, and (c) average return on total assets.

3. Give your evaluation and recommended ranking of the three alternatives.

CASE 11-4   Which machine should the company buy? Changing cash flows

Jackson Manufacturing Company plans to buy a new machine for one of its factory departments. Two competing machines from different suppliers are under consideration. The following reliable data have been developed:

	MACHINE A	MACHINE B
Investment (cash cost)	$26,653	$26,563
Annual estimated income after depreciation and income taxes		
Year 1	$ 687	$ 4,687
Year 2	1,687	3,687
Year 3	2,687	2,687
Year 4	3,687	1,687
Year 5	4,689	689
Total	$13,437	$13,437

Estimated life—straightline (years)	5	5
Estimated residual value	0	0
Estimated average income tax rate	30%	30%
Minimum desired rate of return—16 percent		

REQUIRED

1. Compute the net cash inflow on each machine for each year and the total. Assume depreciation is the only noncash expense included in the above data.
2. Compute the following measures of economic value or investment worth: (a) DCF, net present value method, (b) payback method, and (c) average return on total investment.
3. Prepare an evaluation of the results.

CASE 11-5   *Should the company keep the old machine or buy a new one? A cost-savings analysis*

Ajax Company is considering replacing an old machine used in the manufacture of products. Data on the old machine follow:

	PURPOSE	
	BOOK	TAX
Annual cash operating costs	$60,000	$60,000
Cost (cash basis)	30,000	30,000
Accumulated depreciation—straightline	15,000	15,000
Remaining useful life—years	5	5

Residual value—no residual value has been used for book and tax purposes. The machine can be sold now for $6,000. However, it is estimated that five years from now the machine could be sold for only $400 cash. Assume that any gain or loss on sale would be subject to ordinary tax rates (that is, not a long-term capital gain).

The new machine under consideration has the following economic effects:

	PURPOSE	
	BOOK	TAX
Annual cash operating costs	$65,000	$65,000
Cost (cash basis)	45,000	45,000
Residual value	7,000	0
Useful life—years	5	5
Method of depreciation	Straightline	Sum of years digits (no residual value used)*

Hint: Year 1 depreciation: $45,000 × 5/15 = $15,000.

The minimum desired rate of return, after income taxes, is 12 percent, and assume an ordinary tax rate of 40 percent.

REQUIRED

1. Use net present value computations to compare the two alternatives: (a) keep the old machine and (b) replace the old machine.
2. Explain your recommendations and state why your alternative is preferable.

CASE 11-6   *Can you reconcile this disagreement?*

At a recent conference attended by educators and successful managers from a wide range of industries, the topic for one of the seventy-five minute sessions was: Why is it that economic analysis and business practice do not coincide more closely as to how capital budget decisions should be made? The discussions revealed that the educators insisted that the management should, without exception, rely on the results of discounted cash flow techniques in making major capital expenditure decisions. The business people tended to feel that these techniques were useful "when applicable, but there were many situations where managerial judgment can provide the only practical answer." Finally, the discussions turned to a consideration of the reasons for the divergence of opinion on this important point.

REQUIRED

1. Briefly explain what you consider to be the basis for the divergence of opinion.
2. As moderator of the session, what "reconciling" comment would you make?

CASE 11-7   *Capital expenditure decisions about two major projects*

BIG Manufacturing Company uses a comprehensive profit planning and control program. The strategic long-term plan extends ten years into the future. Each year this plan is reevaluated and extended by dropping the oldest year and adding the new year. The tactical short-term profit plan is for one year ending December 31.

The capital expenditures budget is an important element of planning and controlling because BIG has always had a number of replacement and expansion projects in process. The two separate projects given below were selected from the list of projects under consideration by the management. For instructional purposes, consider each case as independent of the other. All amounts are given in thousands, and the projects have been simplified.

Project A—The company is considering a capital expenditure for a large computer that will have an initial cash cost of $600. It will cause an annual net cash saving of $110. It will have a ten-year useful life and no residual value. The target (minimum) rate of return is 12 percent.

REQUIRED   (round to the nearest $000)

1. Compute the payback period.
2. Compute (a) net present value and (b) internal rate of return.
3. Should the company purchase the computer?
4. Should the computer be purchased if its useful life is seven years? Explain why.

Project B—The company is considering a capital expenditures project that will have a $15,000 initial cash cost. It will provide a $2,400 net cash cost saving each year for an estimated useful life of fifteen years and no residual value. The target (minimum) rate of return is 12 percent.

REQUIRED

1. Compute (a) net present value and (b) internal rate of return.
2. A competing project has a useful life of ten years and a target rate of 12%. Compute (a) net present value and (b) internal rate of return.
3. For each requirement, should BIG approve the proposal?

CASE 11-8   *Rank four capital expenditure projects*

The executive management of Alaska-Canada Airlines is evaluating four different capital expenditures for its strategic capital additions budget (time dimension, fifteen years). Data (summarized) have been developed on the proposals as follows:

PROJECT (MACHINES)	CASH ACQUISITION COST	EXPECTED USEFUL LIFE (NO RESIDUAL VALUE)—YEARS	ESTIMATED NET ANNUAL CASH INFLOWS (AFTER INCOME TAX)
A	$120,000	5	$40,000
B	9,500	15	1,500
C	12,000	10	3,300
D	50,000	8	12,000

The target (minimum) rate of return is 14 percent.

REQUIRED

1. Rank the four projects by using (a) net present value and (b) internal rate of return.
2. If the projects are independent (i.e., mutually exclusive), which projects should be included in the long-term plan?
3. If the company must limit its capital additions to $150,000, what projects should be included in the long-term plan?

12 Planning and Controlling Cash Flows

INTRODUCTION AND PURPOSE   One of the major responsibilities of management is to plan, control, and safeguard the resources of the enterprise. Two kinds of resources flow through many businesses—cash and noncash assets. This chapter focuses on cash inflows (i.e., cash received) and cash outflows (i.e., payments of cash). The planning and control of the cash inflows, the cash outflows, and the related financing is important in all enterprises. Cash budgeting is an effective way to plan and control the cash flows, assess cash needs, and effectively use excess cash. A primary objective is to plan the liquidity position of the company as a basis for determining future borrowings and future investments. For example, excess cash, if not invested, incurs an opportunity cost, that is, loss of the interest that could be earned on the excess cash. The timing of cash flows can be controlled in many ways by the management, such as increasing the effectiveness of credit and collection activities, making payments by time drafts rather than by check, making payments on the last day of discount periods, batching payments, and giving discounts on cash sales. Cash management is important in enterprises, whether large or small. Many lending agencies require cash flow projections before granting large loans.

    The comprehensive case, Superior Manufacturing Company, is used for illustrative purposes throughout this chapter.

THE FOCUS OF CASH PLANNING   A cash budget shows the planned cash inflows, outflows, and ending position by interim periods for a specific time span. Most companies should develop both long-term and short-term plans about their cash flows. The short-term cash budget is included in the annual profit plan. A cash budget basically includes two parts: (1) the planned cash receipts (inflows) and (2) the planned cash disbursements (outflows).

    Planning cash inflows and outflows gives the planned beginning and ending cash position for the budget period. Planning the cash inflows and outflows will indicate (1) the need for financing probable cash deficits or (2) the need for investment planning to put excess cash to profitable use. The cash budget is directly related to other plans, such as the sales plan, accounts receivable and the expense budgets, and the capital expenditures budget. Nevertheless, planning and control of these activities do not automatically take care of the cash position. This statement suggests an essential distinction between the cash budget and the other budgets. The cash budget focuses exclusively on the amounts and **timing** of cash inflows and outflows. In contrast, the other budgets focus on the timing of all transactions—both cash and noncash (this is called the accrual basis).

The primary purposes of the cash budget are to

1 Give the probable cash position at the end of each period as a result of planned operations

2 Identify cash excesses or shortages by time periods

3 Establish the need for financing and/or the availability of idle cash for investment

4 Coordinate cash with (a) total working capital, (b) sales revenue, (c) expenses, (d) investments, and (e) liabilities

5 Establish a sound basis for continuous monitoring of the cash position

Preparation of the cash budget should be the responsibility of the company treasurer.

The cash budget is based almost exclusively on the other budgets; therefore, the treasurer must work closely with the other managers whose decisions may directly affect cash flows.

A comprehensive profit planning and control program establishes the foundation for a realistic cash budget. There must be a balance between available cash and the cash-demanding activities—operations, capital expenditures, and so on. Too often the need for additional cash is not realized until the situation becomes an emergency.

TIME HORIZONS IN CASH PLANNING AND CONTROL   The characteristics and importance of the continuing inflows and outflows of cash in a business indicate that cash planning and control should usually involve three different time horizons—long-term, short-term, and immediate-term.

The **long-term** cash horizon should be consistent with the time dimensions of the (a) strategic long-term profit plan and (b) capital expenditures projects. Planning long-range cash inflows (primarily from sales, services, and financing) and long-range cash outflows (primarily for expenses, capital expenditures, and payment of debt) is fundamental to sound financial decisions and to the optimum use of cash and long-term credit. Long-range cash planning focuses on the major outflows and inflows.

The **short-term** cash horizon should be consistent with the tactical short-term profit plan. Cash planning for this time horizon requires detailed plans for cash inflows and outflows that are directly related to the annual profit plan (e.g., cash from sales and cash to pay for new equipment). The short-term cash budget is developed primarily from the various budget schedules discussed in the preceding chapters that are included in the annual profit plan.

The **immediate** time horizon is used in many enterprises primarily to assess, control, and manage cash inflows and outflows, often on a continuing daily basis. Its primary focus is to ensure that cash shortages and excessive cash balances do not occur. It minimizes interest cost by taking all cash discounts on payables and meeting cash-payment deadlines. It minimizes the opportunity cost of excess cash balances by allowing timely investments if cash accumulates.

APPROACHES USED TO DEVELOP A CASH BUDGET   Two primary approaches are used to develop the cash budget. One is the **cash receipts and disbursements approach** (sometimes called the direct or cash-account method). This method is based on a detailed analysis of the increases and decreases in the budgeted cash account that would reflect all cash inflows and outflows from such budgets as sales, expenses, and capital expenditures. It is simple to develop, and it is appropriate when a detailed profit plan is used. It is often used for short-term cash planning as a part of the annual profit plan. This approach is not appropriate for the more general long-term profit plan. The underlying plans (i.e., budgets) that cause cash inflows and outflows are carefully analyzed to translate them from **an accrual basis to a cash basis.** This approach is illustrated at the end of this chapter for Superior Manufacturing Company.

The other approach is called the **financial accounting approach** (sometimes referred to as the indirect or income statement approach). The starting point in this approach is **planned net income** shown on the budgeted income statement. Basically, planned net income is converted from an accrual basis to a cash basis (that is, adjusted for changes in the noncash working capital accounts such as inventories, receivables, prepaid expenses, accruals, and deferrals). Next, the other cash sources and requirements are identified. This approach requires less supporting detail and provides less detail about the cash inflows and outflows. It is useful for making long-range cash projections. For a common set of underlying plans, both approaches will derive the same cash flow results that differ only with respect to the amounts of detail provided.

Cash Receipts and Disbursements Approach
to Compute Cash Receipts (Inflows)

Cash inflows arise from transactions such as cash sales, collections of accounts and notes receivable, interest received on investments, sales of capital assets, and miscellaneous income sources. If these amounts have been included in the profit plan as discussed and illustrated up to this point, planning cash inflows is relatively simple. Cash sales generate immediate cash; therefore, there is no lag between point of sale and realization of cash.

In the case of credit sales, the lag between point of sale and realization of cash causes a problem. The primary approach to the problem is based on past collection experience—the average period between the date of sale and the date of the related cash collection. The manager responsible for credit and collections should regularly determine, for example, the efficiency of collections. Data such as the percentages of credit sales collected in thirty days, sixty days, and so forth, are useful in planning cash inflows from accounts receivable. These planned cash receipts must be reduced or adjusted for the probable effect of uncollectible accounts.

The treasurer will seldom encounter much difficulty in planning miscellaneous cash inflows from income sources such as royalties, rent, interest, and dividends received on investments.

To illustrate the cash receipts approach we will use the comprehensive case, Superior Manufacturing Company. Superior receives cash from several sources including sales and miscellaneous incomes. First, we will look at accounts receivable. Bad debts experience provided the basis for expected losses from doubtful accounts of $.20 per $100 total sales. This estimate was incorporated into the flexible expense budget (see Schedule 44, Chapter 10). Collection experience also provided a basis for planning collections on total sales. The following decisional inputs (i.e., the collection percentages) were estimated for planning collections for 19X2 (the percentages relate to total sales less expected bad debt losses):

- 82% collected in month sold (i.e., at time of sale or before the month-end)
- 10% collected in the first month following sale
- 5% collected in the second month following sale
- 3% collected in the third month following sale
- Quarterly basis—92% collected in quarter sold; 8% collected in next quarter

For planning purposes, Superior assumes that all sales are recorded in accounts receivable. Also, the estimated bad debt losses are based on total sales because all sales are assumed to be on credit.

The treasurer analyzed the 19X1 accounts receivable and the allowance for doubtful accounts to develop the following expected data for the beginning of the 19X2 budget year.

Actual Balances in Accounts Receivable Expected at January 1, 19X2

MONTH OF SALE	UNCOLLECTED ACCOUNTS RECEIVABLE ON 1/1/X2	BALANCE IN ALLOWANCE FOR DOUBTFUL ACCOUNTS 1/1/X2
Prior to October, 19X1	$ 10,000*	$6,000
October, 19X1	20,000	400
November, 19X1	40,000	800
December, 19X1	90,000	1,800
Total	$160,000	$9,000

*It is anticipated on the basis of current collection activities, that $4,000 of this amount will be collected in 19X2 and that $3,000 will be written off as a bad debt; the balance will be held "open" although collection is uncertain at this date.

SCHEDULE 48. Superior Manufacturing Company

Cash Inflow From Sales and Accounts Receivable
For the Year Ending December 31, 19X2

	REF	CREDIT SALES	LESS ALLOWANCE FOR DOUBTFUL ACCOUNTS	BALANCE TO BE COLLECTED	ESTIMATED COLLECTIONS—19X2 FIRST QUARTER JANUARY	FEBRUARY	MARCH	QUARTERS SECOND	THIRD	FOURTH	BALANCE UNCOLLECTED 12/31/X2
Balance in accounts receivable and allowance for doubtful accounts 12/31/X1											
Prior accounts:											
October 19X1	(Given)	$ 10,000	$ 6,000	$ 4,000							$ 4,000
November 19X1	(Given)	20,000	$ 400	19,600	$ 19,600						
December 19X1	(Given)	40,000	800	39,200*		24,500	$ 14,700				
	(Given)	90,000	1,800	88,200	49,000	24,500	14,700				
		160,000	9,000								
19X2 planned sales:	21										
January		500,400	1,001	499,399†	409,507	49,940	24,970	$ 14,982			
February		540,000	1,080	538,920		441,914	53,892	43,114			
March		574,100	1,148	572,952			469,821	103,131			
1st Quarter		1,614,500	3,229	1,591,810							
2nd Quarter		1,595,000	3,190	1,155,684				1,464,465	$ 127,345		
3rd Quarter		1,158,000	2,316	1,724,045					1,063,229	92,455	
4th Quarter		1,727,500	3,455							1,586,121	
Total year		$6,095,000	$12,190								
		$6,255,000	$21,190	$6,233,810	$502,607	$531,054	$563,383	$1,625,692	$1,190,574	$1,682,576	$137,924
Less bad debts to be written off in 19X2		3,000	3,000								
Budgeted balance in allowance for doubtful accounts, end of 19X2			$18,190								
Less balance uncollected on 12/31/19X2				137,924							
Planned cash receipts for 19X2		6,095,886		$6,095,886	$502,607	$531,054	$563,383	$1,625,692	$1,190,574	$1,682,576	$137,924
Balance in Accounts Receivable Dec. 31, 19X2		$ 156,114									

Selected computations:
*$39,200 × 5%/8% = $24,500; $39,200 × 3%/8% = $14,700.
†$499,399 × 82% = $409,507; $499,399 × 10% = $49,940; etc.

Using the above beginning data and the sales plan (Chapter 5, Schedule 21) for Superior Manufacturing Company, the treasurer planned the **cash inflows from sales and receivables** as shown in Schedule 48. Notice the following features of this schedule: (1) effect of the planned ratio for bad debt losses, (2) use of the collection percentages, (3) computation of the **interim** cash inflows, and (4) reconciliation of the planned balances in accounts receivable.

SCHEDULE 49. Superior Manufacturing Company

Planned Cash Inflows from Other Incomes
For the Year Ending December 31, 19X2

TIME	BUDGETED AMOUNT
January	$ 3,390
February	2,950
March	3,620
Total 1st Quarter	$ 9,960
2nd Quarter	9,510
3rd Quarter	8,220
4th Quarter	9,430
Total for year	$37,120

The detailed cash inflow plans shown in Schedules 48 and 49 are summarized in Schedule 50.

SCHEDULE 50. Superior Manufacturing Company

Summary of Budgeted Cash Inflows
For the Year Ending December 31, 19X2

			SOURCES OF CASH	
TIME	REF.	TOTAL	ACCOUNTS RECEIVABLE 48	OTHER INCOMES 49
January		$ 505,997	$ 502,607	$ 3,390
February		534,004	531,054	2,950
March		567,003	563,383	3,620
Total 1st Quarter		$1,607,004	$1,597,044	$ 9,960
2nd Quarter		1,635,202	1,625,692	9,510
3rd Quarter		1,198,794	1,190,574	8,220
4th Quarter		1,692,006	1,682,576	9,430
Total for year		$6,133,006	$6,095,886	$37,120

Planning Cash Payments (Outflows)

Cash payments are made primarily for materials, direct labor, expenses, capital additions, retirement of debt, and dividends paid to stockholders. The budgets for these items (already prepared at this point in the planning process as illustrated in previous chapters) provide the basis for computing the planned cash outflows. The **cash receipts and disbursements approach** requires elimination of **noncash items,** such as depreciation, from the appropriate expense budgets already prepared. Experience and company policy on purchase discounts must be taken into account in estimating the time lag between the incurrence of accounts payable and the subsequent cash payment of these payables. Accruals and prepayments must be taken into account to determine the timing of related cash payments. Interest payments on debts and property taxes can be estimated. Cash requirements for dividends may be a problem, but many corporations follow a consistent dividend policy that simplifies this problem. In other cases, cash requirements for dividends must be planned by top management on the basis of all information available. For example, the amount of dividends may depend on the availability of cash. Income taxes cannot be planned until the pretax income is planned. Borrowing and repayment of principal and interest affects both cash flow and income taxes. Therefore, there is a computation sequence (unique to each situation) that must usually be followed in planning cash outflows.

The Superior Manufacturing Company comprehensive case will be continued to illustrate how cash outflows can be planned. The company credits all purchases of raw material to accounts payable. The company takes all cash discounts; therefore, purchases and payables are recorded in the accounts at **net of purchase discount.** Payments are made as a general policy on the last day of the discount period. The result is that, on the average, **one-third** of the purchases during a particular month are carried over to the next month for payment. In a similar manner, the treasurer estimated that **one-ninth** of the purchases for each quarter would not be paid until the next quarter.

The treasurer estimated that the December 31, 19X1, balance in accounts payable would be $52,100. Based on these data inputs and data from the **raw material purchases budget** (Chapter 7, Schedule 26), a schedule of **budgeted cash required for purchases of raw materials** was prepared as shown in budget Schedule 51. The computations are rounded to the nearest $10, and cash requirements are developed by interim periods. Notice that Schedule 51 is primarily computational. This schedule is included in the annual profit plan.

Next, we will focus on the development of the cash outflow required for budgeted expenses by interim period for Superior Manufacturing Company. The expense budgets were previously illustrated in Schedules 32, 33, 34, 39, and 40. These schedules show planned expenses for each department by interim time periods. The **treasurer,** working with the controller, must convert these accrual-basis expense amounts to a **cash basis** by excluding the **noncash**

SCHEDULE 51. Superior Manufacturing Company

Budgeted Cash Required for Purchases of Materials
For the Year Ending December 31, 19X2

TIME	REF.	BEGINNING BALANCES ACCOUNTS PAYABLE	MATERIAL PURCHASES 26	TOTAL PAYABLE	ESTIMATED AMOUNT OF PURCHASES TO BE PAID NEXT MONTH	CASH REQUIRED (INVOICES PAYABLE)
January		$52,100	$ 97,900	$150,000	$32,630*	$ 117,370
February		32,630	129,700	162,330	43,230	119,100
March		43,230	118,900	162,130	39,630	122,500
Total 1st Quarter			$ 346,500	$474,460		$ 358,970
2nd Quarter		39,630	373,000	412,630	41,440	371,190
3rd Quarter		41,440	321,850	363,290	35,760	327,530
4th Quarter		35,760	377,650	413,410	41,960	371,450
Total for year			$1,419,000			$1,429,140
Ending balance in Accounts Payable 12/31/X2					$41,960	

*One-third of $97,900.

expense amounts (including those that will not be paid on a current basis). Schedule 52 shows the **budgeted cash required for expenses.** Notice in particular that the "less noncash" items include such items as depreciation (a noncash expense), taxes, insurance, and audit fee (paid annually or less often). For example, the $2,160 noncash exclusion on the first line (general and administrative overhead) in Schedule 52 includes the following noncash expense amounts from Schedule 33, "Factory Expense Budgets."

Depreciation	$1,560
Insurance	240
Taxes	360
Total	$2,160

In developing Schedule 52, the treasurer included additional planned data as follows:

a Lawyer retainer fee—paid monthly.
Audit fee—paid annually on March 1, that is, the 19X1 audit fee is paid on March 1, 19X2.

b Supplies used—purchases when made are placed in inventory and debited to the supplies inventory account; the expense reflects usage on the accrual basis. Therefore, this item was treated as a noncash item in Schedule 52.

c Stationery and office supplies—purchases are paid for when made and are recorded

SCHEDULE 52. Superior Manufacturing Company

Budgeted Cash Required for Expenses
For the Year Ending December 31, 19X2

| | REF. | TOTAL EXPENSE | LESS NONCASH | TOTAL CASH REQUIRED | CASH REQUIREMENTS | | | | | | |
| | | | | | FIRST QUARTER | | | QUARTERS | | | |
					JANUARY	FEBRUARY	MARCH	FIRST	SECOND	THIRD	FOURTH
Manufacturing Division:											
General and Administrative overhead	33	$116,800	$2,160	$114,640	$9,416	$9,524	$9,532	$28,472	$28,700	$28,548	$28,920
Power Department	33	110,000	7,200	102,800	8,246	8,468	8,468	25,182	25,848	25,404	26,366
Repair Department	33	10,000	1,600	8,400	700	700	700	2,100	2,100	2,100	2,100
Department 1	34	319,280	42,560	276,720	21,652	22,708	22,804	67,164	69,660	68,076	71,820
Department 2	34	29,280	2,568	26,712	2,184	2,226	2,226	6,636	6,678	6,636	6,762
Department 3	34	103,840	20,312	83,528	6,515	6,849	6,880	20,244	21,034	20,532	21,718
Total		$689,200	$76,400	$612,800	$48,713	$50,475	$50,610	$149,798	$154,020	$151,296	$157,686
Buildings Services	32	150,000	66,000	84,000	7,700	6,800	6,720	21,220	19,880	20,500	22,400
Sales Divisions:											
Southern District	39	234,656		234,656	19,746	21,298	20,206	61,250	60,389	51,479	61,538
Eastern District	39	313,391		313,391	25,282	27,032	28,551	80,865	81,446	67,654	83,426
Western District	39	115,120		115,120	9,828	8,783	10,170	28,781	27,964	26,249	32,126
General Sales Overhead	39	296,330	600	295,730	24,563	24,985	25,348	74,896	74,690	70,045	76,099
Total		$959,497	$600	$958,897	$79,419	$82,098	$84,275	$245,792	$244,489	$215,427	$253,189
Administrative Division:											
Accounting	40	54,020	3,000	51,020	4,250	4,258	4,264	12,772	12,770	12,682	12,796
Treasurer	40	56,177	13,990	42,187	3,511	3,538	3,562	10,611	10,587	10,290	10,689
Administrative	40	83,516	3,480	80,036	6,660	6,709	6,751*	20,120	20,096	19,563	20,257
Total		$193,713	$20,470	$173,243	$14,421	$14,505	$14,577	$43,503	$43,463	$42,535	$43,742
Grand total		$1,992,410	$163,470	$1,828,940	$150,253	$153,878	$156,182	$460,313	$461,852	$429,758	$477,017

*Does not include 19X1 audit fee; see Schedule 53.

when made directly as an expense; therefore, there is no inventory. This item was shown as a cash outflow at the amount shown in the expense schedule.

d   The capital expenditures budget illustrated in Chapter 11, Schedule 46, gives the cash requirements for that purpose.

The next items that the treasurer had to consider were deferrals, accruals, dividends, and income taxes that require cash. In large measure, these items reflect the results of the accounting process; therefore, the treasurer and the controller jointly developed the following data for planning purposes:

1   **Unexpired insurance**—balance on December 31, 19X1, $2,532 (four months of remaining premium). Policy renewal date May 1, 19X2; $22,788 cash paid for the three-year premium.

2   **Accrued property taxes**—unpaid taxes as of December 31, 19X1, $4,982, payable during February 19X2. Estimated property taxes for 19X2 shown in the expense schedules already prepared.

3   **Federal income taxes**—19X1 income taxes payable on April 15, 19X2, $279,400. (To simplify, assume that the 19X2 income tax rate is 30 percent of net income.)

4   **Accrued interest expense**—balance on December 31, 19X2, $7,000. (This is ten and one-half months' interest on the $200,000, 4 percent long-term notes—low interest rates are used only for instructional purposes.) The interest is payable each February 15; $150,000 of these notes is due and payable on February 15, 19X2.

5   **Dividends**—an annual dividend of $12,000 is anticipated in June 19X2, payable in August 19X2. (See Schedule 14.)

6   **Interest income**—there is no accrued interest income on December 31, 19X1. However, on December 31, 19X2, the bank will credit $2\frac{1}{2}$ percent interest on the building fund of $20,000 to the fund.

7   **Direct labor and other wages**—no accruals.

8   **Stationery and office supplies**—no inventory.

9   **Supplies used**—inventory on December 31, 19X1, $13,700. Budgeted purchases during 19X2: January, $3,400; February, $3,300; March, $3,500; 2nd Quarter, $10,400; 3rd Quarter, $10,400; and 4th Quarter, $10,140. Supplies used as indicated on expense schedules already prepared. Supplies are paid for as purchased.

10   **Annual audit fee**—the 19X1 audit fee of $2,400 (small amount used for instructional purposes only) is payable on March 1, 19X2. The 19X2 audit fee of $2,400 is payable on March 1, 19X3.

11   **Contingent liabilities**—court litigation currently in progress may result in a payment of approximately $620,000 as an adjustment of prior years' federal income taxes.

These data were used to develop Schedule 53. Notice that because of the simplified illustration, numerous items are included in one schedule. This is not typical; usually, separate schedules and computations are needed for each separate type of expenditure. Although the estimates and requirements for income taxes are shown on the schedule, the schedule must initially be constructed without this expense. The schedule should generally be completed with a rough estimate of income taxes so that the probable cash position can be determined. As soon as net income is computed and the tax estimated, Schedule 52 can be recast as illustrated.

SCHEDULE 53. Superior Manufacturing Company

Cash Requirements for
Deferred and Accrued Items and Income Tax
For the Year Ending December 31, 19X2

	BALANCE 12/31/X1	RENEWALS AND PAYMENTS 19X2	TOTAL	EXPIRATIONS AND ACCRUALS 19X2	BALANCE 12/31/X2	CASH REQUIREMENTS							
						FIRST QUARTER			QUARTERS				
						JANUARY	FEBRUARY	MARCH	FIRST	SECOND	THIRD	FOURTH	TOTAL
	(Given)	(Given)											
Unexpired insurance	$ 2,532	$ 22,788	$25,320	$ 7,596	$ 17,724	$	$	$	$	$22,788	$	$	$ 22,788
Accrued property tax	4,982*	4,982		7,284*	7,284*		4,982		4,982				4,982
Federal income taxes	279,400*	279,400		258,318*	258,318*			279,400	279,400				279,400
Accrued interest expense(a)	7,000* (10½ Mos.)	8,000(b) (12 Mos.)	1,000 (12 Mos.)	2,750* (10½ Mos.)	1,750* (10½ Mos.)		8,000		8,000				8,000
Interest income on building fund ($20,000 at 2½% credited to building fund on December 31)													
Supplies inventory	13,700	41,140	54,840	49,640*	5,200*	3,400	3,300	3,500	10,200	10,400	10,400	10,140	41,140
Audit fee	2,400*	2,400		2,400*	2,400*			2,400	2,400				2,400
Total cash requirements						$3,400	$16,282	$285,300	$304,982	$33,188	$10,400	$10,140	$358,710

*Credit

(a) Notes payable is included in Schedule 54.

(b) The interest is on two notes payable ($7,000 + $1,000 = $8,000) as follows:
  (1) Long-term note, 4%, note payable from 19X1: $200,000 × 4% = 10½/12 months = $7,000. This note matures on February 15, 19X3.
  (2) Short-term note, 6%, March 1 to April 30, 19X2: $100,000 × 6% × 2/12 months = $1,000.

Note: This schedule does not include dividends; see Schedule 54 and 57.

SCHEDULE 54. Superior Manufacturing Company

Summary of Cash Requirements (outflows)
For the Year Ending December 31, 19X2

	REF.	ANNUAL TOTAL	FIRST QUARTER			QUARTERS			
			JANUARY	FEBRUARY	MARCH	FIRST	SECOND	THIRD	FOURTH
Material	51	$1,429,140	$117,370	$119,100	$122,500	$ 358,970	$ 371,190	$ 327,530	$ 371,450
Labor	30	1,752,000	125,400	141,600	142,800	409,800	444,000	421,200	477,000
Expense	52	1,828,940	150,253	153,878	156,182	460,313	461,852	429,758	477,017
Capital additions	46	28,700	200			200			28,500
Accrued and deferred items	53	358,710	3,400	16,282	285,300	304,982	33,188	10,400	10,140
Dividends	14	12,000						12,000	
Notes payable	(input)	150,000		150,000		150,000			
Total		$5,559,490	$396,623	$580,860	$706,782	$1,684,265	$1,310,230	$1,200,888	$1,364,107

Note: This schedule does not include any short-term financing to cover a 19X2 cash deficit.

444

The cash requirements indicated in Schedules 46, 51, 52, and 53 are summarized in Schedule 54. Notes payable, to be paid during the upcoming year, are also included.

Determining Interim Financing Needs

Cash inflows and outflows must next be compared to assess the planned cash position throughout the period. To make this comparison, the treasurer had to develop another input—the probable starting cash balance (actual) on January 1, 19X2. The treasurer estimated it at $54,000 and proceeded to develop Schedule 55, "Comparison of Estimated Cash Receipts and Disbursements," prior to financing.

The last column in Schedule 55, "Ending Cash Balance," indicates a favorable cash position for each period except one. At March 31 there is a cash deficit of $23,261, indicating a need for financing. Estimated cash balances for the following periods suggest that a short-term bank loan would protect the cash position. After consideration of all factors involved, the treasurer decided that the following short-term financing should be included in the cash budget.

Date needed	March 1, 19X2
Amount needed	$100,000
Repayment date	April 30, 19X2
Interest rate	6%
Type of financing	Interest-bearing note

SCHEDULE 55. Superior Manufacturing Company

Comparison of Estimated Cash Receipts and Disbursements
(before interim financing)
For the Year Ending December 31, 19X2

TIME	REF.	BEGINNING CASH BALANCE	CASH RECEIPTS 50	TOTAL	CASH DISBURSEMENTS 54	ENDING CASH BALANCE
January		$ 54,000	$ 505,997	$ 559,997	$ 396,623	$163,374
February		163,374	534,004	697,378	580,860	116,518
March		116,518	567,003	683,521	706,782	23,261*
2nd Quarter		23,261*	1,635,202	1,611,941	1,310,230	301,711
3rd Quarter		301,711	1,198,794	1,500,505	1,200,888	299,617
4th Quarter		299,617	1,692,006	1,991,623	$1,364,107	627,516
Total			$6,133,006		$5,559,490	

*Credit balance indicated, which means a cash shortage.

The short-term financing, its interest thereon, and the effect on cash is shown in Schedule 56, "Budgeted Interim Financing Requirements." Determination of budgeted financing is the last input for the final cash budget. Using the data given in Schedules 55 and 56, the treasurer prepared the **final cash budget** shown in Schedule 57. Of the cash flow schedules illustrated, only this last one is needed in the **formal** profit plan.

SCHEDULE 56. Superior Manufacturing Company

Budgeted Interim Financing Requirements*
For the Year Ending December 31, 19X2

(a) NOTES PAYABLE—SHORT TERM

TIME	BEGINNING ACCOUNT BALANCE	CASH RECEIVED (LOAN INCURRED)	SUBTOTAL	CASH PAYMENT (LOAN PAID)	ENDING ACCOUNT BALANCE
January	—				—
February	—				
March	—	$100,000	$100,000		$100,000
1st Quarter		$100,000	$100,000		$100,000
2nd Quarter	$100,000		$100,000	$100,000	—
3rd Quarter	—				—
4th Quarter	—				—
Total	—	$100,000	$100,000	$100,000	—

(b) INTEREST EXPENSE ON SHORT-TERM NOTES

TIME	BEGINNING ACCOUNT BALANCE	EXPENSE INCURRED	SUBTOTAL	CASH PAYMENTS	ENDING ACCOUNT BALANCE
January	—				—
February	—				
March	—	$ 500	$ 500		$500
1st Quarter	—	$ 500	$ 500		$500
2nd Quarter	$500	$ 500	$1,000	$1,000	—
3rd Quarter	—				—
4th Quarter	—				—

*In view of the fact that only *one* loan is contemplated, this schedule is superfluous. It is included simply to indicate one possible format for situations involving numerous loans and repayments.

SCHEDULE 57. Superior Manufacturing Company

Final Cash Budget
For the Year Ending December 31, 19X2

TIME	REF.	BEGINNING CASH BALANCE	CASH RECEIPTS 50	TOTAL	CASH PAYMENTS 54	ENDING CASH BALANCE
January		$ 54,000	$ 505,997	$ 559,997	$ 396,623	$163,374
February		163,374	534,004	697,378	580,860	116,518
March		116,518	667,003[a]	783,521	706,782	76,739
2nd Quarter		76,739	1,635,202	1,711,941	1,411,230[b]	300,711
3rd Quarter		300,711	1,198,794	1,499,505	1,200,888	298,617
4th Quarter		298,617	1,692,006	1,990,623	1,364,107	626,516
Totals			$6,233,006		$5,660,490	

[a] Includes short-term financing note, $100,000 (i.e., Schedule 50, $567,003 + $100,000 = $667,003).
[b] Includes payment of short-term bank loan and interest, $101,000 (i.e., Schedule 54, $1,310,230 + $101,000 = $1,411,230).

The schedules relating to the cash budget illustrated in this chapter are primarily computation schedules. The format of the cash budget should be adapted to enhance understanding and communications. There is no single universal format.

FINANCIAL ACCOUNTING APPROACH TO COMPUTE CASH FLOWS   The financial accounting approach is used by some companies for analytical purposes to develop the annual cash budget. However, it is used more often for long-term cash planning. This approach requires less detail and fits the approaches commonly used in long-range planning.

Basically, this method develops cash flows starting with *net income*; adjustments to net income are made for noncash items affecting accrual-basis net income. Essentially, net income is converted from the **accrual** basis to a cash basis (e.g., cash flow from operations). The other cash inflows and outflows are estimated for nonoperating items such as sale of fixed assets, capital additions, and payment of debt and dividends. These estimates are computed much like the cash receipts and disbursements method. For a common set of underlying plans, the cash receipts and disbursements approach and the financial accounting approach derive the same cash flow results. The cash receipts and disbursements method provides more detail data that are useful for assessment and control of cash flows.[1]

[1] Glenn A. Welsch and Charles T. Zlatkovich, *Intermediate Accounting,* 8th ed. (Homewood, Ill.: Richard D. Irwin, 1988), Chap. 23.

EXHIBIT 12-1

Financial Accounting Approach Used to Develop an Analysis of Income and Cash

AK Corporation—Budgeted Income and Cash Flow Statement
For the Year Ending December 31, 19XX
(In Thousand Dollars: Only 100% Column Partially Completed with Hypothetical Amounts for Illustrative Purposes)

PART 1—INCOME STATEMENT:	AT 80% CAPACITY AMOUNT	PERCENT	AT 90% CAPACITY AMOUNT	PERCENT	AT 100% CAPACITY AMOUNT	PERCENT	AT 110% CAPACITY AMOUNT	PERCENT	AT 120% CAPACITY AMOUNT	PERCENT
Sales	$ 8,000		$9,000		$10,000	100	$11,000		$12,000	
Variable expenses:										
Direct material										
Direct labor										
Factory overhead										
Distribution expense										
General administrative expense										
Total variable expenses					7,000	70				
Marginal income					3,000	30				
Fixed expenses										
Factory overhead										
Distribution										
General administrative										
Total expenses					2,500	25				
Operating income					500	5				
Provision for income taxes					250	2.5				
Net income					$ 250	2.5				

448

PART 2—CASH FLOW ANALYSIS:

Beginning cash balance		$ 40
Cash sources:		
Net income	250	
Add: Depreciation and amortization	100	
Decrease in inventory	12	
Deduct: Increase in prepaid expenses	(5)	
Increase in receivables	(7)	
Net income converted to cash inflow basis	350	
Financing	100	
Total cash inflow		450
Total cash available		490
Cash requirements:		
Dividends	40	
Decrease in long-term liabilities	30	
Net increase in fixed assets	300	
Total cash required		370
Ending cash balance		$ 120

Exhibit 12-1 shows how one company uses the financial accounting method for analytical purposes when each expense is categorized as either fixed or variable. Notice that (1) the cash flow analysis *starts* with net income ($250,000), (2) this amount is "adjusted" from the accrual basis to the *cash basis* ($350,000), and (3) inflows and outflows not directly related to the income statement are shown separately. You should analyze the adjustments to net income to comprehend how they are handled. For example, the $7,000 increase in receivables is a deduction because income includes this noncash amount of credit sales that will be collected later (i.e., a cash inflow). Two broader features of this illustration should be noted: (a) this company develops a **contribution margin** income statement (Part 1) and cash flow analysis (Part 2) for several capacity levels, and (b) the budgeted income statement and cash flow analysis are shown as a single schedule.

Exhibit 12-2 shows how another company uses the financial statement approach to develop a long-range cash budget. Notice that this exhibit shows less detail and broader plans that are implicit in this approach.

EXHIBIT 12-2

Financial Accounting Approach Used to Develop a Long-term Cash Plan

RB Company Long-Range Plans—Analysis of Cash Flow

ITEM	CURRENT YEAR 19X1	FUTURE PROJECTIONS 19X2	19X3	19X4	19X5	19X6
Beginning cash position (000)	160					
Cash inflows:						
Net income planned (after tax)	400					
Adjustments:						
Add: Depreciation and amortization	70					
Deduct: Increase in working capital other than cash	(10)					
Net income on cash basis	460					
Other sources of cash:						
Capital stock sold	100					
Long-term loans	80					
Sales of fixed assets	30					
Total cash inflow	670					
Cash outflows:						
Sinking fund requirements	20					
Dividend payments	40					
Payment on long-term debt	550					
Additions to fixed assets	150					
Total cash outflow	760					
Ending cash position	70					

CONTROL OF THE CASH POSITION   The company's financial officer (e.g., treasurer) is responsible for control of the cash position. Actual cash receipts and payments during the budget period will usually be somewhat different from those shown in the profit plan. This difference may result from (1) changing variables that affect cash, such as change in tax rates; (2) sudden and unexpected events that influence operations; or (3) lack of cash control.

An effective system of cash control is important because of the potential consequences. Frequently, it is possible for management to make decisions or to alter existing policies so that the cash position is enhanced. For example, an unexpected change in operations may create a serious cash shortage, but management may be able to avoid, or at least to minimize, the undesirable situation by (1) increasing efforts to collect receivables, (2) reducing cash expenses, (3) deferring capital expenditures, (4) deferring payment of selected liabilities, (5) reducing inventories, and (6) altering timing of operations that affect cash. The effect of these kinds of decisions on the cash position is contingent upon their timing. Often the earlier the decision, the greater the opportunity to protect the cash position. Therefore, it is essential that management be fully informed as far in advance as possible about the *probable* cash position.

Assuming effective planning, continuing control of the cash position should usually involve two procedures. One is **continuous evaluation** of both the present and the probable cash position. This procedure involves a periodic evaluation and reporting, usually monthly, of the actual cash position to date. This report is coupled with a **reprojection** of the probable future cash flows for the remainder of the period, taking into account budgeted conditions affected by unexpected developments not originally anticipated and the future outlook. Assume, for example, that at the end of February there was an actual cash balance of $71,000, and the original budgeted balance was $92,000. The factors causing the $21,000 unfavorable variance in cash should be carefully analyzed, with particular emphasis on the probable future effect. Next, the budgeted cash receipts and payments for the **remainder** of the year should be carefully evaluated and **adjusted for any new conditions** that may affect them. The final step, then, in evaluating the probable future cash position is to start with the $11,000 actual cash balance at the end of February by adding to it the reprojected budget receipts for each time period during the remainder of the budget year and by subtracting the reprojected budget payments for the same period. In this way, a completely new evaluation of the probable future cash position can be developed for top management. This dynamic approach gives management a **continuous budget** evaluation of the cash position. This continuous monitoring enhances control through policy decisions that, by the very nature of the situation, must be made some time in advance to have the maximum effect on the cash position. This procedure is shown in Exhibit 12-3, which was adapted from the procedures of a medium-size company.

The other procedure used for cash control maintains data on the day-to-day (or week-to-week) cash position. To minimize interest costs and to ensure

EXHIBIT 12-3

Monthly Report of Cash Position
X Company
At March 31, 19XX

	ACTUAL CASH POSITION		REPROJECTION OF CASH POSITION FOR REMAINDER OF YEAR				
PARTICULARS	MONTH OF MARCH	CUMULATIVE JAN. 1–MAR. 31	APRIL	MAY	JUNE	3RD QUARTER	4TH QUARTER
Cash receipts:							
Accounts receivable							
Trade notes receivable							
Cash sales							
Other sources							
Total cash inflow							
Cash payments:							
Raw material							
Accounts payable							
Current expenses							
Dividends							
Other payments							
Total cash outflow							
Indicated cash position from operations							
Financing require (net of interest):*							
Short-term							
Long-term							
Total							
Indicated cash position (after financing)							

*Indicates payment of debt.

EXHIBIT 12-4

Daily Report on Cash Position
Y Company
For the Month of ___

DATE	DAY	RUNNING CASH BALANCE	CASH INFLOW				CASH OUTFLOW			
			TOTAL CASH INFLOW	COLLECTION ON RECEIVABLES	OTHER SOURCES OF CASH	TOTAL CASH OUTFLOW	PAYMENT CURRENT LIABILITIES	PAYROLL REQUIRE-MENTS	OPERATING EXPENSE	OTHER DISBURSE-MENTS
1	Th									
2	Fri									
3	*									
4	*									
5	Mon									
6	Tue									
7	Wed									
8	Th									
9	Fri									
Etc.										

*Nonworking day.

End of month cash balances analyzed:

Actual:
   Amount $ _____
   Average daily balance (based on the
     number of working days in the month) $ _____

Budgeted:
   Amount $ _____
   Average daily balance (based on the
     number of working days in the month) $ _____

adequate cash, some financial executives develop a daily evaluation of the current cash position as shown in Exhibit 12-4. This approach is particularly useful in companies having widely fluctuating cash demands and widely dispersed branches through which large amounts of cash flow. Many companies are aware of the reduced interest costs that can be attained through daily control of cash. For example, one company estimated that daily control saved approximately $240,000 in interest during one year. Prior to instituting daily control, it was not uncommon for one division of the company to have excess cash of several million dollars while another division was borrowing substantial amounts on a short-term basis and paying 10 percent interest.

Many companies control cash by concurrent use of the two procedures discussed above. Therefore the three primary cash planning and control activities are (1) systematic planning of the cash flows for both the long range and short range, (2) monthly reprojection of the cash position as discussed above, and (3) daily evaluation of the cash position.

TECHNIQUES FOR IMPROVING CASH FLOW   Planning the cash flows of a company should include consideration of how to improve cash flow. Improving cash flow basically involves increasing the amount of available cash on a day-to-day basis. To accomplish this objective, the management should focus on (a) the **cash collection process** to speed up cash collections, (b) the **cash payment process** to slow down the payments of cash, and (c) the **investment policies** for the immediate investment of idle cash balances to maximize interest earnings. Improving the cash collection and payment processes and the investment policies for otherwise idle cash will enhance a company's **liquidity position.** Liquidity refers to the availability of cash to efficiently meet the day-to-day cash demands of a company.

Collectively, these activities are usually called cash management, which in and of itself should be cost effective. Cash management in a large company is so important that the related policies and processes should be subject to internal audits.[2]

Some of the ways often used to improve the efficiency of the **cash collection process** are as follows:[3]

1. Review the lag from the date of sale of goods and services on credit to the mailing of (a) invoices and (b) the first billing. To the extent feasible, invoices should be designed to also be the first billing to encourage immediate payment by the customer. The time lag here can avoid a significant adverse affect on early collection.
2. If cash discounts are given to customers for early payment, review their effect on early cash collections and whether the discount is too high or too low. Also, monitor

---

[2] Leslie Masonson, "Cash Management Audit, How It Can Uncover Outmoded Practices, Reduce Risk, and Cut Costs," *Financial Executive,* February 1987, pp. 30–33.

[3] David L. Shafer, "Cash Management: A Cost-Effective Approach," *Journal of Accountancy,* March 1987, pp. 114–17.

whether the discount policy is being violated in the company (i.e., allowing the discount after its expiration date). Alternatively, if discounts are not given, does the company assess an "interest" penalty for late payment? How much cash inflow is lost by not charging for late payments?

3. Review the credit-granting process to determine whether bad credit risks are being screened out. Also, are delinquent receivables being identified early and collection action taken *before* the receivable becomes an uncollectible (i.e., a bad debt)?

4. Consider ways to decrease the time between the date that customers pay by check and the date that the cash is available for use in the company's bank account. This time is called "float" and it may vary from one day to ten days. Float can be very costly because (a) the cash inflow is slow and (b) the opportunity to earn interest on the cash during the float period is lost. The float lag can be minimized by techniques such as the following:

(a) Use a lockbox system—the purpose of a lockbox system is to reduce the float time of cash from the customer to the company. The way a lockbox system operates has been summarized as follows:

> The essential concept of the lockbox is that the corporation contracts with a bank to receive and process incoming remittances. The corporation then instructs its customers to remit payment to a post office box in a designated city (which may be some distance from the corporation's own offices). Then, each day, the bank collects the contents of the post office box and processes the contents in accordance with the corporation's instructions.
>
> The checks are endorsed "credited to the account of the within named payee" and deposited into the corporation's account at the bank. The bank then forwards all backup documentation (such as invoices, empty envelopes and photocopies of the checks) to the corporation, and may provide the corporation with telephone notification, data transmission and so on.
>
> *From incoming funds to earning assets.* The primary objective of a wholesale lockbox is to accelerate the conversion of incoming funds into earning assets. The lockbox accomplishes this objective for two reasons.
>
> First of all, incoming mail time is often reduced because the bank may collect the contents of the post office box far more often than the corporation would itself. Very often, bank lockbox departments work throughout the evening and on weekends and holidays as well.
>
> Moreover, because the corporation can establish a lockbox in any city, it can place the lockbox close to the customers, thus further reducing mail time.
>
> Second, check clearing time for the incoming checks is reduced. Reasons for this include the location of the lockbox nearer to the customers and the fact that the bank receives the incoming checks at its operations center early in the day, thus enabling the bank to enter the checks into the check collection system as soon as possible.

This process is designed to significantly reduce the mail time for cash inflows. The bank charges the company a specified amount per collection. A lockbox system should be carefully analyzed on a cost-benefit basis because the decrease in float time may not fully compensate for the cost of the system.

(b) Establish bank accounts in outlying areas where a designated company employee receives the customer's payments and immediately deposits the checks in the bank account.

(c) Decrease the check-processing time (check received from customers) within the company and make daily night deposits of all cash and checks received during the day.

(d) Promote timely and frequent billing on all receivables. Do not use month-end billings, bill immediately after sale.

Some of the ways often used to improve the efficiency of the **cash payment process** are as follows:

1 Make all payments on the latest nonpenalty day. Do not pay early.

2 Make all payments by check, preferably on Friday to *maximize* float in favor of the company. Do not use "wire transfer" unless it is necessary. Less-frequent mailing enhances cash flow and reduces clerical effort.

3 Take all cash discounts allowed for early payment.

4 Establish a policy of no cash advances (to both outsiders and employees).

5 Establish policies, and a payment process, to minimize the possibility of fraudulent payments by company employees.

A company should develop a specific policy about the investment of temporarily idle cash. The policy should be specific about such issues as (a) types and mix of acceptable securities, (b) monthly reporting and monitoring of the portfolio, and (c) safeguarding and disposal of temporary investments.

Finally, the responsibilities for cash management should be specified in terms of responsibility centers, with a designated overall responsibility (usually the top financial executive).

PLANNING AND CONTROLLING CASH IN A NONMANUFACTURING COMPANY

In companies of all types, cash management is vital. In retail and wholesale enterprises particularly, cash management is needed because large and costly inventories frequently must be maintained. Also, extensive credit is used to maintain the inventories. A complete plan of operations is essential in developing a realistic cash budget. A line of credit with lending agencies is frequently dependent on a realistic sales plan supported by a comprehensive profit plan. The cash budget in retail and wholesale companies is developed in a manner similar to that already discussed and illustrated for a manufacturing business. Control of the cash position also is exercised in a similar manner.

CHAPTER SUMMARY   The planned statement of cash flows (i.e., the cash budget) is necessarily prepared near the end of the annual planning cycle along with the planned income statement and balance sheet. The cash plan or budget is prepared from the previously completed budgets, such as the sales, materials, labor, overhead, and capital expenditures budgets. Thus, preparing the cash plan (or budget) primarily involves two activities: (a) combining all the planned cash inflows and outflows and (b) making decisions about interim financing, in case of cash shortages, and interim investing, in case of excess cash.

The cash budget can be prepared by using either (a) the cash receipts and cash disbursements approach or (b) the financial accounting approach. The cash receipts and disbursements approach basically involves the use of detailed data from the budgeted cash account. The financial statement approach starts with net income (accrual basis), which is adjusted to a cash basis to compute "cash flow from continuing operations." The remaining cash sources and uses must be determined by using data from the various budgets already prepared. The cash receipts and disbursements approach is usually used for the tactical short-term plan because it provides more details. The financial statement method is usually used for broad analyses of the cash position and for strategic long-range planning.

Controlling cash flows is a daily task in many companies. Cash performance reports monthly, weekly, and even daily identify evolving cash flow problems that often need immediate attention.

Suggested References

ARCHER, STEPHEN H., G. MARC CHOATE, and GEORGE RACETTE, *Financial Management*, Chap. 8. New York: John Wiley, 1983.

BARTON, A. D., *The Anatomy of Accounting*, Chap. 20. New York: University of Queensland Press, 1984.

CHATFIELD, MICHAEL, and DENIS VEILSON, *Cost Accounting*, Chap. 7. New York: Harcourt Brace Jovanovich, 1984.

CIRZ, RAYMOND T., and MICHAEL S. SORICH, "Developing a Better Cash Flow Projection," *Appraisal Journal*, May 1986, p. 2.

COHEN, JEROME B., SIDNEY ROBBINS, and ALLAN YOUNG. *The Financial Manager*, Chap. 6. Columbus, Ohio: Publishing Horizons, 1986.

DAVIS, HENRY A., "Changing Priorities in Corporate Cash Management," *Financial Executives Magazine*, January 1987, p. 18.

DAVIS, JOSEPH M., "Cash Flow Model Analysis: Buy the Assumptions, Not the Investments," *Appraisal Journal*, April 1985, p. 228.

DOMINICK, GERALDINE F., and JOSEPH G. LOUDERBACK III, *Managerial Accounting*, Chap. 7. Boston: Kent Publishing, 1985.

GARRISON, RAY H., *Managerial Accounting: Concepts for Planning, Control, Decision Making*, Chap. 8. Plano, Tex.: Business Publications, 1985.

HEITGER, LESTER E., and SERGE MATULICH, *Managerial Accounting*, Chap. 7. New York: McGraw-Hill, 1986.

"How to Analyze Cash Flow When Buying or Selling a Business," *BUSINESS OWNER*, July 1985, p. 9.

"How to Compute the Real Cost of an Investment or Any Cash Outlay," *Business Owner*, January 1987, p. 6.

KOCHANEK, RICHARD, and CORINE T. NORGAARD, "Why the Focus Has Changed from Working Capital to Cash Flow," *Financial Executives Magazine*, January 1987, p. 27.

LEUNG, LAWRENCE C., and J.M.A. TANCHOCO, "Alternative Methods of Cash Flow Modeling," *Engineering Economist*, Summer 1986, p. 303.

NEVEN, RAYMOND P., *Fundamentals of Managerial Finance*, Chap 4. Cincinnati: South-Western Publishing, 1985.

SWANSON, EDWARD P., "Designing a Cash Flow Statement," *CPA JOURNAL*, January 1986, p. 38.

Discussion Questions

1. Define *cash budget*, and explain its scope and objectives.
2. Which manager or managers should be responsible for planning and controlling cash?
3. What are the two primary approaches used to develop cash flow budgets? Explain each briefly.
4. In planning cash outflows, budgeted expenses must be "adjusted." Explain the general approach and the nature of the adjustment.
5. The financial accounting approach used to develop the cash budget involves the "adjustment" of net income to a cash flow basis. Explain the nature of the adjustment required for each of the following: depreciation, amortization, inventory change, changes in accounts receivable, changes in prepaid items, and changes in accrued items.
6. Assuming adequate planning, the control of and management of cash should usually be based on two procedures. Identify and explain the two procedures.

CASE 12-1 *Compute cash inflow from credit sales*

Evers Company sells its products on both cash and credit terms. For planning purposes, the company has been making rough estimates of its expected cash collections from credit sales. The sales plan for the past several years has been realistic, but cash planning has been unsatisfactory. The management is currently developing the 19X8 annual profit plan. The following budget data (simplified for case purposes) have been developed:

(a) Balance in accounts receivable at December 31, 19X7, $1,000.
(b) Balance in allowance for doubtful accounts at December 31, 19X7, $600.
(c) Planned sales:

19X8	CASH	CREDIT
January	$ 55,000	$10,000
February	65,000	12,120
March	56,000	11,110
2nd Quarter	150,000	30,300
3rd Quarter	170,000	33,330
4th Quarter	160,000	32,320

(d) Estimated losses on accounts receivable due to bad debts—1 percent of sales (rounded to the nearest $10).

(e) Experience indicates that collections, after provision for bad debts, should be: 80 percent in month sold; 10 percent in first month following sale, and 10 percent in second month following sale. On a quarterly basis: 90 percent will be collected in the quarter sold and the balance in the next quarter. One-sixth of the $1,000 balance in accounts receivable at December 31, 19X7, will probably be collected in June; the balance is expected to be collected except for $200 of accounts receivable, which will be written off as a bad debt in 19X8.

REQUIRED

1. Prepare a budget schedule to estimate 19X8 cash inflows from credit sales by time period. Evers Company uses the cash receipts and disbursements approach to develop its cash budget.

2. Prepare a summary budget of planned cash inflow from cash sales, credit sales, and total, by time period.

CASE 12-2   *Use a flexible expense budget to prepare an expense budget and a cash outflow budget*

Doss Department Store uses flexible budget formulas for its selling expense budget (excluding cost of goods sold). The company treasurer uses the expense budget to compute cash requirements for selling expense. The 19X8 flexible budget for selling expense is as follows:

EXPENSE	FIXED (PER MONTH)	VARIABLE RATE (PER $100 SALES)
Salaries (paid each month)	$50,000	
Travel and promotion (paid as incurred)	2,000	
Advertising (paid as incurred)		$3.00
Telephone (paid each month)	300	
Selling supplies (paid as used)		2.00
Depreciation (straightline)	200	
Loss on bad debts (recorded each month)		.50
Property taxes (paid in 19X9)	10	
Insurance (paid on policy date)	5	
Miscellaneous (paid as incurred)	2	.20

PLANNED SALES FOR 19X8	
January	$200,000
February	210,000
March	220,000
Quarter 2	600,000
Quarter 3	450,000
Quarter 4	700,000

REQUIRED

1. Prepare the 19X8 selling expense budget by time periods.

2. Prepare the budget of cash requirements for selling expense, by expense, by time. This budget schedule will be used to help complete the annual cash budget.

CASE 12-3   Prepare an annual cash budget using the cash receipts and disbursements approach

Standish Wholesale Company prepares an annual profit plan for all phases of operations. The plan is developed by quarter, and the first quarter is detailed by months. The following 19X2 planning data have been approved:

a. Capital expenditures budget—Cash requirements as follows: Machinery to be purchased: March, $2,500; 3rd Quarter, $6,000. Contribution to building fund: $30,000 on December 15. Blanket appropriations for minor capital additions: 1st Quarter, $600; 2nd Quarter, $500; 3rd Quarter, $500; 4th Quarter, $700.

b. Sales budget (average 70 percent cash sales)—January, $90,000; February, $85,000; March, $85,000; 2nd Quarter, $250,000; 3rd Quarter, $230,000; 4th Quarter, $300,000.

c. Collections on credit sales, after allowance for doubtful accounts, are expected to be as follows: 80 percent in month sold, 10 percent in first month following sale, 7 percent in second month following sale, and 3 percent in third month. On a quarterly basis, 94 percent collected in the quarter sold and 6 percent in the next quarter.

d. Estimated balances at January 19X2:

Accounts receivable	$20,000	(estimated collections: 2nd
Allowance for doubtful accounts	7,000	Quarter, $5,000; 4th Quarter,
Cash	15,000	$7,000)

e. Planned other incomes and other expenses for 19X2 (cash basis):

TIME	OTHER INCOMES	OTHER EXPENSES
January	$1,500	$2,000
February	1,000	2,000
March	1,000	1,500
2nd Quarter	3,000	5,000
3rd Quarter	3,000	5,000
4th Quarter	4,000	6,000

f. Planned expense for doubtful accounts is one-half of 1 percent of credit sales. (Round to the nearest $10.)

g. Cash required for purchases is estimated to be as follows: January, $14,408; February, $16,272; March, $15,230; 2nd Quarter, $46,380; 3rd Quarter, $39,370; 4th Quarter, $48,496.

h. Expense budget totals are as follows (exclusion for noncash items such as depreciation total $4,500 per month): January, $70,900; February, $67,710; March, $70,120; 2nd Quarter, $200,620; 3rd Quarter, $174,630; and 4th Quarter, $212,010.

i. Planned miscellaneous cash requirements:
   (1) Insurance policy to be renewed on June 1, cost $750.
   (2) Property taxes to be paid in February, $1,400.
   (3) March 15 annual payment of interest (4 percent) on long-term notes payable, principal $50,000; and $20,000 is also paid on the principal at this time.
   (4) Dividends, $20,000 (June).
   (5) Legal retainer fees $150 per month (not included in item h above).
   (6) Audit fee payable, $2,500 (February).
   (7) Federal income taxes: April, $21,000; November, $3,000; and December, $3,000.

j. Recommended interim financing—Use amount of cash shortages (if any) rounded to the nearest $1,000. Therefore, assume the following interim financing at 6 percent: bank loan, $10,000 (3 months) on March 1; bank loan, $20,000 (8 months) on April 1.

REQUIRED   Prepare the following schedules for the annual profit plan:
   1. Planned cash collections from receivables
   2. Summary of cash inflows detailed by source and time periods
   3. Summary of cash outflows—detailed by reason and time periods
   4. Tentative cash budget
   5. Schedule of short-term financing recommended (5 percent interest per year)
   6. Final cash budget—show financing and repayment separately

CASE 12-4   *Prepare a long-range income plan, which is then used to develop a long-range cash plan*

Triple X Industries is a medium-size manufacturer of a limited line of retail items sold through hardware stores. Production is carried on in an old plant; however, management is planning the construction of a new plant in 19X3. The management is currently developing a five-year long-range plan (19X1 through 19X5). The following 19X1 budget plans have been approved:

1. Sales, $800,000: The sales objective is to increase sales $40,000 per year through 19X5.
2. Variable cost objective: 40 percent of sales; fixed cost objective $380,000 with a 10 percent increase in 19X4.
3. Depreciation and amortization expense: 30 percent of the fixed costs given in item 2.
4. Actual cash balance: At the beginning of 19X1, $70,000; working capital other than cash at this date, $150,000. The planned objective for working capital other than cash is to hold it to the same rate of increase as sales.
5. Income tax rate planned: 52 percent (for instructional purposes only).
6. Sources of cash:

   a. Sale of old assets: 19X1, $5,000; 19X2, $5,000; 19X3, $50,000; 19X4, $4,000; 19X5, $4,000.
   b. Sale of treasury stock in 19X3, $100,000 cash.
   c. Borrowing—long-term loan and mortgage in 19X2, $200,000.
7. Cash requirements:
   a. The sinking fund has a balance at the start of 19X1 of $150,000, and $50,000 must be added to it during 19X1.
   b. Payment of bonds amounting to $600,000 from sinking fund and cash in 19X2.
   c. Capital expenditures: 19X1, $40,000; 19X2, $50,000; 19X3, $350,000 (plant); 19X4; $50,000; 19X5; $50,000.
   d. Dividends paid in cash: 19X1 and 19X2, $20,000 per year; 19X3, 19X4 and 19X5, $24,000 per year.
   e. Miscellaneous cash requirements: 19X1, $4,500; 19X2, $6,020; 19X3, $6,540; 19X4, $6,220; and 19X5, $6,740.

REQUIRED

1. Prepare the long-range planned income statement (one column for each of the five years). Use side captions in the following order: sales, variable costs, contribution margin, fixed expenses, pretax income, income tax, and net income.

2. Prepare the long-range cash flow plan (use the financial accounting approach).

3. Comment on any particular problems or suggestions about your income and cash flow budgets.

CASE 12-5   *Prepare an analysis of profit and the cash position for a company that has a cash flow problem*

The executive committee of the Riley Company is trying to develop a profit plan for the company. This is the company's first attempt to develop an annual profit plan. Some estimates for the upcoming year, 19X8, have been made. Attention is now focusing on the cash budget. The controller has asked Sid Pearce, a recent MBA graduate and a new employee, to "develop a cash flow analysis." After considerable effort and numerous discussions, Sid collected the following data from various sources:

a   From the 19X8 tentative sales budget: Planned sales, $400,000 (normal capacity)

b   From the accounting department: Payment on bonds payable to be made during 19X8, $55,000 plus $5,000 bond interest; annual cash dividends per year for the past seven years, $12,000; probable beginning balances at beginning of 19X8:
       Cash, $22,000; accounts receivable, $32,000; and inventory, $62,000; variable costs, 55 percent of sales; fixed costs per year, $120,000 (including depreciation, $40,000; amortization of intangibles, $10,000; and bond interest for the year, $5,000)

c   From the controller: Idle assets to be sold during 19X8 for $10,000 cash (net of tax); accounts receivable at year-end should be approximately 10 percent of sales, and inventory 15 percent of sales

d   From the company engineer: Estimated cost of 19X8 plant addition, $200,000

e   From the executive vice-president: A $140,000 long-term mortgage loan will be obtained in March 19X8

Sid believed that these were the best data obtainable at this time. Therefore, he proceeded to develop a tentative cash flow analysis at three levels of operations, that is, at the "normal" level specified in the tentative sales budget, and at levels 10 percent above and 10 percent below the sales budget. Sid decided upon this strategy because it might stimulate more interest and involvement in the planning process. Also, it would emphasize any cash flow problems "at the margin."

REQUIRED

1. Develop a combined income statement (designate it Part A) and cash flow analysis (Part B) for each of the three levels in the way that you think Sid would have done. For simplicity, assume a 40 percent income tax rate for 19X8.

2. Explain any assumptions that you make, and recommend appropriate management action for each assumption. No major events are anticipated during 19X8 except construction of the new plant. It will not go "on stream" during 19X8.

3. Evaluate the budget cash positions developed in requirement 1.

CASE 12-6   *Prepare a cash performance report and an analysis of cash flows for the remainder of the budget period*

Shadow Retail Company prepares its short-term profit plan on a semiannual basis, detailed by months. The company has been experiencing considerable difficulty with working capital, especially cash. Payments on a serial bond issue are a heavy drain on cash. The last bond payment is to be made in 19X2. Certain data as of March 31, 19X2 are given below.

1 The cash budget for the six months ending June 30, 19X2 is shown on p. 464.

2 Actual results of operations in respect to cash for three months ending March 31, 19X2:
Cash receipts—Cash sales: Jan.–Feb., $173,000 (cumulative): March, $81,000. Receivable collections: Jan.–Feb., $61,000; March $34,000. Notes collected: Jan.–Feb., $8,000; March, $3,000. Other income: Jan.–Feb., $6,200; March, $3,400.
Cash payments—Raw material purchases: Jan.–Feb., $36,000 (cumulative): March, $18,000. Accounts paid: Jan.–Feb., $51,000; March, $28,000. Notes paid: Jan.–Feb., $10,000; March, $10,000. Expenses paid: Jan.–Feb., $115,700; March $68,200. Other expenses: Jan.–Feb., $13,000; March, $5,500. Capital expenditures: Jan.–Feb., $10,500; March, $900.

REQUIRED

1. Prepare a performance report of cash receipts and disbursements as of March 31, 19X2 (March and cumulative). Provide comments where appropriate.

2. Prepare an analysis of the probable cash position for the remainder of the six-month interim financing. The present line of credit is $50,000. Provide comments where appropriate.

Shadow Retail Company Cash Budget
(Six Months Ending June 30, 19X2)

	JANUARY	FEBRUARY	MARCH	APRIL	MAY	JUNE	TOTAL
Beginning cash balance	$ 20,000	$ 33,500	$ 40,800	$ 47,500	($21,300)	($15,300)	$ 20,000
Cash receipts (inflows):							
Cash sales	80,000	90,000	90,000	75,000	70,000	65,000	470,000
Accounts receivable	30,000	35,000	36,000	25,000	20,000	20,000	166,000
Notes receivable	5,000	2,000	3,000	8,000	3,000	6,000	27,000
Other incomes	3,000	3,000	3,500	3,000	2,500	2,500	17,500
Sale treasury stock				18,000			18,000
Total cash receipts	118,000	130,000	132,500	129,000	95,500	93,500	698,500
Total cash available	138,000	163,500	173,300	176,500	74,200	78,200	718,500
Cash payments (outflows):							
Merchandise purchases	15,000	$17,000	16,000	$ 8,000	$ 14,000	13,000	83,000
Accounts payable	25,000	28,000	26,000	12,000	17,300	25,000	133,300
Notes payable	10,000		10,000				20,000
Expenses	48,500	61,700	66,600	54,800	52,700	49,500	333,800
Dividends						15,000	15,000
Bonds				40,000			40,000
Other expenses	5,000	6,000	6,000	4,500	4,500	4,000	30,000
Income taxes				78,000			78,000
Capital expenditures	1,000	10,000	1,200	500	1,000	500	14,200
Total cash payments	104,500	122,700	125,800	$197,800	89,500	107,000	747,300
Ending cash balance (before financing)	33,500	40,800	47,500	($21,300)	(15,300)	(28,800)	(28,800)
Interim financing				35,000*			35,000
Ending cash balance (after financing)	$ 33,500	$ 40,800	$ 47,500	$ 13,700	$ 19,700	$ 6,200	$ 6,200

*Six months' bank loan $35,000 @ 5%.

464

CASE 12-7   *Examine a recommended cash budget; should it be approved?*

The treasurer of Bandy Company received the following 19X8 cash budget summary from a new employee. Attached to it was this note: "I have prepared this summary from the appropriate budget schedules, and it has tentatively been approved by the executive committee. I recommended that you approve it because it agrees with the detailed cash receipts and cash payments attached to it."

Bandy Company
Budget Summary
(000 dollars)

	BEGINNING	COLLECTIONS*	TOTAL	PAYMENTS*	ENDING
January	$ 80*	$ 482	$ 562	$ 430	$ 132
February	132	1,497†	1,629	490	1,139
March	1,193	498	1,691	520	1,171
Second Quarter	1,171	1,239	2,410	914	1,496
Third Quarter	1,496	1,572	3,068	2,423	744
Fourth Quarter	744	1,217	1,961	1,861	100

*These amounts have been verified.
†Sold fixed assets, $1,000.

REQUIRED

1. Would you recommend approval of the above budget summary? Why?
2. If your answer is no, prepare a summary that you would recommend. State any assumptions that you make.

Completion and Application of the Profit Plan

13

INTRODUCTION AND PURPOSE   The planning process coordinates a long-range profit plan and a short-range profit plan. Chapters 4 through 12 discussed the components of the planning process and the resulting profit plans. This chapter discusses completion of the planning cycle. At this point, planned financial statements are developed to report the financial results of the various functional subplans and commitments. Three topics in profit planning and control that were deferred until this point are discussed in the following order:

1   Completion of the profit plan
2   Analysis, evaluation, and choice among alternatives in developing the profit plan
3   Implementation of the completed profit plan

COMPLETION OF THE PROFIT PLAN   The development of an annual profit plan ends with the planned income statement, the planned balance sheet, and the planned statement of cash flows. These three statements summarize and integrate the detailed plans developed by management for the planning period. They also report the primary impacts of the detailed plans on the financial characteristics of the company.

At this point in profit planning, the budget director has an important responsibility. Aside from designing and improving the overall system, the budget director has been described as an adviser to the various managers to help develop plans for each responsibility center. Now the parts must be assembled into a complete profit plan. This is the responsibility of the budget director. Other essential subbudgets not already discussed are the following:

1   Planned statement of cost of goods manufactured
2   Planned statement of cost of goods sold

3 Planned income statements
4 Planned statement of cash flows
5 Planned balance sheet

These subbudgets, which have only been tentatively approved, must now be combined by the budget director to compute planned net income, assets, liabilities, owners' equity and cash flows. These are the final steps in the development of the detailed plans. The last section of this chapter illustrates this combining process for Superior Manufacturing Company.

Prior to distributing the completed profit plan, it is generally desirable to restate certain budget schedules (some of which were previously illustrated as spreadsheets) so that technical accounting mechanics, computations, and jargon can be avoided as much as possible. The redesigned budget schedules should be assembled in a logical order, reproduced, and distributed before the first day of the planned budget period. When assembled, the completed plan is variously referred to as the profit plan, the planning budget, the plan, the master budget, the forecast budget, the financial budget, the operating plan, or the plan of operations. Throughout this book, the terms **tactical** or **short-term profit plan** and **strategic** or **long-term profit plan** have been used. Many organizations drop the word "budget" entirely and use instead such terms as **profit plan** or simply the **plan.** There are behavioral reasons for this terminology. Over the years, many people have tended to associated the word "budget" with restrictions, pressure devices, and limitations. This unfavorable attitude can be traced to a misunderstanding of the purposes and to misuses of budgets. Aside from these attitudinal considerations, terms such as **profit plan** are more descriptive of the characteristics and objectives of comprehensive profit planning and control.

In arranging the schedules to be included in the final profit plan, the budget director should consider management preferences, as well as the principles of effective communication. No one arrangement is best in all situations. As a general rule, however, it is preferable to place the planned financial statements before the supporting subbudgets, such as the sales, expense, cash, and capital additions budgets. The arrangement should emphasize responsibility centers from the top down.

The budget director should have a limited number of copies of the entire profit plan to control its distribution, which should vary from the distribution of specific schedules. It may be desirable to use loose-leaf binding because the budget should be viewed as a flexible document to be revised as circumstances warrant. Revision may involve one or more subbudgets, depending on the extent of the revision. The profit plan completion date is important. Issuance of a profit plan after the beginning of the budget period is one sure way to destroy much of the budget's potential. Timely completion of the budget suggests the need for a budget calendar (see Chapter 4).

ALTERNATIVES IN DEVELOPING THE PROFIT PLAN The clerical and mechanical parts of profit plan development might suggest that once the sales plan is complete, this can be followed by a series of simple clerical activities that result in the production, inventory, purchases, labor, and materials budgets. This view is misleading because it ignores the fundamental importance of decision making, policy formulation, and consideration of alternative actions throughout the planning process. We have emphasized the importance of participation by all members of management in providing the decisional inputs. The development of decisional inputs and the preparation of a subbudget by the manager of each responsibility center is the heart of a comprehensive profit planning and control program.

Management choices among numerous alternatives are essential to building a realistic plan of operations. Throughout the preceding chapters, references were made to tentative approval of the various subbudgets by the executive committee and the president. In giving these tentative approvals, there was step-by-step consideration of numerous alternatives. **Tentative approvals** are given in most cases, because the full impact of a selected alternative may not be fully understood until the profit plan has been completed and the financial statements have been developed.

The buildup of a profit plan will normally not, and probably should not, involve an inflexible flow of planning and decision making from one phase to the next phase. Subsequent development of other parts of the plan may indicate that a previously selected alternative should be discarded and other alternatives considered. Through this process of building, tearing down, and rebuilding, a realistic profit plan can be developed. Sometimes a plan that is almost completed has to be torn down, restudied, and rebuilt. This may be the result, for example, of an unsatisfactory profit margin, return on investment ratio, or cash flow. Management must then develop a strategy that can "turn the plan around." Of course, to be realistic, there may be circumstances where a loss must be planned. Various procedures such as ratio analysis can be used to help management test and evaluate proposed courses of action.

Numerous situations have been cited to show how management, in the process of developing the profit plan, is faced with alternative decisions. Some illustrations demonstrated how to evaluate alternatives and select among them. Other important areas where planning alternatives must be considered and choices made are as follows:

1 **Sales Prices**—Management must set pricing policy and estimate the quantities of goods that can be sold at given prices. Evaluation of such factors as product costs, the market, economic trends, and competitor prices is essential in selecting the optimal price.

2 **General Advertising Policies**—Limitation of advertising expenditures—local versus national, and product versus institutional advertising—are decision areas where alternative choices must be made early in the planning process.

3 **Sales Territory and Sales Force Expansion or Contraction**—Decisions in these functions should be based on knowledgeable studies of market potential, either by company personnel or by outside professionals.

4 **Sales Mix**—Sales mix refers to the relative sales emphasis given to the various products sold by the company. The relative profitability of each product must be assessed. In the analysis of product profitability, it is important that the product costs be realistic. Fixed and variable cost identification, as in the flexible budget, provides a valuable tool for differential cost analysis by product (see Chapter 4).

5 **Balance between Sales, Production, and Inventory Levels**—Mathematical models and computer applications are particularly useful in selecting the preferred economic alternative in this critical coordination problem (see Chapter 6).

6 **Research and Development Expenditures**—This is one of the alternative decision areas that must be based primarily on long-range objectives, judgment, competition, and the company's ability to finance research.

7 **Capital Expenditures**—Cost and income analyses, evaluation of cost and income differentials, and discounted cash flow computations are the primary considerations for assessing alternatives and making capital expenditures decisions (see Chapter 11).

8 **Testing Alternative Decisions**—Perhaps the primary aspect of alternative decisions is projecting the probable profit result while the profit plan is being built, rather than waiting until the budgeted financial statements are developed.

To illustrate decision 8 above, assume that the sales plan, production plan, materials budget, direct labor budget, and flexible expense budgets have tentatively been approved. From these data, for Superior Manufacturing Company, the profit is readily determinable, as shown in Exhibit 13-1. Notice in particular the use of flexible budget totals to compute the summary expense amounts. Trace the data back to the original sources, as indicated in the source column. This procedure illustrates another important use of flexible budgets, that is, to test alternatives. In the absence of flexible expense budgets, estimating expense amounts at various output or sales levels would be a burdensome task. Exhibit 13-1 can show additional columns, frequently developed, to estimate profit for a series of assumed sales levels.

The analysis in Exhibit 13-1 can also be shown graphically as a breakeven chart (see Chapter 14). Many budget directors maintain informal planning spreadsheets and cost-volume-profit graphs throughout the profit planning process. These are continually revised as the various subbudgets are received from the managers of the responsibility centers. The effect of each subbudget on the final income figure is tested. This informal, step-by-step pretesting may highlight potential problems and conflicts at an early date, thereby saving considerable revision of the profit plan at later dates.

Returning to Exhibit 13-1, at this point the indicated operating profit of $827,190 should be evaluated to determine whether it is satisfactory in terms of

1 Past profit trends
2 Long-range profit objectives
3 Industry profits
4 Return on investment and earnings-per-share objectives
5 Cost-volume-profit analysis

If the profit is satisfactory, preparation of the profit plan can be continued. If the profit is unsatisfactory, management should reexamine the alternative decisions (approvals) made to date.

Ratios can also be useful in testing alternative decisions. A ratio test compares selected ratios, based on budget data, with past ratios of the (1) com-

EXHIBIT 13-1

Spreadsheet to Estimate Profit During the Budget Process, Superior Manufacturing Company, 19X2

SOURCE (SCHEDULE NO.)	COMPUTATIONS		AMOUNTS
1	Sales		$6,095,000
	Costs for year:		
29	Direct material	$1,416,600	
30	Direct labor	1,752,000	
	Manufacturing overhead:		
42 and 31	Dept. 1 ($14,000 × 12) + ($31 × 4,880)	319,280	
42 and 31	Dept. 2 ($1,960 × 12) + ($3 × 1,920)	29,280	
42 and 31	Dept. 3 ($4,180 × 12) + ($11 × 4,880)	103,840	
41 and 31	General and Administrative		
	($8,760 × 12) + ($1.00 × 11,680)	116,800	
41 and Estimate	Power ($6,700 × 12) + ($1.48 × 20,000)	110,000	
41 and Estimate	Repair ($720 × 12) + ($.34 × 4,000)	10,000	
Estimated	Building services	90,000	
	Total	$ 779,200	
Estimated	Add inventory	106,800	4,054,600
	Indicated gross margin		2,040,400
	Distribution costs:		
21 and 43	Southern district		
	($9,400 × 12) + ($5.748 × 21,200)	234,656	
21 and 43	Eastern district		
	($12,780 × 12) + ($5.505 × 29,070)	313,391	
21 and 43	Western district		
	($4,750 × 12) + ($5.442 × 10,680)	115,120	
21 and 43	General sales overhead		
	($19,295 × 12) + ($1.063 × 60,950)	296,330	
Estimated	Building services	30,000	
	Total	$ 989,497	
	Administrative costs:		
21 and44	Administrative department		
	($6,340 × 12) + ($.122 × 60,950)	83,516	
21 and 44	Accounting department		
	($4,400 × 12) + ($.02 × 60,950)	54,020	
21 and 44	Treasurer's department		
	($3,310 × 12) + ($.27 × 60,950)	56,177	
Estimated	Building services	30,000	
	Total	$ 223,713	1,213,210
	Estimated operating profit		$ 827,190

pany, (2) industry, and (3) company objectives. Any significant difference between the ratios reflected by the budget data and these target ratios should be investigated to determine the cause. The basic ratios of a company are often difficult to change in the short run. However, if the cause can be related to specific planning decisions, policies, or assumptions that influence planned results, the ratio test has served its purpose.

The budget director should frequently apply ratio tests during the development of the profit plan. When the test shows a particular ratio to be out of line with company objectives, the executive responsible for the particular plan should be informed so that the problem can be studied. Should a preferable alternative be identified, action can be taken to revise all affected parts of the plan. Ratio tests are generally done on an informal spreadsheet maintained by the budget director. One type of ratio analysis on a spreadsheet, adapted from the procedures of an actual company, is shown in Exhibit 13-2. Although this company's budget director applies the tests using a total of sixty-three ratios, only three representative ratios related to operating profit are illustrated. Notice that the ratio test is even more useful in evaluating the plausibility of the quantified results of strategic long-range planning.

EXHIBIT 13-2

Spreadsheet for Ratio Tests of the Budget for 19X2

ITEMS TESTED (RATIO)	HISTORICAL		ANNUAL PROFIT PLAN	STRATEGIC LONG-RANGE PLAN			
	19X0	19X1	19X2	19X3	19X4	19X5	19X6
Sales Ratios:							
Growth trend							
Operating Profit Ratios:							
Profit/sales	6.08	5.92	7.21*	6.20	6.20	6.40	6.40
Sales/investment	1.97	1.96	2.14	2.26	2.25	2.30	2.30
Return on investment	11.98	11.60	15.43*	14.01	13.95	14.72	14.72

*Ratios that appear to be out of line. This potentially indicates either an error or a deficiency in planning.

IMPLEMENTING THE PROFIT PLAN   In the preceding chapters, considerable attention was given to the various segments of the annual profit plan, particularly for control purposes. The ultimate test of whether the effort and cost of developing a profit plan are worthwhile is its usefulness to management; this is a cost-benefit test. This poses some fundamental questions. How should the plans be implemented? Should the plans be followed under all circumstances? Should the profit plan be used as a pressure device? How should it be used by the top, middle, and lower levels of management?

We have emphasized that a profit plan should represent potentially attainable goals, yet the goals should present a challenge to the enterprise. The plan should be developed with the conviction that the enterprise is going to meet or exceed all major objectives. Participation enhances communication (both downward and upward). If this principle is to be effective, the various executives should have a clear understanding of their implementation responsibilities.

After approval of a profit plan, the next step is its distribution to the center managers in the enterprise. In Chapter 4, distribution instructions were illustrated as an important part of the budget manual. Recall that a limited number of copies of the complete profit plan should be prepared. Complete copies of the plan should be distributed to the vice-presidents and to the heads of certain staff groups. The guiding principle in establishing the distribution policy might be to provide one copy to each member of the management team according to his or her overall responsibilities while taking into account the problem of security. Some companies have discovered that a copy of their profit plan found its way into the hands of unauthorized parties—a competitor, for example. Most companies number each copy of the complete profit plan and keep a record of its distribution. At year-end, the copies are returned to the budget director for destruction.

The distribution policy should allow distribution of parts of the profit plan to middle and lower management. For example, a sales district supervisor would not be given a copy of the entire budget but should receive those parts that apply to the sales budget, expense budget, and advertising budget for his or her district. In preceding discussions, we suggested that the budget format should be designed as an integrated unit. However, the budget should also be segregated by responsibility centers which should be explicit by themselves.

After distribution of the profit plan, a series of profit plan conferences should be held. The top executives comprehensively discuss the plans, expectations, and steps in implementation. At this top-level meeting, the importance of action flexibility and continuous control should be emphasized. In particular, each manager must understand that the budget is a tool. The profit plan, regardless of how well designed and how carefully developed, cannot manage. In the final analysis, people, not budgets (or other similar tools), perform the management functions. Use of the profit plan as a guide to action and performance, directed toward attaining or bettering the goals quantified in the annual profit plan, requires continuous management effort and attention.

Budget conferences should be conducted until all levels of management are reached. Managers must clearly understand their responsibilities and how their part of the profit plan fits into the overall company profit plan. These conferences should induce "profit and cost awareness" throughout management and, if conducted properly, will tend to ensure positive support for the objectives. This phase of communication from the top down is an often neglected phase in management.

The profit plan provides the manager of each responsibility center an approved operating plan for the center. For example, the advertising director has an approved advertising plan related to company objectives. Within this plan, the advertising director can make decisions from day to day to execute the advertising function. Similarly, the financial executive has information about such things as expected cash receipts, cash payments, and capital expenditures. Thus, the planning budget becomes the basis for current operations and exerts important coordination and control effects.

USING THE PROFIT PLAN TO CONTROL OPERATIONS   Performance must be measured and reported at all management levels. Execution of the profit plan is ensured through control. Procedures must be established so that implementation or failure of the plan is immediately known. Action can then be taken to correct or minimize any undesirable effects. Short-term performance reporting is essential. For example, one facet in the control of sales is a comparison of actual sales with planned sales by areas of responsibility. Such a comparison at the end of the year would be of little value because it is then too late to take corrective action—what has happened, has happened! On the other hand, daily, weekly, or even monthly sales reports will give a basis for timely action by the management. If January sales are below the quota shown in the sales budget, management should determine the reasons. It may be that the condition is due to circumstances over which the management has no control and little can be done to compensate for it. On the other hand, it may be that management can correct the condition, or compensating action can be taken to increase the sales volume beyond budget figures for subsequent months of the year. It is important that management know about the trouble spots in responsibility centers as they occur so that immediate attention can be given to them. Actual figures standing alone do not indicate trouble spots; they must be compared with a standard (budget) to be identified and evaluated. Chapter 15 discusses performance reports.

One key aspect of budget implementation and control is the principle of flexibility. To view the profit plan as an inflexible blueprint of operations is to invite trouble. During the planning phase, it is impossible to anticipate all contingencies. Therefore, adjustments must be made in the operating plans and the performance reports. The budget should not be viewed as a restriction, but rather as a specification of the goals of the entity. Similarly, performance variances should be viewed flexibly. The primary purposes should be to correct problems and improve implementation. Punishment should not be the purpose of performance reports.

A budget program, viewed and administered in a sophisticated way, does not hamper or restrict management. Instead, it provides definite goals around which day-to-day and month-to-month decisions are made. Through performance reports, it helps implement the exception principle discussed in Chapter 2. Flexibility in the use and application of the profit plan, flexible budgets, and performance reports were also discussed in detail in several other chapters. Flexibility in budget application is essential, and it increases the probability of achieving or bettering the objectives as set forth in the budget.

Comprehensive Demonstration Case

 *SUPERIOR MANUFACTURING COMPANY*

To illustrate the development of the planned financial statements and completion of the short-range profit plan in a typical case, return to Superior Manufacturing Company. We recommend that you now review the subbudgets and trace the development of the following budget statements for Superior Manufacturing Company (the "Ref." column on the various budget schedules provides tracing data).

SCHEDULE NO.	DESIGNATION
58	Budgeted cost of goods manufactured—detailed
59	Budgeted cost of goods manufactured—summary
60	Spreadsheet—cost of goods sold and finished goods inventory
61	Budgeted cost of goods sold—detailed
62	Budgeted cost of goods sold—summary
63	Finished-goods inventory budget
64	Budgeted income statement by time periods
65	Budgeted income statement by sales districts (responsibility)
66	Budgeted income statement by products
67	Budget spreadsheet (for income statement and balance sheet)
68	Budgeted balance sheet—January
69	Cash flow budget

To develop the budgeted financial statements, the first logical step for Superior is preparation of the budgeted cost of goods manufactured. Budgets for materials and parts (Schedule 28), direct labor (Schedule 30), factory overhead applied (Schedule 36), and production (Schedule 22), together with work-in-process inventory, provide data that can be assembled in a schedule for budgeted cost of goods manufactured. This procedure is shown in Schedule 58. Beginning work-in-process inventories (January 1, 19X2) are as follows:

□ Product X—No work-in-process inventory throughout the year.
□ Product Y—10,000 units valued at $13,800. (This inventory is in Department 3 and remains relatively constant throughout the year.)

The budgeted cost of goods manufactured is **detailed** by product and time in Schedule 58. The budgeted cost of goods is **summarized** in Schedule 59. This schedule is developed using data from the budgeted cost of goods manufactured and finished-goods inventories. Superior Manufacturing Company uses the first-in, first-out method to cost finished-goods inventories. To compute cost of goods sold by sales district, Superior assumes that withdrawals from beginning inventories are in the ratio of district unit sales to total unit sales for

SCHEDULE 58. Superior Manufacturing Company

Budgeted Cost of Goods Manufactured—Detailed
For the Year Ending December 31, 19X2

	REF.	ANNUAL TOTAL	FIRST QUARTER				QUARTERS		
			JANUARY	FEBRUARY	MARCH	FIRST	SECOND	THIRD	FOURTH
Product X:									
Materials used	28	$1,156,600	$85,400	$97,600	$97,600	$280,600	$288,000	$276,000	$312,000
Direct labor	30	1,440,000	105,000	120,000	120,000	345,000	360,000	345,000	390,000
Prime cost		2,596,600	190,400	217,600	217,600	625,600	648,000	621,000	702,000
Overhead applied	36	633,600	46,200	52,800	52,800	151,800	158,400	151,800	171,600
Cost of goods manufactured		3,230,200	236,600	270,400	270,400	777,400	806,400	772,800	873,600
Units produced	22	960,000	70,000	80,000	80,000	230,000	240,000	230,000	260,000
Unit cost			$3.38	$3.38	$3.38	$3.38	$3.36	$3.36	$3.36
Product Y:									
Materials used	28	$ 260,000	$17,000	$18,000	$19,000	$54,000	$70,000	$63,500	$72,500
Direct labor	30	312,000	20,400	21,600	22,800	64,800	84,000	76,200	87,000
Prime cost		572,000	37,400	39,600	41,800	118,800	154,000	139,700	159,500
Overhead applied	36	145,600	9,520	10,080	10,640	30,240	39,200	35,560	40,600
Cost of goods manufactured		717,600	46,920	49,680	52,440	149,040	193,200	175,260	200,100
Units produced	22	520,000	34,000	36,000	38,000	108,000	140,000	127,000	145,000
Unit cost			$1.38	$1.38	$1.38	$1.38	$1.38	$1.38	$1.38
All products:									
Materials used	28	$1,416,600	$102,400	$115,600	$116,600	$334,600	$358,000	$339,500	$384,500
Direct labor	30	1,752,000	125,400	141,600	142,800	409,800	444,000	421,200	477,000
Prime cost		3,168,600	227,800	257,200	259,400	744,400	802,000	760,700	861,500
Overhead applied	36	779,200	55,720	62,880	63,440	182,040	197,600	187,360	212,200
Total manufacturing cost		$3,947,800	$283,520	$320,080	$322,840	$926,440	$999,600	$948,060	$1,073,700
Add beginning work-in-process inventory		13,800	13,800	13,800	13,800	13,800	13,800	13,800	13,800
Deduct ending work-in-process inventory		(13,800)	(13,800)	(13,800)	(13,800)	(13,800)	(13,800)	(13,800)	(13,800)
Cost of goods manufactured		$3,947,800	$283,520	$320,080	$322,840	$926,440	$999,600	$948,060	$1,073,700

SCHEDULE 59. Superior Manufacturing Company

Budgeted Cost of Goods Manufactured—Summary

For the Year Ending December 31, 19X2

	REF.	ANNUAL TOTAL	1ST QUARTER			QUARTERS			
			JANUARY	FEBRUARY	MARCH	FIRST	SECOND	THIRD	FOURTH
Product X:									
Cost of goods manufactured	58	$3,230,200	$236,600	$270,400	$270,400	$777,400	$806,400	$772,800	$ 873,600
Units produced	22	960,000	70,000	80,000	80,000	230,000	240,000	230,000	260,000
Unit cost	58		$3.38	$3.38	$3.38	$3.38	$3.36	$3.36	$3.36
Product Y:									
Cost of goods manufactured	58	$ 717,600	$ 46,920	$ 49,680	$ 52,440	$149,040	$193,200	$175,260	$ 200,100
Units produced	22	520,000	34,000	36,000	38,000	108,000	140,000	127,000	145,000
Unit cost	58		$1.38	$1.38	$1.38	$1.38	$1.38	$1.38	$1.38
All products:									
Cost of goods manufactured	58	$3,947,800	$283,520	$320,080	$322,840	$926,440	$999,600	$948,060	$1,073,700

each period. Beginning inventories (January 1, 19X2) of finished goods are estimated to be as follows:

	PRODUCT X	PRODUCT Y
Units	240,000	100,000
Valuation	$806,400	$138,000

Cost of goods sold is developed by product, by time period, and by sales district. A spreadsheet (Schedule 60) is used for this purpose. Detailed results are shown in Schedule 61 (budgeted cost of goods sold) and are summarized in Schedule 62.

Schedule 23 (Chapter 6) illustrated the finished-goods inventory budget. When this schedule was originally developed, only the units were known. Data developed in Schedule 60 (budget spreadsheet) make possible the completion of the finished-goods inventory budget, which is illustrated in Schedule 63.

At this point, the budgeted income statement can be developed by assembling appropriate budget amounts from schedules already developed as shown in Schedule 64 (by time period), Schedule 65 (by sales district), and Schedule 66 (by product).

The budgeted balance sheet can be developed directly from previous schedules much like the income statement. The budgeted balance sheet requires the use of the cash budget, capital expenditures budget, and other budgets to the estimated balances in the accounts at the beginning of the budget year. Thus, the process is more involved than is the development of the income statement. Although it is possible to develop the balance sheet directly from the preceding budget schedules, it is usually preferable to set up a special spreadsheet for this purpose, as shown for Superior Manufacturing Company in Schedule 67. The spreadsheet is developed from the estimated trial balance as of December 31, 19X1, which is shown in the first two columns of the spreadsheet. Remember that this trial balance (December 31, 19X1) is needed before the end of the current operating period (19X1) if the 19X2 budget is to be completed and distributed before the beginning of the budget year. This requirement does not deter completion of the planning budget. This trial balance can usually be estimated with reasonable accuracy by the accounting department by using the November 19X1 actual balance and the current December 19X1 budget. In some cases, it becomes necessary to revise parts of the planning budget after its initial distribution. This revision should be made if the estimated year-end trial balance turns out to have been incorrect by a significant amount.

The resulting annual 19X2 balance sheet for Superior Manufacturing Company was shown in Schedule 17 (Chapter 4). Monthly budgeted balance sheets can also be prepared. Since they require little time to prepare, they may

SCHEDULE 60. Superior Manufacturing Company

Budget Spreadsheet—Cost of Goods Sold and Finished-Goods Inventory

(First-In, First-Out)

For the Year Ending December 31, 19X2

| | TOTAL | | | SALES DISTRICTS | | | | | |
| | | | | SOUTHERN | | EASTERN | | WESTERN | |
	UNITS	UNIT COST	COST	UNITS	COST	UNITS	COST	UNITS	COST
Product X:									
January									
Beginning inventory	240,000	$3.36	$ 806,400						
Production	70,000	3.38	236,600						
Total	310,000		$1,043,000						
Sales at cost	85,000	3.36	285,600	30,000	$ 100,800	40,000	$ 134,400	15,000	$ 50,400
Inventory	155,000	3.36	757,400						
	70,000	3.38							
February production	80,000	3.38	270,400						
Total	155,000	3.36	$1,027,800						
	150,000	3.38							
Sales at cost	90,000	3.36	302,400	35,000	117,600	45,000	151,200	10,000	33,600
Ending inventory	65,000	3.36	725,400						
	150,000	3.38							
March production	80,000	3.36	270,400						
Total	65,000	3.36	$ 995,800						
	230,000	3.38							

	TOTAL Units	TOTAL Unit cost	TOTAL Cost	SOUTHERN Units	SOUTHERN Cost	EASTERN Units	EASTERN Cost	WESTERN Units	WESTERN Cost
Sales at cost	65,000	3.36	$ 218,400	20,526*	$ 68,967	34,211	$ 114,949	10,263	$ 34,484
	30,000	3.38	101,400	9,474	32,022	15,789	53,367	4,737	16,011
Inventory	200,000	3.38	676,000						
2nd Quarter production	240,000	3.38	806,400						
Total			$1,482,400						
Sales at cost	200,000	3.38	676,000	69,231†	234,000	103,846	351,000	26,923	91,000
	60,000	3.36	201,600	20,769	69,784	31,154	104,677	8,077	27,139
Inventory	180,000	3.36	604,800						
3rd Quarter production	230,000	3.36	772,800						
Total	410,000	3.36	$1,377,600						
Sales at cost	190,000	3.36	638,400	65,000	218,400	90,000	302,400	35,000	117,600
Inventory	220,000	3.36	739,200						
4th Quarter production	260,000	3.36	873,600						
Total	480,000	3.36	$1,612,800						
Sales at cost	280,000	3.36	940,800	90,000	302,400	140,000	470,400	50,000	168,000
Inventory	200,000	3.36	672,000						
Total sales at cost	1,000,000		$3,364,600	340,000	$1,143,973	500,000	$1,682,393	160,000	$538,234
Product Y: January									
Beginning inventory	100,000	$1.38	$ 138,000						
Production	34,000	1.38	46,920						
Total	134,000		$ 184,920						
Sales at cost	34,000	1.38	46,920	15,000	$ 20,700	11,000	$ 15,180	8,000	$ 11,040

SCHEDULE 60. (Continued)

| | TOTAL | | | SALES DISTRICTS | | | | | |
| | | | | SOUTHERN | | EASTERN | | WESTERN | |
	UNITS	UNIT COST	COST	UNITS	COST	UNITS	COST	UNITS	COST
Inventory	100,000	1.38	$ 138,000						
February production	36,000	1.38	49,680						
Total	136,000		$ 187,680						
Sales at cost	41,000	1.38	56,580	16,000	$ 22,080	14,000	$ 19,320	11,000	$ 15,180
Inventory	95,000	1.38	131,100						
March production	38,000	1.38	52,440						
Total	133,000		$ 183,540						
Sales at cost	45,000	1.38	62,100	19,000	26,220	15,000	20,700	11,000	15,180
Inventory	88,000	1.38	121,440						
2nd Quarter production	140,000	1.38	193,200						
Total	228,000		$ 314,640						
Sales at cost	135,000	1.38	186,300	55,000	75,900	45,000	62,100	35,000	48,300
Inventory	93,000	1.38	128,340						
3rd Quarter production	127,000	1.38	175,260						
Total	220,000		$ 303,600						
Sales at cost	95,000	1.38	131,100	40,000	55,200	35,000	48,300	20,000	27,600
Inventory	125,000	1.38	172,500						
4th Quarter production	145,000	1.38	200,100						
Total	270,000		$ 372,600						
Sales at cost	150,000	1.38	207,000	65,000	89,700	50,000	69,000	35,000	48,300
Inventory	120,000	1.38	165,600						
Total sales at cost	500,000		$ 690,000	$210,000	$ 289,800	170,000	$ 234,600	120,000	$165,600

Computations:

*March sales in dist.—Sch. 5 / March total sales—Sch. 5 $\times$ March sales costing $3.36 / 1 = Allocation to district

$\dfrac{30,000}{95,000} \times \dfrac{65,000}{1} = 20,526$

$^\dagger \dfrac{90,000}{260,000} \times \dfrac{200,000}{1} = 69,231$

480

SCHEDULE 61. Superior Manufacturing Company

Budgeted Cost of Goods Sold—Detailed
For the Year Ending December 31, 19X2

	REF.	TOTAL ALL DISTRICTS		SOUTHERN DISTRICT		EASTERN DISTRICT		WESTERN DISTRICT	
		UNITS	COST	UNITS	COST	UNITS	COST	UNITS	COST
		21	60	21	60	21	60	21	60
Product X:									
January		85,000	$ 285,600	30,000	$ 100,800	40,000	$ 134,400	15,000	$ 50,400
February		90,000	302,400	35,000	117,600	45,000	151,200	10,000	33,600
March		95,000	319,800	30,000	100,989	50,000	168,316	15,000	50,495
Total 1st Quarter		270,000	907,800	95,000	319,389	135,000	453,916	40,000	134,495
2nd Quarter		260,000	877,600	90,000	303,785	135,000	455,677	35,000	118,138
3rd Quarter		190,000	638,400	65,000	218,400	90,000	302,400	35,000	117,600
4th Quarter		280,000	940,800	90,000	302,400	140,000	470,400	50,000	168,000
Total Product X		1,000,000	$3,364,600	340,000	$1,143,974	500,000	$1,682,393	160,000	$538,233
Product Y:									
January		34,000	$ 46,920	15,000	$ 20,700	11,000	$ 15,180	8,000	$ 11,040
February		41,000	56,580	16,000	22,080	14,000	19,320	11,000	15,180
March		45,000	62,100	19,000	26,220	15,000	20,700	11,000	15,180
Total 1st Quarter		120,000	165,600	50,000	69,000	40,000	55,200	30,000	41,400
2nd Quarter		135,000	186,300	55,000	75,900	45,000	62,100	35,000	48,300
3rd Quarter		95,000	131,100	40,000	55,200	35,000	48,300	20,000	27,600
4th Quarter		150,000	207,000	65,000	89,700	50,000	69,000	35,000	48,300
Total Product Y		500,000	$ 690,000	210,000	$ 289,800	170,000	$ 234,600	120,000	$165,600
All Products:									
January			$ 332,520		$ 121,500		$ 149,580		$ 61,440
February			358,980		139,680		$ 170,520		48,780
March			381,900		127,209		189,016		65,675
Total 1st Quarter			1,073,400		388,389		509,116		175,895
2nd Quarter			1,063,900		379,685		517,777		166,438
3rd Quarter			769,500		273,600		350,700		145,200
4th Quarter			1,147,800		392,100		539,400		216,300
Total for year			$4,054,600		$1,433,774		$1,916,993		$703,833

SCHEDULE 62. Superior Manufacturing Company

Budgeted Cost of Goods Sold—Summary
For the Year Ending December 31, 19X2

| | | TOTAL ALL DISTRICTS | | SALES DISTRICTS | | | | | |
| | | | | SOUTHERN | | EASTERN | | WESTERN | |
	REF.	UNITS	COST	UNITS	COST	UNITS	COST	UNITS	COST
Products:									
X	60	1,000,000	$3,364,600	340,000	$1,143,974	500,000	$1,682,393	160,000	$538,233
Y	60	500,000	690,000	210,000	289,800	170,000	234,600	120,000	165,600
Total Cost			$4,054,600		$1,433,774		$1,916,993		$703,833

SCHEDULE 63. Superior Manufacturing Company

Finished-Goods Inventory Budget
For the Year Ending December 31, 19X2

	Ref.	TOTAL COST	PRODUCT X			PRODUCT Y		
			UNITS 23	UNIT COST 60	TOTAL COST	UNITS 23	UNIT COST 60	TOTAL COST
January 1, 19X2		$944,400	240,000	$3.36	$806,400	100,000	$1.38	$138,000
January 31, 19X2		895,400	225,000	*	$757,400	100,000	1.38	138,000
February 28, 19X2		856,400	215,000	†	725,400	95,000	1.38	131,100
March 31, 19X2		797,440	200,000	3.38	676,000	88,000	1.38	121,440
End of 2nd Quarter		733,140	180,000	3.36	604,800	93,000	1.38	128,340
End of 3rd Quarter		911,700	220,000	3.36	739,200	125,000	1.38	172,500
End of 4th Quarter		837,600	200,000	3.36	672,000	120,000	1.38	165,600

*70,000 units at $3.38, and 155,000 units at $3.36.
†150,000 units at $3.38, and 65,000 units at $3.36.

SCHEDULE 64. Superior Manufacturing Company

Budgeted Income Statement—By Time Periods
For the Year Ending December 31, 19X2

| | REF. | ANNUAL | FIRST QUARTER | | | QUARTERS | | | |
			JANUARY	FEBRUARY	MARCH	FIRST	SECOND	THIRD	FOURTH
Sales (net)	21	$6,095,000	$500,400	$540,000	$574,100	$1,614,500	$1,595,000	$1,158,000	$1,727,500
Less cost of goods sold	61	4,054,600	332,520	358,980	381,900	1,073,400	1,063,900	769,500	1,147,800
Gross margin		2,040,400	167,880	181,020	192,200	541,100	531,100	388,500	579,700
Less:									
Selling expenses	39	989,497	82,109	84,608	86,769	253,486	251,915	222,977	261,119
Administrative expenses	40	223,713	18,752	18,735	18,859	56,346	55,999	54,321	57,047
Total		1,213,210	100,861	103,343	105,628	309,832	307,914	277,298	318,166
Operating income		827,190	67,019	77,677	86,572	231,268	223,186	111,202	261,534
Add:									
Interest income	53	500	42	41	42	125	125	125	125
Other income	49	37,120	3,390	2,950	3,620	9,960	9,510	8,220	9,430
		864,810	70,451	80,668	90,234	241,355	232,821	119,547	271,089
Less interest expense	53	3,750	667	416	667	1,750	1,000	500	500
Income before income tax		861,060	$ 69,784	$ 80,252	$ 89,567	$ 239,603	$ 231,821	$ 119,047	$ 270,589
Percent of sales		14.13	13.9	14.8	15.6	14:8	14.5	10.3	15.7
Federal income taxes	53	258,318							
Net Income		$ 602,742							

SCHEDULE 65. Superior Manufacturing Company

Budgeted Income Statement—By Sales Districts
For the Year Ending December 31, 19X2

	REF.	TOTAL	SALES DISTRICT		
			SOUTHERN	EASTERN	WESTERN
Sales (net)	21	$6,095,000	$2,120,000	$2,907,000	$1,068,000
Cost of goods sold	61	4,054,600	1,433,773	1,916,993	703,834
Gross margin		2,040,400	686,227	990,007	364,166
District sales expenses	39	663,167	234,656	313,391	115,120
District direct operating profit		1,377,233	451,571	676,616	249,046
Percent of net sales		22.6	21.3	23.3	23.3
Allocations:					
General sales overhead	39	296,330			
Administrative expenses	40	193,713			
Building services	32	60,000			
To be allocated		550,043	191,305	262,370	96,368
Allocation basis*			(34.78%)	(47.70%)	(17.52%)
District operating income		827,190	$ 60,266	$ 414,246	$ 152,678
Percent of net sales		13.57	12.3	14.2	14.3
Add net of other incomes and expenses	49 & 53	33,870			
Income before income tax		861,060			
Federal income tax	53	258,318			
Net income		$ 602,742			

*On basis of net sales

be justified. The January balance sheet is shown in Schedule 68. Notice the contingent liability explained in the footnote and the way that manufacturing overhead (overapplied and underapplied) is reported on the monthly balance sheet. The latter item does not appear on the annual balance sheet because by that time its balance is zero. Preparation of the monthly balance sheets can be facilitated through the use of a spreadsheet like Schedule 67.

The cash flow budget, detailed by month is shown in Schedule 69. The cash budget summary was shown in Schedule 55 (Chapter 12).

Superior Manufacturing Company prepares a budgeted statement of cash flows. After completion of the above remaining schedules, the annual profit plan is given to the executive committee and to the chief executive for approval. Upon final approval, the budget director reproduces it for distribution to specified managers.

SCHEDULE 66. Superior Manufacturing Company

Budgeted Income Statement—By Products
For the Year Ending December 31, 19X2

	REF.	TOTAL	PRODUCT	
			X	Y
Sales	21	$6,095,000	$5,066,000	$1,029,000
Cost of goods sold	61	4,054,600	3,364,600	690,000
Gross margin		2,040,400	1,701,400	339,000
Allocations:				
District sales expenses	39	663,167		
General sales overhead	39	296,330		
Administrative expenses	40	193,713		
Building services	32	60,000		
Total to be allocated		1,213,210		
Allocation basis*			1,008,420	204,790
			(83.12%)	(16.88%)
Operating income		827,190	$ 692,980	$ 134,210
Percent of sales		13.57	13.68	12.07
Add net of other incomes and expenses	49& 53	33,870		
Income before income tax		861,060		
Federal income tax	53	258,318		
Net income		$ 602,742		

* On basis of net sales.

SCHEDULE 67. Superior Manufacturing Company

Budget Spreadsheet
For the Year Ending December 31, 19X2

	TRIAL BALANCE DEC. 31, 19X1		BUDGET ENTRIES* FOR 19X2		WORK IN PROCESS		INCOME STATEMENT		BALANCE SHEET DEC. 31, 19X2	
	DR	CR	DR	CR	DR	CR	DR	CR	DR	CR
Cash	54,000		17—6,133,006	17—5,560,490					626,516	
Accounts receivable	160,000		1—6,095,000	10—6,095,886 11—3,000					156,114	
Allowance for doubtful accounts		9,000	11—3,000	9—12,190						18,190
Material inventory	257,600		2—1,419,000	3—1,416,600					260,000	
Work-in-process inventory	13,800				13,800				13,800	
Finished-goods inventory	944,400					13,800	944,400	837,600	837,600	
Prepaid insurance	2,532		15—22,788	5—3,600 6—3,036 9—960					17,724	
Supplies inventory	13,700		15—41,140	6—49,640					5,200	
Land	25,000								25,000	
Building, machinery, and equipment	2,080,000		14—8,700						2,088,700	
Accumulated depreciation		443,380		5—60,000 6—19,560 8—600 9—4,200						527,740
Building fund	20,000		14—20,000 18—500						40,500	
Accounts payable		52,100	13—1,429,140	2—1,419,000						41,960
Audit fee payable		2,400	15—2,400	9—2,400						2,400
Accrued interest expense		7,000	15—8,000	19—2,750						1,750
Property taxes payable		4,982	15—4,982	5—2,400 6—4,164 9—720						7,284

SCHEDULE 67. (Continued)

	TRIAL BALANCE DEC. 31, 19X1		BUDGET ENTRIES* FOR 19X2		WORK IN PROCESS		INCOME STATEMENT		BALANCE SHEET DEC. 31, 19X2	
	DR	CR	DR	CR	DR	CR	DR	CR	DR	CR
Income taxes payable		279,400	15—279,400	20—258,318						258,318
Notes payable—long-term		200,000	15—150,000							50,000
Common stock		2,000,000								2,000,000
Retained earnings		522,770	15—12,000							510,770
Premium on stock		50,000								50,000
	3,571,032	3,571,032								
Sales				1—6,095,000				6,095,000		
Material used			3—1,416,600		1,416,600					
Building services			5—150,000	7—150,000						
Factory overhead			6—689,200 7—90,000		779,200					
Direct labor			4—1,752,000		4—1,752,000					
Selling expenses			7—30,000 8—959,497				989,497			
Administrative expenses			9—193,713 7—30,000				223,713			
Interest expense			16—1,000 19—2,750				3,750			
Interest income				18—500				500		
Other income				12—37,120				37,120		
Income tax expense			20—258,318				258,318			
Cost of goods manufactured						3,947,800	3,947,800			
					3,961,600	3,961,600	602,742			602,742
Net income							6,970,220	6,970,220	4,071,154	4,071,154

*The reference numbers are schedule numbers that provide the data needed for the budget.

SCHEDULE 68. Superior Manufacturing Company

Budgeted Balance Sheet—January[*]
For the Month Ending January 31, 19X2

ASSETS			
Current assets:			
Cash	$	$ 163,374	
Accounts receivable	157,793		
Less allowance for doubtful accounts	10,001	147,792	
Raw material inventory		253,100	
Work-in-process inventory		13,800	
Finished-goods inventory		895,400	
Prepaid insurance		1,899	
Supplies inventory		13,457	$1,488,822
Funds:			
Building fund			20,042
Operational (fixed) assets:			
Land		25,000	
Building	1,800,000		
Less accumulated depreciation	365,000	1,435,000	
Machinery and equipment	280,200		
Less accumulated depreciation	85,261	194,939	1,654,939
Deferred charges:			
Factory overhead underapplied			6,637
Total assets			$3,170,440

LIABILITIES AND CAPITAL			
Current liabilities:			
Accounts payable	$	$ 32,630	$
Audit fee payable		2,600	
Property taxes payable		5,589	
Accrued interest expense		7,667	
Income taxes payable[†]		300,335	348,821
Long-term liabilities:			
Long-term notes payable			200,000
Stockholders' equity			
Common stock		2,000,000	
Premium on common stock		50,000	
Retained earnings	522,770		
Add January net income	48,849	571,619	2,621,619
Total liabilities and stockholders' equity			$3,170,440

[*]See Schedule 17 for annual balance sheet.
[†]Litigation currently in progress may result in payment of approximately $620,000 as an adjustment of prior years' federal income taxes.

SCHEDULE 69. Superior Manufacturing Company

Cash Flow Budget—Detailed (By Month and Quarters)
For the Year Ending December 31, 19X2

	REF.	YEAR	JANUARY	FEBRUARY	MARCH	1ST QUARTER	2ND QUARTER	3RD QUARTER	4TH QUARTER
Beginning cash balance	57	$ 54,000	$ 54,000	$163,374	$116,518	$ 54,000	$ 76,739	$ 300,711	$ 298,617
Budgeted cash receipts (inflow)									
Collections of accounts receivable (sales)	50	6,095,886	502,607	531,054	563,383	1,597,044	1,625,692	1,190,574	1,682,576
Other income	50	37,120	3,390	2,950	3,620	9,960	9,510	8,220	9,430
Proceeds of short-term notes payable	56	100,000			100,000	100,000			
Total budgeted receipts (inflow)	55	6,233,006	505,997	534,004	667,003	1,707,004	1,635,202	1,198,794	1,692,006
Total (beginning balance + receipts)	55	6,287,006	559,997	697,378	783,521	1,761,004	1,611,941	1,500,505	1,991,623
Budgeted cash payments (outflows)									
Material purchases—accounts payable	54	1,429,140	117,370	119,100	122,500	358,970	371,190	327,530	371,450
Direct labor	54	1,752,000	125,400	141,600	142,800	409,800	444,000	421,200	477,000
Factory overhead costs	52	612,800	48,713	50,475	50,610	149,798	154,020	151,296	157,686
Distribution expenses	52	958,897	79,419	82,098	84,275	245,792	244,489	215,427	253,189
Administrative expenses	52	173,243	14,421	14,505	14,577	43,503	43,463	42,535	43,742
Building services	52	84,000	7,700	6,800	6,720	21,220	19,880	20,500	22,400
Capital expenditures	54	28,700	200			200			28,500
Notes payable	56 & 57	250,000		150,000*		150,000	100,000		
Dividends	54	12,000						12,000	
Accrued and deferred items (excluding dividends)	53	359,710	3,400	16,282	285,300	304,982	34,188	10,400	10,140
Total budgeted payments	55	5,660,490	396,623	580,860	706,782	1,684,265	1,411,230	1,200,888	1,364,107
Ending cash balance, Dec. 31, 19X2	55	$ 626,516	$163,374	$116,518	$ 76,739	$ 76,739	$ 300,711	$ 298,617	$ 626,516

*Long-term note payable.

CHAPTER SUMMARY   The planning process involves a long-range profit plan and a short-range profit plan. In developing these plans, many budget schedules are prepared to detail plans for each phase of a company's operations. The final step in the planning process is to complete the profit plan by combining the component schedules and preparing planned financial statements. Planned statements of financial position, income, and cash flows are prepared in order to determine the implications of the company's plans for its future financial condition.

The profit plan or a subset of its parts is then distributed to appropriate managerial personnel to guide them in conducting operations throughout the planning period.

Although some retail firms budget only sales, stock levels, and purchases, a comprehensive profit planning and control program extending to all phases of operations is desirable. In such cases, the several subbudgets (sales, stock, purchases, expenses, capital expenditure, cash, and so on) are summarized in the budgeted income statement, budgeted balance sheet, and cash flow budget.

Discussion Questions

1. Why should planned financial statements be developed as part of the profit plan?
2. What should be the budget director's responsibility for completing and assembling the components of the annual profit plan?
3. During the planning process, why should the various subbudgets usually be given tentative, rather than final, approval?
4. Explain how flexible expense budgets can be used in "testing" the appropriateness of the profit plan during the process of its development.
5. What is meant by a ratio test? Explain its applicability with respect to (a) development of the annual profit plan and (b) long-range planning.
6. The annual profit plan should be completed prior to the beginning of the period for which the budget is being made. To complete it, the trial balance as of the end of the current year is needed before that period ends. What can be done to resolve this apparent inconsistency?
7. Outline the distribution of the annual profit plan in a typical situation.
8. Why should the annual profit plan and the flexible expense budgets be assembled under separate covers?
9. Discuss the advantages of two alternatives concerning distribution of the annual profit plan: alternative 1—distribute through company mail; alternative 2—distribute through line channels supplemented with conferences.
10. Why is it essential that management apply the annual profit plan in a flexible manner?

11. How could computers, and in particular personal computers, assist management in doing ratio tests and investigating the impact of alternative operational plans on the budget?

CASE 13-1   *Develop policies for distribution of the annual profit plan*

The annual profit plan for 19X2 for Superior Manufacturing Company was completed on December 17, 19X1, as illustrated in this and the preceding chapters. The staff assistant to the president is developing a distribution policy for the annual profit plan (including the flexible expense budgets). Assume you are the staff assistant and have been asked to give your recommendations.

REQUIRED
1. Give your recommendations about the following:
   a. What responsibilities should be assigned for distribution of the profit plan?
   b. How should the budget be distributed?
   c. On what date should the budget be distributed?
   d. What special management activities should be initiated immediately after the budget distribution? Give dates, chairperson, participants, and purpose.
2. What should be included in the packages for the various managers? In response to this problem, the president has requested that you indicate for each of the following groups the package by schedule numbers (1 through 69). Thus, you are to list the following and indicate after each the appropriate schedule numbers:
   a. President
   b. Vice-presidents
   c. Controller
   d. Treasurer
   e. Sales district supervisor (list each district separately)
   f. Factory supervisors (list each department separately)
   g. Other individuals or groups (list each)
   h. Schedules not to be distributed
   Prior to making your recommendations, you should review the organization chart for the company, the budget manual, and each of the 69 schedules previously illustrated.

CASE 13-2   *Develop the budgets for cost of goods sold and finished-goods inventory*

Royce, Incorporated, is currently developing its budget for 19X2. Some of the plans developed to date follow.

Budgeted Cost of Goods Manufactured

	PRODUCT A	
TIME	UNITS	UNIT COST
January	20,000	$1.00
February	20,000	1.00
March	21,000	1.00
April	23,000	1.00
May	23,000	1.00
June	23,000	1.00

Sales Budget (Units)

	PRODUCT A	
TIME	DISTRICT 1	DISTRICT 2
January	10,000	7,000
February	12,000	8,000
March	13,000	11,000
April	15,000	12,000
May	14,000	11,000
June	9,000	8,000

Beginning inventory: product A, 20,000 units @ $.90. The company uses FIFO.

REQUIRED

1. Prepare a budget spreadsheet to compute cost of goods sold by product and by sales district. Assume shipments to districts from stock are to be in the ratio of budgeted sales on a unit basis.
2. Prepare a budget for cost of goods sold by product, district, and time period.
3. Prepare a budget of finished-goods inventories by product and time period.
4. Give the sources of the input budget data used in requirements 1, 2, and 3. Is the assumption in requirement 1 sound? Why?

CASE 13-3   *An implementation problem—what revisions should be made to this budget for an airline company?*

Chesapeake Commuter Airlines, Inc., operates a commuter service in Virginia, Maryland, and Delaware. The company has been in operation for more than twenty years and is owned by thirty-one stockholders. The board of directors, consisting of four members of the active management and three other stockholders, meets monthly to review operations and to formulate basic policy. The company has experienced a steady growth in service revenue, having increased aproximately 180 percent to an annual volume of about $18 million.

For several years, the company has budgeted revenue and, to a limited extent, cash flows. During the past year, a complete profit plan was used for the first time. The management was generally pleased with the results even though some aspects of the plan had evidently been unrealistic. During the past year, numerous suggestions were made that some part of the budget be changed. The president took the position that no changes should be made in the plan of operations during the year under any circumstances. This policy caused some concern, especially when the monthly performance reports were distributed.

The budget for the coming year has just been completed and is being considered by the executive committee (composed of the four top operating executives, who are also on the board of directors). The company followed what was considered good budget procedures by bringing intermediate members of the management into the budget planning activities. It appeared that these managers were interested in the budget program, although they were frank to admit that they needed to know more about the whole picture.

The executive committee first considered the revenue budget, which the committee had discussed previously and tentatively approved. In view of the experience during the past several years, there was general agreement that the budget was realistic. The inventory policy appeared to be realistic. The operating expense budgets were considered next. At this stage of the discussions, Ray Crandall, the executive in charge of operations, remarked: "The expense budgets bother me just as they did last year. My department managers, who worked on them, have recommended that our revision policy be relaxed. Once we set the budget, there appears to be a firm policy that it cannot be changed. It seems to me that we should establish a more realistic policy on this matter. Because, now the expenses shown in the budget are the master."

"Well, Ray," replied Harry Rapides, the president, "we have held the line on all revisions (and not only expense) in the past year because requests for budget changes can very quickly become a habit. Every time someone falls down on the job we get a request for a change in the budget. Before long the budget means nothing because some department managers can anticipate an unfavorable report on their operations and, for self-protection, request a budget change before the report is prepared. We have operated under the concept that we will build a good sound plan and that we should know where and when we fall down. As top management, we need a clear-cut plan with some force behind it. We need to know where we are heading. If we continually change the budget, our plan becomes so vague and changeable that it will be of little use to us. If we keep changing our goals, we will lose sight of where we should be going. In fact, we will be wandering in the dark just as if we had no plan at all. Besides we can't be revising the budget at every whipstitch; we have other things to do. What do you think, Rich?"

"I'm not sure just what we should set as policy on this matter, Harry," replied Glen Richards, the executive in charge of ticket sales. "We spend a lot of time developing our budget. Obviously we can't foresee all events and conditions; yet we can't be changing our plans all the time. If conditions get too far from those anticipated in our budget, comparisons won't mean much. If we are willing to look carefully at the variations to determine those causes beyond our control and those due to inefficiency, we might get along without too much revision."

Benny Hughes, the executive in charge of finance and accounting, had responsibility for coordinating the budget activities. Benny had very definite ideas about the issue and said, "We should be very reluctant to change the budget. Only when major events that were unforeseen occur should we consider revision."

Rapides then noticed that it was about lunch time. "Let's knock off until tomorrow at two o'clock. At that time, let's get together and agree on a basic policy about budget revision for the coming year. Remember we are experimenting. We can always change the policy for the next year. In the meantime, I would like each of you to do some serious thinking about this problem."

REQUIRED

What policy would you recommend for this company about the budget revision policy? Give support for your recommendations.

CASE 13-4   *Apply flexible expense budgets to prepare income statements; two alternatives*

The executive committee of Fulton Metals Company has had one meeting to discuss the sales budget proposed by the sales division. During the meeting, there was considerable discussion about income. Profits for the past several years have been low, averaging 4 percent of sales, whereas the industry average is 6 percent. Tentative planning data already developed are as follows:

a Annual sales plan (tentative):

DISTRICT	AMOUNT
1	$6,000,000
2	4,000,000

b Material cost averages 21 percent of sales.
c Direct labor cost averages 30.6 percent of sales.
d Flexible expense budget formulas are (summarized for instructional purposes):

RESPONSIBILITY CENTER	FIXED EXPENSE PER MONTH	VARIABLE EXPENSE RATE
Producing Dept. 1	$50,000	$2.00 per 100 direct machine hours
Producing Dept. 2	40,000	$1.00 per 100 direct machine hours
Service Dept. 21	20,000	$ .20 per 100 total direct machine hours
Administrative Dept. 30	30,000	$ .003 per total sales dollar
Sales:		
Home office	40,000	$ .004 per total sales dollar
District 1	15,000	$ .06 per district sales dollar
District 2	10,000	$ .07 per district sales dollar

e Inventory changes—none.

f Assume federal income tax average rate of 35 percent.

g Output data for the producing departments:

	AT SALES PLAN LEVEL
Direct machine hours (hundreds):	
Department 1	150,000
Department 2	120,000

REQUIRED

1. Prepare a tentative income statement (summarized) at the tentative planned level of sales. Detail the expenses by department.

2. What would be the income if sales volume (not sales price) were increased by 10 percent? Assume direct machine hours will increase by the same percentage.

CASE 13-5   Sales revenue increases unexpectedly; should the profit plan be changed?

Dakota Tooling is a manufacturer of machine tools distributed in a ten-state area. Sales are relatively stable throughout the year. Therefore, the company maintains a stable labor force and plant capacity. Three years ago, the plant capacity was substantially increased. However, the company has not been able to utilize more than 60 percent of that capacity, although there has been a 7 percent increase in sales volume each year since the plant expansion. The company prepares an annual profit plan detailed by months. Internal performance reports are distributed to each responsibility center on a monthly basis. These performance reports compare actual revenues, expenses, and other quantitative performance measurements with the original profit plan.

The company is in the fourth month of the year, and cumulative sales volume is approximately 20 percent above the level anticipated in the annual profit plan. This unexpected increase in sales was due to a contract with a new distributor in a new sales area. Although the salespeople had been working with this distributor for some time, they were not optimistic about new business. Therefore, they did not plan this new development when the profit plan was devised. As a result of this significant increase in sales volume, variations between actual results and the profit plan reflected on the monthly performance reports are, as one manager said, "becoming somewhat ridiculous." In view of the stability of operations in the past, the company had not previously faced this particular budget problem. Several suggestions have been made to resolve the problem. One vice-president stated: "We should completely revise the profit plan for the remainder of the year." Another vice-president stated: "I see no reason for taking all the time that is required to revise the profit plan. My suggestion would be that we continue reporting as we have in the past and then consider the variations as explained. That is, we won't pay much attention to the variations because they are caused by an event that is certainly in our favor."

The financial vice-president has not made a recommendation except for the following statement at the last meeting of the top management: "We must not get in the habit of changing the profit plan at every whipstitch and on the request of anyone and everyone, because our goals cease to have meaning and the profit planning approach to managing would be undermined."

REQUIRED

Evaluate this situation, and give your recommendations about the revision policy posed by this specific problem. Explain the basis for your recommendations.

14

Cost-Volume-Profit and Contribution Analysis

INTRODUCTION AND PURPOSE   Chapter 10 discussed the concept of expense variability and its application in developing flexible expense budgets. That chapter also discussed and illustrated the use of flexible expense budgets to provide (a) expense data for the annual profit plan and (b) expense data adjusted to actual output for the periodic performance reports. The continuing demonstration case—Superior Manufacturing Company—uses flexible expense budgets in each responsibility center (see Schedules 41–45).

This chapter continues our discussion of the concept of expense variability to show its application in analyzing and planning profits. This application usually is called cost-volume-profit analysis. For discussion purposes, we will make a distinction between (a) contribution analysis and (b) breakeven analysis. These concepts require separate identification and measurement of the fixed and variable components of costs (i.e., expenses). The term **volume** means output or productive activity.[1]

FUNDAMENTALS OF CONTRIBUTION ANALYSIS   Contribution analysis involves a series of analytical techniques used to determine and evaluate the effects on profits of changes in sales volume (i.e., units sold), sales prices, fixed costs, and variable costs. It focuses on contribution margin, which is sales revenue minus total variable costs.

Companies that separately identify and measure the fixed and variable components of cost often use a contribution margin approach on their periodic income statements prepared for internal management uses. These income statements provide financial data that are uniquely useful for management planning purposes because of the emphasis on fixed and variable costs. Most

---

[1] Chapter 10 discussed the relationship of expenses to output or productive activity. The term *expense* was used because flexible budgets relate only to expenses. However, in this chapter we also use the alternate term *cost* because it is commonly used in management accounting for the topics discussed herein.

of the managerial decisions that relate to operations (either directly or indirectly) are based in some way on knowledge of the fixed and variable components of cost. A simplified contribution margin income statement for Sierra Company is shown in Exhibit 14-1. For instructional purposes, we assume that Sierra Company sells only one product and that the planned sales level is 10,000 units.

Notice in Exhibit 14-1 that the income statement is based on a **contribution margin approach** and that CONTRIBUTION MARGIN = REVENUE − VARIABLE COST. Total contribution margin will change if any one of the following variables changes: (1) volume (units sold), (2) sales price, or (3) variable cost ratio. For Sierra Company, the contribution margin percentage (or ratio) will always be 40 percent unless the sales price or the variable cost ratio changes. Also, total fixed costs will always be $30,000 within the relevant range unless the management makes discretionary decisions that impact on fixed costs. A budgeted contribution margin income statement makes it possible to answer numerous "what if" questions. Some of these are illustrated in the following independent cases related to Exhibit 14-1:

☐   CASE A—What would profit be if volume (units) is decreased by 5 percent (i.e., to 9,500 units)?
Answer:

$$\text{Profit, } \$10,000 - (\text{CM, } \$40,000 \times 5\% = \$2,000) = \underline{\underline{\$8,000}}.$$

Notice that both sales revenue and variable costs decreased.

☐   CASE B—What would profit be if sales price is increased by 5 percent (i.e., to $10.50)?
Answer:

$$\text{Profit, } \$10,000 + (\text{Sales, } \$100,000 \times 5\% = \$5,000) = \underline{\underline{\$15,000}}.$$

Notice that costs did not change.

EXHIBIT 14-1

Sierra Company, Annual Profit Plan
Income Statement, Contribution Margin Approach

		TOTAL		UNIT BASIS	
	ABBR.	AMOUNT	%	$	%
Sales revenue (10,000 units)*	SR	$100,000	100%	$10	100%
Less variable costs†	VC	60,000	60%	6	60%
Contribution margin	CM	40,000	40%	$ 4	40%
Less fixed costs†	FC	30,000			
Profit	P	$ 10,000			

*The relevant range for cost variability is 7,000 to 11,000 units.
†Based on flexible expense budget formulas already developed.

- ☐ CASE C—What would profit be if fixed costs are increased by $3,000 (i.e., by 10 percent)?
  Answer:

$$\text{Profit, } \$10,000 - \text{FC, } \$3,000 = \underline{\$7,000.}$$

Notice that revenue and variable costs did not change.

- ☐ CASE D—What would profit be if variable costs are decreased by 5 percent (i.e., decreased to $5.70)?
  Answer:

$$\text{Profit, } \$10,000 + (\text{VC, } \$60,000 \times 5\% = \$3,000) = \underline{\$13,000.}$$

Notice that sales revenue and fixed costs did not change.

- ☐ CASE E—What would profit be if all the four changes given in the above cases were made?
  Answer:

Sales revenue (10,000 units × 95%) × ($10 × 105%)	$99,750
Less variable costs [9,500 units × ($6 × 95%)]	54,150
Contribution margin	45,600
Less fixed costs ($30,000 + $3,000)	33,000
Profit	$12,600

- ☐ CASE F—How much budgeted profit is there on each unit sold in Exhibit 14-1? (Disregard Cases A through E.)
  Answer:
  The contribution margin earned is $4 per unit, but no profit will be earned until all the fixed costs ($30,000) are recovered (paid). This would require sales of 7,500 units (i.e., FC, $30,000 ÷ CM per unit, $4 = 7,500 units, or $75,000). This is called the breakeven point (i.e., no profit or loss), which is discussed in the next section.

For internal management purposes, a contribution margin income statement is preferable. Exhibit 14-2 emphasizes the differences between traditional and contribution margin income statements. Notice that the traditional income statement is static, whereas the contribution income statement is dynamic. Only the latter method provides the data needed to readily answer most "what if" questions, such as those illustrated above.

The traditional method is discussed in financial accounting courses that focus on external reporting. This method does not apply the concept of expense variability. In contrast, a contribution margin income statement emphasizes expense variability because of its relevance in the managerial responsibilities of planning and control.

BREAKEVEN ANALYSIS   Cost-volume-profit analysis includes both contribution analysis and breakeven analysis. Breakeven analysis uses the same concepts as contribution analysis; however, it emphasizes the level of output or productive

EXHIBIT 14-2

Income Statement, Western Company

Comparison of the Traditional and Contribution Margin Methods

TRADITIONAL FINANCIAL ACCOUNTING METHOD COSTS REPORTED BY FUNCTIONS		CONTRIBUTION MARGIN METHOD FIXED AND VARIABLE COSTS REPORTED SEPARATELY	
Sales revenue	$90,000	Sales revenue	
Less cost of goods sold*	40,500	Less variable costs:	$90,000
Gross margin	49,500	Production costs	24,300
Less operating expenses:		Administrative costs	1,800
Administrative expenses*	15,300	Distribution costs	900
Distribution expenses*	25,200	Total variable costs	27,000
Total operating expenses*	40,500	Contribution margin	63,000
Net income (loss)	$ 9,000	Less fixed costs:	
		Production costs	16,200
		Administrative costs	13,500
*Includes both fixed and variable costs. If this were a merchandising or a service company, cost of goods sold would all be variable.		Distribution costs	24,300
		Total fixed costs	54,000
		Net income (loss)	$ 9,000

activity at which sales revenue exactly totals costs; that is, there is no profit or loss. Breakeven analysis rests upon the foundation of cost variability—separate identification and measurement of the fixed and variable components of cost. Breakeven analysis is usually applied on a "total company" basis.

Breakeven analysis usually incorporates both (a) breakeven analyses and (b) breakeven graphs. Exhibit 14-3 gives a contribution margin income statement for Hudson Company which will be used to illustrate several applications of breakeven analysis.

Preparing Breakeven Graphs

To introduce the concepts that underlie breakeven analysis, we will first "graph" the contribution margin income statement given in Exhibit 14-3. The graph (or chart) is shown in Exhibit 14-4. The vertical scale on the graph represents dollars of revenue and cost. The horizontal scale represents the activity base—volume or output—in this case, measured in **units of volume.** The three lines representing total fixed costs, total costs, and sales may be readily located by marking the **profit plan** vertically at the budgeted volume of 200,000 units and marking the budget level of (1) fixed costs ($1.8 million), (2) total costs ($4.4 million), and (3) sales dollars ($5.0 million). The fixed cost line is drawn **horizontally** through the fixed cost point of $1.8 million. The total cost line is drawn through (1) the total cost point of $4.4 million and (2) the intersection of the fixed cost line with the left vertical scale. The sales line is drawn through

EXHIBIT 14-3

Hudson Company, Annual Profit Plan
Income Statement, Contribution Margin Method

Sales revenue (volume, 200,000 units × $25)		$5,000,000	(100%)
Less variable costs:			
Direct material	$ 900,000		
Direct labor	1,000,000		
Factory overhead	300,000		
Administrative costs	100,000		
Distribution costs	300,000		
Total variable costs		$2,600,000	(52%)
Contribution margin		2,400,000	(48%)
Less fixed costs:			
Factory overhead	700,000		
Administrative costs	600,000		
Distribution costs	500,000		
Total fixed costs		1,800,000	
Profit		$ 600,000	

Notes:
  a. Capacity production, 240,000 units.
  b. Relevant range, 140,000 to 220,000 units.

the budget sales point ($5.0 million) to the origin point at the lower left. If the same distance is used on the horizontal scale for volume of sales as on the vertical scale for the revenue at that volume, the sales line will connect opposite corners of the graph.

The point at which the **sales revenue** and **total cost** lines intersect is the breakeven point ($3.75 million). The area between the two lines: to the right of this point represents the profit potential, and the area between the two lines to the left represents the loss potential. Notice that variable costs were graphed above fixed costs.

From the point of view of graphing technique, two additional variations of the breakeven graph can be used as shown in Exhibit 14-5. The first variation shows fixed costs **above** variable costs. This graph has the advantage of showing the recovery of fixed costs at various volume levels before profits are realized. Also, notice that output or volume is expressed in **budgeted sales dollars** rather than in units. The units were converted to sales dollars at the budgeted unit sales price of $25. Exhibit 14-5 shows another format in which the various fixed and variable costs are graphed in a particular sequence, such as those shown on the income statement. The breakeven point is the same in each of the three methods of graphing. Exhibit 14-4 shows the breakeven volume in both units (150,000) and dollars ($3.75 million), whereas Exhibit 14-5 shows the breakeven volume in dollars only ($3.75 million).

EXHIBIT 14-4

Breakeven Graph, Hudson Company
(Variable Costs above Fixed Costs)

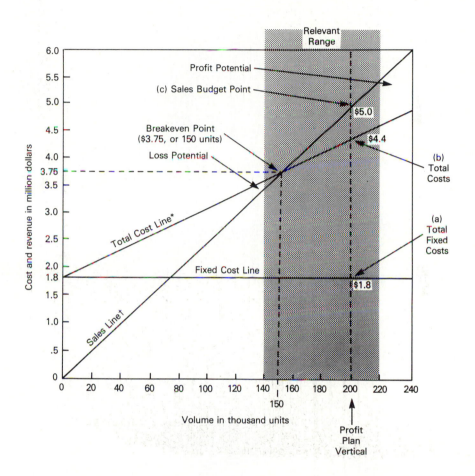

Computing the Breakeven Point

The breakeven point, as well as other important information, can be computed by using simple mathematical procedures. A number of formulas can be used for these computations; the two usually employed are as follows.[2]

[2] Harold Bierman, Jr., Thomas Dyckman, and Ronald Hilton, *Cost Accounting: Concepts and Managerial Applications* (New York: Macmillan, 1990); and Charles T. Horngren and George Foster, *Cost Accounting: A Managerial Emphasis* (Englewood Cliffs, N.J.: Prentice-Hall, 1987).

EXHIBIT 14-5

Different Formats for Breakeven Graphs, Hudson Company

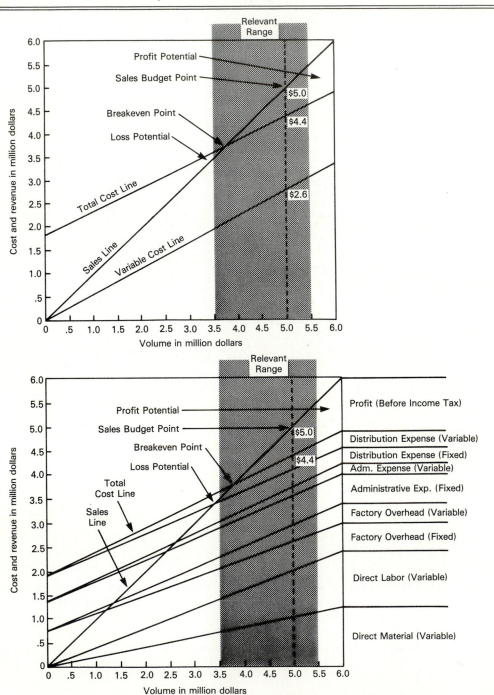

Breakeven computation based on budget totals:

$$BE = \frac{\text{Fixed costs}}{\text{Contribution margin ratio}} = \frac{\text{Fixed costs}}{1 - \dfrac{\text{Variable costs}}{\text{Corresponding sales}}}$$

Substituting the data given in Exhibit 14-3, we get:

$$BE = \frac{\$1.8 \text{ million}}{1 - \dfrac{\$2.6 \text{ million}}{\$5.0 \text{ million}}} = \frac{\$1.8 \text{ million}}{1 - .52} = \frac{\$1.8 \text{ million}}{.48 \text{ (contribution margin ratio)}}$$

$$= \$3.75 \text{ million (breakeven point in dollars)}$$

$$= \$3.75 \text{ million} \div \$25 = \underline{150,000} \text{ (breakeven point in units)}$$

This computation is often simplified as follows:

$$BE = \text{Fixed costs} \div \text{Contribution margin}$$

$$= \$1.8 \text{ million} - .48$$

$$= \underline{\$3.75 \text{ million (or 150,000 units)}}$$

The above formula provides an insight into the characteristics of breakeven analysis.[3] Dividing variable costs by sales gives the **variable cost ratio.** For example, the .52 (that is, $2.6 million ÷ $5.0 million) computed above shows that variable costs are 52 percent of sales, or to express it differently, $.52 of each sales dollar is needed to recover exactly the variable costs. Subtracting the variable cost ratio from one gives the **contribution margin ratio.** For example, the contribution margin ratio means that .48 (that is, 1 − .52) derived in the illustration above indicates that 48 percent of sales are available

---

[3] The formula is derived as follows:

(1) Sales = Fixed costs + Variable costs + Profit

(2) Adapted:

   Breakeven volume = Fixed costs + Variable costs at breakeven volume + Profit at zero

(3) Therefore:

$$BE = FC + \frac{VC}{S}(BE) + \text{Zero profit}$$

(4) Rearranged:

$$BE = \frac{FC}{CM \text{ ratio}} = \frac{FC}{1 - \dfrac{VC}{S}}$$

to cover fixed costs (and generate profit), or differently, $.48 of each sales dollar is available to first cover fixed costs and then to make a profit. Profit at breakeven is zero; therefore, dividing fixed costs by the contribution margin ratio (.48) (also referred to as the P/V ratio) gives the number of dollars of sales revenue necessary to exactly recover fixed costs (i.e., $1.8 million ÷ .48 = $3.75 million). The computation can be verified as follows (see Exhibit 14-3):

Breakeven sales (as computed)		$3,750,000
Less budgeted costs:		
Fixed costs	$1,800,000	
Variable costs ($3,750,000 × .52)	1,950,000	
Total costs		3,750,000
Profit		$ -0-

Computation of the breakeven point shown above was based on total sales and cost data. When there is only one product, the breakeven computation can be based on *unit* prices and costs as follows:

Unit sales price ($5.0 million ÷ 200,000 units)	$25
Unit variable cost ($2.6 million ÷ 200,000 units)	13
Contribution of each unit sold to cover fixed costs and profits	$12

Fixed costs of $1.8 million to be recovered, divided by $12 recovery per unit, gives a breakeven volume of 150,000 units. The breakeven point in dollars then is: 150,000 × $25 = $3.75 million. These computations can be set as a formula as follows:

1 Sales = Variable costs + Fixed costs + Profit

2 Adapted:
Let X = Units at the breakeven point
Therefore:

$$\$25X = \$13X + \$1,800,000 + \$0$$

$$\$12X = \$1,800,000$$

$$X = 150,000 \text{ (units at the breakeven point)}$$

Computations based on unit prices and unit costs can be used only for a single product, or in the case of multiple products, for each product separately.[4]

---

[4] Notice that computations based on total cost give the breakeven point in dollars of sales, whereas the unit cost approach gives the breakeven point in units.

Basic Assumptions That Underlie Contribution and Breakeven Analyses

Contribution analysis and breakeven analysis are based on a specific set of assumptions that should be clearly understood. These underlying assumptions are:

1   That the concept of cost variability is valid; therefore, costs can be classified and measured realistically as fixed and variable.

2   That there is a relevant range of validity (i.e., activity) for using the results of the analysis.

3   That sale price does not change as units of sales change.

4   That there is only one product, or in the case of multiple products, that sales mix among the products remains constant.

5   That basic management policies about operations will not change materially in the short run.

6   That the general price level (i.e., inflation and deflation) will remain essentially stable in the short run.

7   That sales and production levels are synchronized; that is, inventory remains essentially constant or is zero.

8   That efficiency and productivity per person will remain essentially unchanged in the short run.

If any of these assumptions are changed, a revised budget (see Exhibit 14-1) would be needed for a new analysis. This process was briefly illustrated on page 499 and will be emphasized in the remaining discussion in this chapter. Next we will describe each of the above assumptions in the order listed.

CONCEPT OF COST VARIABILITY   All the illustrations in this chapter use the fixed and variable components of cost. The validity of the illustration rests primarily upon the reliability of estimates of cost variability.

The concept of cost variability was discussed in Chapter 10 with respect to flexible expense budgets. Fixed and variable costs were also defined and illustrated there. The concepts of cost variability, fixed costs, and variable costs discussed in Chapter 10 are the same for contribution and breakeven analyses.

Identification of Fixed and Variable Costs Components

If flexible expense budgets are used, cost variability has already been planned; therefore, the flexible budget formulas can readily be used for contribution and breakeven analyses. This relationship of flexible budgets with these analyses means that once reliable flexible budgets are developed, numerous analyses can be used with little effort and cost. This relationship is demonstrated at the end of the chapter for Superior Manufacturing Company.

If the fixed and variable components of costs are not determined, a rough estimate of a company's contribution margin and breakeven point can be made. This can be done by plotting historical revenue and cost data for several prior periods and then extrapolating those results for the upcoming year. Such an estimate may give a general view of the economic characteristics of a company. However, this unsophisticated approach must be viewed skeptically because, in most cases, each set of historical data represents varying conditions such as changes in management policies, accounting classification, productivity, methods of manufacturing, and products. Because this approach uses only historical relationships, there is an implicit assumption that past trends will continue. Some companies use this approach to approximate competitor breakeven points for comparison with their own.

Straightline Cost Variability

The formulas and graphs used in contribution and breakeven analyses usually assume straightline relationships. The assumption that the fixed costs remain constant at all output levels, and that the variable costs vary proportionally at all output levels, is seldom, if ever, literally true. A casual glance at a breakeven graph may convey this impression; however, a practical analyst will know that such is not the case. In Exhibits 14-4 and 14-5, a portion of the breakeven graph was shaded to indicate a **relevant range.** The concept of relevant range was discussed in Chapter 10 (flexible expense budgets). The relevant range of output or volume may be thought of as the area of validity or significance. Although the lines on a breakeven graph may be extended to the left and right of the relevant range, the analysis has meaning only within this range.[5] The analysis shows what fixed costs **should be** and how variable costs **should vary** within the relevant range determined by existing policies. Within this relevant range, operational conditions and management policies are assumed to be relatively consistent; therefore, the results should be predictable on a straightline basis. Outside this range, different operational conditions and management policies will usually cause a completely new pattern of cost variability and, consequently, new revenue, cost, and profit relationships.[6]

SALES PRICE AND SALES MIX CONSIDERATIONS   Cost-volume-profit analysis assumes a constant unit sales price; therefore, the graphical revenue line is straight. This simplifying assumption is made for two practical reasons. First,

---

[5] T. P. Goggans, "Breakeven Analysis with Curvilinear Functions," *Accounting Review,* October 1985, pp. 867–71.

[6] Alfred Rappaport, ed., *Information for Decision Making: Readings in Cost and Managerial Accounting,* Reading No. 8, "Cost-Volume-Profit Under Conditions of Uncertainty" (Englewood Cliffs, N.J.: Prentice-Hall, 1982).

the effect of the budgeted sales price should be shown. Second, because the sales line shows the combined results of volume (units) and sales price, any attempt to show the effect of changes in unit selling prices on sales volume would involve price and demand theory. However, if it is possible to make a reliable estimate of the net effect of a price increase or decrease on units that could be sold, the analyst could show a nonlinear sales plan with a nonlinear sales line. There is no reason why the sales line cannot be expressed as a curve or in steps, provided a realistic determination can be made of the characteristics of the revenue line. Contribution and breakeven analyses can be developed for each product separately or for multiple products. If only one product or similar products are involved, the complication of sales mix is avoided. *Sales mix* refers to the relative quantities and amounts of the various products sold by a company during a given period. Exhibit 14-6, Case I, shows the original budget for a company with a quantity sales mix of 10 to 7.5. The effects of this particular sales mix are included in the budgeted amounts for sales, fixed costs, variable costs, and profit. The breakeven graph for this budget is shown in Exhibit 14-7, Case I. Notice that the breakeven point is $13,640, and profit is $3,500.

Now assume that management is considering the effect of a change in sales mix. One objective is to determine which product should be "pushed." Casual observation of the budget data provides no direct clue as to which product is potentially more profitable. In fact, it may appear that they are equal in profit potential ($.20 profit per unit for each product) and that the budgeted sales mix is appropriate. To demonstrate the effect of a change in sales mix, assume the controller developed Cases II and III shown in Exhibits 14-6 and 14-7.

The analysis of sales mix in Exhibits 14-6 and 14-7 shows that pushing product A (Case II) increased profits. However, it would be desirable to push product B because (1) in Case III a higher profit is indicated than in Case II, and (2) the breakeven point is lower than in either Case I or Case II. Notice that new contribution and breakeven analyses can be developed for each new sales mix ratio, wherein both the sales and cost amounts (and the graphical lines) are based on the new sales mix or quantity ratio between the two products at all points up and down the volume scale. This application provides useful information that shows how the promoting of the more profitable products can affect profit and the breakeven point. Therefore, the sales mix assumptions inherent in cost-volume-profit analysis, if viewed properly, are an advantage rather than a disadvantage. The breakeven points summed for the two products computed separately (which assumes independence) will not equal the breakeven point based on combined data (which assumes a dependence imposed by the budgeted sales mix).[7]

[7] G. L. Johnson and S. S. Simik, "The Use of Probability Inequalities in Multiproduct C-V-P Analysis Under Uncertainty," *Journal of Accounting Research*, Spring 1974, pp. 67–79.

EXHIBIT 14-6
Analysis of Changes in Sales Mix

CASE I—Original budget
(sales mix: product A, 10,000 units; product B, 5,000 units)

	PRODUCT A		PRODUCT B		
	UNITS	AMOUNT	UNITS	AMOUNT	TOTAL
Sales planned	10,000	$10,000	7,500	$10,000	$20,000
Costs budgeted:					
Fixed		2,000		5,500	7,500
Variable		6,000		3,000	9,000
Total		8,000		8,500	16,500
Profit		$ 2,000		$ 1,500	$ 3,500

CASE II—Twenty percent increase in product A units;
no change in product B

	PRODUCT A			PRODUCT B			
	UNITS	PER UNIT	AMOUNT	UNITS	PER UNIT	AMOUNT	TOTAL
Sales	12,000	$1.00	$12,000	7,500	1.33\frac{1}{3}$	$10,000	$22,000
Costs:							
Fixed			2,000			5,500	7,500
Variable		.60	7,200		.40	3,000	10,200
Total			9,200			8,500	17,700
Profit			$ 2,800			$ 1,500	$ 4,300

CASE III—Twenty percent increase in product B
no change in product A

	PRODUCT A			PRODUCT B			
	UNITS	PER UNIT	AMOUNT	UNITS	PER UNIT	AMOUNT	TOTAL
Sales	10,000	$1.00	$10,000	9,000	1.33\frac{1}{3}$	$12,000	$22,000
Costs:							
Fixed			2,000			5,500	7,500
Variable		.60	6,000		.40	3,600	9,600
Total			8,000			9,100	17,100
Profit			$ 2,000			$ 2,900	$ 4,900

Comparison of results

	ORIGINAL BUDGET	20% INCREASE IN PRODUCT A	20% INCREASE IN PRODUCT B
Profit	$ 3,500	$ 4,300	$ 4,900
Percentage profit change			
(increase-decrease)		23%	40%
Breakeven point	$13,640	$13,980	$13,300

EXHIBIT 14-7

Breakeven Graphs—Changes in Sales Mix

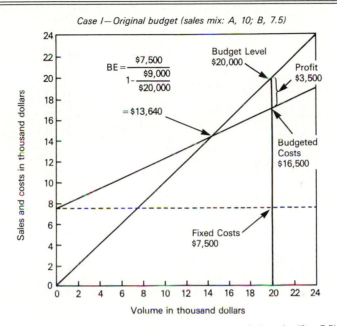

Case I—Original budget (sales mix: A, 10; B, 7.5)

$$BE = \frac{\$7,500}{1 - \dfrac{\$9,000}{\$20,000}}$$

$$= \$13,640$$

Budget Level
$20,000

Profit
$3,500

Budgeted
Costs
$16,500

Fixed Costs
$7,500

Sales and costs in thousand dollars

Volume in thousand dollars

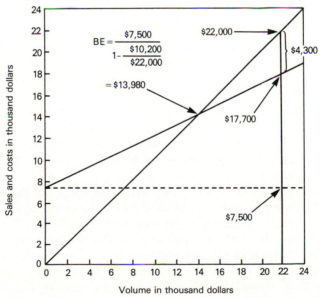

Case II—20 percent increase in units of product A (sales mix: 12 to 7.5)

$$BE = \frac{\$7,500}{1 - \dfrac{\$10,200}{\$22,000}}$$

$$= \$13,980$$

$22,000

$4,300

$17,700

$7,500

Sales and costs in thousand dollars

Volume in thousand dollars

EXHIBIT 14-7

(continued)

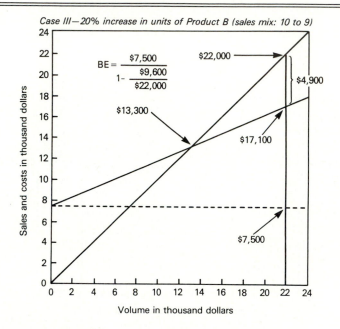

Case III—20% increase in units of Product B (sales mix: 10 to 9)

$$BE = \frac{\$7,500}{1 - \dfrac{\$9,600}{\$22,000}}$$

MANAGEMENT POLICIES   Cost-volume-profit analysis carries implicit assumptions about basic management policies. The revenue data used in the computations imply definite policies on such items as sales prices, sales mix, and products. The fixed cost data imply specific policies on such items as salary scales, number of indirect employees on fixed salaries, depreciation methods, insurance coverage, research, advertising, and plant capacity—that is, those policies that determine the fixed cost structure of a company. The variable cost data imply specific policies that determine the variable cost structure of a company, such as quality of raw materials, production technology, wage rates for direct labor employees, and sales commissions.

Because breakeven analysis implies a definite set of management policies affecting the revenue and cost characteristics of a company—and this is one of its most important applications—it tells management in effect, "Here are the approximate results to be expected at varying volume levels of operations presuming a **specific set** of policies and decisions." For example, if a company is approaching the breakeven point in operations or profits are dropping, management action should be taken to lower the breakeven point **before it is reached.** This distinction is important because management must know what the financial effect of present policies is in order to know when and why they should be changed, how they should be changed, and what the probable effect would be. A series of contribution and breakeven analyses under varying management policy assumptions can help decision making.

Evaluation of Assumptions

The last three assumptions listed on page 507—price stability, stable inventory levels, and worker efficiency, usually have a minimal effect on cost-volume-profit analyses because they are short-term analyses. They usually assume a stable price level. This assumption, of course, is not valid when inflation or deflation is significant.

The assumption of efficiency and productivity per individual is particularly important in the long run. However, these seldom change materially in the short run. If they do, the existing relationships between volume and costs will change and a new analysis is required.

Should a material change in the inventory be anticipated during the budget period, appropriate adjustment must be made in the computations for the inventory increase or decrease along the lines suggested in a later section of this chapter.

Most criticisms of cost-volume-profit analyses are directed at one or more of the eight assumptions listed on page 507. Although some of them are justified in specific situations, none is beyond reasonable resolution in most cases. Whether they can be validated in a particular case will depend to a large degree on the abilities and judgment of the analyst.

SPECIAL PROBLEMS IN COST-VOLUME-PROFIT ANALYSIS   Cost-volume-profit analyses are applied to (a) individual products or parts of a business and (b) all the products or activities combined. In the latter case, three problems may be encountered: (a) the activity base, (b) inventory changes, and (c) nonoperating expenses and incomes.

Activity Base

When two or more products or activities are combined for breakeven analysis, the activity base is usually net sales dollars. Product units are preferable if the analysis is applied to one product. For multiple products, the activity base must be in additive units using a common denominator of volume or output. Therefore, for the company as a whole, net sales dollars are usually the only satisfactory common denominator because manufacturing, selling, and administrative activities are expressed in combination.

If flexible expense budgets are used, they can be summed for cost-volume-profit purposes. This process may cause some complications because the different departmental flexible budgets are related to different activity bases. For example, selling expenses may be related to sales dollars, factory overhead related to direct labor or machine hours, and power department costs related to kilowatt hours. To add the flexible expense budget amounts, it must be assumed that the departmental activity factors correlate reasonably well with the overall activity base selected for breakeven purposes. The usual procedure in developing breakeven analysis based on flexible expense budgets is to add the **fixed cost** components shown in the flexible budget amounts and to treat the remaining costs (determined by subtraction from total costs) as variable. This procedure is illustrated subsequently for Superior Manufacturing Company. Selection of an appropriate activity base for different types of responsibility centers was discussed in Chapter 10.

Inventory Changes

Usually the budgeted changes in inventories (that is, finished goods and work in process) are immaterial in amount and thus may be disregarded in cost-volume-profit analyses. On the other hand, when the change in budgeted inventory is significant, it should be included in the analysis.[8]

Including the effect of inventory changes in cost-volume-profit analyses requires subjective judgments about (1) what management might do (about making inventory changes) at different volume levels and (2) the conceptual precision that is desired. We will consider two practical approaches often used: (a) disregard the inventory change and (b) include the inventory change. These approaches overlook some conceptual issues in favor of pragmatic simplicity. Exhibit 14-8 gives simplified data that will be used for discussion purposes. Notice that (1) only one product is involved (so that the effects may be clearly shown), and (2) there is a budgeted increase in inventory equal to 10 percent of production. We will assume that the increase in inventory is at the same unit cost as budgeted production ($1.40 per unit).

INVENTORY CHANGE DISREGARDED   If it is desired to disregard the inventory change in computing the breakeven point (which is a common practice), the breakeven point can be computed as follows:

a   **Based on budget totals:**

$$BE = \frac{\$80,000 + \$10,000}{1 - \dfrac{\$60,000 + \$9,000 - \$6,000^*}{\$180,000}} = \underline{\underline{138,462}} \text{ (or 69,231 units)}\dagger$$

---

*The variable costs and the sales figures must always relate to the same level of activity. The subtraction of $6,000 (10,000 units at $.60) reduces the variable costs to a 90,000-unit basis, which is necessary in this case because the $180,000 sales figure is based on 90,000 units, whereas the production costs are based on 100,000 units.

†$138,462 ÷ $2 = 69,231 units at breakeven.

[8] R. Lee Brummet, *Overhead Costing* (Bureau of Business Research, School of Business Administration, University of Michigan, 1957); and Roy E. Tuttle, "The Effect of Inventory Change on Breakeven Analysis," *NAA Bulletin*, January 1959, pp. 77–87.

or more simply,

$$BE = (FC + P) \div CM$$

$$= \$90,000 \div .65$$

$$= \$138,462$$

EXHIBIT 14-8

HYP Company—Budgeted Income Statement (with inventory change)

Budgeted sales (90,000 units × $2)		$180,000
Budgeted production (100,000 units):		
Fixed costs	$ 80,000	
Variable costs ($.60 per unit)	60,000	
Total costs	140,000	
Less inventory increase (10,000 units × $1.40)	14,000*	126,000
Gross margin		54,000
Less administrative and distribution costs:		
Fixed costs	10,000	
Variable costs ($.10 per unit)	9,000	19,000
Budgeted profit		$ 35,000

*This amount is composed of:

Variable costs (10,000 units × $.60)	$ 6,000
Fixed costs ($80,000 × 10%)	8,000
	$14,000

Because there is only one product, the following computations give the same results:

b   Based on budgeted unit prices and costs:

Unit sales price		$2.00
Less unit variable costs:		
Factory	$.60	
Administrative and selling	.10	.70
Contribution to cover fixed costs and profit		$1.30

Fixed cost to be recovered $90,000 divided by unit recovery of $1.30 gives 69,231 units at breakeven, or $138,462.

The computations can be verified by disregarding the inventory change:

Breakeven sales (69,231 units × $2)		$138,462
Less production costs:		
Fixed	$80,000	
Variable (69,231 × $.60)	41,539	121,539
Gross margin		16,923
Less administrative and selling:		
Fixed	10,000	
Variable (69,231 × $.10)	6,923	16,923
Profit or loss		$ -0-

INVENTORY CHANGE INCLUDED   If the inventory change involves a material amount, it must be included in the analysis. In this case, we must assume either (1) that management will maintain a constant **ratio** of inventory change to production—that is, in the above example the inventory increase will approximate 10 percent of production at all levels of operations, or (2) that the inventory change will be constant in units—that is, in the above example management will maintain the 10,000 unit increase in inventory regardless of the level of operations. We may also assume (1) that the beginning inventory is, in effect, a fixed cost or (2) that it is in part a fixed cost and in part a variable cost. The conceptual aspects are complicated by these assumptions and the additional factor of **overapplied or underapplied factory overhead.**

To avoid complexity, yet to derive a reasonable approximation, many companies assume (1) that the inventory increase or decrease will be proportional to changes in production, and (2) that the inventory change has the same ratio of fixed and variable costs to total cost as is budgeted for current production.

Returning to Exhibit 14-8, the inventory change (increase of 10,000 units; that is, 10 percent of production) can be analyzed as follows:

Cost in the inventory increase:

Fixed component:	$\dfrac{10,000 \text{ units}}{100,000 \text{ units}} \times \$80,000 =$	$ 8,000
Variable component:	$\dfrac{10,000 \text{ units}}{100,000 \text{ units}} \times \$60,000 =$	6,000
Total (10,000 units)		$14,000

Accepting the two simplifying assumptions given above, the breakeven point can be computed as follows:

a **Based on budget totals:**

$$BE = \frac{\$80,000 + \$10,000 - \$8,000}{1 - \dfrac{\$60,000 + \$9,000 - \$6,000}{\$180,000}}$$

$$= \frac{\$82,000}{.65}$$

$$= \$126,154, \text{ or } 63,077 \text{ units (that is, } \$126,154 \div \$2)$$

Because there is only one product, the following computations give the same results:

b **Based on budgeted unit prices and costs:**

Unit sales price		$2.00
Less unit variable cost:		
Factory	$.60	
Administrative and selling	.10	.70
Contribution to cover fixed costs and profit		$1.30

$$BE = \frac{\$80,000 + \$10,000 - \$8,000}{\$1.30} = \frac{\$82,000}{\$1.30}$$

$$= 63,077 \text{ units, or } \$126,154 \,(63,077 \times \$2)$$

Note that the $8,000 (computed above) subtracted from fixed costs in both computations represents the **fixed cost** component of the inventory change. It is subtracted because the inventory is **increased** and this fixed cost belongs in inventory rather than in cost of goods sold.

The breakeven computations given above can be verified in terms of the two simplifying assumptions as follows:

Breakeven sales (63,077 units × $2)		$126,154
Less costs:		
Production (63,077 ÷ .90 = 70,085 units)		
Fixed costs	$ 80,000	
Variable costs (70,085 × $.60)	42,051	
Total production costs	122,051	
Less inventory (10% of production)	12,205	
Cost of goods sold		109,846
Gross margin		16,308
Less selling and administrative costs		
Fixed	$ 10,000	
Variable (63,077 × $.10)	6,308	16,308
Profit or loss		$ -0-

Alternatively, if we assume the budget given in Exhibit 14-8 with the exceptions that (1) budgeted sales are 110,000 units and (2) production is 100,000 units, a 10,000 **decrease** in inventory results. The breakeven point under the two simplifying assumptions would require that the $8,000 fixed costs **withdrawn** from inventory be added to fixed costs as follows:

$$BE = \frac{\$90,000 + \$8,000}{\$1.30} = \frac{\$98,000}{\$1.30}$$

$$= 75,385 \text{ units (or } \$150,769)$$

Application of this **practical** method is illustrated for Superior Manufacturing Company at the end of this chapter. When dealing with the heterogeneous and detailed data common to an actual situation, some practical approach is generally preferable to a complicated, conceptual approach, assuming that the practical approach provides a reasonable approximation of the results.

Nonoperating Incomes and Expenses

Nonoperating incomes (gains) and expenses (losses), and extraordinary gains and losses, if material in amount, cause another problem in cost-volume-profit analysis. The basic issue is whether they should be included or excluded. Extraordinary gains and losses are nonrecurring and unusual; therefore, they should be excluded. Nonoperating incomes (and gains) and expenses (and losses) are recurring, but they are not related to ongoing operations. For example, interest income and expense, and gains and losses on the sale of operational (fixed) assets, are viewed as nonoperational items. Usually they are excluded from cost-volume-profit analyses. However, if they are included, it is preferable to include the net of other income and other expenses. If the excess is expense, it should be added to fixed expense; whereas if the excess is income, it should be deducted from the fixed expense. When graphed, the effect of these amounts should be indicated with additional lines to show the company's economic characteristics before and after the nonoperating items.

Exhibit 14-9 gives an illustrative situation that shows how to compute the breakeven point for three different cases and includes the related graph.

USE AND APPLICATION OF BREAKEVEN ANALYSIS   Breakeven analysis provides additional insights into the economic characteristics of a company. It can be used to assess the approximate effect of various alternatives. Breakeven analysis is usually based on planned data. The analysis can be characterized appropriately as a "slide-rule" approach that can be used to develop and test, with minimum effort, the approximate effect that several kinds of management decisions have on costs and profits.

EXHIBIT 14-9

Cost-Volume-Profit Analysis—Nonoperating Items

Situation

Budgeted sales (10,000 units × $3)		$30,000
Less:		
Fixed costs	$18,000	
Variable costs	9,000	27,000
Income from operations		3,000
Add nonoperating items:		
Other incomes	$ 3,000	
Less other expenses	1,000	2,000
Budgeted net income		$ 5,000

Computation of Breakeven Points

☐ CASE A—Omitting other incomes and expenses:

$$BES = \frac{\$18,000}{1 - \dfrac{\$9,000}{\$30,000}}$$

$$= 18,000 \div CM, .70$$

$$= \underline{\underline{25,714}}$$

☐ CASE B—Including other incomes and expenses:

$$BES = \frac{\$18,000 - \$2,000}{1 - \dfrac{\$9,000}{\$30,000}}$$

$$= \$16,000 \div CM, .70$$

$$= \underline{\underline{\$22,857}}$$

☐ CASE C—Assuming other incomes of $1,000 and other expenses of $3,000; that is, excess expense of $2,000:

$$BES = \frac{\$18,000 + \$2,000}{1 - \dfrac{\$9,000}{\$30,000}}$$

$$= \$20,000 \div CM, .70$$

$$= \underline{\underline{\$28,571}}$$

EXHIBIT 14-9
(continued)

Verification

The computation can be verified for each case. For example, the verification for Case B is as follows:

Sales (at breakeven)		$22,857
Less:		
Fixed costs	$18,000	
Variable costs (.30 × $22,857)	6,857	24,857
Loss from operations		($ 2,000)
Add:		
Other income	$ 3,000	
Less other expenses	1,000	2,000
Net income		$ -0-

Breakeven Graph:

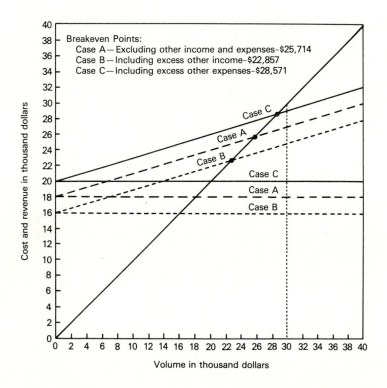

Breakeven analysis can indicate the following economic characteristics of a company:

1   Fixed expenses, variable expenses, and total expenses at varying volumes
2   The profit and loss potential, before and after income taxes, at varying volumes
3   The margin of safety; that is, the relationship of budget sales to breakeven sales
4   The breakeven sales amount (often called the breakeven point)
5   The preferred dividend or danger point; that is, the point below which preferred dividends are not earned
6   The dead point; that is, the sales amount at which the company earns only the "going" rate on the investment
7   The common dividend or unhealthy point; that is, the sales amount below which earnings are insufficient to pay the preferred dividends and the expected dividend on the common stock

All of these sales amounts, and others, can be computed if cost variability data are available. The remaining sections of this chapter discuss some typical applications of breakeven analysis.

Evaluation of Alternatives Using Breakeven Analysis

The first part of this chapter emphasized contribution analysis. Exhibit 14-1 gave data that were used to illustrate how certain "what if" questions could be answered (page 499). Those questions focused on the effects of certain changes on profit. Now we will extend those discussions to include breakeven analysis. Recall that Exhibit 14-1 showed sales revenue as 10,000 units, $100,000 ($10 per unit); variable expenses, $60,000 ($6 per unit); fixed expenses, $30,000; and profit, $10,000. Exhibit 14-10 shows the breakeven analysis for each of the four alternative cases A, B, C, and D given on page 499. Each of the four breakeven graphs shows (a) the original budget (dark lines) and (b) the effects of the alternative "what if" question (dashed lines).

Graph A shows that a change in unit volume does not change the breakeven sales amount; the only effects are to reduce sales revenue and variable expenses proportionately and, as a consequence, contribution margin and profit are decreased.

Graph B shows that a change in sales price does change the breakeven sales point, sales revenue, contribution margin, and profit. It does not change either the fixed or variable expense amounts.

Graph C shows that a change in fixed expenses changes only profit and the breakeven point; contribution margin is not affected.

Graph D shows that a change in variable expenses does change the breakeven point, contribution margin, and profit. It does not change fixed expenses or sales revenue.

EXHIBIT 14-10

Breakeven Analysis—Effects of Changing Variables (Based on data given in Exhibit 14-1)

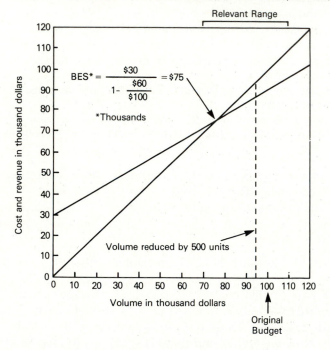

Graph A—Original budget and a 5 percent decrease in units (to 9,500 units)

$$BES^* = \frac{\$30}{1 - \frac{\$60}{\$100}} = \$75$$

*Thousands

Volume reduced by 500 units

Relevant Range

Original Budget

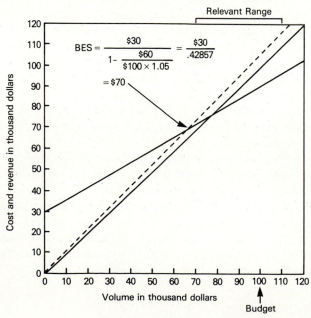

Graph B—5 percent increase in sales price (to $10.50)

$$BES = \frac{\$30}{1 - \frac{\$60}{\$100 \times 1.05}} = \frac{\$30}{.42857}$$

$$= \$70$$

Relevant Range

Budget

EXHIBIT 14-10
(continued)

Graph C—Original budget and a $3,000 increase in fixed costs (by 10%)

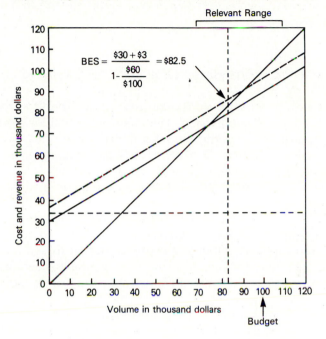

Graph D—Original budget and 5 percent decrease in variable costs (to $5.70)

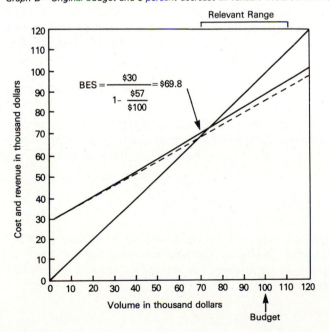

These illustrations indicate the application of cost-volume-profit analyses for testing the effect of proposed alternative management decisions. For example, the technique can help determine the profit potential of replacing old machinery with new machinery, which change may result in a shift of fixed and variable expenses.

Cost-Volume-Profit Analysis by Organizational Subdivision or Product

In many cases, it is useful to develop cost-volume-profit analyses by product, plant, or some other subdivision. The following actual incident dramatizes this kind of application. A particular sales division executive, whose variable expenses to sales ratio was 75 percent, was contemplating an increase in divisional **fixed** expenses. The president asked how much sales would have to be to maintain the present profit position after the increase in fixed expenses. The sales executive replied that for each dollar increase in fixed expenses, sales volume would have to be increased one dollar to maintain the same dollar profit. Needless to say, the sales executive was not nearly so enthusiastic about increasing fixed expenses when told by the controller (based on the cost-volume-profit analysis) that "for each $1 increase in fixed expenses, sales volume must be increased by $4 in order to maintain exactly the present dollar profit position ($1 ÷ 25% = $4)."

Breakeven analysis by organizational subdivisions or by products poses a special problem because of indirect expenses. An indirect expense is one that does not have a traceable relationship to the particular responsibility center under consideration. For example, general administrative expenses are indirect when considering responsibility centers in selling and production. It is generally preferable to develop an analysis (1) before and (2) after allocation of the indirect expenses. Better allocations can frequently be obtained if the allocation basis used for fixed expenses is different from the one used for variable expenses. This is because of the different characteristics of these two kinds of expenses.

One application of breakeven analysis by sales district is shown in Exhibit 14-11. For preparation of a breakeven graph, it is helpful to plot the data on the same graph for before and after the allocation of indirect costs.

Margin of Safety

The margin of safety is the relationship of planned (or actual sales) to the breakeven sales. It shows management how close to the breakeven sales point the company is operating. For example, assume the following data for two companies:

EXHIBIT 14-11

Breakeven Analysis of Sales Districts—Budget Data

	EASTERN DISTRICT			WESTERN DISTRICT			COMPANY		
	FIXED	VARIABLE	TOTAL	FIXED	VARIABLE	TOTAL	FIXED	VARIABLE	TOTAL
Sales revenue			$300,000			$200,000			$500,000
Cost of goods sold	$36,000	$ 84,000	120,000	$24,000	$ 56,000	$ 80,000	$ 60,000	$140,000	200,000
Gross margin			180,000			120,000			300,000
Direct district sales costs	30,000	99,000	129,000	20,000	64,000	84,000	50,000	163,000	213,000
Direct district operating profit			51,000			36,000			87,000
Cost subtotals	66,000	183,000		44,000	120,000		110,000	303,000	
Allocated general sales and administrative costs*	21,600	14,400	36,000	14,400	9,600	24,000	36,000	24,000	60,000
Total costs	87,600	197,400		58,400	129,600		146,000	327,000	
Net income			$ 15,000			$ 12,000			$ 27,000

Breakeven computation:

Before allocations:

EASTERN DISTRICT

$$BE = \frac{\$66,000}{1 - \dfrac{\$183,000}{\$300,000}}$$

$$= \$169,231$$

WESTERN DISTRICT

$$BE = \frac{\$44,000}{1 - \dfrac{\$120,000}{\$200,000}}$$

$$= \$110,000$$

COMPANY

$$BE = \frac{\$146,000}{1 - \dfrac{\$327,000}{\$500,000}}$$

$$= \$421,965$$

After allocations:

$$BE = \frac{\$87,600}{1 - \dfrac{\$197,400}{\$300,000}}$$

$$= \$256,140$$

$$BE = \frac{\$58,400}{1 - \dfrac{\$129,600}{\$200,000}}$$

$$= \$165,909$$

*Indirect cost—allocated herein on same basis to simplify.

ITEM	COMPANY A	COMPANY B
Planned sales	$100,000	$100,000
Planned costs:		
Fixed	70,000	20,000
Variable	20,000	70,000
Planned income	$ 10,000	$ 10,000
Breakeven point (sales)	$ 87,500	$ 66,667

Although the two companies planned the same income amount, a basic difference exists in their economic characteristics. Company A is much closer to the breakeven sales point than Company B. Whereas Company A will operate at a loss if sales drop more than $12\frac{1}{2}$ percent, Company B will earn a profit until sales drop more than $33\frac{1}{3}$ percent. In other words, they have different margins of safety. The margin of safety can be expressed (1) as the ratio or percentage of the difference between planned sales and breakeven sales. The following figures illustrate this concept for Companies A and B:

COMPUTATION	COMPANY A	COMPANY B
Margin of safety expressed as the percentage of the difference between planned sales and breakeven sales:		
($100,000 − $87,500 = $12,500) ÷ $100,000	$12\frac{1}{2}\%$	
($100,000 − $66,667 = $33,333) ÷ $100,000		$33\frac{1}{3}\%$

Another extension of cost-volume-profit analysis is the concept of operating leverage, which is used to measure the sensitivity of operating income to changes in sales volume. The degree of operating leverage specifies how much income will change given an increase or decrease in revenue. Company A and Company B are used again to demonstrate the effects of a 10 percent decrease in sales:

	COMPANY A	COMPANY B
Sales	$90,000	$90,000
Costs:		
Fixed	70,000	20,000
Variable	18,000	63,000
Income	$ 2,000	$ 7,000
Operating Leverage $= \dfrac{\%\text{ change in income}}{\%\text{ change in sales}}$	8.0	3.0

The operating leverage measure can be interpreted as the percentage change in income for a 1 percent change in sales. In the case of Company A, sales decreased 10 percent, operating leverage is 8, so we would expect profits to change by (-10×8) or -80 percent.

Comprehensive Demonstration Case

   *SUPERIOR MANUFACTURING COMPANY*

The 19X2 income budgeted statement for Superior Manufacturing Company is recast for cost-volume-profit purposes in Schedule 70. It assumes that the inventory contains the same ratio of fixed to variable cost as in current production (e.g., total manufacturing cost). This schedule provides the data needed to compute four different breakeven points, each with different assumptions, as follows:

1 Omit inventory change, but include other incomes and expenses.
2 Omit both inventory change and other incomes and expenses.
3 Include inventory change, but omit other incomes and expenses.
4 Include both inventory change and other incomes and expenses.

Representative computations are shown below for the first and second assumptions. The related breakeven graph is shown in Schedule 71. Note that for practical reasons the volume scale at the left does not extend to zero.

Computation of breakeven point:

Assumption 1—Omit inventory change, but include other incomes and expenses.

$$BE = \frac{\$1,309,140 - \$33,870}{1 - \dfrac{\$3,851,870 + \$92,916}{\$6,095,000}}$$

$$= \frac{\$1,275,270}{1 - .6472} = \$1,275,270 \div CM, .3528$$

$$= \underline{\underline{\$3,614,710}}$$

Assumption 2—Omit both inventory change and other incomes and expenses.

$$BE = \frac{\$1,309,140}{1 - \dfrac{\$3,851,870 + \$92,916}{\$6,095,000}}$$

(continued on p. 530)

SCHEDULE 70. Superior Manufacturing Company

Income Statement Data for Cost-Volume-Profit Analysis
For year ending December 31, 19X2

	REF.	TOTAL	FIXED COSTS COMPUTED REF.	AMOUNT	VARIABLE COSTS (TOTAL MINUS FIXED)
Budgeted sales	1	$6,095,000			
Manufacturing costs:					
Material	29	1,416,600			$1,416,600
Labor	30	1,752,000			1,752,000
Prime cost		3,168,600			3,168,600
Manufacturing overhead:					
General factory	33	116,800	41	$ 8,760 × 12 = $ 105,120	11,680
Power	33	110,000	41	6,700 × 12 = 80,400	29,600
Repair	33	10,000	41	720 × 12 = 8,640	1,360
Production Dept. 1	36	319,280	42	14,000 × 12 = 168,000	151,280
Production Dept. 2	34	29,280		1,960 × 12 = 23,520	5,760
Production Dept. 3	34	103,840		4,180 × 12 = 50,160	53,360
Building services	32	90,000		90,000	
Total manufacturing overhead cost		779,200		525,840	253,600
Total manufacturing cost		3,947,800		525,840	3,421,960
Percent of fixed and variable to total		100%		13%	87%
Add decrease in finished goods inventory*		106,800		13,884	92,916
Cost of goods sold	60	4,054,600		539,724	3,514,876
Gross margin		2,040,400			

Distribution:					
General sales overhead	39	296,330	$19,295 \times 12 =$	231,540	64,790
District	39	663,167	$26,930 \times 12 =$	323,160	340,007
Building service	32	30,000		30,000	
Total distribution		989,497		584,700	404,797
Administrative:					
Administrative Department	40	83,516	$6,340 \times 12 =$	76,080	7,436
Treasurer's Department	40	56,177	$3,310 \times 12 =$	39,720	16,457
Accounting Department	40	54,020	$4,400 \times 12 =$	52,800	1,220
Building services	32	30,000		30,000	
Total administrative		223,713		198,600	25,113
Total selling and administrative expense		1,213,210		783,300	429,910
Operating profit		827,190			
Add net of other income and expense	13	33,870			
Net profit before income taxes	13	861,060			
Less federal income taxes	13	258,318			
Net income	13	$ 602,742			
Total fixed costs *excluding*				$1,309,140	
Inventory decrease					
Total variable costs *excluding*					$3,851,870
Inventory decrease					

*Computation of fixed and variable components of the inventory change:
To determine percentages based on the preceding line—cost of goods sold $525,840 ÷ $3,947,800 = 13%, fixed: $106,800 × 13% = $13,884, fixed: $106,800 − $13,884 = $92,916 (87%), variable.

$$= \frac{\$1,309,140}{1 - \dfrac{\$3,944,786}{\$6,095,000}}$$

$$= \frac{\$1,309,140}{1 - .6472} = \$1,309,140 \div CM, .3528$$

$$= \underline{\underline{\$3,710,714}}$$

Points plotted on Schedule 71 for Assumption 2:

SCHEDULE 71. Breakeven Graph—Superior Manufacturing Company

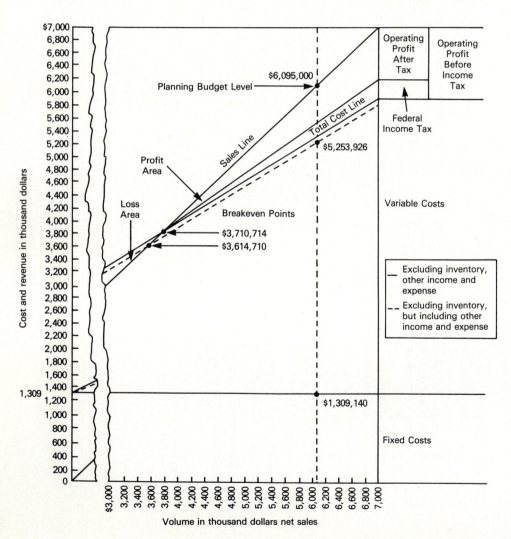

Sales	$6,095,000
Fixed costs	1,309,140
Total costs	
($1,309,140 + $3,944,786)	5,253,926

CHAPTER SUMMARY   Cost-volume-profit analysis includes the related concepts of (a) contribution analysis and (b) breakeven analysis. These concepts entered the mainstream of management accounting starting in the 1930s, with major emphasis in the 1950s. Both concepts rest upon the concept of cost variability (i.e., flexible or variable expense budgets—discussed in Chapter 10). Contribution analysis involves a series of analytical techniques to determine and evaluate the effects on profits of changes in sales volume, sales prices, fixed expenses, and variable expenses. Basically, it applies the concept of a contribution margin income statement: Revenues minus variable expenses equals contribution margin, and contribution margin minus fixed expenses equals profit. Breakeven analysis focuses on the breakeven point: Fixed expenses divided by the contribution margin equals breakeven sales volume (the point at which profit is zero because revenues equal total cost). The results of breakeven analysis are usually graphed to show the relationships between revenue (i.e., sales), fixed expenses, and variable expenses, within a relevant range of sales volume.

Suggested References

BIERMAN, HAROLD, JR., THOMAS DYCKMAN, and RONALD HILTON, *Cost Accounting: Concepts and Managerial Applications*. New York: Macmillan, 1990.

CHAMBERLAIN, NEIL W., *The Firm: Micro-Economic Planning and Action* (a classic). New York: McGraw-Hill, 1962.

GARDNER, FRED V., *Profit Management and Control* (an early classic). New York: McGraw-Hill, 1955.

GIVENS, H. R., "An Application of Curvilinear Breakeven Analysis," *Accounting Review*, January 1966, pp. 141–43.

HORNGREN, CHARLES T., and GEORGE FOSTER, *Cost Accounting: A Managerial Emphasis*. Englewood Cliffs, N.J.: Prentice-Hall, 1987.

MONTGOMERY, A. THOMPSON, *Management Accounting Information*, Chap. 6. Reading, Mass.: Addison-Wesley, 1979.

Discussion Questions

1. Define contribution analysis and contribution margin, and explain how they relate to the concept of cost (or expense) variability.
2. VU Company sells one product. The budgeted amounts are: planned

sales, 20,000 units at $30 per unit; total fixed costs, $250,000; and variable costs per unit, $14.

   a. Prepare a contribution margin income statement that shows contribution margin and profit.

   b. What is the contribution margin percent and the variable cost percent (or ratio)?

3. Refer to the data given in question 2. How much profit should be budgeted if planned sales are (a) 22,000 units and (b) 15,000 units?

4. DW Company sells one product. The budgeted amounts are: planned sales, 10,000 units at $20 per unit; variable costs, $10 per unit; and fixed costs, $80,000.

   a. Prepare the company's contribution margin budget.

   b. How much would budgeted profit be if the sale price is changed to $22 and planned unit sales is not changed?

5. Explain the relationships between budgeting and cost-volume-profit analysis.

6. Explain the concept of breakeven analysis.

7. BE Company's budget showed the following summarized data: fixed costs, $3,200; sales price per unit, $50; variable costs, $6,000; and planned unit sales, 200.

   a. Compute the variable cost ratio (or percent).

   b. Compute the contribution margin ratio (or percent).

   c. Compute the breakeven point in (1) units and (2) dollars.

   d. Compute the planned profit.

8. Discuss the advantages and disadvantages of the three principal methods of graphical presentation of breakeven analysis.

9. Explain the (a) variable cost ratio and (b) profit-volume (pv) ratio, and relate them to breakeven analysis.

10. List and briefly explain the primary assumptions underlying breakeven analysis.

11. Why is it important to define clearly the relevant range in breakeven analysis?

12. Why is the assumption of straightline variability of cost usually considered sufficiently valid for cost-volume-profit analysis?

13. What is the relationship between management policies and cost-volume-profit analysis?

14. Should nonoperating incomes and expenses be included in the breakeven analysis? Explain.

15. When a breakeven analysis is being prepared from budget data that include an inventory change in finished goods, what recognition should be given to the change?

16. What is meant by the margin of safety? Why is it important to management?

17. What are the two primary uses of cost-volume-profit analysis?

CASE 14-1   *An overview of contribution analysis and breakeven analysis*

OV Company has just completed its 19X8 annual profit plan. Summary data from the profit plan: sales revenue goal, $500,000 (units, 10,000); planned fixed costs, $240,000; planned profit per unit sold, $6. Planned sales by months reflect a seasonal variation in sales volume, above and below the monthly average, of 15 percent.

REQUIRED

1. Reconstruct the 19X8 planned income statement (contribution margin basis).
2. Compute the variable cost ratio and the contribution margin ratio.
3. Compute the unit (a) sales price, (b) variable cost, (c) contribution margin, (d) fixed cost, and (e) profit.
4. What is the (a) activity base and (b) relevant range?
5. Compute the breakeven point in (a) dollars and (b) units. Prove your answers.
6. Prepare a breakeven graph with all labels.
7. What is the amount of the "profit pickup" per unit?

CASE 14-2   *An overview of cost-volume-profit analysis*

Symrex Corporation has prepared its budgeted annual income statement as follows:

Sales (400,000 units)		$20,000,000
Manufacturing costs:		
Material	$1,700,000	
Labor	1,600,000	
Fixed overhead	2,650,000	
Variable overhead	4,050,000	
Distribution costs:		
Fixed	3,400,000	
Variable	1,900,000	
Administrative costs:		
Fixed	1,750,000	
Variable	350,000	
Total costs		17,400,000
Profit		$ 2,600,000

The company considers the relevant range to be 300,000 to 420,000 units. Monthly sales vary within 15 percent of the monthly average. Flexible expense budgets are used to develop (a) the planned income statements and (b) the monthly performance reports.

REQUIRED

1. Recast the annual income statement on a contribution margin basis. Show all costs combined into two totals—fixed and variable.

2. What is the (a) activity base and (b) relevant range (annual and monthly basis)?

3. Compute the (a) variable cost ratio, (b) contribution margin ratio, and (c) breakeven point (in units and dollars).

4. Prepare an annual breakeven graph and enter thereon all significant amounts and the related labels.

5. Compute the monthly breakeven point in dollars and units.

6. (a) Prepare a revised profit plan assuming: fixed costs are increased 10 percent, sales price is increased 5 percent, and variable costs are increased 3 percent. (b) Compute the new breakeven point.

CASE 14-3   *Relevant cost; effects of alternative decisions in profit planning*

The executives of Samson Company are developing the annual profit plan. The effect on budgeted profit of several contemplated decisions is being assessed. Some of these decisions will affect fixed costs; others will affect variable costs; and still others relate to sales price and sales volume (number of units). The profit goal set by the management is $25,000. The following preliminary income statement data (summarized) have been developed:

Sales (at $20 per unit)		$100,000
Costs:		
Fixed	$49,600	
Variable	38,000	87,600
Profit		$ 12,400

REQUIRED   (Each alternative is independent, and assume no change in units unless specifically stated otherwise.)

1. Compute the planned contribution margin, profit, and breakeven point based on the preliminary plan.

2. Compute the planned contribution margin, profit, and breakeven point assuming management makes a decision that will cause fixed costs to increase 10 percent.

3. Compute the planned contribution margin, profit, and breakeven point assuming instead that the decision will cause only variable costs to increase 10 percent.

4. Compute the planned contribution margin, profit, and breakeven point assuming a decision is made to increase the sales price by 10 percent.

5. Compute the planned contribution margin, profit, and breakeven point assuming the planned sales volume (units) is increased by 10 percent.

6. There is the possibility that all the above alternatives will be included in the final profit plan—that is, a 10 percent increase in fixed costs, a 10 percent increase in variable costs, a 10 percent increase in sales price, and a 10 percent increase in sales units. Compute the budgeted contribution margin, profit, and breakeven point considering the combined effect of these four changes.

7. How many units would have to be sold under requirement 6 to exactly meet the profit goal?

8. Prepare a summary of the comparative results. Use the following headings:

		CONTRIBUTION MARGIN			BREAKEVEN		
		AMOUNT	RATIO		UNITS	DOLLARS	
REQ.	ALTERNATIVE	AMOUNT	RATIO	PROFIT	UNITS	DOLLARS	COMMENTS

Be prepared to discuss the comparative results. Use the "Comments" column to outline your major points.

CASE 14-4   *Let's consider some alternatives to meet the profit target*

The executives of Fleck Company, a small manufacturer of one product, are developing the annual profit plan. They have just reviewed the "first cut" at the annual income statement and are concerned about the $11,000 indicated profit on a sales volume of 20,000 units. The fixed cost total of $99,000 appears to be high, and they have some doubts about departing from the unit sales price of $10. There is general agreement that the "profit target should be $30,000." This case focuses on several alternatives suggested during the meeting of the executive committee that just reviewed the tentative profit plan.

REQUIRED

1. Prior to the suggested alternatives under consideration, respond to the following (show detailed computations):
   a. Prepare a summarized income statement using the contribution margin approach.
   b. Compute the breakeven point in sales and the margin of safety.
   c. Prepare a breakeven graph that shows the basic characteristics and budget amounts.
   Be prepared to discuss all aspects of the above requirements.

2. Respond directly to each of the following alternatives under consideration by management. Each alternative is independent of the others; state any assumptions that you make.

☐   **Alternative 1**—A sales price increase of 20 percent is contemplated; the sales executive estimates that this will cause a drop in units that can be sold by approximately 15 percent. What would be the new contribution margin and profit? What would be the new breakeven point and margin of safety? How many units would have to be sold to earn the target profit?

☐ **Alternative 2**—A decrease in fixed costs of $5,500 is contemplated. What would be the new contribution margin, profit, breakeven point, and margin of safety?

☐ **Alternative 3**—A decrease in variable costs of 6 percent is contemplated. What would be the new contribution margin, profit, breakeven point, and margin of safety?

☐ **Alternative 4**—A decrease in fixed costs of $5,500 and a decrease in variable costs of 6 percent are contemplated. What would be the new contribution margin, profit, breakeven point, and margin of safety?

3. Set up a table to compare the various alternatives. Use the following headings:

	SALES				BREAKEVEN	MARGIN OF
ALTERNATIVE	UNITS	$	CM	PROFIT	$ UNITS	SAFETY

4. Evaluate the several budgets. What would you recommend? Justify.

CASE 14-5   *Cost-volume-profit analyses for five separate plants*

York Manufacturing Company has five plants dispersed nationally. Each plant uses flexible expense budgets and prepares cost-volume-profit analyses.

REQUIRED

1. Plant 1 manufactures two similar products. The annual profit plan for Plant 1 shows: fixed costs, $120,000; variable costs, $84,000; and sales value of production, $220,000 (assume all units are sold). Allocated home-office planned costs, $32,000.

   Prepare a plant income statement using the contribution margin approach. Also, prepare an analysis that shows the breakeven points before and after cost allocations. Explain any concerns that you have.

2. Plant 2 produces one product that sells at $4.00 and costs $4.25 when produced in quantities of 15,000, and $3.8125 per unit when produced in quantities of 20,000. Allocated home-office costs, $10,000. What is the contribution margin, profit, and breakeven point in dollars and in units at 15,000 units minimum and at 20,000 units maximum?

3. Plant 3 produces three similar products. Its planned income and cost estimates are as follows:

Sales (annual)		$100,000
Costs:		
Fixed	$ 40,000	
Variable	30,000	
Home-office allocated	35,000	105,000
Profit (loss)		$ (5,000)

Compute the contribution margin, profit, and breakeven point.

Sale of Plant 3 for $200,000 is under consideration. What is your recommendation based on the data given? Justify your recommendation.

4. Plant 4 produces one product; the planned income and cost estimates are as follows:

Sales (annual) at $20		$200,000
Costs:		
Fixed	$ 74,750	
Variable	135,000	
Home-office allocated	20,250	230,000
Profit (loss)		$ (30,000)

Compute the contribution margin, profit, and breakeven point. How many additional units must be manufactured in the plant in order to break even, assuming no change in selling price? What would be the profit pickup per unit above breakeven? Explain.

5. Plant 5 produces two products. It is a new plant that is highly automated with low variable costs and high fixed costs. Its plan is as follows:

Sales (annual)	$390,000	100%
Variable costs	69,750	18%
Contribution margin	320,250	82%
Fixed costs	120,000	
Profit (before home office)	200,250	
Home-office allocation	35,000	
Net (after allocation)	$165,250	

Breakeven point:
$120,000 ÷ .82 = $146,342.

No additional analysis is needed in this requirement.

6. Prepare a schedule that shows each plant's plan and the total company plan. Assume that $30,250 of total home-office allocated overhead is variable. Use the following format.

ITEM	PLANT 1	PLANT 2	PLANT 3	PLANT 4	PLANT 5	TOTAL COMPANY
Sales						
VC						
CM						
FC						
Profit						
Breakeven point:						
Margin of safety:						

Be prepared to discuss all aspects of this case.

CASE 14-6   *Should we sell below cost to make a profit?*

Howe Company manufactures two products, A and B. The company is having difficulty attaining a sales volume sufficient to use its present plant capacity. A new customer offers a large repeating contract for product A at $10 each and for product B at $18 each. The first order will be for 1,000 units of each product. The following planning data are available (assume the regular market will not be affected):

COSTS	PRODUCT A	PRODUCT B
Direct labor	$ 6,000	$15,000
Direct material	3,000	5,000
Variable factory overhead	3,000	4,000
Fixed factory overhead	12,000	20,000
Packing, shipping, and other variable costs	4,800	1,000
Administrative and sales overhead (fixed)	9,000	15,000
Current planned sales in the regular market (units)	4,000 units	2,500 units
Planned sales price in the regular market	$ 14	$ 20

The new contract will not increase fixed costs and administrative and sales overhead.

REQUIRED

1. Compute the contribution margin, profit, and breakeven point for each product separately and for the company (exclude the contract).

2. Based on the information given, should the contract be accepted? Support your conclusion with computations.

3. What minimum price and volume (units) for each product should be accepted under the new offer? What about the short-term and long-term implications of the contract?

CASE 14-7   *How would you bid on this printing job?*

Snappy Printers, a small job-printing firm, is preparing a bid for ten thousand to fifteen thousand advertising pamphlets, to which the following budget amounts relate:

Estimated cost of setting up and fixed overhead	$390
Estimated cost of material and variable overhead	$5.00 per hundred
Estimated cost of labor	$3.00 per hundred
Estimated selling price	$0.11 each

REQUIRED

1. How many pamphlets must be sold at $0.11 each to break even?

2. What is the profit per pamphlet above breakeven?

3. What should be the bid price for Case A, 10,000 pamphlets, and for Case B, 15,000 pamphlets, if a 20 percent profit on sales is desired?

4. Prepare a contribution margin income statement for Case A and Case B based on your later conversation with the customer, who said, "I will go for the 15,000 if the price is right." You should prepare the statement with two columns: Case A (to earn the 10 percent on sales) and Case B (to have your "right" price).

CASE 14-8   *A hypothetical case—which company would be the better investment?*

John and Jane Enterprises (a partnership) has decided to purchase Company A or Company B. The price is exactly the same for either company, and John and Jane are in full agreement that the price is right. However, Jane wants to buy Company A because its variable costs are low. John wants to buy Company B because its fixed costs are low. The future for both companies looks about the same.

John and Jane have engaged you—known as an expert consultant—to recommend which company they should buy. They want you to provide "solid arguments" to support your recommendation. You will be limited to the following budget data:

	COMPANY A	COMPANY B
Sales revenue (one product)	$200,000	$200,000
Total expenses	180,000	180,000
Variable cost to sales ratio	30%	60%

REQUIRED

1. Prepare all the relevant analyses that you think might support your recommendation.

2. Based on the data available, give your recommendation and pinpoint the primary economic factors that support your conclusion.

CASE 14-9   *Can you improve this company's sales mix to increase profit?*

Mix Company sells three different products—A, B, and C. The top executives are considering changes in the sales mix. The sales goal has been set at $24,000 for all three products combined. Total advertising and selling efforts can be arranged to obtain sales of the various products to agree with the best sales mix. The dollar amounts are simplified for case purposes.

Total fixed costs budgeted is $3,312. The variable cost ratios based on sales are: product A, 70 percent; product B, 80 percent; and product C, 90 percent.

The executives are considering two alternative sales-mix combinations:

ALTERNATIVE	PRODUCT A	PRODUCT B	PRODUCT C	TOTAL
(1)	50%	30%	20%	100%
(2)	70%	20%	10%	100%

REQUIRED

1. Evaluate each sales-mix alternative in terms of (a) contribution margin, (b) profit, (c) breakeven point, and (d) margin of safety. Which sales mix is preferable?
2. Try to develop a better sales mix with a customer-demand constraint that no product can have less than 10 percent or more than 80 percent of sales.

CASE 14-10   Developing a better profit plan

Solid Manufacturing Company produces and sells two similar products. The 19X5 profit plan is being developed. The first tentative plan was as follows:

Sales revenue		$5,000,000
Cost of goods sold:		
Fixed	$1,600,000	
Variable	1,750,000	3,350,000
Gross margin		1,650,000
Selling and general costs:		
Fixed	556,000	
Variable	800,000	1,356,000
Profit		$ 294,000

After the tentative profit plan was developed, the new vice-president of sales developed a sales plan with a sales goal of $7,500,000 with no change in sales prices. This sales plan calls for the following expense increases for 19X5: sales salaries, $200,000; and advertising, $100,000.

The vice-president of manufacturing realized that the increased sales would require major additions to the plant and increases in certain manufacturing expenses as follows for 19X5: salaries, $20,000; and manufacturing overhead (fixed), $60,000.

The vice-president of finance estimated the following additional increases in fixed costs: depreciation, taxes, and insurance on the plant, $220,000 in total; and interest cost, $50,000. Inventory levels remain constant.

REQUIRED

1. Based on the new plans, prepare a revised profit plan for 19X5. Use the contribution margin approach. Also, compute the breakeven point and margin of safety (a) before the expansion (the original budget) and (b) after the expansion (the new budget). (Hint: The new breakeven point is $5,726,531.)

2. Prepare a schedule to compare before and after expansion for the contribution margin, profit, breakeven, and margin of safety.

3. Compute the sales needed after the expansion to earn a $1,000,000 profit assuming no change in selling prices.

4. Prepare an income statement assuming that the $7,500,000 sales revenue in the new budget was due only to a price increase (i.e., no change in units sold implicit in the original plan).

15

Performance Evaluation and Management Control

INTRODUCTION AND PURPOSE   Performance reporting for internal management use is an important part of a comprehensive profit planning and control system. This chapter focuses on the fundamentals of establishing a coordinated set of performance reports. The performance reporting phase of a comprehensive PPC program significantly influences the extent to which the organization's planned goals and objectives are attained.

To indicate the extensive reporting requirements a business needs and to focus on performance reporting, the following overview of financial reports is presented and briefly explained:

1. **Special External Reports**—These are reports to government agencies, regulatory commissions, creditors, investigative agencies, and other groups external to the active management. Frequently, these reports are extensive and constitute a significant portion of the overall reporting activities of the business. Such reports are costly and involve significant management attention.
2. **Report to Owners**—This is the traditional annual report to the owners (to stockholders in the case of a corporation) and other special reports prepared for the owners. These reports, by and large, are based on "generally accepted accounting principles" and generally report data that have been subject to an audit by an independent CPA.
3. **Internal Reports**—These confidential reports are prepared within the company for internal use only. They do not have to meet the needs of external groups, nor the test of "generally accepted accounting principles," but rather the test of internal management needs. For purposes of discussion, this category of reports is subdivided into three different subclassifications:
   a. **Statistical Reports**—These are accounting reports that show the historical statistics about all phases of operations. The data included in these reports constitute the detailed financial and operating history of the firm. The continual accumulation of these data is essential for both contemplated and unforeseen uses in the future. These statistics include the basic data for the two categories of reports outlined above; they also provide the basic data for special-purpose studies that are made from time to time. Separate reports of this type are common and are made on a repetitive basis (usually monthly).
   b. **Special Reports**—These internal reports are not prepared according to any prede-

542

termined schedule. Each one relates to a specific management problem. Their design, scope, and comprehensiveness depend on the particular problem at hand.

c. **Performance Reports**—These reports are usually prepared on a monthly basis and follow a standardized format from period to period (but are not standardized among companies or industries). Such reports are designed to facilitate internal control by the management. They should be composed of carefully selected series of data related to each responsibility center. Fundamentally, they report actual results compared with goals and budget plans. Frequently, they identify problems that require special reports, since these reports are designed to pinpoint both efficient and inefficient performance.

All companies, regardless of their size, have reporting requirements for all the categories listed above. In smaller companies, most of the basic reporting needs may be accomplished by using a single general-purpose report. However, as the size and complexity of the company increase, there is greater need for segmentation of the reporting as suggested above. Many companies fail to use all of these categories despite the increasing size and complexity of operations. As a company changes and grows, the overall system of financial reporting should be adapted to meet its changing needs. It is common to find an antiquated accounting and financial reporting system. In such cases, the full potential of the management and the company is jeopardized. The usual accounting report prepared for external use has limited application for internal management purposes. Accountants who attempt to meet the internal problems of management with reports designed for external purposes are not serving the management properly.

We are concerned here specifically with **performance reports** (item 3c above). This particular phase of reporting is an integral part of a comprehensive budget program. Next we will discuss some of the essential characteristics of performance reports. Later in the chapter we will discuss a typical monthly performance report related to the annual profit plan.

PERFORMANCE REPORTS AND COMMUNICATION

Performance reporting is an important phase of the control process. Our prior discussion of the control process can be summarized as follows:

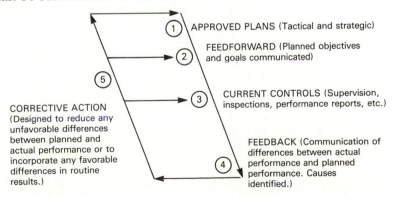

In most businesses, management must rely to a great extent upon information contained in reports developed within the business. These internal reports serve as an important means of communication. One study stated:

> To be useful to management, accounting information must be communicated to management personnel. Communication implies that a person receiving the information understands the nature and significance of material contained in the reports. When communication is genuinely effective, management's actions and decisions are likely to be based on the facts which they receive rather than on untested impressions and guesses. However, there is reason to believe that accounting reports to management have not always achieved their intended purpose because the reports were not understood, recipients lacked time required to grasp the meaning, or the content of reports was not relevant to problems facing the persons who received them.[1]

Reports that communicate effectively to all levels of management stimulate action and influence decisions. Those assigned the responsibility for designing and preparing reports for management should understand all of management's problems, the decision approaches used, and the attitudes of management.

ESSENTIAL FEATURES OF PERFORMANCE REPORTS   Considerable management effort and time is required to develop profit plans for an enterprise. This effort is justified primarily because the activities of all subunits must be focused on enterprise objectives. Each responsibility center in a company fulfills a prescribed and necessary role in attaining enterprise objectives. Attainment of the profit plan is vital. To ensure performance of the objectives, control is necessary. Control has many facets. Among the more important of these are internal performance reports. Therefore, in comprehensive profit planning and control, performance reports are vital. The central objective of performance reports is the communication of performance measurements, actual results, and the related variances. In addition to control implications, performance reports offer management essential insights into all facets of operational efficiencies. Performance reports pose critical behavioral problems because inefficiences, as well as efficiencies, of individuals are pinpointed and reported. Performance reports should be tailored to the characteristics of the particular environment. However, we can generalize about certain criteria in their design and application. Performance reports should be

1 Tailored to the organizational structure and locus of controllability (that is, by responsibility centers).
2 Designed to implement the management-by-exception principle.
3 Repetitive and related to short time periods.

---

[1] "Reports Which Management Find Most Useful," *NAA Bulletin,* Accounting Practice Report, No. 9, Sec. 3.

4 Adapted to the requirements of the primary users.

5 Simple, understandable, and report only essential information.

6 Accurate and designed to pinpoint significant distinctions.

7 Prepared and presented promptly.

8 Constructive in tone.

THE BASIC FORMAT OF PERFORMANCE REPORTS   The first three criteria listed above suggest a basic format in the design and application of performance reports. The performance report system should be tailored to the organizational structure of the enterprise in the same way that we have emphasized for PPC. A separate performance report should be prepared for each responsibility center, starting with those at the lowest level, which in turn feed into summary reports for each higher level. Performance reports should clearly distinguish between controllable and noncontrollable items. Performance measurement requires that actual results be compared with plans, objectives, and standards so that the significant differences (exceptions) call management's attention to high, low, and satisfactory performance. Variances from plans identify for the managers the areas that need investigation and possible action. Management action may be corrective, commendatory, or revisory. Favorable variances justify investigation as well as unfavorable variances. Unfavorable variances may signal danger. Further investigation usually is necessary to pinpoint the precise causes. Performance reports should be prepared periodically, generally on a monthly basis, although certain problems may suggest the need for weekly or even daily reports.

SP Manufacturing Company is used to illustrate the way that performance reports can be (1) related to the organizational structure, (2) designed to identify the exceptional items that are controllable, and (3) related to specific time horizons. Exhibit 15-1 shows the organizational chart for SP Manufacturing Company. Note the four levels of management and the line organization from the president down to the departmental supervisor (manager) of Machining No. 2. The blocked-out segment of the chart is used to illustrate the concepts. Exhibit 15-2 shows the February performance report for each level of management and the integration of these reports. Notice that the lower report (for Machining No. 2) indicates the status of cost control for the month and year to date for each controllable cost in the department. This report is designed especially for the supervisor of Machining No. 2. Similar reports would be prepared for the other producing departments (Machining No. 1, Drill Press, Assembly, and Others). The supervisor of each department normally would receive the performance report that relates only to his or her department.

Moving one step up the organizational ladder (to the production manager), a production department cost summary is prepared. This performance report, shown as Exhibit 15-2, is a summary of the five producing department reports. This report is designed especially for the production manager and pin-

EXHIBIT 15-1

Organization Chart—SP Manufacturing Company

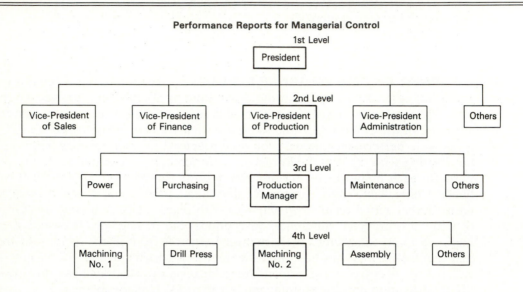

points, by department, weaknesses in cost control. Should the production manager desire to trace the source of either favorable or unfavorable cost control performance to accounts within the department involved, he or she can refer to the appropriate departmental performance reports, each of which should be attached to the summary. For example, the production department cost summary (last column) calls attention to two departments (Machining No. 2 and Assembly) that have unfavorable cost variances. Tracing the $130 unfavorable variance in Machining No. 2, the production manager can immediately identify the specific cost (direct labor) as the primary problem that needs attention.

Noncontrollable costs are not reported in this simplified example. A policy problem exists in this respect; that is, whether to show all costs chargeable to the particular responsibility center or to show only the controllable costs. Although many companies report only controllable costs on departmental performance reports, others prefer to show all costs chargeable to the department, on the basis (in theory) that a department's supervisor should be aware of the full cost of operating the department. In addition to costs, the performance report for a responsibility center should report all controllable items as illustrated in Chapters 6, 7, 8, 9, and 10.

This illustration of SP Manufacturing Company also shows the application of the management-by-exception principle. For example, the production manager does not have to delve into numerous figures to identify the source of trouble (the exception). The manager can check the last column of the summary for significant variances. The exception principle cannot be applied to ac-

EXHIBIT 15-2

Performance Reports—SP Manufacturing Company

SP Manufacturing Company
PERFORMANCE REPORT—February

Division Cost Summary

LEVEL NO. 1

Controllable Costs:	Actual		(Over) or Under Plan	
	This Month	Year to Date	This Month	Year to Date
Sales	$32,900	$ 65,200	$(1,720)	$(3,280)
Finance	3,150	5,990	420	760
Production	21,800	44,740	(200)	(510)
Administration	17,700	35,300	760	980
Others	8,500	15,900	(200)	100
Total	$84,050	$167,130	$ (940)	$(1,950)

$510 etc

SP Manufacturing Company
PERFORMANCE REPORT—February

Factory Cost Summary   Executive M. R. Bryan

LEVEL NO. 2

Controllable Costs:	Actual		(Over) or Under Plan	
	This Month	Year to Date	This Month	Year to Date
Power	$ 3,200	$ 6,650	$210	$350
Purchasing	1,120	2,590	120	170
Production	13,600	27,760	(90)	(310)
Maintenance	2,950	5,850	(360)	(750)
Others	930	1,890	(80)	30
Total	$21,800	$44,740	$(200)	$(510)

SP Manufacturing Company
PERFORMANCE REPORT—February

Dept. Production Department Cost Summary   Supervisor P. M. Cain

$310 etc.

LEVEL NO. 3

Controllable Costs:	Actual		(Over) or Under Plan	
	This Month	Year to Date	This Month	Year to Date
Machining No. 1	$ 3,400	$ 7,000	$120	$ 80
Drill Press	1,850	3,600	80	150
Machining No. 2	4,200	8,600	(90)	(130)
Assembly	2,950	6,100	(250)	(450)
Others	1,200	2,460	50	40
Total	$13,600	$27,760	$ (90)	$(310)

$130 etc.

SP Manufacturing Company
PERFORMANCE REPORT—February

Dept. Machining 2 Cost Report   Foreman A. B. Smith

LEVEL NO. 4

Controllable Costs:	Actual		(Over) or Under Plan	
	This Month	Year to Date	This Month	Year to Date
Direct Labor	$2,150	$4,400	$(70)	$(150)
Direct Material	1,200	2,500	10	30
Supervision	400	800	—	—
Setup	150	310	(10)	(30)
Repair	140	260	(20)	10
Supplies	60	140	—	(10)
Others	100	190	—	20
Total	$4,200	$8,600	$(90)	$(130)

tual (historical) figures standing alone. There must be some standard (plans in this case) against which actual figures may be compared to identify the exceptions.

Moving to level two, the development of the factory cost summary for the vice-president of production is done by listing the summary data for each of the five organizational subdivisions (Power, Purchasing, Production, Maintenance, and Others). The performance summary for the president is developed similarly. The reports are repetitive with monthly and cumulative data. The result of these procedures is an integrated performance reporting system emphasizing (1) the organization structure, (2) the planned objectives and the exception principle, and (3) the specific time dimensions. This system is simple, is easily understood, and enables the managers to keep their fingers on the performance pulse of the company with a minimum of time and effort. This same integrated system should be applied to sales performance reporting and all other responsibility centers.

ADAPT PERFORMANCE REPORTS TO REQUIREMENTS OF USERS   The extent to which the various managers use their performance reports depends on many factors, some behavioral and some technical. One important factor is the extent to which the performance reports serve the measurement and decision-making needs of the users. Communication is a subtle management problem, and it is facilitated by performance reports if the different needs and experiences of the users are taken into account. A department supervisor responds differently than a vice-president.

Top-management personnel need reports that give a complete and readily comprehensible summary of the overall aspects of operations and an identification of major events. The summaries must be supported in sufficient detail to facilitate tracing significant deviations to their source.

Middle management is usually defined as those members of management in charge of the major subdivisions of the business, such as sales, production, and finance. Middle management is responsible for carrying out the responsibilities assigned to the subdivisions within the broad policies and objectives established by top management. Middle management is closer to and more concerned with operations than top management, although it also has important planning functions. Performance reports for middle management, although including summary data, are also characterized by detailed data on day-to-day operations.

Lower-level management (departmental supervisors) is principally concerned with coordination and control of day-to-day operations. Therefore, control reports should principally be concerned with production and cost control. Reports to supervisors should be detailed, simple, understandable, and limited to items that are directly related to the supervisors' operational responsibilities.

The ways of communicating financial information can be broadly classified as follows:

1. Written:
    a. Formal financial statements
    b. Tabulated statistics
    c. Narration and written expositions
    d. Ratios and other performance indicators
2. Graphical:
    a. Charts
    b. Diagrams and pictures
3. Oral:
    a. Group meetings
    b. Conferences with individuals

A company should use a variety of ways for communicating information to management. In most companies, all the ways listed above should be used from time to time. Selection of the appropriate way should depend on such factors as the type of report, data involved, level of management using the report, purpose of the report, background of the principal users, and nature of the operations. Some managers are chart-minded, others are figure-minded, and others prefer written communications. Those designing and preparing performance reports should keep in mind that financial reports are used primarily by nonaccountants with varied backgrounds. In view of these considerations, some companies have adopted combined forms of presentation. One useful combination of ways for recurring reports uses charts, figures, and narrative. To illustrate, assume that the following trend and performance data were taken from a conventional report:

Trend Data—Profits and Sales 19A through 19K

YEAR	OPERATING PROFITS	SALES
19A	$14,000	$150,000
19B	14,000	147,000
19C	14,500	154,000
19D	14,700	160,000
19E	14,400	158,000
19F	14,800	161,000
19G	14,600	164,000
19H	14,500	165,000
19I	14,500	165,000
19J	18,000*	166,000
19K	14,600†	168,000†

*Includes fixed assets sold at a gain of $4,000.
†Budgeted.

Performance Data—Sales March 31, 19L

MONTH	SALES REVENUE		VARIANCE FROM PLAN (UNFAVORABLE)
	ACTUAL	PLANNED	
January	$11,800	$ 12,000	($200)
February	12,100	12,000	100
March	14,300	14,000	300
April		15,000	
May		16,000	
June		15,000	
July		14,000	
August		12,000	
September		13,000	
October		14,000	
November		15,000	
December		16,000	
Total		$168,000	

Although the above data accurately present past profits and sales for a period of years, comparisons and trends are not readily apparent. The same trend on data are presented in a more understandable way in Exhibits 15-3 and 15-5. Similarly, the performance data are presented more clearly in Exhibits 15-4 and 15-6. The reporting formats suggested by this example indicate the advantages of presenting certain types of information both graphically and tabularly. The charts effectively communicate the overall essence of the information; the figures provide exact data when needed. Some companies maintain a "performance report book" for individual executives. The book is usually a loose-leaf binder containing the performance and related reports for the particular executive. If this procedure is used, the graphs can be printed on the back of the page and the corresponding tabulations on the front of the next page so that when the report is opened at any particular page, the graphs are always on the left and the figures are on the right. Exhibits 15-3 through 15-6 are presented in this manner. Many top executives have a strong preference for narrative summaries on internal reports. Words frequently tell the story much more effectively than figures alone. Analyses of the causative factors involved in a performance report showing significant exceptions should usually be presented in narrative form.

Oral presentation should be a significant part of the internal reporting system in all organizations. Controllers and budget directors should encourage the use of executive conferences where the performance report is presented, explained, and discussed. Oral presentation is important because interpretation and emphasis are sometimes difficult in other forms of reporting. Moreover, managers have the opportunity to pose questions and bring up points that are not clear, thereby ensuring understanding and communication.

EXHIBIT 15-3

Line Graph Presentation—Sales and Profits

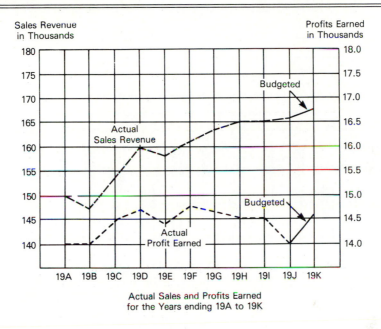

Actual Sales and Profits Earned
for the Years ending 19A to 19K

Keep Reports Simple and Essential

In the design and preparation of performance reports, it is important to keep in mind that the users generally are not accountants. Careful attention to format is important. Titles and headings should be descriptive, column headings and side captions should clearly identify the data, and technical jargon should be avoided.

Reports should not be too long, and complex tabulations should be avoided. Reports should be carefully screened to eliminate all nonessential data. Many performance reports include too much information rather than too little. To simplify, some companies report actual costs and budget variances; planned allowances are omitted. The "Budget" or "Planned" column may add little understanding and tends to make the report bulky. A second technique to simplify reports is to round amounts to the nearest significant figure. Another technique is to use performance indicator ratios, both financial and operational. For example, from a financial perspective, there is return on assets or investment, while from an operational perspective there is capacity utilization, etc. There are practically no limits to the development of appropriate internal performance measurement ratios. Solutions depend entirely on the nature of the operation.

EXHIBIT 15-4

Bar Graph Presentation—Sales and Profits

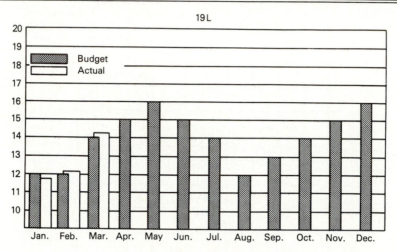

Actual Sales Compared with Planned Sales

Cumulative Sales
Over Plan

Cumulative Sales
Under Plan

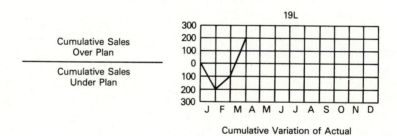

Cumulative Variation of Actual
Sales Over or Under Budget

Performance reports should be standardized to a reasonable degree. Managers become accustomed to certain terminology, formats, and methods of presentation and know where to look to find specific information. Changing report formats and terminology indiscriminately can be a source of annoyance. Despite the desirability of standardizing performance reports, constant attention must be given to improving them. Improvement necessarily involves changes; however, desirable changes, if made at an opportune time and adequately explained, can usually be accomplished with a minimum of confusion.

Reports should be relevant. It is not uncommon to find data in some performance reports (or even entire reports) that serve no useful purpose. Such data sometimes are presented because some manager, months or even years before, requested it for a special purpose. Although there is no further use for the information, no one has taken the initiative to discontinue it. It is not surprising that busy managers, in requesting special information, may not give a

EXHIBIT 15-5

Summary of Actual Sales and Profits Earned from Operations
For Years 19A Through 19K

YEAR	ACTUAL SALES	PROFITS EARNED (EXCLUDING UNUSUAL OR NONOPERATING ITEMS)	PROFITS AS PERCENT OF SALES
19A	$150,000	$14,000	9.3
19B	147,000	14,000	9.5
19C	154,000	14,500	9.4
19D	160,000	14,700	9.1
19E	158,000	14,400	9.1
19F	161,000	14,800	9.2
19G	164,000	14,600	8.9
19H	165,000	14,500	8.8
19I	165,000	14,500	8.8
19J	166,000	14,000	8.4
19K	168,000	14,600	8.7

EXHIBIT 15-6

Summary of Actual Sales Compared with Planned Sales
For Three Months Ending March 31, 19L

MONTH 19L	ACTUAL SALES	BUDGETED SALES	VARIANCE OF ACTUAL SALES FROM PLAN (AMOUNTS BELOW BUDGET) MONTHLY VARIANCE	CUMULATIVE VARIANCE
January	$11,800	$ 12,000	($200)	($200)
February	12,100	12,000	100	(100)
March	14,300	14,000	300	200
April		15,000		
May		16,000		
June		15,000		
July		14,000		
August		12,000		
September		13,000		
October		14,000		
November		15,000		
December		16,000		
Total		$168,000		

date beyond which it will no longer be needed; nor do they necessarily remember to tell someone to discontinue presenting the special data.

Surveys reveal that a considerable portion of the information on internal financial reports is not used. Continuous efforts to simplify reports should include periodic surveys to determine the extent of nonrelevant information being presented to the various levels of management.

Minimize the Time Gap Between the Decision and the Report

As a rule, executives and supervisors are very busy tending to their responsibilities. They must continually make decisions, varying from major decisions to relatively insignificant ones. The quality of these decisions determines the success or failure of the organization. Because of the significance of the decision-making process and its immediate and continuous effect on operations, the time gap between the decision point and the reporting of the effects of decisions should be minimized. In any situation, both effective and ineffective decisions must be expected; the overall effectiveness depends on the ratio of the effective decisions to the total. Advance planning minimizes the risk of an excessive number of ineffective decisions. Efficient performance reporting minimizes this risk. The time gap between the decision point and performance reporting should be minimized. Unfavorable situations and problems are critical to the manager at the time they occur. As time passes, the manager becomes more concerned with new events and less concerned with the past. Moreover, the longer an unfavorable situation continues before correction, the greater the financial loss to the company. Finally, with the passage of time, there is a tendency to regard inefficiency as "normal" or "the best we can do under the circumstances."

Performance reports should be available on a timely basis. To attain a realistic balance between immediate reporting and the costs of detailed reporting, monthly performance reports are widely used in practice. When special problem areas are involved, weekly and even daily performance reporting related to these problem areas may be necessary, at least for some period of time.

The tendency of some accountants to hold up the issuance of performance reports until "all the facts are in" frequently detracts from the usefulness of the performance reports. Because all accounting data will seldom be available (there will always be some estimates, such as depreciation), those preparing performance reports should not hesitate to make reasonable estimates of "actual" items so that a timely report is possible. Even in simple situations, monthly performance reports are often issued after the twentieth of the following month. However, objective analysis will usually find no valid reason for the reports being issued later than the fifth to seventh day in the following month. Some completeness may have to be sacrificed, but not enough to impair the effectiveness of the reporting for management purposes. It bears repeating that external reporting presents communication problems that are significantly different from those of internal reporting.

MANAGEMENT FOLLOW-UP PROCEDURES   Well-managed companies use monthly performance reports covering all aspects of operations. These reports give favorable and unfavorable variances between actual performance and planned performance for the month just ended and, cumulatively, for the year to date. Managers should analyze these monthly reports carefully to be fully knowledgeable about both high and low performance in their respective responsibility centers. High and low performances should be given immediate priority to determine the causes. However, the process should not stop at this point. Follow-up is a key phase of effective control. Some companies require written explanations of significant variances. The follow-up procedures preferred by other companies involve conferences to discuss the causes and corrective actions to be taken. Follow-up procedures should begin at the top-management level (in the executive committee meeting, for example), to discuss and analyze both unsatisfactory and satisfactory conditions. Decisions should be made about the ways and means to correct unsatisfactory conditions. Favorable variances should also be analyzed (1) to determine whether the goals were realistic, (2) to commend those responsible for high performances, and (3) to transfer some "know-how" to other responsibility centers.

Group and individual conferences should be held at various management levels to initiate corrective actions. Follow-up procedures should embody constructive action to correct unfavorable conditions rather than punitive action for failure, the results of which obviously cannot be erased. Another important aspect is that follow-up action is strictly a *line* responsibility rather than a staff responsibility. The budget director, controller, or other staff officer should not undertake, or be assigned, the responsibility for enforcing the budget.

TECHNICAL ASPECTS OF CONTROL REPORTS   Some companies issue separate internal "accounting" and "budget" reports. However, separation of these two reports for internal managerial purposes seems illogical, and we assume in this book that they are combined into a single performance reporting system.

The primary value of performance reports is in the comparison of actual results with budget objectives and in the analysis of the resulting variances. There are numerous methods of expressing variances. The expression of variances as absolute amounts is not always satisfactory because an absolute amount standing alone frequently is not meaningful. Variances should also be expressed in relative terms, that is, as a percentage of the planned or budgeted amount. Although statistical control limits can be developed to determine the significance of variances, most companies find it satisfactory to establish a general "rule-of-thumb" policy for this purpose. For example, a small business might establish a policy that variances up to $25, or 5 percent of budget, are to be considered insignificant. A realistic policy to determine significance should be established, because neither actual figures nor budget objectives will be absolutely accurate.

Many companies show actual, budget, dollar variances, and percentage variances on performance reports. Several methods of reporting variances are illustrated as follows.

					RELATIVES	
	1	2	3	4	5	6
			VARIANCE	PERCENT OF VARIANCES	PERCENT OF PLAN	PERCENT OF ACTUAL
ITEM	ACTUAL	PLANNED	IN DOLLARS	TO PLAN	REALIZATION	TO PLAN
			(1 − 2)	(3 ÷ 2)	(2 ÷ 1)	(1 ÷ 2)
Expense	$ 110	$ 100	$ 10*	10%	90.9%	110%
Sales	$11,000	$10,000	$1,000	10%	110%†	110%

*Unfavorable.
†For revenues, the dividend and divisor must be reversed.

Performance reports should normally show actual (column 1). However, there is a question as to which of the remaining columns would be preferable in a particular situation. In most cases, it would seem desirable to report the data shown in columns 1, 3, and either 4, 5, or 6. Column 4 is more generally used than column 5 or 6 because it relates the variance directly to the plan. In the illustration, column 4 indicates that expense was 10 percent over plan (unfavorable). Sales were also 10 percent over plan, which is favorable. To compute this column, the mathematical process is the same for revenues and expenses, that is, column 3 divided by column 2. If the variance is negative (unfavorable), the resulting percentage will be negative (unfavorable). Column 5, "Percent of Plan Realization," is used by some companies because it is easily understood. In the above case, the plan realization of 90.9% ($100 ÷ $110) indicates that the efficiency of cost control was only 90.9 percent. Had actual expense been $100, plan realization would have been 100 percent, that is, exactly "par." On the other hand, had actual expense been $90, plan realization would have been 111 percent. When dealing with revenues, the mathematical process must be reversed, that is, actual is divided by plan. Thus, the plan realization for sales in the illustration is 110 percent because actual sales were 10 percent above planned sales. The latter method is simple to understand because a percentage figure above 100 percent indicates a favorable condition, whereas a percentage figure below 100 percent indicates an unfavorable condition. The method illustrated in column 6 is seldom used.

Monthly performance reports for all responsibility centers should generally show (1) variances for the period being reported and (2) cumulative variances to date. Those preparing performance reports should use footnote comments when the reasons for specific variances are known to them. In addition, footnotes should be used to direct the attention of management to specific conditions that may require attention.

Integrated Performance Reports

A comprehensive performance report for Producing Department X in Stanley Company is shown in Exhibit 15-7. Notice the following features: (1) clear identification of responsibility; (2) distinction between controllable and noncon-

EXHIBIT 15-7

Departmental Performance Report, Stanley Company

	DEPT. PROD. DEPT. X CURRENT MONTH—JANUARY			DATE JANUARY 19A	RESPONSIBILITY OF B. R. SPEER YEAR TO DATE			
			VARIANCE*					VARIANCE*
ACTUAL	PLANNED	AMOUNT	%	DESCRIPTION	ACTUAL	PLANNED	AMOUNT	%
				CONTROLLABLE:				
87,500	100,000	12,500*	13*	Dept. output in units				
				Material A:				
176,000	175,000	1,000*	1*	Units				
$ 35,200	$ 35,000	$ 200*	1*	Cost				
				Direct labor:				
35,357	35,000	357*	1*	Hours				
$ 1.96	$ 2.00	$ .04	2	Average wage rate				
69,300	70,000	700	1	Cost				
				Controllable dept. overhead:				
10,000	10,000	—	—	Salaries				
3,740	3,800	60	2	Indirect materials				
7,550	7,250	300*	4*	Indirect labor				
560	1,000	440	44	Miscellaneous				
$ 21,850	$ 22,050	$ 200	1	Subtotal				
				Service usage:				
530	480	50*	10*	Kilowatt hours (000)				
72	60	12*	20*	Direct repair hours				
$126,350	$127,050	$ 700	1	Total				
				NONCONTROLLABLE:				
				Dept. Overhead:				
$ 2,000	$ 2,000	—	—	Depreciation				
500	500	—	—	Insurance				
200	200	—	—	Taxes				
$ 2,700	$ 2,700	—	—	Total—noncontrollable				

*Unfavorable variance.

COMMENTS:

1. Output was 13 percent below the planned level due to a production scheduling pullback to accommodate a 5,000 unit unfavorable sales volume variance. The department met its production schedule as adjusted.

2. Unfavorable variances in service usage should be carefully investigated to determine the underlying causes.

trollable items; (3) specific time dimensions—month and cumulative to date; (4) method of reporting variances; (5) adjustment of planned to actual outputs (that is, the flexible budget approach); (6) detail on each category (including service usage in units;) and (7) explanatory notes and suggestions. This illustration will be continued in the next chapter where the analysis of variances is discussed.

In summary, this chapter focused on repetitive performance reports. To be of maximum usefulness, the monthly performance report should be carefully designed to show the performance of each responsibility center manager. It is important to integrate performance reports (as shown in Exhibit 15-2) so that (1) the variances can be traced to the source of the problem and (2) the various segments of the report are, within themselves, a complete report. The latter aspect is essential to pinpoint performance areas for distribution of the segments to the respective responsibility centers.

Distribution of the various segments of the annual profit plan was discussed in Chapter 13. Distribution of the monthly performance report (and its segments) should be to the same responsibility centers. The financial officer or budget director should develop (as a part of the budget manual) a performance report distribution schedule. Certain executives need the complete monthly performance report. Other members of management need only those schedules related to their particular responsibility centers. The tendency to provide everyone with a complete copy of the monthly performance report should be discouraged because it is costly and ineffective. The receipt of a bulky financial report by a department supervisor dampens interest in even the part that directly relates to his or her department. Each lower-level manager should receive only one of the detailed segments. On the other hand, the higher the level of management, the greater the need for summaries. Yet these summaries must be supported by adequate detail to identify particular aspects of operations.

A performance report distribution schedule for SP Manufacturing Company could be as follows:

POSITION AND NAME	REPORT TO BE RECEIVED
Foreman, A. B. Smith	Cost Report, Machining No. 2
Supervisor, P. M. Cain	Cost Report, Production Department Summary
	Cost Reports, All Production Departments
Executive, M. R. Bryan	Factory Cost Summary
	Production Department Summary
	Cost Reports, All Production Departments
	Service Department Summary
	Cost Reports, All Service Departments
President	Complete Report

Comprehensive Demonstration Case

SUPERIOR MANUFACTURING COMPANY

Space limitations preclude inclusion of the Superior Manufacturing Company's monthly performance report. The report is completely integrated and includes two types of comparisons: (1) actual results compared with the annual profit plan and (2) actual results compared with planned amounts for costs (that is, flexible budget amounts). The report shows actual, budget, and variances for the month and cumulative for the year to date. Exhibit 15-7, Stanley Company's Performance Report, represents the general format and composition of the various segments of an integrated report.

Exhibit 15-8 lists the various segments of the complete performance report for Superior Manufacturing Company. Notice that the exhibit identification (first column) indicates the relationship of the detailed and summary schedules. For example, Schedule G2 is a summary performance report of distribution expenses that is supported by Schedules G2.1, G2.2, G2.3, and G2.4, which are the separate responsibility center performance reports for the expenses of the four sales districts. The column on the right, "Order of Preparation," is included to suggest that there is a necessary sequence that must usually be followed in developing the various detailed reports, the summaries, and finally the complete performance report. Notice the structure of the complete report in terms of organizational responsibilities.

PERFORMANCE REPORTING IN NONMANUFACTURING FIRMS   The measurement of actual performance relative to planned targets is just as applicable to nonmanufacturing companies as it is to manufacturing enterprises. Service and retail companies also use tactical plans that specify performance standards, measure actual results, and prepare responsibility center performance reports that analyze departures from planned performance. Two examples follow below and on p. 561.

UNITED PARCEL SERVICE

At UPS performance standards are set by industrial engineers for many tasks performed by UPS employees. For example, according to a *Wall Street Journal* article, a UPS driver is expected to walk at a pace of three feet per second when going to a customer's door and knock rather than take the time to look for a doorbell. The *Wall Street Journal* reported that a UPS executive attributes the company's success to its ability to manage and hold labor accountable.[2]

---

[2] "Up to Speed: United Parcel Service Gets Deliveries Done by Driving Its Workers," *Wall Street Journal*, April 22, 1986.

EXHIBIT 15-8

Superior Manufacturing Company

Performance Report—List of Schedules
January Report—Schedules

SCH. NO.	TITLE	DEPARTMENT	SUPERVISOR	ORDER OF PREPARATION
A	Balance Sheet with Budget Comparisons (with Original Plan)			26
B	Income Statement (compared with Original Plan and Adjusted Budget)			23
C	Cost of Goods Sold			—
D	District Income Statements (compared with Adjusted Budget)	By district		25
E	Sales Control Report	By district		22
F	Summary of Manufacturing Costs (by product)	Mfg.	A. B. Works	24
G	Departmental Expense Control Report (summary)	Company	Gen. Management	20
G1	Departmental Expense Control Report (summary)	Gen. Adm.	B. R. Taylor (Ex. VP)	7
G1.1	" " " " (dept. only)	Adm.	P. A. Johnson	4
G1.2	" " " " "	Accounting	H. H. Harrison	5
G1.3	" " " " "	Treasurer	I. M. Cash	6
G2	" " " " (summary)	Sales	G. A. Beloit	12
G2.1	" " " " (dept. only)	Southern	Ray C. Nixon	8
G2.2	" " " " "	Eastern	C. C. Campbell	9
G2.3	" " " " "	Western	W. W. Anderson	10
G2.4	" " " " "	Gen. Sales	T. K. Rielly	11
G3	" " " " (summary)	Factory	A. B. Works	19
G3.1	" " " " (dept. only)	1	K. R. Mason	13
G3.2	" " " " "	2	A. B. Ross	14
G3.3	" " " " "	3	W. E. Cox	15
G3.4	" " " " "	Repair	C. R. Medford	16
G3.5	" " " " "	Power	K. W. Haus	17
G3.6	" " " " "	Gen. Fac.	A. R. Carson	18
G4	" " " " "	Bldg. Serv.	Sam Adams	3
G5	Report of Noncontrollable Expenses at Dept. Level (summary)	Company	Gen. Man.	21
H	Report of Material Purchases	Pur.	T. E. Merton	2
I	Report of Other Income and Expenses (compared with Orig. Plan)	Treasurer	I. M. Cash	1
J	Analysis of Mfg. O. H. Over/Under Applied	Factory	Gen. Man.	27

AMERICAN EXPRESS COMPANY

Profitability has been increased at American Express Company, according to an article in *Business Week*, by a productivity program. In this program, the steps necessary to perform various customer-service tasks were identified and time targets were set for the performance of each step. Not only does the company feel that this program has improved profits, according to the *Business Week* article, but American Express executives also feel the program has increased customer satisfaction.[3]

EXECUTIVE COMPENSATION AND INCENTIVE PLANS   One way in which performance reports are increasingly used is in evaluating and compensating the managers at various levels in a company. Such incentive schemes are widely used for top management. They were first initiated in 1918 with Alfred Sloan's General Motors Bonus Plan. In this bonus plan, compensation was structured so that rewards increased more than proportionately to executives' salaries as the executives were promoted to higher positions. Thus, managers had an incentive first to become eligible for a bonus, and then to perform in such a way as to be promoted to higher levels in the company. Nowadays, bonus plans are common, with over 90 percent of the managers of decentralized profit centers in large corporations eligible for an annual salary bonus.[4]

Bonus plans are sometimes related to the performance of a company's stock in the capital market. Examples include **stock options** and **stock appreciation rights.** Other bonus plans are directly related to managerial performance on such operating measures as profit, return on investment, or sales. Such plans may provide rewards to managers in the form of cash or stock awards. **Performance share plans,** introduced by CBS in 1971, award shares of the company's stock to managers who achieve a particular performance objective and remain with the company. **Participating units,** another type of incentive plan, are cash payments that are tied to meeting planned targets on such operating measures as income, ROI, sales, or backlog.[5]

The important point of this discussion is that the performance reports produced by the profit planning and control system are used to measure the amounts of bonuses by many companies in their managerial incentive plans. To have a positive motivational impact, the performance measures must be ob-

---

[3] "Boosting Productivity at American Express," *Business Week*, October 5, 1981, pp. 66–68.

[4] Robert Kaplan, *Advanced Management Accounting*, (Englewood Cliffs, N.J.: Prentice-Hall, 1982), pp. 565–66.

[5] See Kaplan, *Advanced Management Accounting*, for this and additional material on managerial incentive plans.

jective, accurate, and substantive. Thus, those reports may have a profound effect on the incentives for managers and their ultimate decisions.

CHAPTER SUMMARY   Performance reports constitute an important part of internal management control procedures. These reports serve to motivate managers to perform in conformity with expectations. Moreover, they signal upper management when operations are not proceeding according to the plans. To be effective, performance reports should be (1) tailored to the organizational structure (i.e., by responsibility centers); (2) simple, accurate, and timely; and (3) used to facilitate management by exception.

A control system in all but the very small companies should be based on a performance reporting system that provides a continuing evaluation of actual results compared with plans. Planned goals are used to assess actual performance as the business moves through the planning period. Performance reports should include all significant aspects of operations and be consistent with assigned responsibilities. The discussion of performance reports in this chapter is applicable to both manufacturing and nonmanufacturing companies.

A realistic profit plan is one of the primary functions of management in nonmanufacturing companies. The profit plan must be complemented with a dynamic system of control.

A control system in all but very small companies must be based on a performance reporting system that provides a continuing evaluation of actual results compared with plans. Planned goals permit the evaluation of performance as the business moves through the planning period. The performance reports should (1) include all significant aspects of operations, (2) be consistent with assigned responsibilities, and (3) implement the management by exception principle. The discussion of performance reports in Chapter 15 is applicable to both manufacturing and nonmanufacturing companies.

Suggested References

ANTHONY, ROBERT, and REGINA HERZLINGER, *Management Control in Nonprofit Organizations*, rev. ed. Homewood, Ill.: Richard D. Irwin, 1980.

BIERMAN, HAROLD, THOMAS DYCKMAN, and RONALD HILTON, *Cost Accounting: Concepts and Managerial Applications*. New York: Macmillan, 1990.

JONES, R. L., and H. J. TRENTIN, "Budgeting General and Administrative Expenses: A Planning and Control System," *Management Bulletin 74*. New York: American Management Association, 1966.

KAPLAN, ROBERT, *Advanced Management Accounting*. Englewood Cliffs, N.J.: Prentice-Hall, 1982.

KING, W. R., "Performance Evaluation in Marketing Systems," *Management Science*, July 1964, pp. 659–66.

MILLER, E. L., *Responsibility Accounting and Performance Evaluation*. New York: Van Nostrand Reinhold, 1982.

Sloan, S., "How Milliken Measures Training Program Effectiveness," *Management Accounting*, July 1981, pp. 37–41.

Tucker, F. G. and S. M. Zivian, "A Xerox Cost Center Imitates a Profit Center," *Harvard Business Review*, May–June 1985, pp. 168–74.

Discussion Questions

1. Outline and briefly explain the reporting structure for a medium to large company that recognizes the needs of the major parties involved.

2. Why are financial reports for internal purposes significantly different in structure and content from those for external purposes?

3. What are the primary purposes of internal performance reports?

4. Upon what foundations are performance reports based?

5. Why should performance reports be tailored to the organizational responsibilities in a company?

6. Relate the management-by-exception principle to performance reports.

7. Distinguish between internal reports for (1) top management, (2) middle management, and (3) lower management.

8. Why is it advisable that several different methods of presentation be used in performance reports?

9. What criteria might be used to determine whether a variance is significant?

10. Why is it generally undesirable to distribute the entire monthly performance report for the company to all managers?

11. Assume that a particular performance report shows for item A a $500 unfavorable variance and for item B a $500 favorable variance. Should equal consideration be given to the two variances? Discuss.

CASE 15-1   *A "topsy-turvy" performance reporting system: overview of reporting*

High-Flight Food Services provides many of nation's major airlines with food preparation services ranging from snacks to all major meals. Annual sales approximated $43 million last year. There are two major food preparation facilities in widely separated sections of the United States. The company is composed of fifteen different departments (seven in each facility) including central company administration. The country is divided into five sales districts, each headed by a district sales manager. The company has approximately nine thousand stockholders, and the stock is sold on one of the national stock exchanges. The latest balance sheet showed that approximately 40 percent of the total assets was provided by creditors. Internal management has been changed in recent years, and the company is now viewed as a dynamic organization.

The company is expecting a 12 percent increase in sales for the coming year. The annual profit plan and the five-year profit plan incorporate this planned increase, although a lower average rate is anticipated for the next four years (long-range). Management tentatively plans to incorporate a new food service facility to be constructed in about five years. In planning for changes, and to keep up with "special problems," management has frequently requested special studies by the controller and other functional executives. The accounting system is well organized, and the organization structure of the company is set up on a responsibility-center basis. Due to seasonality and dynamic growth, monthly plans in the annual profit plan frequently are materially different from actual, particularly in planned service output, but the annual plan has been close to target.

Although the profit planning and control program appears to be functioning effectively and is generally accepted by the managers at all levels, there is a continuing concern about the reporting structure of the company. The financial vice-president stated that "a comprehensive analysis of the reporting in the company as it is now carried on must be undertaken. On the basis of that analysis, and following sound concepts and procedures, we should completely overhaul the reporting structure taking into consideration all actual and potential users of our reports." Casual conversation and observation convinced the case writer that the present reporting structure "just grew."

REQUIRED

Assuming that the statement by the financial vice-president confirmed the conclusion reached by the case writer, present your recommendations for a broad and comprehensive approach to financial reporting for the company. Focus on important concepts, approaches, and issues.

CASE 15-2 A challenge: Can you design a comprehensive performance report for one department in this company?

Canning Company is a medium-size manufacturer of automobile parts. Its major customer is a large automotive manufacturer. Seven different products are produced, three of which are sold to outlets other than the major customer. Sales and production necessarily follow the seasonal patterns experienced by the major customer. The company has developed a comprehensive profit planning and control program that incorporates a five-year long-range plan, an annual profit plan (detailed by month), flexible expense budgets in the factory departments, and a comprehensive performance reporting system. The performance reports are developed and distributed on a responsibility basis each month. Each supervisor concerned has the direct responsibility for investigating the causes of all significant variances (both favorable and unfavorable) in the responsibility center and for reporting the results to the immediate supervisor. Each responsibility manager is expected to recommend specific follow-up actions with respect to all significant variances; when approved by the immediate supervisor, these recommendations are implemented.

There are several service and production departments in the factory. This case specifically relates to one of the productive departments—No. 21, supervised by J. K. Campbell. Of the seven products, this particular department works on three of them: A, B, and C. The output of Department 21 is measured in planned direct machine hours. The department uses one raw material, designated Material X. The following data relate to the operations of this department (amounts simplified for case purposes only):

Profit plan data:

1. Planned output in January—A, 800 units; B, 400 units; and C, 500 units.
2. Planned rates and costs:

Raw material X—Planned purchase price per unit, $3
           —Planned usage rates per unit of finished product:
              A requires one unit of raw material X
              B requires three units of raw material X
              C requires two units of raw material X
Direct labor   —Average wage rate in Department 21, $5 per hour
           —Planned direct labor per unit of finished product:
              A requires three direct labor hours
              B requires two direct labor hours
              C requires one and one-half direct labor hours

Flexible expense budget for Department 21:

COST	FIXED COST PER MONTH	VARIABLE COST PER PLANNED DIRECT MACHINE HOUR
Indirect materials		$.10
Indirect labor	$ 400	.75
Miscellaneous	200	.05
Supervisory salaries*	6,000	
Productive salaries	4,000	
Depreciation*	1,000	
Insurance and taxes*	400	

* Noncontrollable in the department.

Service usage planned for January:

Kilowatt hours (000)	650
Direct repair hours	20

Direct machine hours planned: product A, 4; product B, 6; and product C, 10.

3. Actual data provided by the accounting department at the end of January:
   Output in January—A, 800 units; B, 300 units; and C, 400 units.
   Purchases of raw material X in January—9,000 units at $3.05 per unit.
   Units issued to Department 21 in January, 2,640.
   Direct labor costs for January—3,580 hours, cost $18,616.
   Overhead costs for January:

Indirect materials	$ 940
Indirect labor	7,000
Miscellaneous	690
Supervisory salaries	6,000
Productive salaries (two supervisors resigned and were replaced with a salary increase of $100 each.)	4,200
Depreciation	1,000
Insurance and taxes	400

Actual service usage for January:

Kilowatt hours (000)	640
Direct repair hours	28

Actual direct machine hours for January: 9,100

REQUIRED

Use the above data to prepare a complete and comprehensive performance report for January for Department 21. State any assumptions that you make.

CASE 15-3   *Design an overall comprehensive performance reporting structure*

Super Sound, Inc., manufactures a line of products related to the compact disk industry. The products are processed through five production centers. Selected actual and planned data for the month of June are presented below. Use these data to illustrate an integrated performance report system for the company. Identify the primary features of the system that you design.

	JUNE	
COSTS	ACTUAL	BUDGET
Divisions:		
Sales	$65,000	$60,000
Financial	7,000	7,100
General Administrative	16,000	15,700
Research	21,000	22,000
Factory		

| | JUNE | |
COSTS	ACTUAL	BUDGET
Departments (factory only):		
Purchasing	6,000	5,600
Maintenance	4,000	3,500
Factory Administrative	9,000	8,800
Production (five cost centers)		
Production Cost Centers:		
1	18,000	17,700
2	27,000	26,000
3	32,000	30,500
4 (see below)		
5	11,000	10,000
Cost Detail for Production Cost Center 4:		
Salaries	2,500	2,500
Wages	8,000	7,800
Material used	4,500	4,500
Supplies	420	380
Maintenance	200	160
Depreciation*	100	100
Taxes*	20	20
Insurance*	50	50
Power	120	115
Miscellaneous	80	90

*Noncontrollable in this cost center.

CASE 15-4   *Recommendation for improving a performance reporting system*

Rambler, Incorporated, manufactures three lines of products that are sold to companies in the oil industry. The company has been in operation for approximately twenty years; annual sales for the past year approximated $60 million. The company is organized into three basic functions: production, sales, and finance. Each function is under the direction of a vice-president. There are forty-two departments and five sales regions, each headed by a departmental manager. Since its organization, the company has experienced a relatively stable growth; however, profits and return on investment in recent years have decreased substantially. The results for the past two years have been of great concern to the management and to the approximately three thousand stockholders. The stock is sold over the counter, and there has been little turnover. The management of the company is undergoing gradual change due to the retirement of executives who started with the company.

Two years ago, a new financial vice-president (D. C. Thomas) was employed from the outside. This manager decided to initiate a comprehensive profit planning and control program but has encountered a lackadaisical, though not hostile, attitude throughout the management. Thomas realizes the behavioral problems to be overcome but is not discouraged. "I will keep pushing the program," Thomas stated, "improving it, and through education and demonstration of its usefulness make it a very effective management tool." The annual profit plan for the upcoming year has been completed and distributed to selected managers; appropriate component parts have been provided each manager throughout the company. The planning and implementation conferences were viewed by Thomas as being reasonably successful.

The financial vice-president is now trying to improve the performance reporting system. Monthly performance reports, disaggregated by responsibilities, will be prepared and distributed. Actual performance will be compared with planned performance for each responsibility center. With respect to the performance reports, the vice-president is concerned about the following issues:

a   Specific data that should be included in the performance report: actual, planned, variances, monthly, and cumulative.

b   The method to be used for expressing the variances: dollar amounts, percentage of plan, budget realization, and percentage of actual.

c   What to report for productive departments about usage of services from the nonproductive departments: actual dollars of cost allocation, allocation of standard dollars of cost, actual units of service used.

d   How to define significant variances; policy with respect to favorable variances.

e   Policy on rounding of amounts in the performance reports.

f   Policy with respect to the financial staff providing comments on the performance reports.

g   Extent of "graphing" that should be used in the performance report; this could increase preparation time and cost.

h   Deadline date for distribution of the monthly performance report.

i   Distribution schedule for the performance report.

j   Responsibilities for investigation of significant variances and "explanation" of such variances.

REQUIRED

What recommendation would you make on each of these items? Justify your position.

16 Analysis of Budget Variances

INTRODUCTION AND PURPOSE   Comparison of actual results with planned or budget goals has been emphasized as an integral part of the control process. Performance reports were discussed in the preceding chapter. A basic feature of performance reports is the reporting of **variances** between actual results and planned or budget goals. If a variance is significant, a careful management study should be made to determine the **underlying causes.** The underlying causes, rather than the actual results, should lead to remedies through appropriate corrective action by management. The purpose of this chapter is to discuss the analysis of budget (i.e., performance) variances for managerial planning and control purposes within the context of a comprehensive PPC program. This orientation is particularly relevant because the topic is often presented as a separate topic related to cost accounting.

ANALYZING VARIANCES   In studying and evaluating a variance to determine the underlying causes, the following possibilities should be considered:

1   The variance is immaterial.
2   The variance was caused by reporting errors. Both the planned or budget goal and the actual data provided by the accounting department should be examined for clerical errors. For example, a single accounting entry charging the wrong responsibility center may cause an unfavorable variance in one responsibility center and a favorable variance in another responsibility center.
3   The variance was caused by a specific management decision. To improve efficiency or to meet certain contingencies, management will often make decisions that create variances. For example, it may be decided to raise a salary, to meet competitive efforts by another firm to attract a key employee, or to undertake a special advertising project not previously planned. Such discretionary decisions will result in reported variances. Variances of this type must be identified because, once identified, they usually need no further study. When the decision was made, it should have been recognized that a variance from plans would result.

4 Many variances are explainable in terms of the effect of **uncontrollable** factors that are identifiable. An example would be a loss due to a storm.

5 Those variances for which the underlying causes are not known should be of primary concern and should be carefully investigated. In other words, managers must give special attention to the variances that "need explaining." These are the exceptions that usually require corrective action.

There are numerous ways to study or investigate variances to determine the underlying causes. Some of the primary approaches are the following:

1 Conferences with responsibility center managers and supervisors and other employees in the particular responsibility center involved.

2 Analysis of the work situation including the flow of work, coordination of activities, effectiveness of supervision, and other prevailing circumstances.

3 Direct observation.

4 On-the-spot investigations by **line** managers.

5 Investigations by **staff** groups (carefully specified as to responsibilities).

6 Internal audits.

7 Special studies.

8 Variance analysis.

Variance analysis involves a mathematical analysis of two sets of data in order to gain insight into the underlying causes of a variance. One amount is treated as the base, standard, or reference point. Variance analysis has wide application in financial reporting. It is frequently applied in the following situations:

1 Investigation of variances between actual results of the current period and the actual results of a prior period. The prior period is considered the base.

2 Investigation of variances between actual results and standard costs. The standard cost is used as the base (see Chapter 17 for a discussion of standard costs).

3 Investigation of the variances between actual results and planned or budget goals reflected in the profit plans. The planned or budget goals are used as the base.

In each of these three situations, variance analysis involves the same analytical approach. The arithmetic is essentially the same. The only difference is in the data being analyzed. This chapter discusses only the analysis of budget (or plan) variances related to (1) sales, (2) material, (3) direct labor, and (4) manufacturing overhead.

Analysis of Sales Variances

The significance and limitations of the results of variance analysis are best understood if its arithmetic is known. The following simplified example is used to explain the arithmetic of variance analysis and to suggest how the analysis of certain **variances between actual results and planned or budget goals** may give management greater insights into the **causes** of the variances. First, we will discuss sales variances. Assume that the top management of Stanley Company received the performance report shown in Exhibit 16-1.

EXHIBIT 16-1

Sales Performance Report—Summary
Stanley Company
For the month of January

SALES DISTRICT	ACTUAL RESULTS	GOALS FROM THE PROFIT PLAN	VARIANCE UNFAVORABLE*
1	$ 481,500	$ 500,000	$18,500*
2	198,800	200,000	1,200*
3	402,100	400,000	2,100
Total	$1,082,400	$1,100,000	$17,600*

Management attention in Exhibit 16-1 should immediately focus on the *exceptional* items, that is, the $17,600 total sales variance, and then on the $18,500 unfavorable variance in District 1 monthly sales. Each variance is identified with a specific sales district; therefore, responsibility is pinpointed. In this instance, it is the manager of District 1. However, the *causes* of the unfavorable variance are not apparent. Assume management pursues the issue further and examines another schedule in the performance report that details the $18,500 variance as shown in Exhibit 16-2.

EXHIBIT 16-2

Sales Performance Report—District 1
Stanley Company
For the month of January

PRODUCT	ACTUAL RESULTS UNITS	ACTUAL RESULTS AMOUNT	PROFIT PLAN UNITS	PROFIT PLAN AMOUNT	VARIANCE UNFAVORABLE* UNITS	VARIANCE UNFAVORABLE* AMOUNT
M	35,000	$182,000	40,000	$200,000	5,000*	$18,000*
N	49,900	299,500	50,000	300,000	100*	500*
Total		$481,500		$500,000		$18,500*

In Exhibit 16-2, another exceptional item stands out—product M in District 1. An alert manager would ask. What caused the $18,000 unfavorable variance in product M? At this point, variance analysis of the $18,000 may provide causal insights for management. The first arithmetical step is to compute both the actual and planned **average** sales prices, as follows:

Actual: $182,000 ÷ 35,000 units = $5.20 average sales price

Planned: $200,000 ÷ 40,000 units = $5.00 average sales price

We can see that the **quantity** sold was 5,000 units below the planned goal and that the sales **price** was $.20 above the planned goal. The dollar effects of these two variables—quantity and price—can be computed as shown in Exhibit 16-3.

Interpretation of the results of the above analysis can be explained in the following way:

There was an $18,000 unfavorable variance for product M, in District 1, when actual sales were compared with the goal in the profit plan. Analysis of this variance indicates that the number of units sold was 5,000 below plan. When valued at the planned sales price, an unfavorable **sales quantity variance** of $25,000 resulted. This unfavorable quantity variance was offset in part by a favorable **sales price variance** of $.20 per unit on the 35,000 units actually sold.

EXHIBIT 16-3

Computation of Sales Variances

Panel A—Computations

SALES QUANTITY VARIANCE:
    Sales price held constant:
        Actual sales at planned sales price (35,000 × $5) $175,000
        Planned sales at planned sales price (40,000 × $5)   200,000
        Sales quality variance $25,000*
    [The computation can be simplified:
      (40,000 − 35,000) × $5 = $25,000*]
SALES PRICE VARIANCE:
    Sales quantity held constant:
        Actual sales at actual sales price (35,000 × $5.20)   182,000
        Actual sales at planned sales price (35,000 × $5.00)   175,000
        Sales price variance   7,000
    [The computation can be simplified:
      35,000 × ($5.20 − $5.00) = $7,000]
    Total sales variance $18,000*

*Indicates unfavorable variance.

Panel B—Graphical Display of Variances

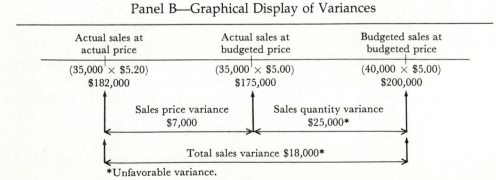

Actual sales at actual price	Actual sales at budgeted price	Budgeted sales at budgeted price
(35,000 × $5.20)	(35,000 × $5.00)	(40,000 × $5.00)
$182,000	$175,000	$200,000

Sales price variance $7,000   Sales quantity variance $25,000*

Total sales variance $18,000*

*Unfavorable variance.

The offset totaled $7,000. The factors causing the large quantity variance should be investigated further.

Note that (1) in computing the quantity variance, the budget *price* factor is held constant and the quantity is variable; (2) in computing the price variance, the actual **quantity** factor is held constant and the price is variable.[1]

Analysis of Material Variances

Material variances are usually shown on two performance reports: (1) one that reports the performance of the **purchasing manager** and (2) one (or more) that reports the performance(s) of the **manager(s)** of the **using department(s)** (review Chapter 7).

First, we will discuss the performance report of the purchasing manager. This manager is responsible for controlling (1) the purchase *prices* of materials and component parts and (2) the **timing** and **quantity** of material purchases. Recall from Chapter 7 that the purchasing manager is also responsible for developing the purchases budget that is included in the annual profit plan.

The performance report on the purchasing function shows a comparison of **actual purchases** with **planned purchases.** The resulting material purchase variance can be analyzed in a manner similar to that shown in Exhibit 16-3 for sales because there are two variables—quantity and price. To illustrate, assume the January performance report for Stanley Company was as shown in Exhibit 16-4, Panel A. The related **variance analysis,** to reflect the two material variances, could be indicated on the performance report as shown in Exhibit 16-4, Panel B. This analysis reveals that the purchasing manager incurred (1) a $5,040 unfavorable price variance by paying $.024 more per unit than planned and (2) a $2,000 unfavorable quantity variance by purchasing 10,000 more units than planned. To focus on the **causes,** the purchasing manager should explain both the unit cost and quantity differences.

Next we discuss the performance report of the **using** department(s). The production manager of a using department is responsible for the **quantity** of raw materials used in producing the actual quantity of department output. Importantly, the production manager has no responsibility for the purchase **cost** of the material used. Management policy determines the **quality,** and hence the planned unit cost, of the raw materials used. Therefore, the using department should be "charged" for the actual number of units used during the pe-

---

[1] Some analysts prefer a three-way analysis rather than the two-way analysis illustrated above. The three-way analysis is shown below.

Quantity variance (40,000 − 35,000) × $5	$25,000*
Price variance ($5.20 − $5.00) × 40,000	8,000
Combined quantity-price variance (40,000 − 35,000) × ($5.20 − $5.00)	$ 1,000*
Total variance	$18,000*

*Unfavorable variance.

EXHIBIT 16-4
Purchasing Performance Report—Purchasing Department
Stanley Company
For the month of January

Panel A—Performance Report for the Month of January (Partial)

	ACTUAL	PLANNED	VARIANCE
Purchase of material A:			
Units	210,000	200,000	
Average price	$ .224	$ .20	
Total cost	47,040	40,000	$7,040*

*Unfavorable.

Panel B—Analysis of the Purchase Variance

Variance analysis—material A:	
Purchase price variance ($.224 − $.200) × 210,000	$5,040*
Purchase quantity variance (210,000 − 200,000) × $.20	2,000*
Total purchase variance	$7,040*

*Unfavorable.

riod, valued at the planned or budgeted price per unit. The resulting amount represents "actual" on the performance report of the using department. In contrast, the budgeted goal should reflect the number of units that should have been used in processing the actual output of the department. These units should be valued at the budgeted unit price. To illustrate, we return to the Stanley Company and Producing Department X, which uses material A. In Chapter 15, Exhibit 15-7 shows the performance report on material A, which is repeated for your convenience as follows:

	ACTUAL	PLANNED	VARIANCE
Units of finished goods (output)	87,500	100,000	
Material A:			
Units (budgeted two units of material per unit of finished goods)	176,000	175,000	
Average unit cost (budgeted $.20)	$ .20	$ .20	
Cost	$ 35,200	$ 35,000	$200*

*Unfavorable.

The $200 unfavorable variance is related to only one variable—material usage; therefore, further analysis is unnecessary. The usage variance can be verified: (176,000-175,000) × $.20 = $200 (unfavorable).

In summary, the purchasing officer is responsible for two subvariances—purchase price and purchase quantity, whereas the *using* manager is responsible for only one variance—material usage.

The material **price** variance is identified at the **time of purchase** and is based on the quantity purchased during the period, whereas the material **usage** variance is identified at the **time of usage** and is based on the planned unit material price. Some companies make a mistake by "charging" the using department with "actual units of raw material used multiplied by the actual price per unit." This procedure creates two effects, both of which are inconsistent with effective control because the material price variance is reflected in the performance report of the using department. The first inconsistency is that the material price variance is identified at the point of **usage** rather than at the point of purchase. The latter is incorrectly viewed as the decisional control point. Identification at the point of usage also incorrectly relates the price variance to the number of units used rather than to the number of units purchased. The second inconsistency is that the procedure incorrectly "charges" the **using** manager rather than the purchasing manager with the material price variance.[2]

Analysis of Direct Labor Variances

The performance report of each producing department using direct labor will usually show a direct labor variance. As with sales and direct materials, the labor variance reflects the effect of two variables—**quantity** (direct labor hours)

[2] For special reasons, it may occasionally be useful to compare (or reconcile) actual cost of materials used for the period with the planned cost of materials reflected in the *original* profit plan. This comparison introduces an additional subvariance to the analysis of the *using* department. To illustrate, the amount of the variance to be analyzed in Department X (Stanley Company) for January would be:

	ACTUAL	ORIGINAL PROFIT PLAN	VARIANCE BETWEEN ACTUAL AND ORIGINAL PROFIT PLAN
Units of finished goods (output)	87,500	100,000	12,500*
Raw material A:			
Units	176,000	200,000	
Cost	$ 35,200	$ 40,000	$ 4,800

The variance analysis for the using department would necessarily identify two subvariances: (1) usage variance and (2) a profit plan volume variance, as follows:

Usage variance 176,000 − (87,500 × 2) × $.20	$ 200*
Profit plan volume variance (200,000 − 175,000) × $.20	5,000
Total variance	$4,800

The profit plan volume variance simply reflects the amount of material that was not used because actual output was 12,500 units less than originally planned, that is, (12,500 × 2) × $.20 = $5,000. This analysis is seldom used because of its limited relevance.

and **price** (average wage rate). Therefore, the direct labor variance can be analyzed mathematically to reflect two subvariances that may add some insight in the management's evaluation of the underlying causes. To illustrate, we return to the Stanley Company and the January performance report for Producing Department X shown in Chapter 15, Exhibit 15-7. The direct labor date from that report are shown below:

	ACTUAL	PLANNED	VARIANCE
Units of finished goods (output)	87,500	100,000	
Direct labor:			
Direct labor hours (budgeted .4 DLH per unit of finished goods)	35,357	35,000	
Average wage rate (budgeted $2.00 per DLH)	$ 1.96	$ 2.00	
Cost	$69,300	$ 70,000	$700

The following variance analysis, to reflect the two subvariances—efficiency or usage (DLHs) and wage rate (price)—could be shown on the performance report of the producing department as additional data for use in identifying the causes:

Variance analysis—direct labor:	
Labor efficiency (usage) variance (35,357 − 35,000) × $2.00	$ 714*
Labor wage rate variance ($2.00 − $1.96) × 35,357	1,414
Total labor variance	$ 700

*Unfavorable.

The analysis of direct labor variances can be shown graphically, as in Exhibit 16-5.

EXHIBIT 16-5

Graphical Display of Direct Labor Variances

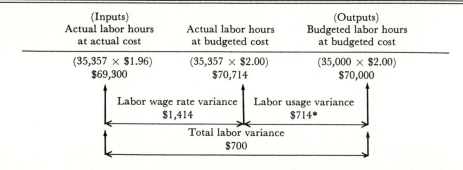

The results of the variance analysis of direct labor can be explained as follows:[3]

The monthly performance report showed a favorable direct labor variance for Department X of $700. This variance resulted from comparing direct labor costs actually incurred in producing 87,500 units of output with the planned cost goal adjusted to this output. Although the total direct labor variance is favorable, further analysis indicates an **unfavorable** labor usage or efficiency variance of $714. This unfavorable condition occurred because the department used 357 more direct labor hours than the planned or budget standard. This situation should be discussed with the manager concerned. However, there was a **favorable** wage rate variance of $1,414 because the average wage rate per hour in the department was $.04 below the standard. This favorable variance should be investigated to determine its cause. It is possible that the manager of the producing department was able to maintain a higher proportion of lower-paid employees, which is desirable assuming product quality and employee relations are not adversely affected. This latter factor may have been the cause of the excess hours used.[4]

Analysis of Manufacturing Overhead Variances

The analysis of manufacturing overhead variances is more complex than the analysis for sales, raw materials, and direct labor. One factor that adds to the the complexity is the kinds of planned or budget data available for the analysis. If flexible expense budget data are available, the overhead fixed and variable components of manufacturing overhead costs are known. In this case, an informative analysis of overhead variances can be done. Alternatively, when only **static** budget data are available (that is, the fixed and variable components of

---

[3] Some analysts prefer a three-way analysis of the direct labor variance as follows:

Labor usage variance $(35,357 - 35,000) \times \$2.00$	$ 714*
Labor wage rate variance $(\$2.00 - \$1.96) \times 35,000$	1,400
Combined usage-rate variance $(357 \times \$.04)$	14
Total labor variance	$ 700

[4] In those special instances where actual direct labor costs are to be reconciled with the original profit plan (as illustrated in a previous footnote for direct materials), direct labor would be analyzed as follows:

Total variance to be analyzed:

Actual direct labor: $35,357$ hours $\times \$1.96 =$	$69,300	
Original profit plan: $100,000 \times .4 \times \$2.00 =$	80,000	
Total variance		$10,700

Variance analysis:

Labor efficiency variance (computed as illustrated above)	714*
Labor wage rate variance (computed as illustrated above)	1,414
Profit plan volume variance $(12,500 \times .4 \times \$2.00)$	10,000
Total variance	$10,700

overhead expenses are not differentiated), attempts to develop a useful analysis are difficult at best. Our discussions and illustrations will be limited to the case when the fixed and variable components of manufacturing overhead costs are known. **The primary purpose of the analysis of manufacturing overhead is to explain the causes of the amount of manufacturing overhead underapplied or overapplied.**

We do not dwell on theoretical distinctions, but rather emphasize the relationship of the analysis of manufaturing overhead variances to the monthly performance report as prepared using a comprehensive profit planning and control program.[5]

To illustrate (1) the mathematical aspects, (2) the interpretation of the results, and (3) the relationship of overhead variance analysis to a comprehensive profit planning and control program, we will refer to Department X of Stanley Company.[6] Focus on the January performance report, and refer again to Chapter 15, Exhibit 15-7. That performance report for Department X reports the variances for each item of controllable and noncontrollable overhead. An overall favorable variance of $200 is reported for January. This variance only partially explains the causes of manufacturing overhead under- or overapplied. To illustrate the analysis of manufacturing overhead under- or overapplied, the following additional data are needed:

1. From the annual profit plan:
   a. Computation of the annual manufacturing overhead rate for Department X (see Chapter 9 for a discussion of this procedure):

	FACTORY OVERHEAD (PLANNED)	OUTPUT (VOLUME) IN DLH (PLANNED)	FACTORY OVERHEAD RATE PLANNED OR BUDGETED (PER DLH)
Fixed costs	$192,000	480,000	$.40
Variable costs	120,000	480,000	.25
Total	$312,000		$.65

   b. Output (volume) in units planned for January, 100,000
   c. Planned direct labor hours for January output, 40,000

[5] Readers interested in an in-depth analysis of manufacturing overhead are referred to one or more of the textbooks on cost accounting. For example, see Harold Bierman, Jr. Thomas Dyckman, and Ronald Hilton, *Cost Accounting: Concepts and Managerial Applications* (New York: Macmillan, 1990).

[6] Throughout this discussion of overhead variance analysis, assume that productive volume (output) is measured in terms of direct labor hours (DLH). Other measures of productive volume might be more appropriate, depending on the circumstance. Assume also that annual predetermined overhead rates are used for accounting purposes and that overhead is applied by multiplying the standard rate by the *standard hours* for the output of the period, as is the practice under standard costing.

2. From the flexible expense budget for Department X:

EXPENSES	FIXED PER MONTH	VARIABLE RATE PER DLH
Salaries	$10,000	
Indirect materials	1,000	$.08
Indirect labor	2,000	.15
Miscellaneous	300	.02
Depreciation	2,000	
Insurance	500	
Taxes	200	
Total	$16,000	$.25

3. Actual Department X data for January provided by the accounting department:
   a. Units produced in January in Department X   87,500
   b. Actual direct labor hours incurred in Department X   35,357
   c. Planned direct labor hours for January at the actual output
      (87,500 × .4 DLH)   35,000
   d. Actual departmental overhead cost incurred in January (debited to
      the manufacturing overhead account) $24,550
   e. Manufacturing overhead applied in January (credited to the
      manufacturing overhead applied account) (35,000 DLH × $.65) $22,750

With these data, we can readily compute the total overhead variance that is to be analyzed for January for Department X. It is the $1,800 **underapplied overhead,** computed as follows:

Actual overhead incurred in the department during January	$24,550
Overhead applied in the department during January	22,750
Underapplied overhead in the department in January	$ 1,800

The objective of overhead variance analysis is to help explain what caused the $1,800 underapplied overhead in Department X in January. The total overhead variance can be analyzed by using either a two-way or a three-way approach. Both approaches compute a **budget (spending) variance** and an **idle capacity (volume) variance.** The three-way approach additionally computes an **efficiency variance.** When the two-way approach is used, the efficiency variance is automatically buried in the budget variance. We will illustrate and compare these two approaches.

Based on the data given above for manufacturing overhead in Department X, Exhibit 16-6 shows: Panel A, the two-way analysis; and Panel B, the three-way analysis.

EXHIBIT 16-6

Analysis of Manufacturing Overhead Variances Stanley Company, Department X

Panel A—Two-Way Approach

(1) Budget (or spending) variance:		
Planned DLH in actual production adjusted using flexible budget formulas, $16,000 + ($.25 × 35,000 DLH)	$24,750[7]	
Actual overhead incurred	24,550	
Budget (or spending) variance		$200
(2) Idle capacity (or volume) variance:		
Department overhead applied (35,000 DLH × $.65)	22,750	
Planned DLH in actual production adjusted using flexible budget formulas (computed above)	24,750	
Idle capacity (or volume) variance		2,000*
Total overhead variance (underapplied overhead)		$1,800*

Panel B—Three-Way Approach

(1) Budget (or spending) variance:		
Actual DLH adjusted using flexible budget formulas, $16,000 + ($.25 × 35,357 DLH)	$24,839	
Actual overhead incurred (at 35,357 DLH)	24,550	
Budget (or spending) variance		$ 289
(2) Idle capacity (or volume) variance (computed as above in the two-way approach)		$2,000*
(3) Overhead efficiency variance:		
Planned DLH in actual production adjusted using flexible budget formulas (computed as above)	24,750	
Actual DLH adjusted using flexible budget formulas (computed as above)	24,839	
Efficiency variance		89*
Total overhead variance (underapplied overhead)		$1,800*

*Unfavorable.

EXPLANATION OF THE TWO-WAY OVERHEAD VARIANCE   The two variances can be evaluated and interpreted as follows.[8]

BUDGET (SPENDING) VARIANCE   This variance is viewed as one valid measure of the effectiveness of overhead **cost control** because actual costs incurred are compared with flexible budget costs **adjusted to the planned work or output of the responsibility center (35,000 DLH in the example).** This variance can be reconciled with departmental variances reported on the departmental performance report if the "Planned" column is adjusted to **planned** output (i.e.,

[7] Some analysts prefer to use for this value the flexible budget allowance adjusted to *actual* hours in production: $16,000 + ($.25 × 35,357) = $24,839.

[8] In some cases, adjustments may have to be made for service department volume differentials.

35,000 DLH in the example). For example, this variance agrees with the $200 favorable variance shown on the January performance report for the department (see Chapter 15, Exhibit 15-7). That report provides the detailed variances that make up the $200 spending variance. However, this variance alone does not "explain" the $1,800 **underapplied overhead.**

IDLE CAPACITY (VOLUME) VARIANCE   This variance measures the **cost of idle plant capacity,** and, as such, it explains the remainder of the **underapplied overhead.** Stanley's annual profit plan anticipated that the average monthly potential capacity of this responsibility center was 40,000 planned DLH (i.e., 480,000 ÷ 12). Actual production volume was equivalent to only 35,000 planned DLH. Therefore, there was idle plant capacity of 5,000 DLH (unfavorable). The idle capacity variance shows the portion of monthly total **fixed cost** related to the idle plant capacity. The 5,000 direct labor hours of idle plant capacity multiplied by the **fixed** component of the overhead rate ($.40) gives this unfavorable variance ($2,000). This can be verified by computing the idle capacity variance as follows:

$$\frac{5,000 \text{ DLH}}{40,000 \text{ DLH}} \times \$16,000 \text{ (monthly fixed costs)} = \underline{\underline{\$2,000}}$$

This variance makes up the remainder of the underapplied factory overhead (total) variance (i.e., $200 favorable plus $2,000 unfavorable equals $1,800 unfavorable).

EXPLANATION OF THE THREE-WAY OVERHEAD VARIANCE   The three-way variance can be evaluated as follows.

BUDGET (SPENDING) VARIANCE   This variance is a valid measure of cost control because actual costs incurred are compared with flexible budget costs adjusted to **actual** output (actual DLH in the example). Notice that in the two-way analysis, this adjustment is based on **planned** DLH. This variance can be reconciled with the "Planned" column of the departmental performance report only if that column is based on actual DLH in actual production (i.e., 35,357 DLH in the example). For this reason, in Exhibit 16-6 the three-way analysis shows this variance as $289, whereas it was $200 in the two-way analysis.

IDLE CAPACITY (VOLUME) VARIANCE   This variance is always the same in the three-way analysis compared with the two-way analysis. Notice that this variance is $2,000 unfavorable in both analyses shown in Exhibit 16-6.

OVERHEAD EFFICIENCY VARIANCE   This variance measures the **excess overhead costs** ($89 unfavorable in the illustration) that were incurred because more actual direct labor hours (35,357 DLH) were used than the budget plan for the actual units produced (35,000 DLH). This means that 357 excess DLH were used. Variable costs (not fixed costs) increase and decrease as direct labor hours increase and decrease; therefore, the efficiency variance should be measured in variable costs only. The variance precisely fits these specifications and can be demonstrated as follows:[9]

Planned hours in actual production	35,000
Actual hours incurred in actual production	35,357
Difference—inefficient hours	357*
Multiply by variable portion of overhead rate	$.25
Overhead efficiency variance (wholly variable)	$ 89*

*Unfavorable.

To emphasize, notice in Exhibit 16-6 that in the three-way analysis, the budget (spending) variance of $289 favorable plus the efficiency variance of $89 unfavorable equals the budget (spending) variance in the two-way analysis of $200 favorable. To summarize, manufacturing overhead under- or overapplied can be "explained" by computing either two variances or three variances. The three-way analysis is preferable because it identifies one of the effects of using inefficient efforts in the productive process (i.e., efficiency overhead variance).

FORMATS TO SYSTEMATIZE VARIANCE ANALYSES To systematize, the computations can be conveniently organized in either a spreadsheet or a graphical format, as illustrated in Exhibit 16-7, for both the two-way and the three-way approaches.

USE OF VARIANCE ANALYSIS In developing and reporting the analyses discussed in this chapter, the analyst should remember that the *results* must (1) deal with relevant distinctions, (2) be understandable, (3) measure with reasonable accuracy what they are supposed to measure, and (4) be presented and explained concisely. It is unrealistic to expect top managers to devote time and attention to esoteric and overly technical analyses.

Whether the additional analyses discussed in this chapter are useful depends to some extent on the situation. These analyses can be useful when carefully developed, interpreted in a practical way, and wisely applied. However, these analyses involve distinctions that are often difficult to express simply and concisely; therefore, they should be used with caution.

---

[9] It may be convincingly argued that the overhead efficiency variance should include some fixed costs, since workers who waste time also waste the cost of space, machinery, supervisory effort, and so forth. If this position is accepted, the computations in the example could be made so that the portion of fixed costs related to the 357 hours of inefficiency are also included in the efficiency variance and excluded from the idle capacity or volume variance. This amount of fixed costs (to be taken from the idle capacity variance and added to the efficiency variance) can be readily computed as follows: $16,000 \times (357/40,000) = 143$.

EXHIBIT 16-7

Systematized Formats to Compute Variances

Panel A—Spreadsheet Format

COMPUTATION OF THE REQUIRED AMOUNTS:

1. Actual overhead incurred (given)	$24,550
2. Flexible budget allowance adjusted to *actual* hours in production	
$16,000 + ($.25 × 35,357)	24,839
3. Flexible budget allowance adjusted to *standard* hours in production	
$16,000 + ($.25 × 35,000)	24,750
4. Overhead applied (35,000 × $.65)	22,750

COMPUTATION OF THE VARIANCES:

VARIANCE	TWO-WAY ANALYSIS COMPUTATION	AMOUNT	THREE-WAY ANALYSIS COMPUTATION	AMOUNT
Budget variance		$ 200		$ 289
Efficiency variance				89*
Idle capacity variance		2,000*		2,000*
Total variance		$1,800*		$1,800*

* Unfavorable

Panel B—Graphical Format

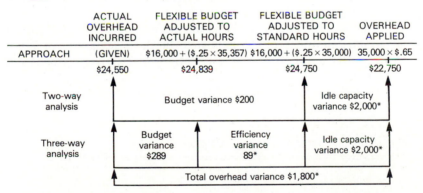

*Unfavorable.

To present the results of variance analyses, two approaches are available. First, the results of the analyses can be reported in a **special report** that focuses on specific (but not recurring) problems with which management is concerned. Second, the results can be included on the **monthly performance report.** The results usually are best reported as supplementary comments in the performance reports.

VARIANCE INVESTIGATION   After all the variances have been calculated for a reporting period, management must decide which variance should be investigated. The concept of **management by exception** typically is employed here, with management investigating only those variances that appear to be significant. The question is, What constitutes a significant variance? The approach commonly used in practice is to investigate all variances (favorable and unfavorable) above a certain limit. This limit can be expressed either in absolute dollars or as a percentage of the budgeted amount. Generally, these **control limits** are set intuitively by management without a sophisticated analysis.

If a more sophisticated method for setting the control limits is desired, management can assume a probability distribution for the variance that will result from random causes if the production system is generally under control. Exhibit 16-8 displays the normal probability distribution for a raw material usage variance.

The control limit beyond which the variance will be investigated is often set at two standard deviations (denoted by s in Exhibit 16-8). If the variance is normally distributed when the production process is under control, the probability of getting either an unfavorable or a favorable variance as large as two standard deviations from the mean or expected value is just under 5 percent. Therefore, it is unlikely that such a large variance would occur if the production process were in control. If such a large variance occurs, the management should investigate the variance to determine its cause and take corrective action if indicated. It may be that the production process is not under control, or there may be other causes.

For example, suppose management believes that when the production process is under control, the material usage variance is normally distributed with a mean of 100 and a standard deviation of 20. If the reported variance is greater than 140 (mean of 100 plus two standard deviations of 20) or less than 60 (mean of 100 less two standard deviations of 20), management should investigate the variance.

The decision to investigate a variance is inherently a cost/benefit decision.

EXHIBIT 16-8

Normal Probability Distribution for Material Usage Variance

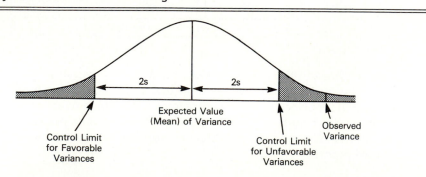

Such an investigation may be costly in terms of management time. The potential benefit is to learn the causes of an unfavorable or a favorable variance. For example, investigation of unfavorable variances may result in "correcting" the production process to prevent such variances from recurring. Investigation of favorable variances may result in management incorporating the cause of the favorable result into the production process, thereby ensuring its recurrence.[10]

CHAPTER SUMMARY   Variance analysis is an important tool that can increase the usefulness of periodic performance reports. Rather than taking action only on the basis of a difference between actual and planned or budgeted costs or sales, variance analysis enables management to decompose such differences into smaller subvariances. Each of these subvariances relates to a particular type of cause for the overall variance. Variance decomposition helps management to better understand the causes of variances from planned performance and take corrective action through management by exception. The decision to investigate a variance is a cost/benefit decision. The benefit derives from the possibility of returning the production system to its efficient state. The cost is the use of management time to investigate the cause of the variance. Management time is usually viewed as a scarce resource with a high cost per hour. However, variances, if not corrected, tend to persist and even increase in significance. This tendency can be very costly because variances accumulate over time.

Suggested References

BARNES, J., "How to Tell If Standard Costs Are Really Standard," *Management Accounting*, June 1983, pp. 50–54.

BIERMAN, HAROLD, THOMAS DYCKMAN, and RONALD HILTON, *Cost Accounting: Concepts and Managerial Applications*. New York: Macmillan, 1990.

DEMSKI, JOEL S., "Decision-Performance Control," *Accounting Review*, October 1969, pp. 669–79.

———, and STANLEY BAIMAN, "Economically Optimal Performance Evaluation and Control Systems," *Journal of Accounting Research*, Supplement, 1980, pp. 184–220.

DOPUCH, NICHOLAS, JACOB BIRNBERG, and JOEL DEMSKI, "An Extension of Standard Cost Analysis," *Accounting Review*, July 1967, pp. 526–36.

DYCKMAN, THOMAS, "The Investigation of Cost Variances," *Journal of Accounting Research*, Autumn 1969, pp. 215–44.

[10] For further discussion of variance investigation, see R. Kaplan, "The Significance and Investigation of Cost Variance," *Journal of Accounting Research*, Autumn 1975, pp. 311–37; and R. Lambert, "Variance Investigation in Agency Settings," *Journal of Accounting Research*, 1985, pp. 633–47.

KAPLAN, ROBERT S., "The Significance and Investigation of Cost Variances," *Journal of Accounting Research*, Autumn 1975, pp. 311–37.

———, *Advanced Management Accounting*. Englewood Cliffs, N.J.: Prentice-Hall, 1982.

LAMBERT, RICHARD, "Variance Investigation in Agency Settings," *Journal of Accounting Research*, Autumn 1985, pp. 633–47.

MAGEE, ROBERT P., *Advanced Managerial Accounting*. New York: Harper & Row, 1986.

Discussion Questions

1. Explain the relationship between the analysis of budget variances and the monthly performance report.

2. What primary approaches are used to determine the underlying causes of variances?

3. Define (1) sales quantity variance and (2) sales price variance.

4. Assume that a performance report showed the following data for product T:

		ACTUAL	PLANNED	VARIANCE
Sales		$9,690	$10,000	$310*
Average sales price		.95	1.00	
Volume variance	$200			
Price variance	$510*			

*Unfavorable.

Explain how the sales quantity and price variances were computed, and give the interpretation of each.

5. Identify and explain the two different responsibilities involved in the analysis of material variances.

6. Why should the using department be "charged" for the actual number of raw material units used multiplied by the planned or budgeted unit cost rather than by the actual unit cost of the material?

7. Explain the direct labor usage variance and the wage rate variance.

8. In the analysis of manufacturing overhead variances, what particular amount is normally subject to variance analysis? Explain.

9. Define the following: (1) budget (or spending) variance, (2) idle capacity variance (or volume variance), and (3) efficiency variance.

10. Why should variance analysis be used with caution?

11. Why is the decision to investigate variances a cost/benefit decision?

CASE 16-1   *You are to improve a performance report and the included variance analysis*

Dryden Company is a medium-size manufacturer of a single line of sports products. There are four different models in the line. There are two plants (located widely apart), and the United States is divided into seven sales districts. The manufacturing vice-president stated that "the Eastern plant (an old plant) has been experiencing difficulty in getting costs in line with the budget." The monthly performance report in some of the departments has consistently shown significant unfavorable variances. The management has undertaken a number of steps to get at this cost problem. Included was a recent decision to use flexible budgets for overhead expenses throughout the plants. The vice-president remarked that "the performance report approaches are being reviewed and improved, and more attention will be given to determination of the underlying causes of significant variances; we have too many excuses now." This case focuses on a suggestion made by a newly employed accountant in the controller's department that "variance analyses should be incorporated in the monthly performance report of each department." Simplified data from one of the producing departments are provided below for case purposes.

REQUIRED

a. Develop a two-way variance analysis of direct materials and direct labor, and a three-way analysis of department overhead.

b. Evaluate the results of your analysis and identify any weaknesses in the departmental performance report illustrated.

Performance Report

DEPT. PRODUCING NO. 4	DATE JANUARY 19XX		SUPERVISOR K.W. MASON	
	ACTUAL		PLANNED	VARIANCE
Department output—measured in direct machine hours:				
Actual hours in output	18,400			
Planned hours in output			18,000	
Direct material A	6,300 at $2.15 = $13,545		6,000 at $2.00 = $12,000	$1,545*
Direct labor	4,160 at $5.10 = 21,216		4,000 at $5.00 = 20,000	1,216
Department overhead	$23,000		$21,000†	2,000*
*Over/under applied overhead:				
Actual incurred	$23,000			
Applied ($1.10 × 18,000 DMH)‡			$19,800‡	
*Underapplied for January				$3,200*
Service usage				
Etc.				

*Unfavorable variance.
†Computation based on the flexible budget: fixed—$12,000 + ($.50 × 18,000) = $21,000.
‡Computation of overhead rate: $264,000 ÷ 240,000 DMH = $1.10 per DMH.

c. Explain and illustrate your recommended method of incorporating the variance analysis developed in a monthly performance report of the department.

d. Should the company incorporate the variance analysis in the regular performance report? Explain the advantages and disadvantages involved.

CASE 16-2   Prepare a performance report for a sales district

Chesapeake Wholesalers is a major distributor of three products in a fourteen-state region. There are four sales districts, each headed by a district sales manager. The company uses a profit planning and control program, including monthly performance reports. Recently the financial vice-president decided that variance analyses would be incorporated into the monthly performance report. The following data for one of the sales districts (Inland) for June have been developed for performance report purposes:

	INLAND DISTRICT		
	PROD. X	PROD. Y	PROD. Z
Planned data:			
Units	15,000	30,000	50,000
Average unit price	$ 2.00	$ .70	$ 1.10
Actual data:			
Units	14,000	25,000	62,000
Amount	$28,560	$18,750	$62,620

REQUIRED

Use the above data for illustrative purposes to prepare appropriate performance schedules for the June performance report. Show by illustration, the integrative relationships and the variance analysis that should be reflected in the report. Limit your illustration to sales. Include a brief evaluation of the results of your variance analysis.

CASE 16-3   Prepare a performance report for a production department

Super-Beam manufactures two major products, "Super" and "Beam." The company uses a profit planning and control program including monthly performance reports. This case relates to one responsibility center—Production Department 8—which works only on Super. The following data are available to develop the Department Performance Report for March (third month in the fiscal period):

Budget data for March:

Units to be manufactured	150,000
Units of material 1 required (based on planned usage rates)	495,000
Planned purchases of material 1—units	540,000
Average unit cost of material 1—$.80	
Direct labor hours planned per unit of finished good	$\frac{3}{4}$
Direct labor cost (total)	$299,250

Actual data at the end of March:

Units actually manufactured during March	160,000
Material 1 cost (purchase cost based on units actually issued)	$434,190
Material 1 (purchase cost based on units actually purchased)	$451,000
Average unit cost of material 1—$.82	
Total direct labor hours for March	125,000
Total direct labor cost for March	$337,500

REQUIRED

1. Prepare a performance report for March for Production Department 8. Include the March data and variances. (Manufacturing overhead and service usage are not included in the above data; therefore, you should indicate how they would be reported without using illustrative amounts.) Also, develop a variance analysis of direct materials and direct labor and incorporate the results in the performance report.

2. Compute and explain any implied variances that should appear on the performance report of another department.

CASE 16-4   *An analysis of manufacturing overhead*

Gem Company manufactures a line of products distributed through local hardware stores. The company uses a profit planning and control program, including monthly performance reports. This case focuses on Production Department 3 in the factory. The activity factor (measure of output) in the department is direct machine hours (DMH) because it processes a number of products simultaneously. Departmental overhead is applied to production on the basis of planned production hours. This case focuses on analysis of the department overhead variance. The following data relating to Department 3 have been extracted from the company records and reports:

From the annual profit plan:

Departmental overhead:	
Fixed per year	$1,080,000
Variable for year (from the flexible budget)	$ 720,000
Direct labor hours planned for the year	144,000
Direct machine hours planned for the year	2,400,000
Direct labor hours planned for January	12,000
Direct machine hours planned for January	200,000

From the accounting records for January (actual data):

Departmental overhead incurred:	Fixed	$ 90,500
	Variable	$ 64,500
Direct labor hours in January:	Actual	13,000
	Planned hours in actual output	12,500
Direct machine hours in January:	Actual	207,000
	Planned hours in actual output	205,000

REQUIRED

An analysis of the departmental overhead variance is to be developed. To establish the background for this analysis, answer the following (show computations in each instance):

a.   What is the annual overhead rate for the department?

b.   How much overhead was applied in January?

c.   What is the amount of over/underapplied overhead in the department for January? Is it favorable or unfavorable?

d.   What is the amount of the total departmental overhead variance to be analyzed for January? Explain.

e.   Give a two-way analysis of the total departmental overhead variance identified in requirement 4.

f.   Present a narrative explanation of the two subvariances developed in requirement 5.

g.   How would the two variances developed in requirement 5 be reflected on the January performance report for Department 3?

CASE 16-5   Can you compute material, labor, and manufacturing overhead variances?

The January performance report for the Tower Company is being developed. It is complete except for the variance analyses. Based on the extracted data given below from the performance report, develop the variance analyses for each schedule (show your computations). Also evaluate each analysis.

Schedule A—Sales Performance Report—Central Sales Division

	ACTUAL		PROFIT PLAN		VARIANCE
	UNITS	AMOUNT	UNITS	AMOUNT	UNFAVORABLE*
Product AK	109,000	$182,030	100,000	$180,000	$2,030
Variance analysis:					
Evaluation:					

Schedule B—Purchasing Department Performance Report

| | ACTUAL | | PROFIT PLAN | | VARIANCE |
	UNITS	AMOUNT	UNITS	AMOUNT	UNFAVORABLE*
Purchase material X	7,000	$11,410	6,000	$10,200	$1,210*
Variance analysis:					
Evaluation:					

Schedule C—Production Department No. 1
Performance Report

	ACTUAL	BUDGET ADJUSTED TO ACTUAL OUTPUT	VARIANCE UNFAVORABLE*
Department output:			
Actual DLH in output	2,900		
Planned DLH in output		2,500	
Raw material	5,300 units, $ 9,010	5,000 units, $ 8,500	$ 510*
Direct labor	2,900 DLH, 11,310	2,500 DLH, 10,000	1,310*
Department overhead:			
Controllable:			
Production salaries	$ 2,600	$ 2,500	$ 100*
Indirect material	4,180	4,000	180*
Indirect labor	3,120	2,900	220*
Noncontrollable:			
Depreciation	2,600	2,600	
Insurance and taxes	400	400	
Supervisory salaries	1,600	1,600	
Total overhead	$14,500	$14,000	$ 500*
Variance Analysis:			
Raw material X			
Evaluation:			
Direct labor			
Evaluation:			
Department overhead:			
Predetermined overhead rate per DLH		$	
Actual overhead incurred			$
Overhead applied			$
Difference—over- or underapplied			$
Variance analysis of overhead (two-way):			
Variance analysis of overhead (three-way):			
Evaluation:			

Additional data are available:

1   From the annual profit plan—Department 1:

Planned annual output in DLH		36,000
Planned annual overhead:	Fixed	$108,000
	Variable	$ 72,000

2   Department 1 flexible budget:

	FIXED PER MONTH	VARIABLE PER DLH
Production salaries	$2,500	
Indirect material	500	$1.40
Indirect labor	1,400	.60
Depreciation	2,600	
Insurance and taxes	400	
Supervisory salaries	1,600	
Total	$9,000	$2.00

17

Coordinating Accounting Systems with Profit Planning and Control

INTRODUCTION AND PURPOSE   The preceding chapters emphasize the usefulness of historical accounting information in the planning and control functions of management. Profit plans and control performance reports should be structured by responsibility centers, products, and time periods. Therefore, the accounting system should be organized to provide actual accounting data (as opposed to planned data) by responsibility centers, products, and time periods. This is called management accounting. Also, the accounting system should be organized to provide actual accounting data for external reporting to investors, creditors, and governmental agencies (e.g., for the income tax return). This is called financial accounting.

The accounting system should be structured to provide information that satisfies the needs of both managerial accounting and financial accounting. However, there should not be two separate accounting systems. The demands of managerial accounting are broader and more fundamental to enterprise success than are those of financial accounting. Therefore, the accounting system should be designed primarily to provide management accounting information; and secondarily, to provide the needed financial accounting information. An emphasis in the accounting system to provide data only for external reporting purposes cannot be cost effective in also meeting the demands of both managerial accounting and PPC.

This chapter (a) emphasizes the importance of an accounting system designed to provide the information needed for **management** planning and control and to identify the characteristics of such a system, (b) discusses product-costing systems related to inventory and cost of goods sold (absorption costing, variable costing, and standard costing), and (c) describes the relationships between these three accounting systems and a comprehensive profit planning and control program (including flexible expense budgets).

593

IMPORTANCE AND CHARACTERISTICS OF A COST-EFFECTIVE ACCOUNTING SYSTEM TO SUPPORT A PROFIT PLANNING AND CONTROL PROGRAM   An accounting system is used to record the economic effects that completed transactions have on an enterprise. This means that a typical accounting system primarily accumulates and reports **actual historical data** about an enterprise period by period. An accounting system also provides some of the data needed to develop (a) internal financial reports that are useful for management planning and control and (b) external financial reports that are useful for investors, creditors, government agencies, and other interested groups. Our focus in this book is on management accounting. Exhibit 17-1 shows the broad characteristics of an accounting system. One author identified the major distinctions between management and financial accounting essentially as follows:[1]

Differences:

1 Managerial accounting focuses on providing data for internal uses by the manager.
2 Managerial accounting places much more emphasis on the future.
3 Managerial accounting is not governed by generally accepted accounting principles.
4 Managerial accounting emphasizes the relevance and flexibility of data.
5 Managerial accounting places less emphasis on precision and more emphasis on nonmonetary data.
6 Managerial accounting emphasizes the segments of an organization, rather than just looking at the organization as a whole.
7 Managerial accounting draws heavily from other disciplines.
8 Managerial accounting is not mandatory.

Similarities:

1. Both rely heavily on a single accounting system.
2. Both rely heavily on the concept of responsibility or stewardship:
   a. Financial accounting is concerned with stewardship responsibility for the company as a whole.
   b. Management accounting is concerned with stewardship responsibility over the parts (responsibility centers) of the company.

This book focuses on management accounting because its purpose is to provide relevant information for the planning and control functions of management. **Management accounting** has been defined as follows: "Management accounting is the identification, measurement, accumulation, analysis, preparation, interpretation, and communication of information that assists executives in fulfilling organizational objectives. A synonym is internal accounting."[2]

---

[1] Ray H. Garrison, *Managerial Accounting, Concepts for Planning, Control, Decision* 4th ed. (Plano, Tex.: Business Publications, 1985), p. 14.

[2] Charles T. Horngren and George Foster, *Cost Accounting: A Managerial Emphasis,* 6th ed. (Englewood Cliff., N.J.: Prentice-Hall, 1987), p. 2.

EXHIBIT 17-1

Broad Characteristics of an Accounting System

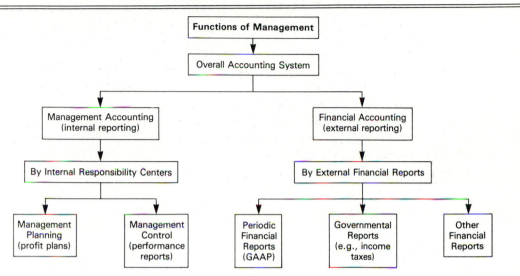

The discussion in the preceding chapters emphasized profit planning and control as an effective way to organize and implement the management functions—primarily planning and control. In this chapter, we emphasize that the accounting system must be tailored to these planning and control responsibilities of management.

The actual historical information provided by an accounting system is often useful in **managerial planning.** Throughout the preceding chapters, we emphasized uses of historical accounting data such as in developing planned revenue, inventory levels, capital expenditures, and expense standards. The method of least squares (illustrated in Chapter 10) used historical accounting data to develop flexible expense budget formulas. Historical accounting data about operations in each responsibility center are often used during the development of the strategic and tactical profit plans both as a launching pad for tentative estimates and as a check on the reasonableness of estimates (that become plans) developed independently of actual historical data. Consider the following possible scenario:

The most important and pervasive use of actual historical data provided by the accounting system is for management control. Effective short-term (e.g., monthly) performance reports by responsibility centers should compare planned amounts with actual amounts to report performance variances. These performance variances should lead to (a) positive motivations when favorable and (b) corrective action and replanning when unfavorable. This element of management control was emphasized throughout the preceding chapters, and especially in Chapter 15.

The implication is that the accounting system must provide relevant and timely information on a responsibility-center basis. If this result does not occur, a profit planning and control system will not be useful. A recent book summarized the importance of accounting data in a somewhat different way, as shown in Exhibit 17-2.[3]

EXHIBIT 17-2

Relationship of Accounting Techniques to Management Needs

	PLANNING	MANAGEMENT CONTROL	OPERATING CONTROL	FINANCIAL REPORTING
Cost estimation methods	X	X	X	
Master budgets		X		X
Cost allocation methods				X
Product-Cost-Determination system				X
Standard costing and variance analysis		X	X	X
Cost-Volume-Profit analysis	X	X	X	
Capital budgeting, cost/benefit analysis	X	X		
Responsibility accounting		X	X	
Performance evaluation methods		X	X	
Scarce resource allocation techniques		X	X	
Inventory management techniques		X	X	
Special decision analysis	X	X		

COST, PROFIT, AND INVESTMENT CENTERS   In a decentralized company, the responsibility centers can be designated as either cost, profit, or investment centers as follows:

---

[3] Reprinted by permission from *Cost Accounting* by Killough & Leininger; Copyright © 1984 by West Publishing Company. All rights reserved.

Responsibility Centers
{
Cost center—the center manager is responsible for expenses (or costs).
Profit center—the center manager is responsible for revenues, expenses, and profit.
Investment center—the center manager is responsible for revenues, expenses, profit, and invested capital.
}

Garrison gives an excellent example of a decentralized company structure that uses the three types of responsibility centers as shown in Exhibit 17-3.[4] In such cases, the profit planning and control program and the accounting system must be coordinated to accommodate each of these three types of responsibility centers.

EXHIBIT 17-3

Investment, Profit, and Cost Centers—General Products, Inc.

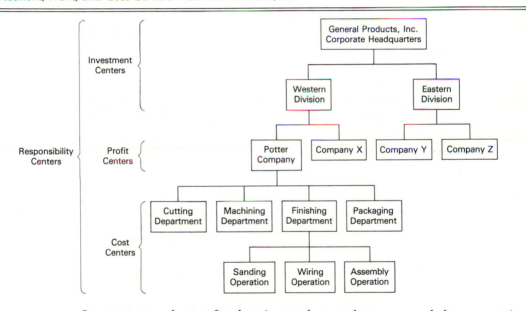

In summary, the profit planning and control process and the accounting process must be in harmony. Also, it should be recognized (see Chapter 15 on performance reports) that the several reporting needs—external and internal—can best be satisfied with significantly different types of reports. This requirement necessitates organization of the accounting function to meet those diverse needs. Industry characteristics can determine to some extent the profit planning and control program and the accounting system used in a given enterprise. However, regardless of the industry or the "system" used, the concept of responsibility accounting dominates the management planning and control point of view.

[4] Garrison, *Managerial Accounting*, p. 452.

SELECTED ACCOUNTING SYSTEMS RELEVANT TO PROFIT PLANNING AND CONTROL   This section discusses various product costing methods used in management accounting as follows:

Type of production activity	$\begin{cases} \text{Job-order costing} \\ \text{Process costing} \end{cases}$
Treatment of fixed overhead	$\begin{cases} \text{Variable costing} \\ \text{Absorption costing} \end{cases}$
Type of costs	$\begin{cases} \text{Actual costing} \\ \text{Normal costing} \\ \text{Standard costing} \end{cases}$

Any combination of methods from these three basic characteristics is possible, thus yielding twelve fundamental types of product-costing systems. These methods apply primarily to a manufacturing company. They focus on average **unit manufacturing costs** used to determine inventory cost (an asset) and cost of goods sold (an expense). Each method reflects a different concept (i.e., definition) of what average unit manufacturing cost should be. Each method can be applied to the different kinds of manufacturing activities in a company as follows:

1   **Process manufacturing**—a single main product is produced during the annual accounting period. Examples are flour milling, petroleum refining, cement, paints, electricity, and chemical products. In these cases, the product flows through a series of consecutive processes that are seldom changed. This is called process costing. In this case, the average unit cost is computed as follows:

$$\text{AVERAGE COST PER UNIT} = \frac{\text{TOTAL MANUFACTURING (PROCESSING) COST}}{\text{TOTAL UNITS PRODUCED (PROCESSED)}}$$

2   **Job-order manufacturing**—several different products, or jobs, are separately produced during the accounting period. Examples are printing jobs, separate contracts, word processing, construction, and customized products. In these cases, an average unit cost for each job or product is computed. This is called job-order costing. Separate unit costs must be computed for each product or job.

Both the profit planning and control format and the accounting format must be consistent with the kinds of manufacturing activities in the company. Because of diverse operations, many companies use process costing in some centers and job-order costing in other centers. Next, we discuss absorption costing and variable costing.

Absorption Costing

Manufacturing cost includes (a) direct materials and component parts, which are a variable cost (see Chapter 7); direct labor, which is a variable cost (see Chapter 8); and manufacturing overhead, which includes both fixed and variable costs (see Chapter 9).

Absorption costing (also called **full costing**) assigns all direct and indirect manufacturing costs, both fixed and variable, to the average unit cost of product. Refer to the comprehensive case in each chapter—Superior Manufacturing Company. This company uses absorption *or* full costing to value inventory and cost of goods sold, but it uses the concept of cost variability to supplement absorption costing in the development of flexible budgets. A portion of Superior's tactical profit plan for January 19X2 is shown as follows:

		JANUARY AVERAGE COST FOR	
SCH. NO.	MANUFACTURING COST	PRODUCT X	PRODUCT Y
28	Direct material	$ 85,400	$17,000
30	Direct labor	105,000	20,400
36	Factory overhead	46,200	9,520
58	Total cost	$236,600	$46,920
22	Production (units)	70,000	34,000
59	Average unit cost	$3.38	$1.38

The profit plan is developed using absorption costing; therefore, Superior's accounting system should be tailored to use the same system for costing inventory and cost of goods sold. Notice that absorption costing does not distinguish between fixed and variable costs to compute unit costs. However, the company does use flexible expense budgets for the monthly performance reports (see Chapter 10), but the fixed and variable amounts are not incorporated into the accounting system per se.

Most companies use absorption costing for external reporting because (a) full cost closely conforms to GAAP, (b) they are reluctant to separately record the fixed and variable components of costs in the accounts, (c) it can be compared with that of other companies, and (d) they question the practical validity of the concept of cost variability.

Absorption costing can be effectively adapted to use the cost variability concept. Under this adaptation, the concept of fixed and variable costs is used only for planning and control purposes. This often extends to separation of the fixed and variable cost components on the internal income statements. Such a supplementation is illustrated in the comprehensive case—Superior Manufacturing Company.

Variable Costing

Variable costing (also called **direct costing**) is applied in the same manner as absorption costing except for one major difference. For costing inventory and cost of goods sold, all the **fixed** manufacturing costs are **excluded** from the average unit cost of inventory (and cost of goods sold). Instead the fixed manufacturing costs are accounted for as a periodic expense when incurred each period rather than being included in inventory cost as an asset, which is later recognized as expense when the goods are sold. Also, the fixed and variable components of administrative and selling expenses are separately recorded in the accounting system and separately reported on the income statement. Variable costing has the following four distinct characteristics:

1   The fixed and variable components of all costs (manufacturing, administrative, and selling) are *formally segregated* in the accounts at initial recording. This segregation of the fixed and variable cost components requires special provision in the chart of accounts. For example, the manufacturing overhead control accounts might appear as follows:
    14191   Variable manufacturing overhead control
    14192   Fixed manufacturing overhead control

2   Only variable costs (direct material, direct labor, and variable manufacturing overhead) are treated as costs of production; therefore, cost of goods sold, inventories of work in process, and finished goods are accounted for and reported at *variable cost* only. Fixed costs are viewed as *period costs* rather than production costs. Therefore, all fixed costs are written off and reported as direct expense deductions on the income statement for the period in which they are incurred. No fixed costs are included in cost of goods sold or capitalized in inventory.

3   The income statement is rearranged to emphasize the *contribution margin,* as discussed in Chapter 14. Contribution margin is the excess of sales revenue over *variable* production, distribution, and administrative costs. The fixed costs are deducted in full as period expenses.

4   Reported contribution margin and pretax operating income fluctuates directly with increases and decreases in revenue from period to period (assuming no changes in selling prices). This effect contrasts with absorption costing, which causes pretax income to be significantly affected by the amount of increase or decrease in inventories. For example, one company recently reported the following comparative results (amounts simplified for illustrative purposes) when the inventory of finished goods changed significantly from month to month:

		REPORTED NET INCOME UNDER	
PERIOD	NET SALES	ABSORPTION COSTING	VARIABLE COSTING
January	$30,000	$ 5,000	$ 5,000
February	27,000	5,600	3,200
March	27,000	800	3,200
Total for quarter		$11,400	$11,400

Exhibit 17-4 shows a variable or direct cost income statement. In this statement, 60 percent (that is, the variable cost ratio) of each sales dollar was required to pay variable costs and 40 percent (the P/V ratio) was available to "cover fixed costs and make a profit." The breakeven point was: $70,000 ÷ .40 = $175,000. The income statement shown can be expanded to report contribution margins by major segments (e.g., divisions or products) of the company (also see Chapter 14).

EXHIBIT 17-4

Variable or Direct Cost Income Statement

Sales revenue			$200,000	100‰
Less variable costs:				
Beginning inventory (at variable cost)		$10,000		
Variable costs:				
Direct material	$50,000			
Direct labor	40,000			
Variable manufacturing overhead	20,000			
Variable administrative expenses	5,000			
Variable distribution expenses	6,000	121,000		
Total		131,000		
Less ending inventory (at variable cost)		11,000		
Total variable costs			120,000	60 (variable cost ratio)
Marginal income (or contribution margin)			80,000	40 (P/V ratio)
Less period (fixed) costs:				
Fixed manufacturing overhead		$ 10,000		
Fixed administrative expenses		25,000		
Fixed distribution expenses		35,000		
Total fixed costs			70,000	
Operating income (pretax)			$ 10,000	

The primary **advantages** of variable or direct costing usually cited are the following:

1 In long-range planning, costs are best projected separately in fixed and variable categories; variable costing provides a sound foundation for this distinction in planning.
2 In short-range profit planning, a distinction between fixed and variable costs is imperative; variable costing provides historical data on this basis, which facilitates projections.
3 The financial statements provided by the accounting system harmonize (format and results) with those developed in the planning process.
4 Income statements, both planned and actual, can be developed and compared on a contribution margin basis.
5 Troublesome allocations of fixed costs to products are largely avoided for both planning and accounting purposes.
6 Control is enhanced; if variable expense budgets are used, the problem of determining the variability of planned expenses is simplified, because the historical expense data will be differentiated between fixed and variable components.
7 The accounting system must be evaluated, and an appropriate activity factor (that is, measure of output) for each responsibility center must be chosen.
8 The comparison of actual costs with planned or budgeted costs by responsibility is enhanced, because allocation of indirect costs is de-emphasized in the accounting system, as it must be in the budget program.
9 The historical data from the accounting system emphasize cost-volume-profit relationships; therefore, these relationships can be projected.
10 Perhaps most important, cost variability provides management with information on the diverse effects of fixed and variable costs on the financial outcomes. The fact that both

planned and **actual** financial data focus on the behavior of costs enhances management's sophistication in considering alternatives when volume varies.

The primary **disadvantages** of variable or direct costing usually cited are ⁺hat (1) it is difficult to realistically segregate actual costs into fixed and variable categories, and (2) costing inventory and cost of goods sold at variable cost is not acceptable under GAAP or current income tax regulations for external financial reporting.[5]

In summary, variable or direct costing incorporated into an accounting system makes a basic distinction and emphasizes an important complementary relationship. The basic distinction is that the fixed and variable cost components are recorded in the accounts; this is not the case in absorption costing. The complementary relationship is that the fixed and variable cost components (not specific amounts) are the same in both the accounting system (historical data) and the profit plan (planned data). Thus, the complementary relationship means that the format of profit plans and the format of the actual results harmonize for internal and external reporting purposes.

One cost accounting book summarized the distinction between absorption costing and variable costing as shown in Exhibit 17-5.[6]

EXHIBIT 17-5

Comparison of Absorption Costing and Variable Costing

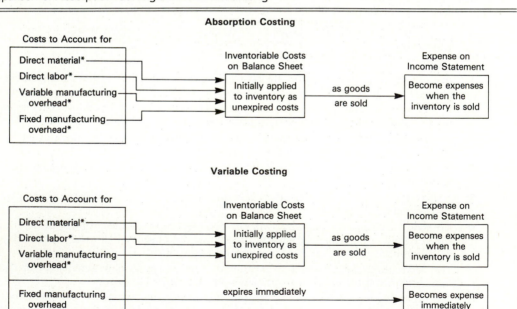

*As goods are manufactured, the costs are "applied" to inventory, usually via the use of unit costs.

[5] Michael Schiff, "Variable Costing: A Closer Look," *Management Accounting,* February 1987, p. 36.
[6] Horngren and Foster, *Cost Accounting,* p. 56.

Standard Costing

Standard costing is a way to introduce the concept of planned (i.e., standard) costs into the accounting system and to compare the standard costs with actual costs. Therefore, standard costing involves (for certain transactions) currently recording in the accounts three different amounts: (a) actual cost, (b) standard cost, and (c) variances between items a and b. Standard costing is applied to the three manufacturing costs—direct material, direct labor, and manufacturing overhead—in both process and job-order manufacturing. Standard costing focuses on *quantity* and *price* differences between actual cost and standard cost (defined later).

STANDARD COSTING FOR DIRECT MATERIALS   To illustrate the nature of the accounting entries for standard costing, assume that Able Company produces one product (i.e., product P). This product moves through two departments (1 and 2). Raw material R is used in Department 1, and raw material M is used in Department 2. Direct labor is required in both departments. Standard manufacturing overhead rates based on departmental direct labor hours are used to allocate manufacturing overhead to the product as it passes through each department.

The predetermined standard costs for Able Company are specified in Exhibit 17-6. Assume that during January, Able Company purchased 2,100 units of material R at $1.55 per unit and 4,200 units of material M at $.49. These purchases would be recorded in the accounts of a standard costing system as follows:

For Material R Purchase:		
Raw materials inventory control (2,100 units × $1.50)	3,150	
Material price variance (2,100 units × $ .05)	105[*]	
Cash (2,100 units at $1.55)		3,255
For Material M Purchase:		
Raw materials inventory control (4,200 units × $ .50)	2,100	
Material price variance (4,200 units × $ .01)		42[*]
Cash (4,200 units at $ .49)		2,058

[*]Formula for price variance:
  Actual units × Price difference

The Raw Materials Control account is debited with the **standard cost of material purchased;** the **difference** between standard cost and actual cost is debited or credited to a Material Price Variance account. Reference to the above entries shows that the Material Price Variance Control account has a debit balance of $63, which represents an unfavorable standard cost variance (a credit balance would be a favorable variance). Notice that material R showed an unfavorable price variance of $105, and material M showed a favorable price variance of $42. Detailed records supporting the control account would indicate the amount of variance for **each item or class of raw material** and specifically which purchases caused the variation. It is not necessary to wait unit the end of the reporting period to determine the material price variance. Variances on weekly or even on individual purchases can be determined and reported to management so that appropriate corrective action can be taken when necessary. The purchasing manager is responsible for controlling material price variances. If the amount is not significant, the Material Price Variance account is usually closed at the end of the accounting period to the Income Summary account and shown as an expense on the income statement because it represents a *loss* due to inefficiency (or gain due to efficiency) rather than a cost of production. However, if the amount of the variance is significant, the amount must be allocated to the inventories (raw material, work-in-process, finished goods) and the cost of goods sold, usually in proportion to the ending balances in the accounts. The price variance would be shown on the monthly performance report of the purchasing manager.

Materials used in production are recorded in the Materials in Process account at standard quantities valued at standard prices. For example, assume that 1,000 units of product P (Exhibit 17-6) were produced in January and that raw material issues were: 2,050 units of raw material R; 4,020 units of raw material M. The entries for standard costing would be:

For Raw Material R:		
Material in process—Dept. 1 (2,000 units × $1.50)	3,000	
Material quantity variance (50 units × $1.50)	75*	
Raw materials inventory control (2,050 units × $1.50)		3,075
For Raw Material M:		
Material in process—Dept. 2 (4,000 units × $.50)	2,000	
Material quantity variance (20 units × $.50)	10*	
Raw materials inventory control (4,020 units × $.50)		2,010

*Formula for the quantity variance:
Standard price × Quantity difference

In the above entries, the Work-in-Process inventory account was debited for the standard quantities of raw material required to produce 1,000 units of product produced multiplied by the standard unit cost. The Material inventory account is credited for the actual quantities used valued at the standard material prices. The material Quantity Variance account has a debit balance of $85, which represents the standard cost of excess material used. This variance measures the effectiveness with which raw materials were used. The variance is expressed in terms of the standard material unit cost rather than of the actual material unit cost because the departmental supervisors (factory Departments 1 and 2) have no control over material prices but do have control over material *usage*. The material usage variances are reported on the monthly performance reports of the respective department managers.

EXHIBIT 17-6

Standard Cost Specification—Able Company (Practical expected standard cost)

		COMPUTATION	STANDARD COST PER UNIT	
Product:	P		Date:	1/1/19X1
Specifications:	Attached			

	COMPUTATION	STANDARD COST PER UNIT	
Department 1:			
Material R	2 units × $1.50	$3.00	
Direct labor	3 hours × 2.00	6.00	
Manufacturing overhead	3 hours × 1.00	3.00	$12.00
Department 2:			
Material M	4 units × $ .50	2.00	
Direct labor	2 hours × 3.00	6.00	
Manufacturing overhead	2 hours × 2.50	5.00	13.00
Total standard cost			$25.00

The Raw Materials Inventory Control account shows the ending inventory of raw materials costed at standard prices. The Material Quantity Variance account is closed at the end of the period to the Income Summary and is reported on the income statement as an expense because the debit balance represents a *loss* due to inefficiency; therefore, it is not a proper cost of production. A credit balance would indicate a favorable variance. As explained under materials purchases, any significant variances must be allocated.

A distinct advantage of standard material costing is that the accounting is simplified for inventories of raw material and work in process. If raw material purchases are recorded in the Materials Inventory Control account at standard unit prices, the problem of costing individual issues on an inventory record (using some method such as FIFO, LIFO, or Average) is avoided for internal reporting. Moreover, perpetual inventory records can be kept in terms of units only, because both issues and inventories are valued at the same standard unit material price. The use of standards for material reduces the cost of the accounting function and at the same time increases control through both accounting and budgeting.

The flow of accounting data through a standard costing system is diagramed in Exhibit 17-7. Notice in particular (a) the dominance of **standard cost** over actual cost and (b) the six variance accounts.

STANDARD COSTING FOR DIRECT LABOR   Standard costing for direct labor is the same as for direct materials except that quantity is measured as direct labor hours and price is measured as the average hour wage rate. Refer to Exhibit 17-6 for typical labor standards. Continuing the assumption for Able Company that 1,000 units of product P are produced in January, assume further that actual direct labor data were: Department 1, 3,100 actual direct labor hours at an average hourly actual rate of $2.05; Department 2, 1,960 actual direct labor

EXHIBIT 17-7

Flow of Accounting Data Through a Standard Costing System

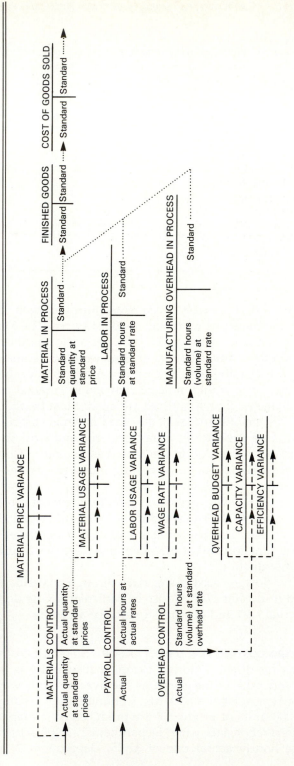

hours at an average hourly actual rate of $3.10. The accounting entries would be:

Department 1:
  Labor in process—Dept. 1 (3,000 DLH × $2.00)   6,000
  Labor usage variance (100 DLH × $2.00)   200*
  Wage rate variance (3,100 DLH × $.05)   155†
    Wages payable (3,100 DLH × $2.05)   6,355

Department 2:
  Labor in process—Dept. 2 (2,000 DLH × $3.00)   6,000
  Wage rate variance (1,960 DLH × $.10)   196†
    Labor usage variance (40 DLH × $3.00)   120*
    Wages payable (1,960 DLH × $3.10)   6,076

Variance formulas:
  * Quantity—labor usage: Standard wage rate × DLH difference
  † Price—wage rate variance: Actual DLH × Wage rate difference

The work-in-process accounts are debited at the standard cost of direct labor (i.e., standard hours times the standard rate). The differences between actual and standard cost are debited or credited to appropriately titled *variance accounts* for usage and rate variances. The labor variance accounts are closed at the end of the period to the Income Summary and reported on the income statement like the material variance accounts. The wage rate and labor usage variances are reported on the monthly performance report of the responsibility center. Inclusion in the ledger accounts (and the income statement) of standard costs for labor and the resulting variances increase management attention to an even higher level. Direct labor variances are a responsibility of the managers of the productive responsibility centers. Labor usage and wage rate variances should be analyzed by cost center, shifts, and groups of workers. By using standard costs, labor usage variances can be measured and reported on a monthly, weekly, or even daily basis for control purposes. Daily and cumulative reports of labor variances are often posted on bulletin boards or charts in the factory in order to emphasize their importance.

The analysis of standard cost variances for material and labor should not cease with the identification of time and responsibility. Significant variances should be investigated to determine precisely **what caused the variances** so that timely management action is possible.

STANDARD COSTING FOR MANUFACTURING OVERHEAD   Standard costs for manufacturing overhead should be based on the overhead budgets for the manufacturing function. Budgeting is essential because **standard overhead rates** must be developed in advance for both profit planning and cost accounting purposes for each responsibility center. A predetermined manufacturing overhead rate is computed as follows (see Chapter 9):

$$\frac{\text{Budgeted overhead for the year}}{\text{Budgeted volume for the year}} = \text{Standard overhead rate per unit of output}$$

This formula requires that (1) annual volume (output) and (2) annual manufacturing overhead costs be budgeted for each responsibility center. It is generally thought that these estimates should be more carefully analyzed when standard costs are being developed than when they are to be used in historical cost systems. There is no logic for the distinction. When a budget program is used, the volume projections and overhead cost budgets should be used as the basis for computation of the standard overhead rate for accounting purposes.

Standard costing procedures for manufacturing overhead can be shown by referring to Exhibit 17-6 for budget data and standard overhead rates. Continuing the assumption that 1,000 units of product P are produced in January, we assume further the following data for overhead: actual overhead incurred for January in Department 1, $3,500; and in Department 2, $5,373. Direct labor hours are given on page 607. Accounting (journal) entries for a standard cost system would be:

Actual Manufacturing Overhead Incurred:

Manufacturing overhead control—Department 1	3,500	
Manufacturing overhead control—Department 2	5,373	
Various accounts		8,873

Manufacturing Overhead Applied—Department 1:

Manufacturing overhead in process (3,000 DLH × $1.00)	3,000	
Manufacturing overhead control—Department 1		3,000

Manufacturing Overhead Applied—Department 2:

Manufacturing overhead in process (2,000 DLH × $2.50)	5,000	
Manufacturing overhead control—Department 2		5,000

Manufacturing Overhead Variances—Department 1:[*]

Manufacturing overhead budget variance	200	
Manufacturing overhead idle capacity variance	300	
Manufacturing overhead control—Department 1		500

Manufacturing Overhead Variances—Department 2:[*]

Manufacturing overhead budget variance	40	
Manufacturing overhead idle capacity variance	333	
Manufacturing overhead control—Department 2		373

[*]Computations:

MANUFACTURING OVERHEAD ITEMS	DEPT. 1	DEPT. 2
1. Actual overhead incurred	$3,500	$5,373
2. Flexible budget adjusted to actual hours:		
Fixed, $2,100 + variable (3,100 × $.40)	$3,340	
Fixed, $2,333 + variable (1,960 × $1.50)		$5,273
3. Flexible budget adjusted to standard hours:		
Fixed, $2,100 + variable (3,000 × $.40)	$3,300	
Fixed, $2,333 + variable (2,000 × $1.50)		$5,333
4. Overhead applied (from above entries)	$3,000	$5,000
Variations:		
Overhead budget variance (1 − 3)	$ 200†	$ 40†
Overhead idle capacity variance (4 − 3)	300†	333†
Total variance (4 − 1)	$ 500†	$ 373†

†Unfavorable.
See the later section on flexible expense budgets.
Note: This analysis is identical conceptually and mathematically with the analysis discussed and illustrated in Chapter 16. The interpretations given there are appropriate for the standard cost variances illustrated above.

Completion of 1,000 units of Product P:*

Finished goods inventory (1,000 units × $25)	25,000	
Material in process (1,000 units × $5)		5,000
Labor in process (1,000 units × $12)		12,000
Manufacturing overhead in process (1,000 units × $8)		8,000

*Standard unit costs from Exhibit 17-6.

Sale of 1,000 units at $40 per unit (finished goods inventory balance, zero):

Cash (1,000 units × $40)	40,000	
Sales revenue		40,000
Cost of goods sold	25,000	
Finished goods inventory (1,000 units × $25)		25,000

Notice that, as with direct material and labor, the Manufacturing Overhead-in-Process account is debited at standard cost (i.e., standard hours times the standard overhead rate). The three Work-in-Process accounts (material, direct labor, and overhead) are **credited** at standard cost for goods completed, leaving the work-in-process inventory valued at standard cost (i.e., $25 per unit from Exhibit 17-6). In the above example, the overhead **underapplied** for January was $500 (that is, $3,500 − $3,000) for Department 1, and $373 (that is, $5,373 − $5,000) for Department 2. In standard costing overhead, over/underapplied is analyzed and recorded in separate variance accounts as illustrated.

Either two-way or three-way analysis can be used (see Chapter 16). The above entries show the two-way analysis, which is more commonly used.

The budget variance represents a loss due to inefficiency; therefore, it is reported on the performance report of the responsibility center to which it relates. On the income statement it is deducted as an expense. The idle capacity variance tends to balance out during the year; therefore, on a monthly reporting basis it is usually reflected on a deferred basis on the balance sheet rather than as an income statement item.

To complete the illustration developed thus far for Able Company, a simplified income statement reflecting the standard costing concept is presented in Exhibit 17-8.

EXHIBIT 17-8

Able Company

Income Statement—Standard Cost Approach
(Based on Standard Cost Data)
For the Month of January 19X2

Sales revenue—product P (1,000 units × $40)		$40,000
Less: standard cost of goods sold (1,000 units × 25)		25,000
Standard gross margin		15,000
Deduct standard cost variances (unfavorable*):		
Material price variance—material R	$105*	
Material price variance—material M	42	
Material quantity variance—material R	75*	
Material quantity variance—material M	10*	
Labor usage variance—Department 1	200*	
Wage rate variance—Department 1	155*	
Labor usage variance—Department 2	120	
Wage rate variance—Department 2	196*	
Mfg. overhead budget variance—Department 1	200*	
Mfg. overhead budget variance—Department 2	40*	
		819*
Actual gross margin		$14,181
Selling and administrative expenses		9,261
Income (pretax)		$ 4,920

Note: On monthly statements, idle capacity variance is usually shown as a deferred item on the balance sheet.

Notice that the variances, except for idle capacity, are written off and reported as expense in the period in which they were incurred. Thus, the losses due to inefficiency do not affect cost of goods sold, nor are they carried forward in inventory as an asset. The monthly performance report would incorporate this income statement, and the variances would be shown in the performance reports by a responsibility center in a manner similar to that illustrated in Chapter 15.

DEFINITION OF STANDARD COST   A primary issue is to define what is meant by standard costs for direct materials, direct labor, and manufacturing overhead. First, a widely used and broad definition is that **standard costs are predetermined or estimated costs of direct material, direct labor, and manufacturing overhead under specified conditions.** For practical applications, standard cost is defined as either (a) ideal (theoretical) costs that are attainable only under the best possible conditions or (b) practical (expected) costs that are challenging, but yet attainable, under normal expected conditions. Practical or expected costs are generally viewed the same as the cost (and expense) goals incorporated into the tactical profit plan and the flexible expense budget formulas. Practical expected standard costs are used in most standard costing systems. Ideal standard costs are useful for special analytical and decision-making purposes, but they cannot be used in tactical profit planning. Moreover, they pose some behavorial (motivation) problems in control through performance reports.

A standard cost specification as shown in Exhibit 17-8 is a basic component of a standard cost system. Notice that it shows, for each manufacturing department (i.e., responsibility center), the unit cost for direct materials, direct labor, and manufacturing overhead. For Able Company, the 19X1 total standard manufacturing cost per unit of product P is $25.

A standard cost specification gives the standard costs of material, labor, and overhead for each product or job. The standard cost specification usually emerges from a series of cost analyses and engineering studies to develop reliable standards. In process manufacturing, each standardized product would have a standard cost specification. In job-order manufacturing, a standard cost specification is developed for each job. Developing standard cost for each job or product involves predetermination of the requirements for raw material, labor, and overhead, taking into account the various responsibility centers through which the work must flow from start to completion. For large jobs, many companies find it practicable to develop a separate standard specification for each major component, operation, or assembly so that the total standard cost can be determined by summing the various standard costs for the component operations. Standard cost specifications should be designed to fit each particular situation.

Standard costing can be used in conjunction with either variable or absorption costing. In a standard variable costing system, the standard cost of direct material and direct labor and the predetermined variable overhead cost are entered into work in process. In a standard absorption costing system, the standard cost of direct material and direct labor and the predetermined cost of both variable and fixed overhead are entered into work in process.

Actual and Normal Costing

Whereas standard costing systems enter standard or predetermined costs into work in process, actual costing systems enter actual (historical) costs into work in process. In normal costing systems, the actual costs of direct material and direct labor are entered into work in process, but overhead is entered into work in process at a predetermined rate. Both actual and normal costing can be combined with either variable or absorption costing.

Exhibit 17-9 highlights the differences between actual, normal, and standard costing systems as well as those between variable and absorption costing systems.

FLEXIBLE EXPENSE BUDGETS RELATED TO STANDARD COSTS   Flexible expense budgets, as discussed in Chapter 10, complement standard cost procedures because they provide data (1) for computation of the predetermined overhead rates and (2) for overhead variance analyses. Predetermined overhead rates were discussed in Chapter 9. The same procedures apply to standard costs. For example, the standard manufacturing overhead rates shown in the cost specification (Exhibit 17-6) and used in the illustrations on pages 609 and 610 were computed as follows:

	DEPT. 1	DEPT. 2
Budgeted data:		
Direct labor hours budgeted for the year	42,000	28,000
Flexible budgets:		
Fixed cost per month	$ 2,100.00	$ 2,333.33
Variable rate per DLH	.40	1.50

Computation of the standard overhead rates for the year:
Dept. 1

$$\frac{(12)(\$2,100) + (42,000 \times \$.40)}{42,000} = \$1.00 \text{ per DLH}$$

Dept. 2

$$\frac{(12)(\$2,333.33) + (28,000 \times \$1.50)}{28,000} = \$2.50 \text{ per DLH}$$

In the analysis of standard cost overhead variances, information from the flexible budget was used as shown in the computations on page 609. The procedures used there are the same as those discussed in Chapter 16. The discussions and illustrations in Chapter 16 concluded that relevance of variance analysis (whether budget data or standard cost data) depends on whether the fixed and variable components of cost are known.

INTEGRATION OF STANDARD COSTING AND PROFIT PLANNING AND CONTROL

Standard costing and profit planning and control have some common objectives and applications. The extent of these similarities depends on whether standard costs are defined as (a) practical expected costs or (b) ideal costs.

Profit planning and control (PPC) focuses on the strategic and tactical profit plans and control through performance reports by responsibility centers. PPC considers all revenues, expenses, cash flows, assets, and liabilities. In contrast, standard costing focuses on unit and total costs for direct materials, direct labor, and manufacturing overhead. The standard costs for each of these inputs determine the inventory valuations (at standard) and cost of goods sold (at standard). PPC is much broader in scope than standard costing.

The planned (i.e., budgeted) direct materials, direct labor, and manufacturing costs are **not recorded** in the accounting system when a PPC program is used with absorption costing. In contrast, when a standard costing system is used, the standard costs and the resulting variances for these three cost elements are recorded in the accounting system and reported on the standard costing income statement.

Profit planning and control uses **performance reports** by responsibility centers for control purposes. These performance reports encompass all phases of operations. They compare actual revenues and costs with planned (i.e., budgeted) revenues and costs to compute performance measurements (i.e., variances) in each responsibility center. PPC uses flexible expense budgets to adjust planned expenses to match the actual level of output or activity in each responsibility center. In contrast, standard costing reports expense variances only for manufacturing costs. These variances between standard costs and actual costs are reported on the income statement for both internal and external reporting. Flexible expense budgets can be used as a supplement with standard costing.

Now we come to a major issue—should the standard costs be the same as the planned PPC costs for direct material, direct labor, and manufacturing overhead? If the standard costs and PPC costs are the same, the variances on the PPC performance reports and the variances on the standard costing income statement are consistent in all respects except for the amount of detail. The PPC performance reports give detailed variances for each expense in each responsibility center, whereas the standard costing income statement shows only summary variances by responsibility centers. This conformity between PPC and standard costing exists only when **practical expected standard costs** are used.

In contrast, when standard costs represent ideal (theoretical) costs, the PPC variances and the standard costing variances usually are significantly different. The differences between budgeted costs (PPC) and standard costs can be measured and reported as "budget variances between practical expected costs and ideal theoretical costs." The problem of reporting these additional variances, and the associated complexities, causes most companies to define both PPC and standard costs as **practical expected costs.**

EXHIBIT 17-9

Differences Between Product Costing Systems

	ACTUAL COSTING WORK IN PROCESS	NORMAL COSTING WORK IN PROCESS	STANDARD COSTING WORK IN PROCESS
	Actual direct material cost	Actual direct material cost	Standard direct material cost
VARIABLE COSTING[*]	Actual direct labor cost	Actual direct labor cost	Standard direct labor cost
	Actual variable overhead cost	Predetermined variable overhead cost	Predetermined variable overhead cost

[*]Under variable costing, fixed overhead is not entered into work in process. It is treated as a period expense.

ABSORPTION COSTING

WORK IN PROCESS		
Actual direct material cost		
Actual direct labor cost		
Actual variable overhead cost		
Actual fixed overhead cost		

WORK IN PROCESS		
Actual direct material cost		
Actual direct labor cost		
Predetermined variable overhead cost		
Predetermined fixed overhead cost		

WORK IN PROCESS		
Standard direct material cost		
Standard direct labor cost		
Predetermined variable overhead cost		
Predetermined fixed overhead cost		

The integration of direct costing and standard costing based on practical expected costs, with a comprehensive profit planning and control program, is an effective approach to comprehensive planning, coordinating, and controlling. However, many companies believe that a comprehensive profit planning and control program based on practical expected standards coupled with a responsibility accounting system, absorption costing, and performance reports for each responsibility center is the most cost-effective combination. This is the planning and control combination illustrated in the demonstration case—Superior Manufacturing Company.

Suggested References

BIERMAN, HAROLD, JR., THOMAS DYCKMAN, and RONALD HILTON, *Cost Accounting: Concepts and Managerial Applications.* New York: Macmillan, 1990.

DEAKIN, EDWARD B., and MICHAEL W. MAHER, *Cost Accounting.* Englewood Cliffs, N.J.: Prentice-Hall, 1987.

HORNGREN, CHARLES T., and GEORGE FOSTER, *Cost Accounting: A Managerial Emphasis,* Chaps. 19 and 20. Englewood Cliffs, N.J.: Prentice-Hall, 1987.

KILLOUGH, LARRY N., and WAYNE E. LEININGER, *Cost Accounting: Concepts and Techniques for Management.* St. Paul, Minn.: West Publishing, 1984.

MATZ, ADOLPH, and MILTON F. USRY, *Cost Accounting, Planning and Control.* Cincinnati: South-Western Publishing, 1984.

Discussion Questions

1. Why should the accounting system be in harmony with the profit planning and control program?
2. Distinguish between responsibility, cost, profit, and investment centers in a business.
3. What is the primary focus of absorption costing, variable or direct costing, and standard costing?
4. Distinguish between process and job-order costing.
5. Define *absorption accounting* and explain its primary features.
6. Define *variable costing* and explain its primary features.
7. Define *standard costs* and compare them conceptually with historical costs.
8. What are standard cost specifications?
9. What are the two standard cost variances with respect to raw materials? Relate them to budget variations for raw material assuming practical expected standards.
10. What are the two standard cost variances with respect to direct labor? Relate them to the budget variances for labor assuming practical expected standards.

11. Briefly explain how manufacturing overhead is assigned to product unit cost when standard costing is used.

12. Which variances are usually associated with manufacturing overhead in standard costing? Relate them to budget variances for overhead.

13. Explain the integration of standard costing and a PPC program.

CASE 17-1   *An accountant's fable!*

Once upon a time a company was losing money. Although its plant had a normal capacity of 30,000 widgets, it was selling only 10,000 a year, and its operating figures looked like this:

Price per unit	$ 10
Total fixed cost	60,000
Fixed cost per unit	6
Variable cost per unit	6.50
Total unit cost	12.50
Total manufacturing cost	125,000
Value of closing inventory	0
Cost of goods sold	125,000
Sales revenue	100,000
Operating loss	(25,000)

Then one day a bearded stranger came to the board of directors and said: "Make me president, pay me half of any operating profit I produce, and I'll put you on easy street."

"Done," they said.

So the bearded stranger set the factory running full tilt, making 30,000 widgets a year. So his figures looked like this:

Total fixed cost	$ 60,000
Fixed cost per unit	2
Variable unit cost	6.50
Total unit cost	8.50
Total manufacturing cost	255,000
Value of closing inventory	170,000
Cost of goods sold	85,000
Sales revenue	100,000
Operating profit	15,000

"Pay me," said the bearded stranger.
"But we're going broke," said a director.

"So what?" said the stranger. "You can read the figures, can't you?" What is your reply?

CASE 17-2   *Adapting standard costing to use the concept of cost variability*

Snow Company is a small manufacturer of a single product sold through auto parts stores in a five-state region. Manufacturing is relatively simple, and only four producing departments are required in the one plant. Manufacturing operations are repetitive, and production is fairly stable throughout the year. The company has experienced steady growth since its organization in 1948, and profits have been slightly above average for the industry. The company has been using a full absorption cost system for plant operations. The accounting department (comprised of three individuals) each year computes a standard overhead rate for the plant. This rate is multiplied by actual plant output to apply overhead for each month. The accounting department has developed some informal standards for direct material and labor. These standards were not a part of the accounting system but have been used as a "gauge of actual performance" on the monthly financial report that was prepared for the management.

The company was organized into a sales division and a manufacturing division. The sales division is comprised of a home office and seven sales districts. Including sales districts, plant departments (four producing and three service), and administrative departments, there are a total of twenty responsibility centers. The company is owned by ten stockholders, and the shares are not for sale. The accounting department develops a quarterly summarized financial statement for the stockholders.

Two years ago, the longtime president retired at the age of seventy-two, and C. A. Snow, son of the founder of the company, was appointed president. He had received a college degree in engineering and two years later an MBA from a large midwestern university. Snow explained numerous plans to "expand the company and to introduce the latest managerial approaches." He perceived that the accounting function was "solid but not up to date in its approaches." The three employees in that department are longtime employees without formal education in management and accounting. The head of the department will retire in two years. Rather than waiting, Snow decided to employ a recent MBA graduate as his "first assistant," and among other responsibilities asked this new employee to "develop a dynamic profit planning and control program." S. T. Baker, the newly employed first assistant, has just completed the first draft of the annual profit plan for the upcoming year. Baker worked closely with the managers of the twenty responsibility centers but had to "do much of the work because this was an entirely new concept to them." The historical accounting data and the informal standards were useful; however, there had never been any effort to categorize costs as fixed and variable. Baker decided to establish the planning process for the plant on the "variable-standard cost basis." Conversations with the plant supervisors and the head of the accounting department convinced Baker that it would be best not to insist on major changes in the accounting system prior to the retirement of the present accounting manager. After the manager's retirement, Baker expected that the accounting system would be placed on a variable-standard cost basis in harmony with the profit planning approach. In the meantime, Baker decided to concentrate on improving the accounting on a responsibility basis and revising the performance reports to be issued monthly, to reflect, by responsibility, *actual, planned,* and *variances* (based on the flexible budget concept). The president agreed with this approach; it was progressive and, in his opinion, would not unduly upset the longtime employees.

To illustrate the approach taken initially in the annual profit plan, the planned income statement for January of the first budget year is given in Exhibit 1 including some explanatory data (amounts have been simplified for case purposes).

EXHIBIT 1

Snow Company, Planned Income Statement—January 19XX (Only)

	UNITS	UNIT PRICE	AMOUNT	PERCENT
Sales revenue	9,000	$10.00	$90,000	100%
Variable standard costs:				
Material	10,000	.90	$ 9,000	
Labor	10,000	1.20	12,000	
Plant overhead	10,000	1.30	13,000	
Total variable mfg. costs at standard	10,000	3.40	34,000	
Less: inventory increase	1,000	3.40	3,400	
Variable cost of goods sold at standard	9,000	3.40	30,600	
Variable distribution expenses	9,000	.40	3,600	
Variable administrative expenses	9,000	.20	1,800	
Total variable expenses	9,000	4.00	36,000	40
Contribution margin	9,000	$ 6.00	54,000	60
Fixed expenses				
Plant overhead			12,000	
Distribution expenses			14,000	
Administrative expenses			16,000	
Total fixed expenses			42,000	
Variances from standard			None	
Total fixed expenses and variances			42,000	
Income (pretax)			$12,000	13%

Additional data from annual profit plan:

1 Annual output planned—120,000 units of product (including 10,000 planned for January)

2 Annual manufacturing overhead rate per unit of output:

COSTS	AMOUNT	UNITS	RATE PER UNIT
Fixed	$144,000	120,000	$1.20
Variable	156,000	120,000	1.30
Total	$300,000	120,000	$2.50

At the end of January of the budget year, the accounting department, following the old approach, prepared the usual financial reports. The income statement portion of the reports is shown in Exhibit 2, including their comments.

Additional actual data for the month of January:

1 Material usage variance, $80; no price variance.
2 Labor variances: efficiency, $120; rate, $160.
3 Overhead incurred, $26,750; applied, 9,900 units × $2.50 = $24,750, underapplied.
4 Inventory valuation on average basis: $47,900 ÷ 9,900 units = $4.84 per unit.
5 There were no changes in the fixed expenses for distribution and administration during the month.

EXHIBIT 2

Snow Company, Income Statement for the Month of January 19XX

| | JANUARY 19XX OF | | | | INCREASE |
	CURRENT YEAR		LAST YEAR		DECREASE*
Sales (9,200 units)	$92,000	100%	$88,000	100%	$4,000
Cost of goods sold:					
Beginning inventory	None		1,450		1,450*
Manufacturing costs (9,900 units mfg.)					
Material	8,990	10	8,920	10	70
Labor	12,160	13	11,940	14	220
Plant overhead applied	24,750	27	23,870	27	880
Plant overhead underapplied	2,000	2	600	1	1,400
Total manufacturing costs	47,900	52	46,780	53	1,120
Final inventory—700 units @ $4.84	3,388	4	None		3,388
Cost of goods sold	44,512	48	46,780	53	2,268*
Gross profit	47,488	52	41,220	47	6,268
Operating costs:					
Distribution costs	17,880	19	15,900	18	1,980
Administrative costs	17,940	20	17,100	19	840
Total operating costs	35,820	39	33,000	37	2,820
Net profit (pretax)	$11,668	13%	$ 8,220	10%	$3,448

REQUIRED

1. Baker had just received the report (Exhibit 2) from the accounting department and has decided to prepare an income statement for January that compares actual results with planned using a format similar to the format shown in the profit plan (Exhibit 1). You have been asked to prepare this variable-standard performance summary report. You should set up side captions similiar to those in Exhibit 1 and then enter in the first money column the "actual" amounts converted to that format. For example, for materials you should enter the following:

LINE	ACTUAL
Variable standard costs:	
Material (9,900 units × $.90)	$8,910
Variances from standard:	
Material usage variance (given above)	80

After completing the "Actual" column in this manner, you should then complete the "Planned" column by "adjusting" the budget to actual output. Finally, the variances should be entered in the third column. Add any comments that appear appropriate. At this point, it is anticipated that the statement will be appropriate for managerial use. (Hint: The "income" amount shown in your "Actual" column should be $10,660, which is the same as in Exhibit 2 except for the effect of the difference in the inventory valuation.)

2. Evaluate the approach to introducing profit planning and control adopted by Baker. Do you agree with Baker's approach to the "accounting problem"? Compare and evaluate the two income statements.

CASE 17-3   *No good answers today*

Slow Company is a small manufacturer of five products. This case focuses on one of the products that has been of considerable concern to the management. Although there is a wide market for this particular product, the company has tended to stay within a three-state region with all its products. The company has been earning low profits for the last four or five years. Two years ago, the president asked the accounting department to develop a budget. The accounting department was comprised of four individuals headed by the chief accountant, who had been with the company since its organization thirty-two years earlier. Neither the chief accountant nor the others had formal training in accounting. The second budget for the company was recently completed and included the following income statement related to product A (summarized):

	UNIT BASIS	TOTAL COST	PERCENT
Sales (10,000 units)	$20	$200,000	100%
Cost of goods manufactured and sold	12	120,000	60
Gross profit	8	80,000	40
Selling and administrative costs	6	60,000	30
Profit	$ 2	$ 20,000	10%

The company uses a full absorption cost system and allocates actual overhead at the end of each month (predetermined overhead rates are not used). Monthly reports are prepared that compare actual expenses with one-twelfth of the annual budgeted amount.

Immediately after a recent meeting of the president and the two vice-presidents (production and sales), the president asked the chief accountant several questions. The chief accountant told the president that some time would be needed, otherwise the answers would be "off the cuff." The president wanted "some estimates now." Essentially, the questions by the president and "off-the-cuff" answers by the chief accountant were as follows:

QUESTION 1: Horn [vice-president, sales] says we should accept a 2,000 unit order at $10.50 per unit; I said no, our cost is $12 per unit. What do you think?

ANSWER: I agree with you; of course, if we produced 12,000 instead of 10,000, our unit cost would go down some but not that much. I would estimate that it might drop to $11 per unit.

QUESTION 2: What do you think our minimum price should be on this offer? It is from a state outside our market, and they are talking to our number-one competitor.

ANSWER: Well, offhand I would say we should not sell for less than $18, or maybe $17 at the absolute minimum.

QUESTION 3: Horn also mentioned our breakeven point on this item. I suggested that it was around 9,000 units. How was that?

ANSWER: Well, we would have to do a lot of analysis to compute it, but your answer makes sense. We make approximately $20,000 on 10,000 units, that is, 1,000 units for the profit. The 9,000 was a good rough estimate.

QUESTION 4: I feel that we need $30,000 profit on this product. As I read it, we pick up $8 per unit; therefore, to pick up another $10,000 profit, we need to sell 1,250 additional units. Blue [vice-president, manufacturing] says we would have no production problems, although Horn says we would have to reduce the price to increase the volume. I also proposed a 10 percent price increase. Horn says that will knock volume down by 15 percent. What do you think?

ANSWER: Well, there are a lot of factors working here. I suspect Horn is right about the 15 percent drop. If we could hold the price and sell the 1,250 units, your profit target would be all right.

QUESTION 5: Blue wants to produce 15,000 units instead of 10,000. He says the unit cost will go way down and profits up. What would be the effect of this plan? Horn insists on the 10,000 volume at our present price.

ANSWER: Well, let's see; our unit cost might go down to the $10 I mentioned earlier. On the 10,000 units budgeted we would pick up $2 each; so our profits would go up to $40,000. However, we might have an inventory problem next year.

REQUIRED

1. Evaluate the responses of the chief accountant.

2. What changes would you recommend in (1) the budget system and (2) the accounting system? Explain.

3. Following your recommendations in requirement 2, develop responses to each of the questions posed by the president. Use the following additional data if it will be helpful:

   Fixed costs included in cost of goods sold, $40,000.
   Fixed costs included in selling and administrative expenses, $50,000.

CASE 17-4   *Management indecision about how to increase profits*

Midwest Company produces ten different but similar products distributed through the same marketing channels. The sales prices vary within a 20 percent range. Because of product similarities, the manufacturing operations are fairly standardized. The selling price differentials are primarily due to size and use capabilities. For some internal purposes, the products are grouped into five categories.

The company is considered a small manufacturer and has been only moderately successful in terms of profit margin. The company controller stated that they "use a full-cost average cost system; materials and labor are accounted for at actual as used and are charged directly to the using department without regard to product." The controller explained that "factory overhead is accumulated by department during the month, and the actual amounts of service department costs are allocated to the producing departments at the end of each month. The unit cost of producing each product is not determined by the cost system, since we can estimate very closely the material and labor costs; overhead is allocated for this purpose as a load factor related to prime cost." Each month the controller prepares a balance sheet and an income statement. The income statement shows actual results for the month and cumulative to date. The format of the statements follows the traditional pattern with no segmentation by products or departments.

Prior to the beginning of each year the controller, at the request of the company president, prepares an annual budgeted income statement, detailed by quarters. This projection for the first quarter of the upcoming year is shown below (amounts simplified for illustrative purposes only).

Budget of Income and Expenses
For the twelve months ending December 31, 19XX

	THIS YEAR		BUDGET FOR NEXT YEAR		
Sales	$727,272	100%		$800,000	100%
Manufacturing costs:					
Direct material	73,113	10	$ 80,000		10
Direct labor	146,121	20	156,000		19.5
Overhead	341,698	47	360,000		45
Total manufacturing costs	560,932	77		596,000	74.5
Gross profit	166,340	23		204,000	25.5
Selling expenses	109,100	15	120,000		15
General administrative expenses	51,120	7	60,000		7.5
Total selling and administrative	160,220	22		180,000	22.5
Pretax net profit	$ 6,120	1%		$ 24,000	3.0%

Notes: 1. Projected a 10 percent increase in sales volume; no change in sales price.
   2. Projected a slight percentage decrease in manufacturing costs; must push managers to keep costs in line.
   3. Projected same percentage increase for selling costs; vice-president of sales says this is necessary to increase sales volume; administrative costs kept in line with this year.

The president and the VP sales and VP production are discussing the budget and the operation policies for next year.

Although the budget reflected a 3 percent profit margin, compared with 1 percent last year, the president insists on a 5 percent margin. The industry average reported by the trade association was 5.21 percent last year. The discussions focused on steps that might be taken to "get the 5 percent profit margin." During the discussions, the controller was called in to "listen." Incidentally, the controller actually served only as the company accountant. He has been with the company many years, having initially been employed as a bookkeeper. His training in accounting consisted of some correspondence courses.

The following ideas were proposed during the meeting, although no definite decisions were made:

a   The president proposed a price increase. "To get the 5 percent profit margin ($40,000) we need $16,000 more profits; now all we need to do is to raise prices 2 percent." However, Mason (vice-president of sales) reflected that volume would "drop off by 3 or 4 percent if we did that, even with the increase in selling expenses."

b   Mason said that he should be given "$15,000 more than that shown in the budget for selling expenses so that I can get you about $50,000 more in sales at the same price; the way I figure it, that would about do the trick."

c   The assistant to the president (a recent college graduate with a mathematics undergraduate degree and an MBA degree) said that he doubted that "the expenses shown in the budget were realistic. No one here complained about them, so they must be acceptable. They appear to be straightline extrapolations from last year, which itself was unsatisfactory. Perhaps a sophisticated analysis would reveal some avenues for savings." This drew absolutely no comments; just a few moments of noticeable silence! (At least, this was the way the assistant reported it to the case writer.)

d Justin (vice-president of production) suggested that "the more profitable items should be pushed. If those allocations of overhead weren't so troublesome to the accountants, we would be sure which products are the more profitable."

e Mason speculated that at present prices "we would break even at about $700,000 sales, since we made a little profit on last year's sales. The president has stated that we should earn $40,000 next year; I still think we can do it on $850,000 sales if we hold all costs as budgeted except for the material, direct labor, and the additional $15,000 that I need."

f Mason also proposed that "if we drop prices by 2 percent, I can pick up 5 percent more volume with no increase in costs. Let's see, that would reduce sales revenue by $16,000, and the volume would increase it by $40,000. Thus sales would be $824,000, which should give us about $16,000 additional profit; 30 percent of the $24,000 sales would go to pay material and labor costs."

REQUIRED

1. In general, would you say that the estimates given by the several participants were approximately correct? Explain.

2. Evaluate the budget approach. What basic changes would you recommend with respect to the budget program and the accounting system?

3. On the basis of your recommendations, recast the budgeted income statement for internal purposes. For illustrative purposes, if you need additional information, assume that fixed costs included in the expenses are: manufacturing overhead, $240,000; selling expenses, $84,000; and administrative expenses, $60,000.

4. On the basis of your response to requirement 3, develop responses to each of the six proposals discussed in the meeting.

CASE 17-5   *Using standard costing with profit planning and flexible expense budgets*

Standard Products manufactures a line of products known as "Packers." There are eleven different designs and sizes in the line. The company distributes the line over a wide geographical area, and seasonality of sales is a minor factor. The manufacturing operations are primarily repetitive; therefore, the company uses standard cost accounting, profit planning, and flexible budgets for factory expenses (selling and administrative expenses are all fixed for all practical purposes). This case focuses on one product designated as Packer X–1. The following data about this item were extracted from the annual profit plan:

1 Planned costs for one unit of Packer X–1:

	PRODUCING DEPARTMENTS		
	X	Y	Z
Raw materials: 1 ($1.00 per unit)	2 units		
2 ($1.20 per unit)		3 units	
3 ($1.50 per unit)		1 unit	4 units
Direct labor: Hours	1.5	1	2
Average wage rate	$8.00	$8.40	$10.00

2 Planned output for year (all products):

In direct labor hours (DLH)	120,000	50,000	144,000

3 Planned manufacturing overhead costs for the year (activity base DLH):

(All products): Fixed	$120,000	$36,000	$ 86,400
Variable	60,000	50,000	201,600

The following actual data relate to transactions that were completed during the month of January (the first month of the budget year):

1 Actual number of units of X–1 manufactured during January, 2,000.
2 Actual number of units of X–1 sold during January, 1,900 at $110 each.
3 Actual raw material purchases:

> Material 1—4,200 units @ $1.05
> Material 2—5,800 units @ $1.20
> Material 3—10,000 units @ $1.45

4 Actual issues of raw materials:

> Dept. X—4,100 units of material 1
> Dept. Y—6,150 units of material 2
>   1,900 units of material 3
> Dept. Z—8,200 units of material 3

5 Actual direct labor incurred:

> Dept. X—3,125 hours @ $8.24
> Dept. Y—1,950 hours @ $8.20
> Dept. Z—4,000 hours @ $10.10

6   Actual overhead incurred:

$$
\begin{array}{l}
\text{Dept. X—\$14,000} \\
\text{Dept. Y—\$ 7,480} \\
\text{Dept. Z—\$18,600}
\end{array}
$$

7   Departmental overhead is applied on the basis of standard direct labor hours in actual output.

8   The company uses two-way analysis of variances for direct materials, direct labor, and overhead.

9   Actual selling expenses, 22,000; and administrative expenses, $12,000.

Flexible budget formulas (summarized) for the three departments (summarized) were as follows:

	FIXED PER MONTH	VARIABLE PER DLH
Dept. X	$12,000	$ .50
Dept. Y	3,000	1.00
Dept. Z	7,200	1.40

REQUIRED

1. Compute the annual overhead rates for each of the three departments; maintain a distinction between the fixed and variable expenses.
2. Prepare a standard specification (cost per unit) for Packer X–1.
3. Record the actual transactions and overhead application for January; use the standard cost format, and record the variances in appropriate accounts. Assume cash transactions.
4. Prepare a summarized income statement using the standard cost format.
5. Be prepared to discuss the interrelationships in the above requirements between the profit planning and control program and the standard cost system.

CASE 17-6   *The accounting entries, income statement, and summary performance report must be prepared, using standard costing and a flexible expense budget*

Simplex Company is a small manufacturer of a single product that has been successful in a two-state distribution area. The company uses a comprehensive budget program, including flexible expense budgets for factory overhead and monthly performance reports. Since the product is standardized and the operations are repetitive, a standard cost system for manufacturing is used by the accounting department. The budget and standard cost unit cost data are the same. The monthly performance report, by responsibility, includes a monthly income statement prepared on a standard cost basis. Predetermined manufacturing overhead rates per standard direct machine hour are used. Manufacturing overhead is applied on the basis of standard machine hours (DMH) in actual output.

The following data are from the annual profit plan and related documents (data simplified for case purposes only):

1. From the flexible budget:

	FIXED PER MONTH	VARIABLE PER DMH
Manufacturing overhead:		
Indirect materials	$ 1,000	$ .30
Indirect labor	3,000	.50
Salaries	9,000	
Depreciation	1,500	
Insurance and taxes	400	
Remaining	100	.20
Total	$15,000	$1.00
Selling expenses	$ 6,500	
Administrative expenses	5,000	

2. From the annual profit plan:
   a. Annual production planned: in units, 7,500; in DMH, 90,000.
   b. One raw material is used in producing the product. The raw material costs (at standard) are $2 per unit, and 10 units are used for each unit of finished product.
   c. Each unit of finished product requires four direct labor hours (DLH) at a budgeted average rate of $10 per hour.
   d. Planned output for January, 625 units.

The following data relate to actual transactions completed during January, the first month of the budget year:

1. Sales: planned, 610; actual, 590 units at $140 per unit during January.
2. Manufactured 600 units of product.
3. Purchases of raw material, 6,600 at $2.07 per unit.
4. Issues of raw material, 6,150 units.
5. Direct labor incurred, 2,500 hours amounting to $24,875.
6. Actual overhead incurred during January (actual direct machine hours, 7,500):

	AMOUNT
Manufacturing overhead:	
Indirect materials	$ 3,460
Indirect labor	7,200
Salaries	9,300
Depreciation	1,500
Insurance and taxes	400
Remaining	1,740
Total	$23,600

7   Actual selling expenses, $7,000; and actual administrative expenses, $4,800.

REQUIRED

1. Compute the annual predetermined overhead rate.
2. Prepare a standard specification per unit of product.
3. Give the accounting entries for January assuming a standard cost system.
4. Prepare a standard cost income statement for January for internal management purposes.
5. Prepare a summarized performance report for manufacturing costs for January that shows detailed variances (including selling and distribution).
6. Be prepared to discuss the interrelationships between the budget program and the accounting system reflected in the above requirements.

18 Perspectives and Overview

INTRODUCTION AND PURPOSE   Throughout this book, we have emphasized profit planning and control as an integral part of the broad management process. We have also emphasized its conceptual and practical applications in decision making, planning, and control. We stressed (1) the importance of broad management participation, (2) the application of PPC to all phases of operations, and (3) the long-range and short-range planning involved in a comprehensive system of profit planning and control. Throughout these discussions, we also emphasized that PPC is not a financial or an accounting exercise, but rather that PPC must rest upon a firm foundation of management leadership evidenced by realistic objectives, awareness of motivational issues, and dynamic control. This chapter summarizes some of the most important aspects in applying profit planning and control.

ADAPTATION IN THE PROFIT PLANNING AND CONTROL PROCESS   A central problem in developing and applying an effective profit planning and control program is selecting appropriate concepts and techniques for different situations. As the enterprise grows, changes, and becomes more complex, there is the continuing problem of discarding less useful approaches and replacing them with more appropriate ones. Both the budgeting process and the accounting system must be revised as the enterprise changes. It is not uncommon to find a situation where these two systems are internally inconsistent and do not effectively serve the needs of the enterprise. This result usually occurs when a "system" was developed in another enterprise and was literally transplanted without change. It is doubtful that any two profit planning and control systems should be identical, because no two organizations are identical.

Prior to initiating a profit planning and control program, management should conduct studies designed to collect information on the strengths and weaknesses of the enterprise and to assess the economics involved in potential changes. One type of study or survey, called **factual studies,** requires in-depth analysis of present operations. Such a study should constitute critical self-analysis and introspection to determine the internal strengths and weaknesses of the enterprise and of each of its subdivisions. This self-audit provides factual and sometimes unpleasant information essential to the development of a con-structive profit improvement program and the implementation of changes. An-other type of study, frequently characterized as **economic feasibility studies,** focuses on alternatives to correct or minimize the inefficiencies pinpointed in prior **factual studies.** Economic feasibility studies develop alternative courses of action and assess their economic characteristics. Many decisions to pursue selected alternatives are based on persuasion rather than facts. To prevent such a result, these two types of studies—factual studies and feasibility studies—go hand in hand. Studies of these types are fundamental not only in the design but also in the continuing implementation and improvement of a comprehen-sive profit planning and control program.

Appropriate methods of planning sales and other revenue vary among companies, depending on (1) external factors that affect the enterprise, (2) in-ternal characteristics, and (3) level of management sophistication. Similarly, the best approach to plan expenses should necessarily vary among companies. For example, flexible budgeting procedures for expenses do not have universal ap-plication, but the concept of adjusting budget expense allowances to output should be given serious consideration by every management. The flexible bud-get concept may not have application with respect to all costs in a business, yet it may be particularly useful in certain responsibility centers. Cost-volume-profit analysis may have considerable application in one situation but not in another. The design of performance reports should be based on the situation's characteristics and the particular needs of the principal users. A profit planning and control process should not be static; for example, contribution margin anal-ysis may not be useful currently in a particular company, yet five years later it may be imperative. The system of planning sales that is appropriate today may be entirely inadequate a few years hence.

INSTALLATION OF A PPC SYSTEM   System installation can be troublesome for a number of reasons. First, there is a natural tendency on the part of many indi-viduals, regardless of their position in the organization, to resist major changes of any type. This tendency may be due to several factors, such as insecurity, lack of understanding, and fear of the unknown. Second, as a result of unfor-tunate misuse, budgeting has acquired a bad reputation in the minds of some people. Some supervisors may think of budgeting as just another device used by management to increase pressure. Third, budgeting requires time and effort on the part of executives and supervisors. For these reasons, it is imperative that a profit planning and control program be carefully designed and imple-mented.

It has been said that a company should not expect to develop an adequate profit planning and control program in less than two years; generally, by the end of the third year, the program should be satisfactory. Although the company's size and characteristics are the determining factors, it may be undesirable to attempt to budget all phases of operations in the first year. The sales function is often one of the first areas in which budget procedures are initiated. Many companies, through necessity, have initiated budget procedures for capital expenditures and have subsequently extended budget procedures to other phases of operations. Where practicable, however, it is advisable to start on companywide profit planning and control in the first year.

BUDGET EDUCATION   Once the program has started, its development must be enthusiastically supported by top management. Initial resistance can only be overcome through active management participation and continuous **budget education** conducted at all levels of management. The objectives of the profit planning and control program should be explained to executives and supervisors alike. Adequate understanding and appreciation of the program can best be accomplished through conferences and discussions to show how the program cannot only benefit the company but also help the executives and supervisors in meeting their responsibilities. A common mistake is to hire a budget director to "come in and set up a budget program in the shortest possible time." The mistake is compounded when executive management fails to follow through to ensure (1) a positive internal climate, (2) management participation, and (3) effective budget education. In budget education, the idea of some executives that "everyone but me" needs to be educated must frequently be overcome. Line executives should actively participate in conducting budget education within their particular areas of responsibility.

IMPLEMENTING THE PPC PROGRAM   The way in which the budgeting program is initiated will have a marked effect upon its acceptance throughout the enterprise. Psychological (i.e., behavioral) factors are important determinants of budget acceptance. Careful planning by top management prior to budget initiation is essential. It is generally desirable that a committee of top-management officials be appointed to analyze the budgetary needs of the enterprise, to develop the specific objectives of a budget program for the business, and to recommend an approach to budget initiation and implementation.

In designing and implementing a profit planning and control program the following steps are recommended:

1   Appoint a high-level management committee to provide broad recommendations.
2   Analyze the internal environment based on factual studies.
3   Conduct economic feasibility studies.

4   Specify the broad objectives of the program.

5   Specify management responsibilities in planning and controlling (line versus staff).

6   Decide on the basic budgetary approach.

7   Select appropriate concepts, techniques, and approaches.

8   Plan the implementation of the system.

9   Institute budget education.

10 Establish procedures for monitoring the system to ensure its appropriateness and to provide for improvements.

11 Establish guidelines to ensure effective utilization of the system by all levels of management.

MANAGERIAL FLEXIBILITY IN APPLYING PPC   Profit planning and control is an approach for managing future performance consistent with specified management responsibilities. The profit plan results from critical evaluation of many alternatives. These alternatives affect the future of the enterprise under conditions of uncertainty. In accomplishing the management task, broad enterprise objectives must be established—such as target rates of return, profit margins, growth rates, and social programs. An enterprise is seldom involved in profit maximization in the theoretical sense; rather, its broad objectives represent judgments by the management that are generally based on the company's past performance, comparisons with other companies, and to some extent the ambitions and personal whims of executive management.

The profit planning and control concept imposes a self-discipline on the management to specify plans, to evaluate precisely their probable effects on the resource flows of the company, and to measure and evaluate performance on a continuing basis.

Management Attitudes: The Key To Flexibility

Profit planning and control requires a high level of management sophistication. Broad problems of leadership, motivation, judgment, and technical competence are generally encountered. The profit plan should be viewed as a guideline to action; realistic goals and objectives are specified and buttressed with strategies and policies. There must be a strong management commitment to attain the specified objectives and goals. On the other hand, the plans must not be administered inflexibly. One of the most important facets of dynamic management is **rational flexibility** designed to take advantage of all favorable opportunities and minimize the impact of unfavorable events. Flexibility is as much a matter of management attitudes as anything else. The willingness to listen, to evaluate alternatives not covered in the plans, and to change positions are elements of management flexibility. No plan can anticipate all events; thus, a dynamic approach is needed to cope with a dynamic environment.

Replanning To Attain Flexibility

To attain managerial flexibility, many companies employ **current estimates of future performance.** Under this approach, as unanticipated events occur or previously anticipated events become unlikely, the emphasis is not on mechanical revision of the profit plan. Instead, each manager of the responsibility centers directly affected should submit by the end of the current month a reprojection of his or her expectations, taking into account the altered situation. Should this reprojection be materially different in any respect from the original profit plan, a complete explanation of the expectations should be required. In addition to flexibility, this procedure should be used to provide top management with information concerning all developments expected in the immediate future that may have a significant financial effect. Such a procedure puts management in a position to take effective advance action to cope with a changing situation. This concept meets a need that the annual profit plan and the end-of-the-month performance reports do not fully satisfy.

Applied on a broader basis, estimation of future performance constitutes a reappraisal of the primary variable and economic effects in light of present conditions so that the probable results for the remainder of the short-range planning period can be recast. The concept is demonstrated in Exhibits 18-1 and 18-2. Notice in the illustration that, at the end of August, sales were reprojected for the remainder of the planning period. The reprojection is significantly different from the original plan. Thus, by combining the "actuals" for the first eight months with the reprojection for the remaining four months, management has a realistic and valuable estimate of "how we will probably come out by year-end." The application illustrated for sales suggests the potential for applying the concept of replanning to all major areas of operations.

EXHIBIT 18-1

Illustrative Data for Estimation of Future Performance (Illustrative Data Simplified)

	ANNUAL PROFIT PLAN (SALES PLAN)		ACTUAL		REEVALUATION	
	MONTHLY	CUMULATIVE	MONTHLY	CUMULATIVE	MONTHLY	CUMULATIVE
Jan.	10	10	14	14		
Feb.	14	24	16	30		
March	16	40	12	42		
April	10	50	7	49		
May	20	70	19	68		
June	40	110	32	100		
July	30	140	28	128		
Aug.	10	150	7	135		
Sept.	10	160			13	148
Oct.	20	180			20	168
Nov.	40	220			34	202
Dec.	20	240			23	225
Totals	240	240				225

EXHIBIT 18-2

Estimation of Future Performance

Estimation of Probable *Cumulative* Results Compared with the Plan of Operations for
September–December

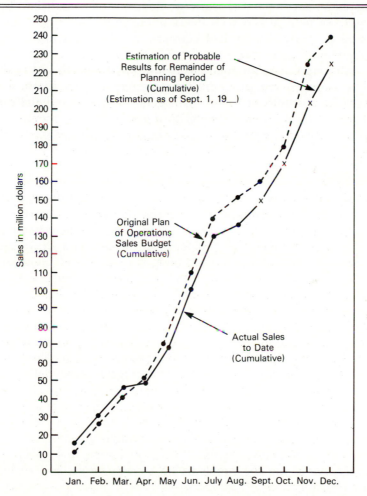

Techniques for Introducing Flexibility

In addition to management attitudes and behavior, flexibility can be introduced
into a profit planning and control program by a number of techniques: estimation of future performance; flexible expense budgets; cost-volume-profit analyses; continuous budgeting; variance analysis and interpretation; and budget revision. Each of these approaches has been discussed in the preceding chapters.

   If unanticipated opportunities arise, this fact should not deter immediate
management action to take advantage of the situation. Similarly, should condi-

tions change so that it appears undesirable to carry out planned projects, such as a costly capital expenditure, there should be no hesitancy to violate the budget. All these suggestions imply that the budget should not be a rigid, inflexible plan, but rather that it should be used as a viable tool that should be adjusted as circumstances warrant. On the other hand, it is essential that the budget not be changed with every whim, nor that it be taken lightly. Implemented properly, the budget becomes an important tool permitting effective management by exception.

Although there are many techniques that tend to add flexibility to a profit planning and control program, we must reemphasize that it is the human element—the attitudes of higher managers—that fundamentally reflects the real and perceived flexibility so vital to dynamic management. Remember also a statement made early in the book: Budgets do not manage; only people manage.

BEHAVIORAL CONSIDERATIONS   We have emphasized the importance of human behavior in profit planning and control. Many of the shortcomings attributed to budget programs can be directly identified with defective management attitudes and other behavioral problems. In the case of a weak or unsophisticated management, techniques such as budgeting frequency are used as the focus of criticism. However, a technique by itself can do nothing; the individuals using it determine its worth. It is the individual manager who commits the error, exerts unfair pressure, establishes unrealistic standards, or exhibits inflexibility. The overriding factors in the management process are the interrelationships between individuals and groups. A key function of the manager is the positive motivation of people through enlightened leadership. The behavioral implications of a profit planning and control program offer both opportunities and problems. In designing and administering the program, the emphasis should be on maximizing the positive motivation of managers at all levels. Focusing on the behavioral impact of PPC, it may be helpful from time to time to distinguish between the viewpoint of the individual manager and that of the enterprise. Each has its own peculiarities, motivations, and goals. A common error is to always blame the problems on someone else. Self-evaluation can solve many problems.

Critical behavioral implications of a comprehensive profit planning and control program were discussed in preceding chapters. By way of summary, it is appropriate to pinpoint selected areas and to suggest that those who may become involved in management should give these areas further study and reflection. Some of the most critical behavioral issues are as follows:

1   **The System**—Management is a leadership or directive effort that sets objectives and goals and measures performance. Profit planning and control is a system that helps management accomplish these responsibilities. Individual managers quickly identify the management approach with the enterprise; the system, as they perceive it, will affect them both positively and negatively. In the case of excessive negative motivation, they may become discouraged, resign, or often sabotage the system. They may even go to the extent of soliciting help from others in sabotage. Alternatively, if the system gains their favor, they will reflect enthusiasm, creativity, and productivity. Thus, the interface between the system and the managers at all levels is loaded with behavioral implications. This point suggests the importance of applying sound behavioral judgment in developing, administering, and improving the management system.

2   Goal Orientation—The goal orientation of the enterprise and that of the individual manager must be harmonized. The enterprise goals must be understood and must be in conformity with the ethical and economic goals of the manager. The manager must be able to reconcile the goals of the enterprise with his or her own personal goals—reward, recognition, social, and ethical.

3   Attitudinal—The attitudes of higher managers permeate from top management down through the organization. The lower managers adopt certain attitudes of the managers above. A critical aspect is the ease with which lower managers distinguish between the claimed and real attitudes of higher managers. Attitudes of importance relate to such factors as participation, flexibility, fairness, openness, goal accomplishment, cost consciousness, productivity, and diligence.

4   Participation—An important behavioral facet is the opportunity of each manager to participate effectively in planning, as opposed to pseudoparticipation. To be effective, participation must be systematic. There are two primary benefits of participation. First, budgetary participation is a means for top management to elicit privately held information from lower-level managers. Information asymmetry between the levels of management can be an obstacle to establishment of effective incentive programs. Second, budgetary participation often results in a greater level of commitment by lower-level managers to achievement of the goals implicit in the budget. Although participation is generally helpful in most situations, there are important cultural, organizational, and personality factors that determine the overall effectiveness of budgetary participation.

5   Line vs. Staff—Many management problems arise because of conflicts between line and staff; the staff is accused of usurping the authority of the line managers, and the line managers are viewed as ineffective by the staff. The solution to this behavioral problem is clear definition, understanding, and observance of the respective roles of the two groups.

6   Aspiration Levels—The level of performance that an individual manager will personally strive for is related to many factors, including his or her own immediate past performance. Past successes and failures significantly affect such attitudes. Top management should strive to raise the aspiration levels of the individual managers and of the enterprise as a whole.

7   Pressure—Individuals and groups react to pressure differently. Systems such as profit planning and control are pressure inducing. Pressure, depending on its characteristics, may create positive or negative motivations. Numerous subtle behavioral implications are involved.

8   Resistance to Change—This reaction is rooted in fear of the effects of change, uncertainty, lack of information, and lack of confidence in the leadership. It can be largely avoided through a budget education process.

9   Performance Measurement—This activity implies a knowledge of what is good and bad performance and the measurement of actual performance. Fairness, relevance, consistency, and rewards (positive and negative) are implicit. There are broad and pervasive behavioral and economic implications in this area, and much additional research is needed.

10   Padding the Budget—This behavioral problem is due to "self-protection." There are many reasons for building slack into budgets, and top management must continually be aware of the tendency.

11 **Budget Approval**—The approach used in approving profit plans is loaded with potential for positive and negative motivation.

12 **Follow-up on Variances**—Management policies, attitudes, and actions on favorable and unfavorable variables have important behavioral implications.

13 **Communication**—The profit planning and control program can serve as an important means of communication between levels of management and between managers on the same level. Since the way in which concepts are communicated often affects the attitude of the recipient of the communication, this aspect can have important behavioral implications throughout an organization.

14 **Risk Sharing**—Organizations operate in a world of uncertainty. All the employees of the organization thus face risk that stems from the environmental and technological uncertainty faced by the organization. To the extent that risk can be shared among the organization's employees, there can be net gains in the welfare of all. The PPC program, with its implicit goals, evaluations, and rewards, is one means by which risk sharing can be accomplished.

Roles of the Controller and Budget Director

The items in the above list suggest the scope and pervasiveness of the behavioral implications of a profit planning and control program. Several of the items indirectly relate to the responsibilities of the controller and budget director. The controller (or chief financial officer) and budget director are staff personnel, and as such they are concerned principally with service. Staff personnel should neither usurp line authority nor give that impression. Staff personnel should not be directed to exercise authority over operating line personnel. The controller and budget director should not provide the decisional inputs to the profit plan; this is strictly a line function. Nor should the controller or budget director reprimand operating personnel for unfavorable results reflected on performance reports.

The duties of the budget director have been outlined. These duties are to design and direct the budget program. The budget director should not provide decisional inputs, nor should he or she have responsibility for enforcing the budget. It is important to make a clear-cut distinction between (1) enforcing the budget and (2) reporting actual results compared with budget goals. The controller and budget director are responsible for reporting to all levels of management the results of operations related to budget goals. Corrective action resulting from either favorable or unfavorable results is strictly a line function. The controller or budget director should not be put in the position of approving budgets or taking line action concerning efficient or inefficient operating results. The controller and budget director should not be responsible for cost control. Instead, they may be properly charged to design an effective system of cost control. In the final analysis, line executives and supervisors should be charged with the direct responsibility for implementing cost control. A careful distinction between line and staff is essential to good management; the distinction must not only be drawn by top management, but there must also be assurance that the distinction is being practiced throughout the organization. The responsibilities for budget planning and control should be carefully specified in written instructions distributed to all managers. A company budget manual is important for disseminating general budget responsibilities and policies.

The behavioral implications of both accounting and profit planning and control are complex. Students and others interested in the subject are encouraged to look into these implications in much greater depth than is possible within the scope of this book.

QUANTITATIVE METHODS AND COMPUTERIZATION   The scope of this book has precluded detailed discussion of mathematical models and data-processing systems important to profit planning and control. The development of operational mathematical models and computerized data-processing systems has imposed an even greater significance on the quantification of management objectives and standards. Since the typical business enterprise is complex and must adapt to change, it requires sophisticated conceptual approaches and information processing. The dynamics of the relevant variables with which a company must cope also frequently demand extensive conceptual and data-processing capacities. Simulation can serve as a partial, although valuable, substitute for actual experience. Quantitative objectives and standards required for profit planning and control are basic foundations for effective application of mathematical models and computer technology. Thus, the greater the sophistication of these two developments, the greater the need for the development by executive management of enterprise objectives and standards of performance. Greater data-processing capacity, as well as related conceptual developments, makes available more background data and current information important to the planning and control functions. Computers have led a number of companies to adapt these techniques to many facets of the budget process. The replacement of manual procedures by computerized methods is significant. However, it must be realized that the computer cannot substitute for the judgment and unique decision-making role of the manager.

In viewing the budget process, one quickly notices the necessity for testing the financial effect of numerous alternatives and processing large quantities of data. The computer is especially useful for these two purposes. The computer can perform mathematical calculations in tremendous quantities at fantastic speeds. It can store vast quantities of data. On the other hand, the computer can only do what it is told to do; that is, a program must tell the computer what data to select and what operations to perform on the selected data. Thus, we have two basic sets of input data: (1) programming input (instructions) and (2) basic data to be used by the computer in connection with the programmed instructions. The latter data are enhanced by the computer only to the extent that mathematical manipulations can improve it. Fundamentally, the output data can be no better than the basic input data and the programmed instructions. Thus, there are two distinct sets of input for data.

Electronic data processing (EDP) aids budgeting by (1) handling the burden of mass calculations, (2) reducing the time span required for such calculations, (3) testing the probable effects of numerous alternatives and sets of assumptions, and (4) providing more time for executive consideration of the basic decisions underlying the budget. While most businesses have placed their accounting system and PPC process on a mainframe computer, the advent of the personal computer has made the quantitative power of computer methods more accessible to small business and to individual managers within organizations. Moreover, electronic spreadsheet programs have provided managers who do not possess extensive computer-programming skills with the capability of easily performing significant quantitative analyses.

Suggested References

BEDEIAN, ARTHUR G., *Management*. New York: Dryden Press, 1985.

COLLINS, FRANK, PAUL MUNTER, and DON W. FINN, "The Budgeting Games People Play," *Accounting Review,* January 1987, pp. 29–49. Includes a comprehensive bibliography.

ITAMI, HIROYUKI, *Adaptive Behavior: Management Control and Information Analysis.* Sarasota, Fla.: American Accounting Association, 1977.

SCHIFF, MICHAEL, and ARIE Y. LEWIN, *Behavioral Aspects of Accounting.* Englewood Cliffs, N.J.: Prentice-Hall, 1974.

CASE 18-1   *Help the company president decide whether to make or buy[1]*

Liquid Chemical Company sells a range of high-grade products, which because of their chemical properties require careful packing. The company had always made a feature of the special properties of the containers used. The containers had a special patented lining made from a material known as GHL. The company operated a department to maintain its containers in good condition and to make new ones to replace those that were not repairable. (Note—The amounts herein were reduced to one-tenth of the original amount only to simplify the computations.)

For some time H. G. Walsh, the company president, had believed that the company might save money and get equally good service by buying its containers outside. After careful inquiries, Walsh approached a company specializing in container production, Packages, Inc., and obtained price quotations

[1] This case was prepared by Professor David Solomons of the University of Pennsylvania as a basis for class discussion. It is reproduced here with the permission of the author.

from them. At the same time, Walsh asked G. A. Dyer, the controller, to prepare a statement of the current cost of operating the container department.

Within a few days, the quotation from Packages was received. Packages was prepared to supply all the new containers required—at that time running at the rate of 3,000 a year—for $60,000 per annum. The contract was to be for a term of five years certain, and thereafter to be renewable from year to year. If the number of containers required increased, the total contract price would be increased proportionately. Additionally, and regardless of whether the above contract was concluded, Packages proposed to perform the maintenance work on containers, short of replacement, for a sum of $17,500 per annum on the same contract terms.

Walsh then compared Packages' proposal with the cost analysis prepared by Dyer covering a year's operations of the container department, as follows:

ITEM	VOLUME—3,000 UNITS	
Direct materials		$20,000
Direct labor		35,000
Container departmental overhead:		
Manager's salary	$8,000	
Rent	1,500	
Depreciation of machinery	6,000	
Maintenance of machinery	1,350	
Remaining expenses	6,300	23,150
		78,150
Allocation of company		
administrative overhead		6,750
Total cost of department for year		$84,900

Walsh's conclusion was that no time should be lost in closing down the container department and in entering into the contracts offered by Packages. However, Walsh decided to give the manager of the department, D. M. Duffy, an opportunity to question this conclusion prior to a decision. Therefore, Walsh called Duffy and laid out the facts, at the same time making it clear that Duffy's own position was not in jeopardy, for even if the department were closed down, another managerial position would be vacant to which Duffy could be moved without loss of pay or future prospects.

Duffy looked thoughtful and asked for time to think the matter over. The next morning, Duffy asked to speak to the president again. Duffy said that there were a number of considerations that ought to be borne in mind before that department was closed down. "For instance," Duffy said, "what will you do with the machinery? It cost $48,000 four years ago, but you'd be lucky if you got $8,000 for it now, even though it's good for another four years at least. And then there's the stock of GHL we bought a year ago. That cost us another $30,000, and at the rate we're using it now, it will last us another three years or so. We used up about a quarter of it last year. Dyer's figure of $20,000 for materials included about $7,500 for GHL. But it will be tricky stuff to handle if we don't use it up. We paid $150 a ton for it, and you couldn't buy it today for less than $180. But you wouldn't have more than $120 a ton left if you sold it, after you'd covered all the handling expenses."

Walsh thought that Dyer ought to be present during this discussion. He called the controller and explained Duffy's points. "I don't much like all this conjecture," Dyer said. "I think my figures are pretty conclusive. Besides, if we are going to have all this talk about 'what will happen if,' don't forget the problem of space we're faced with. We're paying $2,750 a year to rent a warehouse a couple of miles away. If we closed Duffy's department, we'd have all the warehouse space we need without renting."

"That's a good point," said Walsh. "Though I must say, I'm a bit worried about the men if we close the department. I don't think we can find room for any of them elsewhere in the company. I could see whether Packages will take any of them. But two of them are getting on. There's Walters and Hines, for example. They've been with us since they left school forty years ago. I'd feel bound to give them a small pension, say $1,000 a year each."

Duffy showed some relief at this but said, "But I still don't like Dyer's figures. What about this $6,750 for general administrative overhead? You surely don't expect to fire anyone in the general office if I'm closed down, do you?" "Probably not," said Dyer, "but someone has to pay for these costs. We can't ignore them when we look at an individual department because if we do that with each department in turn, we will end by convincing ourselves that general managers, accountants, typists, stationery, and the like, don't have to be paid for. And they do, believe me."

"Well, I think we've thrashed this out pretty fully," said Walsh, "but I've been turning over in my mind the possibility of perhaps keeping on the maintenance work ourselves. What are your views on that, Duffy?" "I don't know," said Duffy, "but it's worth looking into. We shouldn't need any machinery for that, and I could hand the supervision over to a foreman. You could save about $2,000 a year there. You'd only need about one-fifth of the men, but you could keep on the oldest. You wouldn't save any space, so I suppose the rent would be the same. I shouldn't think the other expenses would be more than $2,600 a year." "What about materials?" asked Walsh. "We use about 10 percent of the total on maintenance," Duffy replied.

"Well, I've told Packages that I'd let them know my decision within a week," said Walsh. "I'll let you know what I decide to do before I contact them."

REQUIRED

1. State the primary problem and identify the alternatives that should be considered.

2. Analyze the economics of each alternative.*

3. Based on all relevant quantitative and qualitative factors, give and support your recommendations.

*Assumptions to simplify the arithmetic:

1 Income tax rate, 40%.

2 After-tax discount rate, 10%.

3 Remaining life of equipment, 5 years; fully depreciated after 4 years; straightline depreciation; and no residual value.

4 Constant wages and prices.

5 All gains and losses are ordinary.

CASE 18-2   *Prepare a master budget*

Scarborough Corporation manufactures and sells two products, Thingone and Thingtwo. In July 19X7, Scarborough's budget department gathered the following data in order to project sales and budget requirements for 19X8.

19X8 Projected Sales:

PRODUCT	UNITS	PRICE
Thingone	60,000	$ 70
Thingtwo	40,000	$100

19X8 Inventories—in units:

PRODUCT	EXPECTED JANUARY 1, 19X8	DESIRED DECEMBER 31, 19X8
Thingone	20,000	25,000
Thingtwo	8,000	9,000

In order to produce one unit of Thingone and Thingtwo, the following raw materials are used:

RAW MATERIAL	UNIT	AMOUNT USED PER UNIT THINGONE	THINGTWO
A	lbs.	4	5
B	lbs.	2	3
C	each		1

Projected data for 19X8 with respect to raw materials is as follows:

RAW MATERIAL	ANTICIPATED PURCHASE PRICE	EXPECTED INVENTORIES JANUARY 1, 19X8	DESIRED INVENTORIES DECEMBER 31, 19X8
A	$8	32,000 lbs.	36,000 lbs.
B	$5	29,000 lbs.	32,000 lbs.
C	$3	6,000 each	7,000 each

Project direct labor requirements for 19X8 and rates are as follows:

PRODUCT	HOURS PER UNIT	RATE PER HOUR
Thingone	2	$3
Thingtwo	3	$4

Overhead is applied at the rate of $2 per direct labor hour.

REQUIRED   Based on the above projections and budget requirements for 19X8 for Thingone and Thingtwo, prepare the following budgets for 19X8:

1. Sales budget (in dollars)
2. Production budget (in units)
3. Raw materials purchase budget (in quantities)
4. Raw materials purchase budget (in dollars)
5. Direct labor budget (in dollars)
6. Budgeted finished goods inventory at December 31, 19X8 (in dollars)

(CPA adapted)

CASE 18-3   *Interpret a master budget*

Einhard Enterprises has a comprehensive budgeting program. Proforma statements of earnings and financial position are prepared as the final step in the budget program. Einhard's projected financial position as of June 30, 19X2 is presented below. Various 19X2–19X3 master budget schedules based upon the plans for the fiscal year ending June 30, 19X3, are also provided.

All sales are made on account. Raw material, direct labor, factory over-head, and selling and administrative expenses are credited to vouchers payable. Federal income tax expense is charged to income taxes payable. The federal income tax rate is 40 percent.

EINHARD ENTERPRISES
Proforma Statement of Financial Position
as of June 30, 19X2
($000 omitted)

ASSETS	
Cash	$ 800
Accounts receivable	750
Direct material inventory	506
Finished goods inventory	648
Total current assets	$ 2,704
Land	$ 1,500
Property, plant & equipment	11,400
Less accumulated depreciation	(2,250)
Total long-term assets	$10,650
Total assets	$13,354

LIABILITIES AND EQUITY	
Vouchers payable	$ 1,230
Income taxes payable	135
Notes payable (due 12/30/X2)	1,000
Total liabilities	$ 2,365
Common stock	$10,200
Retained earnings	789
Total equity	$10,989
Total liabilities and equity	$13,354

Cash Receipts and Disbursements Schedule
($000 omitted)

Cash balance 7/1/X2 (estimated)	$ 800	
Cash receipts		
Collection of accounts receivable	33,450	
Total cash available		$34,250
Cash disbursements		
Payment of vouchers payable		
Direct material	$11,900	
Direct labor	8,400	
Manufacturing overhead	4,650	
Selling and administrative expenses	5,200	
Total vouchers payable	$30,150	
Income taxes	1,100	
Purchase of equipment	400	
Cash dividends	820	
Total cash disbursements		$32,470
Excess cash		$ 1,780
Financing		
Repayment of note payable 12/30/X2	$ 1,000	
Interest expense	50	
Total financing cost		$ 1,050
Projected cash balance 6/30/X3		$ 730

Beginning Inventory Schedule in Units and Dollars

	QUANTITY	COST PER UNIT	TOTAL COST
Direct material	184,000 pounds	$ 2.75 per lb	$506,000
Finished goods	54,000 units	$12.00 per unit	$648,000

Sales Schedule in Units and Dollars

UNIT SALES	SELLING PRICE PER UNIT	TOTAL SALES REVENUE
2,100,000	$16	$33,600,000

Production Schedule in Units and Dollars

PRODUCTION IN UNITS	COST PER UNIT	TOTAL MANUFACTURING COST
2,110,000	$12	$25,320,000

Raw Material Purchases Schedule in Units and Dollars

PURCHASES IN POUNDS	COST PER POUND	TOTAL PURCHASE COST
4,320,000	$2.75	$11,880,000

Two pounds of raw material are needed to make one unit of finished product.

Direct Labor Schedule in Units and Dollars

PRODUCTION IN UNITS	DIRECT LABOR COST PER HOUR	TOTAL DIRECT LABOR COST
2,110,000	$8	$8,440,000

Each unit requires one-half hour of direct labor time.

Manufacturing Overhead Schedule in Dollars
(expected activity level—1,055,000 direct labor hours)

Variable expenses	$2,954,000*
Depreciation	600,000
Other fixed expenses	1,721,000*
Total manufacturing overhead	$5,275,000

* All require cash expenditures. The manufacturing overhead rate is $5.00 per direct labor hour ($5,275,000 ÷ 1,055,000).

Selling and Administrative Expense Schedule in Dollars

Selling expenses	$2,525,000
Administrative expenses	2,615,000
Total	$5,140,000

All selling and administrative expenses require the expenditure of cash.

REQUIRED

Construct a planned statement of cash flows for Einhard Enterprises as of June 30, 19X3.

(CMA adapted)

APPENDIX:
Probability and
Decision Making
Under Uncertainty

INTRODUCTION AND PURPOSE   Almost all decision-making, planning, and control activities are conducted under conditions of uncertainty. Environmental uncertainty includes such phenomena as the demand, the actions of competitors, and the regulatory environment. Technological uncertainty includes such factors as the quantity of material required to manufacture a product and the life of a piece of machinery. Many decisions and planning exercises can be improved through the explicit consideration of uncertainty. The purpose of this appendix is to review some fundamentals of probability and decision making under uncertainty. The concepts covered here can be applied to many of the issues and techniques discussed throughout the book.

ELEMENTS OF DECISION MAKING UNDER UNCERTAINTY   All decisions have the following five common elements:

1 **Actions.** The set of actions available (e.g., buy one of four available pieces of equipment).
2 **States of Nature.** The set of possible events that can occur (e.g., different levels of demand for a company's product or service).
3 **Probabilities of the States.** Each state is assigned a probability reflecting its likelihood. Probabilities are all nonnegative, and they sum to one (e.g., the probability of some measurable rainfall tomorrow is .40, and the probability of no measurable rainfall is .60).
4 **Outcomes.** For each action and state of nature, there is a consequence or outcome. For example, if the product price is set at $5 per unit (the action), and the demand is 1,000 units (the state of nature), the outcome is sales revenue of $5,000.
5 **Utility.** The payoff of an outcome may be a *utility* measure associated with the outcome. Utilities should be used when monetary measures are not sufficient to reflect the consequence of an action and a state of nature. For example, a fifty-fifty chance at gaining or losing $100 has an *expected monetary value* of zero [i.e., (−$100)(.50) plus ($100)(.50)]. A fifty-fifty chance at gaining or losing $1,000,000 also has an expected monetary value of

zero. However, most people would not view these gambles as being equivalent. The *risk attitude* of the decision maker has not been taken into account in the expected-monetary-value measure.

MAXIMIZING EXPECTED MONETARY VALUE   In situations where the decision maker is not averse to the risk inherent in a decision under uncertainty, it is appropriate to choose the action that maximizes expected monetary value. In the decision represented in Exhibit A-1, for example, the optimal decision is to select action a_2. The expected monetary value of action a_i is the sum of the products of the outcomes, under action a_i, and the probabilities of those outcomes. Thus, the expected value associated with action a_2 is calculated as $[4][.2] + [1][.5] + [5][.3]$, a total of 2.8.

EXHIBIT A-1

Outcome Table

ACTION	STATE OF NATURE			EXPECTED MONETARY VALUE
	s_1	s_2	s_3	
a_1	2.7	2.7	2.7	2.7
a_2	4.0	1.0	5.0	2.8
a_3	3.0	1.0	1.0	1.4
Probability of State	.2	.5	.3	

MAXIMIZING EXPECTED UTILITY   If the decision maker is averse to the risk inherent in a decision under uncertainty, then the concept of a utility function should be used. A risk-averse decision maker exhibits a concave utility function, such as the one shown in Exhibit A-2.

The utilities associated with the actions and states of nature are displayed in Exhibit A-3. Note that the action with the highest expected utility is action a_1. Why does action a_1 exhibit the highest expected utility even though action a_2 has a higher expected monetary value? The reason is that a_2 is much riskier than action a_1. The monetary outcomes associated with action a_2, under the various states of nature, vary widely. In contrast, the monetary outcomes associated with action a_1 have no variance across the states of nature. Since the decision maker is averse to risk, as evidenced by the utility function in Exhibit A-2, the less risky of the two actions is preferable.[1]

[1] To delve further into decision making under uncertainty, see Howard Raiffa, *Decision Analysis: Introductory Lectures on Choices under Uncertainty* (Reading, Mass.: Addison-Wesley, 1970).

EXHIBIT A-2

Concave Utility Function Exhibiting Risk Aversion

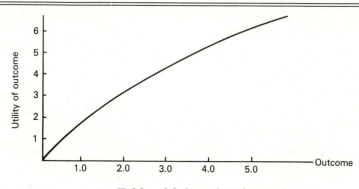

Table of Selected Utility Values

OUTCOME	UTILITY OF OUTCOME
1.0	1.8
2.7	4.0
3.0	4.3
4.0	5.2
5.0	5.9

EXHIBIT A-3

Utility Table for Decision Under Uncertainty

ACTION	STATE OF NATURE			EXPECTED UTILITY
	s_1	s_2	s_3	
a_1	4.0	4.0	4.0	4.00
a_2	5.2	1.8	5.9	3.71
a_3	4.3	1.8	1.8	2.30
Probability of State	.2	.5	.3	

RISK SHARING Risk sharing means that two or more persons share in the risky outcome from a gamble. Insurance is a common example of risk sharing where the insured people pool their risk of accidents or illness through premium payments and the settlement of claims.

Risk-averse people can always be made better off when they share the risks they face. Consider the utility function in Exhibit A-2. Suppose two persons, denoted by X and Y, each face the gamble of a fifty-fifty chance at receiving $1 or $5. Without risk sharing, each person has an expected utility of 3.85 [i.e., (.5)(1.8) + (.5)(5.9)]. Now suppose X and Y pool their risk by agreeing to equally split the combined outcome of their gambles. There are three possible outcomes for the combined gamble faced by the two persons. These outcomes are as follows:

X's OUTCOME	Y's OUTCOME	COMBINED OUTCOME	PROBABILITY
1	1	2	.25
1	5	6	.50
5	1	6	
5	5	10	.25

Since the combined outcome will be split equally by X and Y, each now faces the following gamble:

EACH PERSON'S OUTCOME	UTILITY OF OUTCOME	PROBABILITY
2/2 = 1	1.8	.25
6/2 = 3	4.3	.50
10/2 = 5	5.9	.25

Now each person's expected utility is 4.075 [i.e., (1.8)(.25) + (4.3)(.50) + (5.9)(.25)]. Thus, risk sharing has increased each person's expected utility.

Risk sharing can be an important dimension of the design of incentive contracts and performance evaluation systems. Managers will be more likely to accept risky projects that are in the company's best interest if they are at least partially protected from bearing that risk themselves.[2]

PROBABILISTIC BUDGETS

One way in which probabilities can be explicitly introduced into the profit planning and control program is by the use of probabilistic profit budgets. Under this approach, several estimates are made for each of several key components in the budget, and probabilities are assigned to these estimates. One reasonable approach is to select an **optimistic**, a **pessimistic**, and a **most likely** estimate for each key number in the budget. Exhibit A-4 illustrates this approach.

The result of the approach illustrated in Exhibit A-4 is that management has a probability distribution over the possible profit levels instead of a single point estimate. Moreover, various **summary statistics** can be calculated for this probability distribution. For example, the mean or expected value of the profit distribution is $90. It is, of course, possible to be much more sophisticated in the application of this technique. Complicated probability distributions can be

[2] For further discussion, see Robert S. Kaplan, *Advanced Management Accounting* (Englewood Cliffs, N.J.: Prentice-Hall, 1982).

EXHIBIT A-4

Probabilistic Profit Budget

Estimates and Probabilities

	PESSIMISTIC	MOST LIKELY	OPTIMISTIC
Sales revenue	$100	$150	$200
Cost of goods sold	$ 60	$ 50	$ 40
Selling and administrative expenses	$ 10	$ 10	$ 10
Probabilities*	.25	.50	.25

*These are the probabilities associated with the various estimates of each budget number as an *independent* variable. Thus, sales revenue could be $100 (with probability .25), and cost of goods sold could be $50 (with probability .50). The *joint probability* of both of these events occurring is the product of their individual probabilities, .25 × .50, or .125.

Probabilistic Budget

Sales Revenue	Cost of Goods Sold	S & A Expenses	Profit	Probability
	$60 P = .25	$10	$30	.0625
$100 P = .25	$50 P = .50	$10	$40	.1250
	$40 P = .25	$10	$50	.0625
	$60 P = .25	$10	$80	.1250
$150 P = .50	$50 P = .50	$10	$90	.2500
	$40 P = .25	$10	$100	.1250
	$60 P = .25	$10	$130	.0625
$200 P = .25	$50 P = .50	$10	$140	.1250
	$40 P = .25	$10	$150	.0625

specified for all the important components in the budgeting process. Then a computer can be used to calculate all the possible combinations of budget component values and the probabilities of the resulting profit levels. Many large companies employ this approach using computer **simulations** to ask "what if" questions about the effects of changes in budget components on the bottom line.[3]

OTHER PROBABILISTIC TECHNIQUES   In this appendix we have only scratched the surface of the possible uses of probabilities in profit planning and control. Many other techniques exist. For example, cost-volume-profit analysis can be conducted with probabilistic estimates of the sales price, variable cost, fixed cost, and so forth. Under this approach, instead of a single breakeven point, one calculates a probability of breaking even. Probabilities can also be used in such areas as cost variance investigation, project planning, and capital budgeting—to name only a few.[4] The interested reader can consult the list of suggested references.

Suggested References

DEMSKI, JOEL, and GERALD FELTHAM, *Cost Determination: A Conceptual Approach*. Ames: Iowa State University Press, 1976.

FERRARA, WILLIAM L., and JACK C. HAYYA, "Toward Probabilistic Profit Budgets," *Managment Accounting*, October 1970.

KAPLAN, ROBERT S., *Advanced Management Accounting*. Englewood Cliffs, N.J.: Prentice-Hall, 1982.

MAGEE, ROBERT S., *Advanced Managerial Accounting*. New York: Harper & Row, 1986.

RAIFFA, HOWARD, *Decision Analysis: Introductory Lectures on Choices under Uncertainty*. Reading, Mass.: Addison-Wesley, 1970.

[3] For further discussion, see William L. Ferrara and Jack C. Hayya, "Toward Probabilistic Profit Budgets," *Management Accounting*, October 1970.

[4] See Kaplan, *Advanced Management Accounting;* or Robert Magee, *Advanced Managerial Accounting* (New York: Harper & Row, 1986).

Index